4 SAINT☆YOUNG MEN

C O N T E N T S

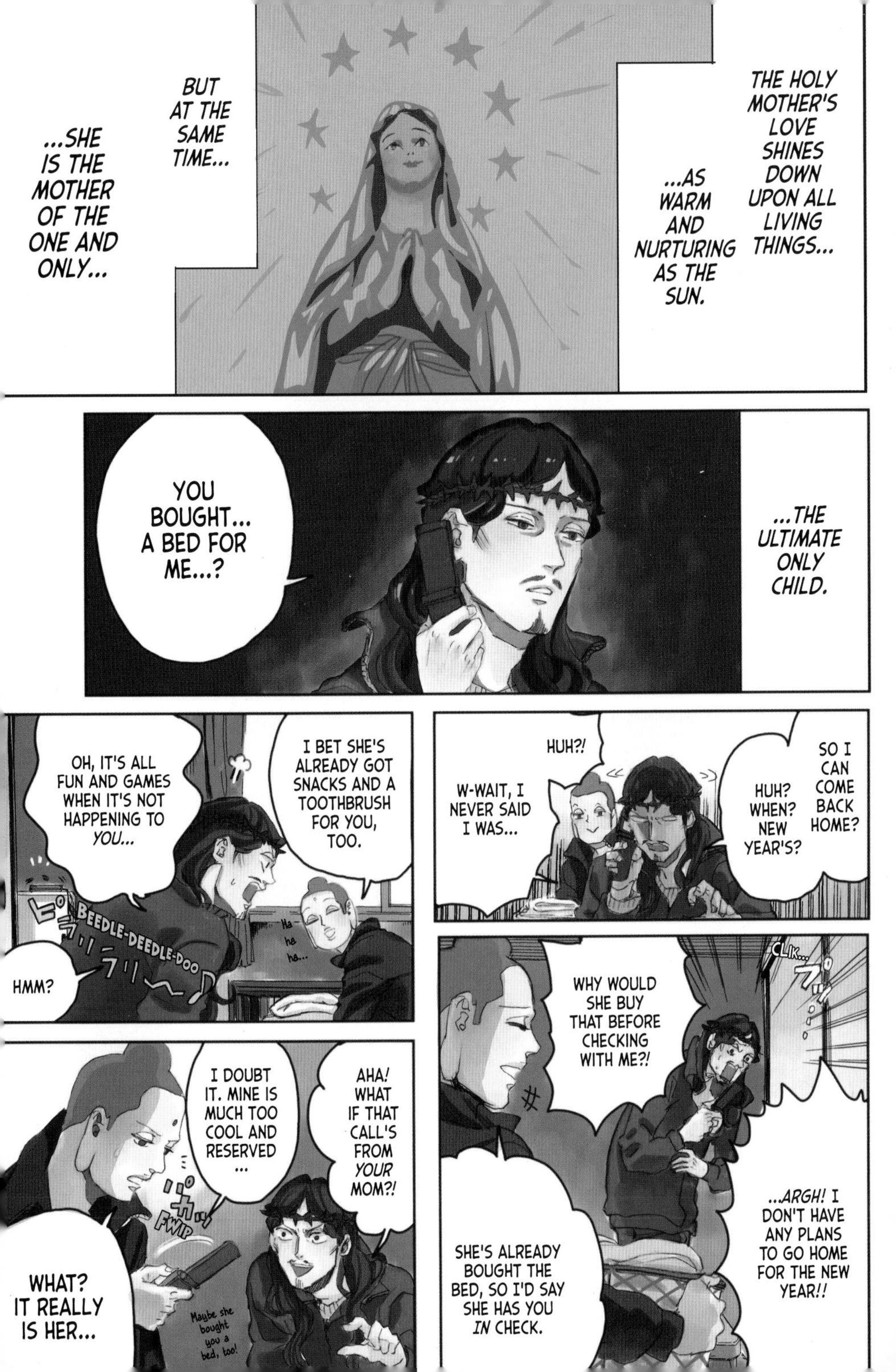
THE HOLY MOTHER'S LOVE SHINES DOWN UPON ALL LIVING THINGS...
...AS WARM AND NURTURING AS THE SUN.
BUT AT THE SAME TIME...
...SHE IS THE MOTHER OF THE ONE AND ONLY...
...THE ULTIMATE ONLY CHILD.
YOU BOUGHT... A BED FOR ME...?
SO I CAN COME BACK HOME?
HUH? WHEN? NEW YEAR'S?
HUH?!
W-WAIT, I NEVER SAID I WAS...
I BET SHE'S ALREADY GOT SNACKS AND A TOOTHBRUSH FOR YOU, TOO.
OH, IT'S ALL FUN AND GAMES WHEN IT'S NOT HAPPENING TO *YOU*...
Ha ha ha...
BEEDLE-DEEDLE-DOO
HMM?
CLIK...
WHY WOULD SHE BUY THAT BEFORE CHECKING WITH ME?!
...*ARGH!* I DON'T HAVE ANY PLANS TO GO HOME FOR THE NEW YEAR!!
SHE'S ALREADY BOUGHT THE BED, SO I'D SAY SHE HAS YOU *IN* CHECK.
AHA! WHAT IF THAT CALL'S FROM *YOUR* MOM?!
I DOUBT IT. MINE IS MUCH TOO COOL AND RESERVED...
FWIP
WHAT? IT REALLY IS HER...
Maybe she bought you a bed, too!

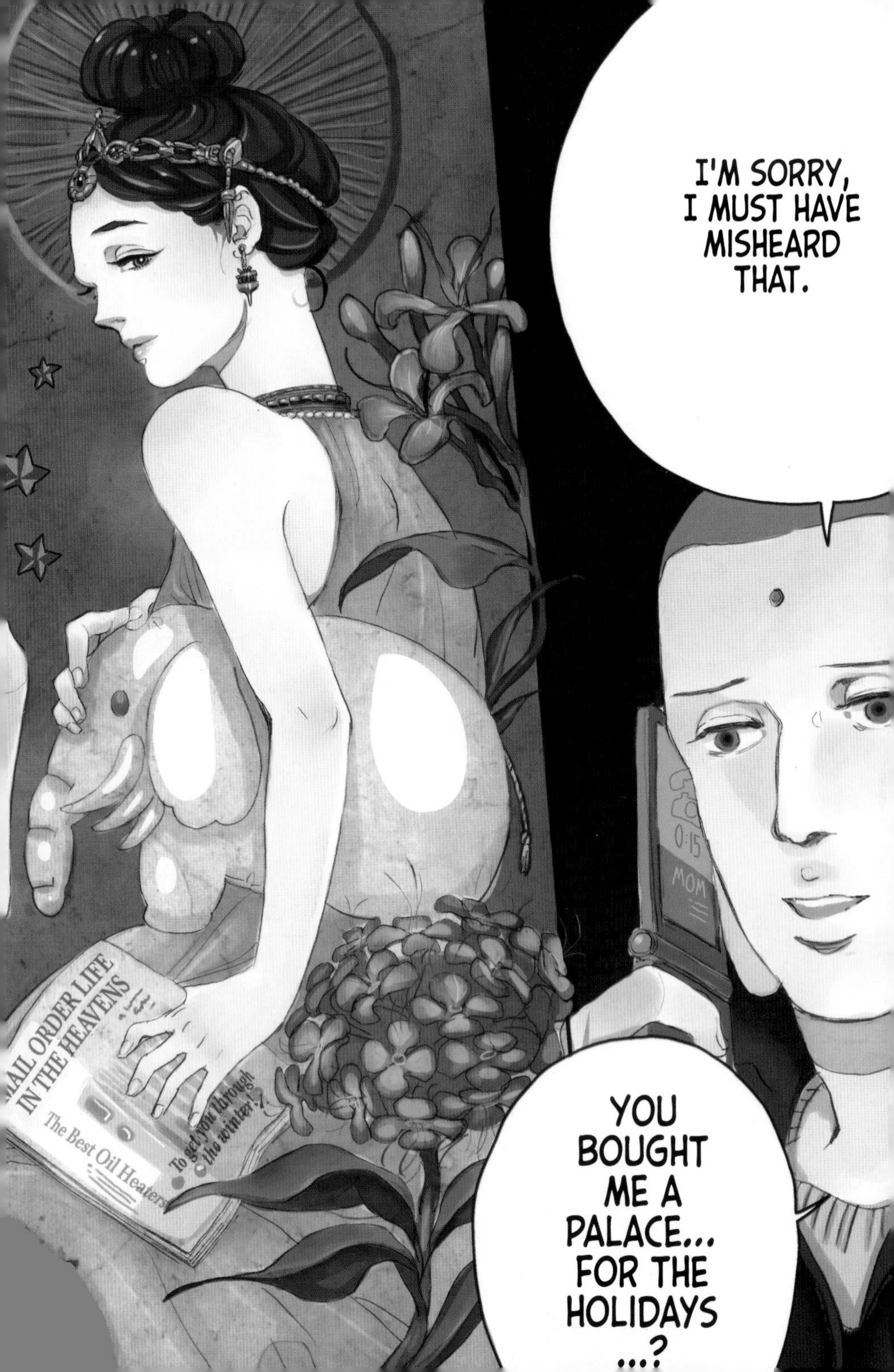
I'M SORRY, I MUST HAVE MISHEARD THAT.
0:15
MOM
YOU BOUGHT ME A PALACE... FOR THE HOLIDAYS ...?
MAIL ORDER LIFE IN THE HEAVENS
The Best Oil Heaters
To get you through the winter!

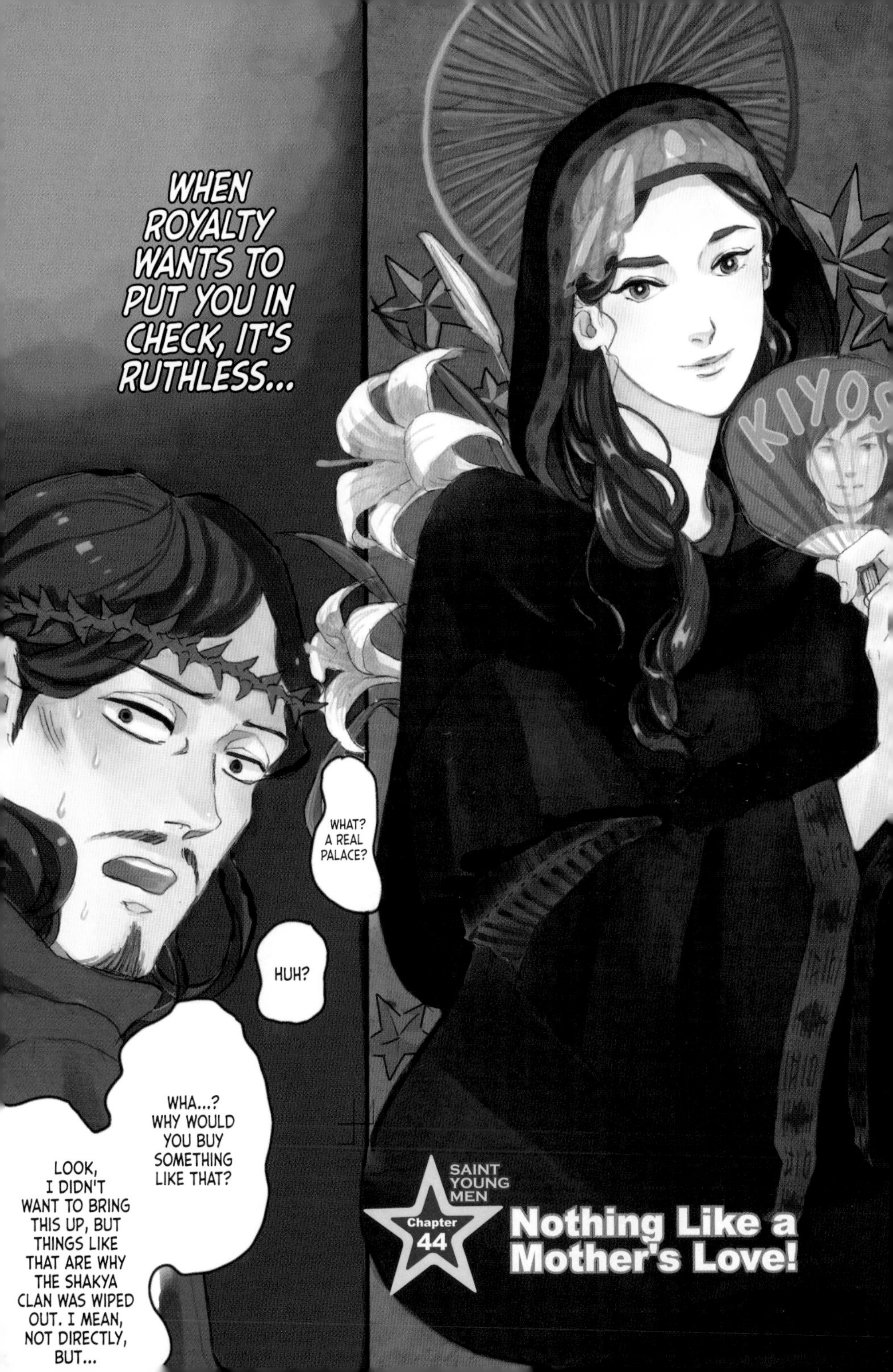
KIYOS
SAINT YOUNG MEN
Chapter 44
Nothing Like a Mother's Love!
WHEN ROYALTY WANTS TO PUT YOU IN CHECK, IT'S RUTHLESS...
WHAT? A REAL PALACE?
HUH?
WHA...? WHY WOULD YOU BUY SOMETHING LIKE THAT?
LOOK, I DIDN'T WANT TO BRING THIS UP, BUT THINGS LIKE THAT ARE WHY THE SHAKYA CLAN WAS WIPED OUT. I MEAN, NOT DIRECTLY, BUT...

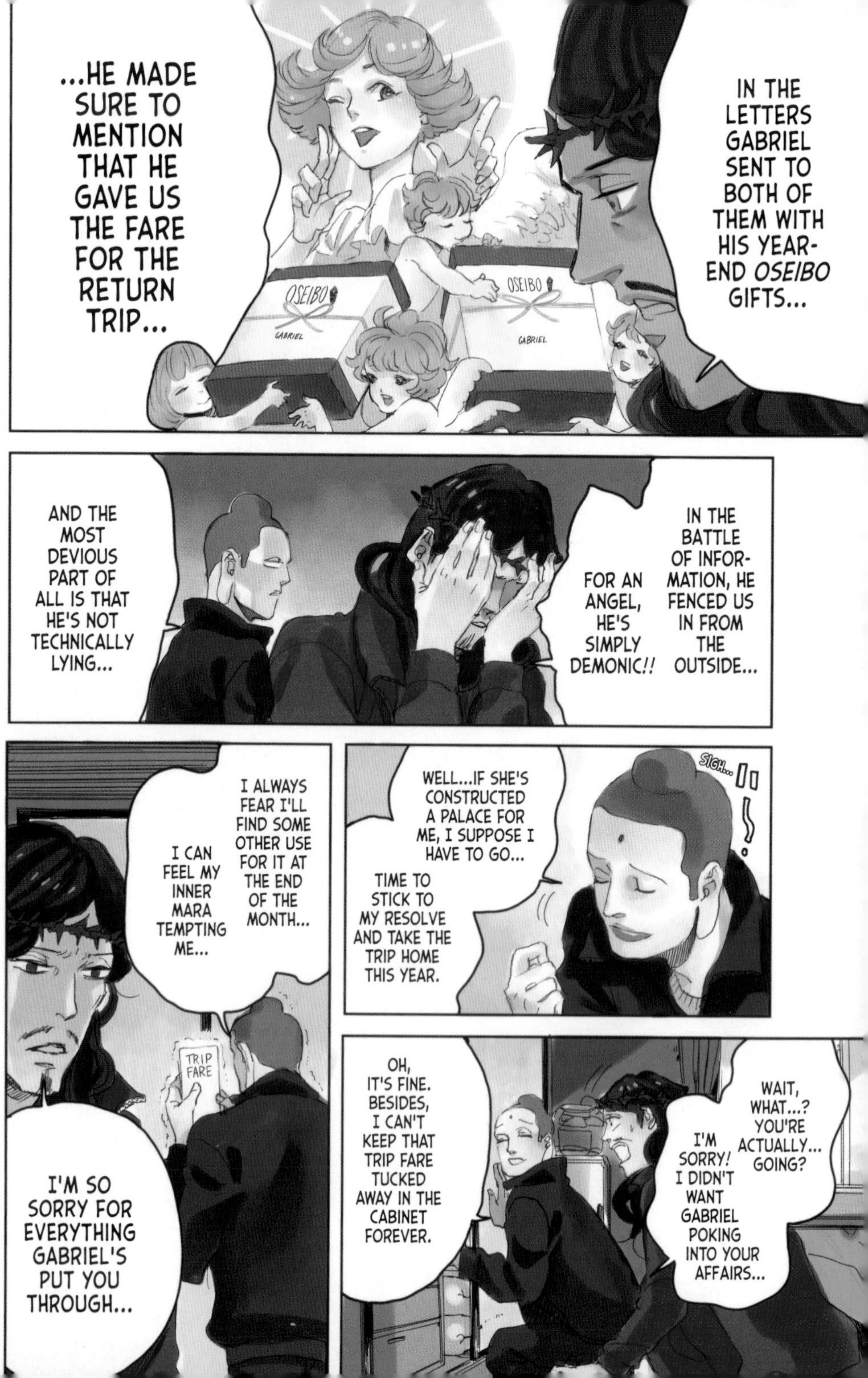
IN THE LETTERS GABRIEL SENT TO BOTH OF THEM WITH HIS YEAR-END *OSEIBO* GIFTS...
...HE MADE SURE TO MENTION THAT HE GAVE US THE FARE FOR THE RETURN TRIP...
OSEIBO
GABRIEL
OSEIBO
GABRIEL
IN THE BATTLE OF INFORMATION, HE FENCED US IN FROM THE OUTSIDE...
FOR AN ANGEL, HE'S SIMPLY DEMONIC!!
AND THE MOST DEVIOUS PART OF ALL IS THAT HE'S NOT TECHNICALLY LYING...
SIGH...
WELL...IF SHE'S CONSTRUCTED A PALACE FOR ME, I SUPPOSE I HAVE TO GO...
TIME TO STICK TO MY RESOLVE AND TAKE THE TRIP HOME THIS YEAR.
WAIT, WHAT...? YOU'RE ACTUALLY... GOING?
I'M SORRY! I DIDN'T WANT GABRIEL POKING INTO YOUR AFFAIRS...
OH, IT'S FINE. BESIDES, I CAN'T KEEP THAT TRIP FARE TUCKED AWAY IN THE CABINET FOREVER.
I ALWAYS FEAR I'LL FIND SOME OTHER USE FOR IT AT THE END OF THE MONTH...
I CAN FEEL MY INNER MARA TEMPTING ME...
TRIP FARE
I'M SO SORRY FOR EVERYTHING GABRIEL'S PUT YOU THROUGH...

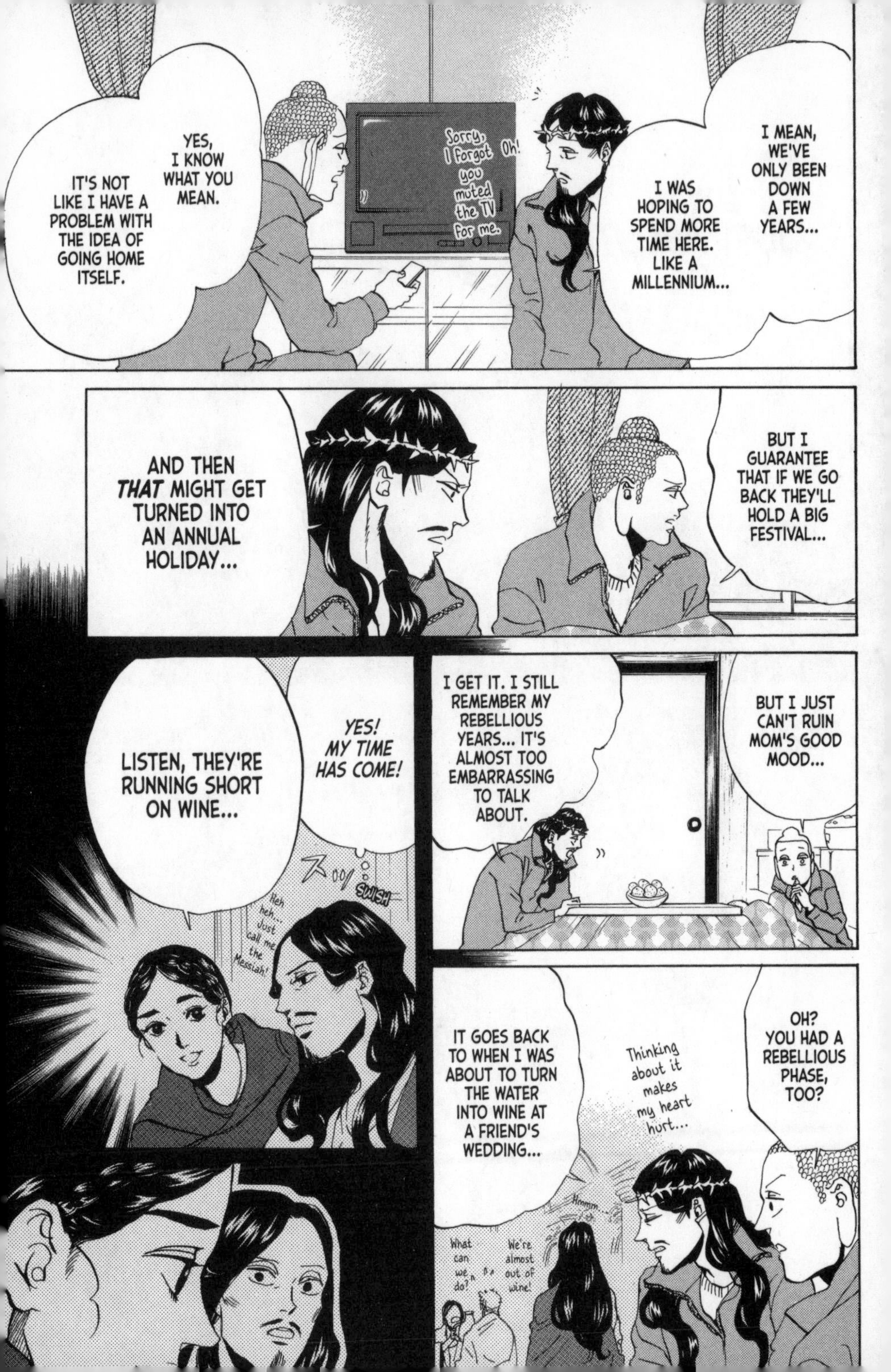

I MEAN, WE'VE ONLY BEEN DOWN A FEW YEARS...
I WAS HOPING TO SPEND MORE TIME HERE. LIKE A MILLENNIUM...
Oh!
Sorry, I forgot you muted the TV for me.
YES, I KNOW WHAT YOU MEAN.
IT'S NOT LIKE I HAVE A PROBLEM WITH THE IDEA OF GOING HOME ITSELF.
BUT I GUARANTEE THAT IF WE GO BACK THEY'LL HOLD A BIG FESTIVAL...
AND THEN *THAT* MIGHT GET TURNED INTO AN ANNUAL HOLIDAY...
BUT I JUST CAN'T RUIN MOM'S GOOD MOOD...
I GET IT. I STILL REMEMBER MY REBELLIOUS YEARS... IT'S ALMOST TOO EMBARRASSING TO TALK ABOUT.
OH? YOU HAD A REBELLIOUS PHASE, TOO?
Thinking about it makes my heart hurt...
IT GOES BACK TO WHEN I WAS ABOUT TO TURN THE WATER INTO WINE AT A FRIEND'S WEDDING...
Hmmm...
We're almost out of wine!
What can we do?
YES! MY TIME HAS COME!
LISTEN, THEY'RE RUNNING SHORT ON WINE...
SWISH
Heh heh... Just call me the Messiah!

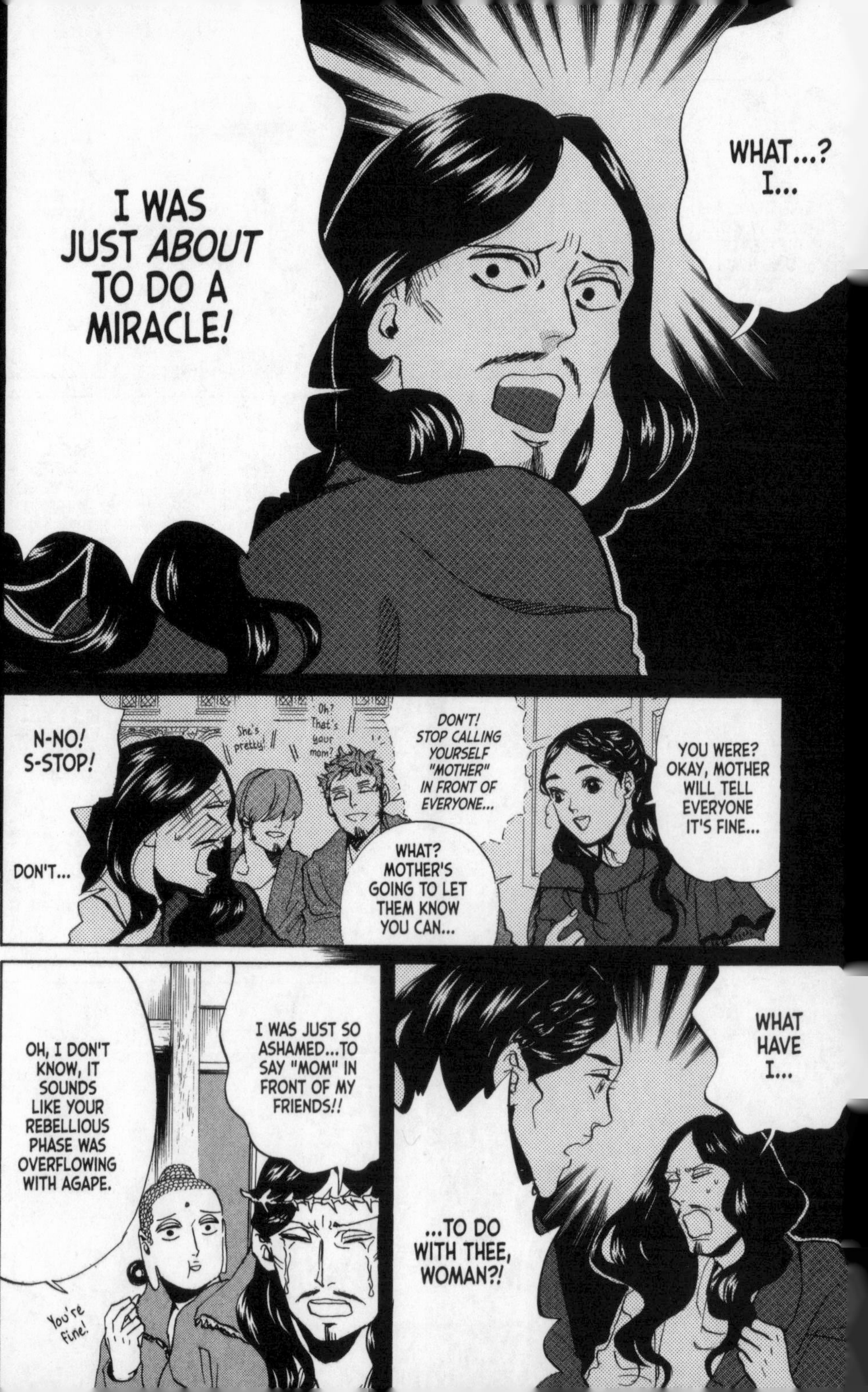
WHAT...? I...
I WAS JUST *ABOUT* TO DO A MIRACLE!
YOU WERE? OKAY, MOTHER WILL TELL EVERYONE IT'S FINE...
DON'T! STOP CALLING YOURSELF "MOTHER" IN FRONT OF EVERYONE...
WHAT? MOTHER'S GOING TO LET THEM KNOW YOU CAN...
Oh? That's your mom?
She's pretty!
N-NO! S-STOP!
DON'T...
WHAT HAVE I...
...TO DO WITH THEE, WOMAN?!
I WAS JUST SO ASHAMED...TO SAY "MOM" IN FRONT OF MY FRIENDS!!
OH, I DON'T KNOW, IT SOUNDS LIKE YOUR REBELLIOUS PHASE WAS OVERFLOWING WITH AGAPE.
You're fine!

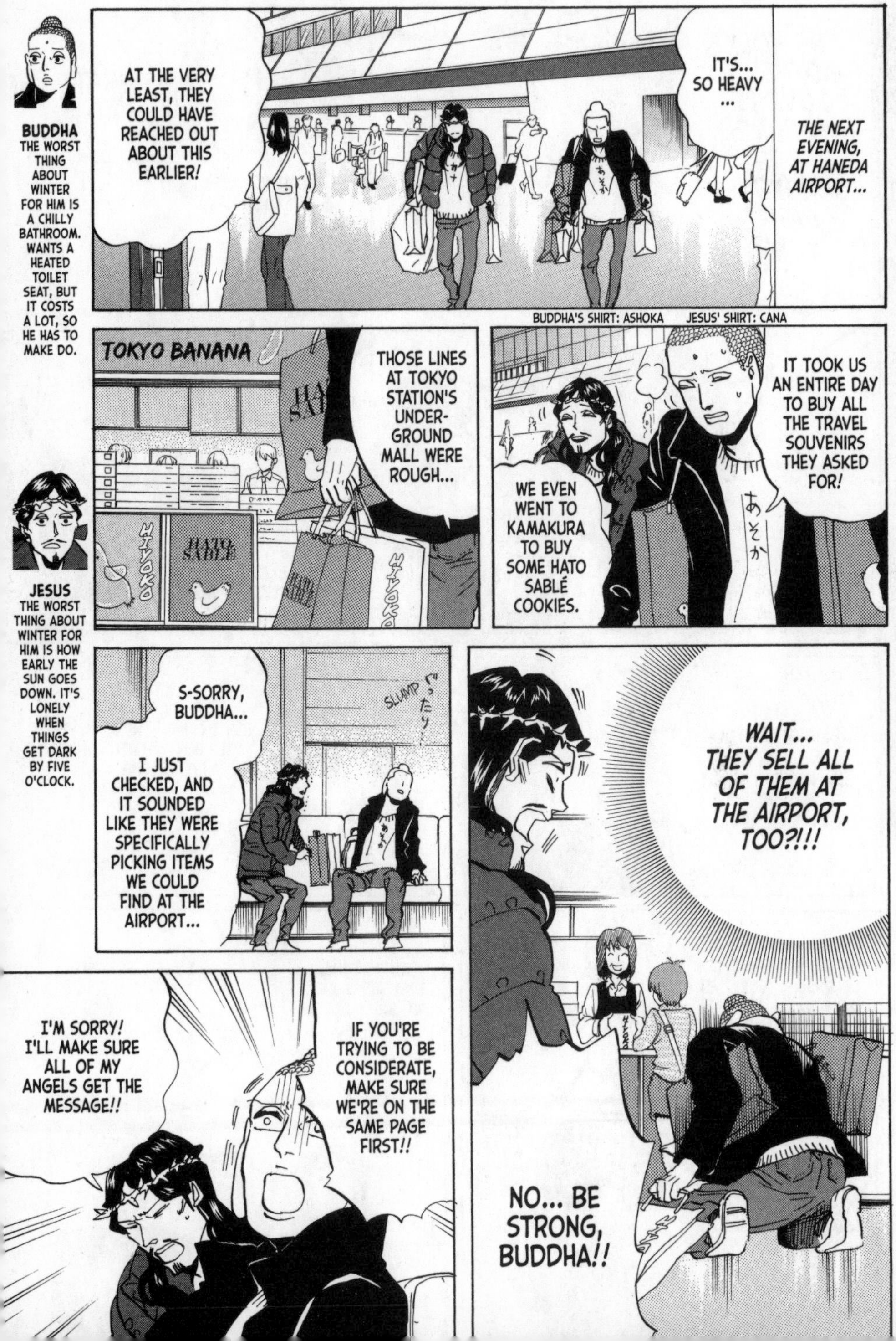
BUDDHA
THE WORST THING ABOUT WINTER FOR HIM IS A CHILLY BATHROOM. WANTS A HEATED TOILET SEAT, BUT IT COSTS A LOT, SO HE HAS TO MAKE DO.
JESUS
THE WORST THING ABOUT WINTER FOR HIM IS HOW EARLY THE SUN GOES DOWN. IT'S LONELY WHEN THINGS GET DARK BY FIVE O'CLOCK.
THE NEXT EVENING, AT HANEDA AIRPORT...
IT'S... SO HEAVY...
AT THE VERY LEAST, THEY COULD HAVE REACHED OUT ABOUT THIS EARLIER!
BUDDHA'S SHIRT: ASHOKA JESUS' SHIRT: CANA
IT TOOK US AN ENTIRE DAY TO BUY ALL THE TRAVEL SOUVENIRS THEY ASKED FOR!
WE EVEN WENT TO KAMAKURA TO BUY SOME HATO SABLÉ COOKIES.
THOSE LINES AT TOKYO STATION'S UNDER-GROUND MALL WERE ROUGH...
TOKYO BANANA
HIYOKO
HATO SABLÉ
WAIT... THEY SELL ALL OF THEM AT THE AIRPORT, TOO?!!!
NO... BE STRONG, BUDDHA!!
S-SORRY, BUDDHA...
I JUST CHECKED, AND IT SOUNDED LIKE THEY WERE SPECIFICALLY PICKING ITEMS WE COULD FIND AT THE AIRPORT...
SLUMP
IF YOU'RE TRYING TO BE CONSIDERATE, MAKE SURE WE'RE ON THE SAME PAGE FIRST!!
I'M SORRY! I'LL MAKE SURE ALL OF MY ANGELS GET THE MESSAGE!!

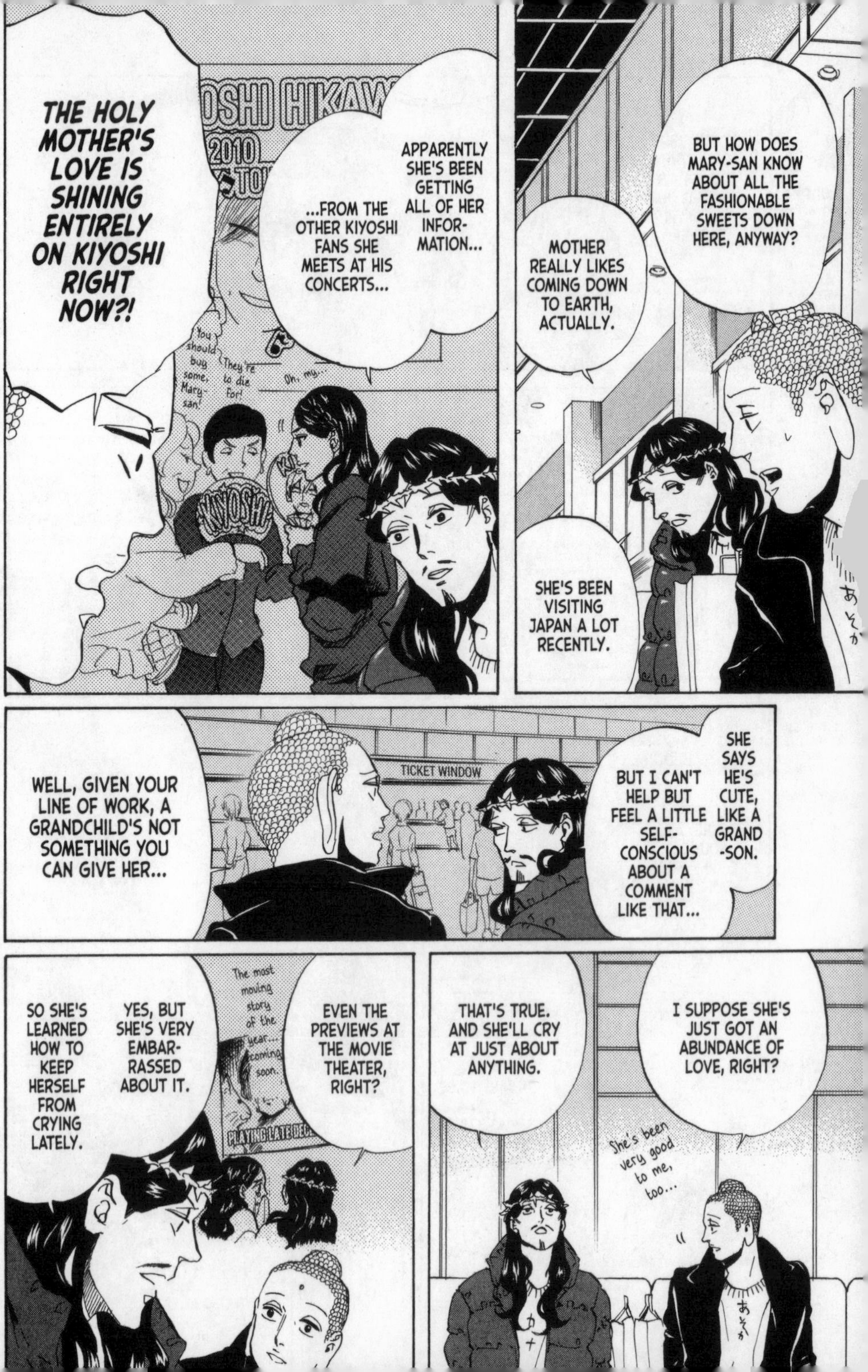
BUT HOW DOES MARY-SAN KNOW ABOUT ALL THE FASHIONABLE SWEETS DOWN HERE, ANYWAY?
MOTHER REALLY LIKES COMING DOWN TO EARTH, ACTUALLY.
SHE'S BEEN VISITING JAPAN A LOT RECENTLY.
あそか
APPARENTLY SHE'S BEEN GETTING ALL OF HER INFORMATION...
...FROM THE OTHER KIYOSHI FANS SHE MEETS AT HIS CONCERTS...
2010
You should buy some, Mary-san!
They're to die for!
Oh, my...
KIYOSHI
THE HOLY MOTHER'S LOVE IS SHINING ENTIRELY ON KIYOSHI RIGHT NOW?!
SHE SAYS HE'S CUTE, LIKE A GRAND-SON.
BUT I CAN'T HELP BUT FEEL A LITTLE SELF-CONSCIOUS ABOUT A COMMENT LIKE THAT...
TICKET WINDOW
WELL, GIVEN YOUR LINE OF WORK, A GRANDCHILD'S NOT SOMETHING YOU CAN GIVE HER...
I SUPPOSE SHE'S JUST GOT AN ABUNDANCE OF LOVE, RIGHT?
She's been very good to me, too...
THAT'S TRUE. AND SHE'LL CRY AT JUST ABOUT ANYTHING.
EVEN THE PREVIEWS AT THE MOVIE THEATER, RIGHT?
The most moving story of the year... coming soon.
YES, BUT SHE'S VERY EMBARRASSED ABOUT IT.
SO SHE'S LEARNED HOW TO KEEP HERSELF FROM CRYING LATELY.

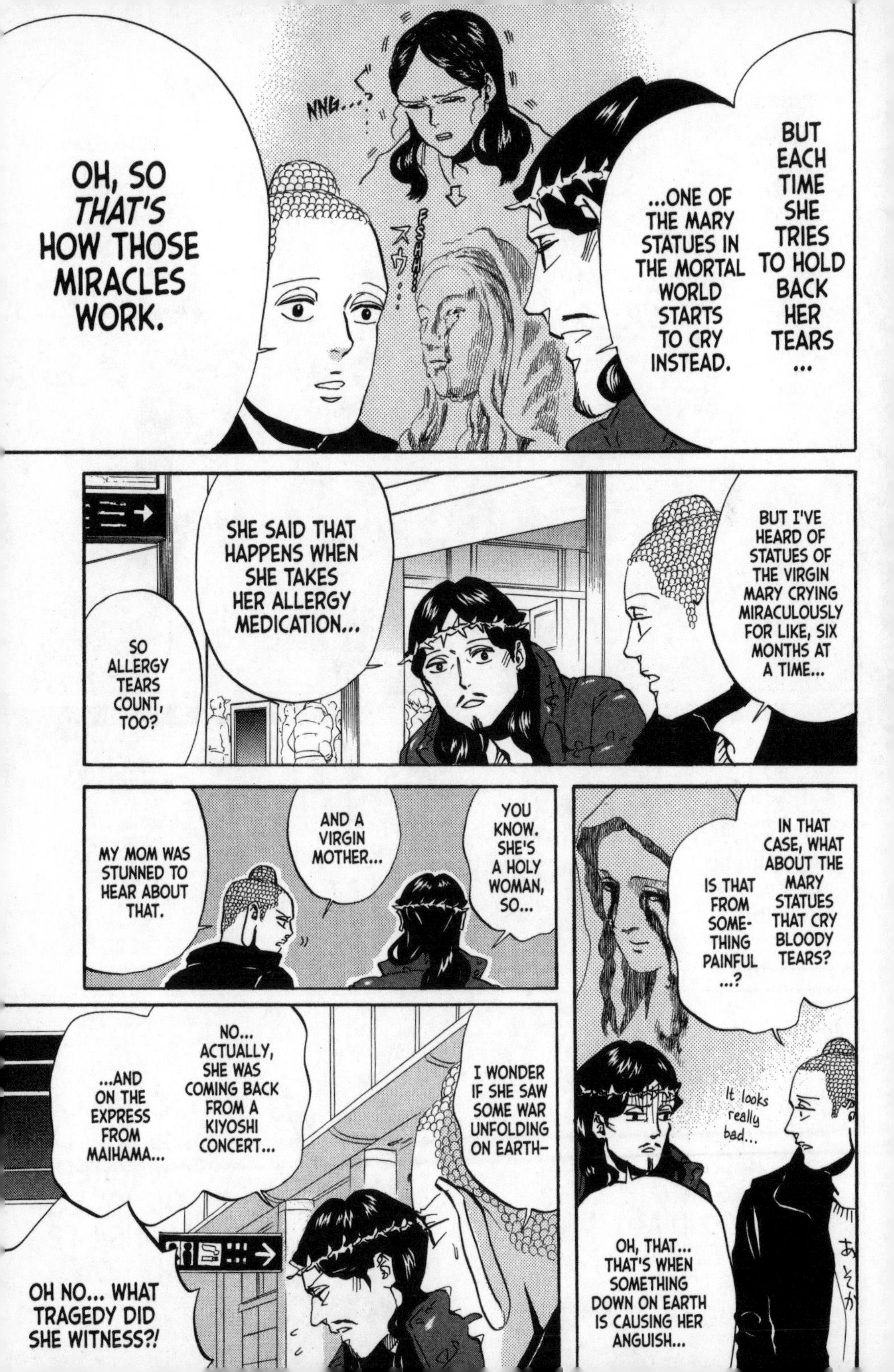
BUT EACH TIME SHE TRIES TO HOLD BACK HER TEARS ...
...ONE OF THE MARY STATUES IN THE MORTAL WORLD STARTS TO CRY INSTEAD.
NNG...
FSHH...
OH, SO *THAT'S* HOW THOSE MIRACLES WORK.
BUT I'VE HEARD OF STATUES OF THE VIRGIN MARY CRYING MIRACULOUSLY FOR LIKE, SIX MONTHS AT A TIME...
SHE SAID THAT HAPPENS WHEN SHE TAKES HER ALLERGY MEDICATION...
SO ALLERGY TEARS COUNT, TOO?
IN THAT CASE, WHAT ABOUT THE MARY STATUES THAT CRY BLOODY TEARS?
IS THAT FROM SOME-THING PAINFUL ...?
It looks really bad...
OH, THAT... THAT'S WHEN SOMETHING DOWN ON EARTH IS CAUSING HER ANGUISH...
YOU KNOW. SHE'S A HOLY WOMAN, SO...
AND A VIRGIN MOTHER...
MY MOM WAS STUNNED TO HEAR ABOUT THAT.
I WONDER IF SHE SAW SOME WAR UNFOLDING ON EARTH-
NO... ACTUALLY, SHE WAS COMING BACK FROM A KIYOSHI CONCERT...
...AND ON THE EXPRESS FROM MAIHAMA...
OH NO... WHAT TRAGEDY DID SHE WITNESS?!

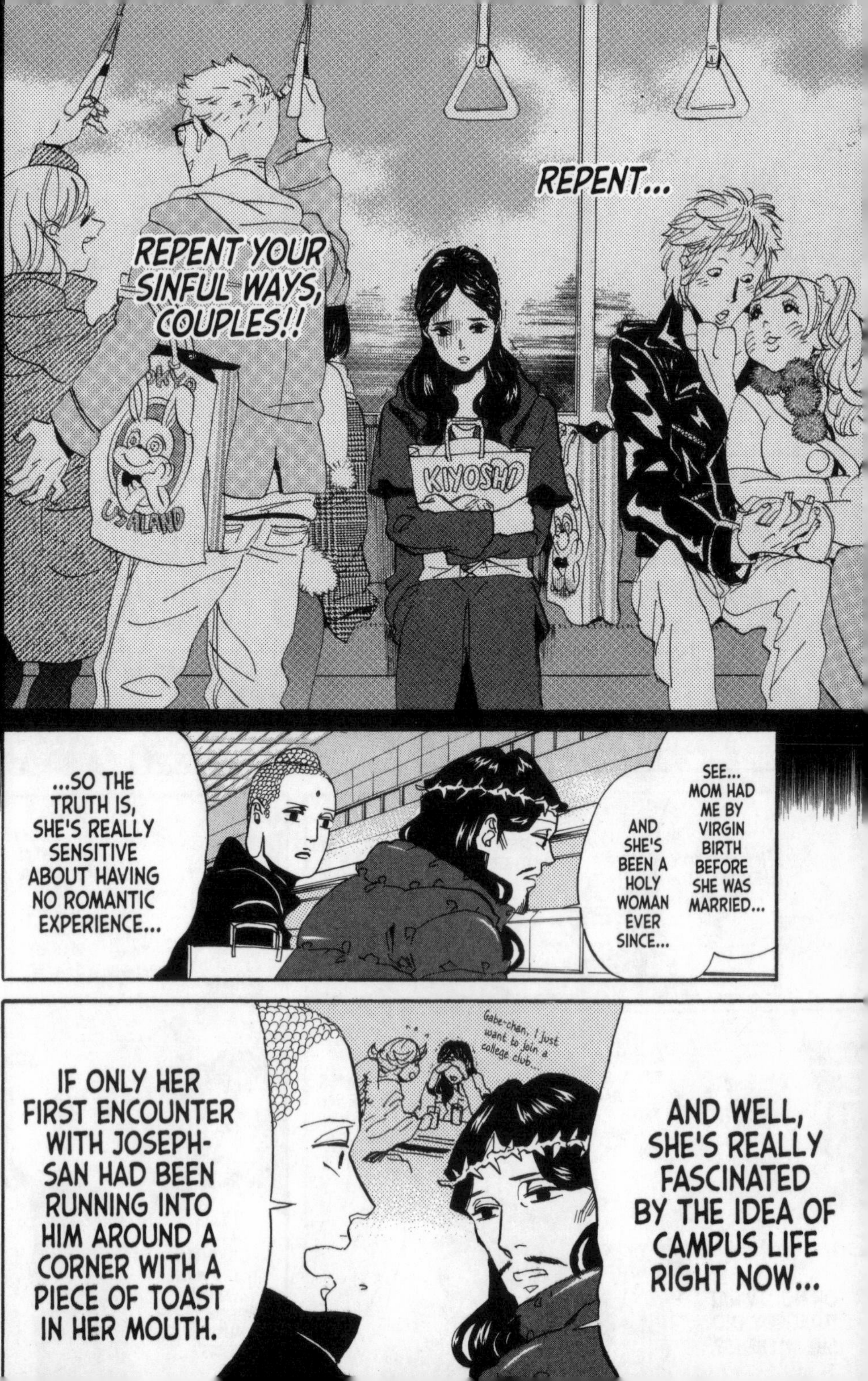
REPENT...
REPENT YOUR SINFUL WAYS, COUPLES!!
KIYOSHI
USALAND
SEE... MOM HAD ME BY VIRGIN BIRTH BEFORE SHE WAS MARRIED...
AND SHE'S BEEN A HOLY WOMAN EVER SINCE...
...SO THE TRUTH IS, SHE'S REALLY SENSITIVE ABOUT HAVING NO ROMANTIC EXPERIENCE...
AND WELL, SHE'S REALLY FASCINATED BY THE IDEA OF CAMPUS LIFE RIGHT NOW...
Gabe-chan, I just want to join a college club...
IF ONLY HER FIRST ENCOUNTER WITH JOSEPH-SAN HAD BEEN RUNNING INTO HIM AROUND A CORNER WITH A PIECE OF TOAST IN HER MOUTH.

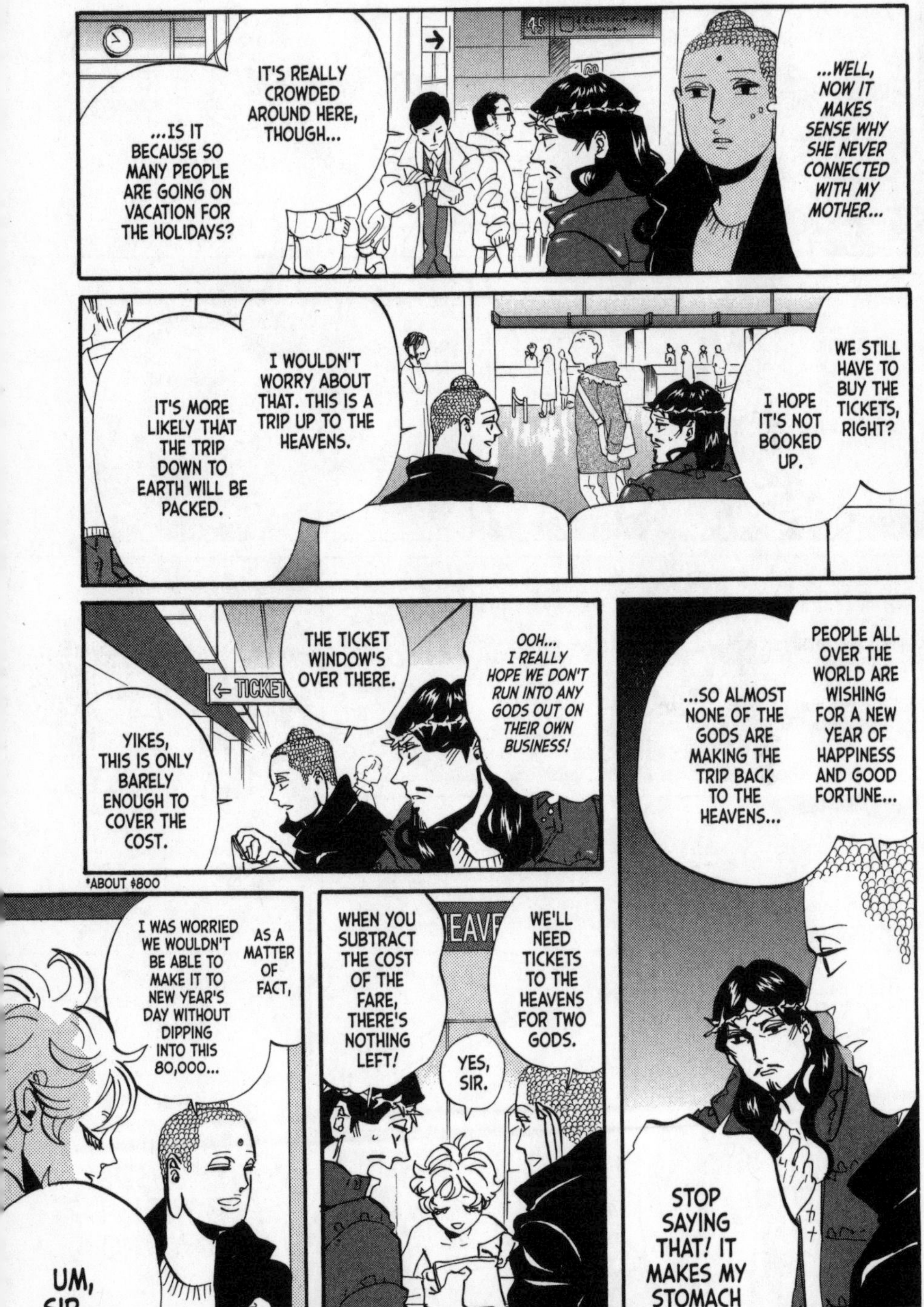
...WELL, NOW IT MAKES SENSE WHY SHE NEVER CONNECTED WITH MY MOTHER...
IT'S REALLY CROWDED AROUND HERE, THOUGH...
...IS IT BECAUSE SO MANY PEOPLE ARE GOING ON VACATION FOR THE HOLIDAYS?
WE STILL HAVE TO BUY THE TICKETS, RIGHT?
I HOPE IT'S NOT BOOKED UP.
I WOULDN'T WORRY ABOUT THAT. THIS IS A TRIP UP TO THE HEAVENS.
IT'S MORE LIKELY THAT THE TRIP DOWN TO EARTH WILL BE PACKED.
PEOPLE ALL OVER THE WORLD ARE WISHING FOR A NEW YEAR OF HAPPINESS AND GOOD FORTUNE...
...SO ALMOST NONE OF THE GODS ARE MAKING THE TRIP BACK TO THE HEAVENS...
STOP SAYING THAT! IT MAKES MY STOMACH HURT!
OOH... I REALLY HOPE WE DON'T RUN INTO ANY GODS OUT ON THEIR OWN BUSINESS!
THE TICKET WINDOW'S OVER THERE.
YIKES, THIS IS ONLY BARELY ENOUGH TO COVER THE COST.
WE'LL NEED TICKETS TO THE HEAVENS FOR TWO GODS.
WHEN YOU SUBTRACT THE COST OF THE FARE, THERE'S NOTHING LEFT!
YES, SIR.
AS A MATTER OF FACT,
I WAS WORRIED WE WOULDN'T BE ABLE TO MAKE IT TO NEW YEAR'S DAY WITHOUT DIPPING INTO THIS 80,000...
UM, SIR...

*ABOUT $800

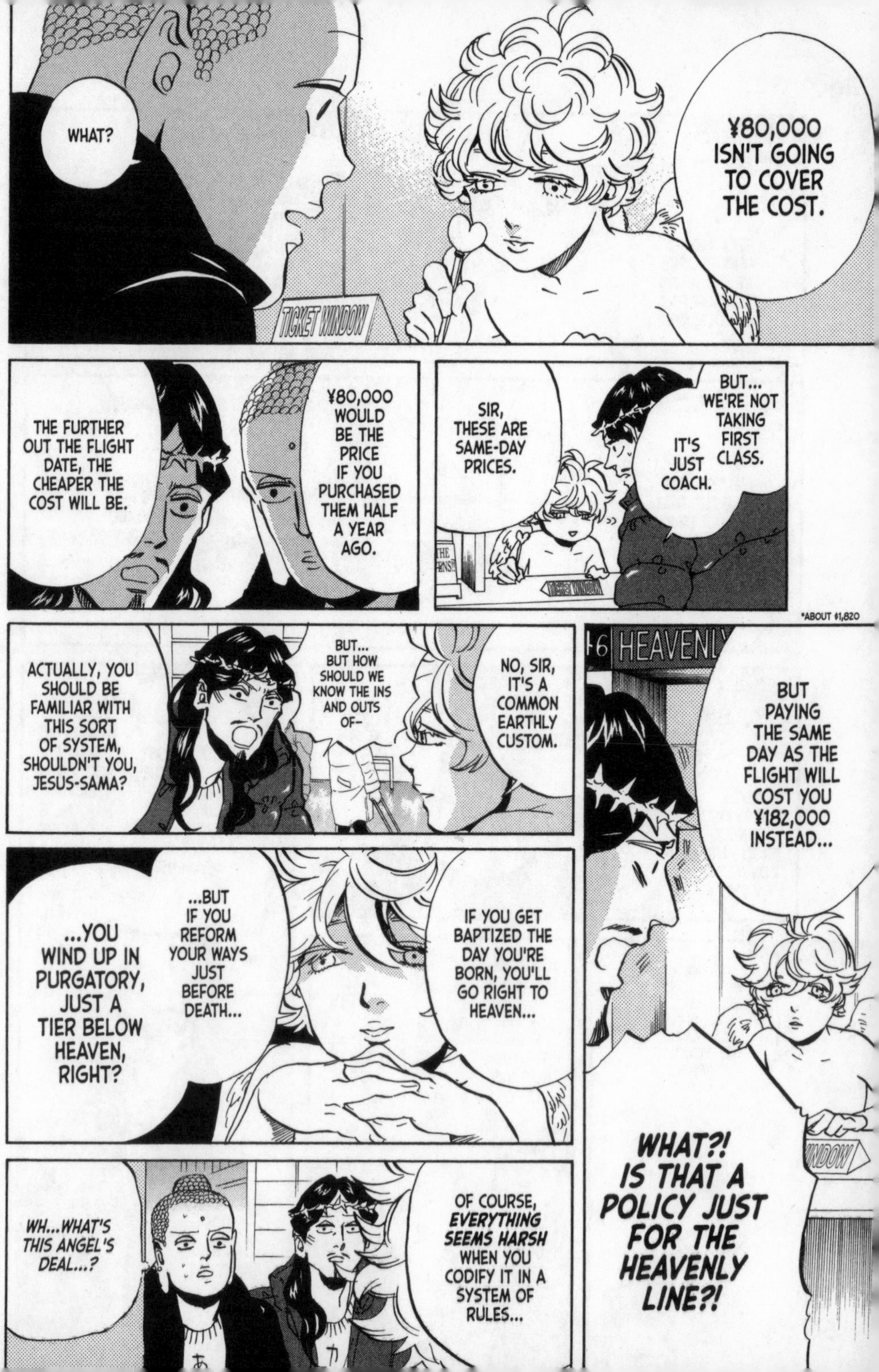
¥80,000 ISN'T GOING TO COVER THE COST.
WHAT?
TICKET WINDOW
BUT... WE'RE NOT TAKING FIRST CLASS.
IT'S JUST COACH.
SIR, THESE ARE SAME-DAY PRICES.
TICKET WINDOW
¥80,000 WOULD BE THE PRICE IF YOU PURCHASED THEM HALF A YEAR AGO.
THE FURTHER OUT THE FLIGHT DATE, THE CHEAPER THE COST WILL BE.
*ABOUT $1,820
46 HEAVENLY
BUT PAYING THE SAME DAY AS THE FLIGHT WILL COST YOU ¥182,000 INSTEAD...
WHAT?! IS THAT A POLICY JUST FOR THE HEAVENLY LINE?!
NO, SIR, IT'S A COMMON EARTHLY CUSTOM.
BUT... BUT HOW SHOULD WE KNOW THE INS AND OUTS OF–
ACTUALLY, YOU SHOULD BE FAMILIAR WITH THIS SORT OF SYSTEM, SHOULDN'T YOU, JESUS-SAMA?
IF YOU GET BAPTIZED THE DAY YOU'RE BORN, YOU'LL GO RIGHT TO HEAVEN...
...BUT IF YOU REFORM YOUR WAYS JUST BEFORE DEATH...
...YOU WIND UP IN PURGATORY, JUST A TIER BELOW HEAVEN, RIGHT?
OF COURSE, EVERYTHING SEEMS HARSH WHEN YOU CODIFY IT IN A SYSTEM OF RULES...
WH...WHAT'S THIS ANGEL'S DEAL...?

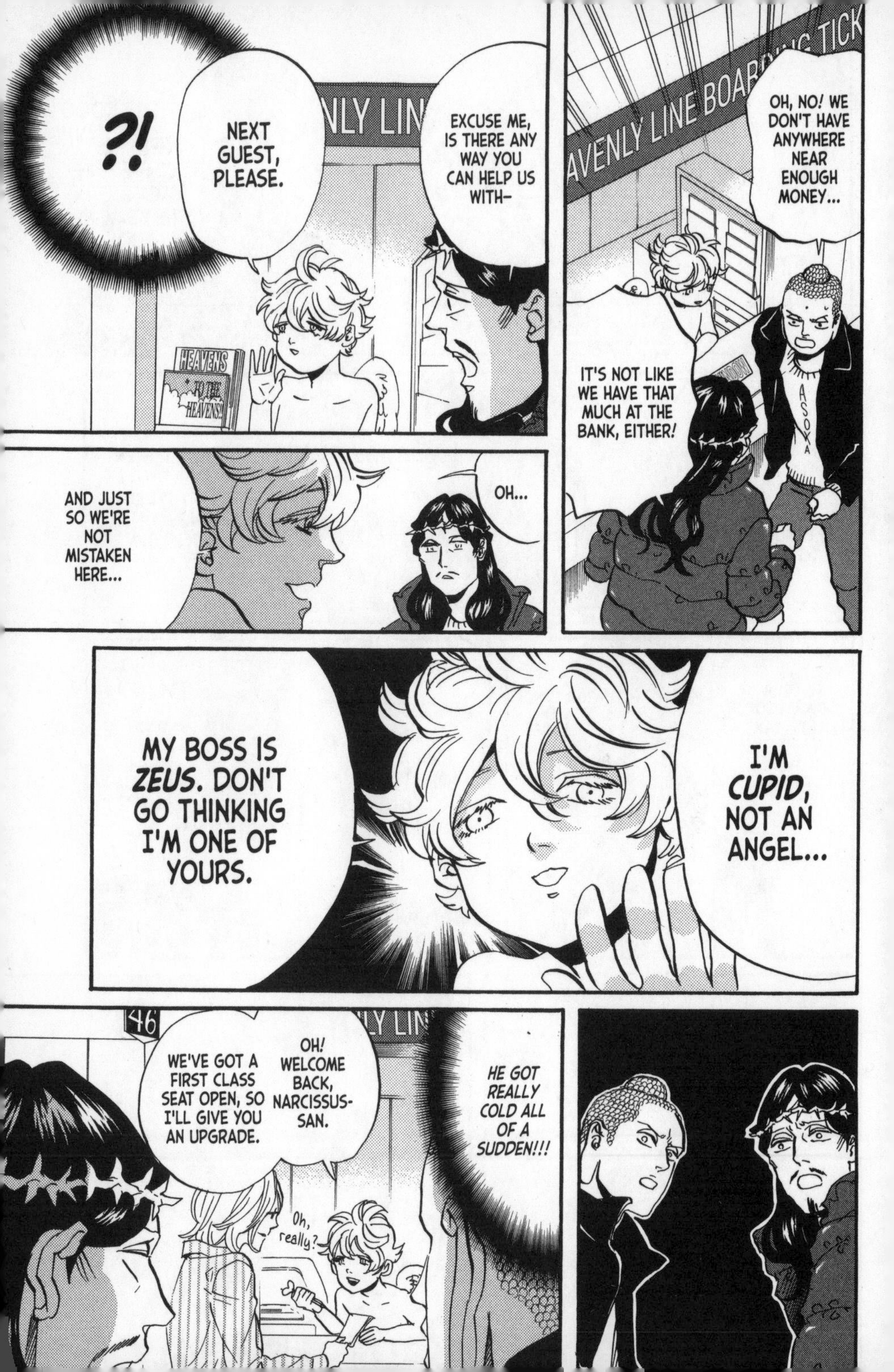
AVENLY LINE BOARDING TICK
OH, NO! WE DON'T HAVE ANYWHERE NEAR ENOUGH MONEY...
IT'S NOT LIKE WE HAVE THAT MUCH AT THE BANK, EITHER!
ASOYA
EXCUSE ME, IS THERE ANY WAY YOU CAN HELP US WITH–
NEXT GUEST, PLEASE.
?!
HEAVENS TO THE HEAVENS!
OH...
AND JUST SO WE'RE NOT MISTAKEN HERE...
I'M CUPID, NOT AN ANGEL...
MY BOSS IS ZEUS. DON'T GO THINKING I'M ONE OF YOURS.
HE GOT REALLY COLD ALL OF A SUDDEN!!!
46
OH! WELCOME BACK, NARCISSUS-SAN.
WE'VE GOT A FIRST CLASS SEAT OPEN, SO I'LL GIVE YOU AN UPGRADE.
Oh, really?

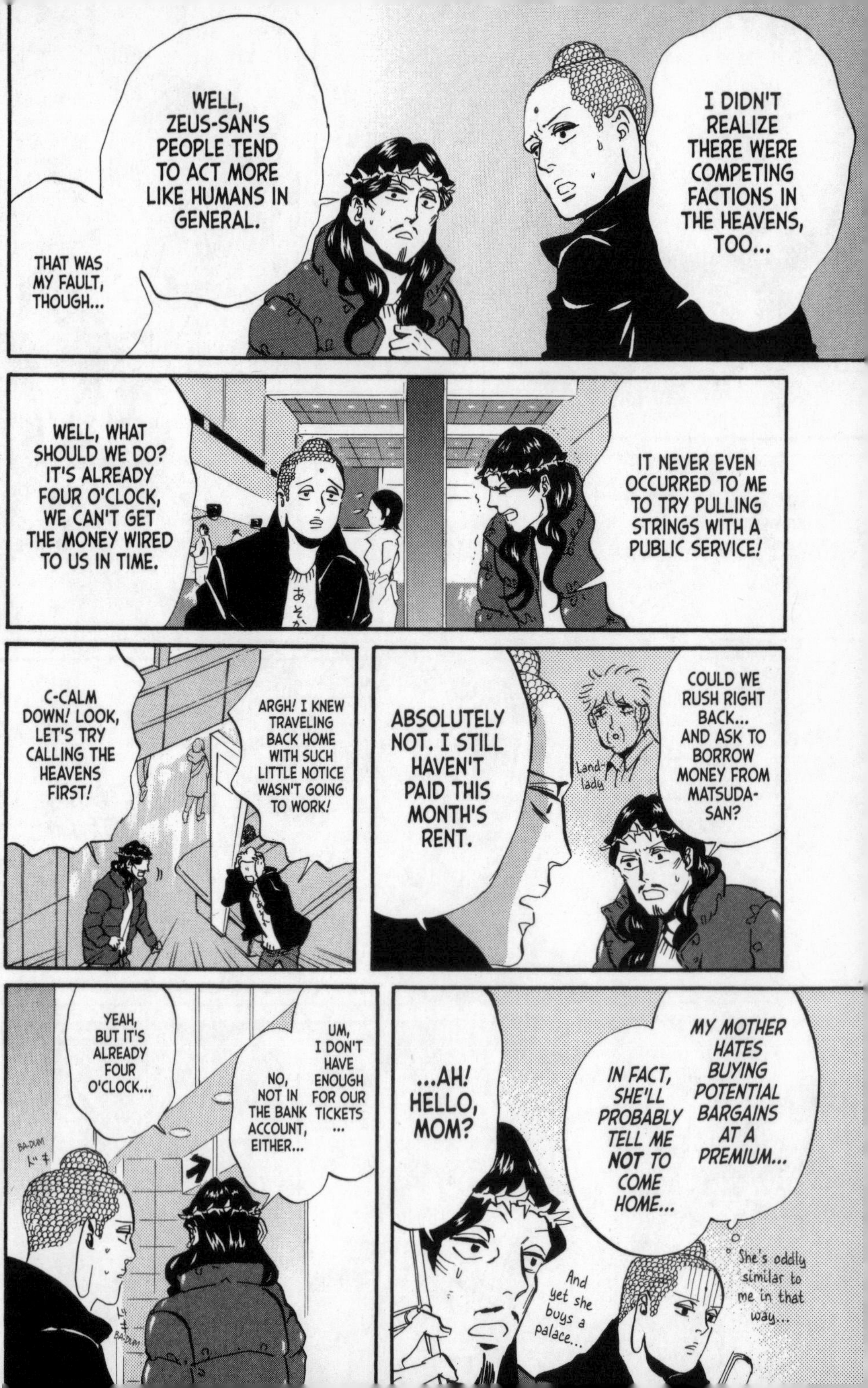
I DIDN'T REALIZE THERE WERE COMPETING FACTIONS IN THE HEAVENS, TOO...
WELL, ZEUS-SAN'S PEOPLE TEND TO ACT MORE LIKE HUMANS IN GENERAL.
THAT WAS MY FAULT, THOUGH...
IT NEVER EVEN OCCURRED TO ME TO TRY PULLING STRINGS WITH A PUBLIC SERVICE!
WELL, WHAT SHOULD WE DO? IT'S ALREADY FOUR O'CLOCK, WE CAN'T GET THE MONEY WIRED TO US IN TIME.
COULD WE RUSH RIGHT BACK... AND ASK TO BORROW MONEY FROM MATSUDA-SAN?
Land-lady
ABSOLUTELY NOT. I STILL HAVEN'T PAID THIS MONTH'S RENT.
ARGH! I KNEW TRAVELING BACK HOME WITH SUCH LITTLE NOTICE WASN'T GOING TO WORK!
C-CALM DOWN! LOOK, LET'S TRY CALLING THE HEAVENS FIRST!
MY MOTHER HATES BUYING POTENTIAL BARGAINS AT A PREMIUM...
IN FACT, SHE'LL PROBABLY TELL ME NOT TO COME HOME...
...AH! HELLO, MOM?
She's oddly similar to me in that way...
And yet she buys a palace...
UM, I DON'T HAVE ENOUGH FOR OUR TICKETS...
NO, NOT IN THE BANK ACCOUNT, EITHER...
YEAH, BUT IT'S ALREADY FOUR O'CLOCK...
BA-DUM ドキ
BA-DUM ドキ

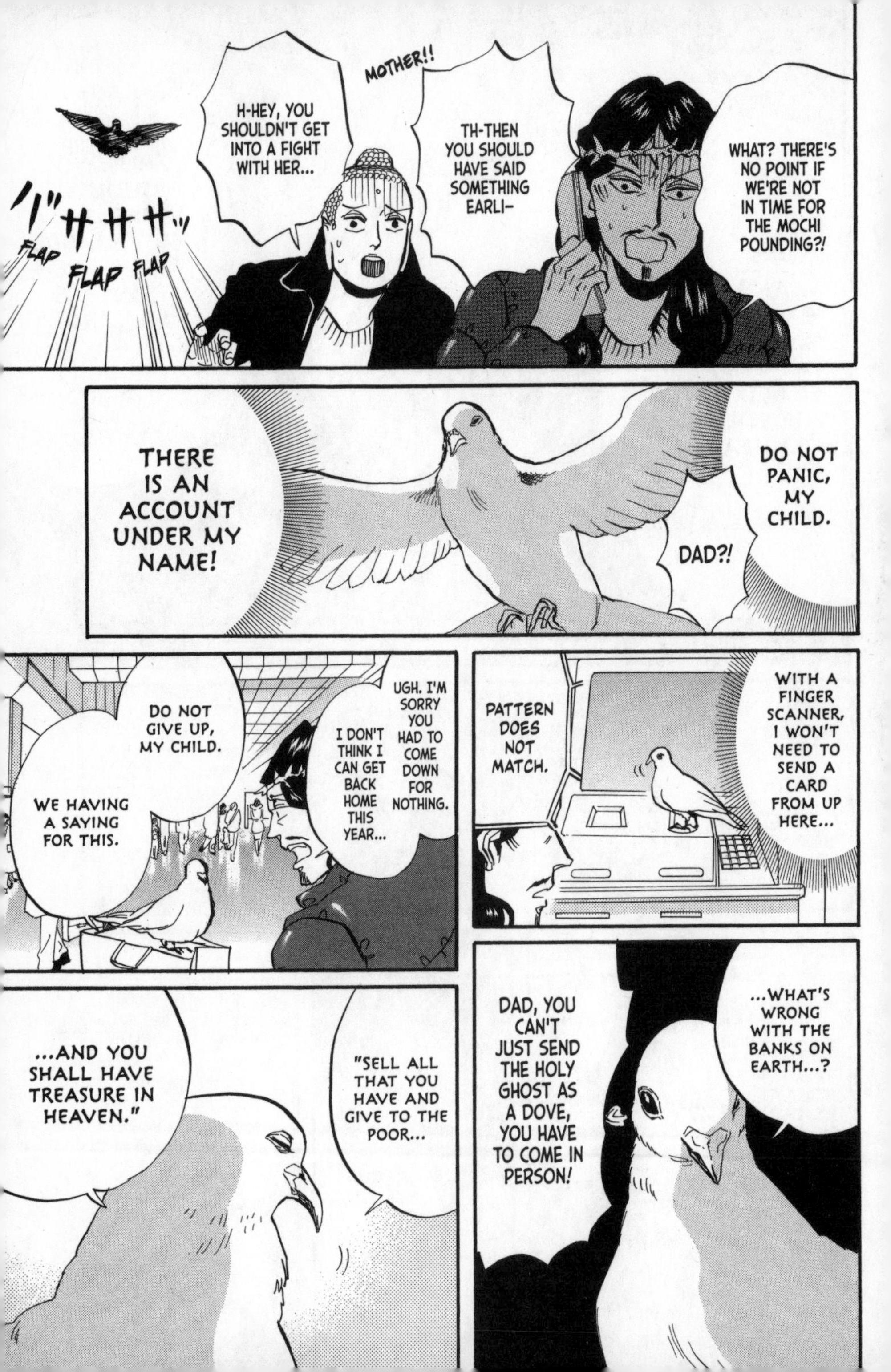
WHAT? THERE'S NO POINT IF WE'RE NOT IN TIME FOR THE MOCHI POUNDING?!
TH-THEN YOU SHOULD HAVE SAID SOMETHING EARLI–
MOTHER!!
H-HEY, YOU SHOULDN'T GET INTO A FIGHT WITH HER...
バサササッ
FLAP FLAP FLAP
DO NOT PANIC, MY CHILD.
DAD?!
THERE IS AN ACCOUNT UNDER MY NAME!
WITH A FINGER SCANNER, I WON'T NEED TO SEND A CARD FROM UP HERE...
PATTERN DOES NOT MATCH.
UGH. I'M SORRY YOU HAD TO COME DOWN FOR NOTHING.
I DON'T THINK I CAN GET BACK HOME THIS YEAR...
DO NOT GIVE UP, MY CHILD.
WE HAVING A SAYING FOR THIS.
...WHAT'S WRONG WITH THE BANKS ON EARTH...?
DAD, YOU CAN'T JUST SEND THE HOLY GHOST AS A DOVE, YOU HAVE TO COME IN PERSON!
"SELL ALL THAT YOU HAVE AND GIVE TO THE POOR...
...AND YOU SHALL HAVE TREASURE IN HEAVEN."

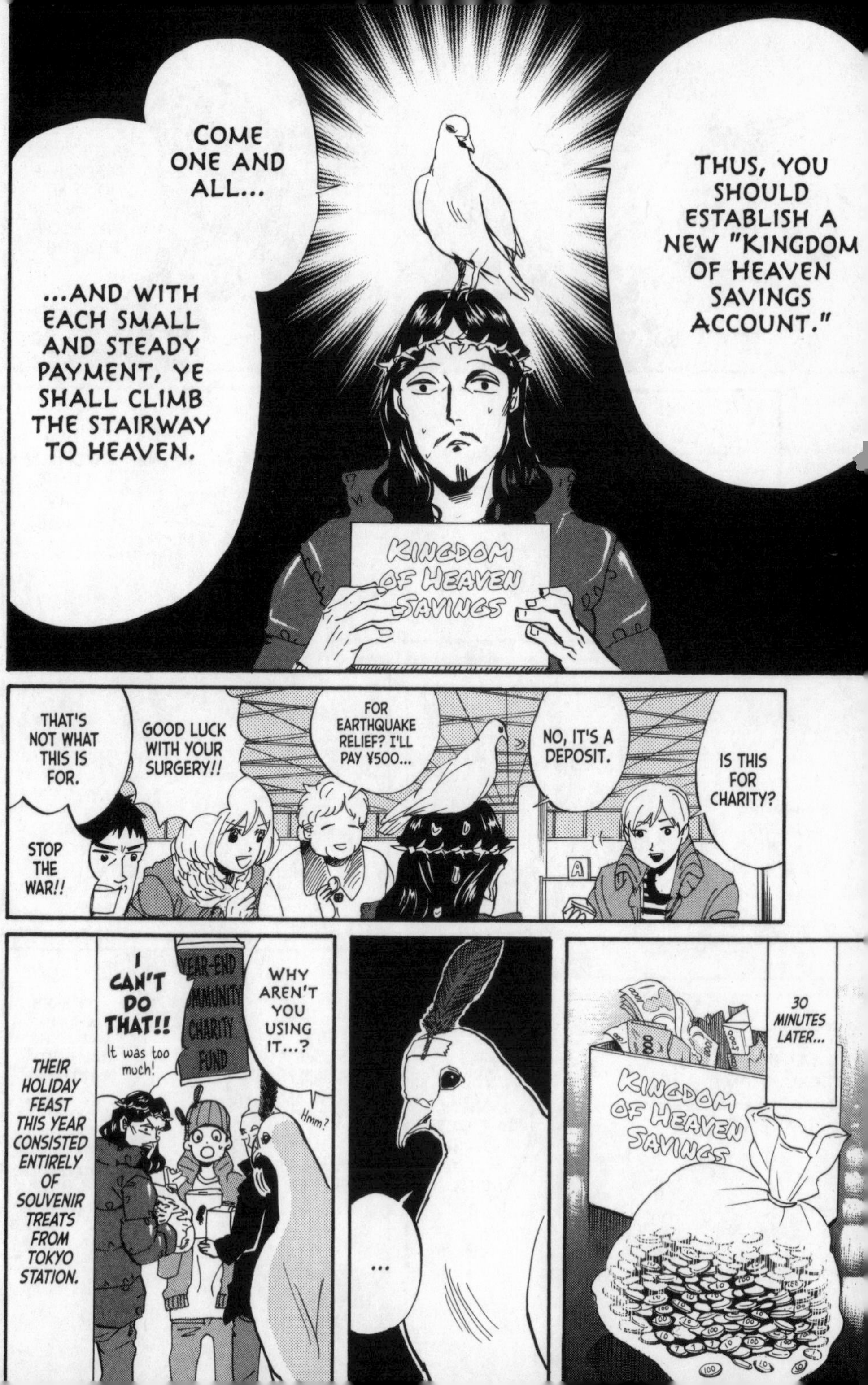

THUS, YOU SHOULD ESTABLISH A NEW "KINGDOM OF HEAVEN SAVINGS ACCOUNT."
COME ONE AND ALL...
...AND WITH EACH SMALL AND STEADY PAYMENT, YE SHALL CLIMB THE STAIRWAY TO HEAVEN.
KINGDOM OF HEAVEN SAVINGS
IS THIS FOR CHARITY?
NO, IT'S A DEPOSIT.
FOR EARTHQUAKE RELIEF? I'LL PAY ¥500...
GOOD LUCK WITH YOUR SURGERY!!
THAT'S NOT WHAT THIS IS FOR.
STOP THE WAR!!
30 MINUTES LATER...
KINGDOM OF HEAVEN SAVINGS
...
WHY AREN'T YOU USING IT...?
Hmm?
I CAN'T DO THAT!!
It was too much!
EAR-END MMUNITY CHARITY FUND
THEIR HOLIDAY FEAST THIS YEAR CONSISTED ENTIRELY OF SOUVENIR TREATS FROM TOKYO STATION.

Buddha's Palace For his Trip Home
Big, isn't it?
If I go there, they'll never let me back out...
GULP...

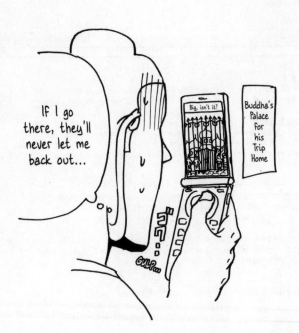

CHAPTER 44 TRANSLATION NOTES

Shakya Clan, page 3
The Shakya clan to which Siddhartha Gautama (the Buddha) was born were held to be a proud and arrogant people by their neighbors, and were eventually destroyed by a rival clan.

Oseibo, **page 4**
A traditional mid-December gift tradition in Japan, *oseibo* is a formal type of present typically packed into ceremonial boxes and given to those to whom you are indebted, such as relatives, arranged-marriage matchmakers, work superiors, etc. The gift is most often something that will aid the New Year celebration, such as alcohol, ham, sausage, fish, and so on.

What have I to do with thee?, page 6
A quote that is attributed to Jesus in John 2:4, when he performed the miracle of turning water into wine. This was said to be the first of Jesus's miracles. The wedding was in a place called Cana (the name on Jesus's shirt in this chapter) in Galilee.

Ashoka, page 7
The name of the type of tree, *Saraca asoca*, that the Buddha is said to have been born underneath. Ashoka are prized for their beautiful and fragrant flowers. Ashoka is also the name of one of the more famous rulers of pre-modern South Asia, who is said to have converted to Buddhism after reflecting on the toll of his violent military campaigns, and then spread the teachings of the Buddha across the expanse of his new empire that occupied present day India, Nepal, Pakistan and Bengal.

Hato sablé, Hiyoko, Tokyo Banana, page 7
All of the items seen here are types of treats considered local to Tokyo. Hato sablé is a dove-shaped butter cookie sold in Kamakura. Hiyoko pastries are shaped like chicks. Tokyo Banana is a brand of soft banana sponge cakes that resemble Twinkies.

Kiyoshi, page 8
A reference to popular enka (a subgenre of popular songs resembling traditional Japanese music) singer Kiyoshi Hikawa. For being a younger man in the more old-fashioned and traditional enka style, his handsome looks earned him the title of the "Prince of Enka."

Weeping statues, page 9
A widely-reported phenomenon of statues of the Virgin Mary shedding tears, sometimes of blood or oil. When such a statue is sighted it can bring many pilgrims hoping to witness its miraculous power.

Toast in the mouth, page 10
An oft-parodied form of the "meet cute" trope in romantic manga for girls. A typical situation would be a girl running late to school with a piece of toast in her mouth. She bumps into a boy around a blind corner, and when she arrives at school later, he is introduced as a new transfer student. Despite being initially repulsed by him, she eventually falls in love.

Purgatory, page 12
An concept of the afterlife most associated with Catholicism. Purgatory is a place where those who are "imperfectly purified" can be cleansed before they are ready to go into Heaven.

Cupid, page 13
The Roman god of desire and erotic love, often associated with the bow and arrow. Over time, Cupid's iconography was absorbed into Christian art, such that he is typically depicted today as a kind of cherub most active on Valentine's Day as a matchmaker.

Narcissus, page 13
A figure in Greek mythology who was so beautiful that he gazed at his own reflection in the water. The source of the word "narcissism."

Mochi **pounding, page 15**
Mochi are glutinous rice cakes that are most associated with the new year. The traditional method of making *mochi* is called *mochitsuki*, or "*mochi* pounding." The kneaded rice is placed in a mortar and mashed with a large wooden mallet by one person, while a second person flips the *mochi* and keeps it wet in between strikes. It is done quickly, so rhythm is essential to avoid injury.

Sell all that you have and give to the poor, page 15
A quote attributed to Jesus in an episode recorded in the gospels of Matthew, Mark, and Luke. When a rich man asks Jesus what he can do to enter heaven, Jesus advises him to give away all his wealth. In Luke, this is the source of the famous quote that it is easier for a camel to pass through the eye of a needle than for a rich man to enter the kingdom of heaven.

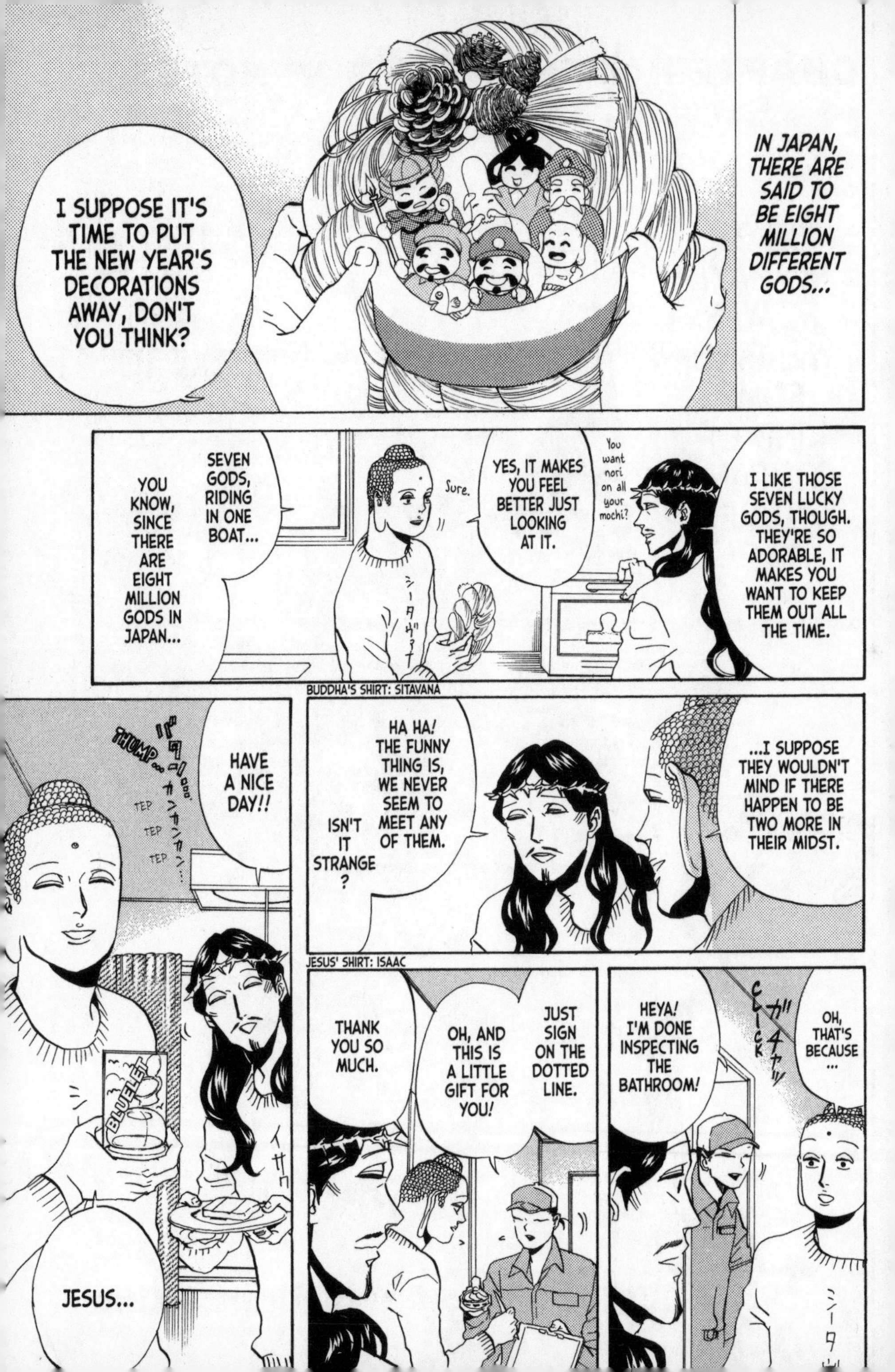
IN JAPAN, THERE ARE SAID TO BE EIGHT MILLION DIFFERENT GODS...
I SUPPOSE IT'S TIME TO PUT THE NEW YEAR'S DECORATIONS AWAY, DON'T YOU THINK?
I LIKE THOSE SEVEN LUCKY GODS, THOUGH. THEY'RE SO ADORABLE, IT MAKES YOU WANT TO KEEP THEM OUT ALL THE TIME.
You want nori on all your mochi?
YES, IT MAKES YOU FEEL BETTER JUST LOOKING AT IT.
Sure.
SEVEN GODS, RIDING IN ONE BOAT...
YOU KNOW, SINCE THERE ARE EIGHT MILLION GODS IN JAPAN...
BUDDHA'S SHIRT: SITAVANA
...I SUPPOSE THEY WOULDN'T MIND IF THERE HAPPEN TO BE TWO MORE IN THEIR MIDST.
HA HA! THE FUNNY THING IS, WE NEVER SEEM TO MEET ANY OF THEM.
ISN'T IT STRANGE?
JESUS' SHIRT: ISAAC
OH, THAT'S BECAUSE...
CLICK
HEYA! I'M DONE INSPECTING THE BATHROOM!
JUST SIGN ON THE DOTTED LINE.
OH, AND THIS IS A LITTLE GIFT FOR YOU!
THANK YOU SO MUCH.
HAVE A NICE DAY!!
THUMP...
TEP
TEP
TEP
BLUELET
JESUS...

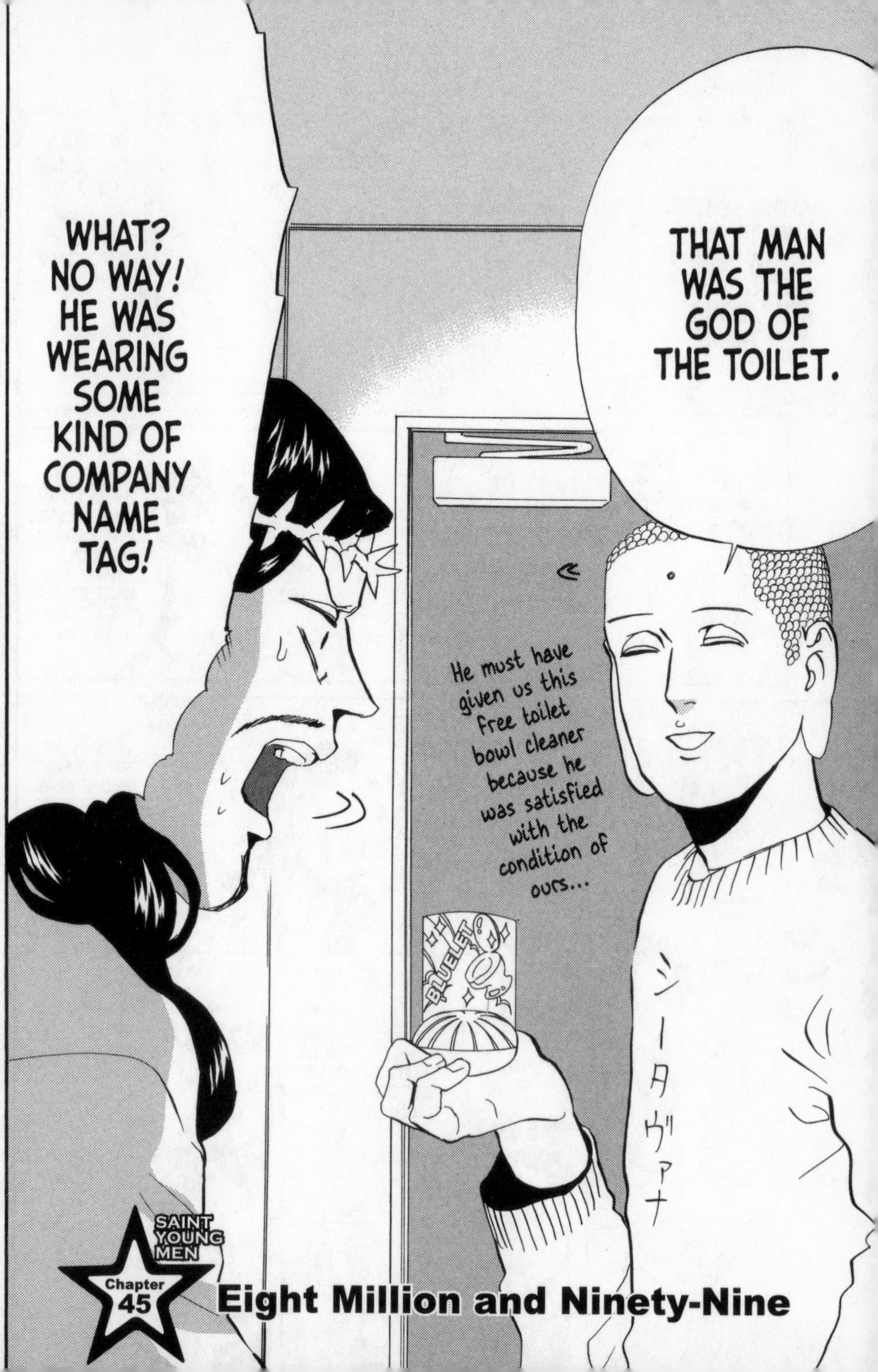
THAT MAN WAS THE GOD OF THE TOILET.
He must have given us this free toilet bowl cleaner because he was satisfied with the condition of ours...
シータヴァナ
BLUELET
WHAT? NO WAY! HE WAS WEARING SOME KIND OF COMPANY NAME TAG!
SAINT YOUNG MEN
Chapter 45
Eight Million and Ninety-Nine

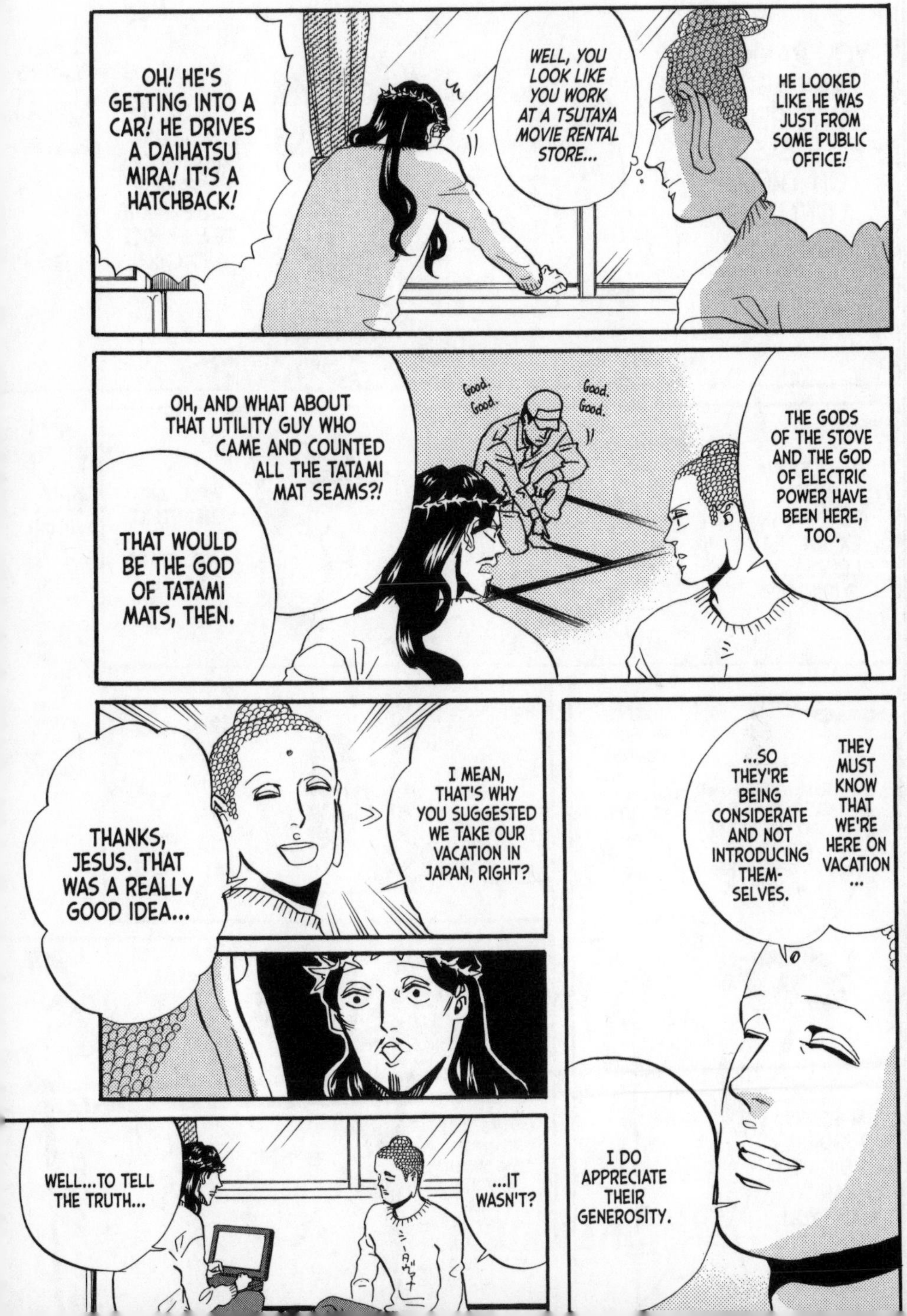
HE LOOKED LIKE HE WAS JUST FROM SOME PUBLIC OFFICE!
WELL, YOU LOOK LIKE YOU WORK AT A TSUTAYA MOVIE RENTAL STORE...
OH! HE'S GETTING INTO A CAR! HE DRIVES A DAIHATSU MIRA! IT'S A HATCHBACK!
THE GODS OF THE STOVE AND THE GOD OF ELECTRIC POWER HAVE BEEN HERE, TOO.
Good. Good.
Good. Good.
OH, AND WHAT ABOUT THAT UTILITY GUY WHO CAME AND COUNTED ALL THE TATAMI MAT SEAMS?!
THAT WOULD BE THE GOD OF TATAMI MATS, THEN.
THEY MUST KNOW THAT WE'RE HERE ON VACATION...
...SO THEY'RE BEING CONSIDERATE AND NOT INTRODUCING THEM-SELVES.
I DO APPRECIATE THEIR GENEROSITY.
I MEAN, THAT'S WHY YOU SUGGESTED WE TAKE OUR VACATION IN JAPAN, RIGHT?
THANKS, JESUS. THAT WAS A REALLY GOOD IDEA...
...IT WASN'T?
WELL...TO TELL THE TRUTH...

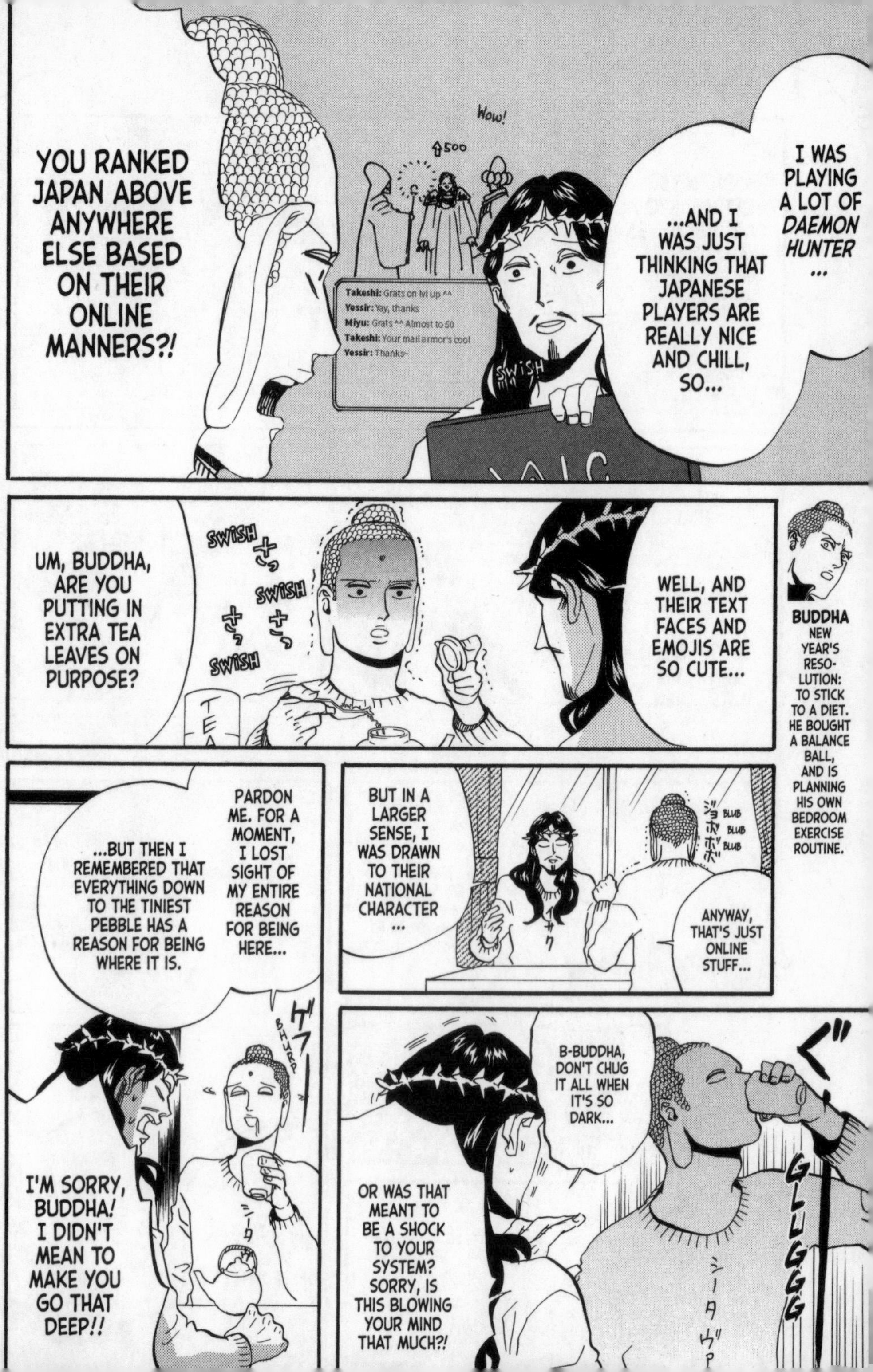
I WAS PLAYING A LOT OF *DAEMON HUNTER*...
...AND I WAS JUST THINKING THAT JAPANESE PLAYERS ARE REALLY NICE AND CHILL, SO...
SWISH
Wow!
⇧500
Takeshi: Grats on lvl up ^^
Yessir: Yay, thanks
Miyu: Grats ^^ Almost to 50
Takeshi: Your mail armor's cool
Yessir: Thanks~
YOU RANKED JAPAN ABOVE ANYWHERE ELSE BASED ON THEIR ONLINE MANNERS?!
BUDDHA NEW YEAR'S RESOLUTION: TO STICK TO A DIET. HE BOUGHT A BALANCE BALL, AND IS PLANNING HIS OWN BEDROOM EXERCISE ROUTINE.
WELL, AND THEIR TEXT FACES AND EMOJIS ARE SO CUTE...
SWISH
SWISH
SWISH
UM, BUDDHA, ARE YOU PUTTING IN EXTRA TEA LEAVES ON PURPOSE?
TEA
BLUB BLUB BLUB
ANYWAY, THAT'S JUST ONLINE STUFF...
BUT IN A LARGER SENSE, I WAS DRAWN TO THEIR NATIONAL CHARACTER...
PARDON ME. FOR A MOMENT, I LOST SIGHT OF MY ENTIRE REASON FOR BEING HERE...
...BUT THEN I REMEMBERED THAT EVERYTHING DOWN TO THE TINIEST PEBBLE HAS A REASON FOR BEING WHERE IT IS.
GLUGG
B-BUDDHA, DON'T CHUG IT ALL WHEN IT'S SO DARK...
OR WAS THAT MEANT TO BE A SHOCK TO YOUR SYSTEM? SORRY, IS THIS BLOWING YOUR MIND THAT MUCH?!
BHURP
I'M SORRY, BUDDHA! I DIDN'T MEAN TO MAKE YOU GO THAT DEEP!!

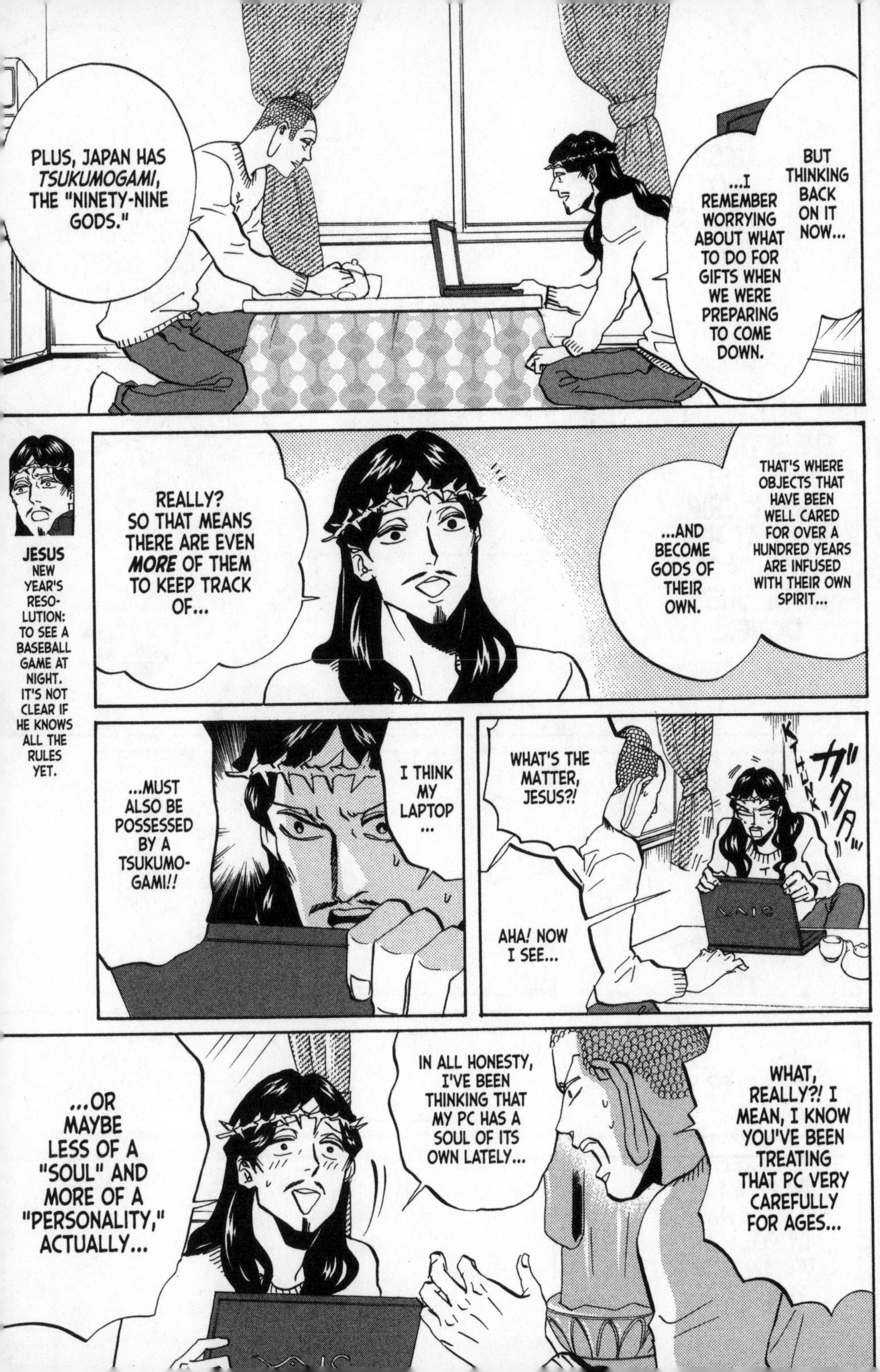
BUT THINKING BACK ON IT NOW...
...I REMEMBER WORRYING ABOUT WHAT TO DO FOR GIFTS WHEN WE WERE PREPARING TO COME DOWN.
PLUS, JAPAN HAS *TSUKUMOGAMI*, THE "NINETY-NINE GODS."
THAT'S WHERE OBJECTS THAT HAVE BEEN WELL CARED FOR OVER A HUNDRED YEARS ARE INFUSED WITH THEIR OWN SPIRIT...
...AND BECOME GODS OF THEIR OWN.
REALLY? SO THAT MEANS THERE ARE EVEN *MORE* OF THEM TO KEEP TRACK OF...
KATHUNK
WHAT'S THE MATTER, JESUS?!
AHA! NOW I SEE...
I THINK MY LAPTOP ...
...MUST ALSO BE POSSESSED BY A TSUKUMO-GAMI!!
WHAT, REALLY?! I MEAN, I KNOW YOU'VE BEEN TREATING THAT PC VERY CAREFULLY FOR AGES...
IN ALL HONESTY, I'VE BEEN THINKING THAT MY PC HAS A SOUL OF ITS OWN LATELY...
...OR MAYBE LESS OF A "SOUL" AND MORE OF A "PERSONALITY," ACTUALLY...
JESUS
NEW YEAR'S RESOLUTION: TO SEE A BASEBALL GAME AT NIGHT. IT'S NOT CLEAR IF HE KNOWS ALL THE RULES YET.

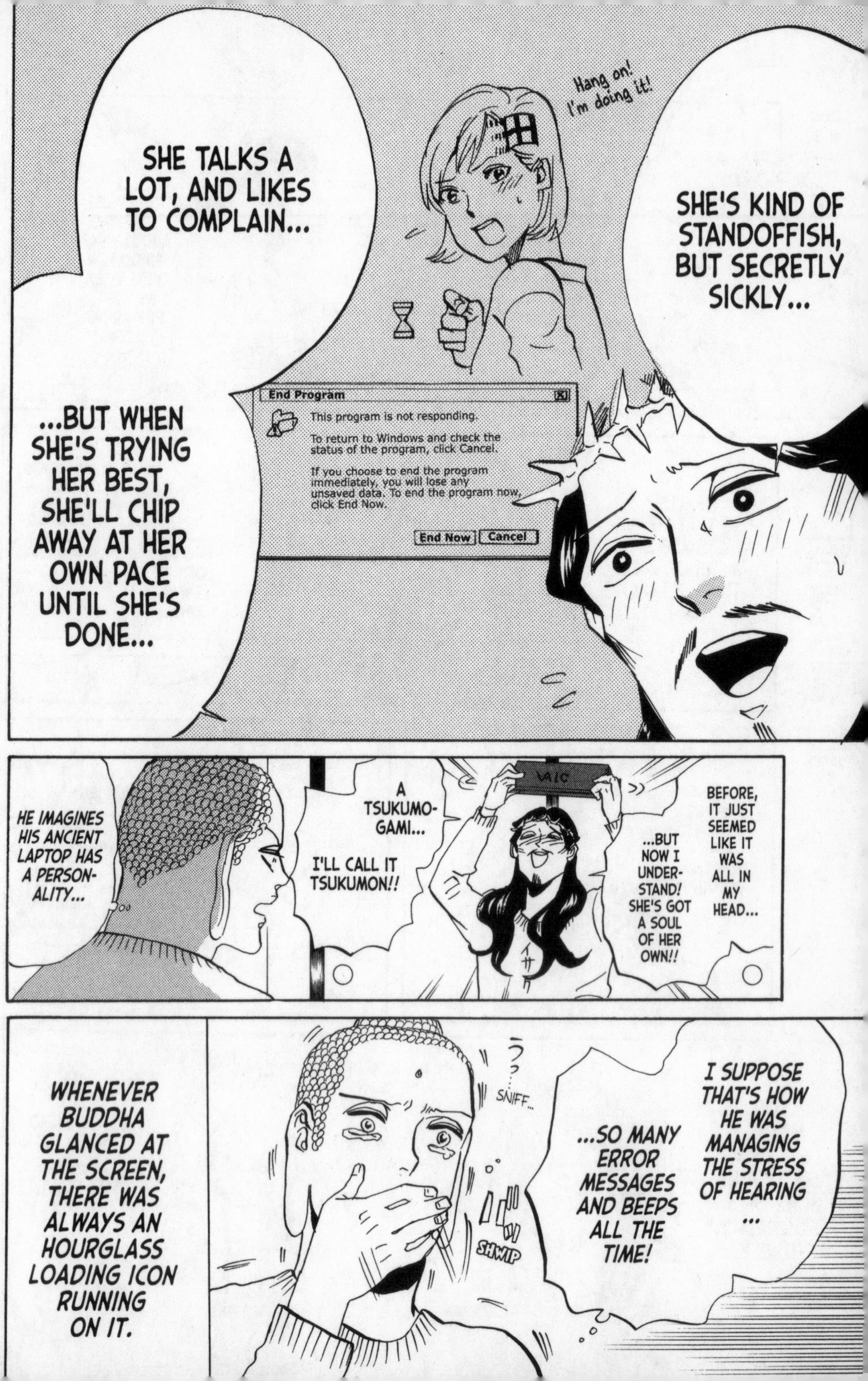
SHE'S KIND OF STANDOFFISH, BUT SECRETLY SICKLY...
Hang on! I'm doing it!
SHE TALKS A LOT, AND LIKES TO COMPLAIN...
End Program
This program is not responding.
To return to Windows and check the status of the program, click Cancel.
If you choose to end the program immediately, you will lose any unsaved data. To end the program now, click End Now.
End Now
Cancel
...BUT WHEN SHE'S TRYING HER BEST, SHE'LL CHIP AWAY AT HER OWN PACE UNTIL SHE'S DONE...
BEFORE, IT JUST SEEMED LIKE IT WAS ALL IN MY HEAD...
...BUT NOW I UNDER-STAND! SHE'S GOT A SOUL OF HER OWN!!
A TSUKUMO-GAMI...
I'LL CALL IT TSUKUMON!!
HE IMAGINES HIS ANCIENT LAPTOP HAS A PERSON-ALITY...
I SUPPOSE THAT'S HOW HE WAS MANAGING THE STRESS OF HEARING ...
...SO MANY ERROR MESSAGES AND BEEPS ALL THE TIME!
SNIFF...
SHWIP
WHENEVER BUDDHA GLANCED AT THE SCREEN, THERE WAS ALWAYS AN HOURGLASS LOADING ICON RUNNING ON IT.

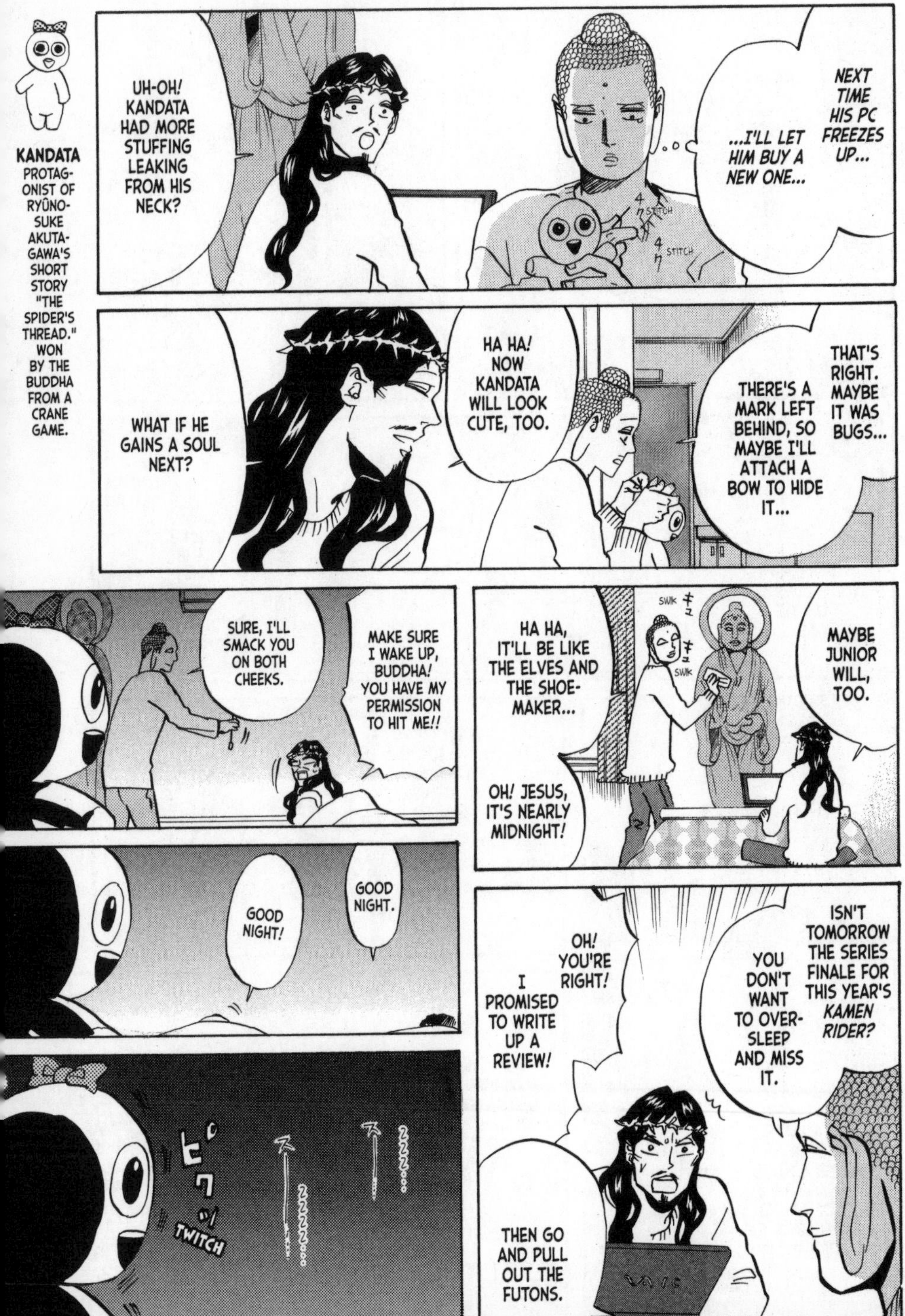
KANDATA
PROTAGONIST OF RYŪNOSUKE AKUTAGAWA'S SHORT STORY "THE SPIDER'S THREAD." WON BY THE BUDDHA FROM A CRANE GAME.
NEXT TIME HIS PC FREEZES UP...
...I'LL LET HIM BUY A NEW ONE...
STITCH
STITCH
UH-OH! KANDATA HAD MORE STUFFING LEAKING FROM HIS NECK?
THAT'S RIGHT. MAYBE IT WAS BUGS...
THERE'S A MARK LEFT BEHIND, SO MAYBE I'LL ATTACH A BOW TO HIDE IT...
HA HA! NOW KANDATA WILL LOOK CUTE, TOO.
WHAT IF HE GAINS A SOUL NEXT?
MAYBE JUNIOR WILL, TOO.
HA HA, IT'LL BE LIKE THE ELVES AND THE SHOEMAKER...
SWIK
SWIK
OH! JESUS, IT'S NEARLY MIDNIGHT!
ISN'T TOMORROW THE SERIES FINALE FOR THIS YEAR'S *KAMEN RIDER?*
YOU DON'T WANT TO OVERSLEEP AND MISS IT.
OH! YOU'RE RIGHT!
I PROMISED TO WRITE UP A REVIEW!
THEN GO AND PULL OUT THE FUTONS.
MAKE SURE I WAKE UP, BUDDHA! YOU HAVE MY PERMISSION TO HIT ME!!
SURE, I'LL SMACK YOU ON BOTH CHEEKS.
GOOD NIGHT.
GOOD NIGHT!
TWITCH

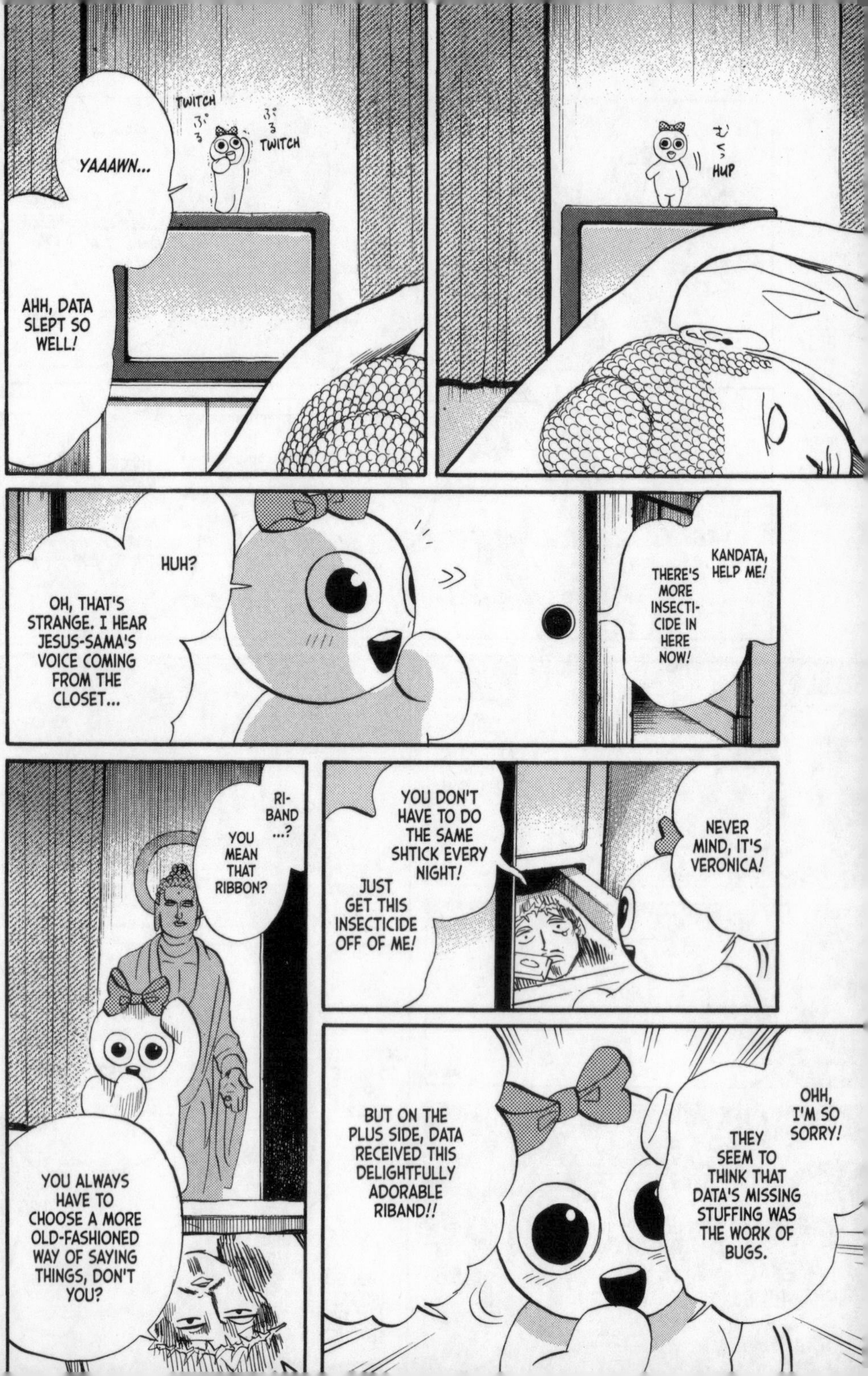

むく
HUP
TWITCH
ぷる
ぷる
TWITCH
YAAAWN...
AHH, DATA SLEPT SO WELL!
KANDATA, HELP ME!
THERE'S MORE INSECTICIDE IN HERE NOW!
HUH?
OH, THAT'S STRANGE. I HEAR JESUS-SAMA'S VOICE COMING FROM THE CLOSET...
NEVER MIND, IT'S VERONICA!
YOU DON'T HAVE TO DO THE SAME SHTICK EVERY NIGHT!
JUST GET THIS INSECTICIDE OFF OF ME!
OHH, I'M SO SORRY!
THEY SEEM TO THINK THAT DATA'S MISSING STUFFING WAS THE WORK OF BUGS.
BUT ON THE PLUS SIDE, DATA RECEIVED THIS DELIGHTFULLY ADORABLE RIBAND!!
RI-BAND ...?
YOU MEAN THAT RIBBON?
YOU ALWAYS HAVE TO CHOOSE A MORE OLD-FASHIONED WAY OF SAYING THINGS, DON'T YOU?

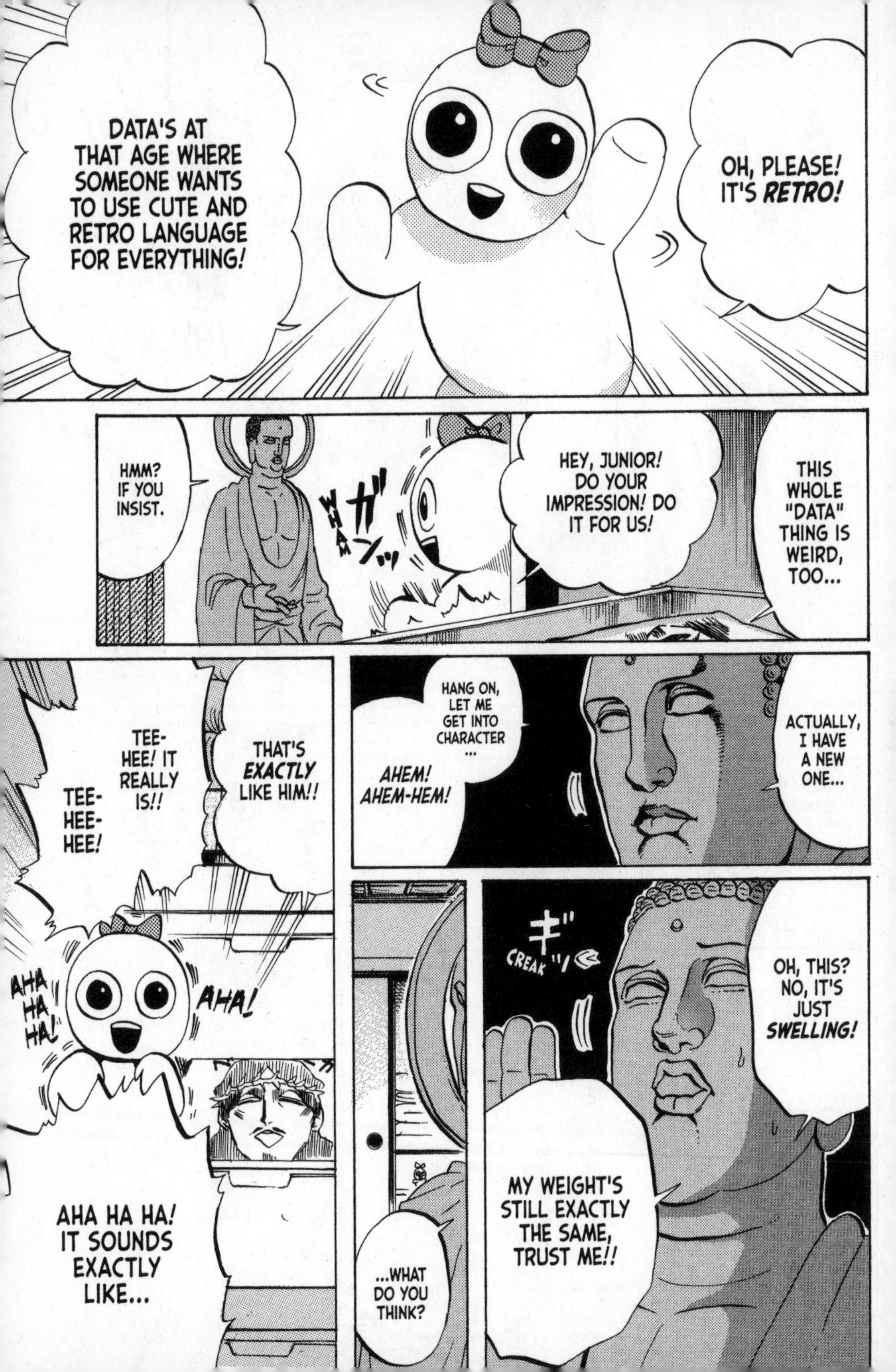
OH, PLEASE! IT'S *RETRO!*
DATA'S AT THAT AGE WHERE SOMEONE WANTS TO USE CUTE AND RETRO LANGUAGE FOR EVERYTHING!
THIS WHOLE "DATA" THING IS WEIRD, TOO...
HEY, JUNIOR! DO YOUR IMPRESSION! DO IT FOR US!
WHAM ガンッ
HMM? IF YOU INSIST.
ACTUALLY, I HAVE A NEW ONE...
HANG ON, LET ME GET INTO CHARACTER...
AHEM! AHEM-HEM!
OH, THIS? NO, IT'S JUST *SWELLING!*
ギ CREAK
MY WEIGHT'S STILL EXACTLY THE SAME, TRUST ME!!
...WHAT DO YOU THINK?
THAT'S *EXACTLY* LIKE HIM!!
TEE-HEE! IT REALLY IS!!
TEE-HEE-HEE!
AHA!
AHA HA HA!
AHA HA HA! IT SOUNDS EXACTLY LIKE...

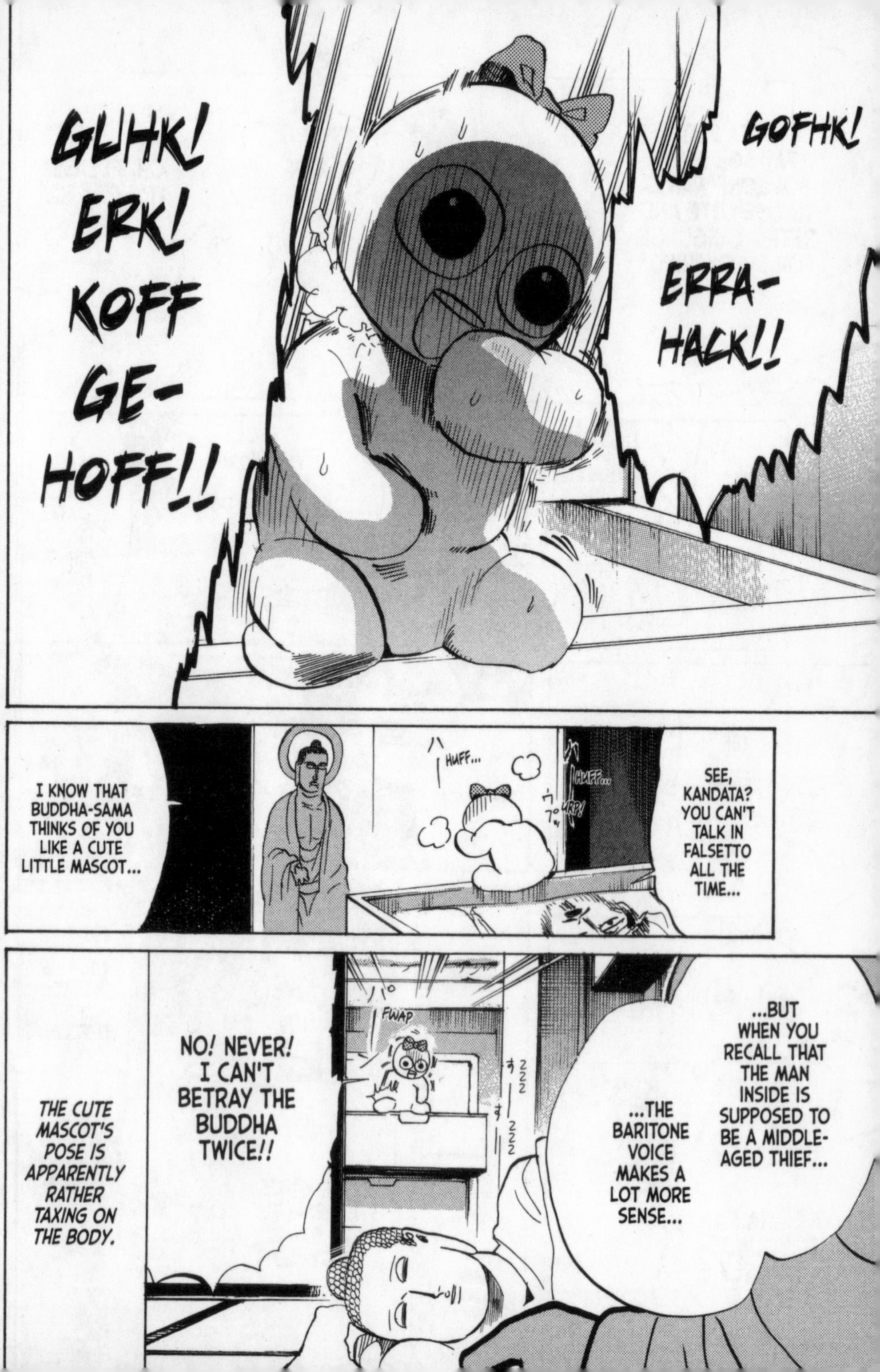
GOFHK!
ERRA-HACK!!
GUHK! ERK! KOFF GE-HOFF!!
SEE, KANDATA? YOU CAN'T TALK IN FALSETTO ALL THE TIME...
HUFF...
HUFF...
URP!
I KNOW THAT BUDDHA-SAMA THINKS OF YOU LIKE A CUTE LITTLE MASCOT...
...BUT WHEN YOU RECALL THAT THE MAN INSIDE IS SUPPOSED TO BE A MIDDLE-AGED THIEF...
...THE BARITONE VOICE MAKES A LOT MORE SENSE...
FWAP
NO! NEVER! I CAN'T BETRAY THE BUDDHA TWICE!!
THE CUTE MASCOT'S POSE IS APPARENTLY RATHER TAXING ON THE BODY.

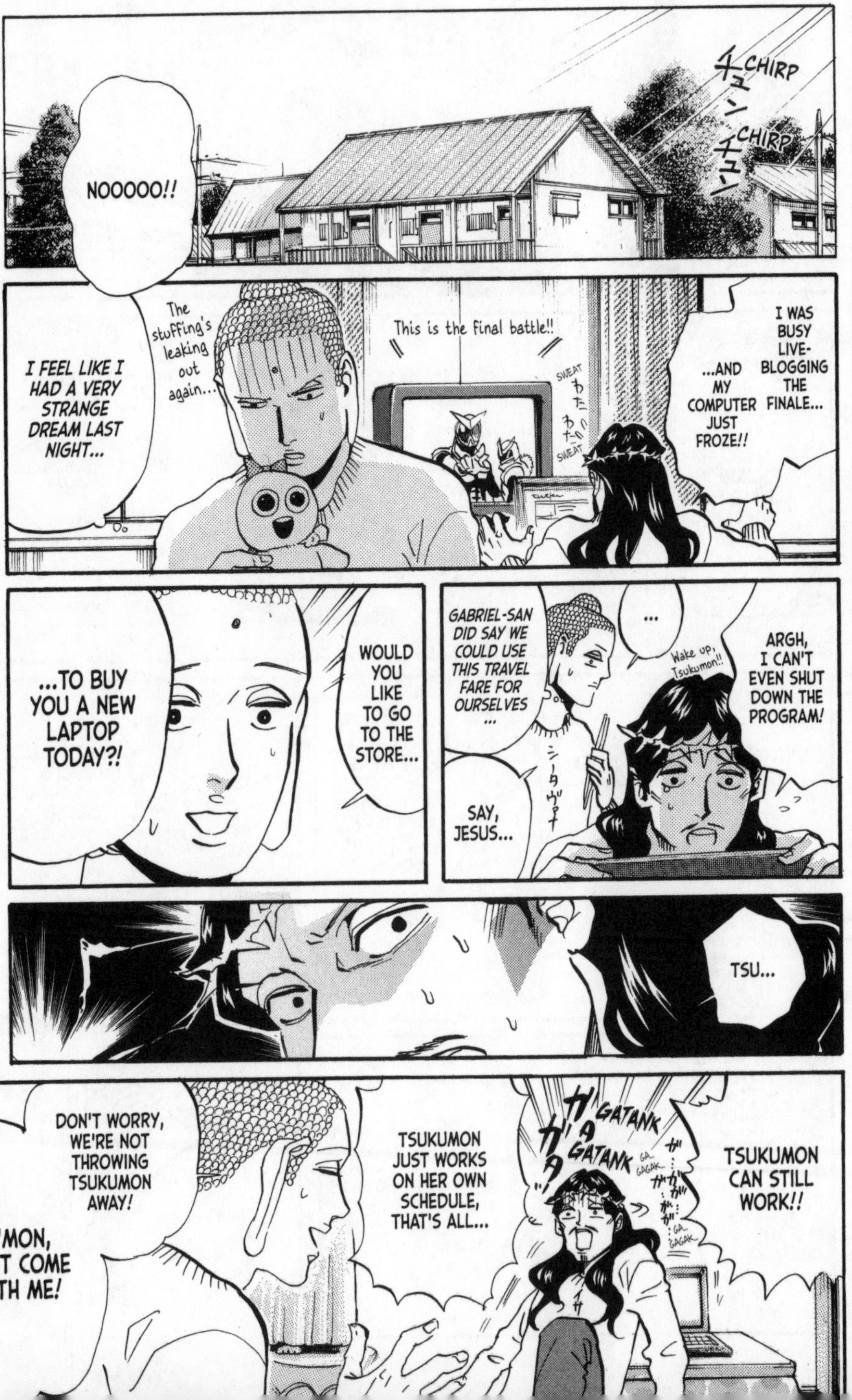
CHIRP
CHIRP
NOOOOO!!
I WAS BUSY LIVE-BLOGGING THE FINALE...
...AND MY COMPUTER JUST FROZE!!
SWEAT
SWEAT
This is the final battle!!
The stuffing's leaking out again...
I FEEL LIKE I HAD A VERY STRANGE DREAM LAST NIGHT...
ARGH, I CAN'T EVEN SHUT DOWN THE PROGRAM!
Wake up, Tsukumon!!
...
GABRIEL-SAN DID SAY WE COULD USE THIS TRAVEL FARE FOR OURSELVES ...
SAY, JESUS...
WOULD YOU LIKE TO GO TO THE STORE...
...TO BUY YOU A NEW LAPTOP TODAY?!
TSU...
TSUKUMON CAN STILL WORK!!
GATANK
GATANK
GA GAGAK
GA GAGAK
TSUKUMON JUST WORKS ON HER OWN SCHEDULE, THAT'S ALL...
DON'T WORRY, WE'RE NOT THROWING TSUKUMON AWAY!
C'MON, JUST COME WITH ME!

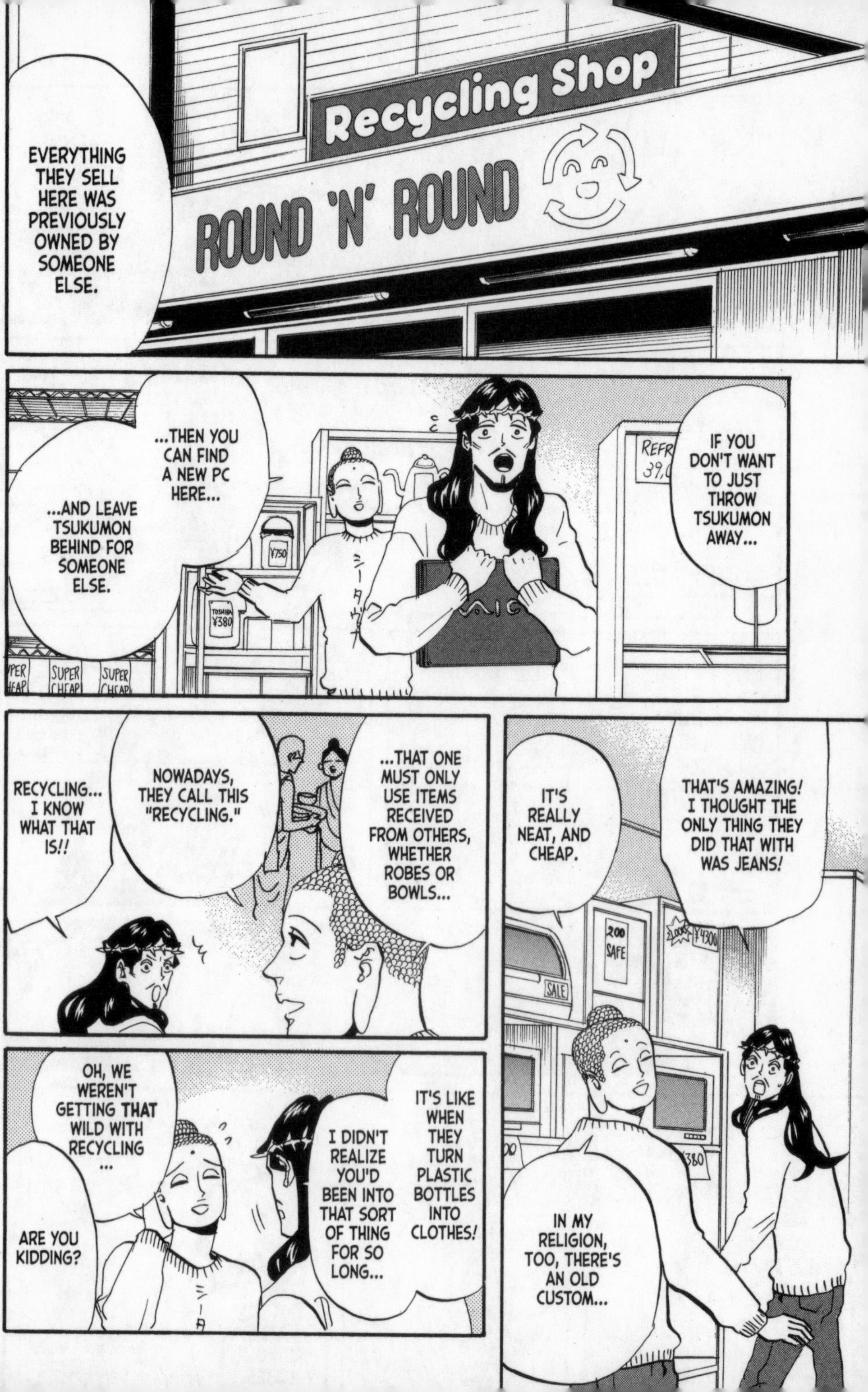
Recycling Shop
ROUND 'N' ROUND
EVERYTHING THEY SELL HERE WAS PREVIOUSLY OWNED BY SOMEONE ELSE.
IF YOU DON'T WANT TO JUST THROW TSUKUMON AWAY...
...THEN YOU CAN FIND A NEW PC HERE...
...AND LEAVE TSUKUMON BEHIND FOR SOMEONE ELSE.
¥750
TOSHIBA ¥380
SUPER CHEAP
THAT'S AMAZING! I THOUGHT THE ONLY THING THEY DID THAT WITH WAS JEANS!
IT'S REALLY NEAT, AND CHEAP.
200 SAFE
SALE
¥4300
IN MY RELIGION, TOO, THERE'S AN OLD CUSTOM...
...THAT ONE MUST ONLY USE ITEMS RECEIVED FROM OTHERS, WHETHER ROBES OR BOWLS...
NOWADAYS, THEY CALL THIS "RECYCLING."
RECYCLING... I KNOW WHAT THAT IS!!
IT'S LIKE WHEN THEY TURN PLASTIC BOTTLES INTO CLOTHES!
I DIDN'T REALIZE YOU'D BEEN INTO THAT SORT OF THING FOR SO LONG...
OH, WE WEREN'T GETTING THAT WILD WITH RECYCLING ...
ARE YOU KIDDING?

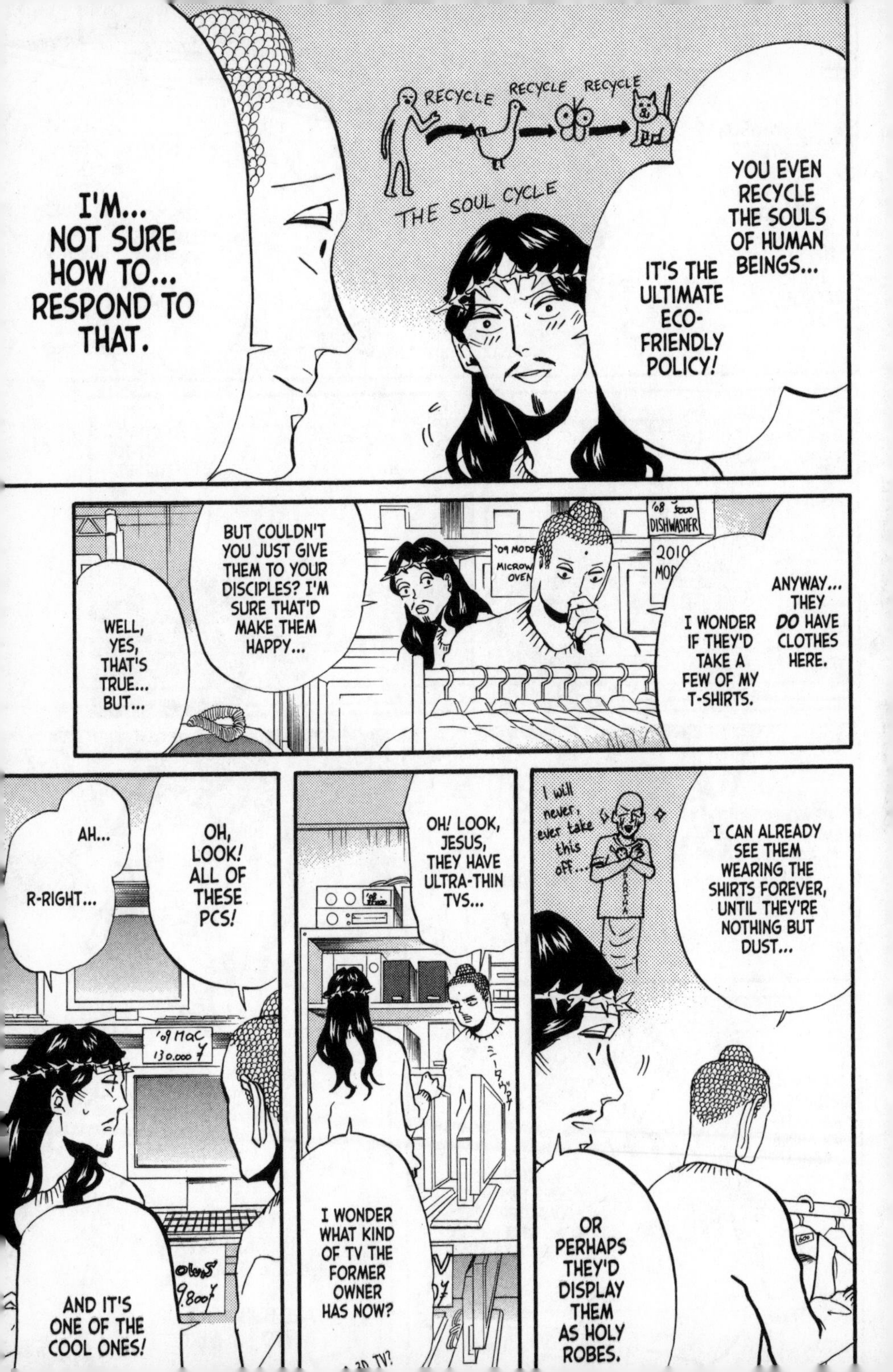
YOU EVEN RECYCLE THE SOULS OF HUMAN BEINGS...
IT'S THE ULTIMATE ECO-FRIENDLY POLICY!
RECYCLE RECYCLE RECYCLE
THE SOUL CYCLE
I'M... NOT SURE HOW TO... RESPOND TO THAT.
ANYWAY... THEY *DO* HAVE CLOTHES HERE.
I WONDER IF THEY'D TAKE A FEW OF MY T-SHIRTS.
DISHWASHER
BUT COULDN'T YOU JUST GIVE THEM TO YOUR DISCIPLES? I'M SURE THAT'D MAKE THEM HAPPY...
WELL, YES, THAT'S TRUE... BUT...
I CAN ALREADY SEE THEM WEARING THE SHIRTS FOREVER, UNTIL THEY'RE NOTHING BUT DUST...
I will never, ever take this off...
OR PERHAPS THEY'D DISPLAY THEM AS HOLY ROBES.
OH! LOOK, JESUS, THEY HAVE ULTRA-THIN TVS...
I WONDER WHAT KIND OF TV THE FORMER OWNER HAS NOW?
OH, LOOK! ALL OF THESE PCS!
'09 MaC 130,000¥
AH...
R-RIGHT...
AND IT'S ONE OF THE COOL ONES!

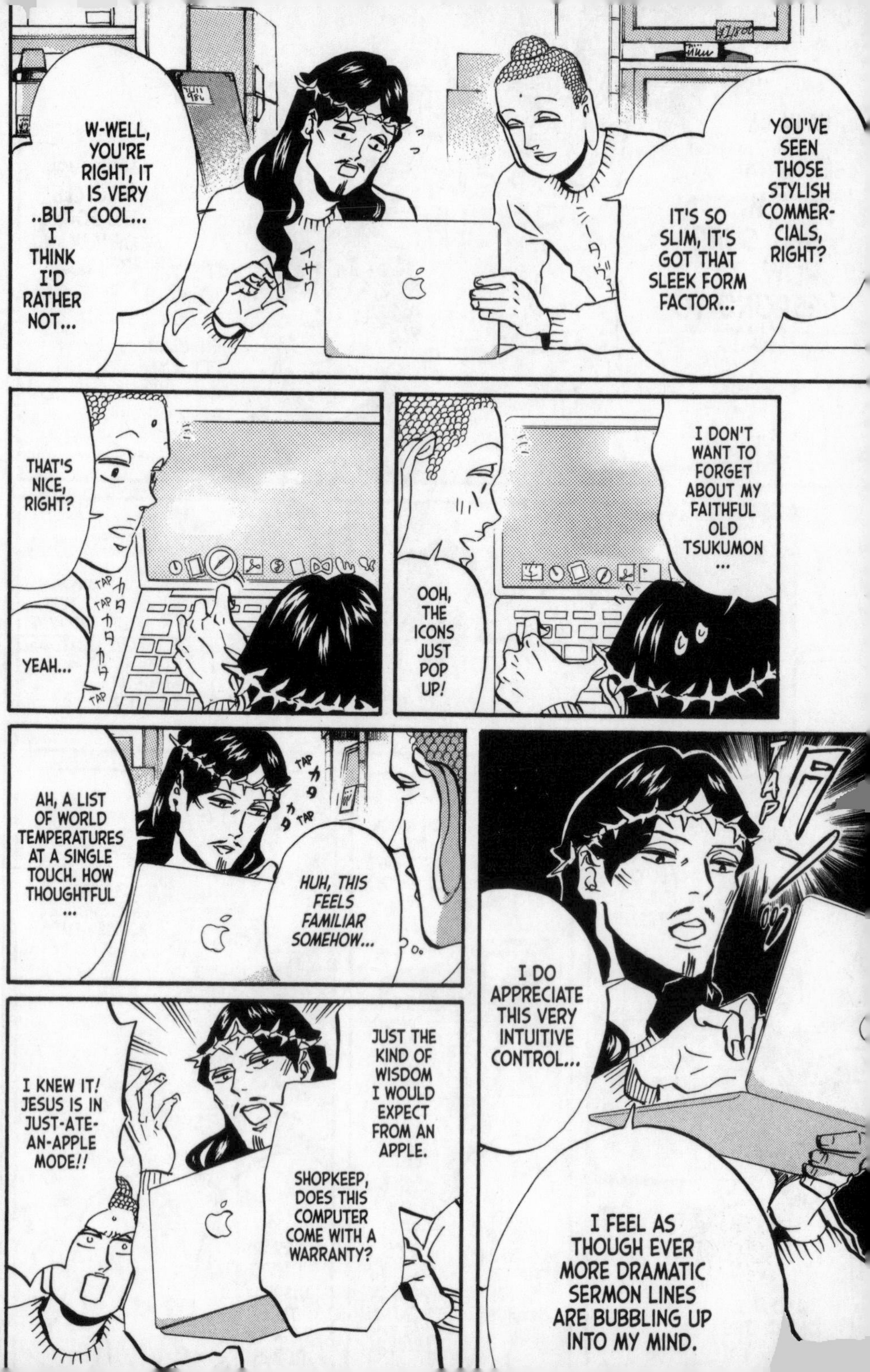

YOU'VE SEEN THOSE STYLISH COMMERCIALS, RIGHT?
IT'S SO SLIM, IT'S GOT THAT SLEEK FORM FACTOR...
W-WELL, YOU'RE RIGHT, IT IS VERY COOL...
..BUT I THINK I'D RATHER NOT...
I DON'T WANT TO FORGET ABOUT MY FAITHFUL OLD TSUKUMON...
OOH, THE ICONS JUST POP UP!
THAT'S NICE, RIGHT?
TAP TAP TAP
YEAH...
TAP
TAP
I DO APPRECIATE THIS VERY INTUITIVE CONTROL...
I FEEL AS THOUGH EVER MORE DRAMATIC SERMON LINES ARE BUBBLING UP INTO MY MIND.
TAP TAP
HUH, THIS FEELS FAMILIAR SOMEHOW...
AH, A LIST OF WORLD TEMPERATURES AT A SINGLE TOUCH. HOW THOUGHTFUL...
JUST THE KIND OF WISDOM I WOULD EXPECT FROM AN APPLE.
SHOPKEEP, DOES THIS COMPUTER COME WITH A WARRANTY?
I KNEW IT! JESUS IS IN JUST-ATE-AN-APPLE MODE!!

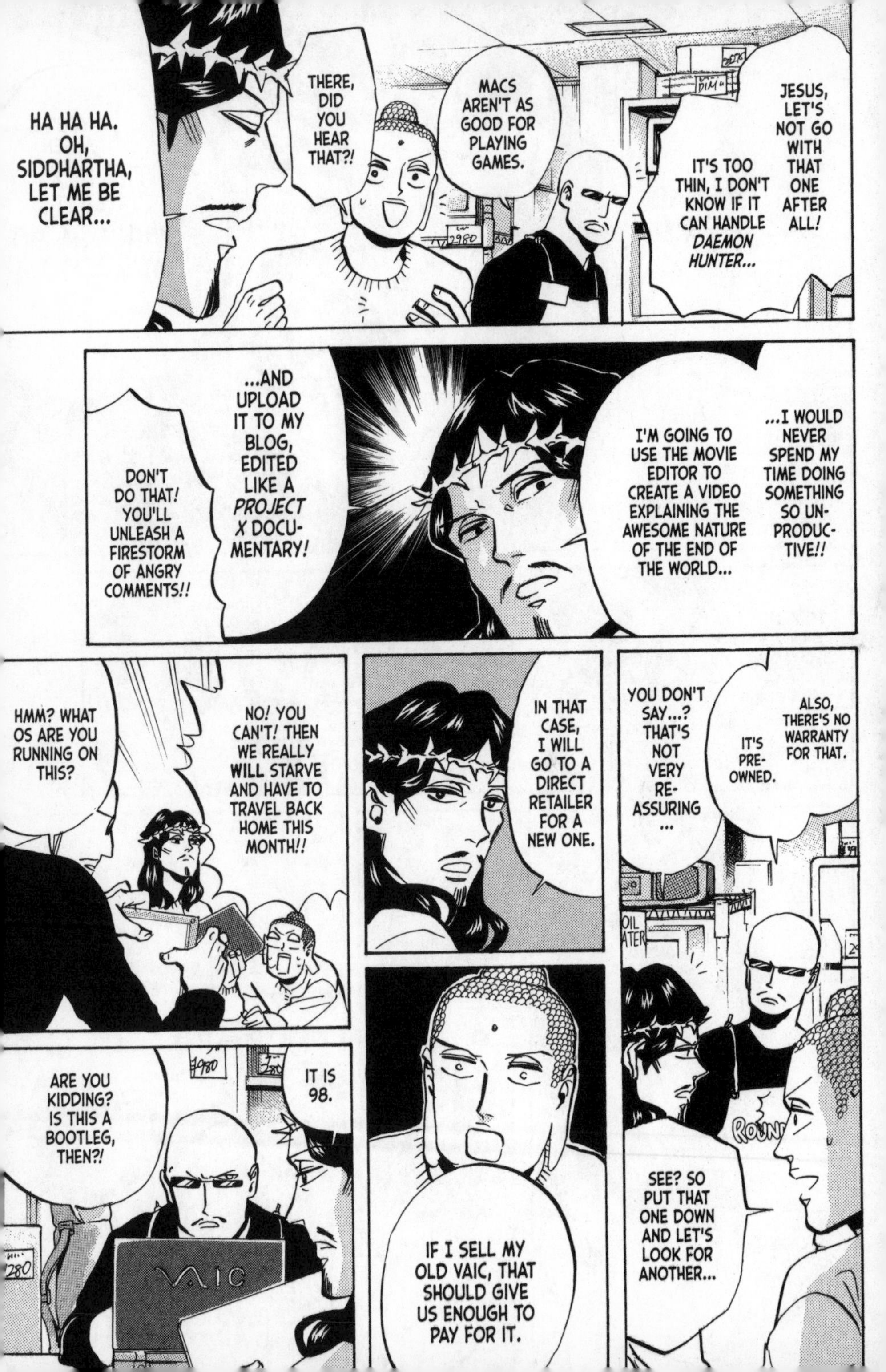
JESUS, LET'S NOT GO WITH THAT ONE AFTER ALL!
IT'S TOO THIN, I DON'T KNOW IF IT CAN HANDLE *DAEMON HUNTER*...
MACS AREN'T AS GOOD FOR PLAYING GAMES.
THERE, DID YOU HEAR THAT?!
HA HA HA. OH, SIDDHARTHA, LET ME BE CLEAR...
...I WOULD NEVER SPEND MY TIME DOING SOMETHING SO UN-PRODUC-TIVE!!
I'M GOING TO USE THE MOVIE EDITOR TO CREATE A VIDEO EXPLAINING THE AWESOME NATURE OF THE END OF THE WORLD...
...AND UPLOAD IT TO MY BLOG, EDITED LIKE A *PROJECT X* DOCU-MENTARY!
DON'T DO THAT! YOU'LL UNLEASH A FIRESTORM OF ANGRY COMMENTS!!
ALSO, THERE'S NO WARRANTY FOR THAT.
IT'S PRE-OWNED.
YOU DON'T SAY...? THAT'S NOT VERY RE-ASSURING ...
SEE? SO PUT THAT ONE DOWN AND LET'S LOOK FOR ANOTHER...
IN THAT CASE, I WILL GO TO A DIRECT RETAILER FOR A NEW ONE.
IF I SELL MY OLD VAIC, THAT SHOULD GIVE US ENOUGH TO PAY FOR IT.
NO! YOU CAN'T! THEN WE REALLY **WILL** STARVE AND HAVE TO TRAVEL BACK HOME THIS MONTH!!
HMM? WHAT OS ARE YOU RUNNING ON THIS?
IT IS 98.
ARE YOU KIDDING? IS THIS A BOOTLEG, THEN?!
VAIC

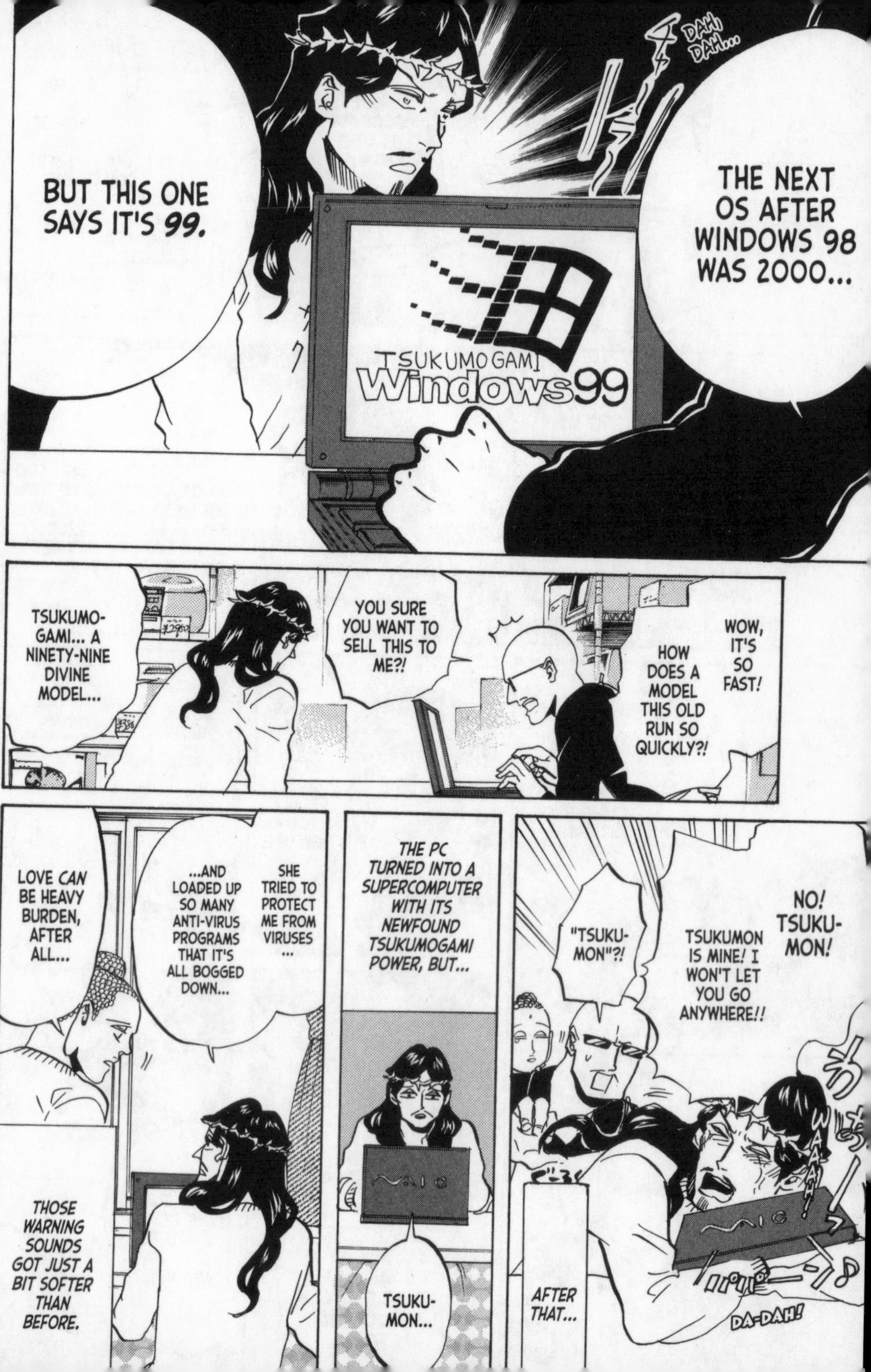
THE NEXT OS AFTER WINDOWS 98 WAS 2000...
DAH! DAH...
BUT THIS ONE SAYS IT'S 99.
TSUKUMOGAMI
Windows99
WOW, IT'S SO FAST!
HOW DOES A MODEL THIS OLD RUN SO QUICKLY?!
YOU SURE YOU WANT TO SELL THIS TO ME?!
TSUKUMO-GAMI... A NINETY-NINE DIVINE MODEL...
NO! TSUKU-MON!
TSUKUMON IS MINE! I WON'T LET YOU GO ANYWHERE!!
"TSUKU-MON"?!
WAAAH!
DA-DAH!
AFTER THAT...
THE PC TURNED INTO A SUPERCOMPUTER WITH ITS NEWFOUND TSUKUMOGAMI POWER, BUT...
TSUKU-MON...
SHE TRIED TO PROTECT ME FROM VIRUSES...
...AND LOADED UP SO MANY ANTI-VIRUS PROGRAMS THAT IT'S ALL BOGGED DOWN...
LOVE CAN BE HEAVY BURDEN, AFTER ALL...
THOSE WARNING SOUNDS GOT JUST A BIT SOFTER THAN BEFORE.

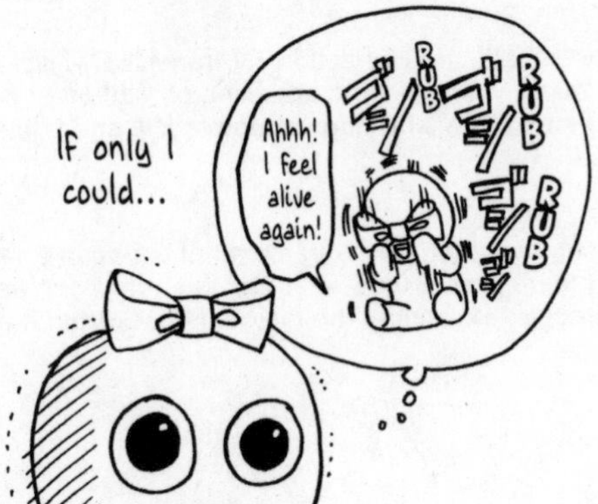

If only I could...
Ahhh! I feel alive again!
RUB
RUB
RUB

CHAPTER 45 TRANSLATION NOTES

Eight million, page 19
While the literal number for eight million in Japanese would be *happyaku-man*, in the context of Shinto gods the same kanji are read *yaoyorozu*, which is understood to mean simply a myriad, or plethora.

Sitavana, page 19
A burial ground in the ancient Maghada kingdom of India. Because its colder temperature made it ideal for storing bodies, its Sanskrit name is translated into Japanese and Chinese as "cold forest," which is therefore a poetic term for a graveyard.

Seven lucky gods, page 19
A collection of seven gods often depicted together in Japan. Each is originally based on a figure from either Hinduism or Buddhism (with one originating from Japanese folklore) and they correspond to different professions in society.

Isaac, page 19
A figure from the Old Testament, son of Abraham and Sarah. The story of the binding of Isaac tells of how God ordered Abraham to sacrifice his son as a test. Abraham is interrupted before he can do the deed, God having been satisfied by his obedience, and thus sacrifices a ram instead.

The Elves and the Shoemaker, page 25
A fairy tale contained among *Grimm's Fairy Tales* about a poor, hardworking shoemaker who wakes up to find that helpful elves have cobbled together his remaining leather into a pair of shoes that he can sell to keep his business open.

Kamen Rider, page 25
A long-running *tokusatsu* (heavy on special effects) live action TV franchise, which translates to "Masked Rider." Virtually every year sees the unveiling of a different *Kamen Rider* series, featuring an insect-styled superhero who rides a motorcycle and fights against villains.

Project X, page 33
An NHK documentary series that focuses on various achievements of Japan in a variety of topics, from science and technology to medicine, food, and architecture. Each episode depicts the people behind the achievements, explaining the historical background and the challenges they faced.

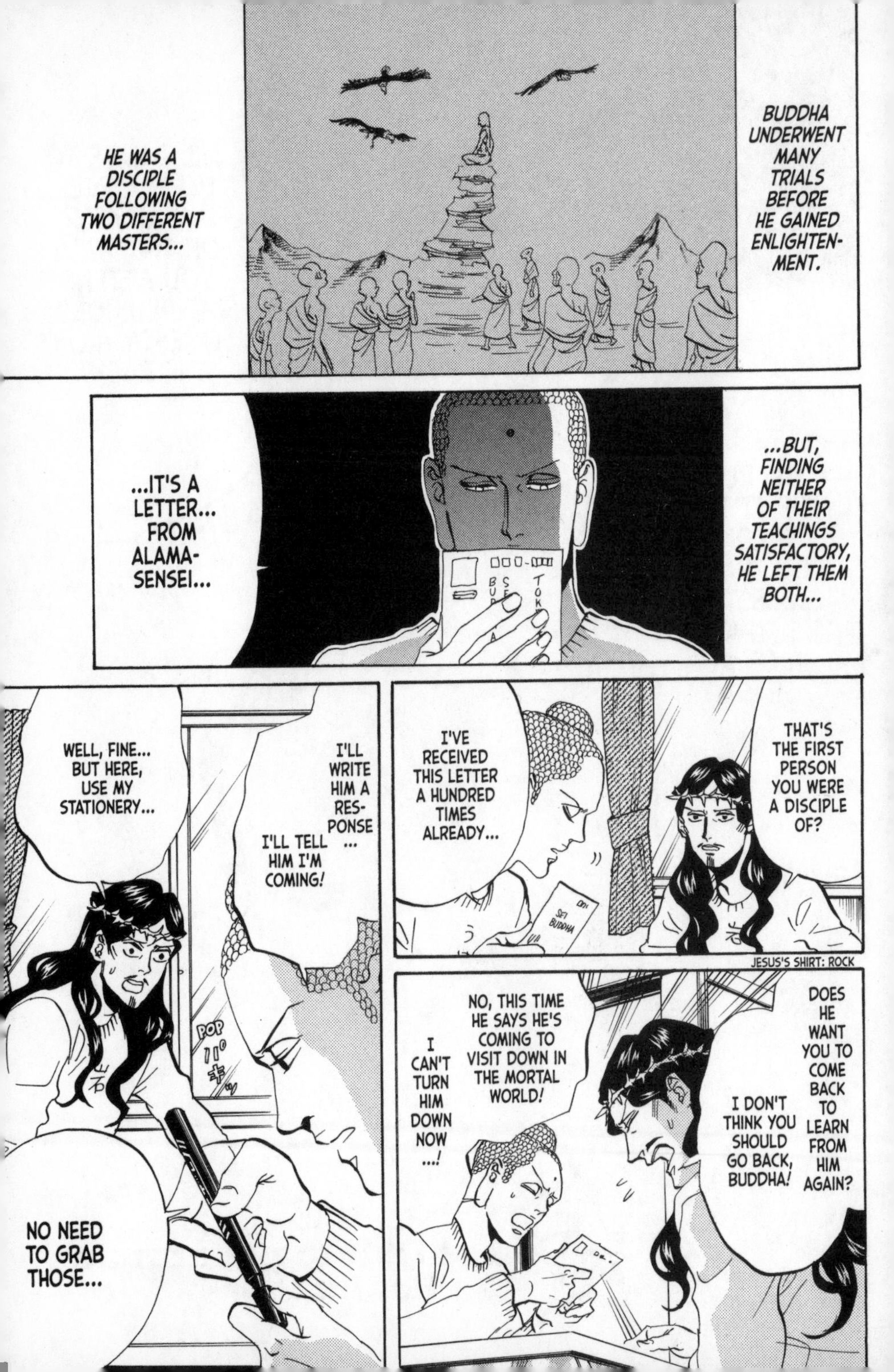
BUDDHA UNDERWENT MANY TRIALS BEFORE HE GAINED ENLIGHTEN-MENT.
HE WAS A DISCIPLE FOLLOWING TWO DIFFERENT MASTERS...
...BUT, FINDING NEITHER OF THEIR TEACHINGS SATISFACTORY, HE LEFT THEM BOTH...
...IT'S A LETTER... FROM ALAMA-SENSEI...
THAT'S THE FIRST PERSON YOU WERE A DISCIPLE OF?
I'VE RECEIVED THIS LETTER A HUNDRED TIMES ALREADY...
JESUS'S SHIRT: ROCK
DOES HE WANT YOU TO COME BACK TO LEARN FROM HIM AGAIN?
I DON'T THINK YOU SHOULD GO BACK, BUDDHA!
NO, THIS TIME HE SAYS HE'S COMING TO VISIT DOWN IN THE MORTAL WORLD!
I CAN'T TURN HIM DOWN NOW ...!
I'LL WRITE HIM A RES-PONSE ...
I'LL TELL HIM I'M COMING!
WELL, FINE... BUT HERE, USE MY STATIONERY...
POP
NO NEED TO GRAB THOSE...

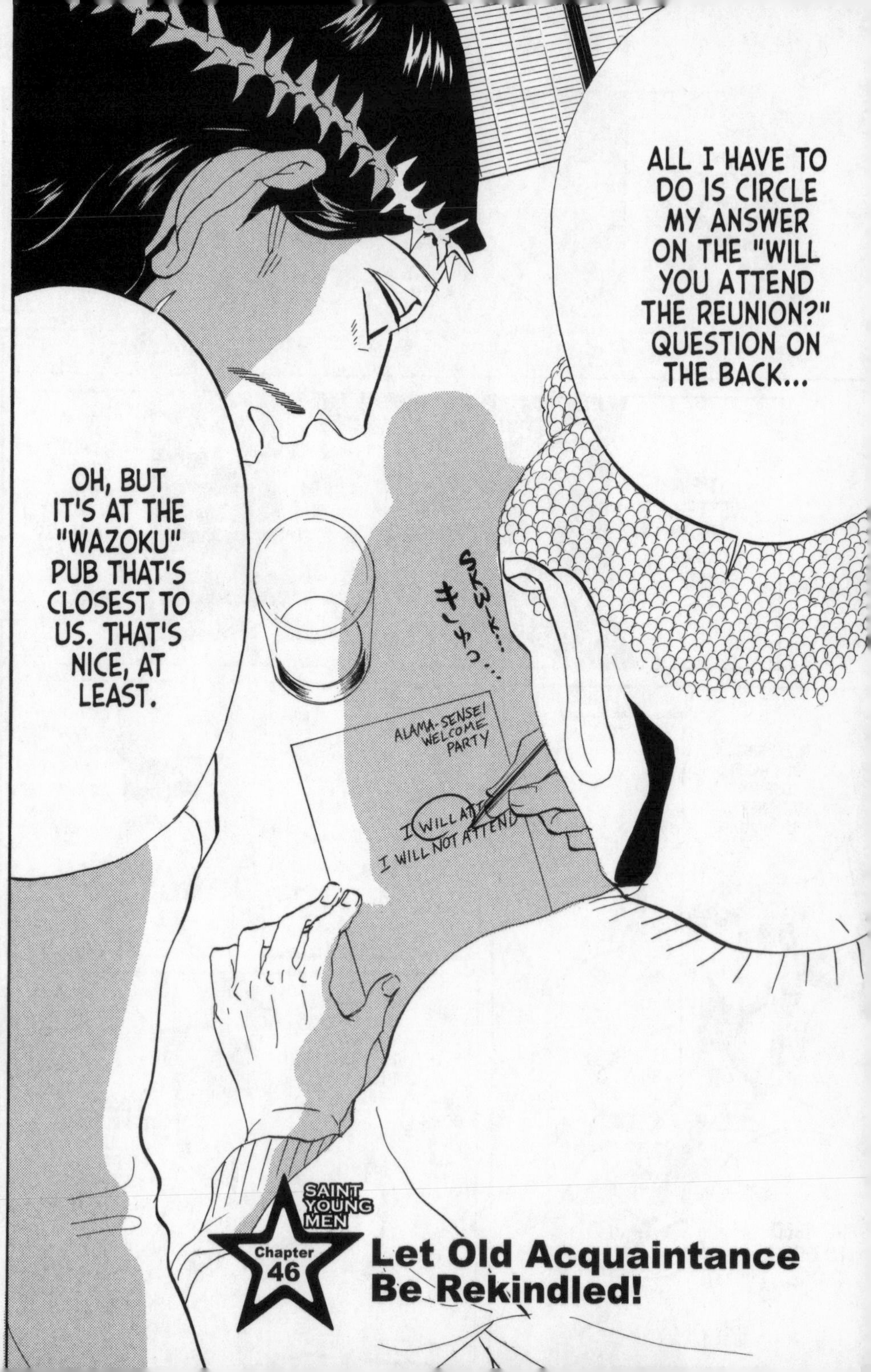
ALL I HAVE TO DO IS CIRCLE MY ANSWER ON THE "WILL YOU ATTEND THE REUNION?" QUESTION ON THE BACK...
OH, BUT IT'S AT THE "WAZOKU" PUB THAT'S CLOSEST TO US. THAT'S NICE, AT LEAST.
SKWIK...
きしゅっ...
ALAMA-SENSEI WELCOME PARTY
I WILL ATTEND
I WILL NOT ATTEND
SAINT YOUNG MEN
Chapter 46
Let Old Acquaintance Be Rekindled!

BUDDHA CAN'T FIGURE OUT WHY FEBRUARY ONLY HAS 28 DAYS. YOU'D THINK JANUARY AND MARCH COULD LEND IT ONE DAY EACH.

JESUS CAN'T FIGURE OUT WHY BARLEY TEA IS CALLED "TEA" WHEN IT'S A GRAIN, NOT A LEAF. BUT YOU WOULDN'T ASK FOR A "HOT CUP OF BARLEY," SO IT'S OKAY.

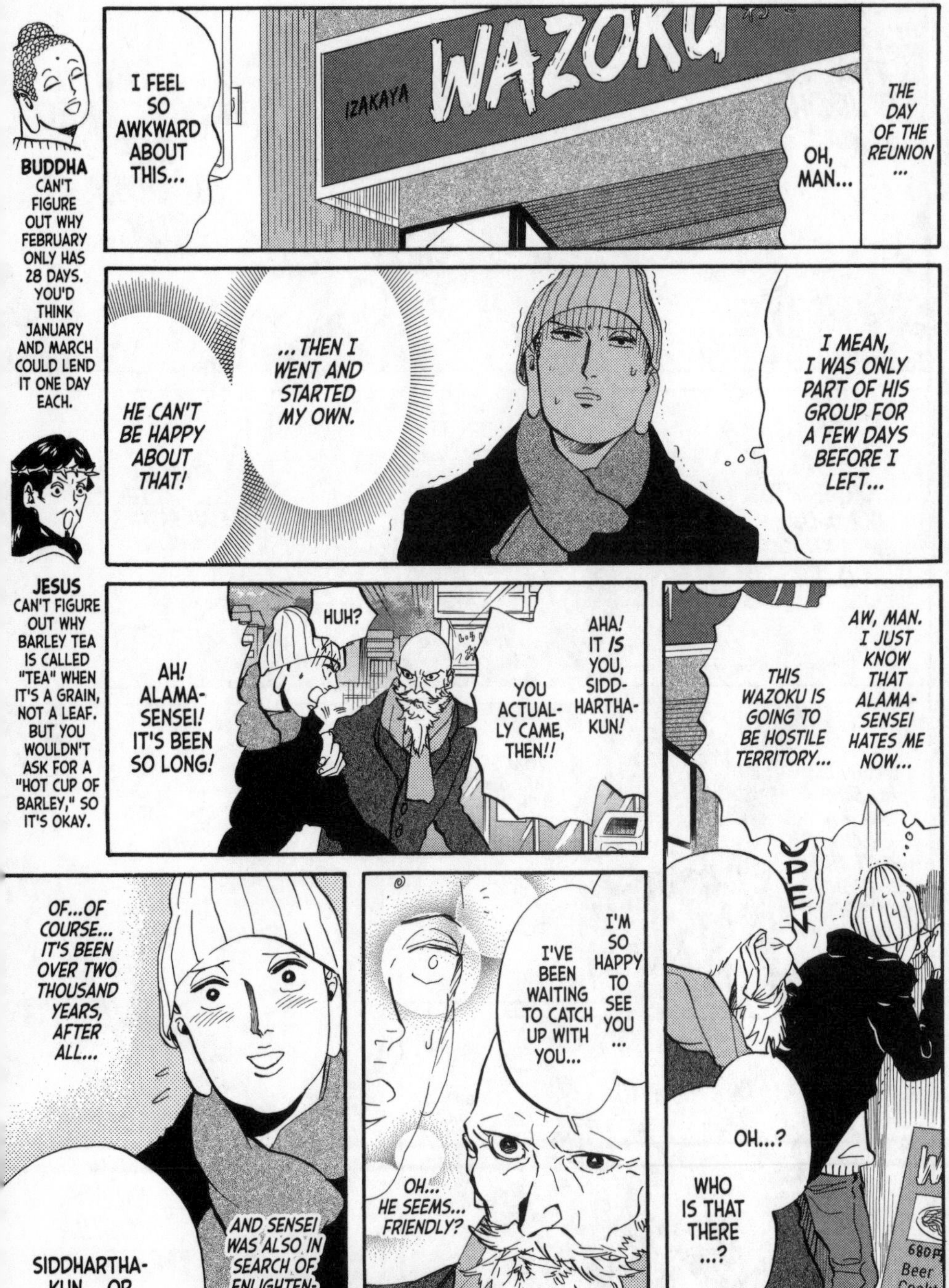
THE DAY OF THE REUNION...
OH, MAN...
IZAKAYA
WAZOKU
I FEEL SO AWKWARD ABOUT THIS...
I MEAN, I WAS ONLY PART OF HIS GROUP FOR A FEW DAYS BEFORE I LEFT...
...THEN I WENT AND STARTED MY OWN.
HE CAN'T BE HAPPY ABOUT THAT!
AW, MAN. I JUST KNOW THAT ALAMA-SENSEI HATES ME NOW...
THIS WAZOKU IS GOING TO BE HOSTILE TERRITORY...
OPEN
OH...?
WHO IS THAT THERE ...?
680円
Beer
AHA! IT IS YOU, SIDDHARTHA-KUN!
YOU ACTUALLY CAME, THEN!!
HUH?
AH! ALAMA-SENSEI! IT'S BEEN SO LONG!
I'M SO HAPPY TO SEE YOU ...
I'VE BEEN WAITING TO CATCH UP WITH YOU...
OH... HE SEEMS... FRIENDLY?
OF...OF COURSE... IT'S BEEN OVER TWO THOUSAND YEARS, AFTER ALL...
AND SENSEI WAS ALSO IN SEARCH OF ENLIGHTENMENT...
SIDDHARTHA-KUN... OR SHOULD I SAY...

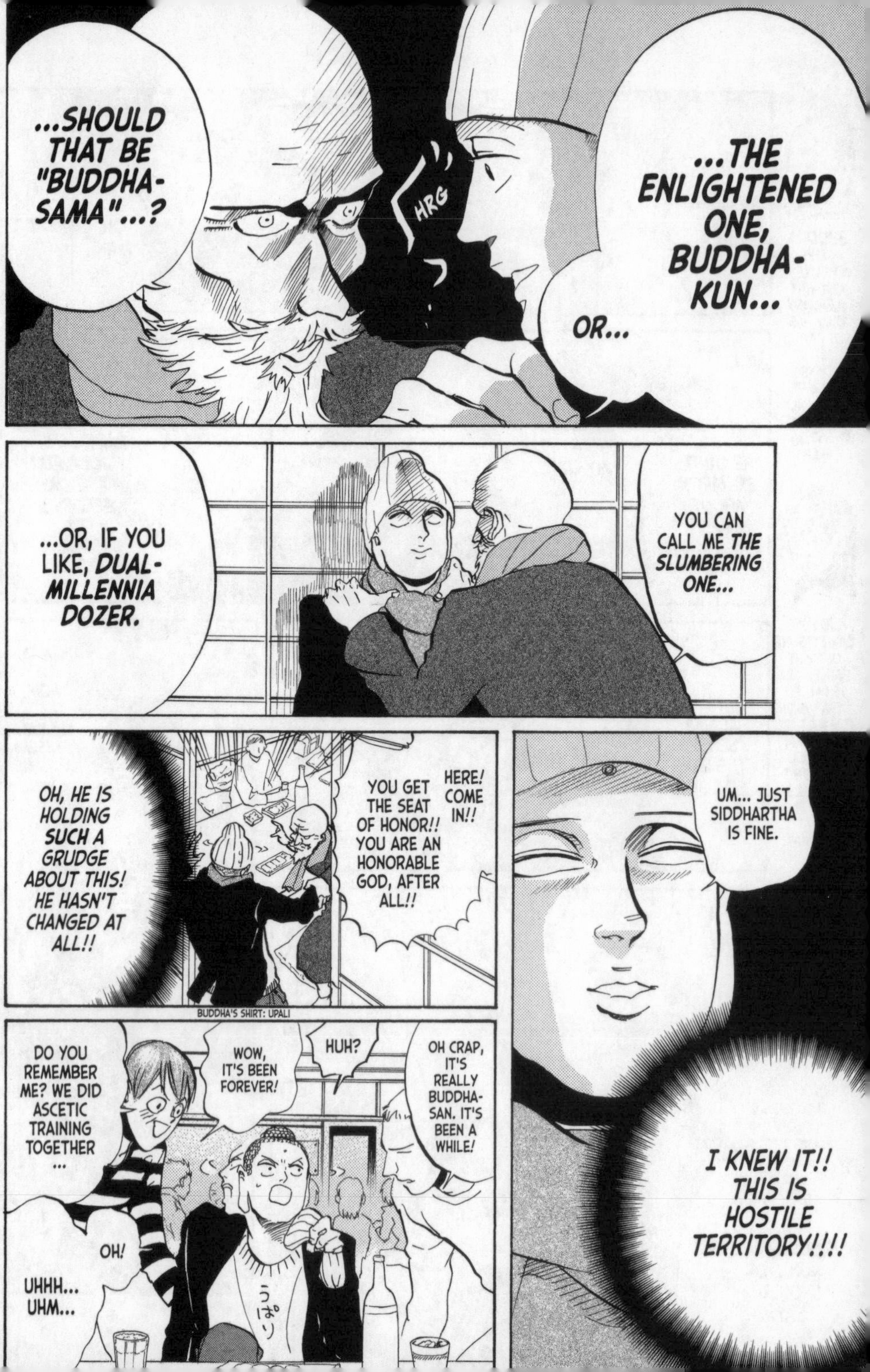
...THE ENLIGHTENED ONE, BUDDHA-KUN...
OR...
HRG
...SHOULD THAT BE "BUDDHA-SAMA"...?
YOU CAN CALL ME THE SLUMBERING ONE...
...OR, IF YOU LIKE, DUAL-MILLENNIA DOZER.
UM... JUST SIDDHARTHA IS FINE.
I KNEW IT!! THIS IS HOSTILE TERRITORY!!!!
HERE! COME IN!!
YOU GET THE SEAT OF HONOR!! YOU ARE AN HONORABLE GOD, AFTER ALL!!
OH, HE IS HOLDING SUCH A GRUDGE ABOUT THIS! HE HASN'T CHANGED AT ALL!!
BUDDHA'S SHIRT: UPALI
OH CRAP, IT'S REALLY BUDDHA-SAN. IT'S BEEN A WHILE!
HUH?
WOW, IT'S BEEN FOREVER!
DO YOU REMEMBER ME? WE DID ASCETIC TRAINING TOGETHER ...
OH!
UHHH... UHM...
うぱり

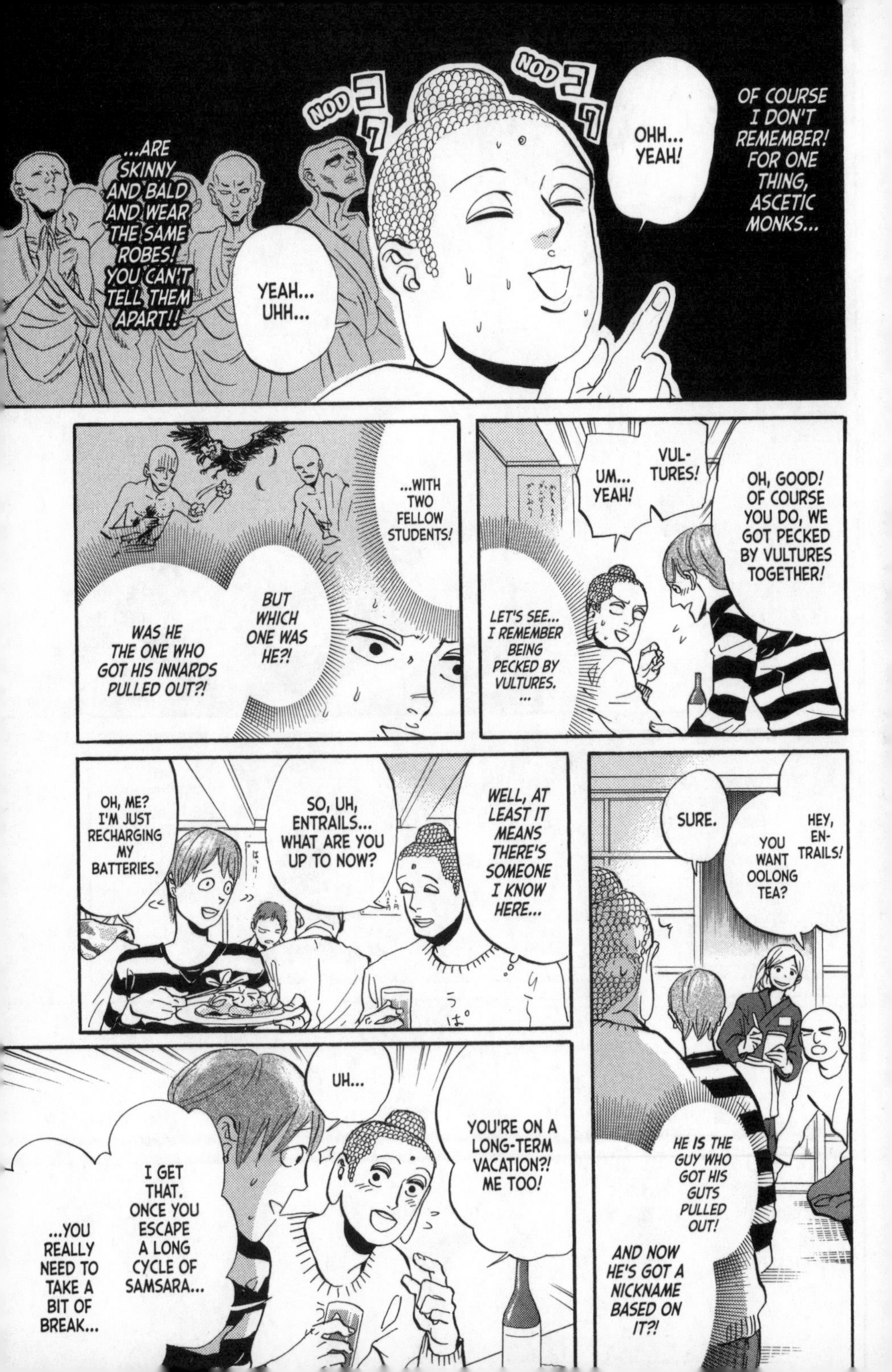
OF COURSE I DON'T REMEMBER! FOR ONE THING, ASCETIC MONKS...
OHH... YEAH!
NOD コク
NOD コク
YEAH... UHH...
...ARE SKINNY AND BALD AND WEAR THE SAME ROBES! YOU CAN'T TELL THEM APART!!
OH, GOOD! OF COURSE YOU DO, WE GOT PECKED BY VULTURES TOGETHER!
VUL-TURES!
UM... YEAH!
LET'S SEE... I REMEMBER BEING PECKED BY VULTURES. ...
...WITH TWO FELLOW STUDENTS!
BUT WHICH ONE WAS HE?!
WAS HE THE ONE WHO GOT HIS INNARDS PULLED OUT?!
HEY, EN-TRAILS!
YOU WANT OOLONG TEA?
SURE.
HE IS THE GUY WHO GOT HIS GUTS PULLED OUT!
AND NOW HE'S GOT A NICKNAME BASED ON IT?!
WELL, AT LEAST IT MEANS THERE'S SOMEONE I KNOW HERE...
SO, UH, ENTRAILS... WHAT ARE YOU UP TO NOW?
OH, ME? I'M JUST RECHARGING MY BATTERIES.
YOU'RE ON A LONG-TERM VACATION?! ME TOO!
UH...
I GET THAT. ONCE YOU ESCAPE A LONG CYCLE OF SAMSARA...
...YOU REALLY NEED TO TAKE A BIT OF BREAK...

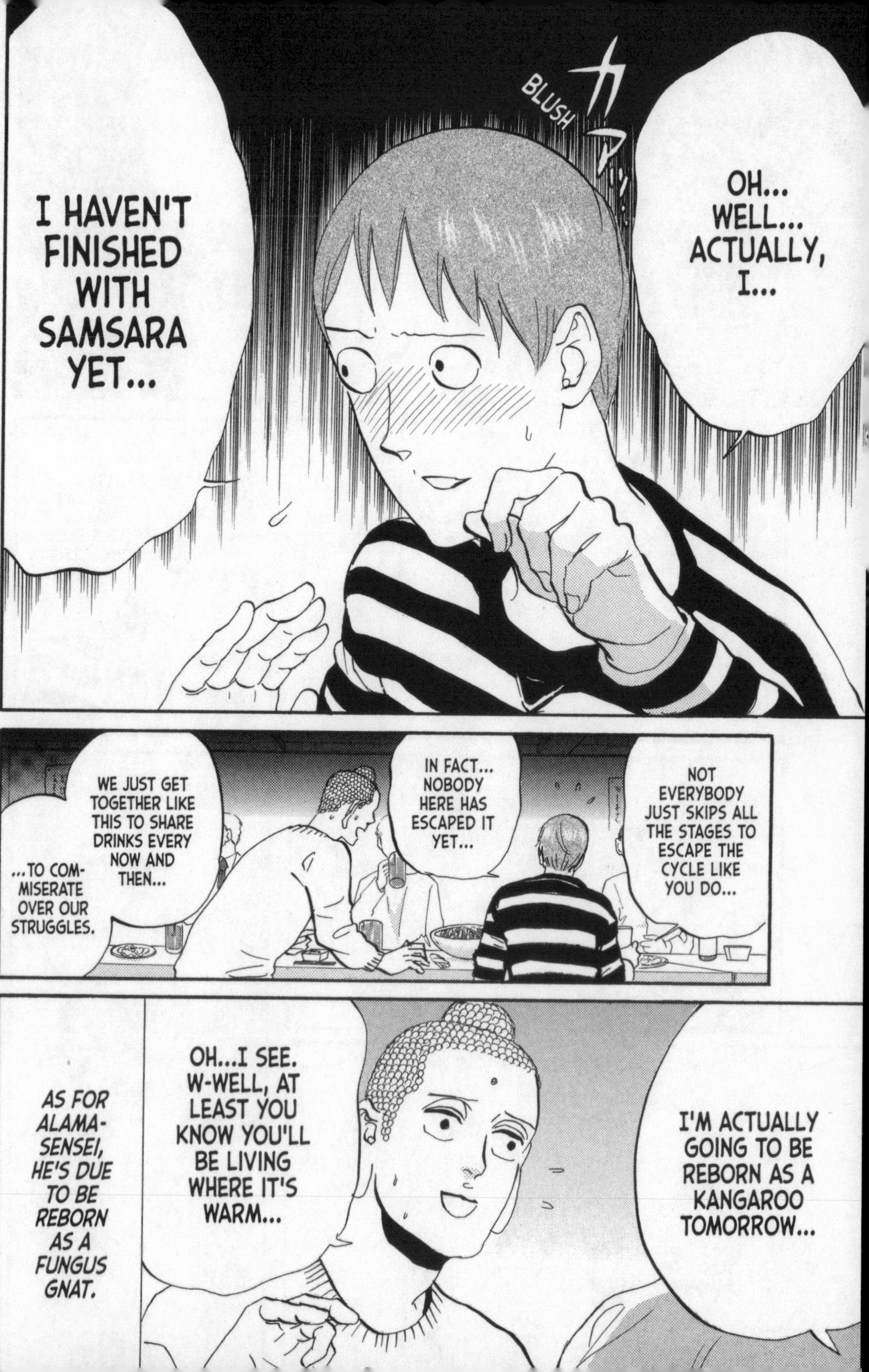
OH... WELL... ACTUALLY, I...
BLUSH
I HAVEN'T FINISHED WITH SAMSARA YET...
NOT EVERYBODY JUST SKIPS ALL THE STAGES TO ESCAPE THE CYCLE LIKE YOU DO...
IN FACT... NOBODY HERE HAS ESCAPED IT YET...
WE JUST GET TOGETHER LIKE THIS TO SHARE DRINKS EVERY NOW AND THEN...
...TO COM-MISERATE OVER OUR STRUGGLES.
I'M ACTUALLY GOING TO BE REBORN AS A KANGAROO TOMORROW...
OH...I SEE. W-WELL, AT LEAST YOU KNOW YOU'LL BE LIVING WHERE IT'S WARM...
AS FOR ALAMA-SENSEI, HE'S DUE TO BE REBORN AS A FUNGUS GNAT.

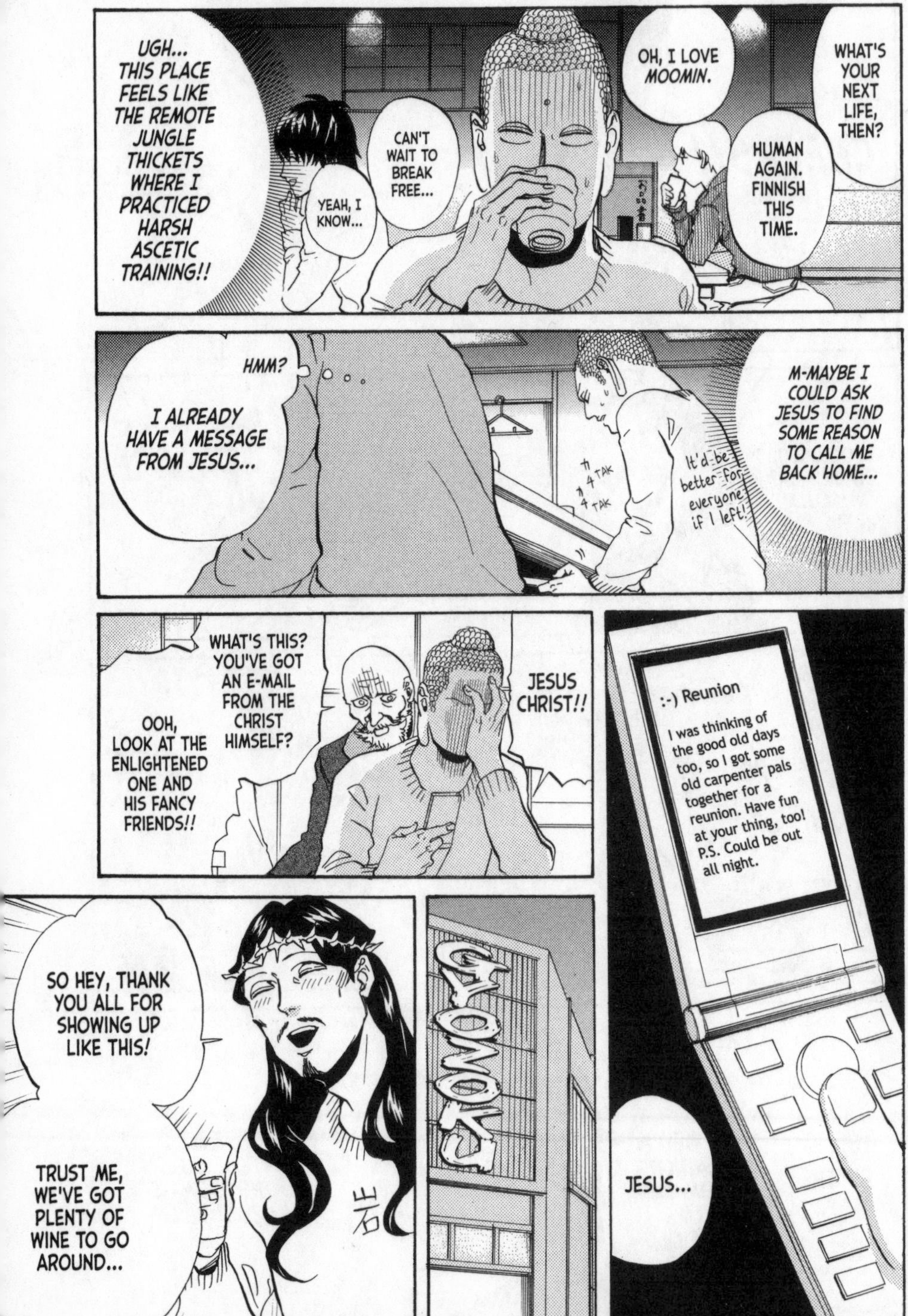
WHAT'S YOUR NEXT LIFE, THEN?
HUMAN AGAIN. FINNISH THIS TIME.
OH, I LOVE MOOMIN.
CAN'T WAIT TO BREAK FREE...
YEAH, I KNOW...
UGH... THIS PLACE FEELS LIKE THE REMOTE JUNGLE THICKETS WHERE I PRACTICED HARSH ASCETIC TRAINING!!
M-MAYBE I COULD ASK JESUS TO FIND SOME REASON TO CALL ME BACK HOME...
It'd be better for everyone if I left!
TAK
TAK
HMM?
I ALREADY HAVE A MESSAGE FROM JESUS...
:-) Reunion
I was thinking of the good old days too, so I got some old carpenter pals together for a reunion. Have fun at your thing, too! P.S. Could be out all night.
JESUS...
JESUS CHRIST!!
WHAT'S THIS? YOU'VE GOT AN E-MAIL FROM THE CHRIST HIMSELF?
OOH, LOOK AT THE ENLIGHTENED ONE AND HIS FANCY FRIENDS!!
SO HEY, THANK YOU ALL FOR SHOWING UP LIKE THIS!
TRUST ME, WE'VE GOT PLENTY OF WINE TO GO AROUND...

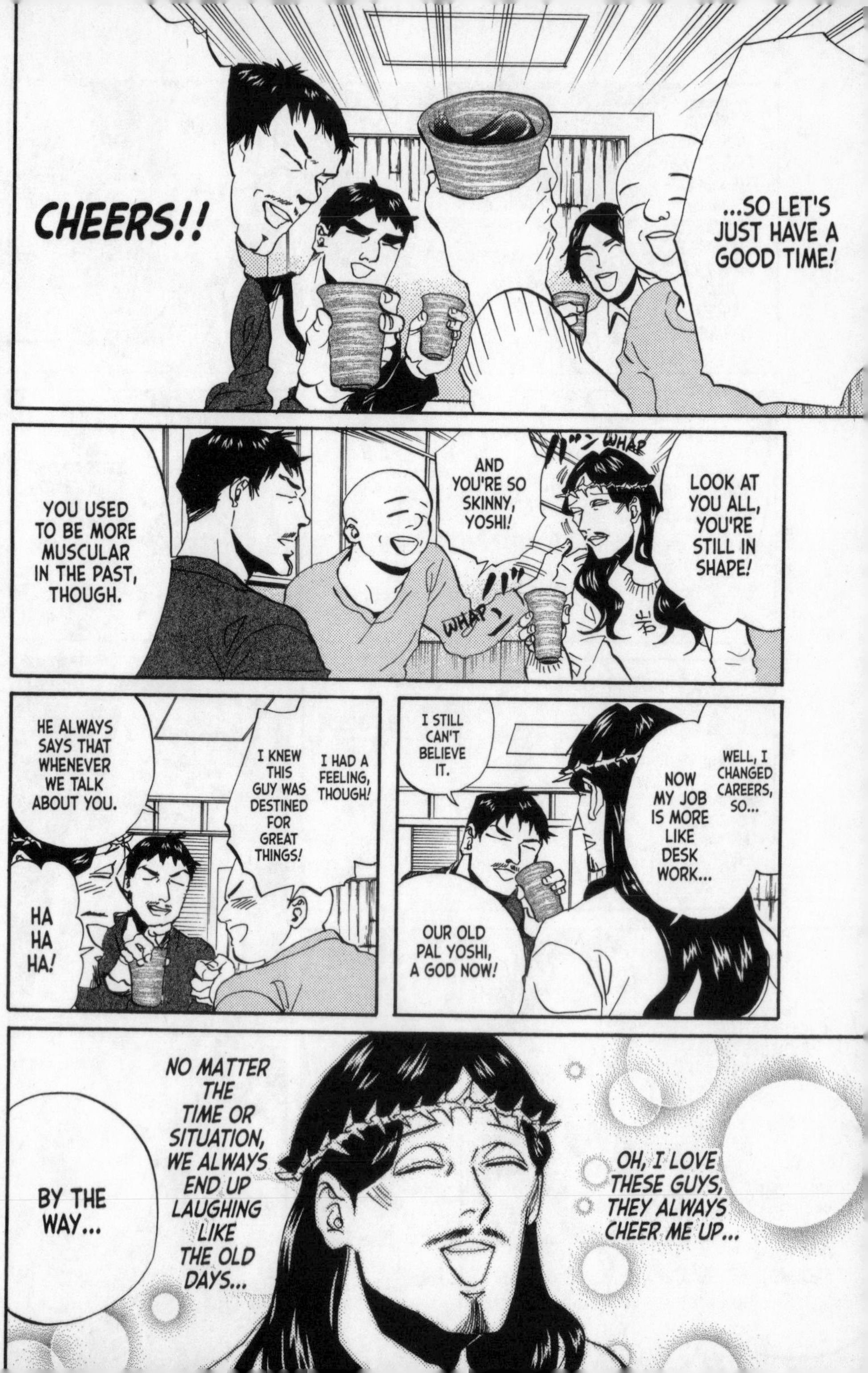
...SO LET'S JUST HAVE A GOOD TIME!
CHEERS!!
LOOK AT YOU ALL, YOU'RE STILL IN SHAPE!
WHAP
AND YOU'RE SO SKINNY, YOSHI!
WHAP
YOU USED TO BE MORE MUSCULAR IN THE PAST, THOUGH.
WELL, I CHANGED CAREERS, SO...
NOW MY JOB IS MORE LIKE DESK WORK...
I STILL CAN'T BELIEVE IT.
OUR OLD PAL YOSHI, A GOD NOW!
I HAD A FEELING, THOUGH!
I KNEW THIS GUY WAS DESTINED FOR GREAT THINGS!
HE ALWAYS SAYS THAT WHENEVER WE TALK ABOUT YOU.
HA HA HA!
OH, I LOVE THESE GUYS, THEY ALWAYS CHEER ME UP...
NO MATTER THE TIME OR SITUATION, WE ALWAYS END UP LAUGHING LIKE THE OLD DAYS...
BY THE WAY...

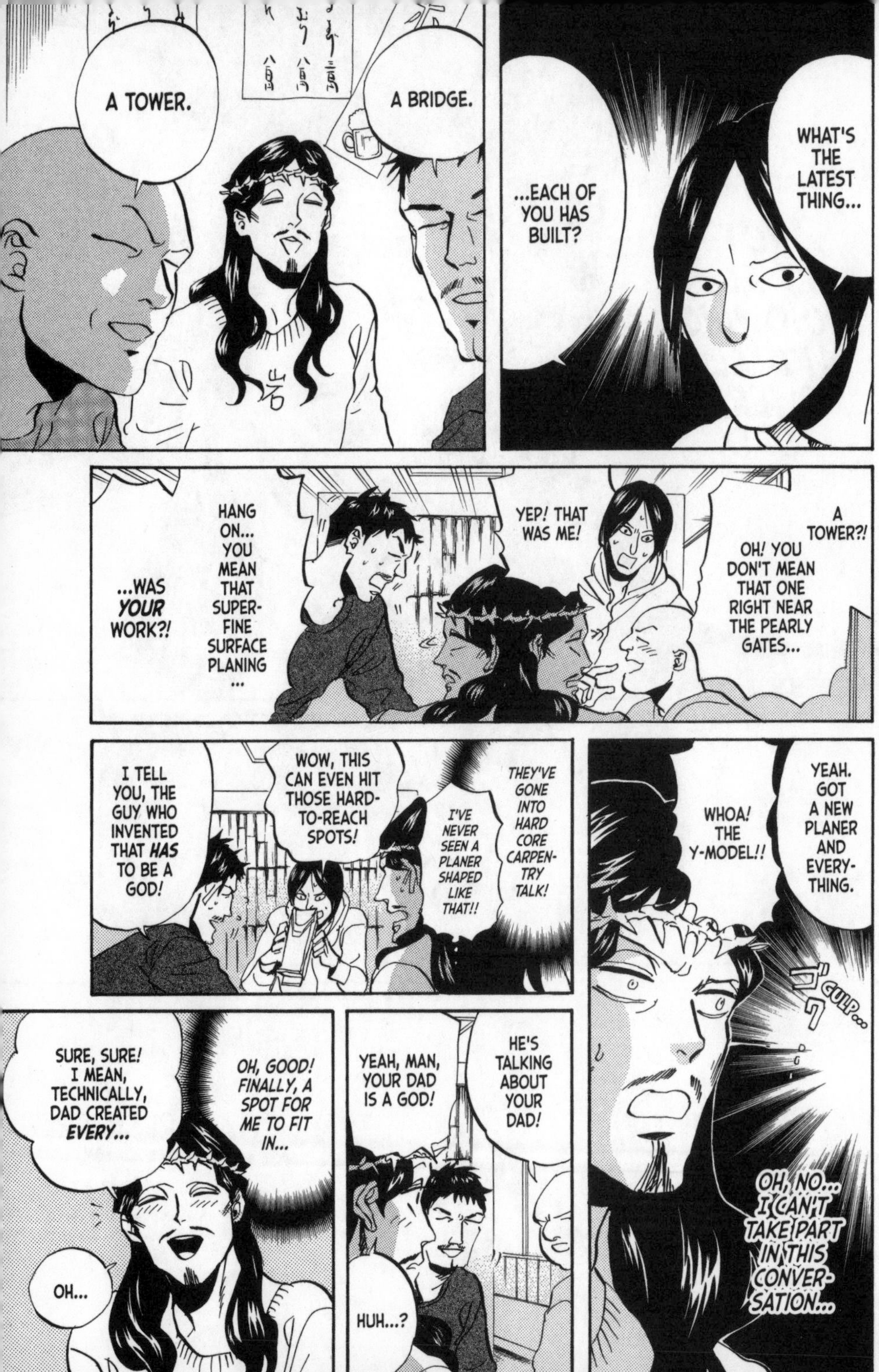
WHAT'S THE LATEST THING...
...EACH OF YOU HAS BUILT?
A BRIDGE.
A TOWER.
A TOWER?!
OH! YOU DON'T MEAN THAT ONE RIGHT NEAR THE PEARLY GATES...
YEP! THAT WAS ME!
HANG ON... YOU MEAN THAT SUPER-FINE SURFACE PLANING...
...WAS *YOUR* WORK?!
YEAH. GOT A NEW PLANER AND EVERY-THING.
WHOA! THE Y-MODEL!!
ゴク GULP...
OH, NO... I CAN'T TAKE PART IN THIS CONVER-SATION...
THEY'VE GONE INTO HARD CORE CARPEN-TRY TALK!
I'VE NEVER SEEN A PLANER SHAPED LIKE THAT!!
WOW, THIS CAN EVEN HIT THOSE HARD-TO-REACH SPOTS!
I TELL YOU, THE GUY WHO INVENTED THAT *HAS* TO BE A GOD!
HE'S TALKING ABOUT YOUR DAD!
YEAH, MAN, YOUR DAD IS A GOD!
HUH...?
OH, GOOD! FINALLY, A SPOT FOR ME TO FIT IN...
SURE, SURE! I MEAN, TECHNICALLY, DAD CREATED *EVERY...*
OH...

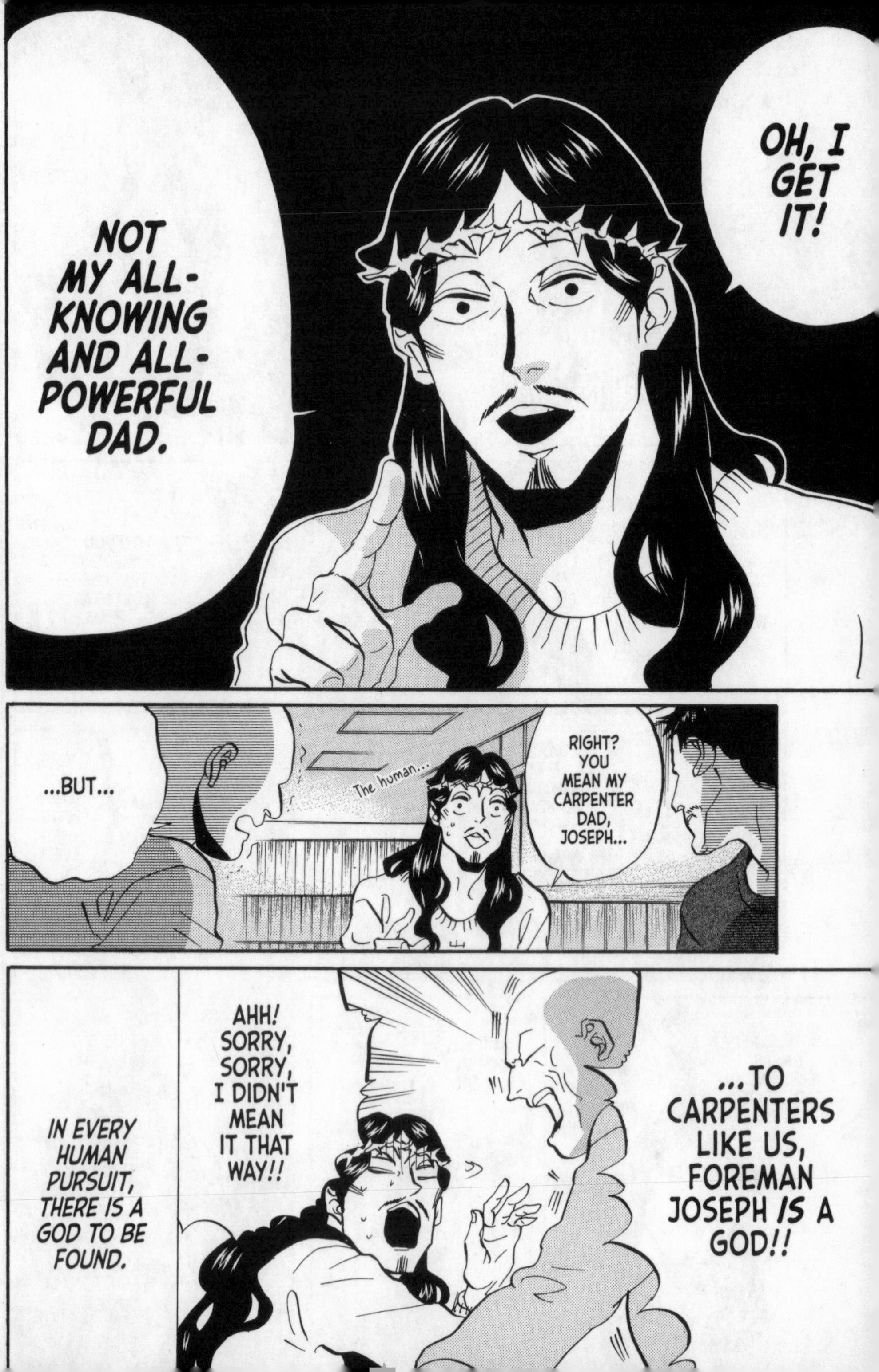
OH, I GET IT!
NOT MY ALL-KNOWING AND ALL-POWERFUL DAD.
RIGHT? YOU MEAN MY CARPENTER DAD, JOSEPH...
The human...
...BUT...
...TO CARPENTERS LIKE US, FOREMAN JOSEPH *IS* A GOD!!
AHH! SORRY, SORRY, I DIDN'T MEAN IT THAT WAY!!
IN EVERY HUMAN PURSUIT, THERE IS A GOD TO BE FOUND.

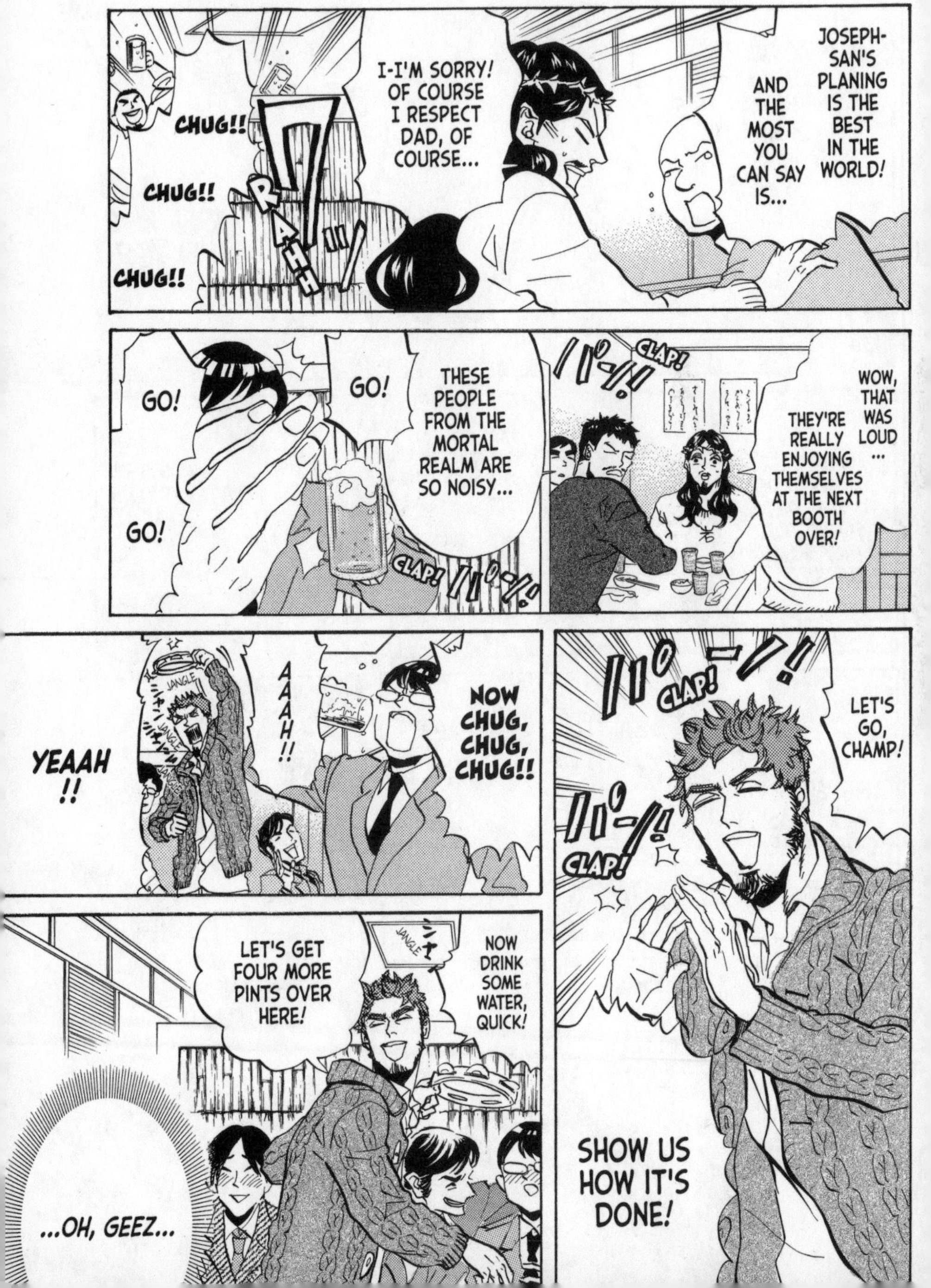
JOSEPH-SAN'S PLANING IS THE BEST IN THE WORLD!
AND THE MOST YOU CAN SAY IS...
I-I'M SORRY! OF COURSE I RESPECT DAD, OF COURSE...
RAHHH
CHUG!!
CHUG!!
CHUG!!
WOW, THAT WAS LOUD ...
THEY'RE REALLY ENJOYING THEMSELVES AT THE NEXT BOOTH OVER!
CLAP!
THESE PEOPLE FROM THE MORTAL REALM ARE SO NOISY...
GO!
GO!
GO!
CLAP!
CLAP!
LET'S GO, CHAMP!
CLAP!
SHOW US HOW IT'S DONE!
NOW CHUG, CHUG, CHUG!!
AAAAH!!
JANGLE
JANGLE
YEAAH!!
NOW DRINK SOME WATER, QUICK!
JANGLE
LET'S GET FOUR MORE PINTS OVER HERE!
...OH, GEEZ...

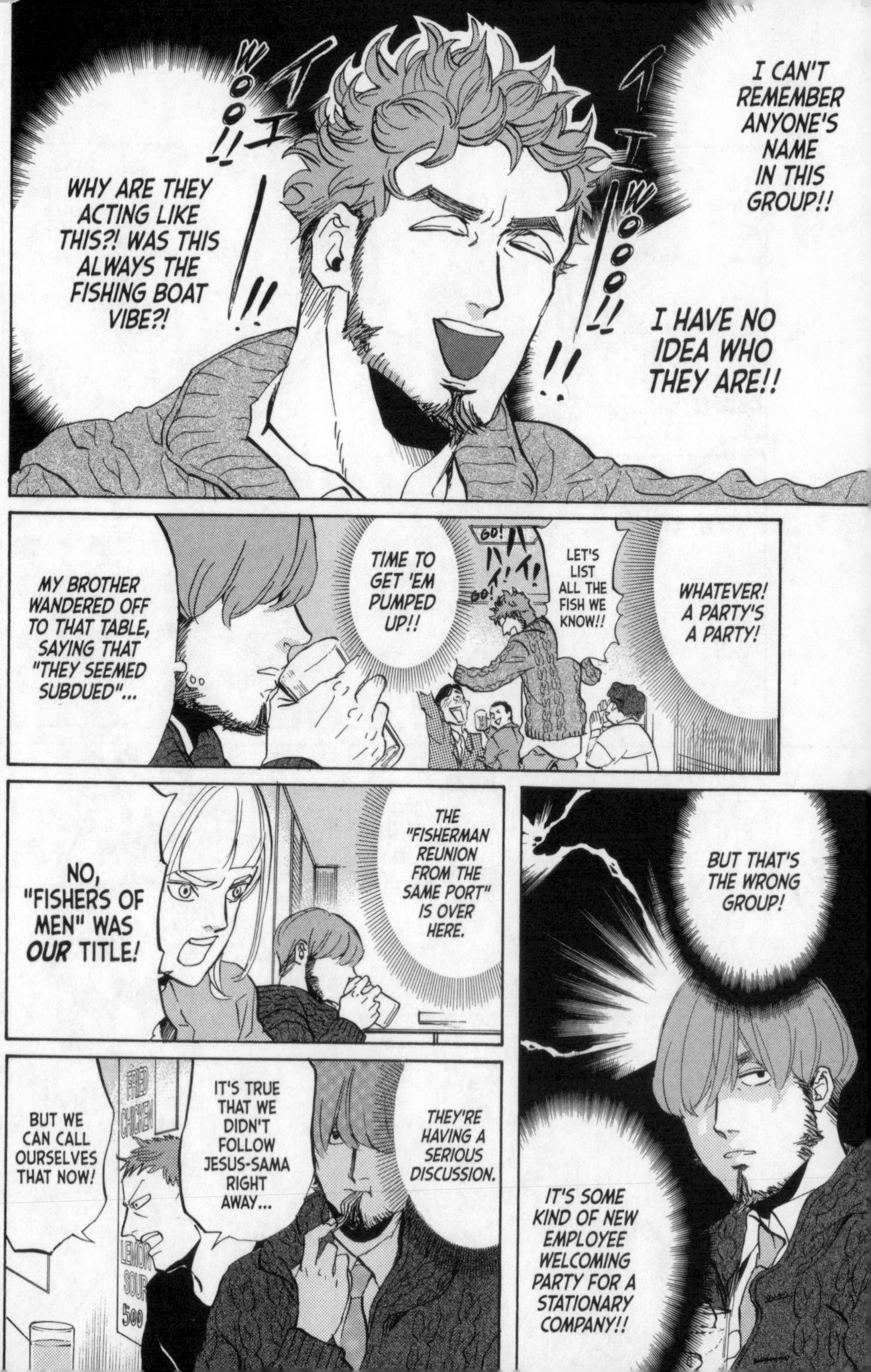
I CAN'T REMEMBER ANYONE'S NAME IN THIS GROUP!!
I HAVE NO IDEA WHO THEY ARE!!
イエー!!
WOOOO!!
イエー!!
WOO!!
WHY ARE THEY ACTING LIKE THIS?! WAS THIS ALWAYS THE FISHING BOAT VIBE?!
WHATEVER! A PARTY'S A PARTY!
LET'S LIST ALL THE FISH WE KNOW!!
GO! ハイ! ハイ! GO!
TIME TO GET 'EM PUMPED UP!!
MY BROTHER WANDERED OFF TO THAT TABLE, SAYING THAT "THEY SEEMED SUBDUED"...
BUT THAT'S THE WRONG GROUP!
IT'S SOME KIND OF NEW EMPLOYEE WELCOMING PARTY FOR A STATIONARY COMPANY!!
THE "FISHERMAN REUNION FROM THE SAME PORT" IS OVER HERE.
NO, "FISHERS OF MEN" WAS OUR TITLE!
THEY'RE HAVING A SERIOUS DISCUSSION.
IT'S TRUE THAT WE DIDN'T FOLLOW JESUS-SAMA RIGHT AWAY...
FRIED CHICKEN
BUT WE CAN CALL OURSELVES THAT NOW!
LEMON SOUR 500

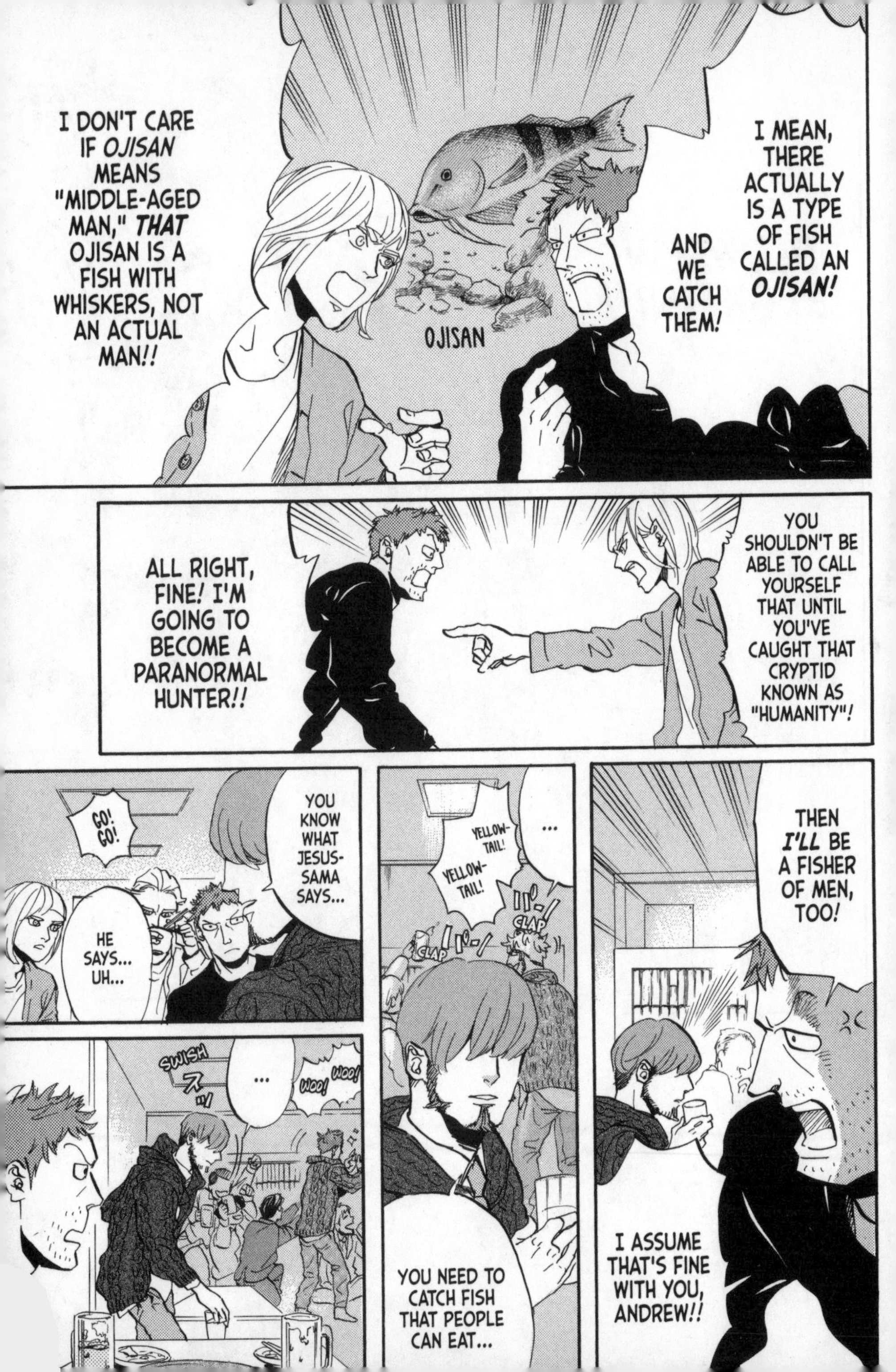
I MEAN, THERE ACTUALLY IS A TYPE OF FISH CALLED AN *OJISAN!*
AND WE CATCH THEM!
OJISAN
I DON'T CARE IF *OJISAN* MEANS "MIDDLE-AGED MAN," ***THAT*** OJISAN IS A FISH WITH WHISKERS, NOT AN ACTUAL MAN!!
YOU SHOULDN'T BE ABLE TO CALL YOURSELF THAT UNTIL YOU'VE CAUGHT THAT CRYPTID KNOWN AS "HUMANITY"!
ALL RIGHT, FINE! I'M GOING TO BECOME A PARANORMAL HUNTER!!
THEN ***I'LL*** BE A FISHER OF MEN, TOO!
I ASSUME THAT'S FINE WITH YOU, ANDREW!!
...
YELLOW-TAIL!
YELLOW-TAIL!
CLAP
CLAP
YOU NEED TO CATCH FISH THAT PEOPLE CAN EAT...
YOU KNOW WHAT JESUS-SAMA SAYS...
GO! GO!
HE SAYS... UH...
WOO!
WOO!
...
SWISH

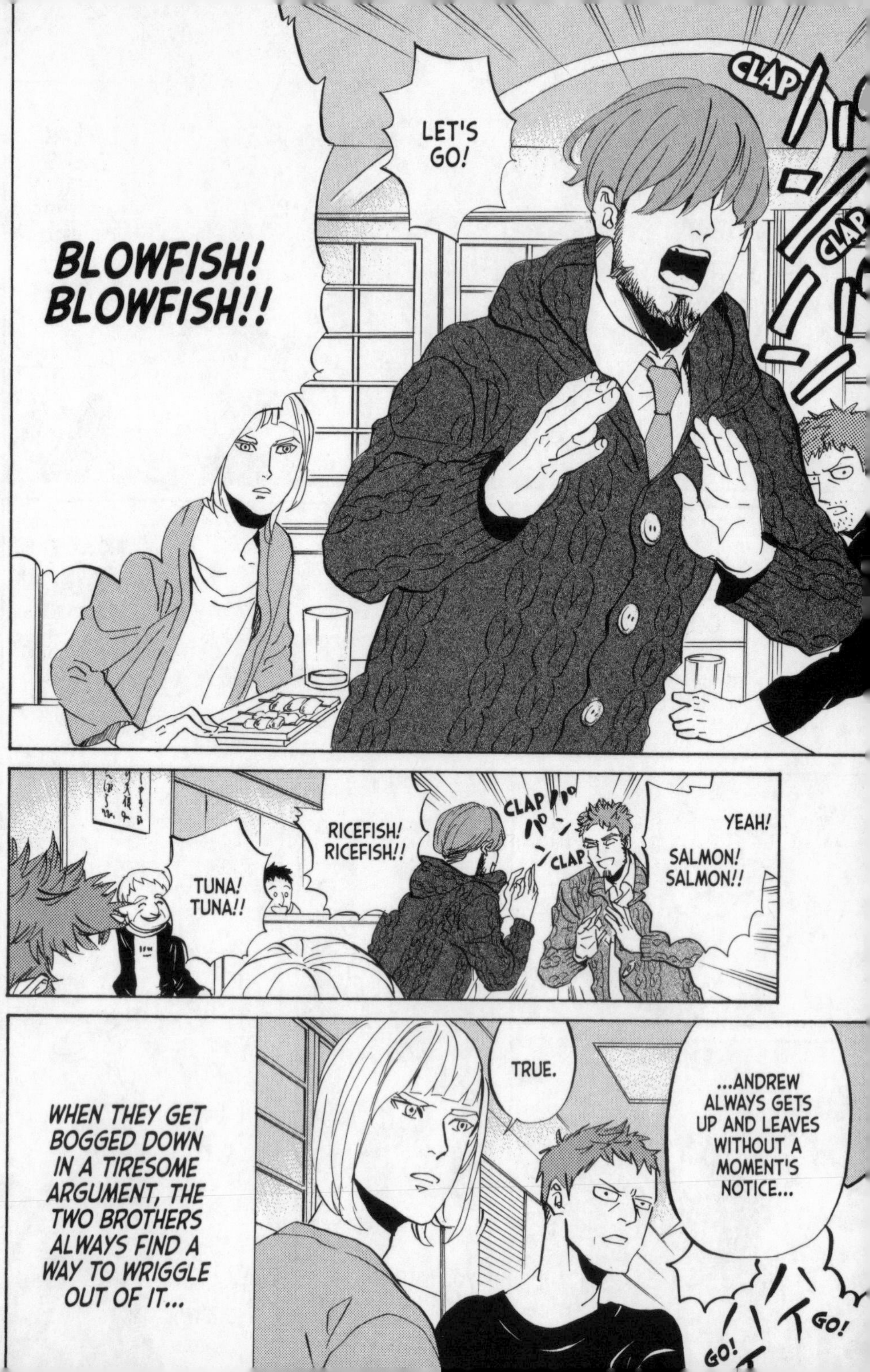
CLAP
CLAP
LET'S GO!
BLOWFISH! BLOWFISH!!
YEAH!
SALMON! SALMON!!
CLAP
CLAP
RICEFISH! RICEFISH!!
TUNA! TUNA!!
...ANDREW ALWAYS GETS UP AND LEAVES WITHOUT A MOMENT'S NOTICE...
TRUE.
GO!
GO!
WHEN THEY GET BOGGED DOWN IN A TIRESOME ARGUMENT, THE TWO BROTHERS ALWAYS FIND A WAY TO WRIGGLE OUT OF IT...

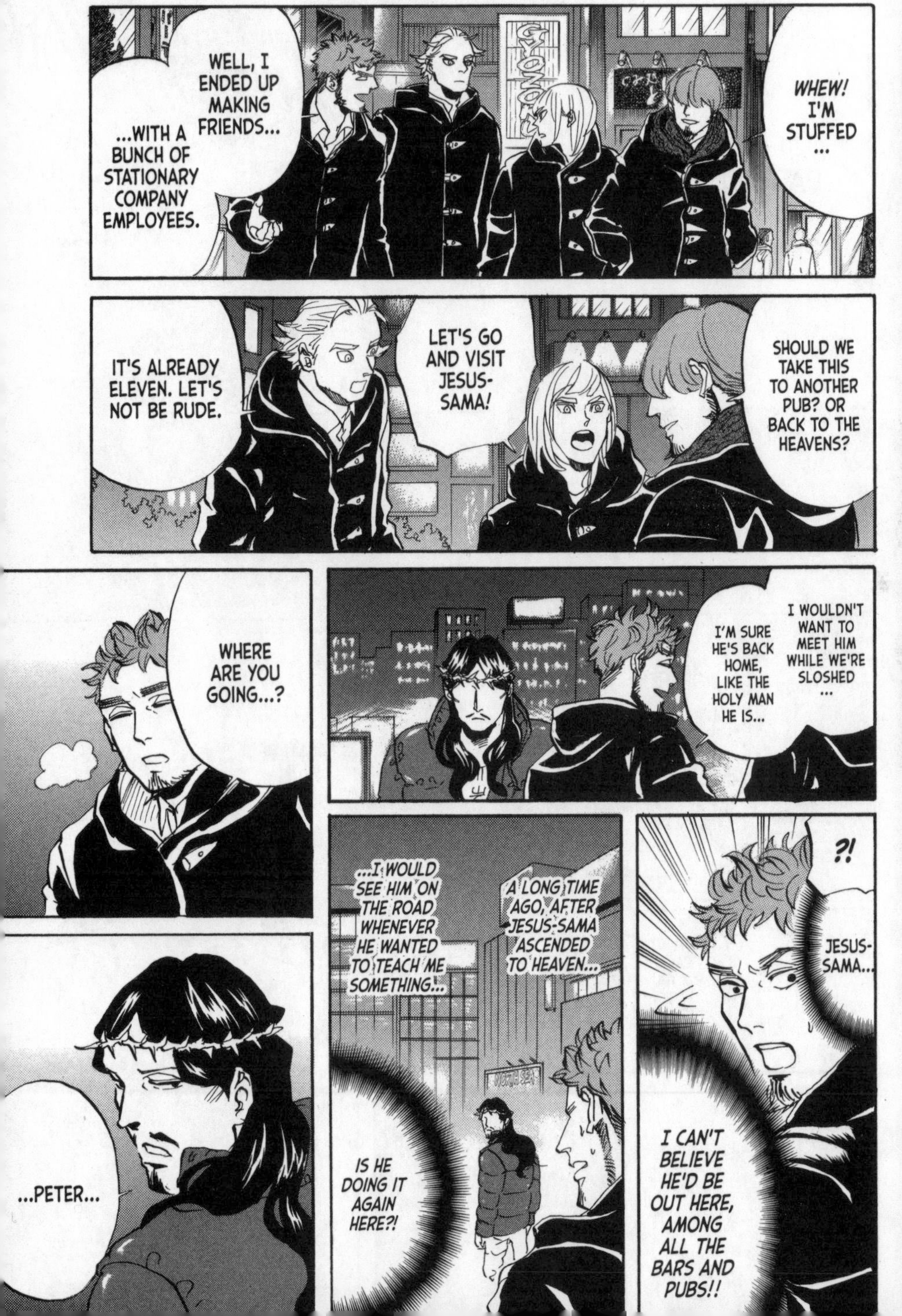
WHEW! I'M STUFFED ...
WELL, I ENDED UP MAKING FRIENDS...
...WITH A BUNCH OF STATIONARY COMPANY EMPLOYEES.
SHOULD WE TAKE THIS TO ANOTHER PUB? OR BACK TO THE HEAVENS?
LET'S GO AND VISIT JESUS-SAMA!
IT'S ALREADY ELEVEN. LET'S NOT BE RUDE.
I WOULDN'T WANT TO MEET HIM WHILE WE'RE SLOSHED ...
I'M SURE HE'S BACK HOME, LIKE THE HOLY MAN HE IS...
WHERE ARE YOU GOING...?
?!
JESUS-SAMA...
I CAN'T BELIEVE HE'D BE OUT HERE, AMONG ALL THE BARS AND PUBS!!
A LONG TIME AGO, AFTER JESUS-SAMA ASCENDED TO HEAVEN...
...I WOULD SEE HIM ON THE ROAD WHENEVER HE WANTED TO TEACH ME SOMETHING...
NORTH SEA
IS HE DOING IT AGAIN HERE?!
...PETER...

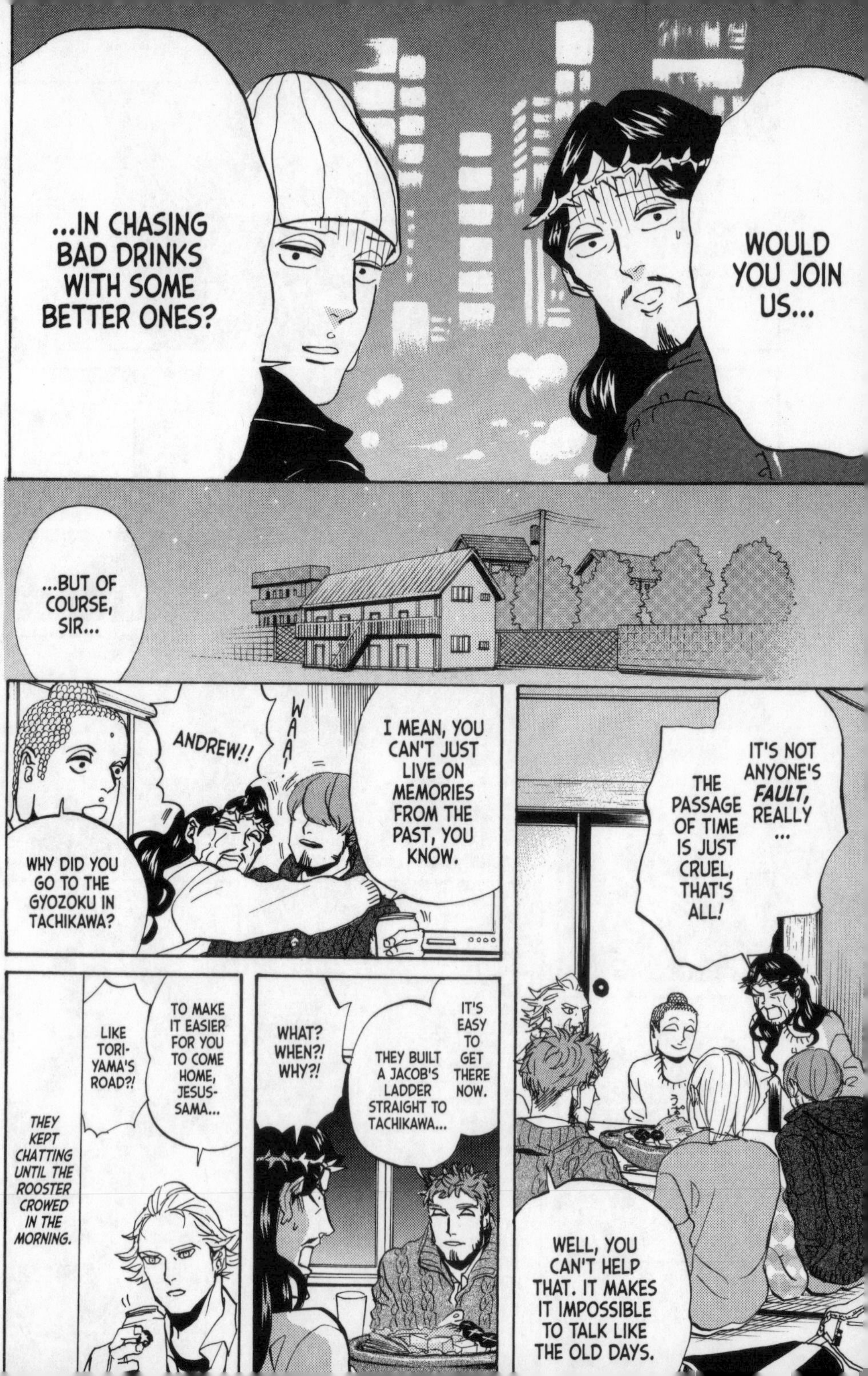
WOULD YOU JOIN US...
...IN CHASING BAD DRINKS WITH SOME BETTER ONES?
...BUT OF COURSE, SIR...
IT'S NOT ANYONE'S *FAULT*, REALLY ...
THE PASSAGE OF TIME IS JUST CRUEL, THAT'S ALL!
WELL, YOU CAN'T HELP THAT. IT MAKES IT IMPOSSIBLE TO TALK LIKE THE OLD DAYS.
I MEAN, YOU CAN'T JUST LIVE ON MEMORIES FROM THE PAST, YOU KNOW.
WAAA!
ANDREW!!
WHY DID YOU GO TO THE GYOZOKU IN TACHIKAWA?
IT'S EASY TO GET THERE NOW.
THEY BUILT A JACOB'S LADDER STRAIGHT TO TACHIKAWA...
WHAT? WHEN?! WHY?!
TO MAKE IT EASIER FOR YOU TO COME HOME, JESUS-SAMA...
LIKE TORI-YAMA'S ROAD?!
THEY KEPT CHATTING UNTIL THE ROOSTER CROWED IN THE MORNING.

I'll give it my all...
next life.
By Entrails

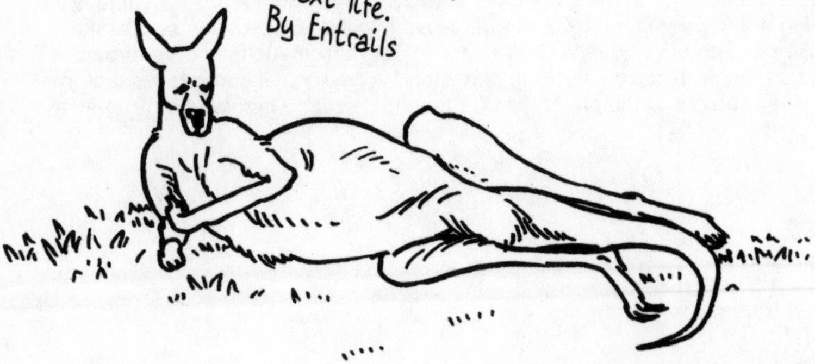

CHAPTER 46 TRANSLATION NOTES

Rock, page 37
God and Jesus are often compared to a rock to describe their supportive qualities beneath one's feet. The phrase "The Lord is my rock" appears in several books of the Bible.

Alama-sensei, page 37
Gautama Buddha's first teacher was a hermit by the name of Alara Kalama, until Gautama ultimately became his equal, and moved on to find a new teacher. Within *Saint Young Men*, this figure is referred to as simply "Alama".

Wazoku, page 38
An in-world chain of *izakaya*, or Japanese-style pubs that serve drinks and smaller food items, ideal for social gatherings. The name *wazoku* literally means "people/clan of harmony."

Upali, page 40
One of the Buddha's ten primary disciples. Upali was born to a low caste in the Buddha's society, and served the Shakya clan as a barber, a very low and disrespected profession within the traditional caste system. Upali became acquainted with Gautama as a child when he shaved the future Buddha's head.

Gyozoku, page 43
After Buddha's trip to the izakaya named Wazoku (harmonious people), Jesus' *izakaya* means "fish people," most likely referring to his instruction to his disciples that they should be "fishers of men."

Ojisan, page 49
The word ojisan literally means "uncle," but is often used in a general sense to refer to any middle-aged man. The fish (a species of goatfish in English) is called *ojisan* because it has the "goatee" feelers that look like an old man's facial hair.

Jacob's ladder, page 52
A ladder going up to heaven that appeared in one of Jacob's dreams, as described in the Book of Genesis.

Toriyama's road, page 52
An urban legend dating back to the glory days of *Dragon Ball*. Artist Akira Toriyama is famous for living in Aichi Prefecture rather than moving to Tokyo like many successful artists. His finished chapters had to be flown back to Tokyo from Aichi, and the urban legend states that the prefecture was so reliant upon his personal income taxes that they built a private road straight to the airport just for him, to dissuade him from moving away.

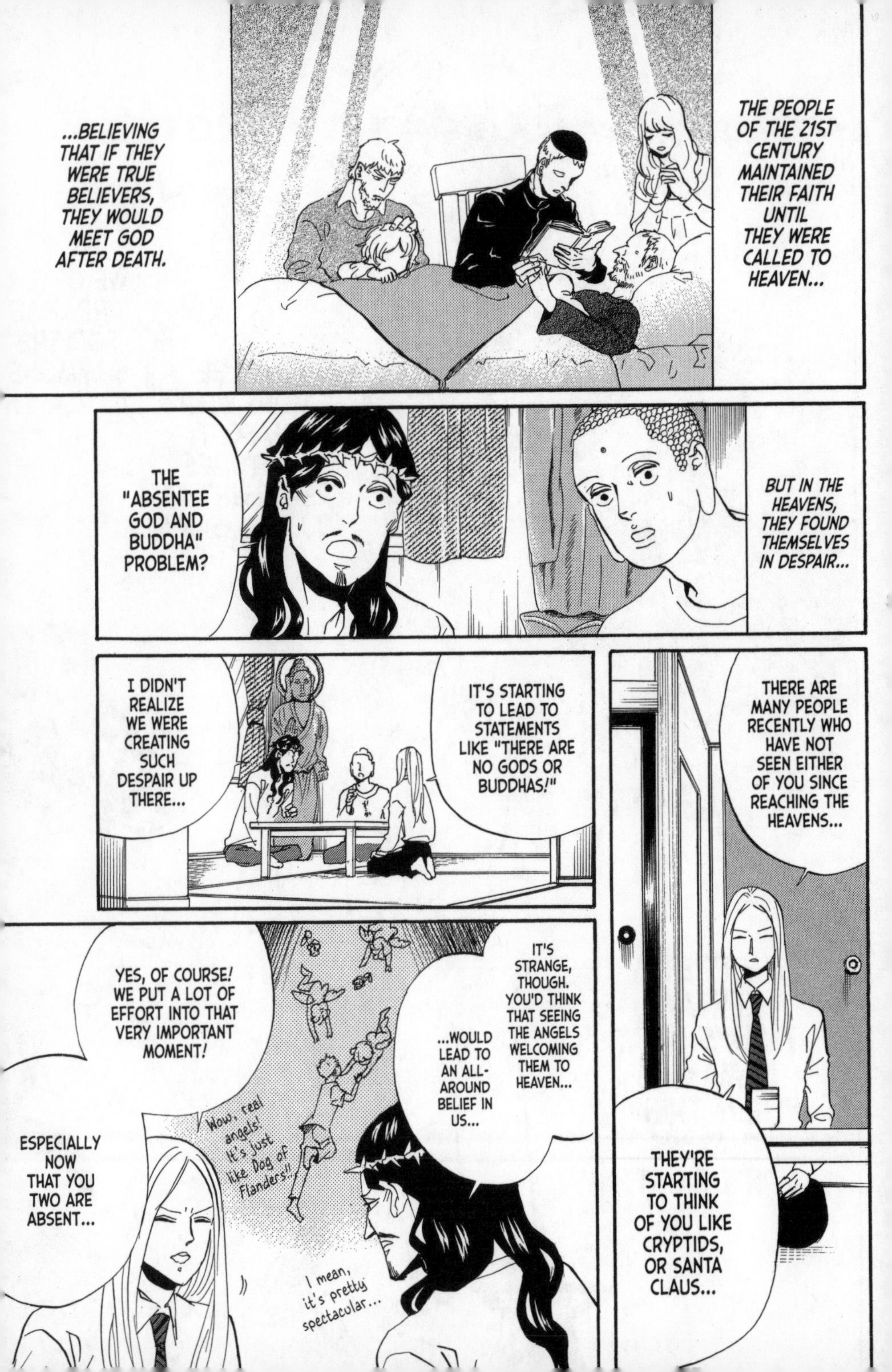
THE PEOPLE OF THE 21ST CENTURY MAINTAINED THEIR FAITH UNTIL THEY WERE CALLED TO HEAVEN...
...BELIEVING THAT IF THEY WERE TRUE BELIEVERS, THEY WOULD MEET GOD AFTER DEATH.
BUT IN THE HEAVENS, THEY FOUND THEMSELVES IN DESPAIR...
THE "ABSENTEE GOD AND BUDDHA" PROBLEM?
THERE ARE MANY PEOPLE RECENTLY WHO HAVE NOT SEEN EITHER OF YOU SINCE REACHING THE HEAVENS...
THEY'RE STARTING TO THINK OF YOU LIKE CRYPTIDS, OR SANTA CLAUS...
IT'S STARTING TO LEAD TO STATEMENTS LIKE "THERE ARE NO GODS OR BUDDHAS!"
I DIDN'T REALIZE WE WERE CREATING SUCH DESPAIR UP THERE...
IT'S STRANGE, THOUGH. YOU'D THINK THAT SEEING THE ANGELS WELCOMING THEM TO HEAVEN...
...WOULD LEAD TO AN ALL-AROUND BELIEF IN US...
YES, OF COURSE! WE PUT A LOT OF EFFORT INTO THAT VERY IMPORTANT MOMENT!
Wow, real angels! It's just like Dog of Flanders!!
ESPECIALLY NOW THAT YOU TWO ARE ABSENT...
I mean, it's pretty spectacular...

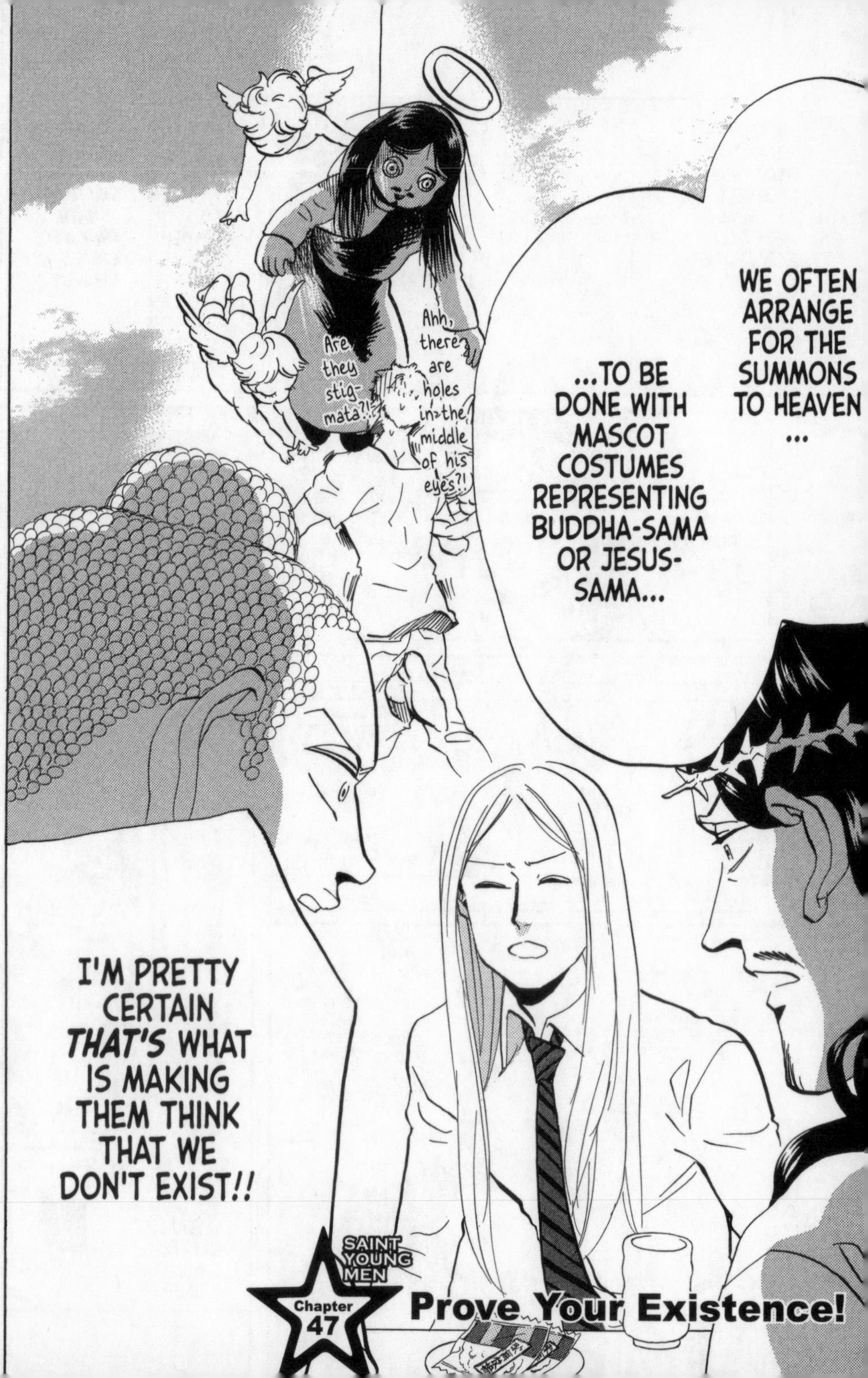
WE OFTEN ARRANGE FOR THE SUMMONS TO HEAVEN...
...TO BE DONE WITH MASCOT COSTUMES REPRESENTING BUDDHA-SAMA OR JESUS-SAMA...
Ahh, there are holes in the middle of his eyes?!
Are they stigmata?!
I'M PRETTY CERTAIN *THAT'S* WHAT IS MAKING THEM THINK THAT WE DON'T EXIST!!
SAINT YOUNG MEN
Chapter 47
Prove Your Existence!

BUDDHA
RECENT DISCOVERY: ACCIDENTALLY LICKED A LOTION TISSUE AND FOUND IT WAS SWEET.

JESUS
RECENT DISCOVERY: IF HE STICKS HIS TONGUE AGAINST HIS UPPER JAW, HE WON'T CRY WHEN CUTTING ONIONS.

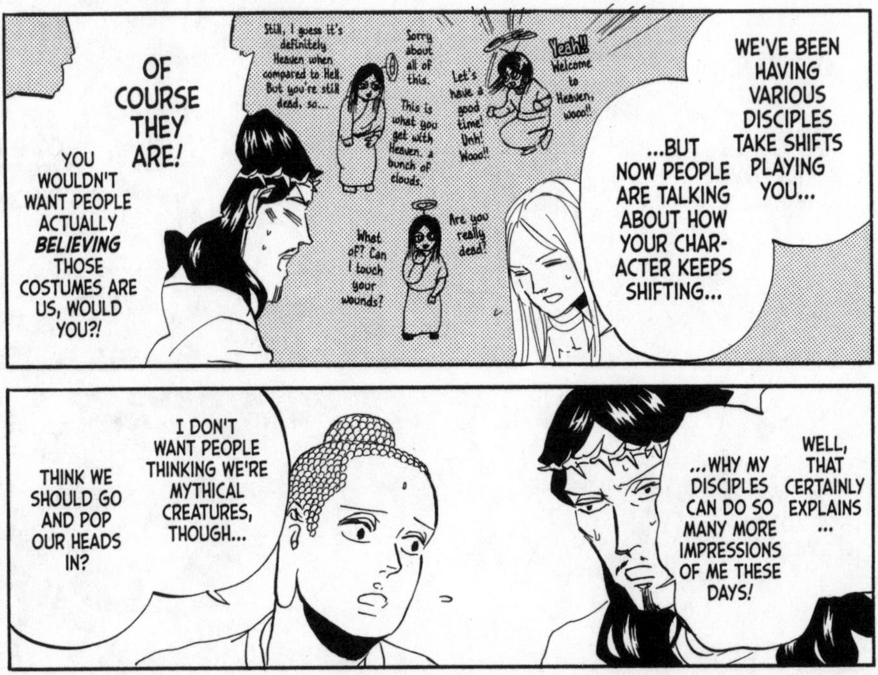
WE'VE BEEN HAVING VARIOUS DISCIPLES TAKE SHIFTS PLAYING YOU...
...BUT NOW PEOPLE ARE TALKING ABOUT HOW YOUR CHARACTER KEEPS SHIFTING...
Yeah!! Welcome to Heaven, wooo!!
Let's have a good time! Unh! Wooo!!
Sorry about all of this.
This is what you get with Heaven, a bunch of clouds.
Still, I guess it's definitely Heaven when compared to Hell. But you're still dead, so...
Are you really dead?
What of? Can I touch your wounds?
OF COURSE THEY ARE!
YOU WOULDN'T WANT PEOPLE ACTUALLY *BELIEVING* THOSE COSTUMES ARE US, WOULD YOU?!
WELL, THAT CERTAINLY EXPLAINS...
...WHY MY DISCIPLES CAN DO SO MANY MORE IMPRESSIONS OF ME THESE DAYS!
I DON'T WANT PEOPLE THINKING WE'RE MYTHICAL CREATURES, THOUGH...
THINK WE SHOULD GO AND POP OUR HEADS IN?

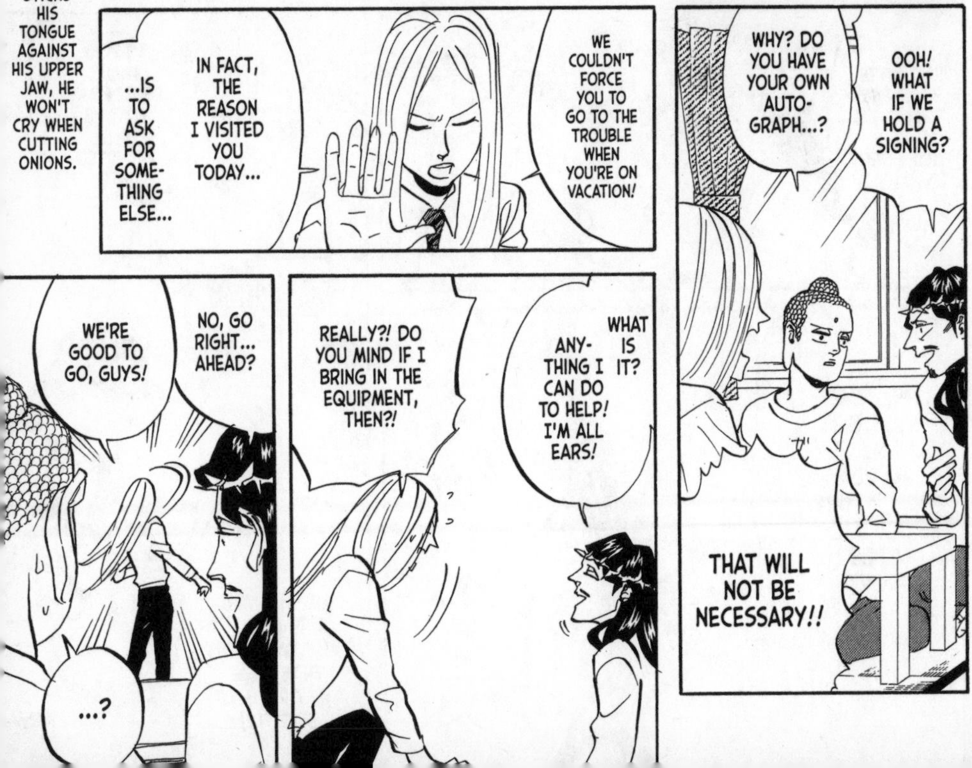
OOH! WHAT IF WE HOLD A SIGNING?
WHY? DO YOU HAVE YOUR OWN AUTOGRAPH...?
THAT WILL NOT BE NECESSARY!!
WE COULDN'T FORCE YOU TO GO TO THE TROUBLE WHEN YOU'RE ON VACATION!
IN FACT, THE REASON I VISITED YOU TODAY...
...IS TO ASK FOR SOMETHING ELSE...
WHAT IS IT?
ANYTHING I CAN DO TO HELP! I'M ALL EARS!
REALLY?! DO YOU MIND IF I BRING IN THE EQUIPMENT, THEN?!
NO, GO RIGHT... AHEAD?
WE'RE GOOD TO GO, GUYS!
...?

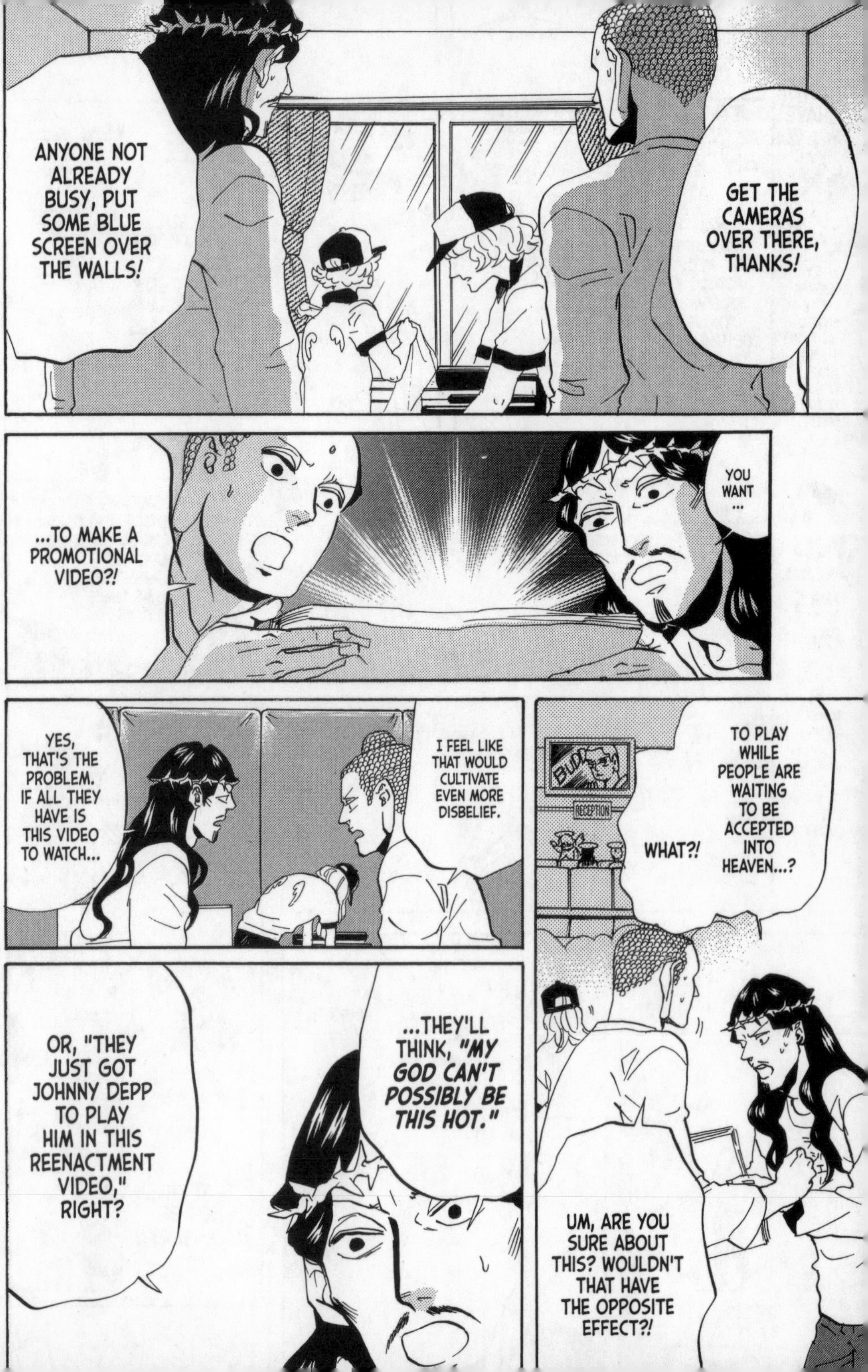
GET THE CAMERAS OVER THERE, THANKS!
ANYONE NOT ALREADY BUSY, PUT SOME BLUE SCREEN OVER THE WALLS!
YOU WANT ...
...TO MAKE A PROMOTIONAL VIDEO?!
TO PLAY WHILE PEOPLE ARE WAITING TO BE ACCEPTED INTO HEAVEN...?
WHAT?!
UM, ARE YOU SURE ABOUT THIS? WOULDN'T THAT HAVE THE OPPOSITE EFFECT?!
I FEEL LIKE THAT WOULD CULTIVATE EVEN MORE DISBELIEF.
YES, THAT'S THE PROBLEM. IF ALL THEY HAVE IS THIS VIDEO TO WATCH...
...THEY'LL THINK, "MY GOD CAN'T POSSIBLY BE THIS HOT."
OR, "THEY JUST GOT JOHNNY DEPP TO PLAY HIM IN THIS REENACTMENT VIDEO," RIGHT?

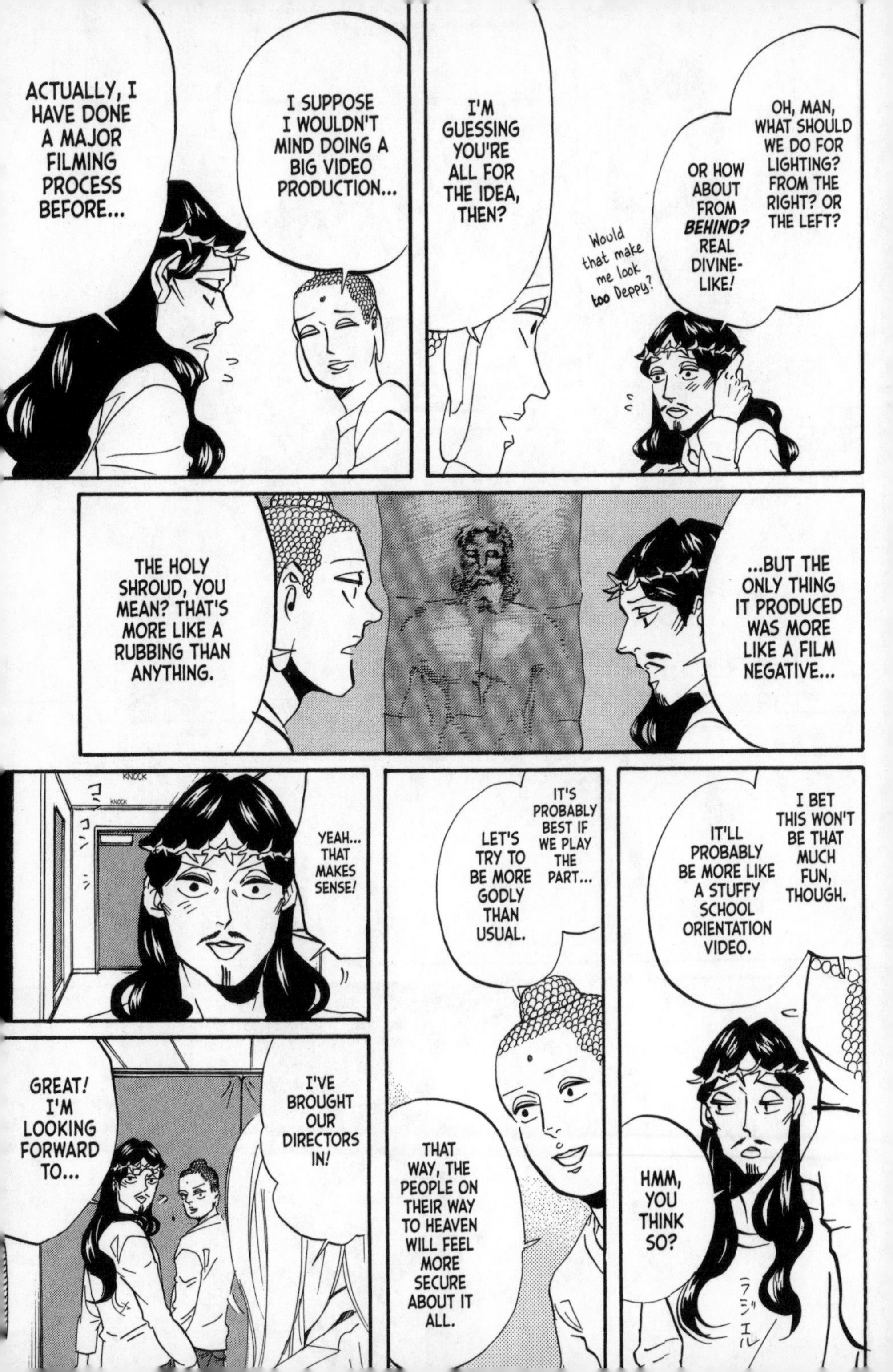
OH, MAN, WHAT SHOULD WE DO FOR LIGHTING? FROM THE RIGHT? OR THE LEFT?
OR HOW ABOUT FROM BEHIND? REAL DIVINE-LIKE!
Would that make me look too Deppy?
I'M GUESSING YOU'RE ALL FOR THE IDEA, THEN?
I SUPPOSE I WOULDN'T MIND DOING A BIG VIDEO PRODUCTION...
ACTUALLY, I HAVE DONE A MAJOR FILMING PROCESS BEFORE...
...BUT THE ONLY THING IT PRODUCED WAS MORE LIKE A FILM NEGATIVE...
THE HOLY SHROUD, YOU MEAN? THAT'S MORE LIKE A RUBBING THAN ANYTHING.
I BET THIS WON'T BE THAT MUCH FUN, THOUGH.
IT'LL PROBABLY BE MORE LIKE A STUFFY SCHOOL ORIENTATION VIDEO.
HMM, YOU THINK SO?
IT'S PROBABLY BEST IF WE PLAY THE PART...
LET'S TRY TO BE MORE GODLY THAN USUAL.
THAT WAY, THE PEOPLE ON THEIR WAY TO HEAVEN WILL FEEL MORE SECURE ABOUT IT ALL.
KNOCK
KNOCK
YEAH... THAT MAKES SENSE!
I'VE BROUGHT OUR DIRECTORS IN!
GREAT! I'M LOOKING FORWARD TO...

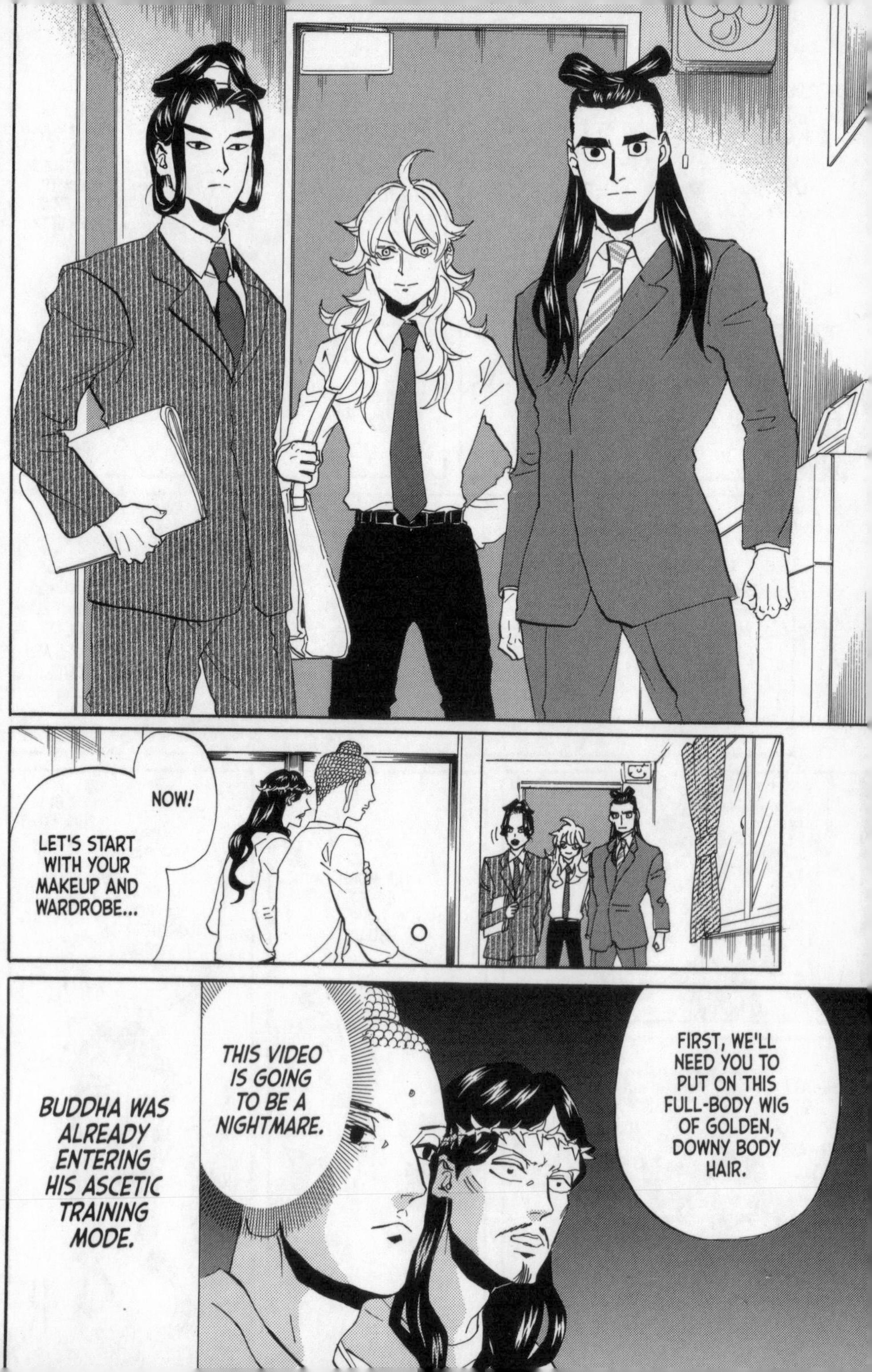
NOW!
LET'S START WITH YOUR MAKEUP AND WARDROBE...
FIRST, WE'LL NEED YOU TO PUT ON THIS FULL-BODY WIG OF GOLDEN, DOWNY BODY HAIR.
THIS VIDEO IS GOING TO BE A NIGHTMARE.
BUDDHA WAS ALREADY ENTERING HIS ASCETIC TRAINING MODE.

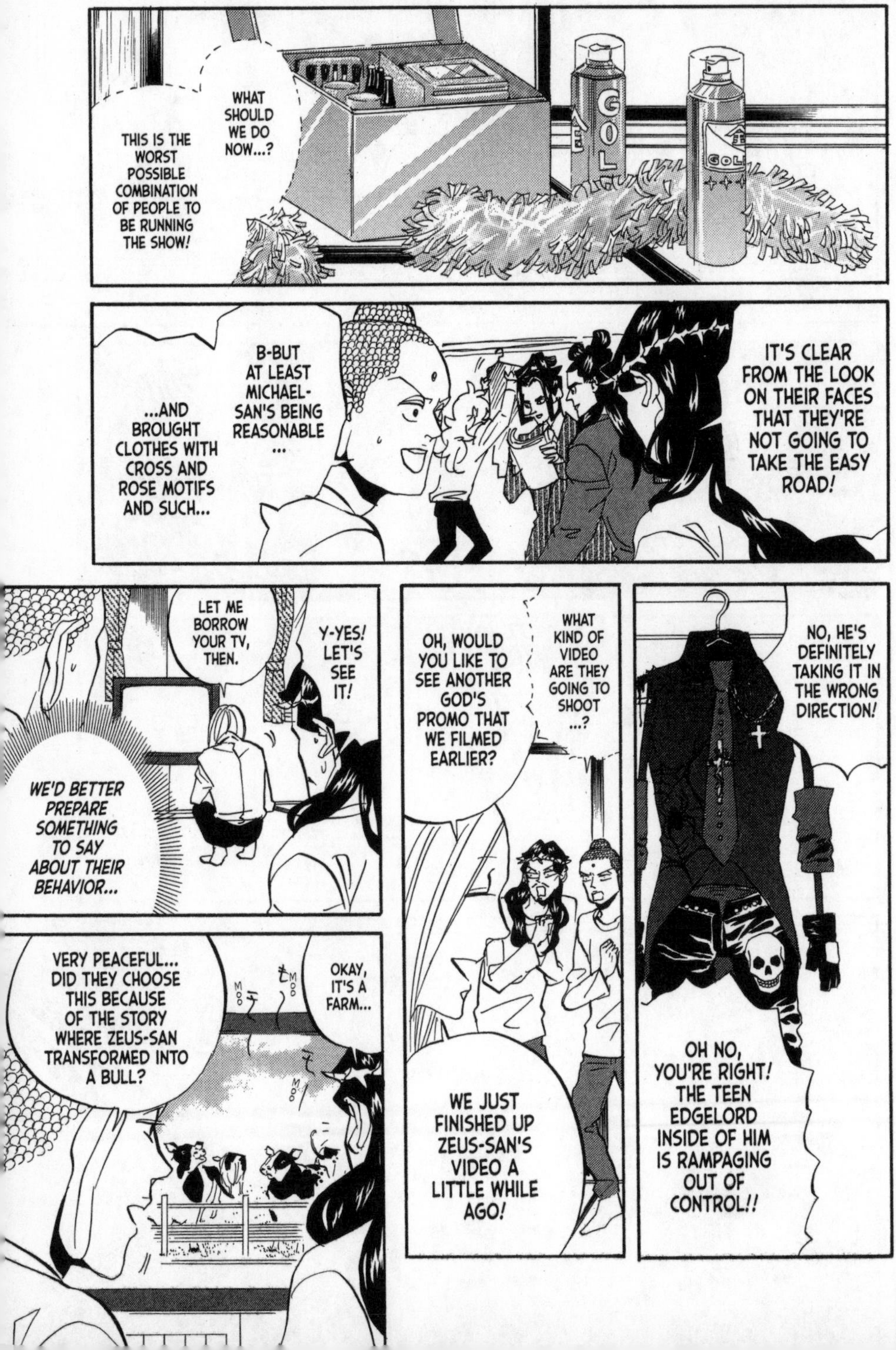
WHAT SHOULD WE DO NOW...?
THIS IS THE WORST POSSIBLE COMBINATION OF PEOPLE TO BE RUNNING THE SHOW!
IT'S CLEAR FROM THE LOOK ON THEIR FACES THAT THEY'RE NOT GOING TO TAKE THE EASY ROAD!
B-BUT AT LEAST MICHAEL-SAN'S BEING REASONABLE...
...AND BROUGHT CLOTHES WITH CROSS AND ROSE MOTIFS AND SUCH...
NO, HE'S DEFINITELY TAKING IT IN THE WRONG DIRECTION!
OH NO, YOU'RE RIGHT! THE TEEN EDGELORD INSIDE OF HIM IS RAMPAGING OUT OF CONTROL!!
WHAT KIND OF VIDEO ARE THEY GOING TO SHOOT...?
OH, WOULD YOU LIKE TO SEE ANOTHER GOD'S PROMO THAT WE FILMED EARLIER?
WE JUST FINISHED UP ZEUS-SAN'S VIDEO A LITTLE WHILE AGO!
Y-YES! LET'S SEE IT!
LET ME BORROW YOUR TV, THEN.
WE'D BETTER PREPARE SOMETHING TO SAY ABOUT THEIR BEHAVIOR...
OKAY, IT'S A FARM...
MOO
MOO
MOO
MOO
VERY PEACEFUL... DID THEY CHOOSE THIS BECAUSE OF THE STORY WHERE ZEUS-SAN TRANSFORMED INTO A BULL?

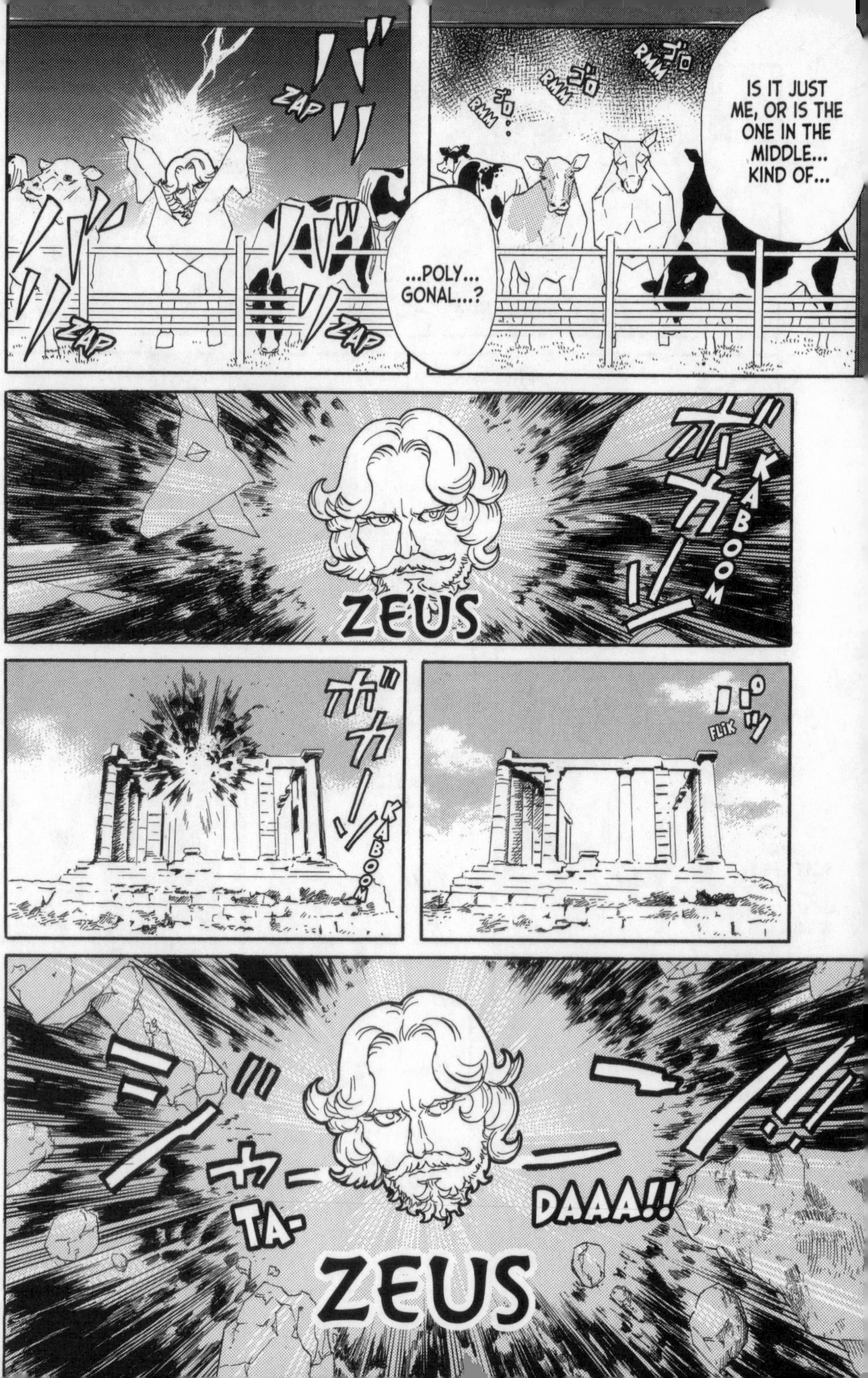
RMM
RMM
RMM
IS IT JUST ME, OR IS THE ONE IN THE MIDDLE... KIND OF...
...POLY... GONAL...?
ZAP
ZAP
ZAP
KABOOM
ZEUS
FLIK
KABOOM
TA-
DAAA!!
ZEUS

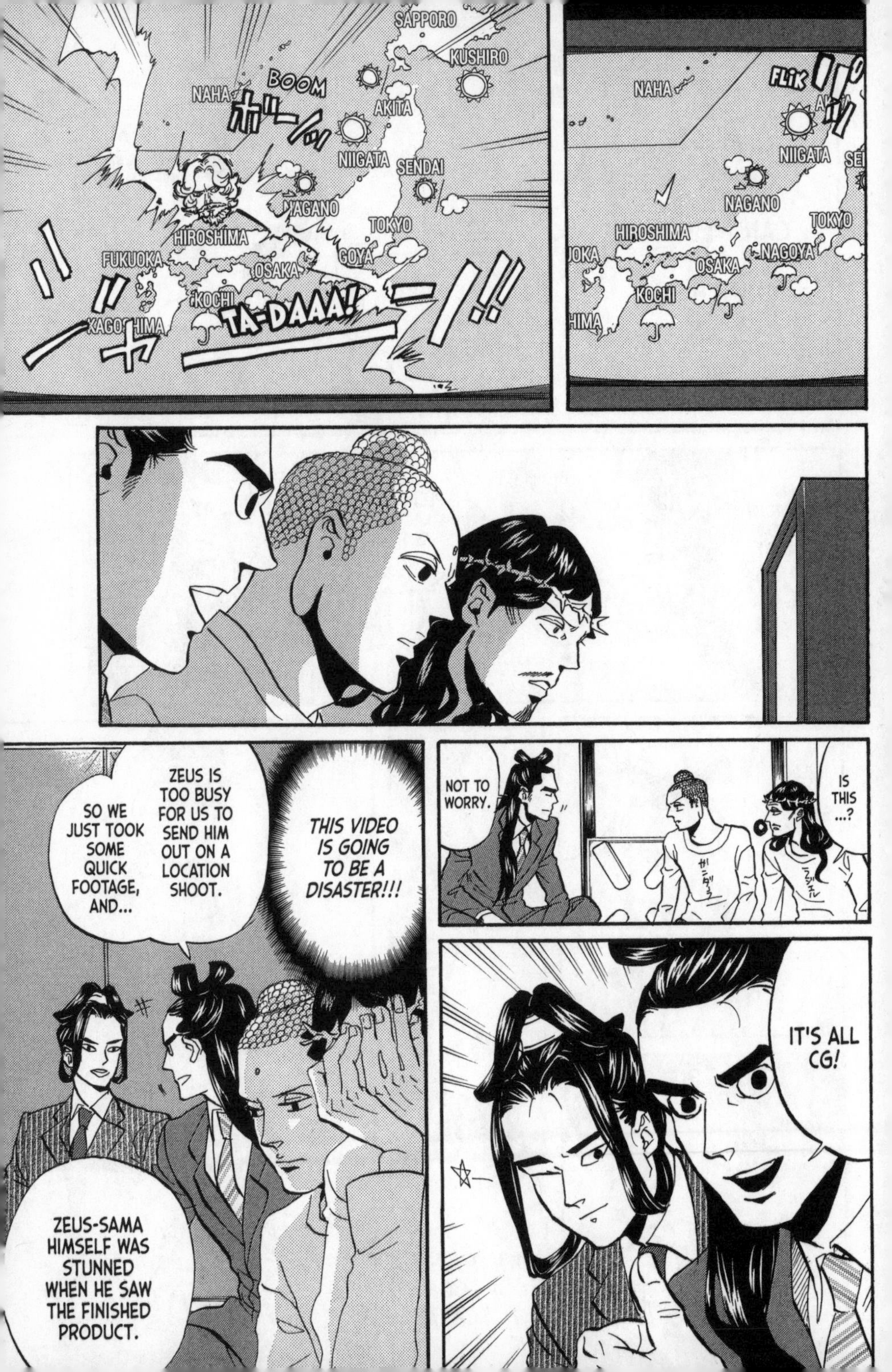
FLIK
NAHA
NIIGATA
NAGANO
TOKYO
HIROSHIMA
NAGOYA
OSAKA
KOCHI
SAPPORO
KUSHIRO
BOOM
NAHA
AKITA
NIIGATA
SENDAI
NAGANO
TOKYO
HIROSHIMA
FUKUOKA
OSAKA
KOCHI
KAGOSHIMA
TA-DAAA!
IS THIS ...?
NOT TO WORRY.
IT'S ALL CG!
THIS VIDEO IS GOING TO BE A DISASTER!!!
ZEUS IS TOO BUSY FOR US TO SEND HIM OUT ON A LOCATION SHOOT.
SO WE JUST TOOK SOME QUICK FOOTAGE, AND...
ZEUS-SAMA HIMSELF WAS STUNNED WHEN HE SAW THE FINISHED PRODUCT.

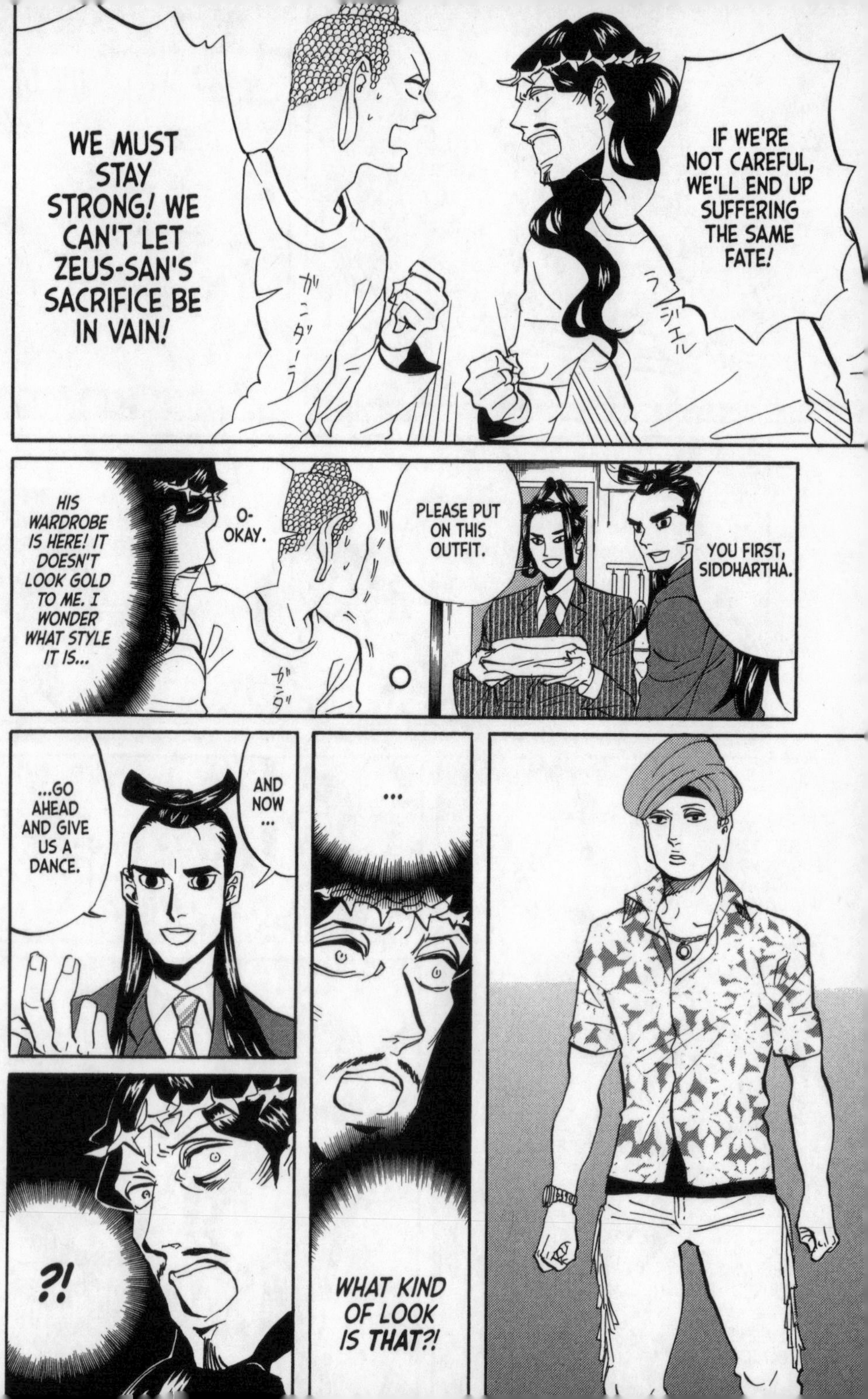
IF WE'RE NOT CAREFUL, WE'LL END UP SUFFERING THE SAME FATE!
WE MUST STAY STRONG! WE CAN'T LET ZEUS-SAN'S SACRIFICE BE IN VAIN!
YOU FIRST, SIDDHARTHA.
PLEASE PUT ON THIS OUTFIT.
O-OKAY.
HIS WARDROBE IS HERE! IT DOESN'T LOOK GOLD TO ME. I WONDER WHAT STYLE IT IS...
...
WHAT KIND OF LOOK IS THAT?!
AND NOW ...
...GO AHEAD AND GIVE US A DANCE.
?!

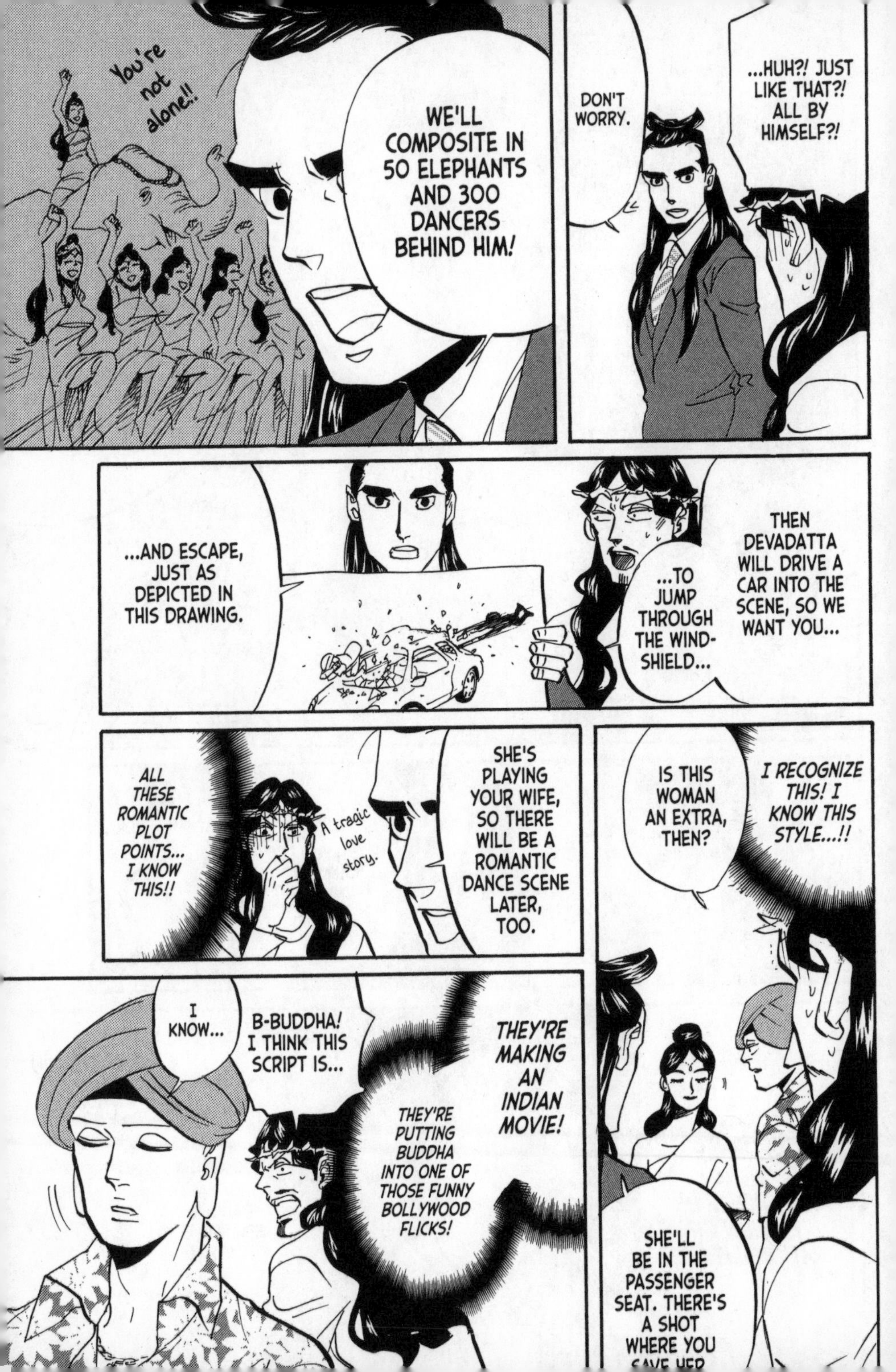
...HUH?! JUST LIKE THAT?! ALL BY HIMSELF?!
DON'T WORRY.
WE'LL COMPOSITE IN 50 ELEPHANTS AND 300 DANCERS BEHIND HIM!
You're not alone!!
THEN DEVADATTA WILL DRIVE A CAR INTO THE SCENE, SO WE WANT YOU...
...TO JUMP THROUGH THE WIND-SHIELD...
...AND ESCAPE, JUST AS DEPICTED IN THIS DRAWING.
I RECOGNIZE THIS! I KNOW THIS STYLE...!!
IS THIS WOMAN AN EXTRA, THEN?
SHE'LL BE IN THE PASSENGER SEAT. THERE'S A SHOT WHERE YOU SAVE HER
SHE'S PLAYING YOUR WIFE, SO THERE WILL BE A ROMANTIC DANCE SCENE LATER, TOO.
A tragic love story.
ALL THESE ROMANTIC PLOT POINTS... I KNOW THIS!!
THEY'RE MAKING AN INDIAN MOVIE!
THEY'RE PUTTING BUDDHA INTO ONE OF THOSE FUNNY BOLLYWOOD FLICKS!
B-BUDDHA! I THINK THIS SCRIPT IS...
I KNOW...

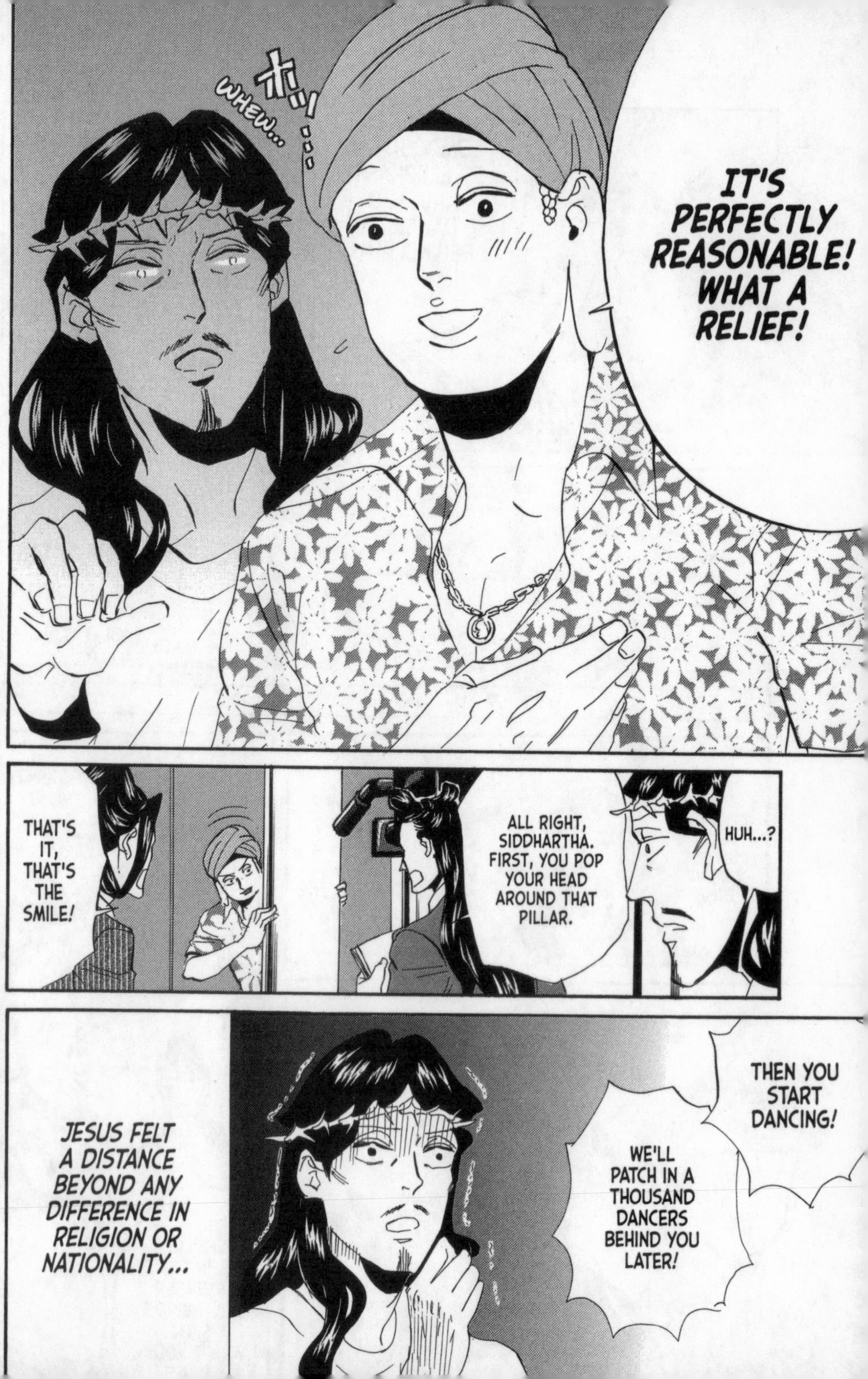
IT'S PERFECTLY REASONABLE! WHAT A RELIEF!
ホッ
WHEW...
HUH...?
ALL RIGHT, SIDDHARTHA. FIRST, YOU POP YOUR HEAD AROUND THAT PILLAR.
THAT'S IT, THAT'S THE SMILE!
THEN YOU START DANCING!
WE'LL PATCH IN A THOUSAND DANCERS BEHIND YOU LATER!
JESUS FELT A DISTANCE BEYOND ANY DIFFERENCE IN RELIGION OR NATIONALITY...

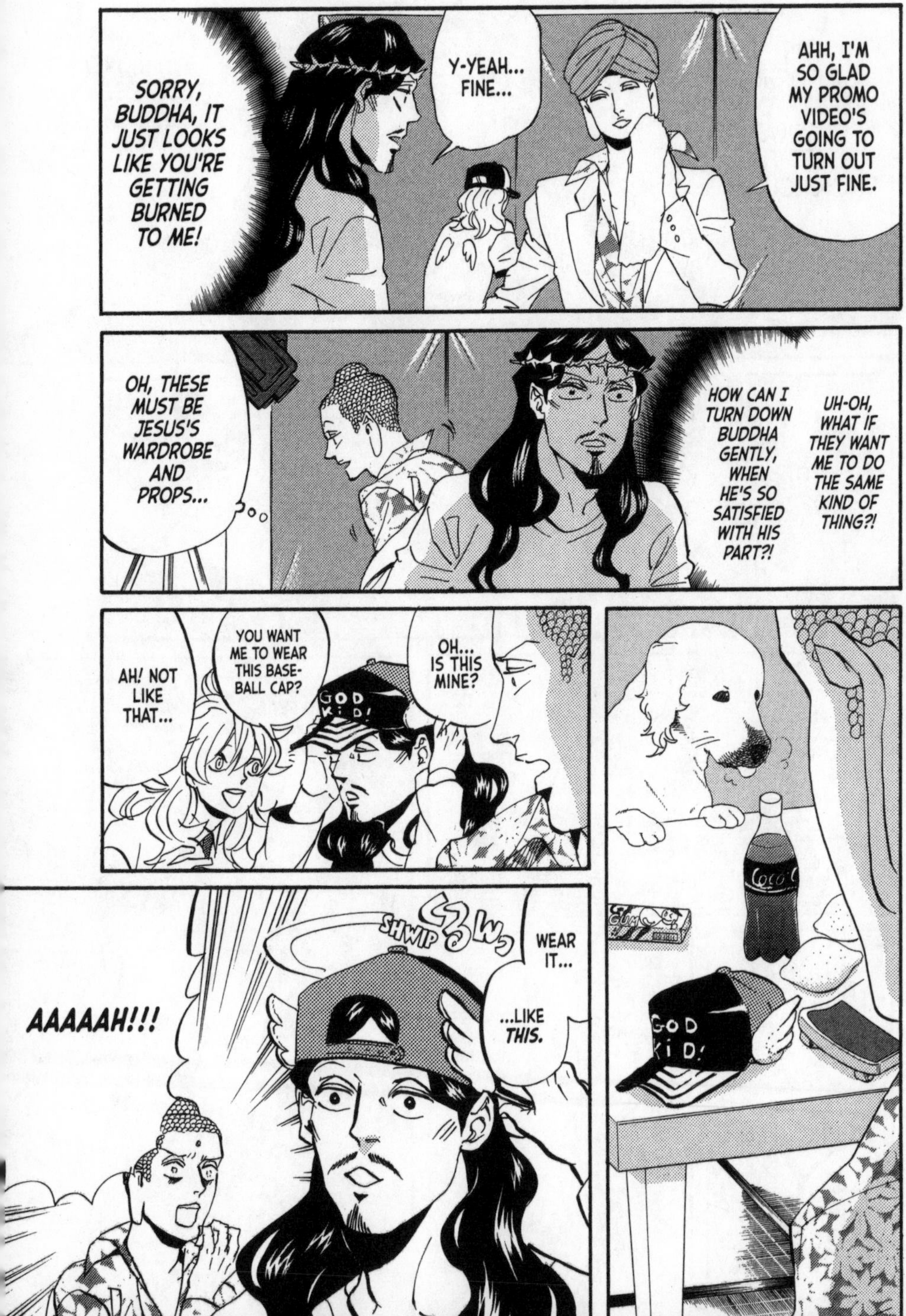
AHH, I'M SO GLAD MY PROMO VIDEO'S GOING TO TURN OUT JUST FINE.
Y-YEAH... FINE...
SORRY, BUDDHA, IT JUST LOOKS LIKE YOU'RE GETTING BURNED TO ME!
UH-OH, WHAT IF THEY WANT ME TO DO THE SAME KIND OF THING?!
HOW CAN I TURN DOWN BUDDHA GENTLY, WHEN HE'S SO SATISFIED WITH HIS PART?!
OH, THESE MUST BE JESUS'S WARDROBE AND PROPS...
GOD KiD!
GUM
OH... IS THIS MINE?
YOU WANT ME TO WEAR THIS BASE-BALL CAP?
GOD KiD!
AH! NOT LIKE THAT...
SHWIP
WEAR IT...
...LIKE *THIS.*
AAAAAH!!!

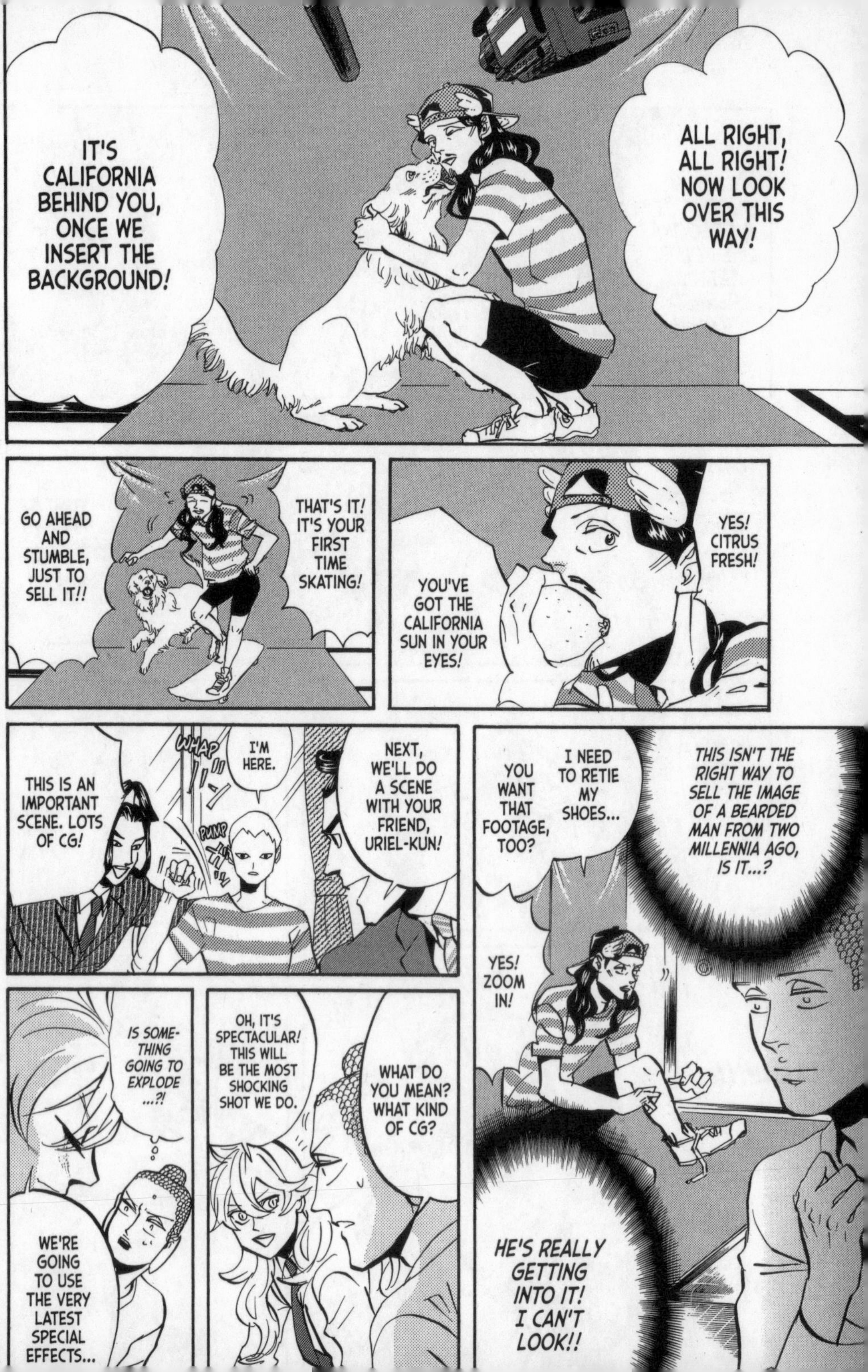
ALL RIGHT, ALL RIGHT! NOW LOOK OVER THIS WAY!
IT'S CALIFORNIA BEHIND YOU, ONCE WE INSERT THE BACKGROUND!
YES! CITRUS FRESH!
YOU'VE GOT THE CALIFORNIA SUN IN YOUR EYES!
THAT'S IT! IT'S YOUR FIRST TIME SKATING!
GO AHEAD AND STUMBLE, JUST TO SELL IT!!
THIS ISN'T THE RIGHT WAY TO SELL THE IMAGE OF A BEARDED MAN FROM TWO MILLENNIA AGO, IS IT...?
I NEED TO RETIE MY SHOES...
YOU WANT THAT FOOTAGE, TOO?
YES! ZOOM IN!
HE'S REALLY GETTING INTO IT! I CAN'T LOOK!!
NEXT, WE'LL DO A SCENE WITH YOUR FRIEND, URIEL-KUN!
I'M HERE.
WHAP
PUMP
THIS IS AN IMPORTANT SCENE. LOTS OF CG!
WHAT DO YOU MEAN? WHAT KIND OF CG?
OH, IT'S SPECTACULAR! THIS WILL BE THE MOST SHOCKING SHOT WE DO.
IS SOME-THING GOING TO EXPLODE ...?!
WE'RE GOING TO USE THE VERY LATEST SPECIAL EFFECTS...

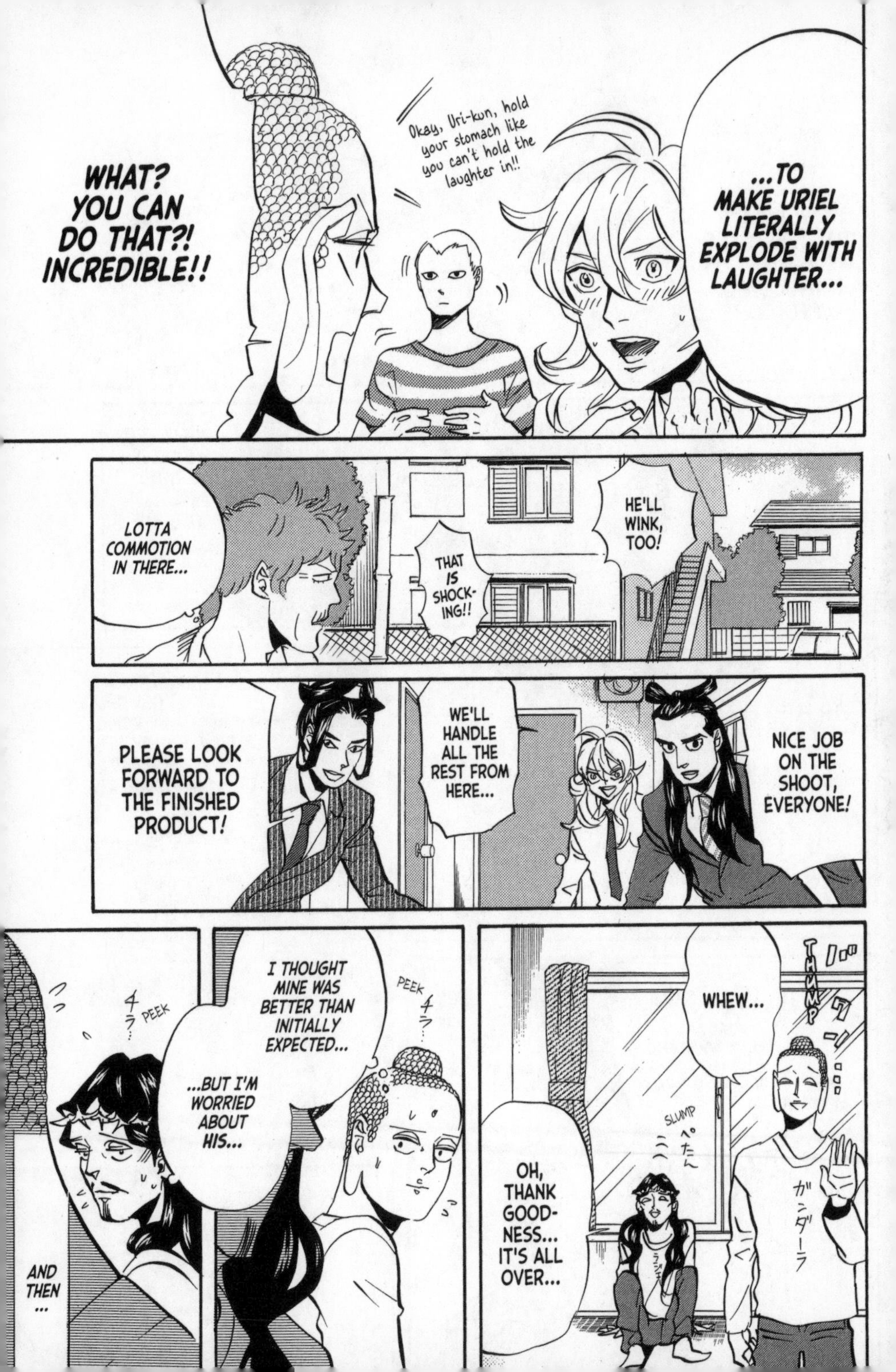
...TO MAKE URIEL LITERALLY EXPLODE WITH LAUGHTER...
Okay, Uri-kun, hold your stomach like you can't hold the laughter in!!
WHAT? YOU CAN DO THAT?! INCREDIBLE!!
HE'LL WINK, TOO!
THAT IS SHOCKING!!
LOTTA COMMOTION IN THERE...
NICE JOB ON THE SHOOT, EVERYONE!
WE'LL HANDLE ALL THE REST FROM HERE...
PLEASE LOOK FORWARD TO THE FINISHED PRODUCT!
THUMP
WHEW...
SLUMP
OH, THANK GOODNESS... IT'S ALL OVER...
ガンダーラ
PEEK
I THOUGHT MINE WAS BETTER THAN INITIALLY EXPECTED...
...BUT I'M WORRIED ABOUT HIS...
PEEK
AND THEN...

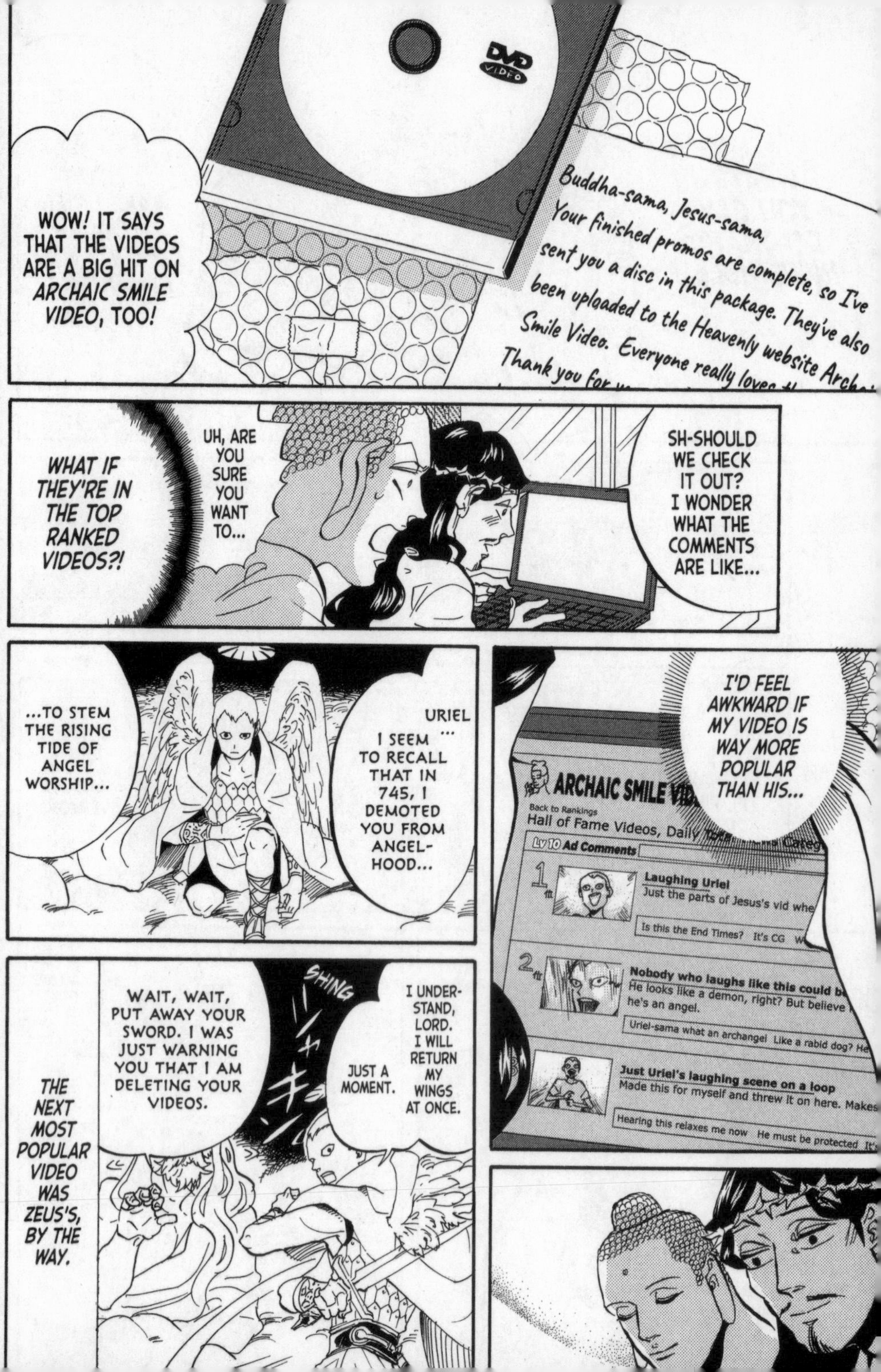
Buddha-sama, Jesus-sama,
Your finished promos are complete, so I've sent you a disc in this package. They've also been uploaded to the Heavenly website Archaic Smile Video. Everyone really loves
Thank you for
DVD VIDEO
WOW! IT SAYS THAT THE VIDEOS ARE A BIG HIT ON ARCHAIC SMILE VIDEO, TOO!
SH-SHOULD WE CHECK IT OUT? I WONDER WHAT THE COMMENTS ARE LIKE...
UH, ARE YOU SURE YOU WANT TO...
WHAT IF THEY'RE IN THE TOP RANKED VIDEOS?!
I'D FEEL AWKWARD IF MY VIDEO IS WAY MORE POPULAR THAN HIS...
ARCHAIC SMILE
Back to Rankings
Hall of Fame Videos, Daily
Lv 10 Ad Comments
1
Laughing Uriel
Just the parts of Jesus's vid
Is this the End Times? It's CG
2
Nobody who laughs like this could
He looks like a demon, right? But believe
he's an angel.
Uriel-sama what an archangel Like a rabid dog?
Just Uriel's laughing scene on a loop
Made this for myself and threw it on here.
Hearing this relaxes me now He must be protected
URIEL ... I SEEM TO RECALL THAT IN 745, I DEMOTED YOU FROM ANGEL-HOOD...
...TO STEM THE RISING TIDE OF ANGEL WORSHIP...
I UNDERSTAND, LORD. I WILL RETURN MY WINGS AT ONCE.
JUST A MOMENT.
SHING
WAIT, WAIT, PUT AWAY YOUR SWORD. I WAS JUST WARNING YOU THAT I AM DELETING YOUR VIDEOS.
THE NEXT MOST POPULAR VIDEO WAS ZEUS'S, BY THE WAY.

I am the Buddha, the Enlightened One!!
My every breath is golden wind, and my voice is the song of the bird of paradise!!!

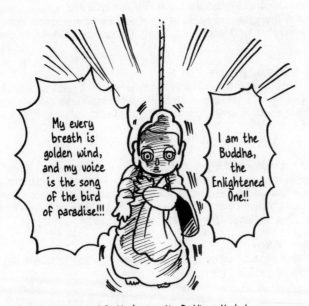

Different disciples of Buddha's wear the Buddha suit, but they pretty much all end up sounding like this.

CHAPTER 47 TRANSLATION NOTES

Dog of Flanders, page 55
A touching and tragic 19th century English novel about a poor Belgian boy named Nello and his dog, Patrasche. Very popular in Japan, it received a 1975 TV anime adaptation that remains one of the most beloved animation series ever. At the tragic end, Nello and Patrasche freeze to death in the winter, and witness cherubim coming to take them up to heaven.

Holy Shroud, page 59
A burial shroud, also known as the Shroud of Turin, which is purportedly what Jesus was buried in after his crucifixion. In the original Japanese, Buddha compares the process to gyotaku (literally "fish printing"), a practice of creating ink rubbings of fish for aesthetic or record-keeping purposes.

Raziel, page 59
A Judeo-Christian archangel, Raziel is known as being a keeper of secret knowledge. In Jewish Kabbalah, one story holds that Raziel gave Adam and Eve his book of knowledge after they ate the forbidden fruit and were exiled from the Garden of Eden.

Gandhara, page 63
The name of an ancient kingdom in present day Pakistan which was a major center of ancient Buddhism. It was the source of some of the oldest Buddhist manuscripts, and also home to a flourishing style of Greco-Buddhist art that combined Hellenistic and Buddhist traditions.

Archaic Smile Video, page 70
The archaic smile is the name of a type of facial expression often seen on ancient Greek sculpture. In this case, it's also a pun on the popular Japanese video-hosting website Nico Nico Video, which is analogous to Youtube, and translates to "Smiley-Smile Video."

Uriel, page 70
The archangel Uriel is not mentioned in any of the books of the Protestant Christian Bible, but does appear in material accepted as canonical in Roman Catholicism and Eastern Orthodox Christianity. Pope St. Zachary forbade obsession with angel worship in 745 to head off certain practices growing in popularity at the time, and held that certain books that heavily mentioned Uriel were not canonical.

***Archaic Smile Video*, page 72**
The "archaic smile" is a type of smile seen on Greek statues from the Archaic period (5th - 6th centuries BCE).

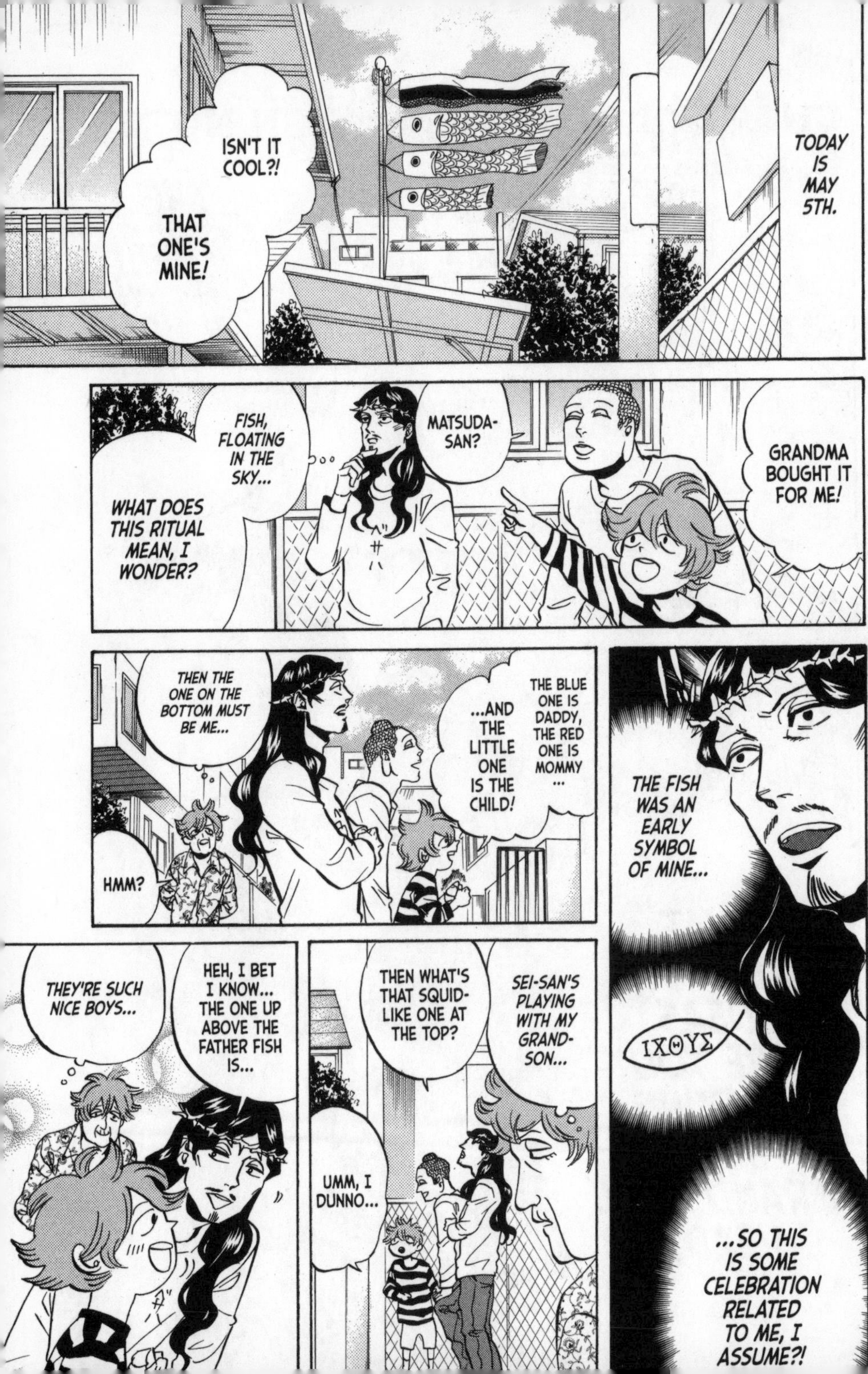

TODAY IS MAY 5TH.
ISN'T IT COOL?!
THAT ONE'S MINE!
GRANDMA BOUGHT IT FOR ME!
MATSUDA-SAN?
FISH, FLOATING IN THE SKY...
WHAT DOES THIS RITUAL MEAN, I WONDER?
THE FISH WAS AN EARLY SYMBOL OF MINE...
ΙΧΘΥΣ
...SO THIS IS SOME CELEBRATION RELATED TO ME, I ASSUME?!
THE BLUE ONE IS DADDY, THE RED ONE IS MOMMY ...
...AND THE LITTLE ONE IS THE CHILD!
THEN THE ONE ON THE BOTTOM MUST BE ME...
HMM?
SEI-SAN'S PLAYING WITH MY GRANDSON...
THEN WHAT'S THAT SQUID-LIKE ONE AT THE TOP?
UMM, I DUNNO...
HEH, I BET I KNOW... THE ONE UP ABOVE THE FATHER FISH IS...
THEY'RE SUCH NICE BOYS...

JESUS' SHIRT: PESACH

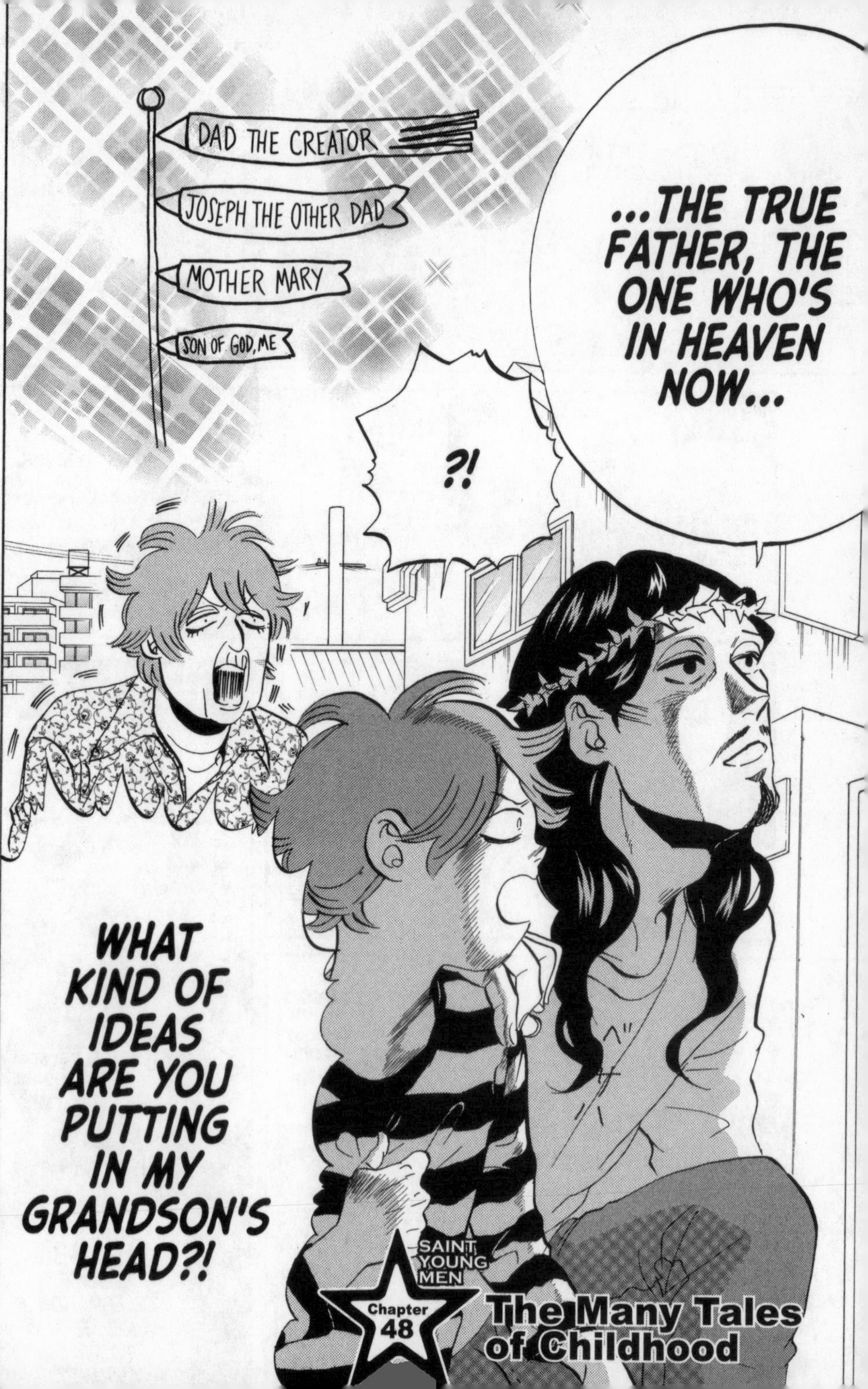
...THE TRUE FATHER, THE ONE WHO'S IN HEAVEN NOW...
DAD THE CREATOR
JOSEPH THE OTHER DAD
MOTHER MARY
SON OF GOD, ME
?!
WHAT KIND OF IDEAS ARE YOU PUTTING IN MY GRANDSON'S HEAD?!
SAINT YOUNG MEN
Chapter 48
The Many Tales of Childhood

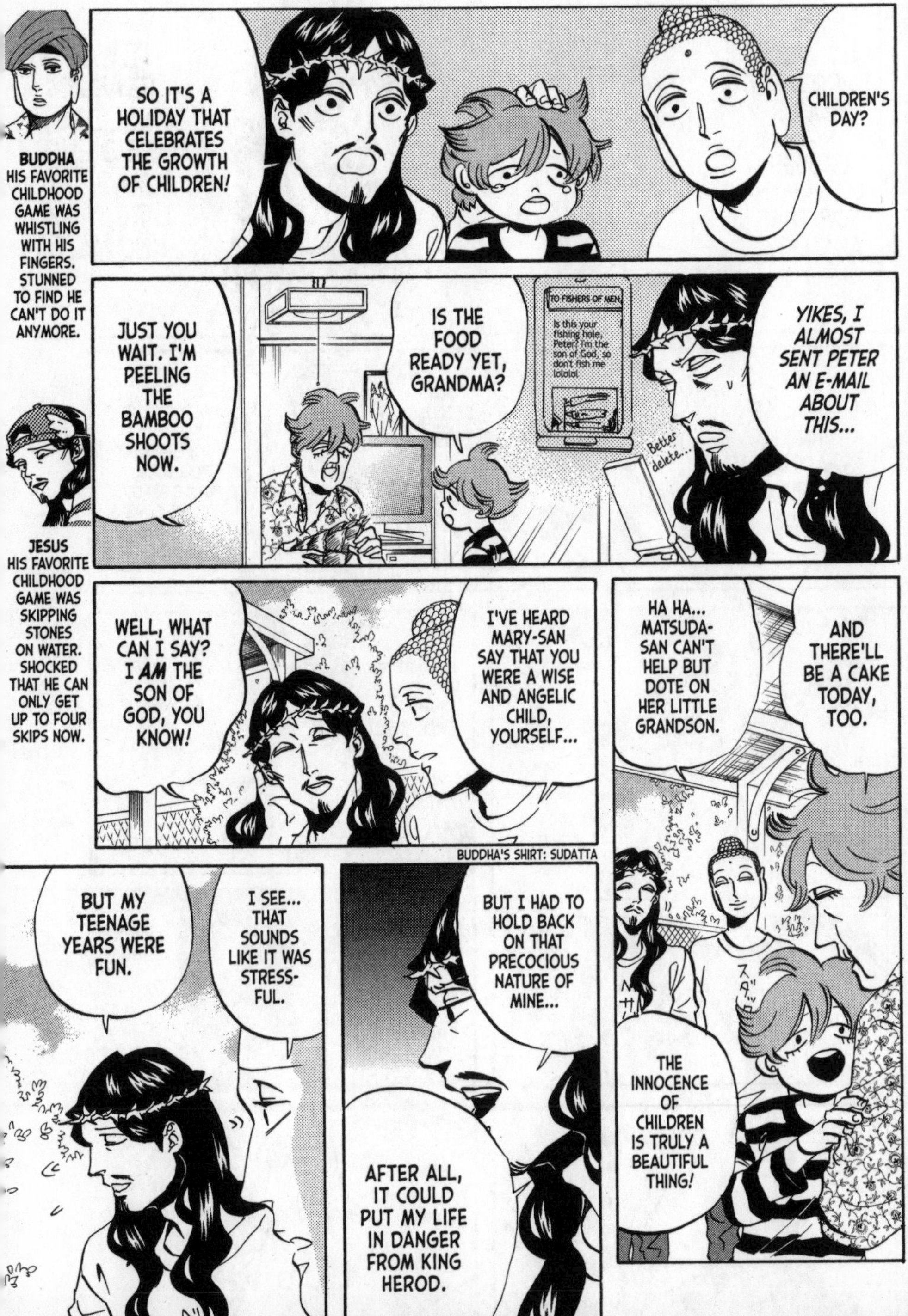
CHILDREN'S DAY?
SO IT'S A HOLIDAY THAT CELEBRATES THE GROWTH OF CHILDREN!
YIKES, I ALMOST SENT PETER AN E-MAIL ABOUT THIS...
TO FISHERS OF MEN
Is this your fishing hole, Peter? I'm the son of God, so don't fish me lololol.
Better delete...
IS THE FOOD READY YET, GRANDMA?
JUST YOU WAIT. I'M PEELING THE BAMBOO SHOOTS NOW.
AND THERE'LL BE A CAKE TODAY, TOO.
HA HA... MATSUDA-SAN CAN'T HELP BUT DOTE ON HER LITTLE GRANDSON.
THE INNOCENCE OF CHILDREN IS TRULY A BEAUTIFUL THING!
I'VE HEARD MARY-SAN SAY THAT YOU WERE A WISE AND ANGELIC CHILD, YOURSELF...
WELL, WHAT CAN I SAY? I *AM* THE SON OF GOD, YOU KNOW!
BUDDHA'S SHIRT: SUDATTA
BUT I HAD TO HOLD BACK ON THAT PRECOCIOUS NATURE OF MINE...
AFTER ALL, IT COULD PUT MY LIFE IN DANGER FROM KING HEROD.
I SEE... THAT SOUNDS LIKE IT WAS STRESS-FUL.
BUT MY TEENAGE YEARS WERE FUN.
BUDDHA HIS FAVORITE CHILDHOOD GAME WAS WHISTLING WITH HIS FINGERS. STUNNED TO FIND HE CAN'T DO IT ANYMORE.
JESUS HIS FAVORITE CHILDHOOD GAME WAS SKIPPING STONES ON WATER. SHOCKED THAT HE CAN ONLY GET UP TO FOUR SKIPS NOW.

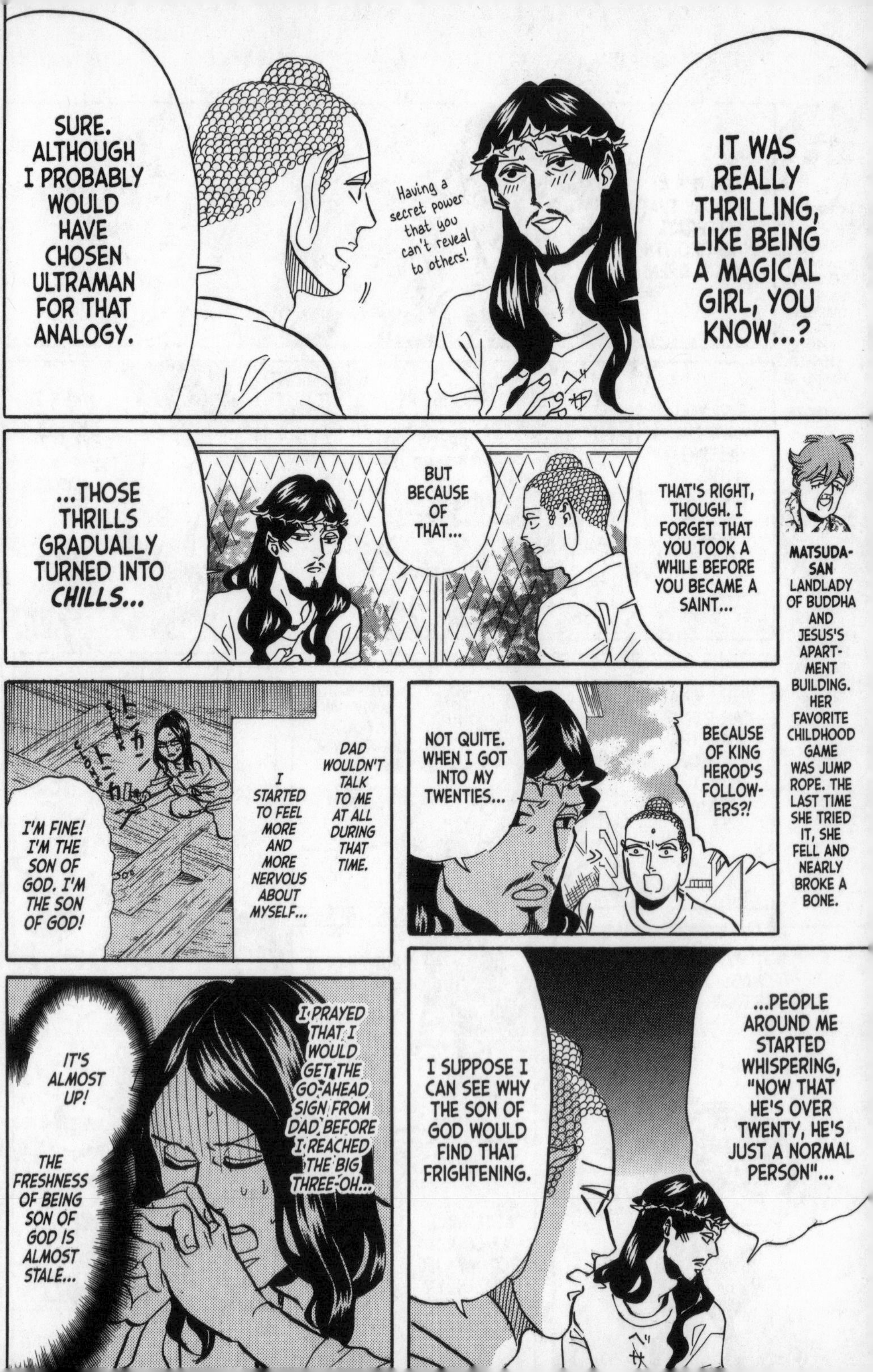
IT WAS REALLY THRILLING, LIKE BEING A MAGICAL GIRL, YOU KNOW...?
Having a secret power that you can't reveal to others!
SURE. ALTHOUGH I PROBABLY WOULD HAVE CHOSEN ULTRAMAN FOR THAT ANALOGY.
MATSUDA-SAN LANDLADY OF BUDDHA AND JESUS'S APARTMENT BUILDING. HER FAVORITE CHILDHOOD GAME WAS JUMP ROPE. THE LAST TIME SHE TRIED IT, SHE FELL AND NEARLY BROKE A BONE.
THAT'S RIGHT, THOUGH. I FORGET THAT YOU TOOK A WHILE BEFORE YOU BECAME A SAINT...
BUT BECAUSE OF THAT...
...THOSE THRILLS GRADUALLY TURNED INTO *CHILLS*...
BECAUSE OF KING HEROD'S FOLLOWERS?!
NOT QUITE. WHEN I GOT INTO MY TWENTIES...
DAD WOULDN'T TALK TO ME AT ALL DURING THAT TIME.
I STARTED TO FEEL MORE AND MORE NERVOUS ABOUT MYSELF...
I'M FINE! I'M THE SON OF GOD. I'M THE SON OF GOD!
...PEOPLE AROUND ME STARTED WHISPERING, "NOW THAT HE'S OVER TWENTY, HE'S JUST A NORMAL PERSON"...
I SUPPOSE I CAN SEE WHY THE SON OF GOD WOULD FIND THAT FRIGHTENING.
I PRAYED THAT I WOULD GET THE GO-AHEAD SIGN FROM DAD BEFORE I REACHED THE BIG THREE-OH...
IT'S ALMOST UP!
THE FRESHNESS OF BEING SON OF GOD IS ALMOST STALE...

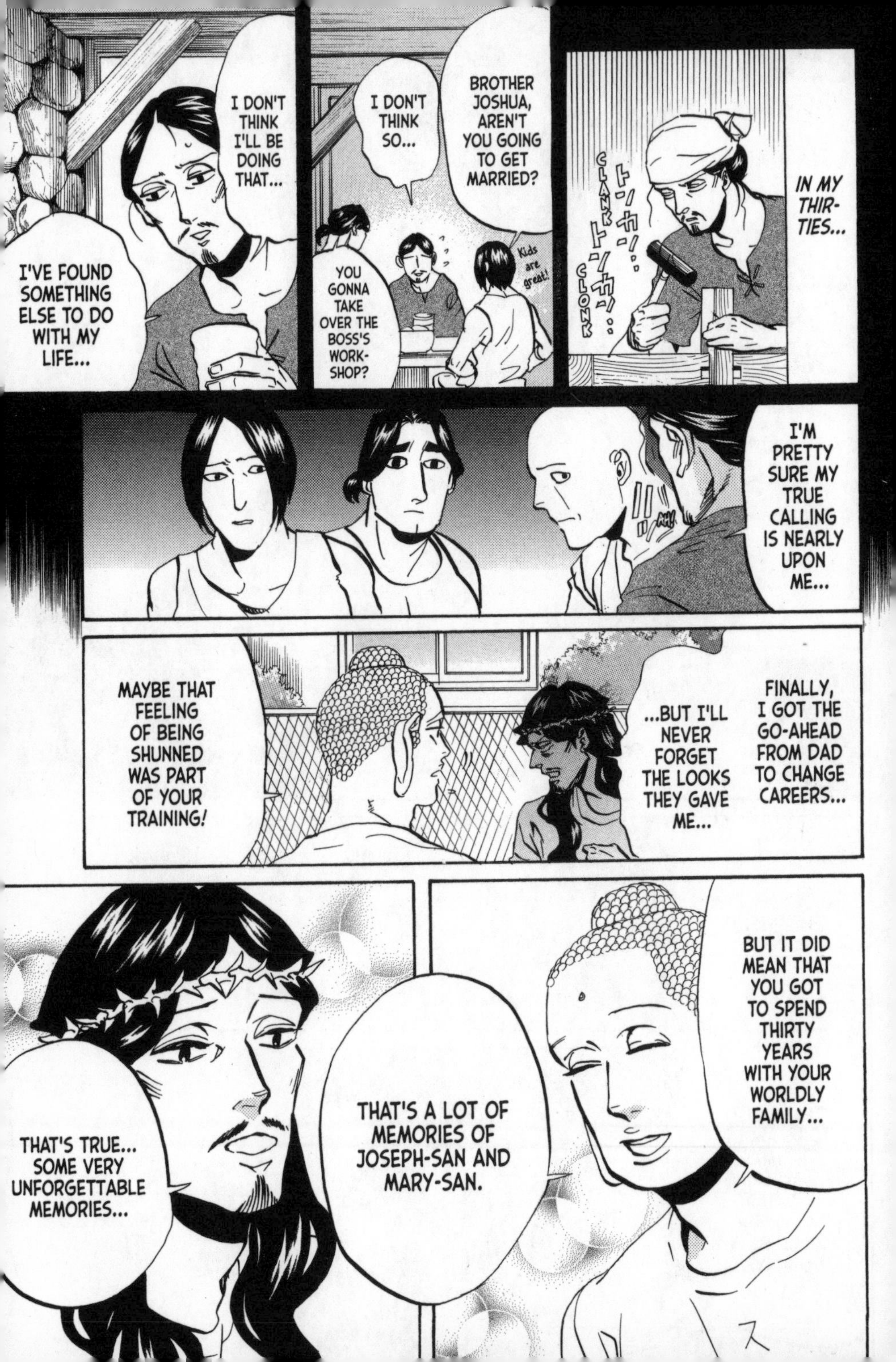
IN MY THIRTIES...
CLANK
CLONK
BROTHER JOSHUA, AREN'T YOU GOING TO GET MARRIED?
I DON'T THINK SO...
Kids are great!
YOU GONNA TAKE OVER THE BOSS'S WORKSHOP?
I DON'T THINK I'LL BE DOING THAT...
I'VE FOUND SOMETHING ELSE TO DO WITH MY LIFE...
I'M PRETTY SURE MY TRUE CALLING IS NEARLY UPON ME...
AH!
FINALLY, I GOT THE GO-AHEAD FROM DAD TO CHANGE CAREERS...
...BUT I'LL NEVER FORGET THE LOOKS THEY GAVE ME...
MAYBE THAT FEELING OF BEING SHUNNED WAS PART OF YOUR TRAINING!
BUT IT DID MEAN THAT YOU GOT TO SPEND THIRTY YEARS WITH YOUR WORLDLY FAMILY...
THAT'S A LOT OF MEMORIES OF JOSEPH-SAN AND MARY-SAN.
THAT'S TRUE... SOME VERY UNFORGETTABLE MEMORIES...

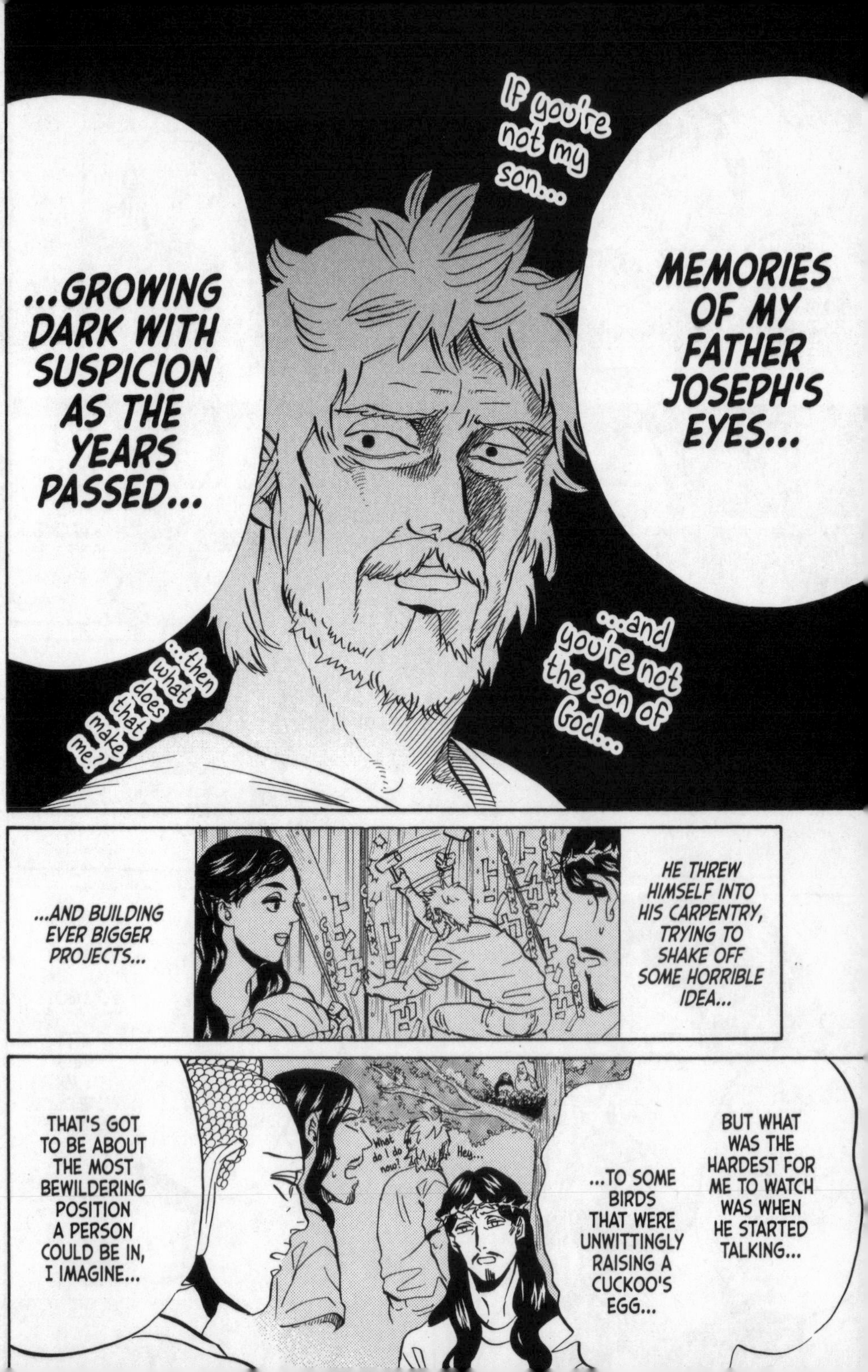
MEMORIES OF MY FATHER JOSEPH'S EYES...
If you're not my son...
...GROWING DARK WITH SUSPICION AS THE YEARS PASSED...
...and you're not the son of God...
...then what does that make me?
HE THREW HIMSELF INTO HIS CARPENTRY, TRYING TO SHAKE OFF SOME HORRIBLE IDEA...
...AND BUILDING EVER BIGGER PROJECTS...
BUT WHAT WAS THE HARDEST FOR ME TO WATCH WAS WHEN HE STARTED TALKING...
...TO SOME BIRDS THAT WERE UNWITTINGLY RAISING A CUCKOO'S EGG...
Hey...
What do I do now?
THAT'S GOT TO BE ABOUT THE MOST BEWILDERING POSITION A PERSON COULD BE IN, I IMAGINE...

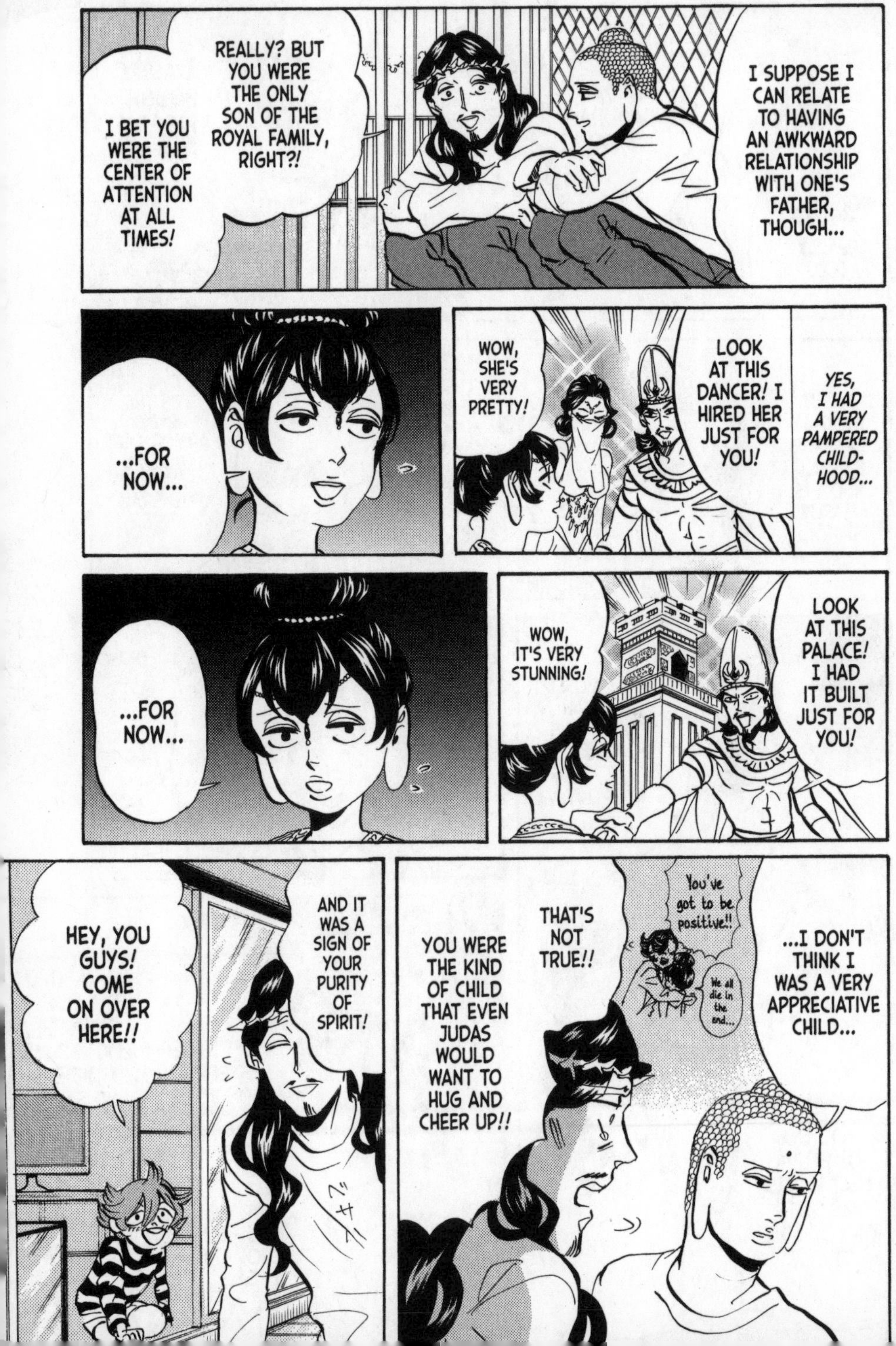
I SUPPOSE I CAN RELATE TO HAVING AN AWKWARD RELATIONSHIP WITH ONE'S FATHER, THOUGH...
REALLY? BUT YOU WERE THE ONLY SON OF THE ROYAL FAMILY, RIGHT?!
I BET YOU WERE THE CENTER OF ATTENTION AT ALL TIMES!
YES, I HAD A VERY PAMPERED CHILDHOOD...
LOOK AT THIS DANCER! I HIRED HER JUST FOR YOU!
WOW, SHE'S VERY PRETTY!
...FOR NOW...
LOOK AT THIS PALACE! I HAD IT BUILT JUST FOR YOU!
WOW, IT'S VERY STUNNING!
...FOR NOW...
...I DON'T THINK I WAS A VERY APPRECIATIVE CHILD...
You've got to be positive!!
We all die in the end...
THAT'S NOT TRUE!!
YOU WERE THE KIND OF CHILD THAT EVEN JUDAS WOULD WANT TO HUG AND CHEER UP!!
AND IT WAS A SIGN OF YOUR PURITY OF SPIRIT!
HEY, YOU GUYS! COME ON OVER HERE!!

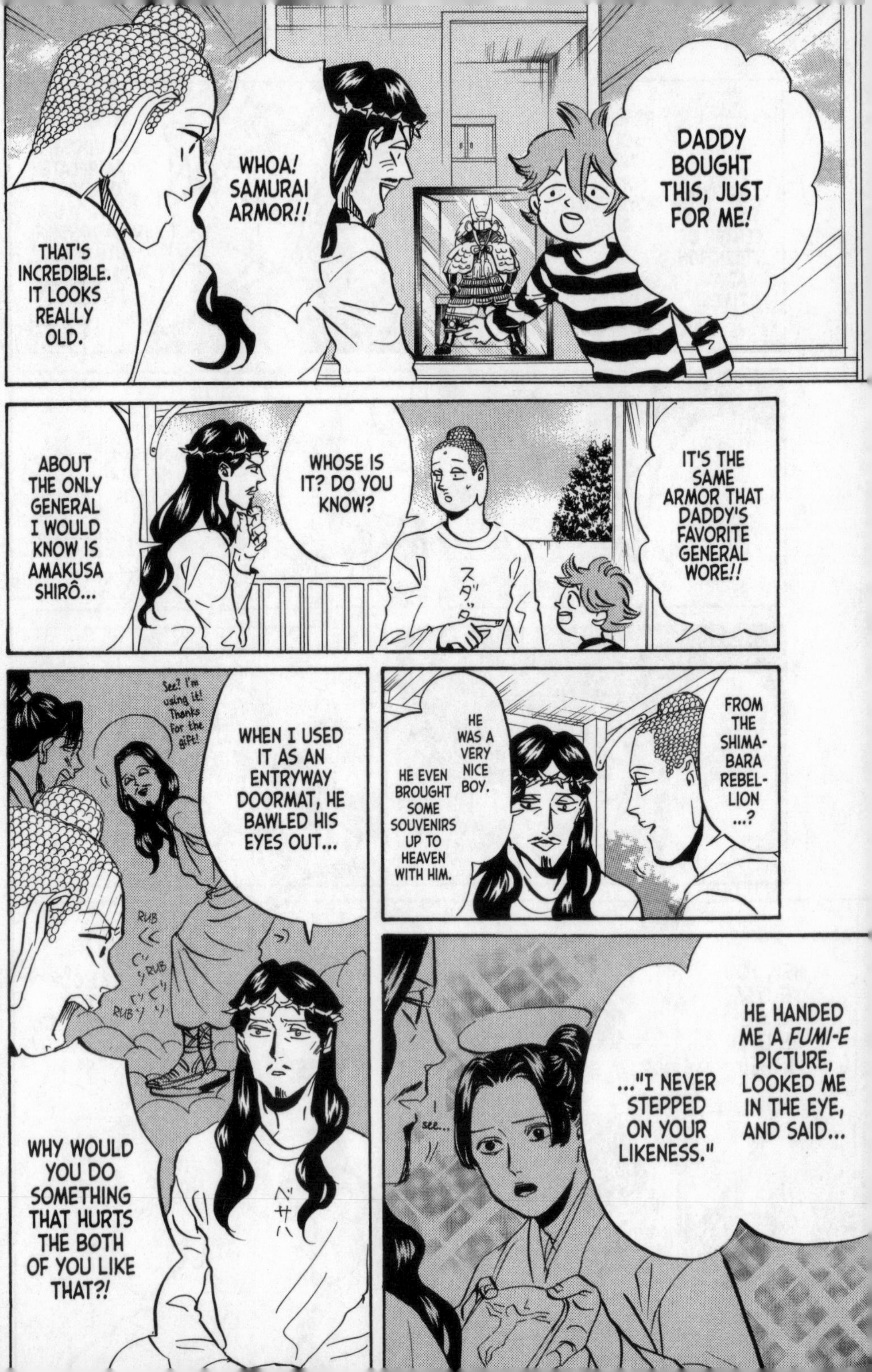
DADDY BOUGHT THIS, JUST FOR ME!
WHOA! SAMURAI ARMOR!!
THAT'S INCREDIBLE. IT LOOKS REALLY OLD.
IT'S THE SAME ARMOR THAT DADDY'S FAVORITE GENERAL WORE!!
WHOSE IS IT? DO YOU KNOW?
ABOUT THE ONLY GENERAL I WOULD KNOW IS AMAKUSA SHIRÔ...
FROM THE SHIMABARA REBELLION...?
HE WAS A VERY NICE BOY.
HE EVEN BROUGHT SOME SOUVENIRS UP TO HEAVEN WITH HIM.
HE HANDED ME A *FUMI-E* PICTURE, LOOKED ME IN THE EYE, AND SAID...
..."I NEVER STEPPED ON YOUR LIKENESS."
I see...
See? I'm using it! Thanks for the gift!
WHEN I USED IT AS AN ENTRYWAY DOORMAT, HE BAWLED HIS EYES OUT...
RUB
RUB
RUB
WHY WOULD YOU DO SOMETHING THAT HURTS THE BOTH OF YOU LIKE THAT?!

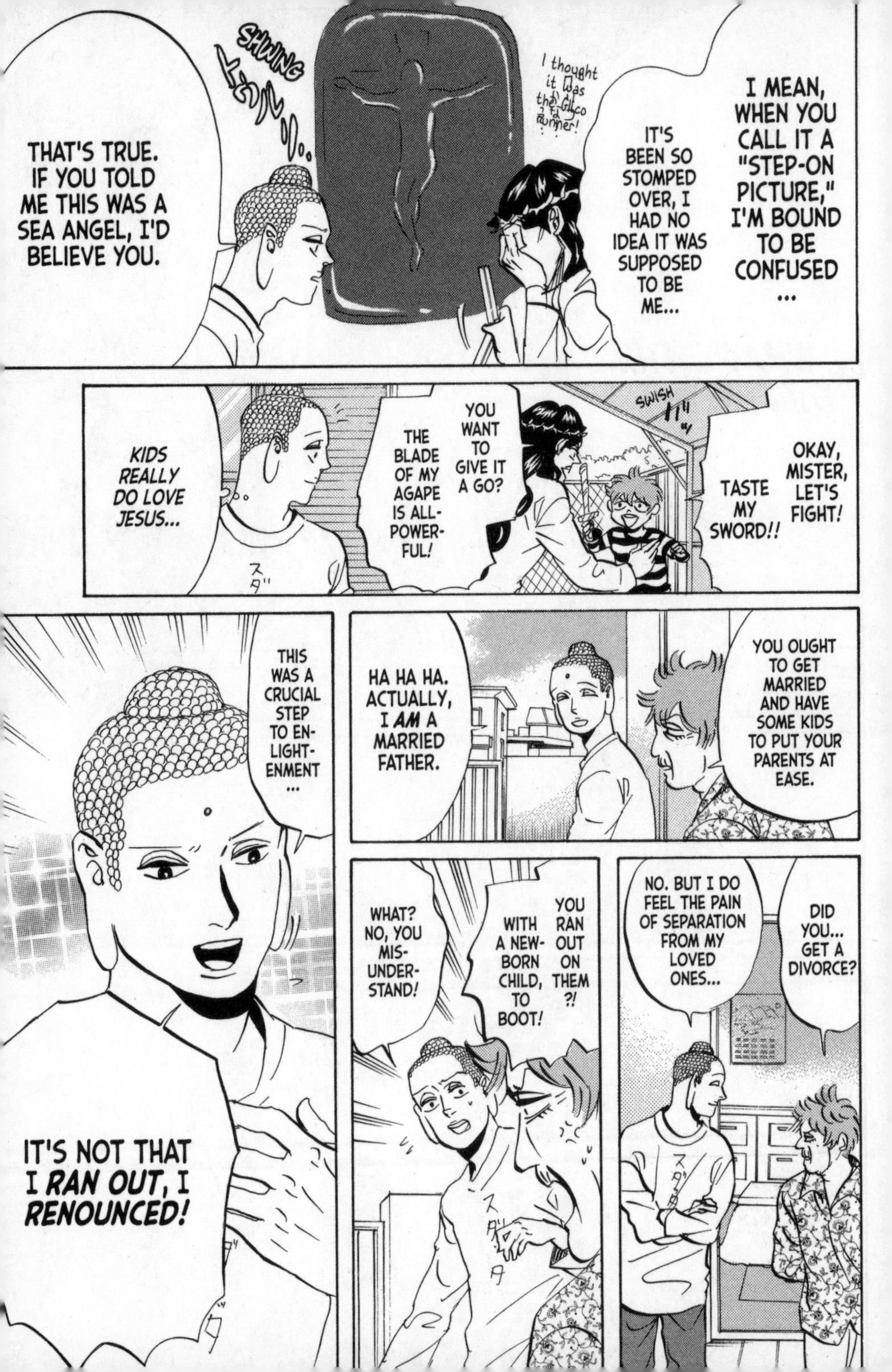
I MEAN, WHEN YOU CALL IT A "STEP-ON PICTURE," I'M BOUND TO BE CONFUSED ...
IT'S BEEN SO STOMPED OVER, I HAD NO IDEA IT WAS SUPPOSED TO BE ME...
I thought it was the Glico runner!
SHWING
THAT'S TRUE. IF YOU TOLD ME THIS WAS A SEA ANGEL, I'D BELIEVE YOU.
OKAY, MISTER, LET'S FIGHT!
TASTE MY SWORD!!
SWISH
YOU WANT TO GIVE IT A GO?
THE BLADE OF MY AGAPE IS ALL-POWERFUL!
KIDS REALLY DO LOVE JESUS...
YOU OUGHT TO GET MARRIED AND HAVE SOME KIDS TO PUT YOUR PARENTS AT EASE.
HA HA HA. ACTUALLY, I *AM* A MARRIED FATHER.
DID YOU... GET A DIVORCE?
NO. BUT I DO FEEL THE PAIN OF SEPARATION FROM MY LOVED ONES...
YOU RAN OUT ON THEM?!
WITH A NEWBORN CHILD, TO BOOT!
WHAT? NO, YOU MISUNDERSTAND!
THIS WAS A CRUCIAL STEP TO ENLIGHTENMENT ...
IT'S NOT THAT I *RAN OUT*, I ***RENOUNCED!***

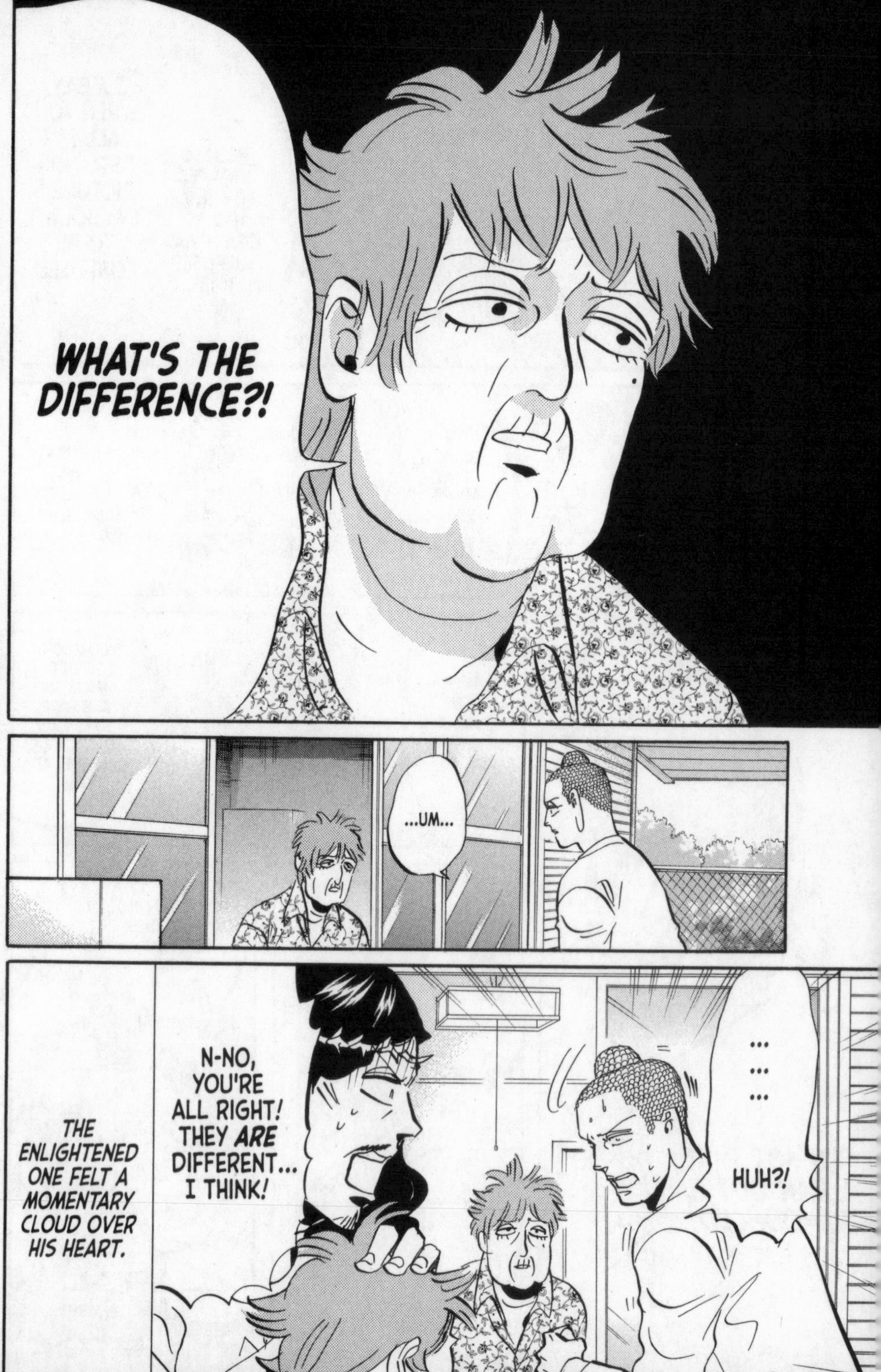

WHAT'S THE DIFFERENCE?!
...UM...
...
...
...
N-NO, YOU'RE ALL RIGHT! THEY ARE DIFFERENT... I THINK!
HUH?!
THE ENLIGHTENED ONE FELT A MOMENTARY CLOUD OVER HIS HEART.

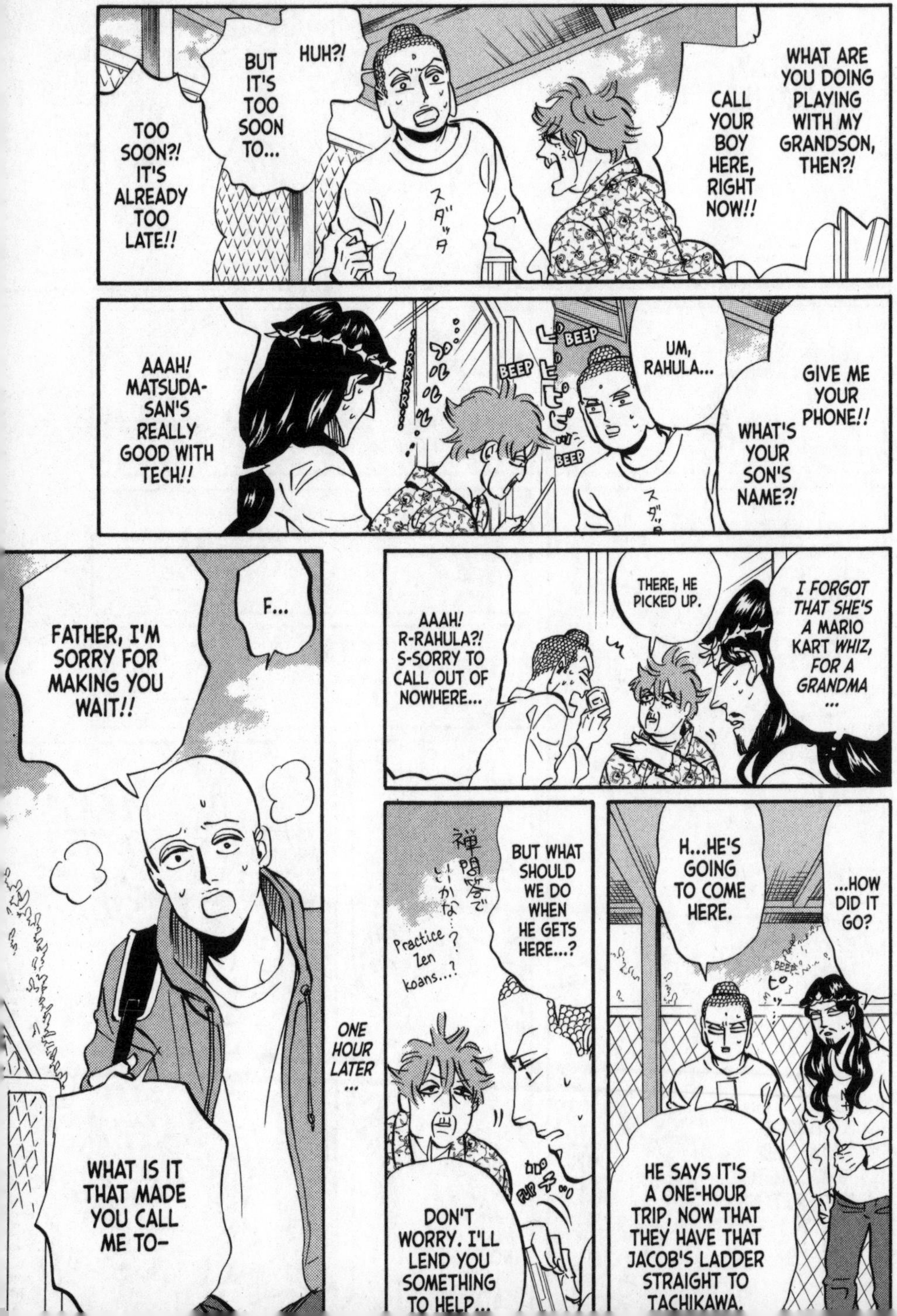
WHAT ARE YOU DOING PLAYING WITH MY GRANDSON, THEN?!
CALL YOUR BOY HERE, RIGHT NOW!!
HUH?!
BUT IT'S TOO SOON TO...
TOO SOON?! IT'S ALREADY TOO LATE!!
スダッタ
GIVE ME YOUR PHONE!!
WHAT'S YOUR SON'S NAME?!
UM, RAHULA...
BEEP
BEEP
BEEP
AAAH! MATSUDA-SAN'S REALLY GOOD WITH TECH!!
I FORGOT THAT SHE'S A MARIO KART WHIZ, FOR A GRANDMA...
THERE, HE PICKED UP.
AAAH! R-RAHULA?! S-SORRY TO CALL OUT OF NOWHERE...
...HOW DID IT GO?
H...HE'S GOING TO COME HERE.
BEEP
HE SAYS IT'S A ONE-HOUR TRIP, NOW THAT THEY HAVE THAT JACOB'S LADDER STRAIGHT TO TACHIKAWA.
BUT WHAT SHOULD WE DO WHEN HE GETS HERE...?
禅問答でいいかな…？
Practice Zen koans...?
DON'T WORRY. I'LL LEND YOU SOMETHING TO HELP...
FLIP
ONE HOUR LATER...
F...
FATHER, I'M SORRY FOR MAKING YOU WAIT!!
WHAT IS IT THAT MADE YOU CALL ME TO-

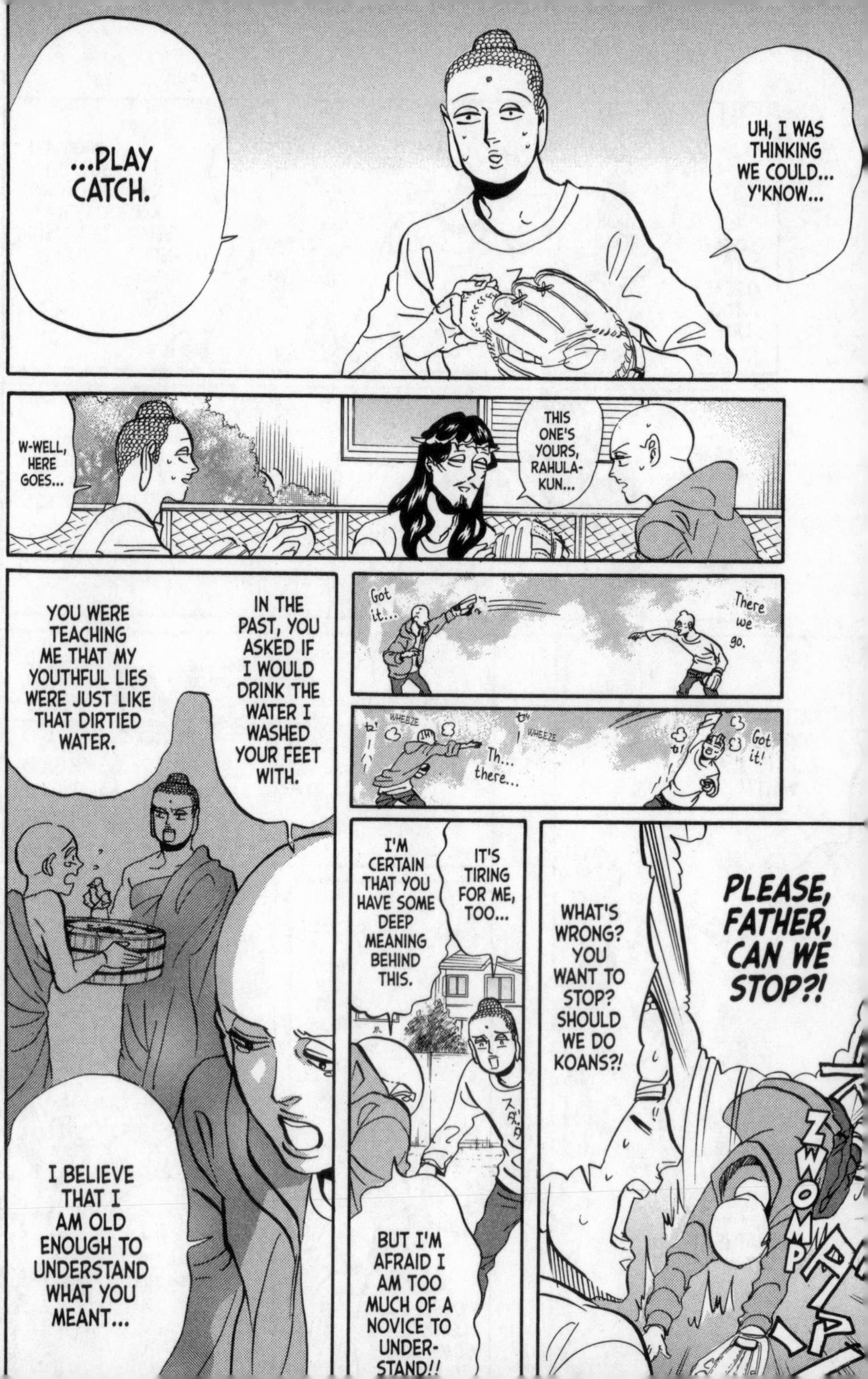
UH, I WAS THINKING WE COULD... Y'KNOW...
...PLAY CATCH.
THIS ONE'S YOURS, RAHULA-KUN...
W-WELL, HERE GOES...
There we go.
Got it...
Got it!
WHEEZE
Th... there...
WHEEZE
PLEASE, FATHER, CAN WE STOP?!
WHAT'S WRONG? YOU WANT TO STOP? SHOULD WE DO KOANS?!
ZWOMP
IT'S TIRING FOR ME, TOO...
I'M CERTAIN THAT YOU HAVE SOME DEEP MEANING BEHIND THIS.
BUT I'M AFRAID I AM TOO MUCH OF A NOVICE TO UNDER-STAND!!
IN THE PAST, YOU ASKED IF I WOULD DRINK THE WATER I WASHED YOUR FEET WITH.
YOU WERE TEACHING ME THAT MY YOUTHFUL LIES WERE JUST LIKE THAT DIRTIED WATER.
I BELIEVE THAT I AM OLD ENOUGH TO UNDERSTAND WHAT YOU MEANT...

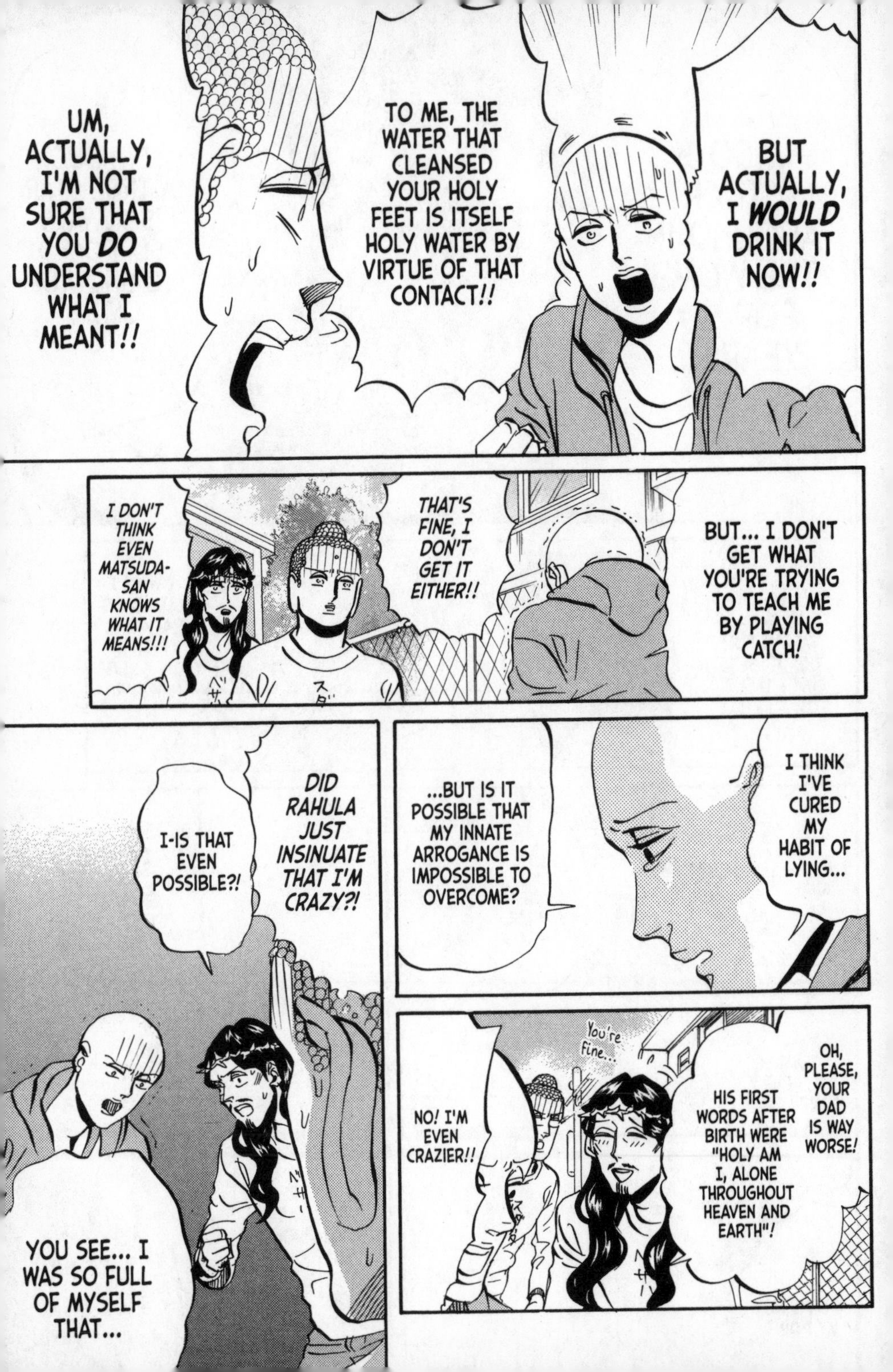
BUT ACTUALLY, I *WOULD* DRINK IT NOW!!
TO ME, THE WATER THAT CLEANSED YOUR HOLY FEET IS ITSELF HOLY WATER BY VIRTUE OF THAT CONTACT!!
UM, ACTUALLY, I'M NOT SURE THAT YOU *DO* UNDERSTAND WHAT I MEANT!!
BUT... I DON'T GET WHAT YOU'RE TRYING TO TEACH ME BY PLAYING CATCH!
THAT'S FINE, I DON'T GET IT EITHER!!
I DON'T THINK EVEN MATSUDA-SAN KNOWS WHAT IT MEANS!!!
I THINK I'VE CURED MY HABIT OF LYING...
...BUT IS IT POSSIBLE THAT MY INNATE ARROGANCE IS IMPOSSIBLE TO OVERCOME?
OH, PLEASE, YOUR DAD IS WAY WORSE!
HIS FIRST WORDS AFTER BIRTH WERE "HOLY AM I, ALONE THROUGHOUT HEAVEN AND EARTH"!
You're fine...
NO! I'M EVEN CRAZIER!!
DID RAHULA JUST INSINUATE THAT I'M CRAZY?!
I-IS THAT EVEN POSSIBLE?!
YOU SEE... I WAS SO FULL OF MYSELF THAT...

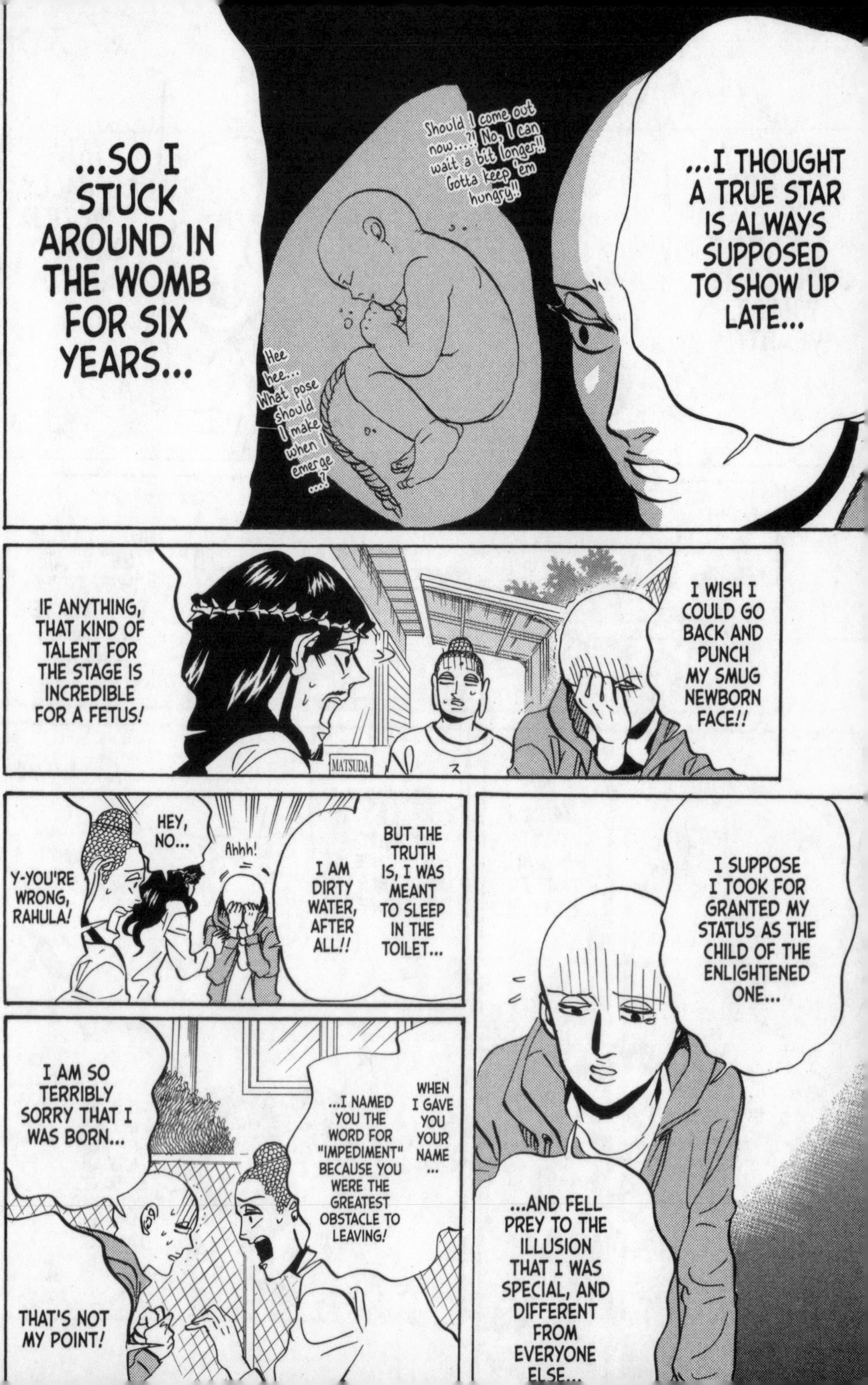
...I THOUGHT A TRUE STAR IS ALWAYS SUPPOSED TO SHOW UP LATE...
Should I come out now...?! No, I can wait a bit longer!! Gotta keep 'em hungry!!
...SO I STUCK AROUND IN THE WOMB FOR SIX YEARS...
Hee hee... What pose should I make when I emerge...?
I WISH I COULD GO BACK AND PUNCH MY SMUG NEWBORN FACE!!
IF ANYTHING, THAT KIND OF TALENT FOR THE STAGE IS INCREDIBLE FOR A FETUS!
MATSUDA
I SUPPOSE I TOOK FOR GRANTED MY STATUS AS THE CHILD OF THE ENLIGHTENED ONE...
...AND FELL PREY TO THE ILLUSION THAT I WAS SPECIAL, AND DIFFERENT FROM EVERYONE ELSE...
BUT THE TRUTH IS, I WAS MEANT TO SLEEP IN THE TOILET...
I AM DIRTY WATER, AFTER ALL!!
Ahhh!
HEY, NO...
Y-YOU'RE WRONG, RAHULA!
WHEN I GAVE YOU YOUR NAME...
...I NAMED YOU THE WORD FOR "IMPEDIMENT" BECAUSE YOU WERE THE GREATEST OBSTACLE TO LEAVING!
I AM SO TERRIBLY SORRY THAT I WAS BORN...
THAT'S NOT MY POINT!

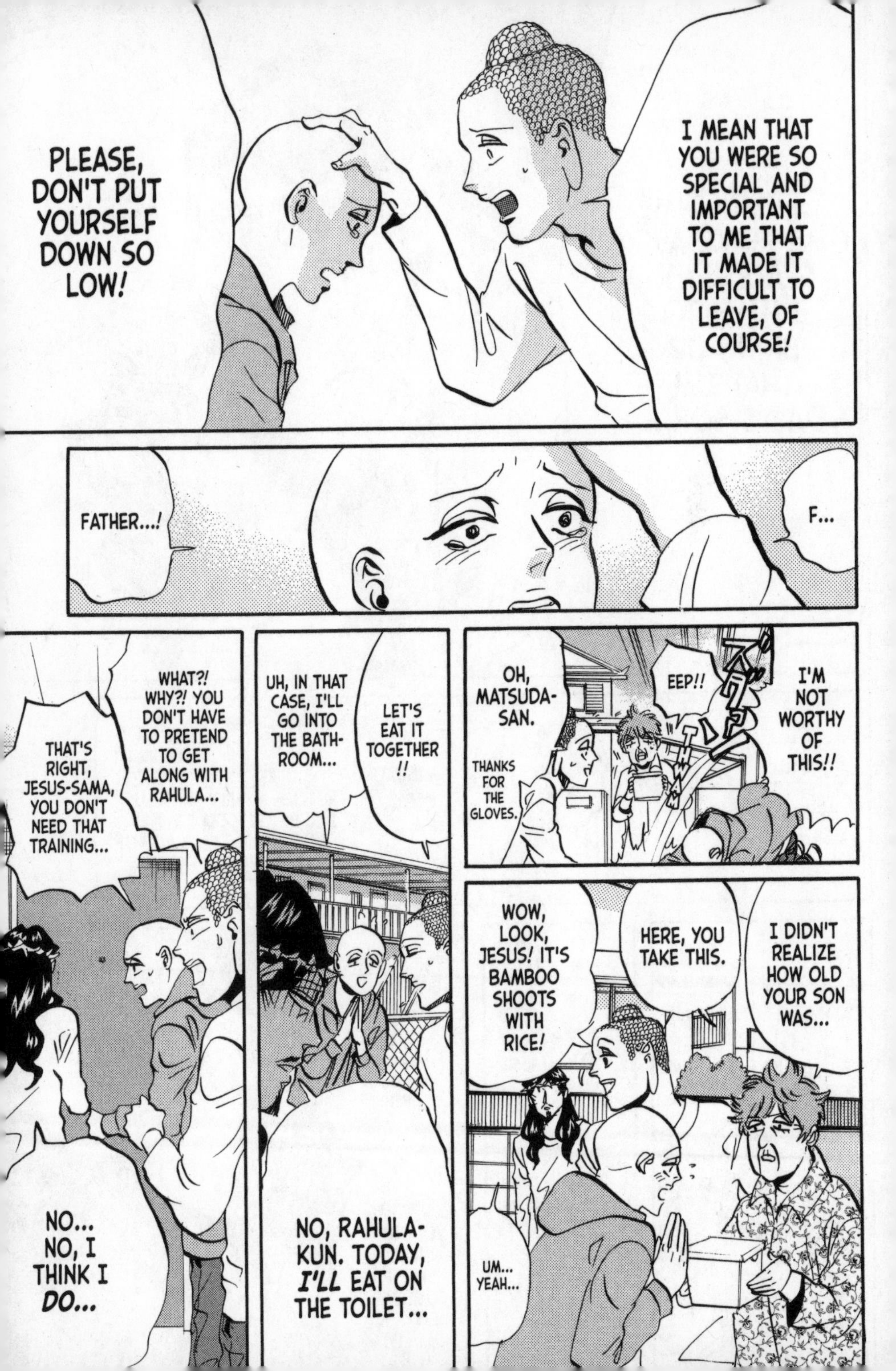
I MEAN THAT YOU WERE SO SPECIAL AND IMPORTANT TO ME THAT IT MADE IT DIFFICULT TO LEAVE, OF COURSE!
PLEASE, DON'T PUT YOURSELF DOWN SO LOW!
F...
FATHER...!
I'M NOT WORTHY OF THIS!!
EEP!!
THWAM
OH, MATSUDA-SAN.
THANKS FOR THE GLOVES.
I DIDN'T REALIZE HOW OLD YOUR SON WAS...
HERE, YOU TAKE THIS.
WOW, LOOK, JESUS! IT'S BAMBOO SHOOTS WITH RICE!
UM... YEAH...
LET'S EAT IT TOGETHER!!
UH, IN THAT CASE, I'LL GO INTO THE BATH-ROOM...
NO, RAHULA-KUN. TODAY, *I'LL* EAT ON THE TOILET...
WHAT?! WHY?! YOU DON'T HAVE TO PRETEND TO GET ALONG WITH RAHULA...
THAT'S RIGHT, JESUS-SAMA, YOU DON'T NEED THAT TRAINING...
NO... NO, I THINK I *DO*...

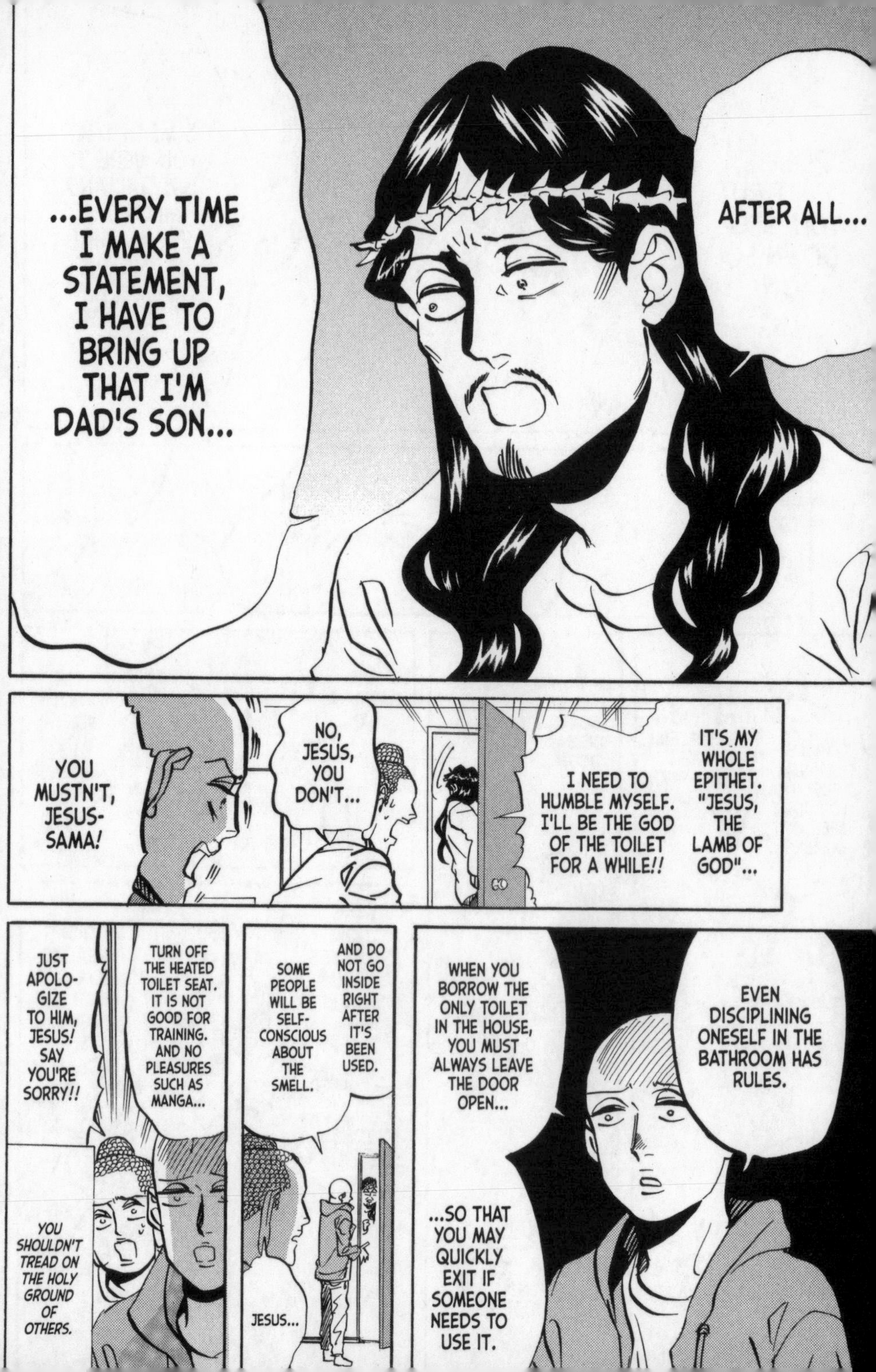
AFTER ALL...
...EVERY TIME I MAKE A STATEMENT, I HAVE TO BRING UP THAT I'M DAD'S SON...
IT'S MY WHOLE EPITHET. "JESUS, THE LAMB OF GOD"...
I NEED TO HUMBLE MYSELF. I'LL BE THE GOD OF THE TOILET FOR A WHILE!!
NO, JESUS, YOU DON'T...
YOU MUSTN'T, JESUS-SAMA!
EVEN DISCIPLINING ONESELF IN THE BATHROOM HAS RULES.
WHEN YOU BORROW THE ONLY TOILET IN THE HOUSE, YOU MUST ALWAYS LEAVE THE DOOR OPEN...
...SO THAT YOU MAY QUICKLY EXIT IF SOMEONE NEEDS TO USE IT.
AND DO NOT GO INSIDE RIGHT AFTER IT'S BEEN USED.
SOME PEOPLE WILL BE SELF-CONSCIOUS ABOUT THE SMELL.
JESUS...
TURN OFF THE HEATED TOILET SEAT. IT IS NOT GOOD FOR TRAINING. AND NO PLEASURES SUCH AS MANGA...
JUST APOLOGIZE TO HIM, JESUS! SAY YOU'RE SORRY!!
YOU SHOULDN'T TREAD ON THE HOLY GROUND OF OTHERS.

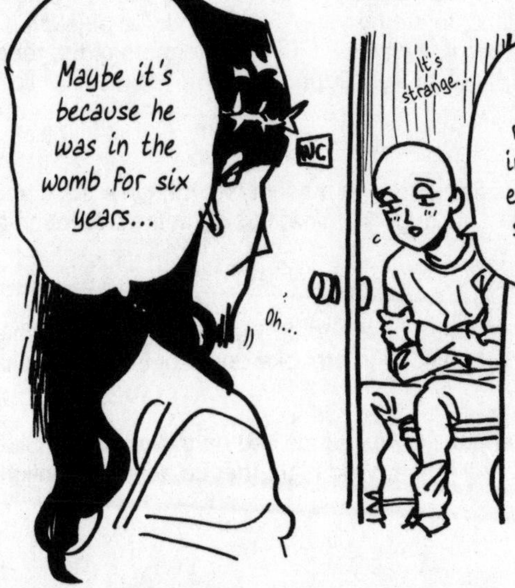
It's strange...
I feel relaxed in dark, enclosed spaces.
WC
Maybe it's because he was in the womb for six years...
Oh...

CHAPTER 48 TRANSLATION NOTES

Pesach, page 73
The Hebrew name for the holiday of Passover, in which God's "passing over" of the Hebrews during the Ten Plagues of Egypt is celebrated.

Ichthys, page 73
The early Christian symbol of the fish, dating back to the 2nd century CE. The letters sometimes seen inside it are the first letters of the Greek words that mean "Jesus Christ, Son of God, Savior."

Sudatta, page 75
One of Gautama Buddha's disciples. Sudatta was born into a wealthy family and was known for his great charity to the needy. He built Jetavana Monastery, one of the chief temples dedicated to the Buddha, and fed all of the monks who stayed there. He was also known by the name Anathapindika.

Ultraman, page 76
A famous *tokusatsu* live action hero who fights against giant monsters that threaten the Earth. A team called the Science Patrol is supposed to fight the monsters, but one of them is secretly an alien named Ultraman who must transform into a giant warrior to save the day without blowing his cover to the rest of the patrol.

Amakusa Shirô, page 80
The young leader of the failed Shimabara Rebellion, an uprising of Japanese Catholics against the Shogunate in 1638, in response to increasing persecution of Christians. *Fumi-e*, or "step-on pictures," were likenesses of Jesus or Mary that were used as a test to identify potential Christians; to step on one's picture would be such a grave insult that no true Christian could do it, it was said. In the aftermath of the rebellion, all European missionaries were expelled from Japan, and the seclusion policy was tightened up until the 1850s.

Glico, page 81
Glico is a Japanese food manufacturer. Its logo mascot is a man in a track and field outfit raising his arms with triumph. Its huge illuminated sign in the Dôtonbori area of Osaka is a landmark of the city.

Zen koan, page 83
A form of dialogue that is meant to test a pupil's understanding of Zen Buddhist thought, using allusion and indirect analogy to provoke doubt or intuitive thinking.

Rahula's birth, page 86
In one tradition of the story of Rahula, he was conceived on the night that Siddhartha Gautama renounced his throne, and born on the night that he achieved enlightenment six years later.

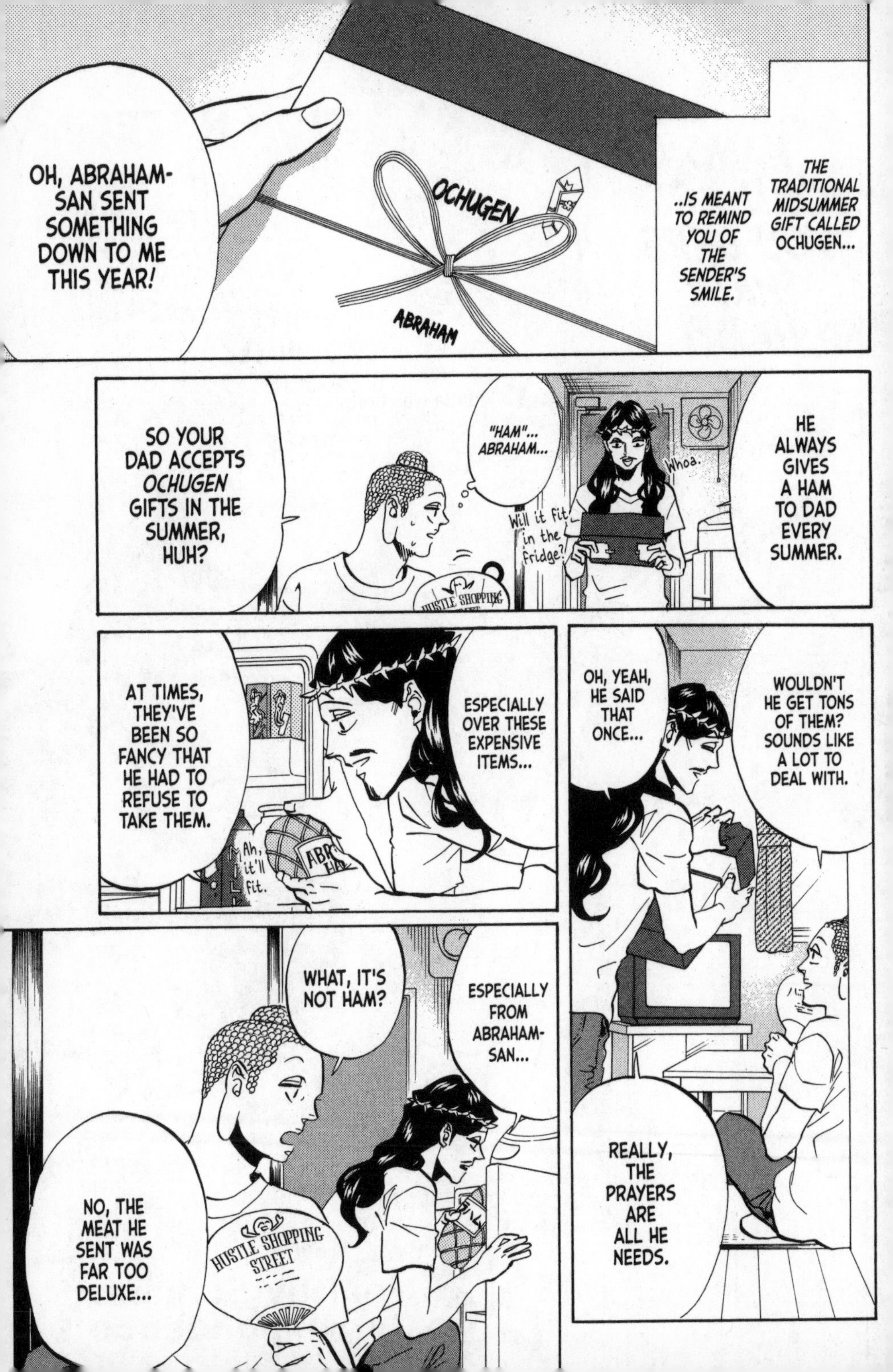
THE TRADITIONAL MIDSUMMER GIFT CALLED OCHUGEN...
..IS MEANT TO REMIND YOU OF THE SENDER'S SMILE.
OCHUGEN
ABRAHAM
OH, ABRAHAM-SAN SENT SOMETHING DOWN TO ME THIS YEAR!
HE ALWAYS GIVES A HAM TO DAD EVERY SUMMER.
Whoa.
Will it fit in the fridge?
"HAM"... ABRAHAM...
SO YOUR DAD ACCEPTS OCHUGEN GIFTS IN THE SUMMER, HUH?
HUSTLE SHOPPING STREET
WOULDN'T HE GET TONS OF THEM? SOUNDS LIKE A LOT TO DEAL WITH.
OH, YEAH, HE SAID THAT ONCE...
REALLY, THE PRAYERS ARE ALL HE NEEDS.
ESPECIALLY OVER THESE EXPENSIVE ITEMS...
AT TIMES, THEY'VE BEEN SO FANCY THAT HE HAD TO REFUSE TO TAKE THEM.
Ah, it'll fit.
ESPECIALLY FROM ABRAHAM-SAN...
WHAT, IT'S NOT HAM?
NO, THE MEAT HE SENT WAS FAR TOO DELUXE...
HUSTLE SHOPPING STREET

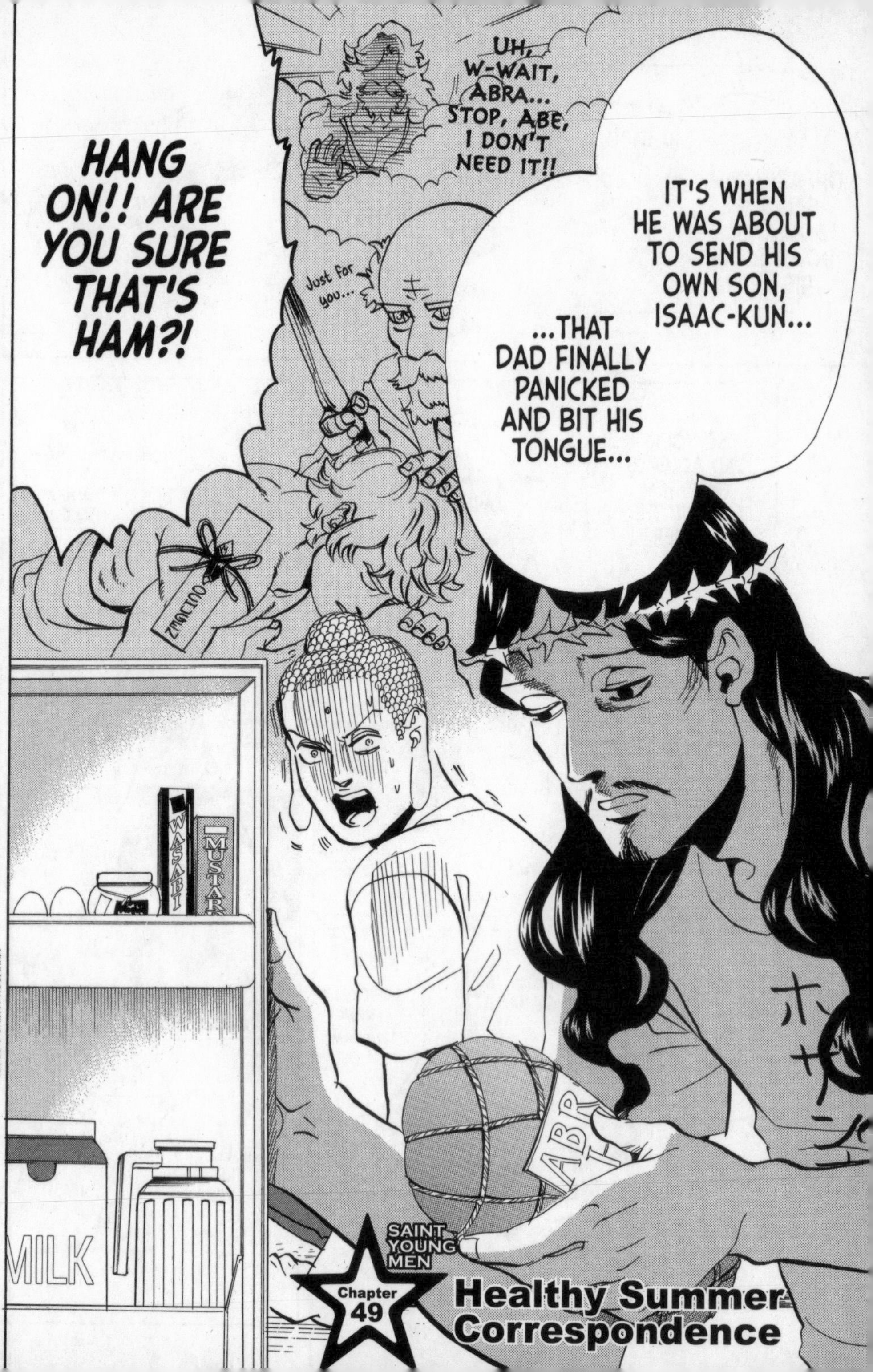
IT'S WHEN HE WAS ABOUT TO SEND HIS OWN SON, ISAAC-KUN...
...THAT DAD FINALLY PANICKED AND BIT HIS TONGUE...
UH, W-WAIT, ABRA... STOP, ABE, I DON'T NEED IT!!
Just for you...
HANG ON!! ARE YOU SURE THAT'S HAM?!
WASABI
MUSTAR
MILK
ABR
SAINT YOUNG MEN
Chapter 49
Healthy Summer Correspondence

JESUS'S SHIRT: HOSANNA

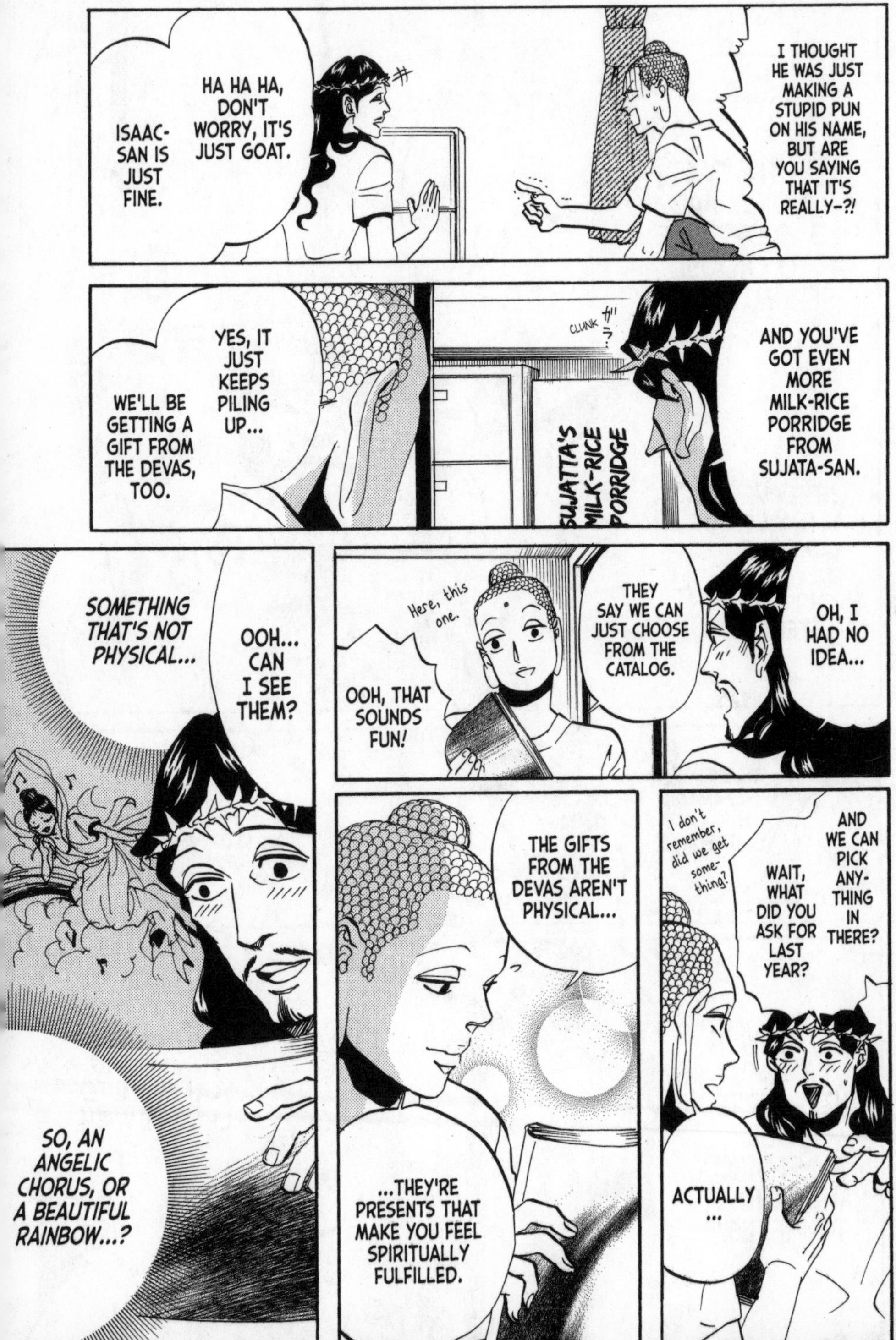
I THOUGHT HE WAS JUST MAKING A STUPID PUN ON HIS NAME, BUT ARE YOU SAYING THAT IT'S REALLY-?!
HA HA HA, DON'T WORRY, IT'S JUST GOAT.
ISAAC-SAN IS JUST FINE.
AND YOU'VE GOT EVEN MORE MILK-RICE PORRIDGE FROM SUJATA-SAN.
CLUNK
SUJATTA'S MILK-RICE PORRIDGE
YES, IT JUST KEEPS PILING UP...
WE'LL BE GETTING A GIFT FROM THE DEVAS, TOO.
OH, I HAD NO IDEA...
THEY SAY WE CAN JUST CHOOSE FROM THE CATALOG.
Here, this one.
OOH, THAT SOUNDS FUN!
AND WE CAN PICK ANYTHING IN THERE?
WAIT, WHAT DID YOU ASK FOR LAST YEAR?
I don't remember, did we get something?
ACTUALLY...
THE GIFTS FROM THE DEVAS AREN'T PHYSICAL...
...THEY'RE PRESENTS THAT MAKE YOU FEEL SPIRITUALLY FULFILLED.
OOH... CAN I SEE THEM?
SOMETHING THAT'S NOT PHYSICAL...
SO, AN ANGELIC CHORUS, OR A BEAUTIFUL RAINBOW...?

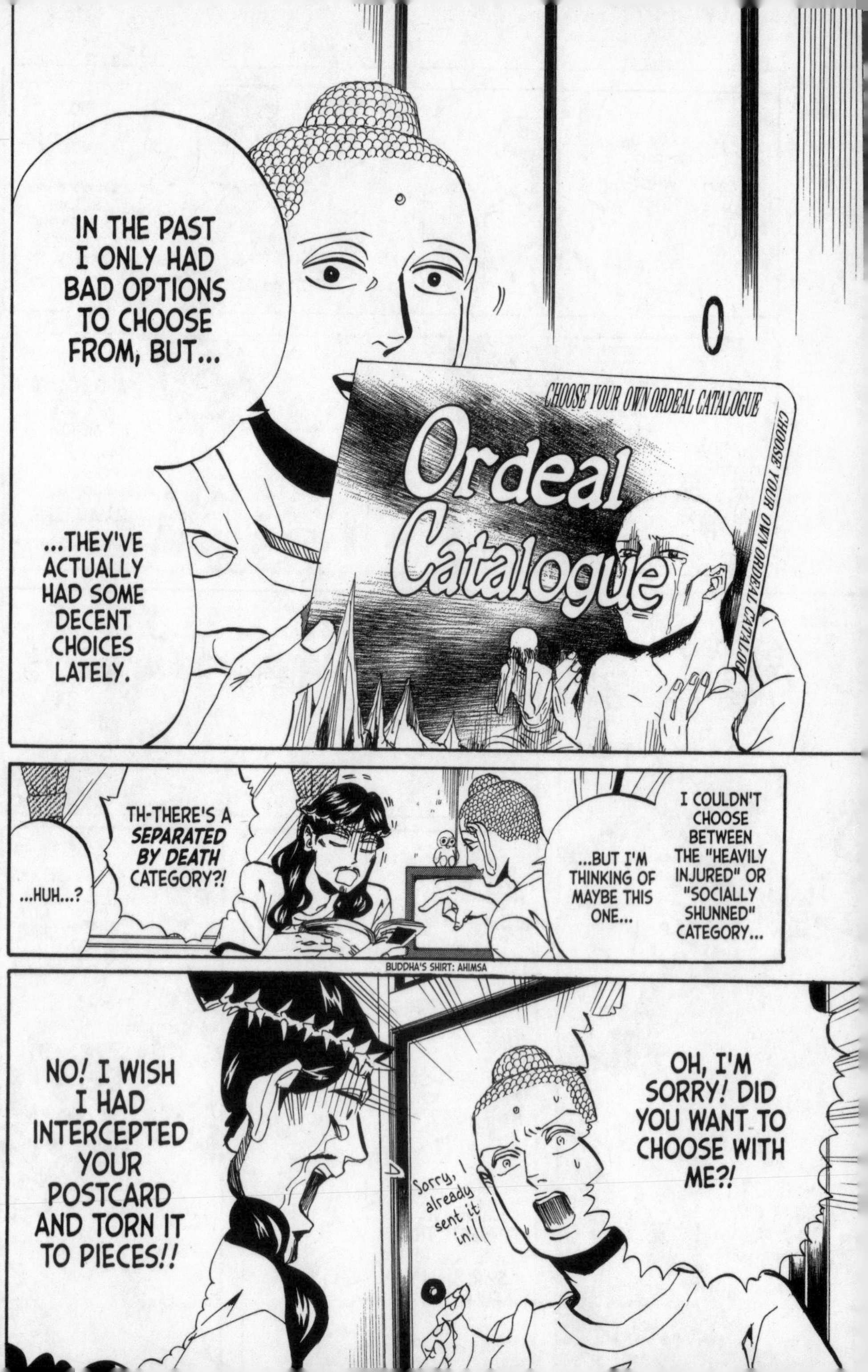
IN THE PAST I ONLY HAD BAD OPTIONS TO CHOOSE FROM, BUT...
...THEY'VE ACTUALLY HAD SOME DECENT CHOICES LATELY.
CHOOSE YOUR OWN ORDEAL CATALOGUE
Ordeal Catalogue
I COULDN'T CHOOSE BETWEEN THE "HEAVILY INJURED" OR "SOCIALLY SHUNNED" CATEGORY...
...BUT I'M THINKING OF MAYBE THIS ONE...
TH-THERE'S A *SEPARATED BY DEATH* CATEGORY?!
...HUH...?
BUDDHA'S SHIRT: AHIMSA
OH, I'M SORRY! DID YOU WANT TO CHOOSE WITH ME?!
Sorry, I already sent it in!!
NO! I WISH I HAD INTERCEPTED YOUR POSTCARD AND TORN IT TO PIECES!!

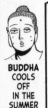

BUDDHA COOLS OFF IN THE SUMMER SEASON BY WATCHING LOTS OF HORROR MOVIES.

JESUS COOLS OFF IN THE SUMMER SEASON BY EATING LOTS OF ICE CREAM.

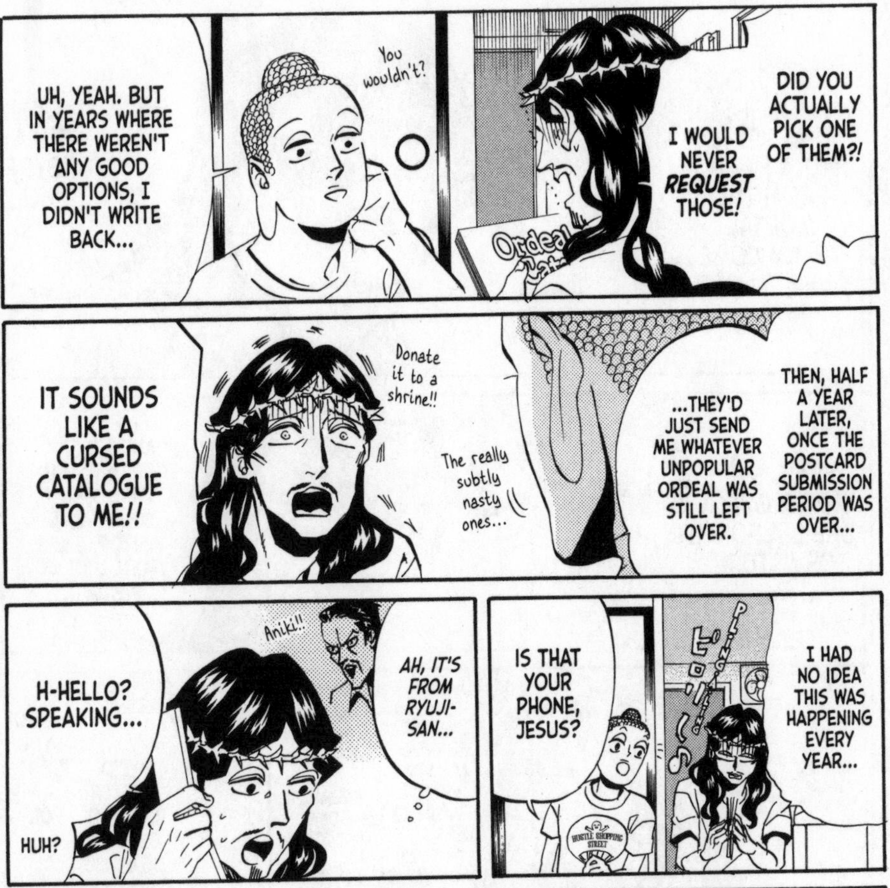
DID YOU ACTUALLY PICK ONE OF THEM?!
I WOULD NEVER REQUEST THOSE!
You wouldn't?
UH, YEAH. BUT IN YEARS WHERE THERE WEREN'T ANY GOOD OPTIONS, I DIDN'T WRITE BACK...
THEN, HALF A YEAR LATER, ONCE THE POSTCARD SUBMISSION PERIOD WAS OVER...
...THEY'D JUST SEND ME WHATEVER UNPOPULAR ORDEAL WAS STILL LEFT OVER.
The really subtly nasty ones...
Donate it to a shrine!!
IT SOUNDS LIKE A CURSED CATALOGUE TO ME!!
I HAD NO IDEA THIS WAS HAPPENING EVERY YEAR...
PLING
IS THAT YOUR PHONE, JESUS?
HUSTLE SHOPPING STREET
AH, IT'S FROM RYUJI-SAN...
Aniki!!
H-HELLO? SPEAKING...
HUH?

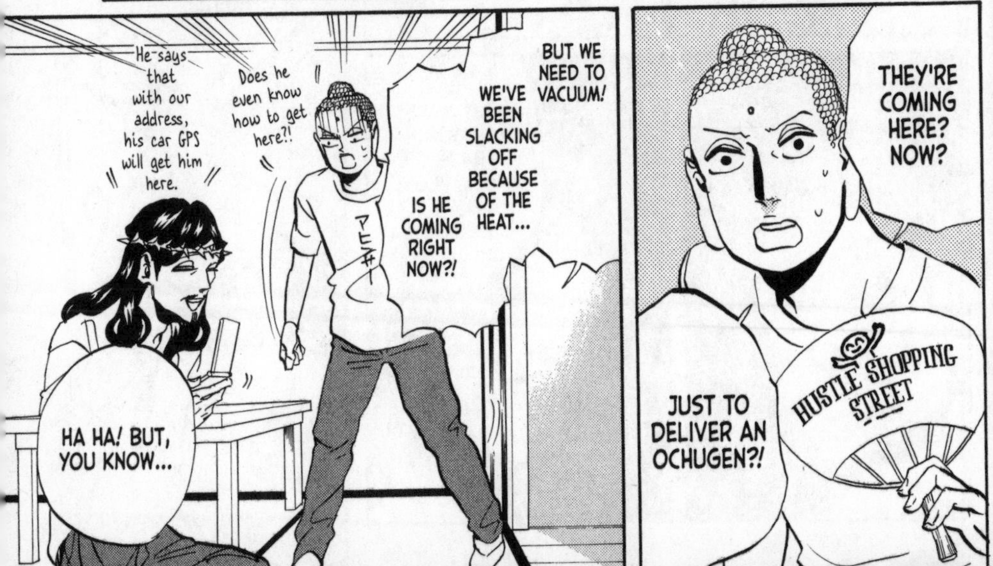
THEY'RE COMING HERE? NOW?
JUST TO DELIVER AN OCHUGEN?!
HUSTLE SHOPPING STREET
BUT WE NEED TO VACUUM!
WE'VE BEEN SLACKING OFF BECAUSE OF THE HEAT...
IS HE COMING RIGHT NOW?!
Does he even know how to get here?!
He says that with our address, his car GPS will get him here.
HA HA! BUT, YOU KNOW...

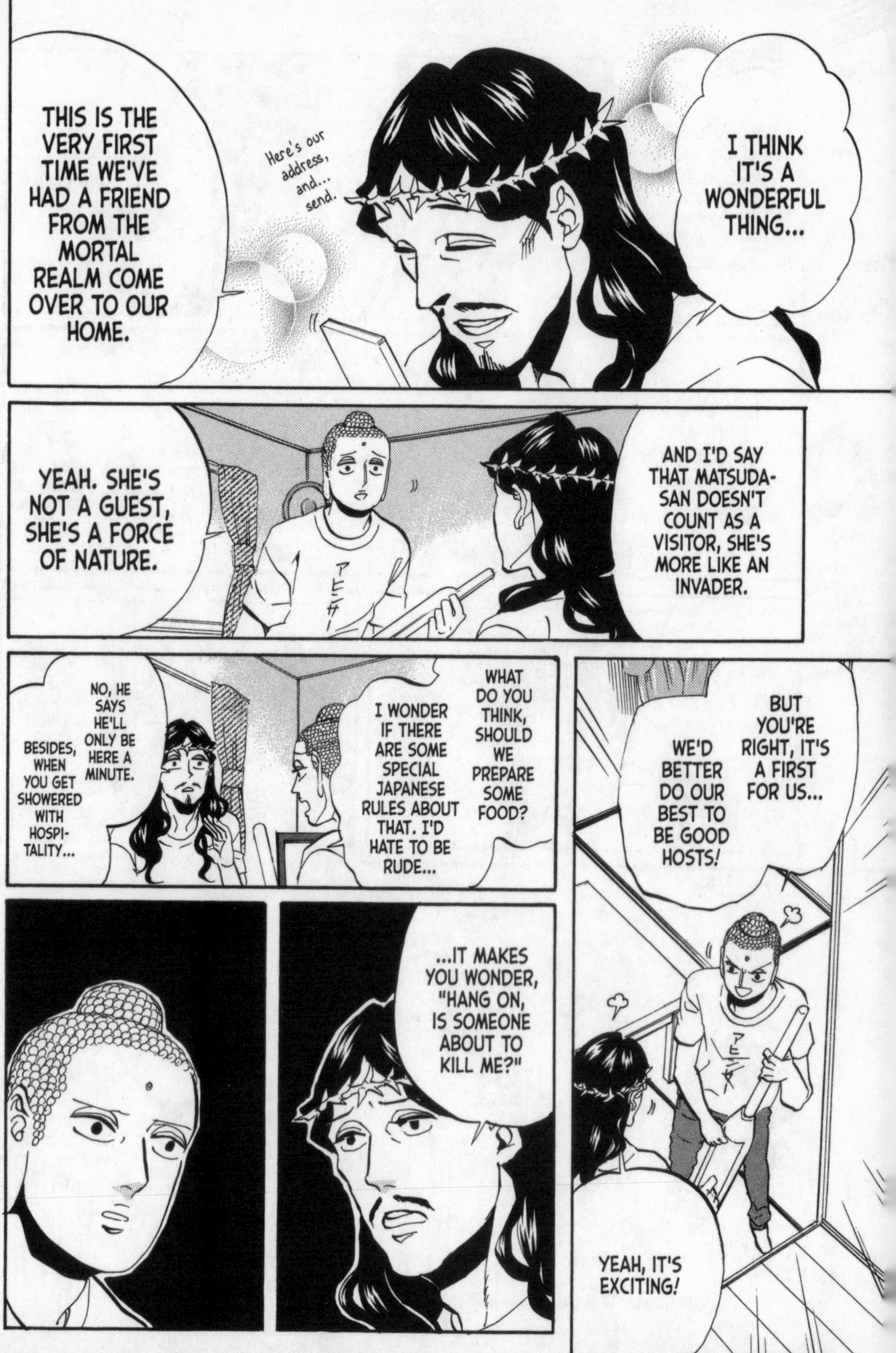
I THINK IT'S A WONDERFUL THING...
Here's our address, and... send.
THIS IS THE VERY FIRST TIME WE'VE HAD A FRIEND FROM THE MORTAL REALM COME OVER TO OUR HOME.
AND I'D SAY THAT MATSUDA-SAN DOESN'T COUNT AS A VISITOR, SHE'S MORE LIKE AN INVADER.
YEAH. SHE'S NOT A GUEST, SHE'S A FORCE OF NATURE.
BUT YOU'RE RIGHT, IT'S A FIRST FOR US...
WE'D BETTER DO OUR BEST TO BE GOOD HOSTS!
YEAH, IT'S EXCITING!
WHAT DO YOU THINK, SHOULD WE PREPARE SOME FOOD?
I WONDER IF THERE ARE SOME SPECIAL JAPANESE RULES ABOUT THAT. I'D HATE TO BE RUDE...
NO, HE SAYS HE'LL ONLY BE HERE A MINUTE.
BESIDES, WHEN YOU GET SHOWERED WITH HOSPITALITY...
...IT MAKES YOU WONDER, "HANG ON, IS SOMEONE ABOUT TO KILL ME?"

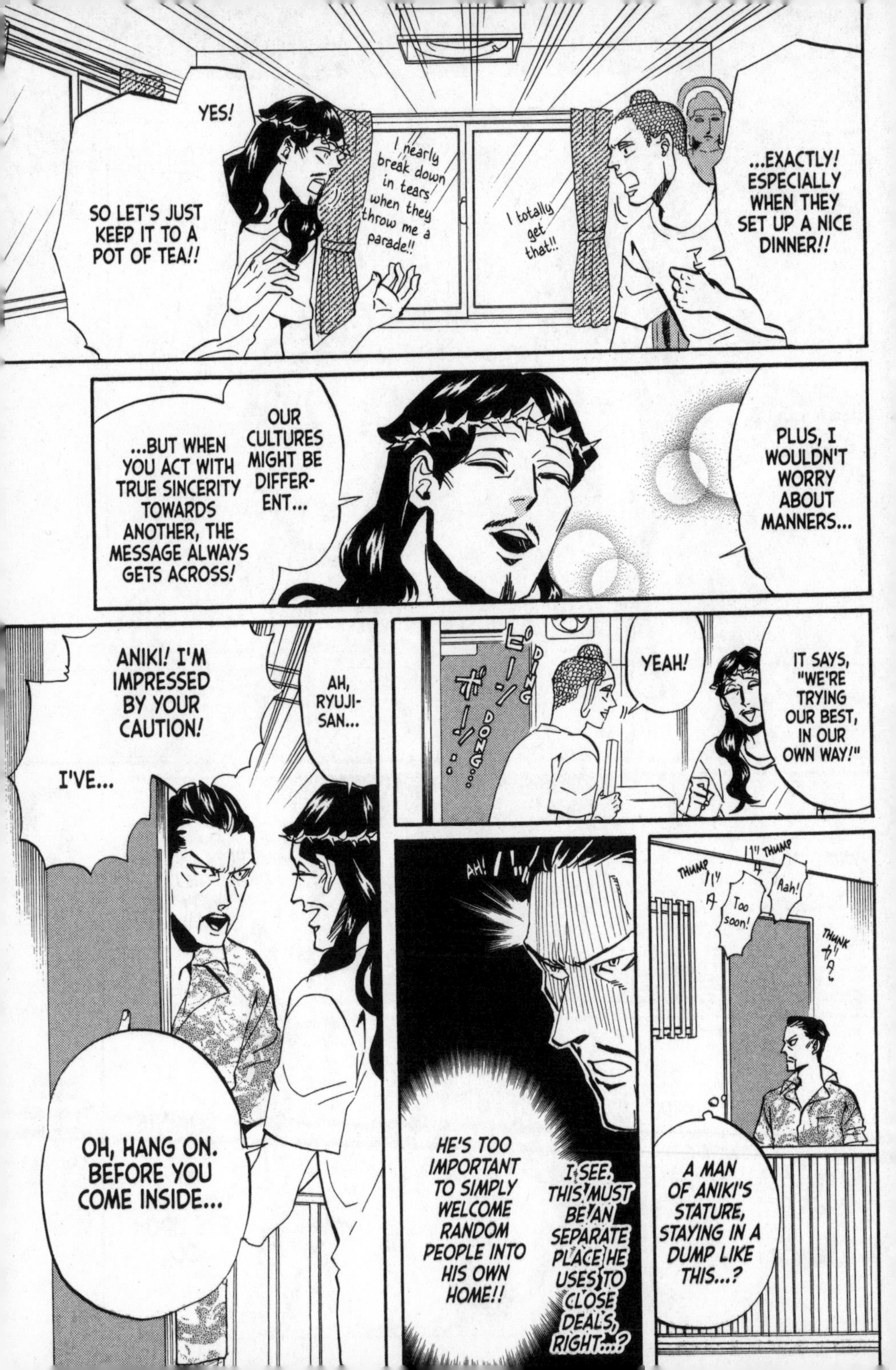
...EXACTLY! ESPECIALLY WHEN THEY SET UP A NICE DINNER!!
I totally get that!!
I nearly break down in tears when they throw me a parade!!
YES!
SO LET'S JUST KEEP IT TO A POT OF TEA!!
PLUS, I WOULDN'T WORRY ABOUT MANNERS...
OUR CULTURES MIGHT BE DIFFER-ENT...
...BUT WHEN YOU ACT WITH TRUE SINCERITY TOWARDS ANOTHER, THE MESSAGE ALWAYS GETS ACROSS!
IT SAYS, "WE'RE TRYING OUR BEST, IN OUR OWN WAY!"
YEAH!
DING DONG...
THUMP THUMP
Aah!
Too soon!
THUNK
A MAN OF ANIKI'S STATURE, STAYING IN A DUMP LIKE THIS...?
AH!
I SEE. THIS MUST BE AN SEPARATE PLACE HE USES TO CLOSE DEALS, RIGHT...?
HE'S TOO IMPORTANT TO SIMPLY WELCOME RANDOM PEOPLE INTO HIS OWN HOME!!
AH, RYUJI-SAN...
ANIKI! I'M IMPRESSED BY YOUR CAUTION!
I'VE...
OH, HANG ON. BEFORE YOU COME INSIDE...

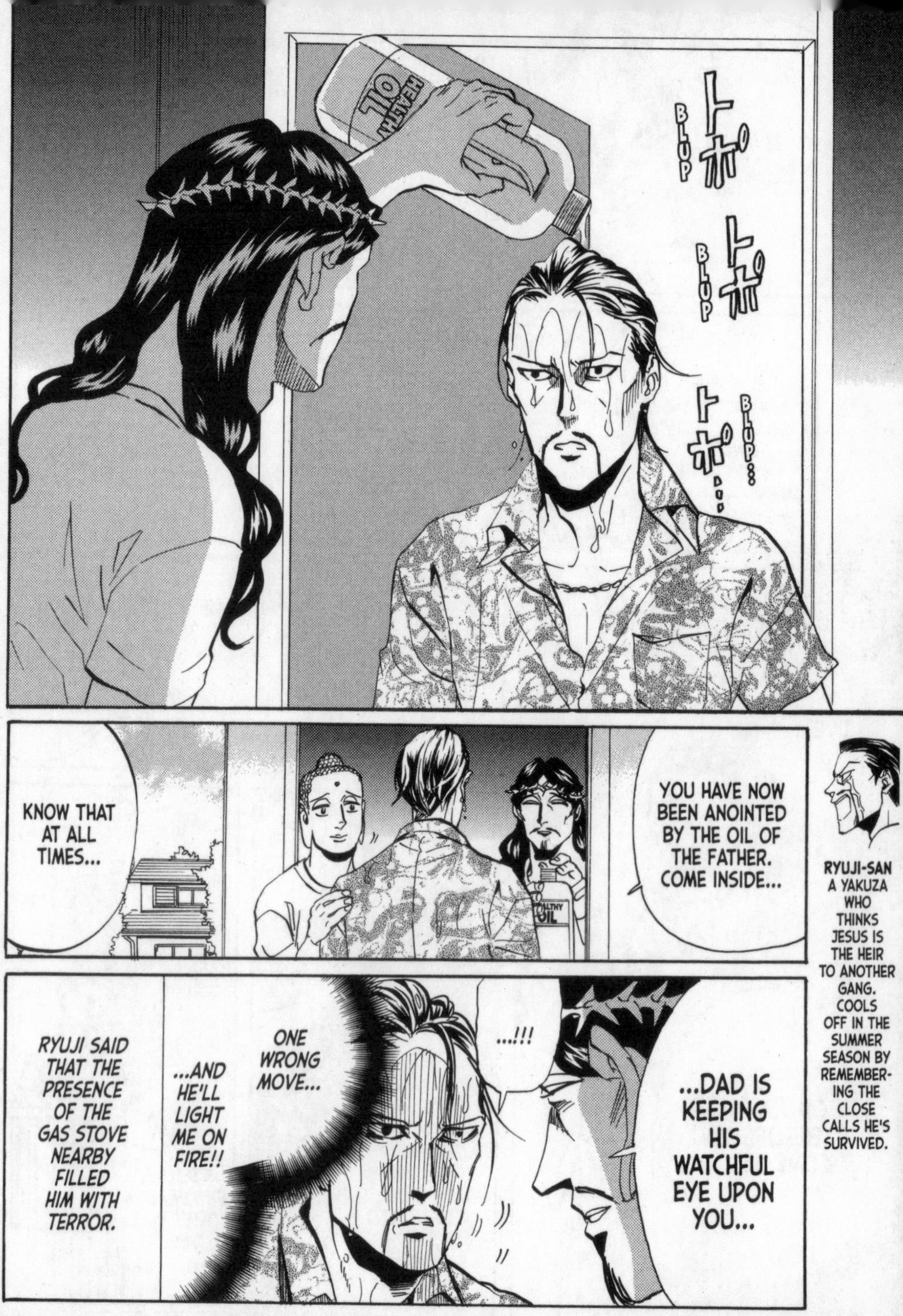
トポ
BLUP
トポ
BLUP
トポ...
BLUP...
RYUJI-SAN
A YAKUZA WHO THINKS JESUS IS THE HEIR TO ANOTHER GANG. COOLS OFF IN THE SUMMER SEASON BY REMEMBERING THE CLOSE CALLS HE'S SURVIVED.
YOU HAVE NOW BEEN ANOINTED BY THE OIL OF THE FATHER. COME INSIDE...
KNOW THAT AT ALL TIMES...
...DAD IS KEEPING HIS WATCHFUL EYE UPON YOU...
...!!!
ONE WRONG MOVE...
...AND HE'LL LIGHT ME ON FIRE!!
RYUJI SAID THAT THE PRESENCE OF THE GAS STOVE NEARBY FILLED HIM WITH TERROR.

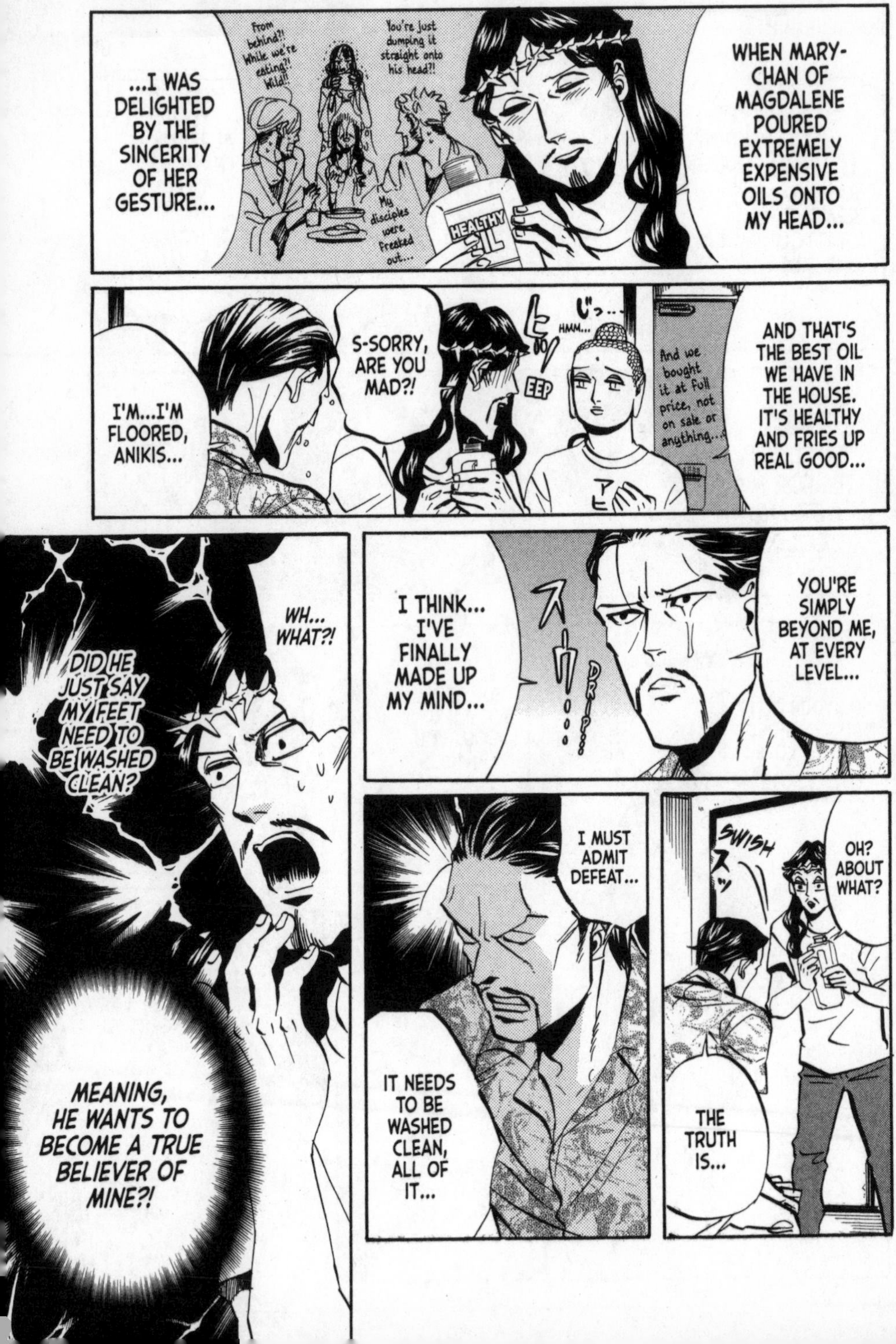
WHEN MARY-CHAN OF MAGDALENE POURED EXTREMELY EXPENSIVE OILS ONTO MY HEAD...
You're just dumping it straight onto his head?!
From behind?! While we're eating?! Wild!!
My disciples were freaked out...
HEALTHY OIL
...I WAS DELIGHTED BY THE SINCERITY OF HER GESTURE...
AND THAT'S THE BEST OIL WE HAVE IN THE HOUSE. IT'S HEALTHY AND FRIES UP REAL GOOD...
And we bought it at full price, not on sale or anything...
じっ...
HMM...
ヒッ
EEP
S-SORRY, ARE YOU MAD?!
I'M...I'M FLOORED, ANIKIS...
YOU'RE SIMPLY BEYOND ME, AT EVERY LEVEL...
スゥ
DRIP...
I THINK... I'VE FINALLY MADE UP MY MIND...
SWISH
スッ
OH? ABOUT WHAT?
THE TRUTH IS...
I MUST ADMIT DEFEAT...
IT NEEDS TO BE WASHED CLEAN, ALL OF IT...
WH... WHAT?!
DID HE JUST SAY MY FEET NEED TO BE WASHED CLEAN?
MEANING, HE WANTS TO BECOME A TRUE BELIEVER OF MINE?!

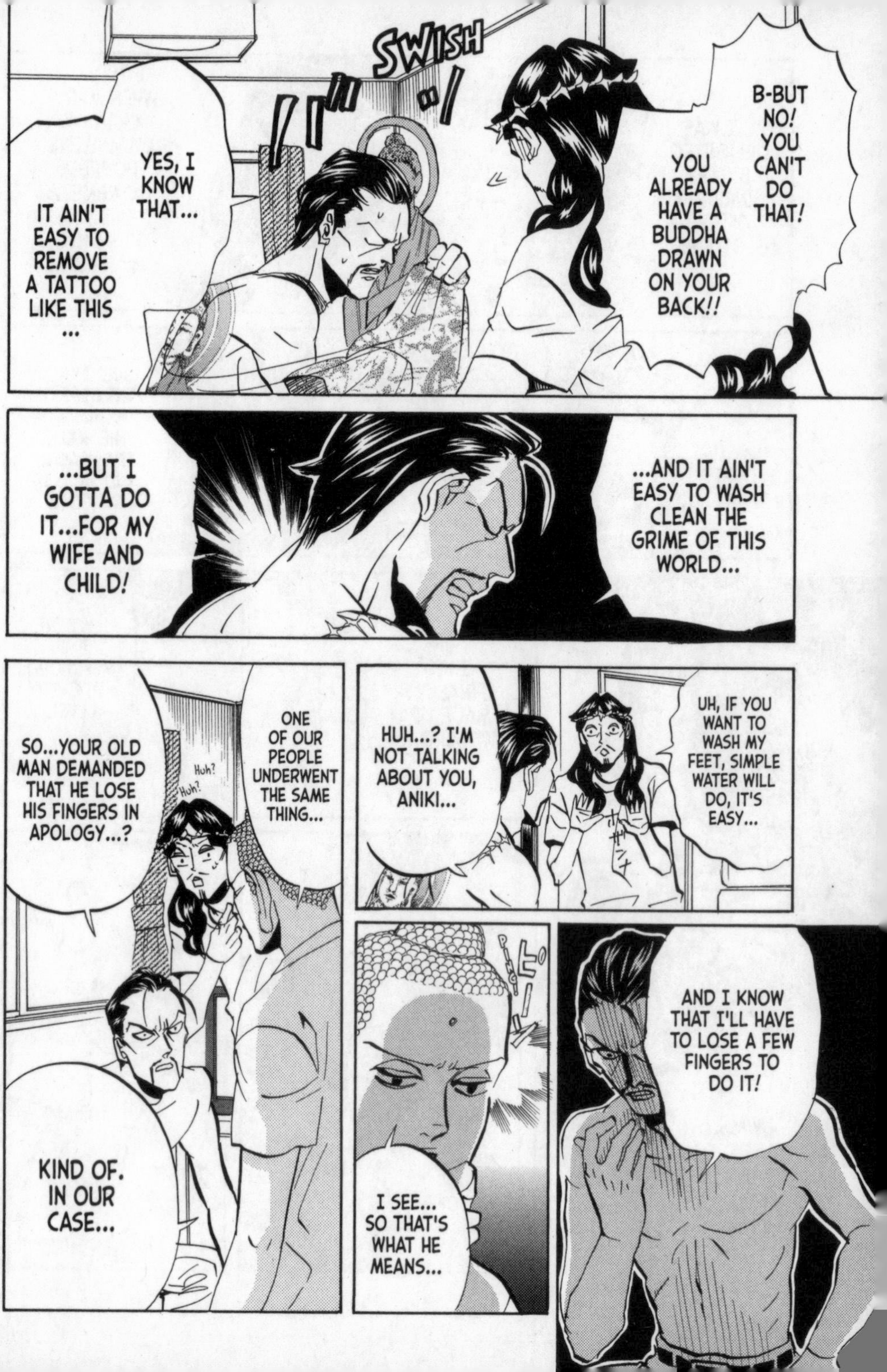

B-BUT NO! YOU CAN'T DO THAT!
YOU ALREADY HAVE A BUDDHA DRAWN ON YOUR BACK!!
SWISH
YES, I KNOW THAT...
IT AIN'T EASY TO REMOVE A TATTOO LIKE THIS ...
...AND IT AIN'T EASY TO WASH CLEAN THE GRIME OF THIS WORLD...
...BUT I GOTTA DO IT...FOR MY WIFE AND CHILD!
UH, IF YOU WANT TO WASH MY FEET, SIMPLE WATER WILL DO, IT'S EASY...
HUH...? I'M NOT TALKING ABOUT YOU, ANIKI...
AND I KNOW THAT I'LL HAVE TO LOSE A FEW FINGERS TO DO IT!
PING!
I SEE... SO THAT'S WHAT HE MEANS...
ONE OF OUR PEOPLE UNDERWENT THE SAME THING...
Huh?
Huh?
SO...YOUR OLD MAN DEMANDED THAT HE LOSE HIS FINGERS IN APOLOGY...?
KIND OF. IN OUR CASE...

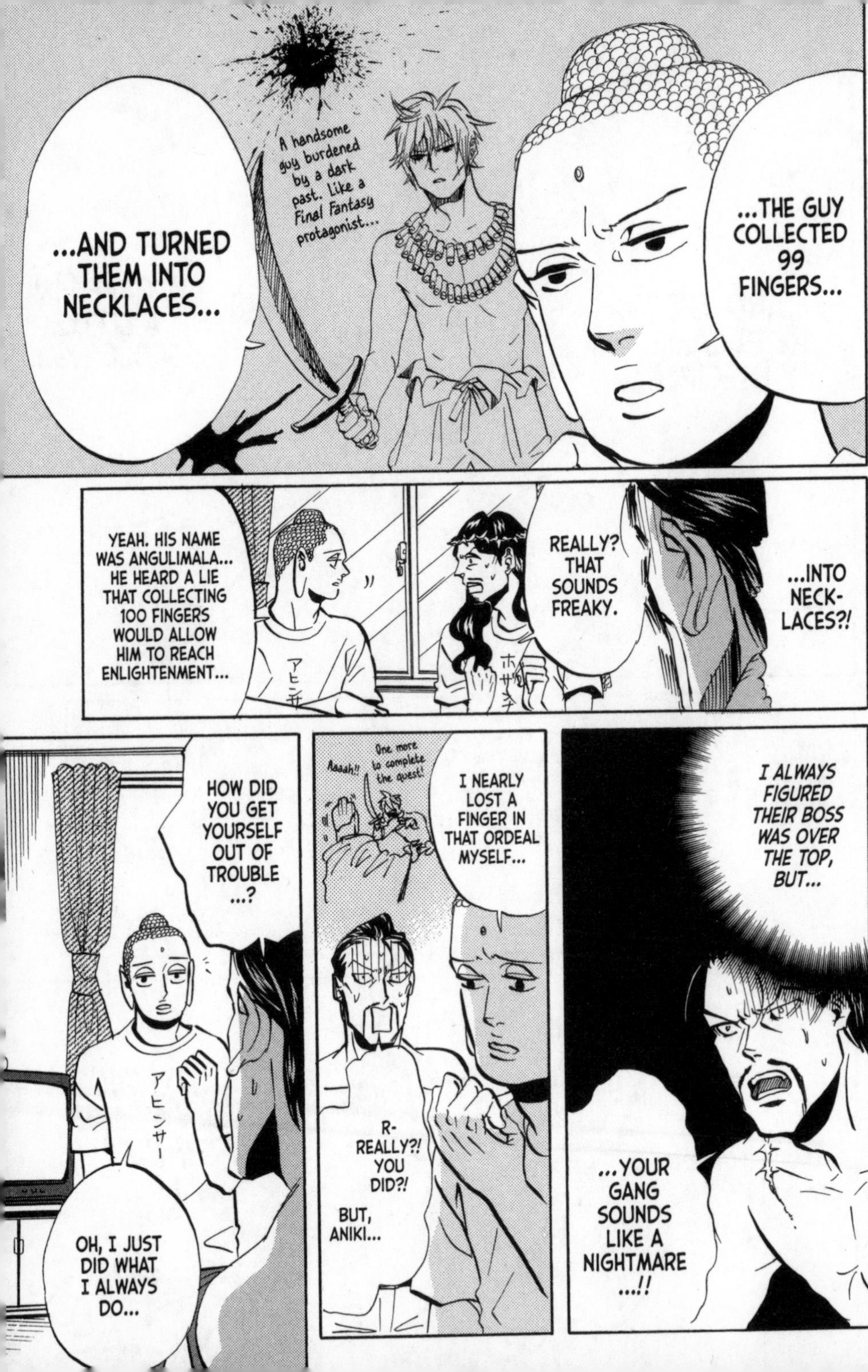
...THE GUY COLLECTED 99 FINGERS...
A handsome guy burdened by a dark past. Like a Final Fantasy protagonist...
...AND TURNED THEM INTO NECKLACES...
...INTO NECK-LACES?!
REALLY? THAT SOUNDS FREAKY.
YEAH. HIS NAME WAS ANGULIMALA... HE HEARD A LIE THAT COLLECTING 100 FINGERS WOULD ALLOW HIM TO REACH ENLIGHTENMENT...
I ALWAYS FIGURED THEIR BOSS WAS OVER THE TOP, BUT...
...YOUR GANG SOUNDS LIKE A NIGHTMARE ...!!
I NEARLY LOST A FINGER IN THAT ORDEAL MYSELF...
One more to complete the quest!
Aaaah!!
R-REALLY?! YOU DID?!
BUT, ANIKI...
HOW DID YOU GET YOURSELF OUT OF TROUBLE ...?
アヒンサー
OH, I JUST DID WHAT I ALWAYS DO...

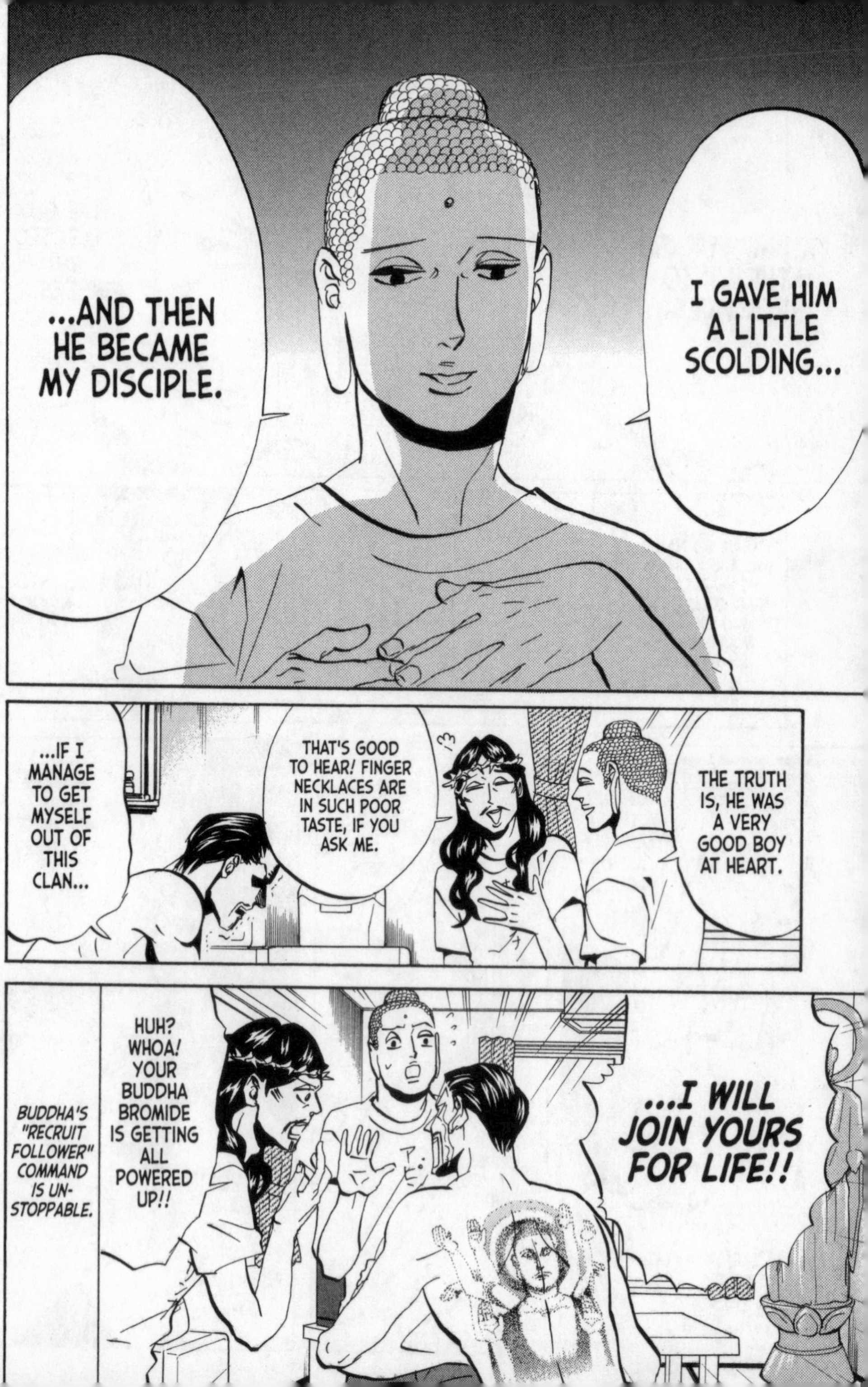
I GAVE HIM A LITTLE SCOLDING...
...AND THEN HE BECAME MY DISCIPLE.
THE TRUTH IS, HE WAS A VERY GOOD BOY AT HEART.
THAT'S GOOD TO HEAR! FINGER NECKLACES ARE IN SUCH POOR TASTE, IF YOU ASK ME.
...IF I MANAGE TO GET MYSELF OUT OF THIS CLAN...
...I WILL JOIN YOURS FOR LIFE!!
HUH? WHOA! YOUR BUDDHA BROMIDE IS GETTING ALL POWERED UP!!
BUDDHA'S "RECRUIT FOLLOWER" COMMAND IS UN-STOPPABLE.

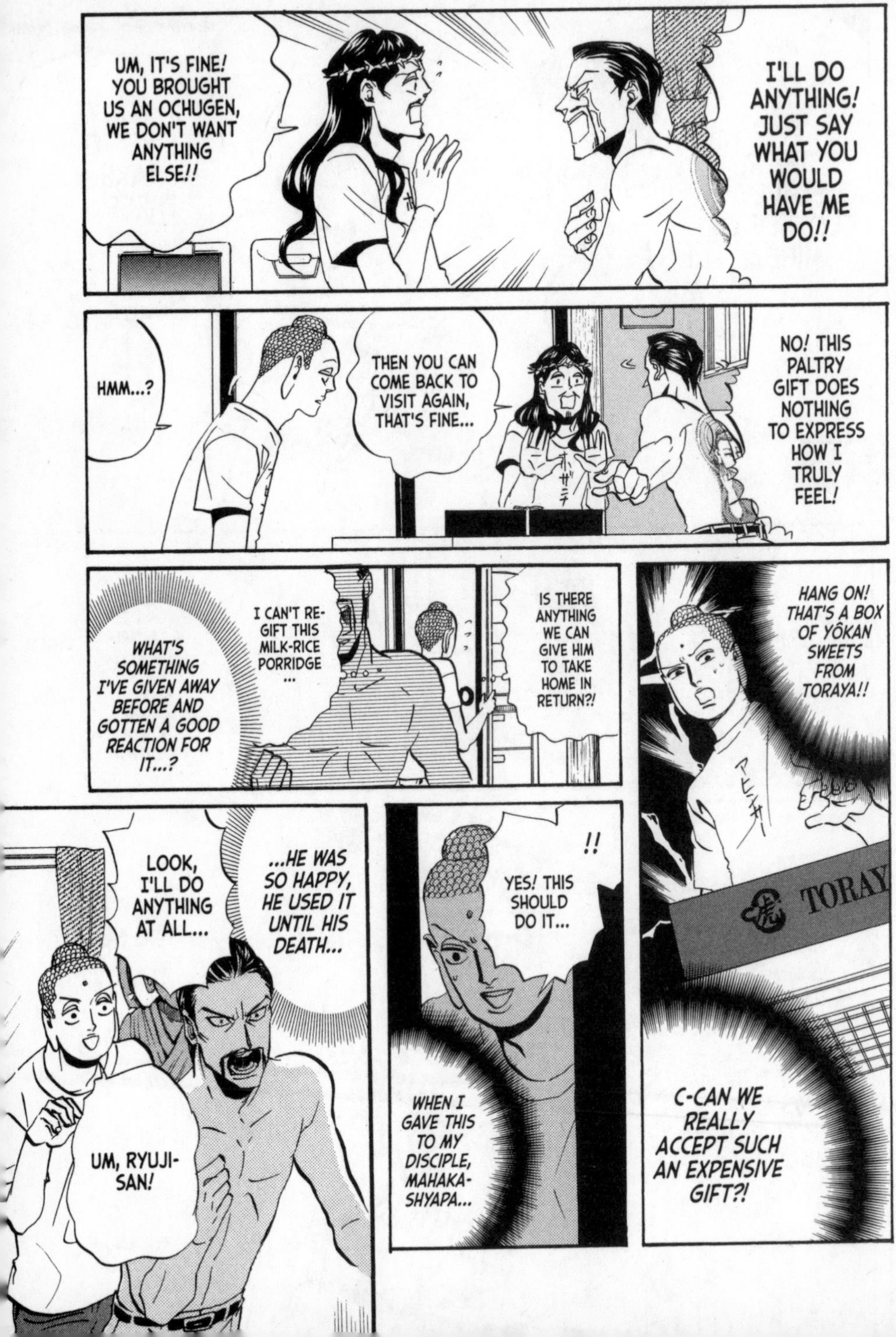
I'LL DO ANYTHING! JUST SAY WHAT YOU WOULD HAVE ME DO!!
UM, IT'S FINE! YOU BROUGHT US AN OCHUGEN, WE DON'T WANT ANYTHING ELSE!!
NO! THIS PALTRY GIFT DOES NOTHING TO EXPRESS HOW I TRULY FEEL!
THEN YOU CAN COME BACK TO VISIT AGAIN, THAT'S FINE...
HMM...?
HANG ON! THAT'S A BOX OF YÔKAN SWEETS FROM TORAYA!!
TORAY
C-CAN WE REALLY ACCEPT SUCH AN EXPENSIVE GIFT?!
IS THERE ANYTHING WE CAN GIVE HIM TO TAKE HOME IN RETURN?!
I CAN'T RE-GIFT THIS MILK-RICE PORRIDGE ...
WHAT'S SOMETHING I'VE GIVEN AWAY BEFORE AND GOTTEN A GOOD REACTION FOR IT...?
!!
YES! THIS SHOULD DO IT...
WHEN I GAVE THIS TO MY DISCIPLE, MAHAKA-SHYAPA...
...HE WAS SO HAPPY, HE USED IT UNTIL HIS DEATH...
LOOK, I'LL DO ANYTHING AT ALL...
UM, RYUJI-SAN!

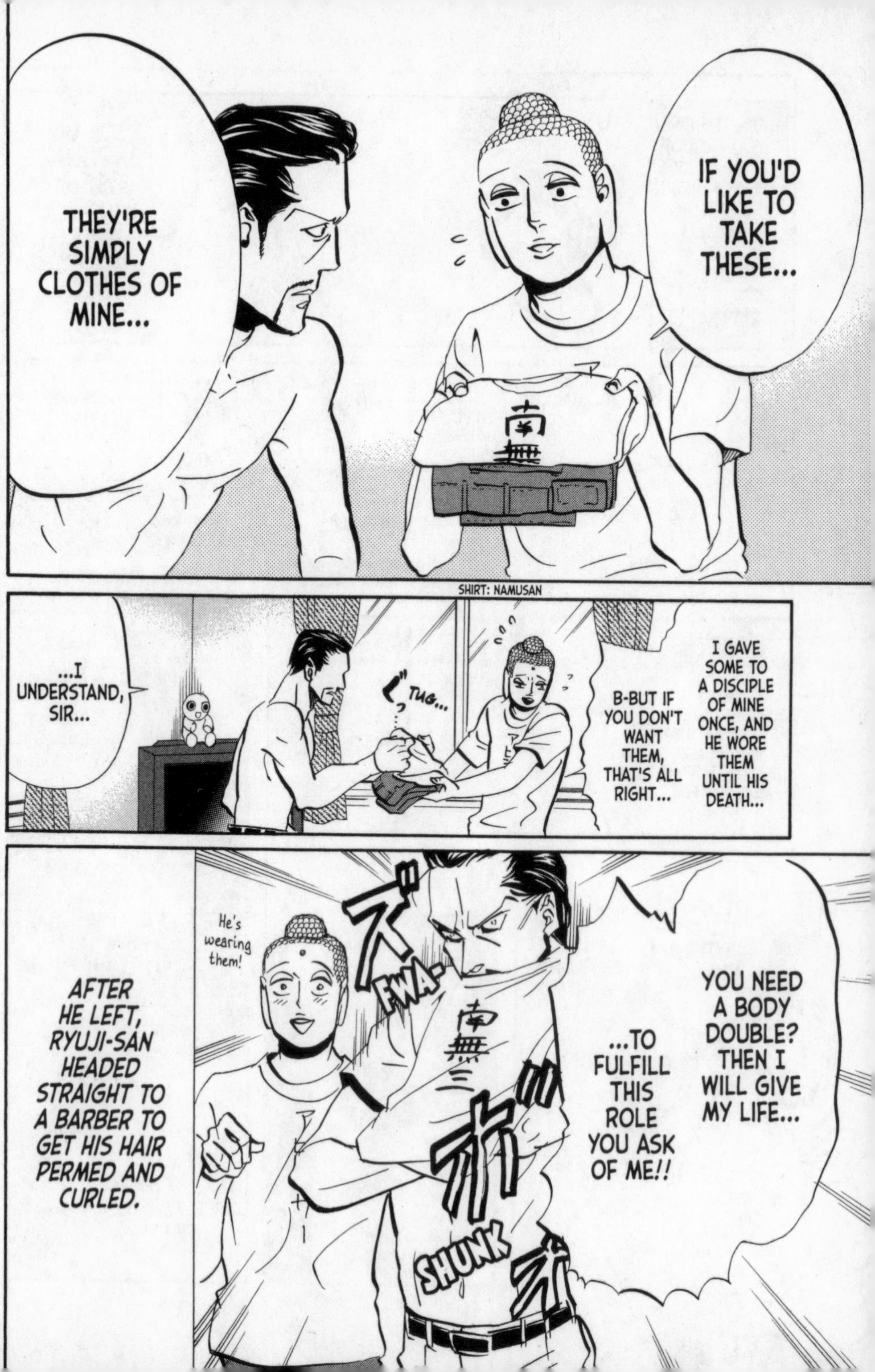
IF YOU'D LIKE TO TAKE THESE...
THEY'RE SIMPLY CLOTHES OF MINE...
SHIRT: NAMUSAN
I GAVE SOME TO A DISCIPLE OF MINE ONCE, AND HE WORE THEM UNTIL HIS DEATH...
B-BUT IF YOU DON'T WANT THEM, THAT'S ALL RIGHT...
TUG...
...I UNDERSTAND, SIR...
YOU NEED A BODY DOUBLE? THEN I WILL GIVE MY LIFE...
...TO FULFILL THIS ROLE YOU ASK OF ME!!
FWA-
SHUNK
He's wearing them!
AFTER HE LEFT, RYUJI-SAN HEADED STRAIGHT TO A BARBER TO GET HIS HAIR PERMED AND CURLED.

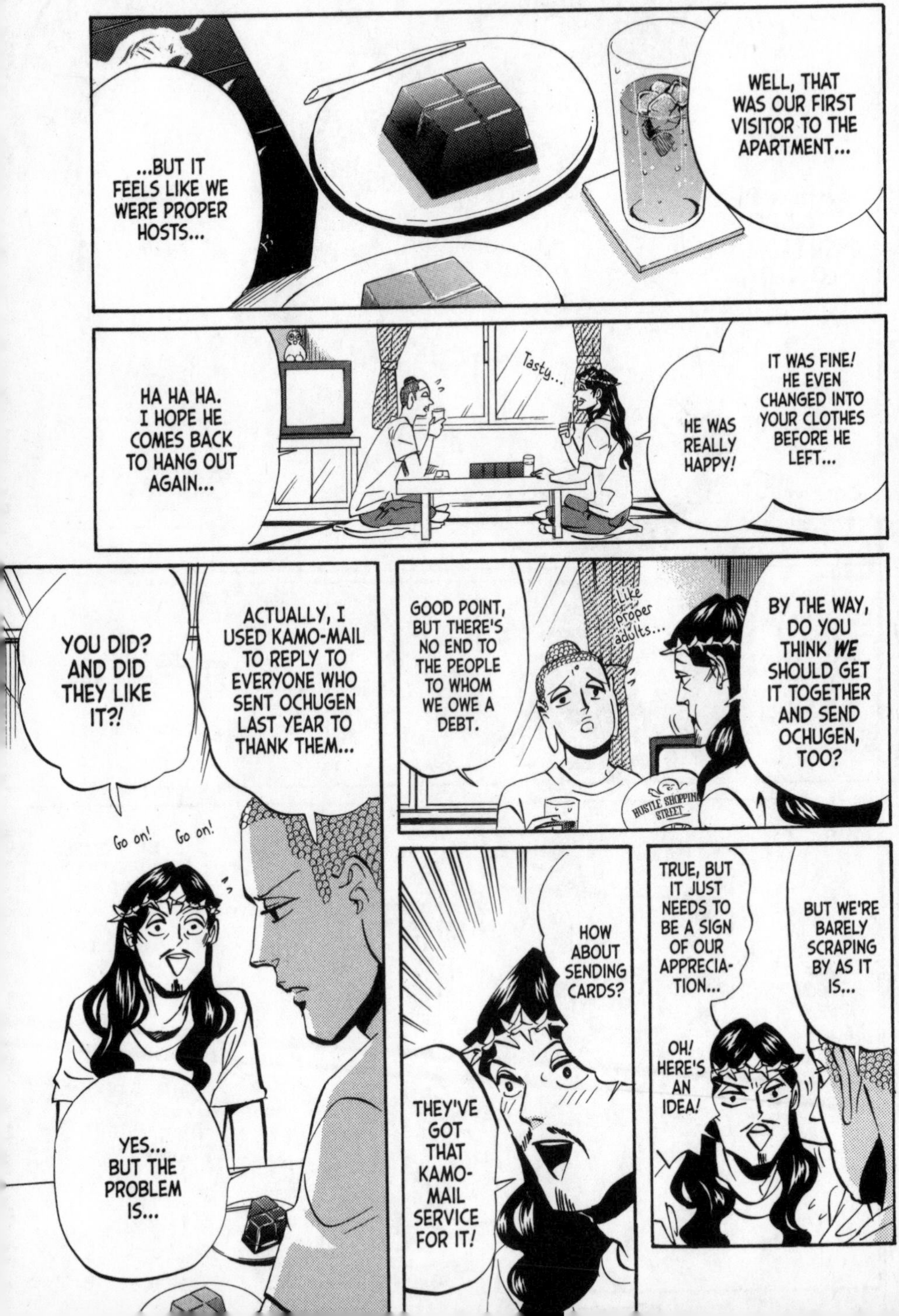
WELL, THAT WAS OUR FIRST VISITOR TO THE APARTMENT...
...BUT IT FEELS LIKE WE WERE PROPER HOSTS...
IT WAS FINE! HE EVEN CHANGED INTO YOUR CLOTHES BEFORE HE LEFT...
HE WAS REALLY HAPPY!
Tasty...
HA HA HA. I HOPE HE COMES BACK TO HANG OUT AGAIN...
BY THE WAY, DO YOU THINK *WE* SHOULD GET IT TOGETHER AND SEND OCHUGEN, TOO?
HUSTLE SHOPPING STREET
Like proper adults...
GOOD POINT, BUT THERE'S NO END TO THE PEOPLE TO WHOM WE OWE A DEBT.
BUT WE'RE BARELY SCRAPING BY AS IT IS...
TRUE, BUT IT JUST NEEDS TO BE A SIGN OF OUR APPRECIA-TION...
OH! HERE'S AN IDEA!
HOW ABOUT SENDING CARDS?
THEY'VE GOT THAT KAMO-MAIL SERVICE FOR IT!
ACTUALLY, I USED KAMO-MAIL TO REPLY TO EVERYONE WHO SENT OCHUGEN LAST YEAR TO THANK THEM...
YOU DID? AND DID THEY LIKE IT?!
Go on! Go on!
YES... BUT THE PROBLEM IS...

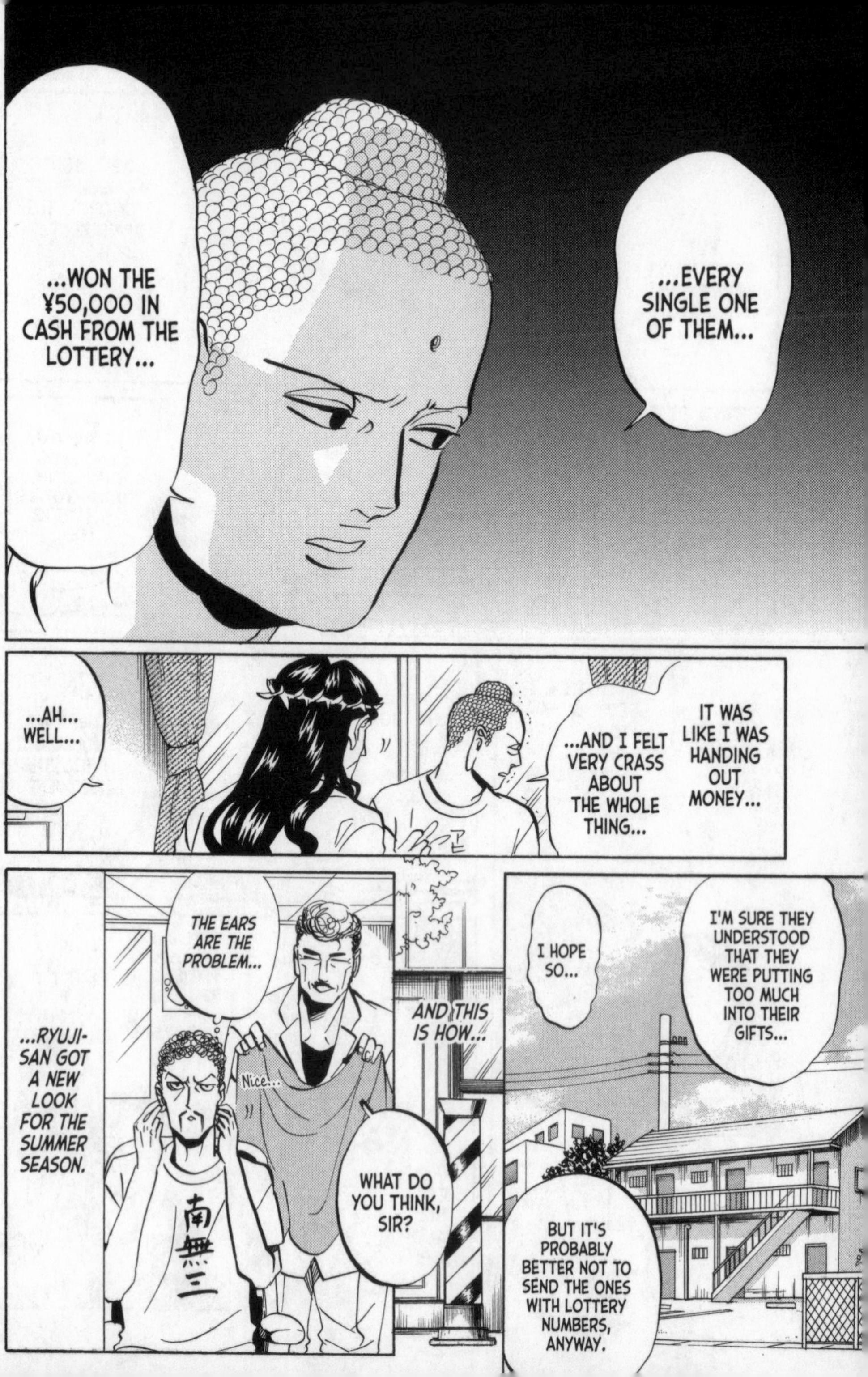
...EVERY SINGLE ONE OF THEM...
...WON THE ¥50,000 IN CASH FROM THE LOTTERY...
IT WAS LIKE I WAS HANDING OUT MONEY...
...AND I FELT VERY CRASS ABOUT THE WHOLE THING...
...AH... WELL...
I'M SURE THEY UNDERSTOOD THAT THEY WERE PUTTING TOO MUCH INTO THEIR GIFTS...
I HOPE SO...
BUT IT'S PROBABLY BETTER NOT TO SEND THE ONES WITH LOTTERY NUMBERS, ANYWAY.
AND THIS IS HOW...
THE EARS ARE THE PROBLEM...
WHAT DO YOU THINK, SIR?
Nice...
南無三
...RYUJI-SAN GOT A NEW LOOK FOR THE SUMMER SEASON.

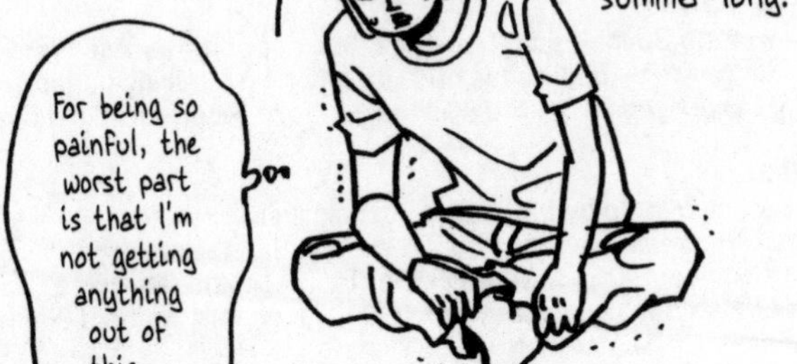
The ordeal of having mosquitoes bite your pinky toes all summer long.
HUFF...
HUFF...
For being so painful, the worst part is that I'm not getting anything out of this...

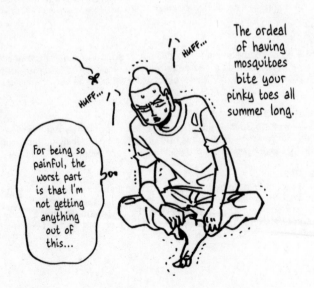

CHAPTER 49 TRANSLATION NOTES

Hosanna, page 92
A religious word that comes from a Hebrew term for "save." In a Christian context it appears as a word of praise in recognition of Jesus' entry into Jerusalem.

Ahimsa, page 95
The virtue of nonviolence observed in several South Asian religions, including Buddhism. A central facet of Ahimsa is that harming others harms oneself due to its karmic effects.

Anointing, page 98
To baptize a person with fragrant oils, or "anoint" them, is the greatest of honors. The Greek word *christos* means "anointed one," and is the root for the title of Christ.

"Dad," page 98
Yakuza hierarchies are based loosely on a family concept, and the titles with which they refer to each other reflect that. The boss is the *oyaji*, or "Dad," while the rank and file are his "sons." Any member speaking to a senior within the group will usually call him *aniki*, which means "older brother."

Feet washing, page 99
The phrase "to wash one's feet" in Japanese means to give up a life of crime, however this is also a custom of humility and commitment to Jesus Christ as an object of veneration, as related in John 13:1.

Angulimala, page 101
A brigand who collected fingers before he met the Buddha and became a follower, reforming himself. According to the story, Angulimala's old teacher tried to get rid of him by claiming that finding human fingers (the story ranges from 100 to 1,000) would bring him enlightenment. When the Buddha convinces him before he can kill his very last victim, he demonstrates that anyone can change their life for the better.

Yôkan, page 103
A traditional dessert made of an (red bean paste) solidified with agar and sugar. It's presented in neat little cubes that can be easily picked up and eaten with a toothpick. The kind mentioned here is mizu-yôkan, or "water yôkan" which is made with extra water and can be served chilled in the summer.

Mahakashyapa, page 104
One of the principal disciples of the Buddha and a foremost teacher of his ascetic practices. The Buddha exchanged robes with him to symbolize his passing off of the teachings after death. Later, at the end of his own life, Mahakashyapa wore the Buddha's robe to receive his final alms.

Kamo-mail, page 105
A special summer-season service offered by the Japan Post exclusively for traditional summer greeting cards known as *shochu-mimai* (greetings during summer heat) or *zansho-mimai* (greetings during lingering heat) depending on whether they're sent in the late July to early August period, or later in the summer. Kamo-mail postcards have serial numbers on them that will later be entered into a lottery that is drawn in September.

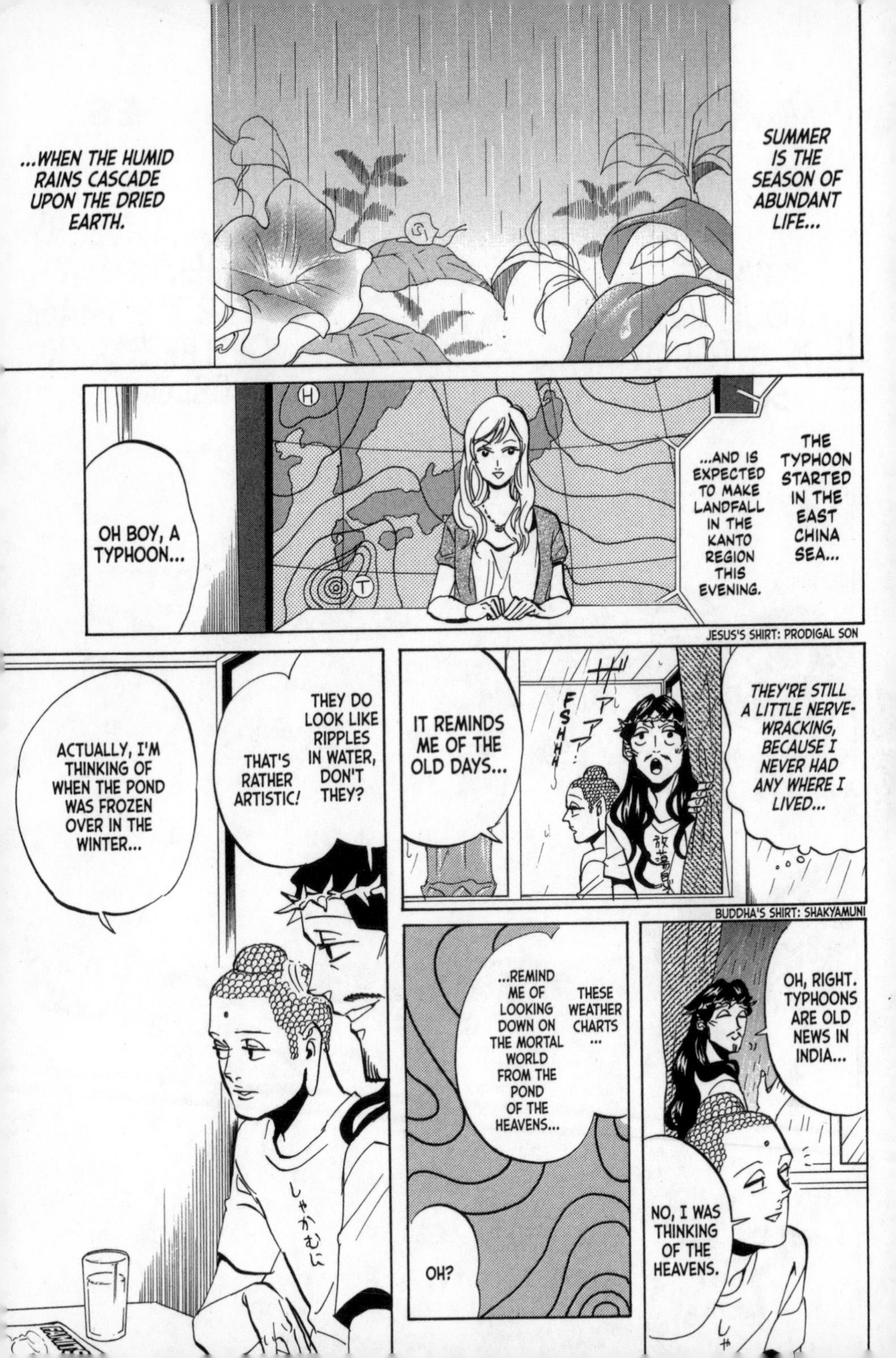
SUMMER IS THE SEASON OF ABUNDANT LIFE...
...WHEN THE HUMID RAINS CASCADE UPON THE DRIED EARTH.
THE TYPHOON STARTED IN THE EAST CHINA SEA...
...AND IS EXPECTED TO MAKE LANDFALL IN THE KANTO REGION THIS EVENING.
OH BOY, A TYPHOON...
JESUS'S SHIRT: PRODIGAL SON
THEY'RE STILL A LITTLE NERVE-WRACKING, BECAUSE I NEVER HAD ANY WHERE I LIVED...
ザアアア
FSHHH
IT REMINDS ME OF THE OLD DAYS...
BUDDHA'S SHIRT: SHAKYAMUNI
OH, RIGHT. TYPHOONS ARE OLD NEWS IN INDIA...
NO, I WAS THINKING OF THE HEAVENS.
THESE WEATHER CHARTS...
...REMIND ME OF LOOKING DOWN ON THE MORTAL WORLD FROM THE POND OF THE HEAVENS...
OH?
THEY DO LOOK LIKE RIPPLES IN WATER, DON'T THEY?
THAT'S RATHER ARTISTIC!
ACTUALLY, I'M THINKING OF WHEN THE POND WAS FROZEN OVER IN THE WINTER...
しゃかむに

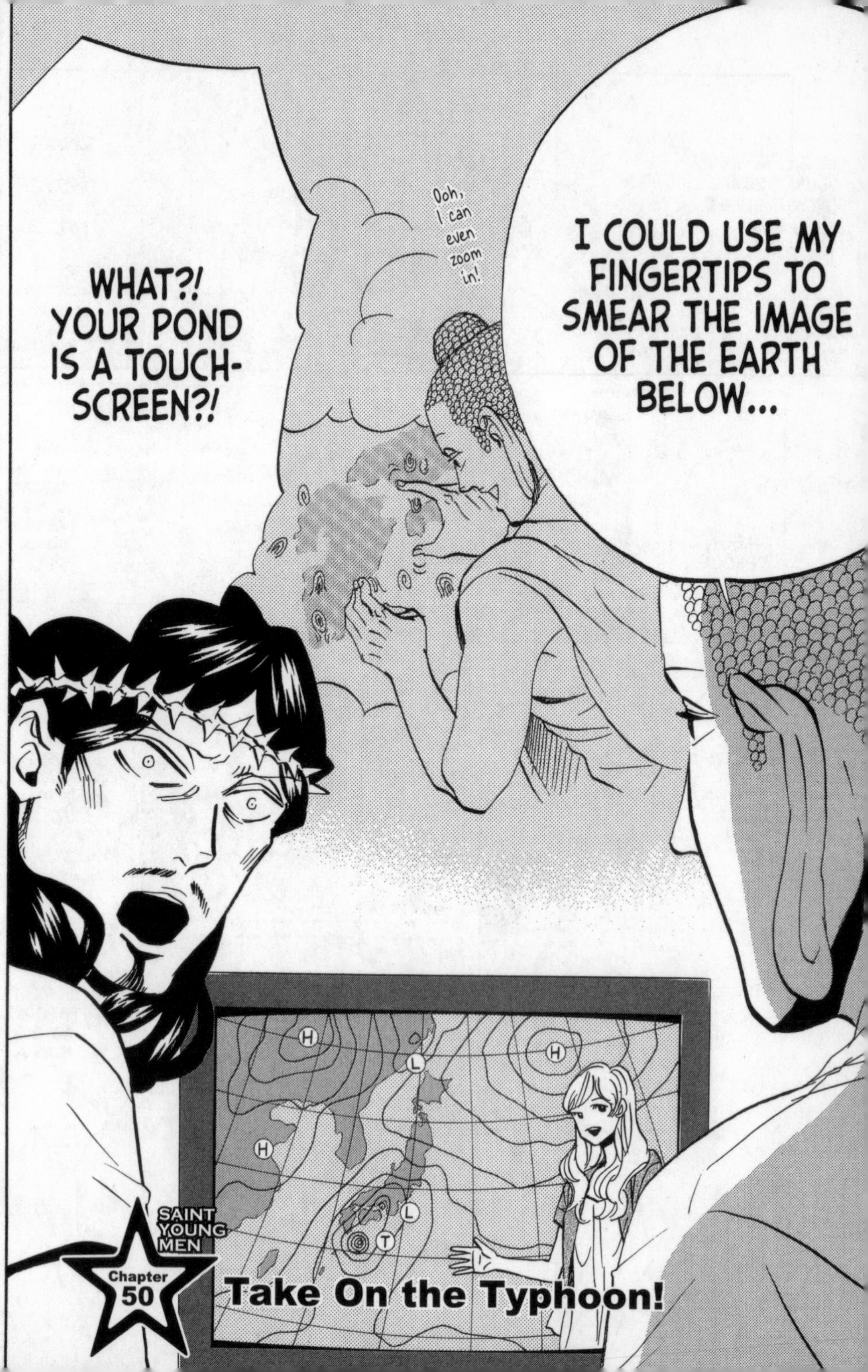
I COULD USE MY FINGERTIPS TO SMEAR THE IMAGE OF THE EARTH BELOW...
Ooh, I can even zoom in!
WHAT?! YOUR POND IS A TOUCH-SCREEN?!
SAINT YOUNG MEN

Chapter 50 Take On the Typhoon!

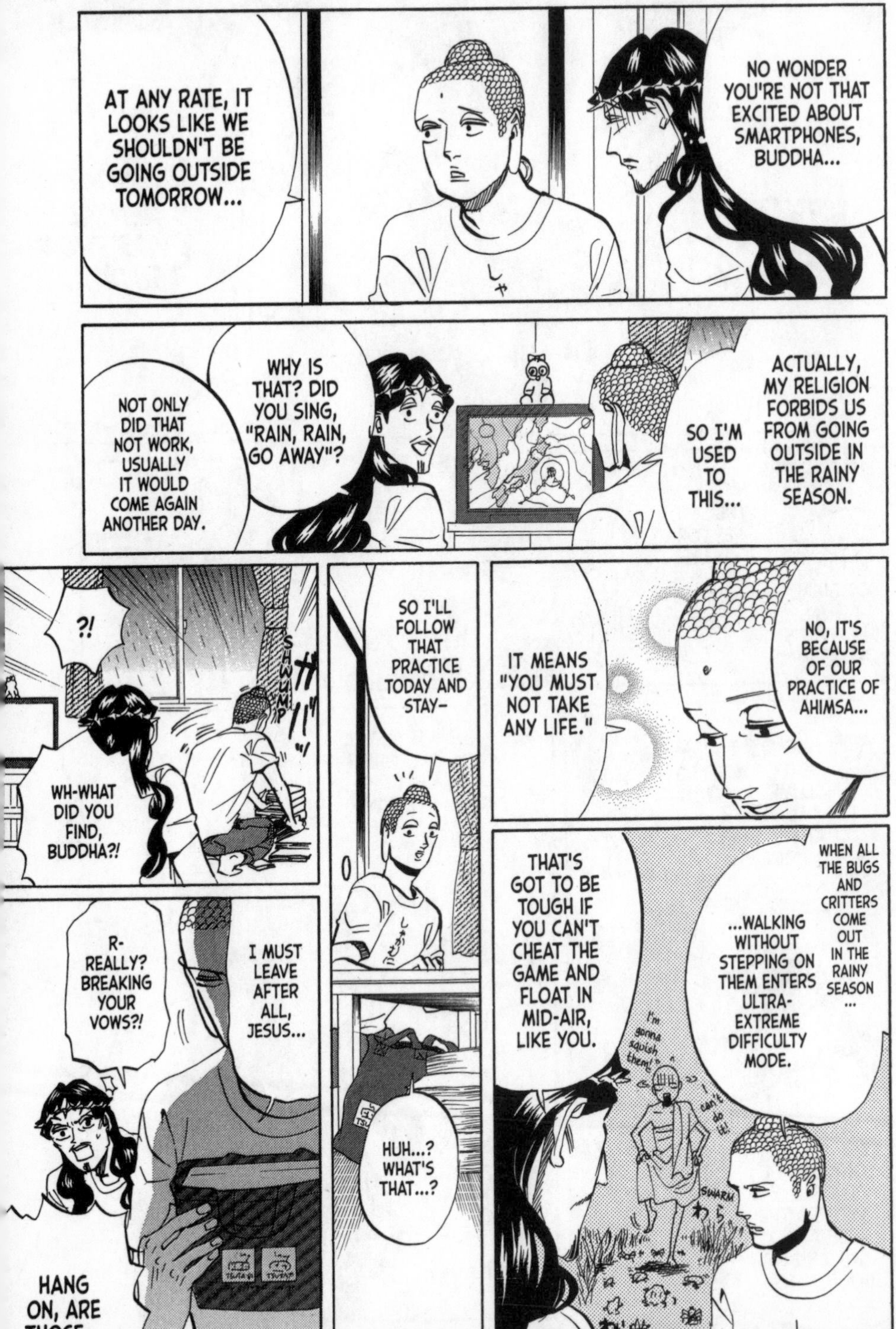
NO WONDER YOU'RE NOT THAT EXCITED ABOUT SMARTPHONES, BUDDHA...
AT ANY RATE, IT LOOKS LIKE WE SHOULDN'T BE GOING OUTSIDE TOMORROW...
ACTUALLY, MY RELIGION FORBIDS US FROM GOING OUTSIDE IN THE RAINY SEASON.
SO I'M USED TO THIS...
WHY IS THAT? DID YOU SING, "RAIN, RAIN, GO AWAY"?
NOT ONLY DID THAT NOT WORK, USUALLY IT WOULD COME AGAIN ANOTHER DAY.
NO, IT'S BECAUSE OF OUR PRACTICE OF AHIMSA...
IT MEANS "YOU MUST NOT TAKE ANY LIFE."
WHEN ALL THE BUGS AND CRITTERS COME OUT IN THE RAINY SEASON...
...WALKING WITHOUT STEPPING ON THEM ENTERS ULTRA-EXTREME DIFFICULTY MODE.
I'm gonna squish them!
I can't do it!
SWARM
SWARM
THAT'S GOT TO BE TOUGH IF YOU CAN'T CHEAT THE GAME AND FLOAT IN MID-AIR, LIKE YOU.
SO I'LL FOLLOW THAT PRACTICE TODAY AND STAY-
HUH...? WHAT'S THAT...?
?!
SHWUMP
WH-WHAT DID YOU FIND, BUDDHA?!
I MUST LEAVE AFTER ALL, JESUS...
R-REALLY? BREAKING YOUR VOWS?!
HANG ON, ARE THOSE...

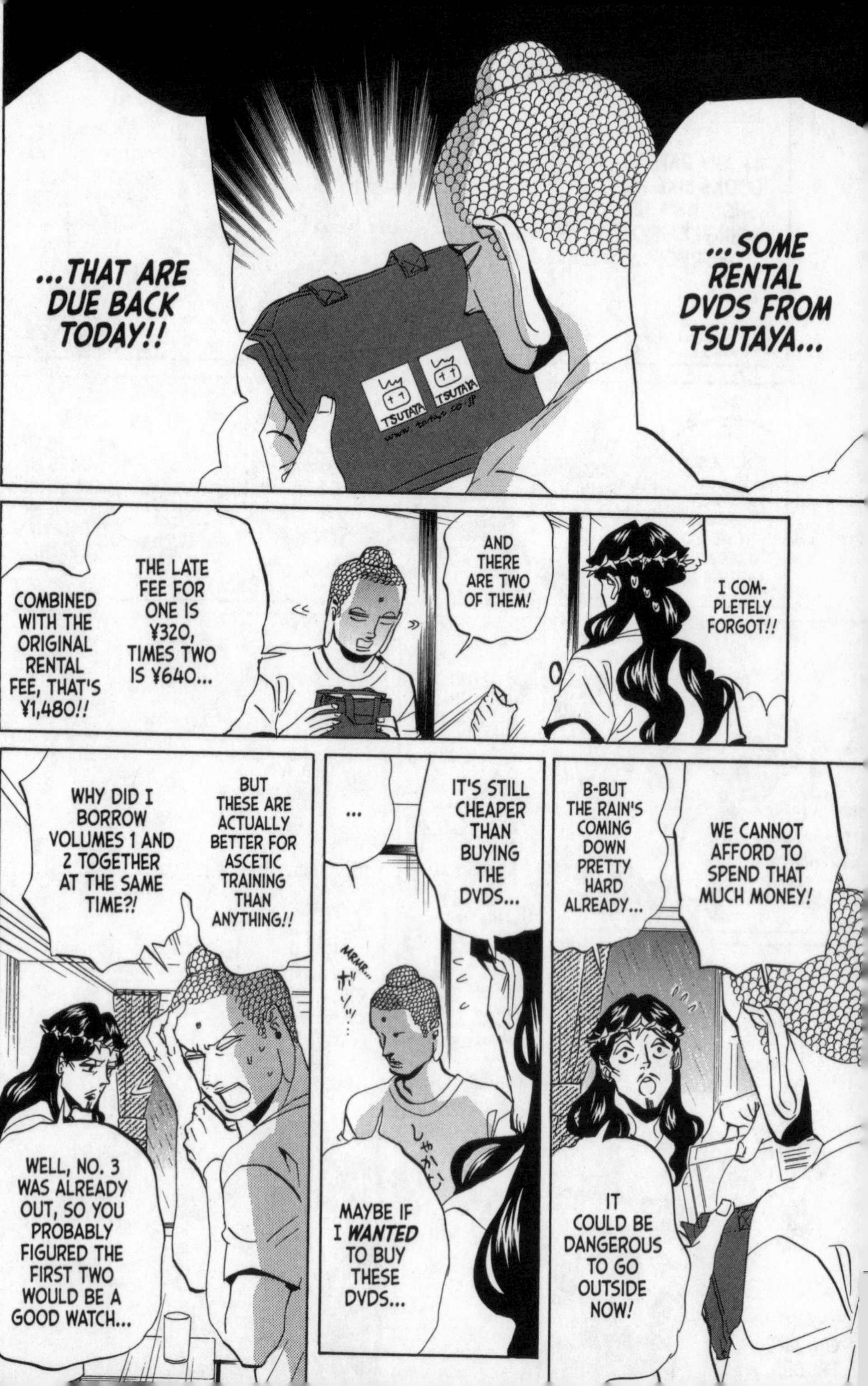
...SOME RENTAL DVDS FROM TSUTAYA...
...THAT ARE DUE BACK TODAY!!
TSUTAYA
TSUTAYA
I COMPLETELY FORGOT!!
AND THERE ARE TWO OF THEM!
THE LATE FEE FOR ONE IS ¥320, TIMES TWO IS ¥640...
COMBINED WITH THE ORIGINAL RENTAL FEE, THAT'S ¥1,480!!
WE CANNOT AFFORD TO SPEND THAT MUCH MONEY!
B-BUT THE RAIN'S COMING DOWN PRETTY HARD ALREADY...
IT COULD BE DANGEROUS TO GO OUTSIDE NOW!
IT'S STILL CHEAPER THAN BUYING THE DVDS...
...
MRMR... ボソッ...
しゃかし
MAYBE IF I *WANTED* TO BUY THESE DVDS...
BUT THESE ARE ACTUALLY BETTER FOR ASCETIC TRAINING THAN ANYTHING!!
WHY DID I BORROW VOLUMES 1 AND 2 TOGETHER AT THE SAME TIME?!
WELL, NO. 3 WAS ALREADY OUT, SO YOU PROBABLY FIGURED THE FIRST TWO WOULD BE A GOOD WATCH...

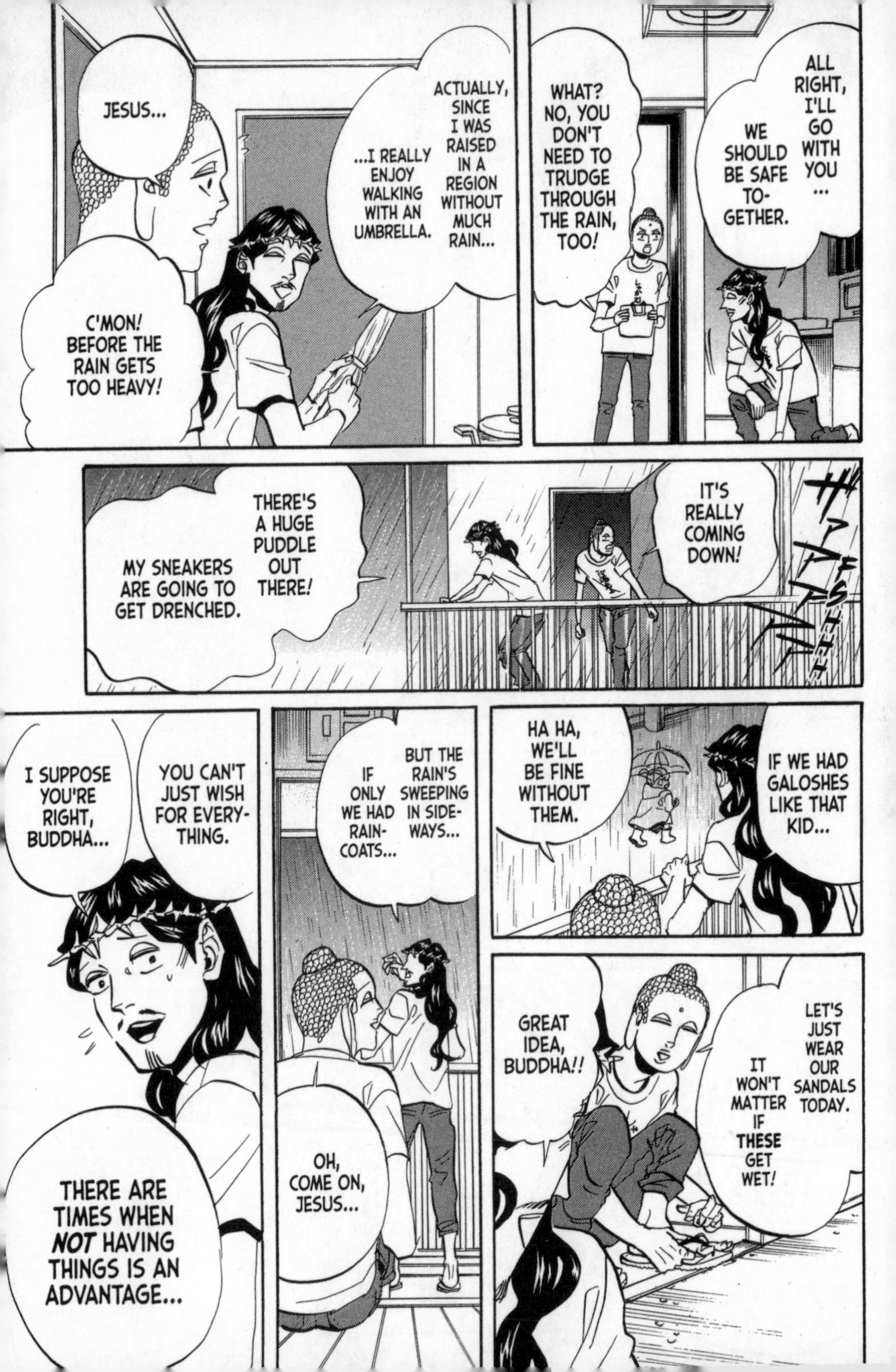
ALL RIGHT, I'LL GO WITH YOU ...
WE SHOULD BE SAFE TOGETHER.
WHAT? NO, YOU DON'T NEED TO TRUDGE THROUGH THE RAIN, TOO!
ACTUALLY, SINCE I WAS RAISED IN A REGION WITHOUT MUCH RAIN...
...I REALLY ENJOY WALKING WITH AN UMBRELLA.
JESUS...
C'MON! BEFORE THE RAIN GETS TOO HEAVY!
FSHHH
IT'S REALLY COMING DOWN!
THERE'S A HUGE PUDDLE OUT THERE!
MY SNEAKERS ARE GOING TO GET DRENCHED.
IF WE HAD GALOSHES LIKE THAT KID...
HA HA, WE'LL BE FINE WITHOUT THEM.
LET'S JUST WEAR OUR SANDALS TODAY.
IT WON'T MATTER IF THESE GET WET!
GREAT IDEA, BUDDHA!!
BUT THE RAIN'S SWEEPING IN SIDEWAYS...
IF ONLY WE HAD RAINCOATS...
OH, COME ON, JESUS...
YOU CAN'T JUST WISH FOR EVERYTHING.
I SUPPOSE YOU'RE RIGHT, BUDDHA...
THERE ARE TIMES WHEN *NOT* HAVING THINGS IS AN ADVANTAGE...

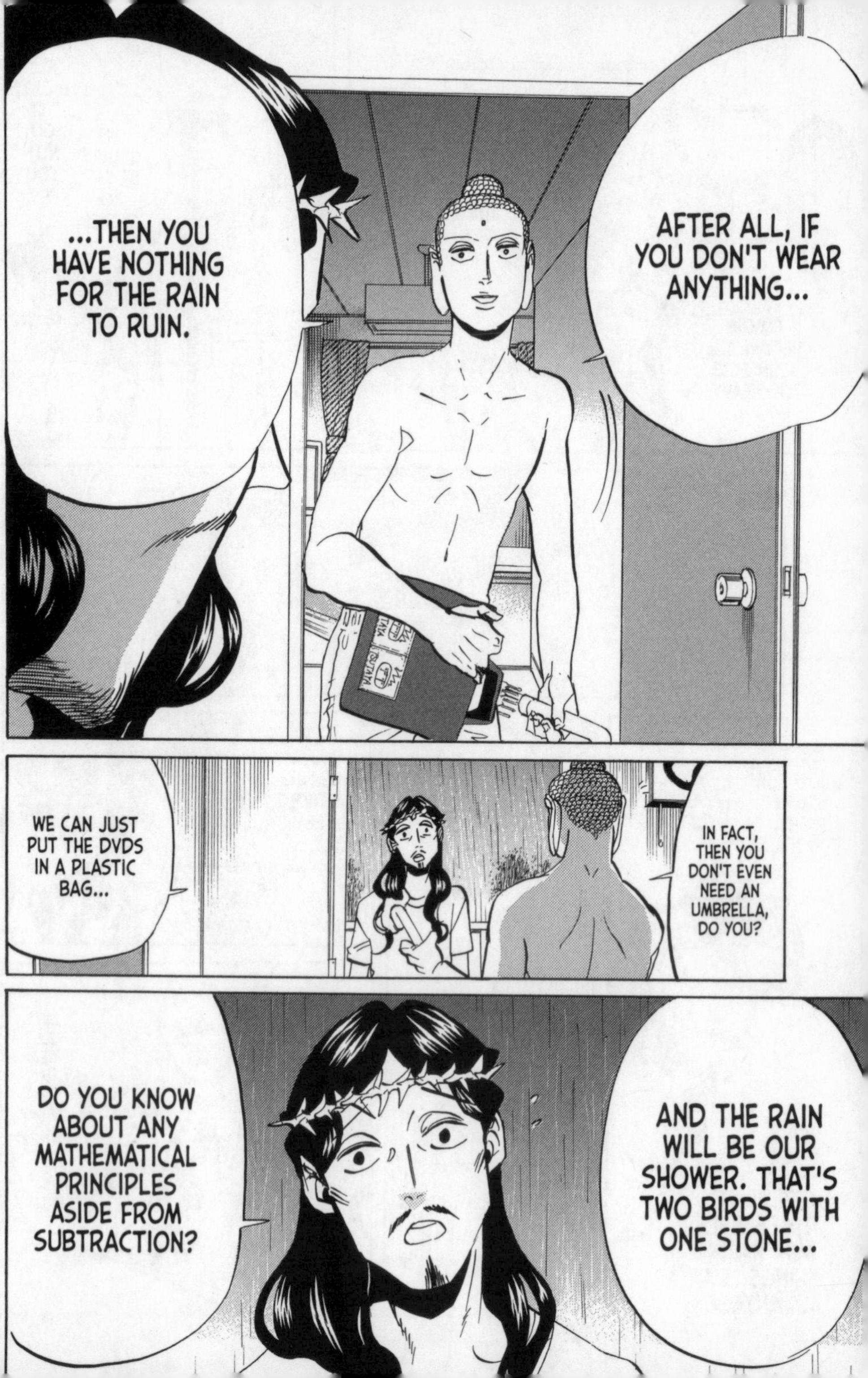
AFTER ALL, IF YOU DON'T WEAR ANYTHING...
...THEN YOU HAVE NOTHING FOR THE RAIN TO RUIN.
IN FACT, THEN YOU DON'T EVEN NEED AN UMBRELLA, DO YOU?
WE CAN JUST PUT THE DVDS IN A PLASTIC BAG...
AND THE RAIN WILL BE OUR SHOWER. THAT'S TWO BIRDS WITH ONE STONE...
DO YOU KNOW ABOUT ANY MATHEMATICAL PRINCIPLES ASIDE FROM SUBTRACTION?

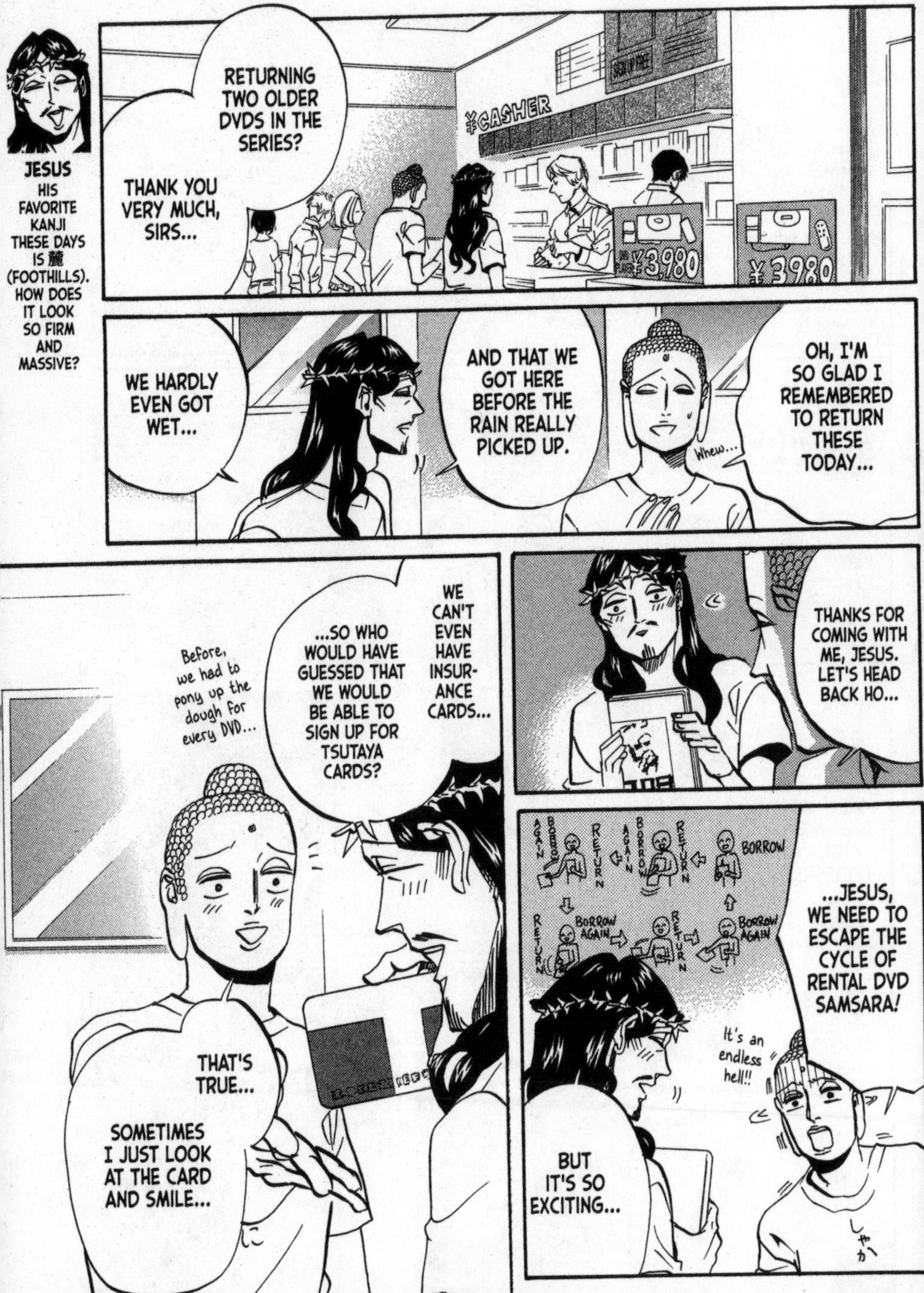

RETURNING TWO OLDER DVDS IN THE SERIES?
THANK YOU VERY MUCH, SIRS...
¥CASHER
¥3980
¥3980
OH, I'M SO GLAD I REMEMBERED TO RETURN THESE TODAY...
Whew...
AND THAT WE GOT HERE BEFORE THE RAIN REALLY PICKED UP.
WE HARDLY EVEN GOT WET...
THANKS FOR COMING WITH ME, JESUS. LET'S HEAD BACK HO...
BORROW
RETURN
BORROW AGAIN
RETURN
BORROW AGAIN
RETURN
BORROW AGAIN
RETURN
BORROW AGAIN
...JESUS, WE NEED TO ESCAPE THE CYCLE OF RENTAL DVD SAMSARA!
It's an endless hell!!
BUT IT'S SO EXCITING...
しゃか
WE CAN'T EVEN HAVE INSUR-ANCE CARDS...
...SO WHO WOULD HAVE GUESSED THAT WE WOULD BE ABLE TO SIGN UP FOR TSUTAYA CARDS?
Before, we had to pony up the dough for every DVD...
THAT'S TRUE...
SOMETIMES I JUST LOOK AT THE CARD AND SMILE...
JESUS
HIS FAVORITE KANJI THESE DAYS IS 麓 (FOOTHILLS). HOW DOES IT LOOK SO FIRM AND MASSIVE?

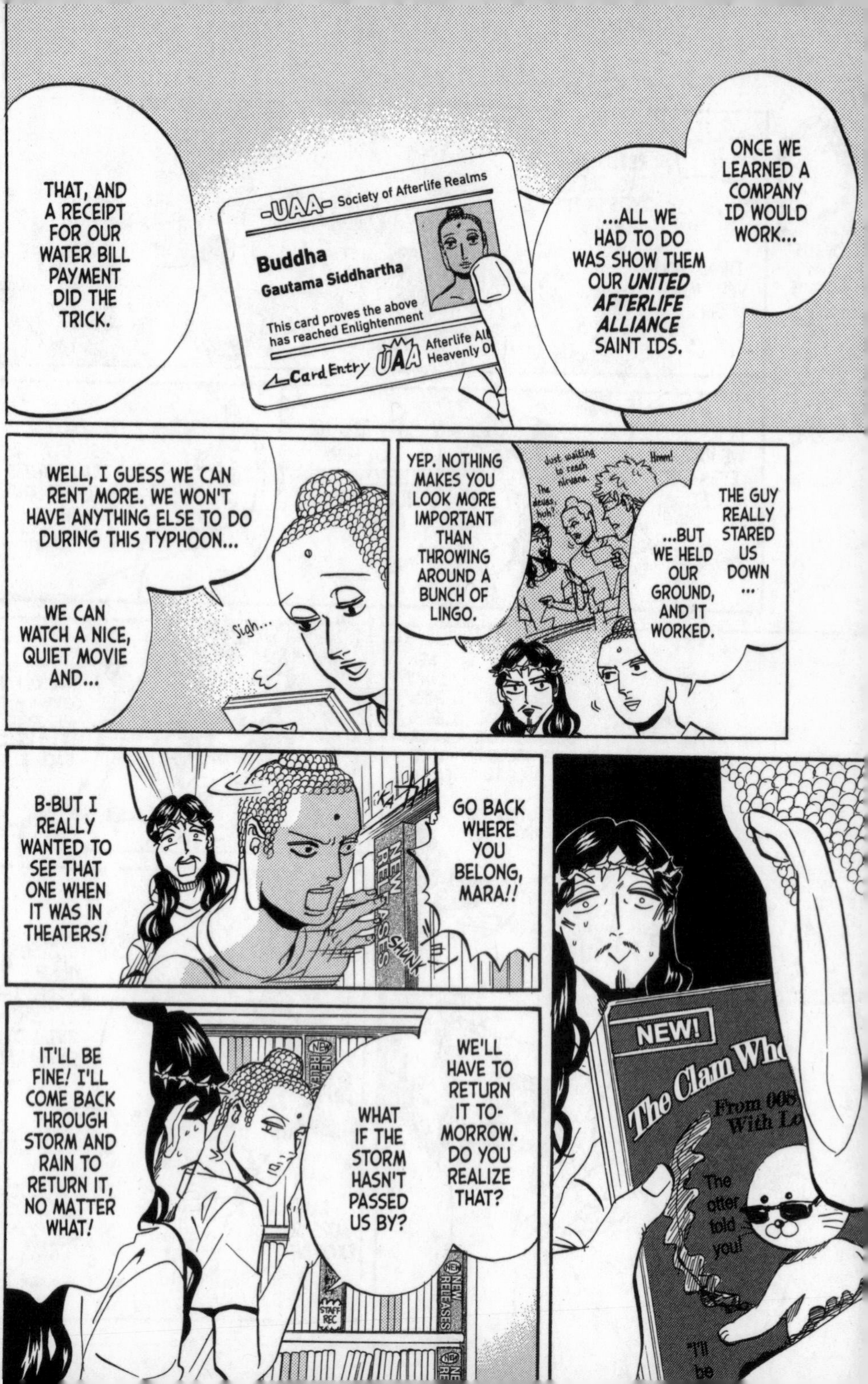
ONCE WE LEARNED A COMPANY ID WOULD WORK...
...ALL WE HAD TO DO WAS SHOW THEM OUR *UNITED AFTERLIFE ALLIANCE* SAINT IDS.
-UAA- Society of Afterlife Realms
Buddha
Gautama Siddhartha
This card proves the above has reached Enlightenment
Card Entry
UAA
THAT, AND A RECEIPT FOR OUR WATER BILL PAYMENT DID THE TRICK.
THE GUY REALLY STARED US DOWN ...
...BUT WE HELD OUR GROUND, AND IT WORKED.
Hmm!
Just waiting to reach nirvana.
The devas, huh?
YEP. NOTHING MAKES YOU LOOK MORE IMPORTANT THAN THROWING AROUND A BUNCH OF LINGO.
WELL, I GUESS WE CAN RENT MORE. WE WON'T HAVE ANYTHING ELSE TO DO DURING THIS TYPHOON...
WE CAN WATCH A NICE, QUIET MOVIE AND...
Sigh...
NEW!
The otter told you!
I'll be
GO BACK WHERE YOU BELONG, MARA!!
SHUNK
NEW RELEASES
B-BUT I REALLY WANTED TO SEE THAT ONE WHEN IT WAS IN THEATERS!
WE'LL HAVE TO RETURN IT TO-MORROW. DO YOU REALIZE THAT?
WHAT IF THE STORM HASN'T PASSED US BY?
IT'LL BE FINE! I'LL COME BACK THROUGH STORM AND RAIN TO RETURN IT, NO MATTER WHAT!

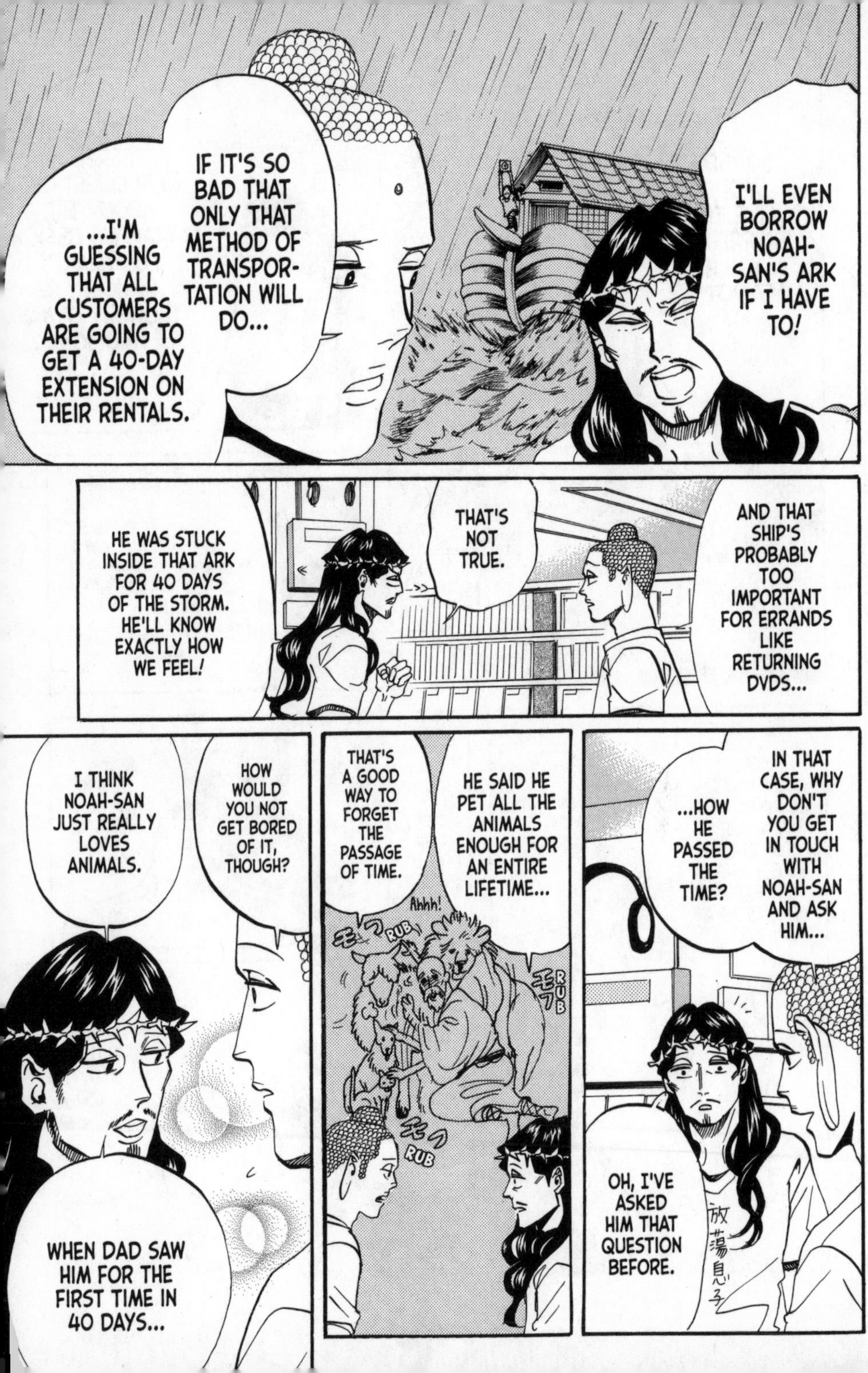
I'LL EVEN BORROW NOAH-SAN'S ARK IF I HAVE TO!
IF IT'S SO BAD THAT ONLY THAT METHOD OF TRANSPORTATION WILL DO...
...I'M GUESSING THAT ALL CUSTOMERS ARE GOING TO GET A 40-DAY EXTENSION ON THEIR RENTALS.
AND THAT SHIP'S PROBABLY TOO IMPORTANT FOR ERRANDS LIKE RETURNING DVDS...
THAT'S NOT TRUE.
HE WAS STUCK INSIDE THAT ARK FOR 40 DAYS OF THE STORM. HE'LL KNOW EXACTLY HOW WE FEEL!
IN THAT CASE, WHY DON'T YOU GET IN TOUCH WITH NOAH-SAN AND ASK HIM...
...HOW HE PASSED THE TIME?
OH, I'VE ASKED HIM THAT QUESTION BEFORE.
放蕩息子
HE SAID HE PET ALL THE ANIMALS ENOUGH FOR AN ENTIRE LIFETIME...
THAT'S A GOOD WAY TO FORGET THE PASSAGE OF TIME.
Ahhh!
RUB
RUB
RUB
HOW WOULD YOU NOT GET BORED OF IT, THOUGH?
I THINK NOAH-SAN JUST REALLY LOVES ANIMALS.
WHEN DAD SAW HIM FOR THE FIRST TIME IN 40 DAYS...

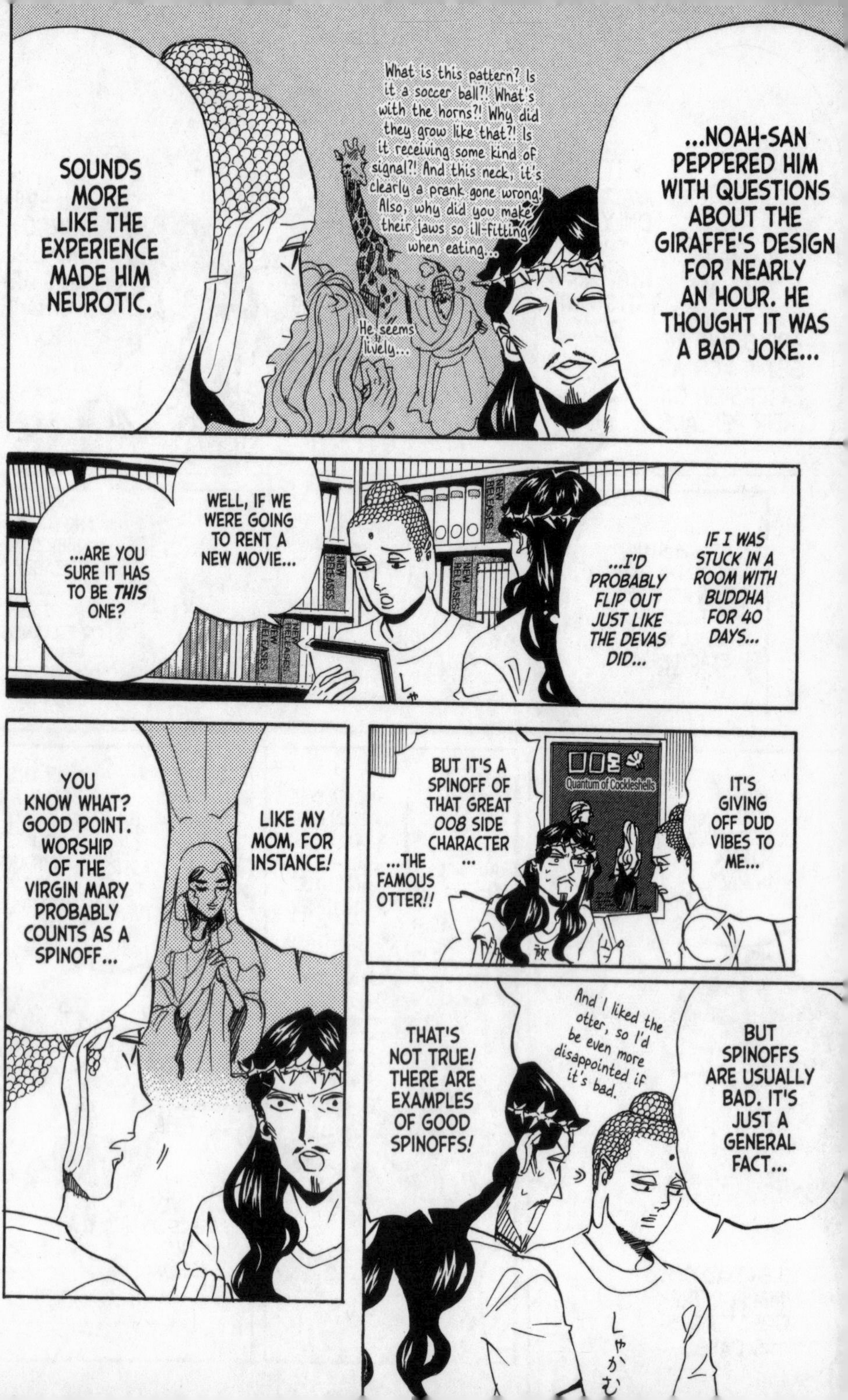
...NOAH-SAN PEPPERED HIM WITH QUESTIONS ABOUT THE GIRAFFE'S DESIGN FOR NEARLY AN HOUR. HE THOUGHT IT WAS A BAD JOKE...
What is this pattern? Is it a soccer ball?! What's with the horns?! Why did they grow like that?! Is it receiving some kind of signal?! And this neck, it's clearly a prank gone wrong! Also, why did you make their jaws so ill-fitting when eating...
He seems lively...
SOUNDS MORE LIKE THE EXPERIENCE MADE HIM NEUROTIC.
IF I WAS STUCK IN A ROOM WITH BUDDHA FOR 40 DAYS...
...I'D PROBABLY FLIP OUT JUST LIKE THE DEVAS DID...
WELL, IF WE WERE GOING TO RENT A NEW MOVIE...
...ARE YOU SURE IT HAS TO BE *THIS* ONE?
NEW RELEASES
IT'S GIVING OFF DUD VIBES TO ME...
Quantum of Cockleshells
BUT IT'S A SPINOFF OF THAT GREAT *008* SIDE CHARACTER ...
...THE FAMOUS OTTER!!
BUT SPINOFFS ARE USUALLY BAD. IT'S JUST A GENERAL FACT...
And I liked the otter, so I'd be even more disappointed if it's bad.
THAT'S NOT TRUE! THERE ARE EXAMPLES OF GOOD SPINOFFS!
しゃかむ
LIKE MY MOM, FOR INSTANCE!
YOU KNOW WHAT? GOOD POINT. WORSHIP OF THE VIRGIN MARY PROBABLY COUNTS AS A SPINOFF...

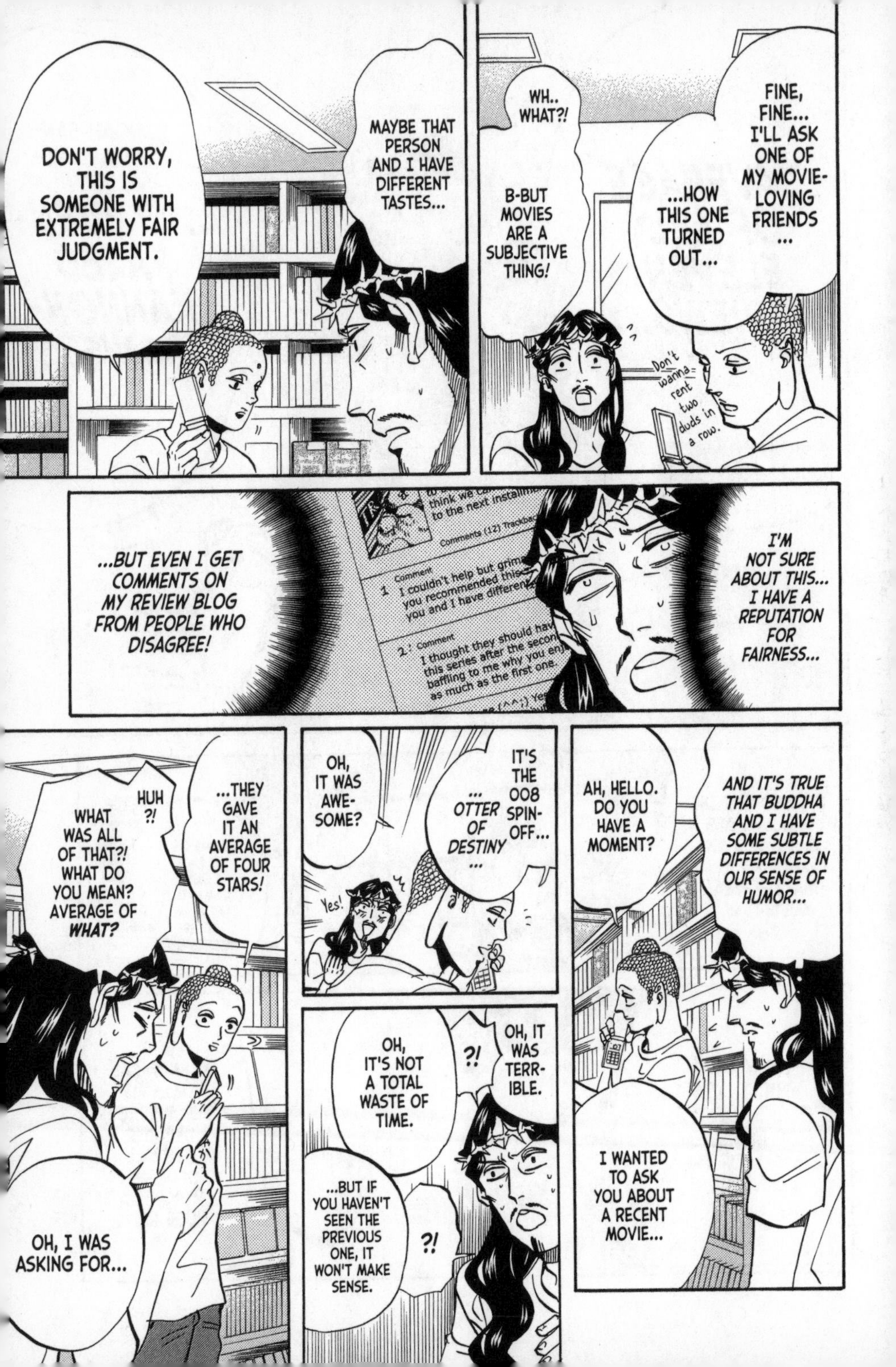
FINE, FINE... I'LL ASK ONE OF MY MOVIE-LOVING FRIENDS ...
...HOW THIS ONE TURNED OUT...
WH.. WHAT?!
B-BUT MOVIES ARE A SUBJECTIVE THING!
Don't wanna rent two duds in a row.
MAYBE THAT PERSON AND I HAVE DIFFERENT TASTES...
DON'T WORRY, THIS IS SOMEONE WITH EXTREMELY FAIR JUDGMENT.
I'M NOT SURE ABOUT THIS... I HAVE A REPUTATION FOR FAIRNESS...
...BUT EVEN I GET COMMENTS ON MY REVIEW BLOG FROM PEOPLE WHO DISAGREE!
AND IT'S TRUE THAT BUDDHA AND I HAVE SOME SUBTLE DIFFERENCES IN OUR SENSE OF HUMOR...
AH, HELLO. DO YOU HAVE A MOMENT?
I WANTED TO ASK YOU ABOUT A RECENT MOVIE...
IT'S THE 008 SPIN-OFF...
...OTTER OF DESTINY...
OH, IT WAS AWE-SOME?
Yes!
OH, IT WAS TERRIBLE.
?!
OH, IT'S NOT A TOTAL WASTE OF TIME.
...BUT IF YOU HAVEN'T SEEN THE PREVIOUS ONE, IT WON'T MAKE SENSE.
?!
...THEY GAVE IT AN AVERAGE OF FOUR STARS!
HUH ?!
WHAT WAS ALL OF THAT?! WHAT DO YOU MEAN? AVERAGE OF WHAT?
OH, I WAS ASKING FOR...

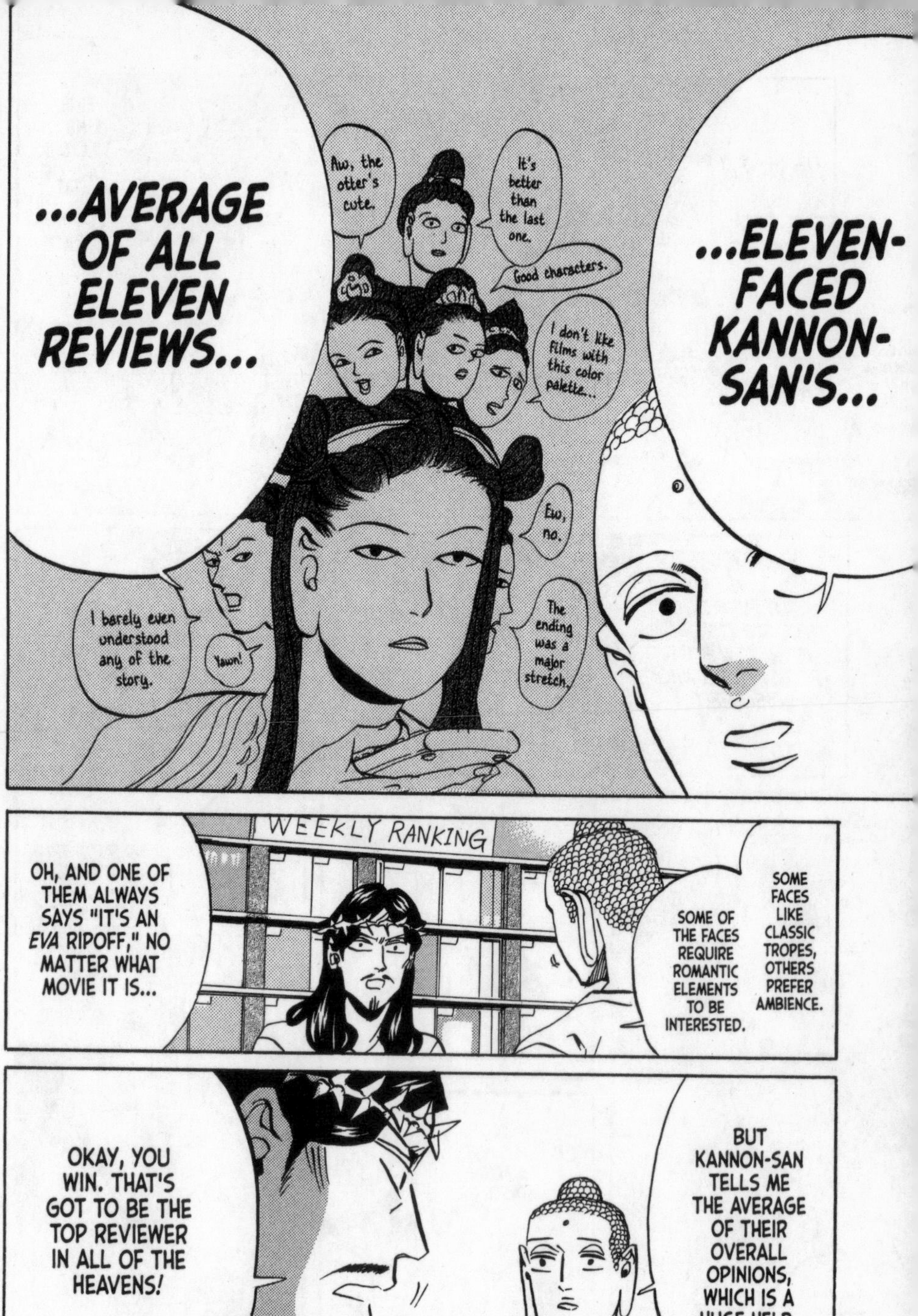
...ELEVEN-FACED KANNON-SAN'S...
...AVERAGE OF ALL ELEVEN REVIEWS...
It's better than the last one.
Aw, the otter's cute.
Good characters.
I don't like films with this color palette...
Ew, no.
The ending was a major stretch.
Yawn!
I barely even understood any of the story.
SOME FACES LIKE CLASSIC TROPES, OTHERS PREFER AMBIENCE.
SOME OF THE FACES REQUIRE ROMANTIC ELEMENTS TO BE INTERESTED.
WEEKLY RANKING
OH, AND ONE OF THEM ALWAYS SAYS "IT'S AN *EVA* RIPOFF," NO MATTER WHAT MOVIE IT IS...
BUT KANNON-SAN TELLS ME THE AVERAGE OF THEIR OVERALL OPINIONS, WHICH IS A HUGE HELP.
OKAY, YOU WIN. THAT'S GOT TO BE THE TOP REVIEWER IN ALL OF THE HEAVENS!

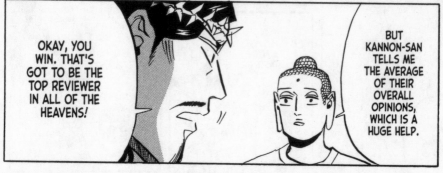

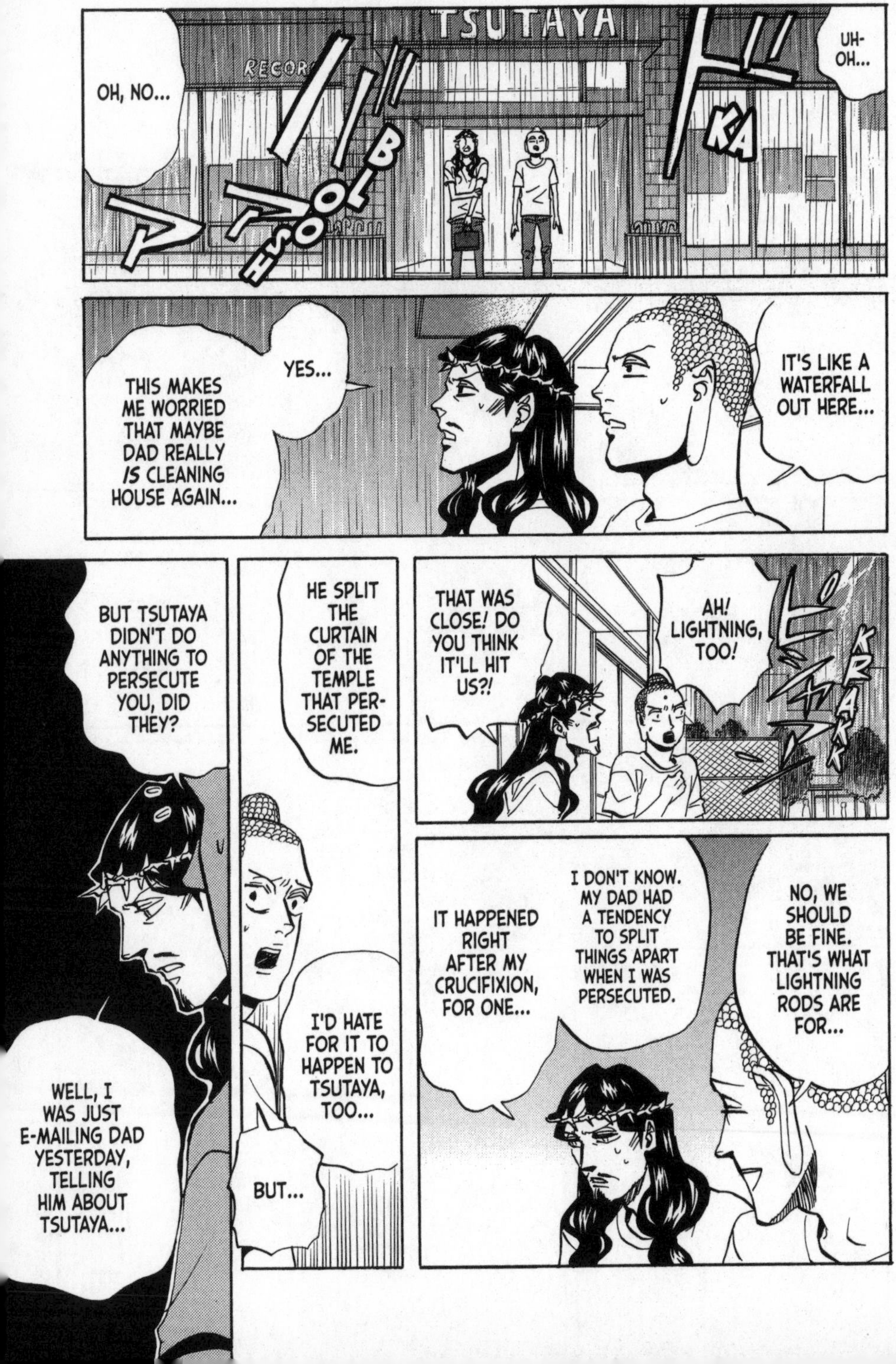
TSUTAYA
UH-OH...
KA
OH, NO...
BOLOSH
IT'S LIKE A WATERFALL OUT HERE...
YES...
THIS MAKES ME WORRIED THAT MAYBE DAD REALLY *IS* CLEANING HOUSE AGAIN...
KRAKK
AH! LIGHTNING, TOO!
THAT WAS CLOSE! DO YOU THINK IT'LL HIT US?!
NO, WE SHOULD BE FINE. THAT'S WHAT LIGHTNING RODS ARE FOR...
I DON'T KNOW. MY DAD HAD A TENDENCY TO SPLIT THINGS APART WHEN I WAS PERSECUTED.
IT HAPPENED RIGHT AFTER MY CRUCIFIXION, FOR ONE...
HE SPLIT THE CURTAIN OF THE TEMPLE THAT PER-SECUTED ME.
I'D HATE FOR IT TO HAPPEN TO TSUTAYA, TOO...
BUT...
BUT TSUTAYA DIDN'T DO ANYTHING TO PERSECUTE YOU, DID THEY?
WELL, I WAS JUST E-MAILING DAD YESTERDAY, TELLING HIM ABOUT TSUTAYA...

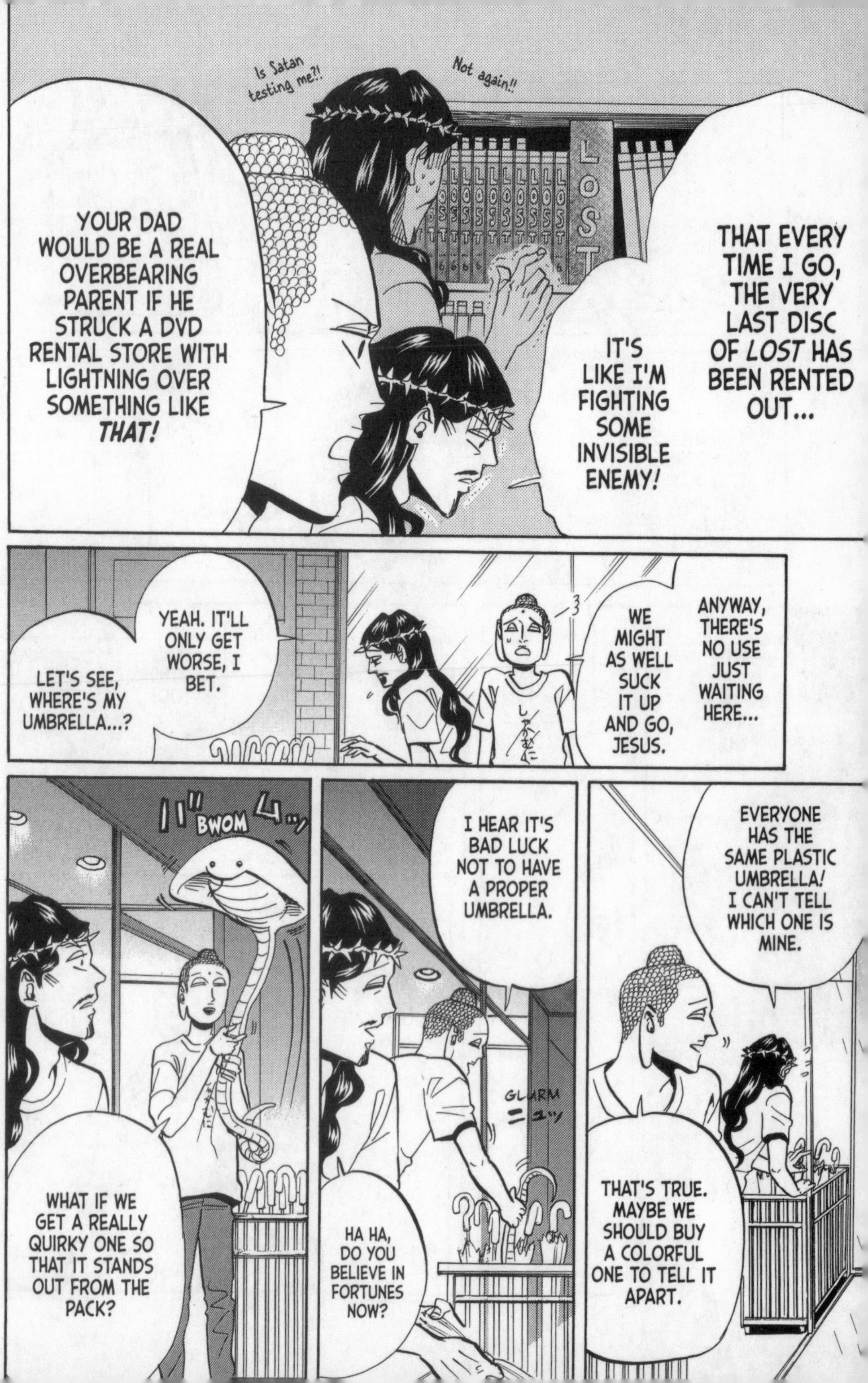

THAT EVERY TIME I GO, THE VERY LAST DISC OF *LOST* HAS BEEN RENTED OUT...
IT'S LIKE I'M FIGHTING SOME INVISIBLE ENEMY!
Not again!!
Is Satan testing me?!
YOUR DAD WOULD BE A REAL OVERBEARING PARENT IF HE STRUCK A DVD RENTAL STORE WITH LIGHTNING OVER SOMETHING LIKE *THAT!*
LOST
ANYWAY, THERE'S NO USE JUST WAITING HERE...
WE MIGHT AS WELL SUCK IT UP AND GO, JESUS.
YEAH. IT'LL ONLY GET WORSE, I BET.
LET'S SEE, WHERE'S MY UMBRELLA...?
EVERYONE HAS THE SAME PLASTIC UMBRELLA! I CAN'T TELL WHICH ONE IS MINE.
THAT'S TRUE. MAYBE WE SHOULD BUY A COLORFUL ONE TO TELL IT APART.
I HEAR IT'S BAD LUCK NOT TO HAVE A PROPER UMBRELLA.
GLURM
HA HA, DO YOU BELIEVE IN FORTUNES NOW?
BWOM
WHAT IF WE GET A REALLY QUIRKY ONE SO THAT IT STANDS OUT FROM THE PACK?

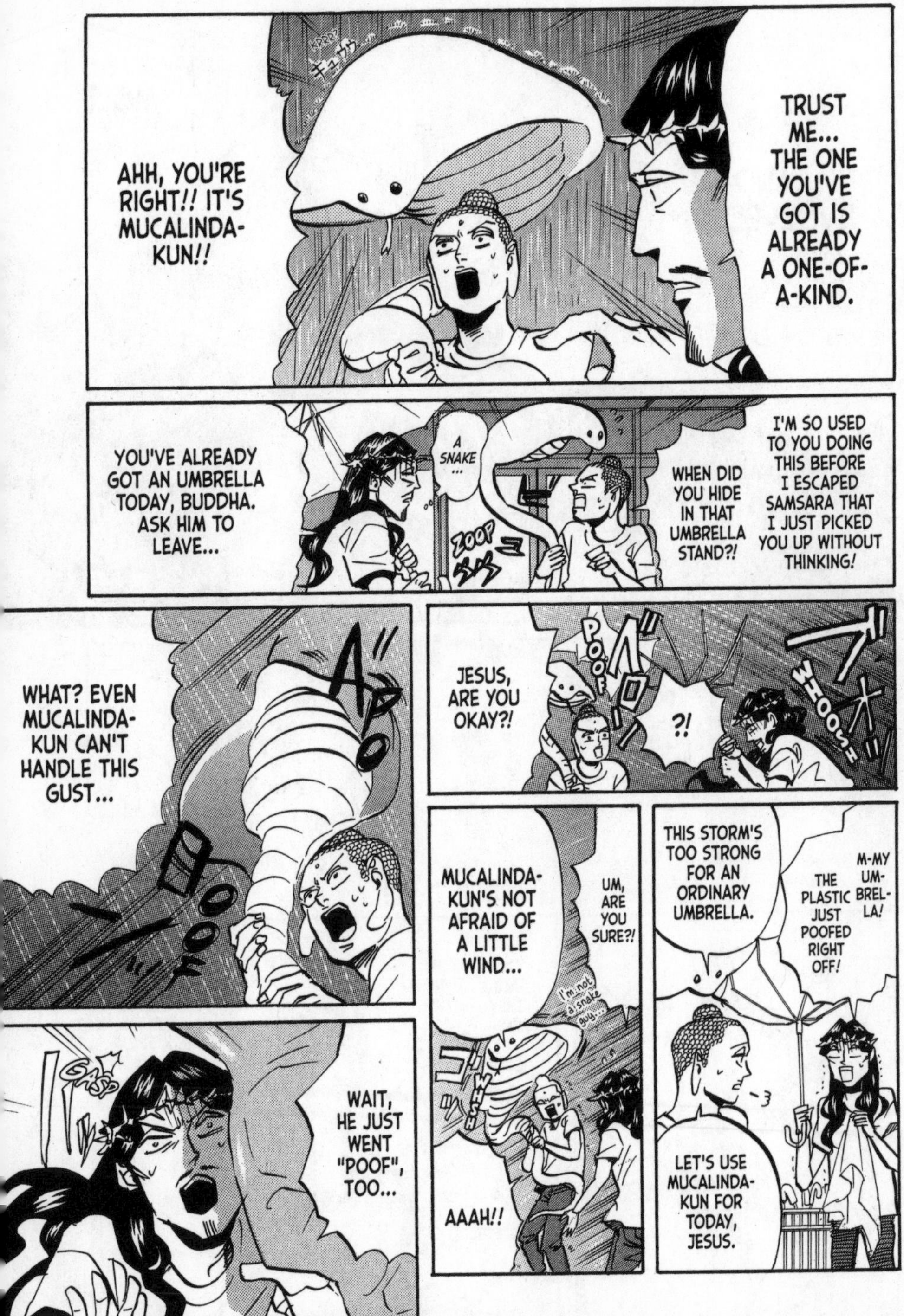
TRUST ME... THE ONE YOU'VE GOT IS ALREADY A ONE-OF-A-KIND.
KRRR?
キュウウ
AHH, YOU'RE RIGHT!! IT'S MUCALINDA-KUN!!
I'M SO USED TO YOU DOING THIS BEFORE I ESCAPED SAMSARA THAT I JUST PICKED YOU UP WITHOUT THINKING!
WHEN DID YOU HIDE IN THAT UMBRELLA STAND?!
A SNAKE...
ZOOP
YOU'VE ALREADY GOT AN UMBRELLA TODAY, BUDDHA. ASK HIM TO LEAVE...
WHOOSH
POOF
?!
JESUS, ARE YOU OKAY?!
M-MY UM-BREL-LA!
THE PLASTIC JUST POOFED RIGHT OFF!
THIS STORM'S TOO STRONG FOR AN ORDINARY UMBRELLA.
LET'S USE MUCALINDA-KUN FOR TODAY, JESUS.
UM, ARE YOU SURE?!
MUCALINDA-KUN'S NOT AFRAID OF A LITTLE WIND...
I'm not a snake guy...
WHSH
AAAH!!
POOF
WHAT? EVEN MUCALINDA-KUN CAN'T HANDLE THIS GUST...
WAIT, HE JUST WENT "POOF", TOO...
GASP

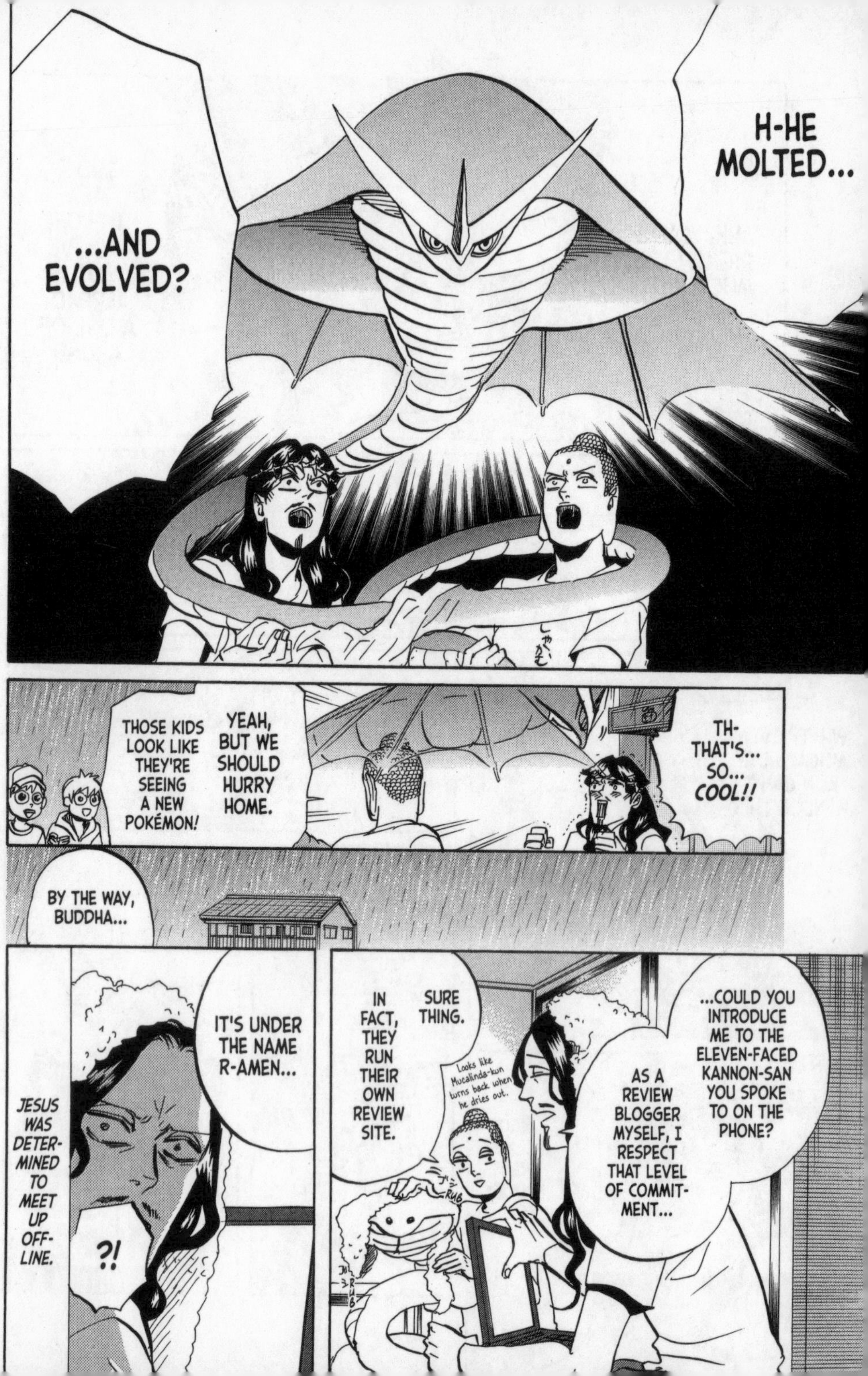
H-HE MOLTED...
...AND EVOLVED?
TH- THAT'S... SO... COOL!!
THOSE KIDS LOOK LIKE THEY'RE SEEING A NEW POKÉMON!
YEAH, BUT WE SHOULD HURRY HOME.
BY THE WAY, BUDDHA...
...COULD YOU INTRODUCE ME TO THE ELEVEN-FACED KANNON-SAN YOU SPOKE TO ON THE PHONE?
SURE THING.
IN FACT, THEY RUN THEIR OWN REVIEW SITE.
AS A REVIEW BLOGGER MYSELF, I RESPECT THAT LEVEL OF COMMITMENT...
Looks like Mucalinda-kun turns back when he dries out.
RUB
RUB
IT'S UNDER THE NAME R-AMEN...
?!
JESUS WAS DETERMINED TO MEET UP OFF-LINE.

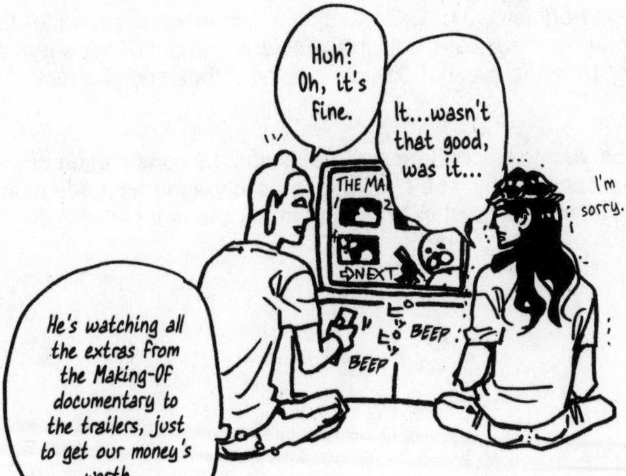
It...wasn't that good, was it...
I'm sorry...
Huh? Oh, it's fine.
THE MA
NEXT
ピッ BEEP
ピッ BEEP
He's watching all the extras from the Making-Of documentary to the trailers, just to get our money's worth...

CHAPTER 50 TRANSLATION NOTES

Prodigal son, page 109
One of Jesus's parables. In it, a man has two sons, and gives one of them his inheritance. The prodigal (wasteful) son squanders his money and returns home to beg for forgiveness, and to his surprise, his father welcomes him, saying that he "was lost and now is found." In this parable, the all-encompassing love of the father reflects the mercy of God.

Shakyamuni, page 109
A title given to the Buddha that means "Sage of the Shakyas," referring to his clan.

"Rain, Rain, Go Away," page 111
The original reference here was to a Japanese nursery song about a fictional King Hamehameha on a southern island, a play on the actual Hawaiian king Kamehameha. One of the verses is about Hamehameha's children, and contains the lines: The king of the southern island's / kids are also named Hamehameha / They hate going to school / When the wind blows, they show up late / When the rain falls, they don't go at all.

Noah's ark, page 117
In the Book of Genesis, God commands Noah to build an ark and fill it with two of every animal so that the world may be flooded and remade. When the flood arrives, the ark floats on top of the water for forty days and nights before it recedes and reveals land once again.

Eleven-Faced Kannon, page 120
One of the forms of the Bodhisattva of Compassion, Kannon. One legend for the eleven-faced form states that her head split into eleven faces out of her sheer desire to help those suffering from the cycle of Samsara, to hear their cries better.

Eva, page 120
The seminal sci-fi robot anime Neon Genesis Evangelion. Its combination of giant robot tropes, religious iconography, and challenging psychoanalysis made it one of the most influential anime series of all time, and many series created in its wake suffered the accusation of "ripping it off."

SAINT☆YOUNG MEN

SAINT☆YOUNG MEN

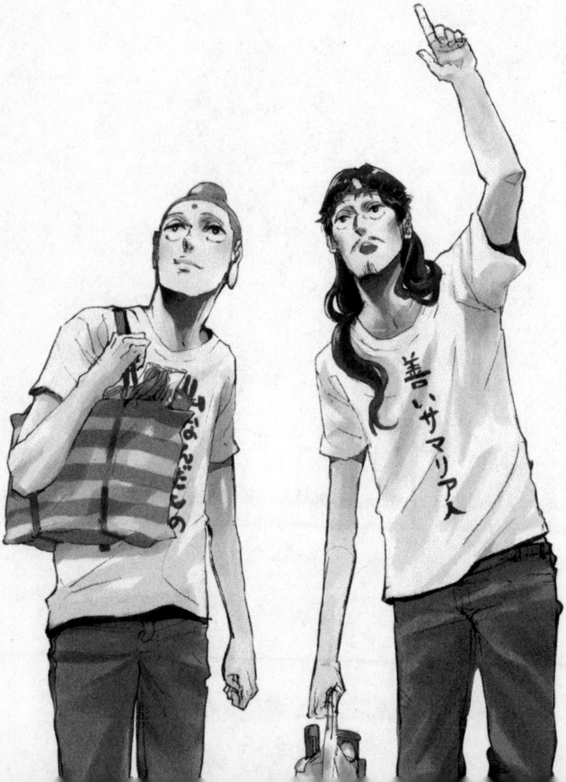
善いサマリア人

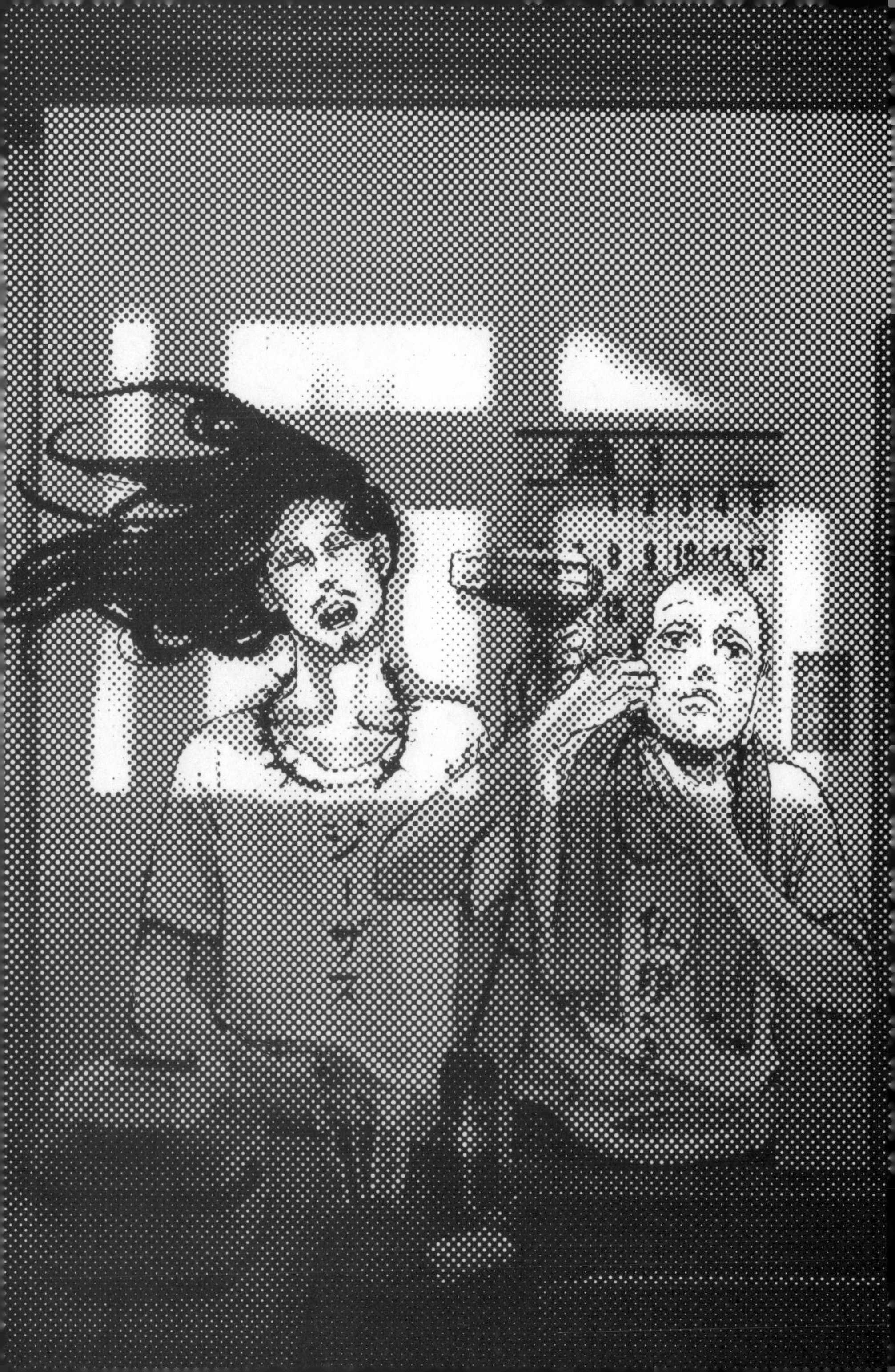

SAINT☆YOUNG MEN

SAINT☆YOUNG MEN

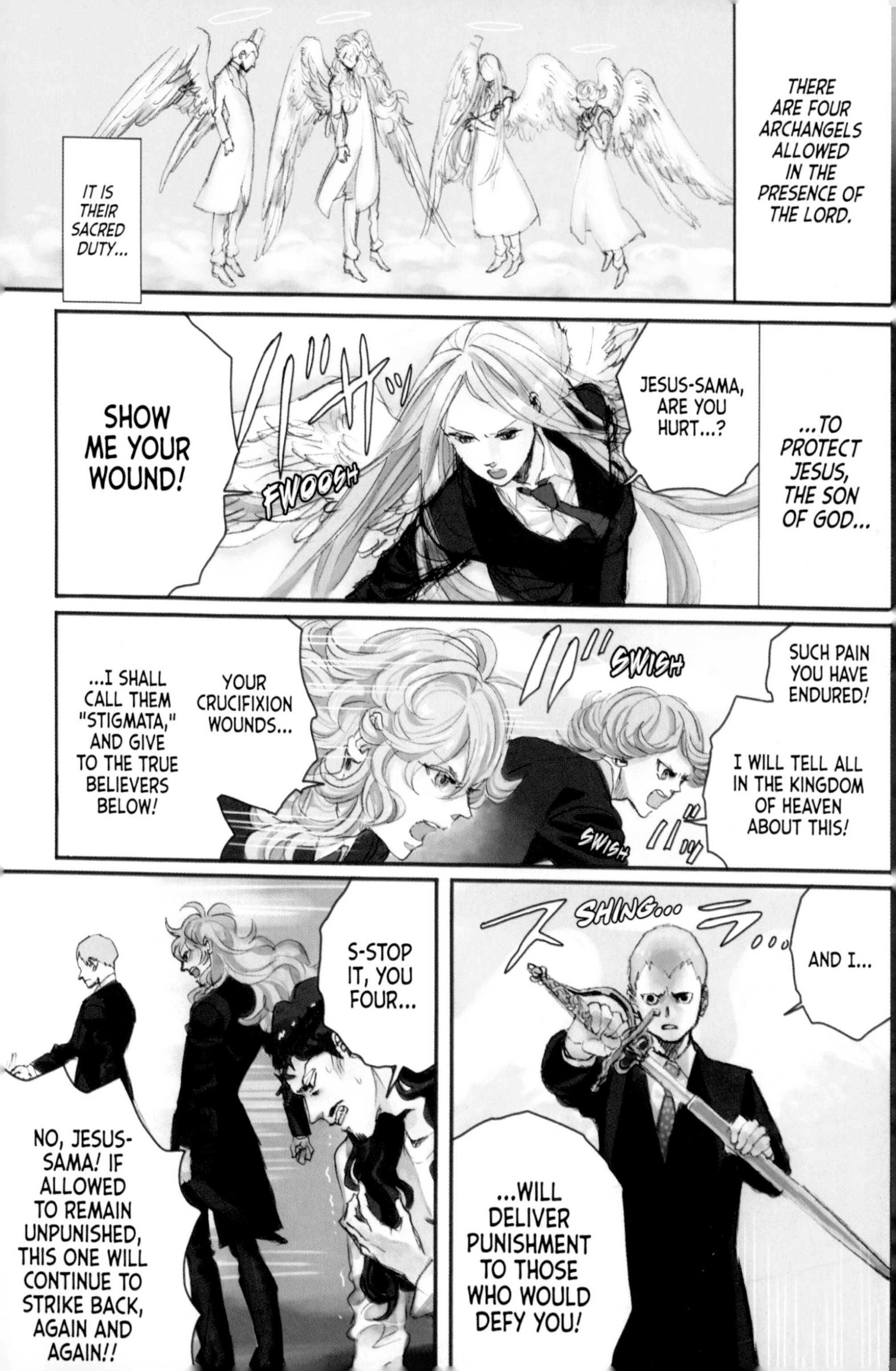
THERE ARE FOUR ARCHANGELS ALLOWED IN THE PRESENCE OF THE LORD.
IT IS THEIR SACRED DUTY...
...TO PROTECT JESUS, THE SON OF GOD...
JESUS-SAMA, ARE YOU HURT...?
FWOOSH
SHOW ME YOUR WOUND!
SUCH PAIN YOU HAVE ENDURED!
I WILL TELL ALL IN THE KINGDOM OF HEAVEN ABOUT THIS!
SWISH
SWISH
YOUR CRUCIFIXION WOUNDS...
...I SHALL CALL THEM "STIGMATA," AND GIVE TO THE TRUE BELIEVERS BELOW!
SHING...
AND I...
...WILL DELIVER PUNISHMENT TO THOSE WHO WOULD DEFY YOU!
S-STOP IT, YOU FOUR...
NO, JESUS-SAMA! IF ALLOWED TO REMAIN UNPUNISHED, THIS ONE WILL CONTINUE TO STRIKE BACK, AGAIN AND AGAIN!!

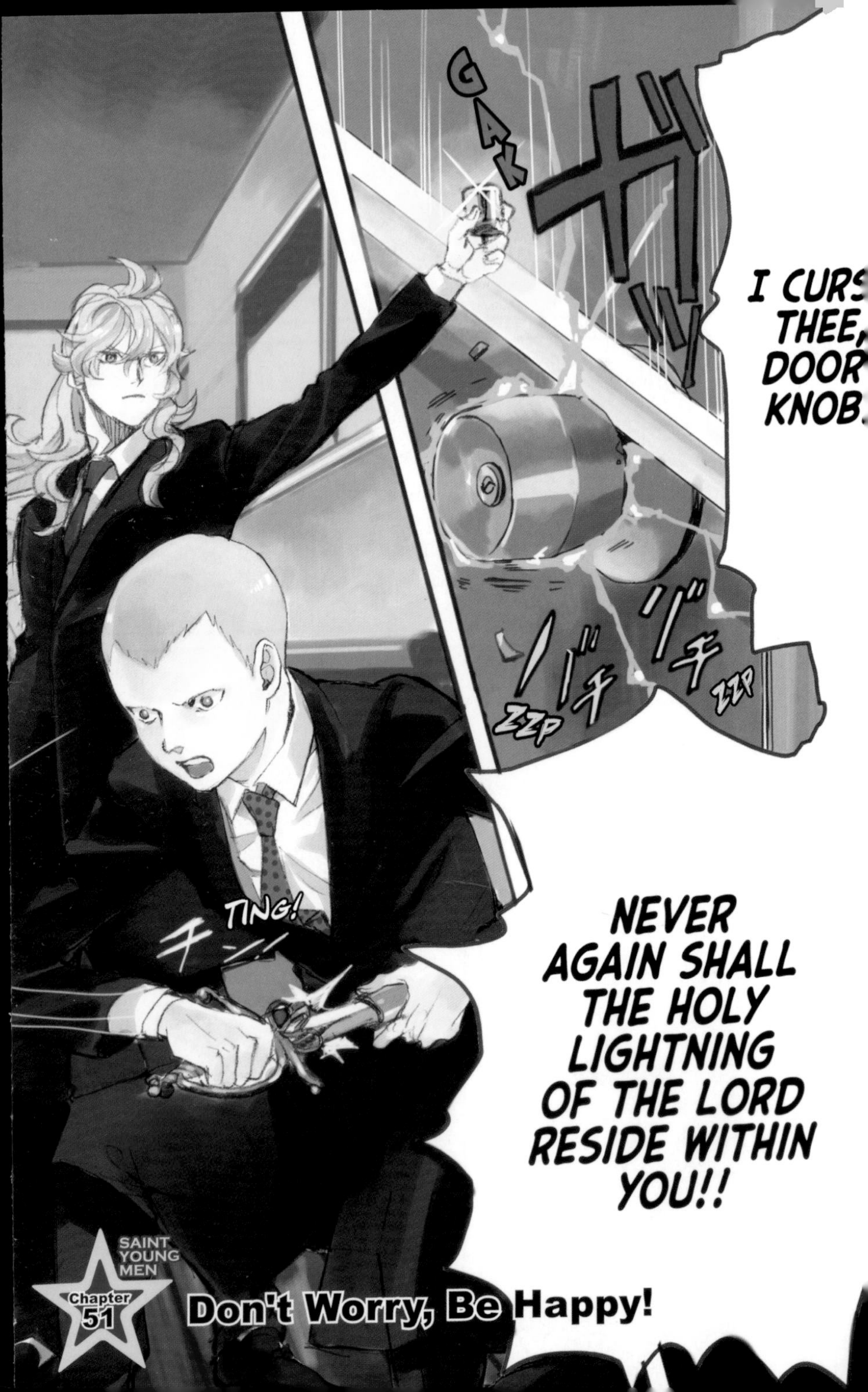
I CURS
THEE,
DOOR
KNOB
GAK
ZZP
ZZP
NEVER AGAIN SHALL THE HOLY LIGHTNING OF THE LORD RESIDE WITHIN YOU!!
TING!
SAINT YOUNG MEN
Chapter 51
Don't Worry, Be Happy!

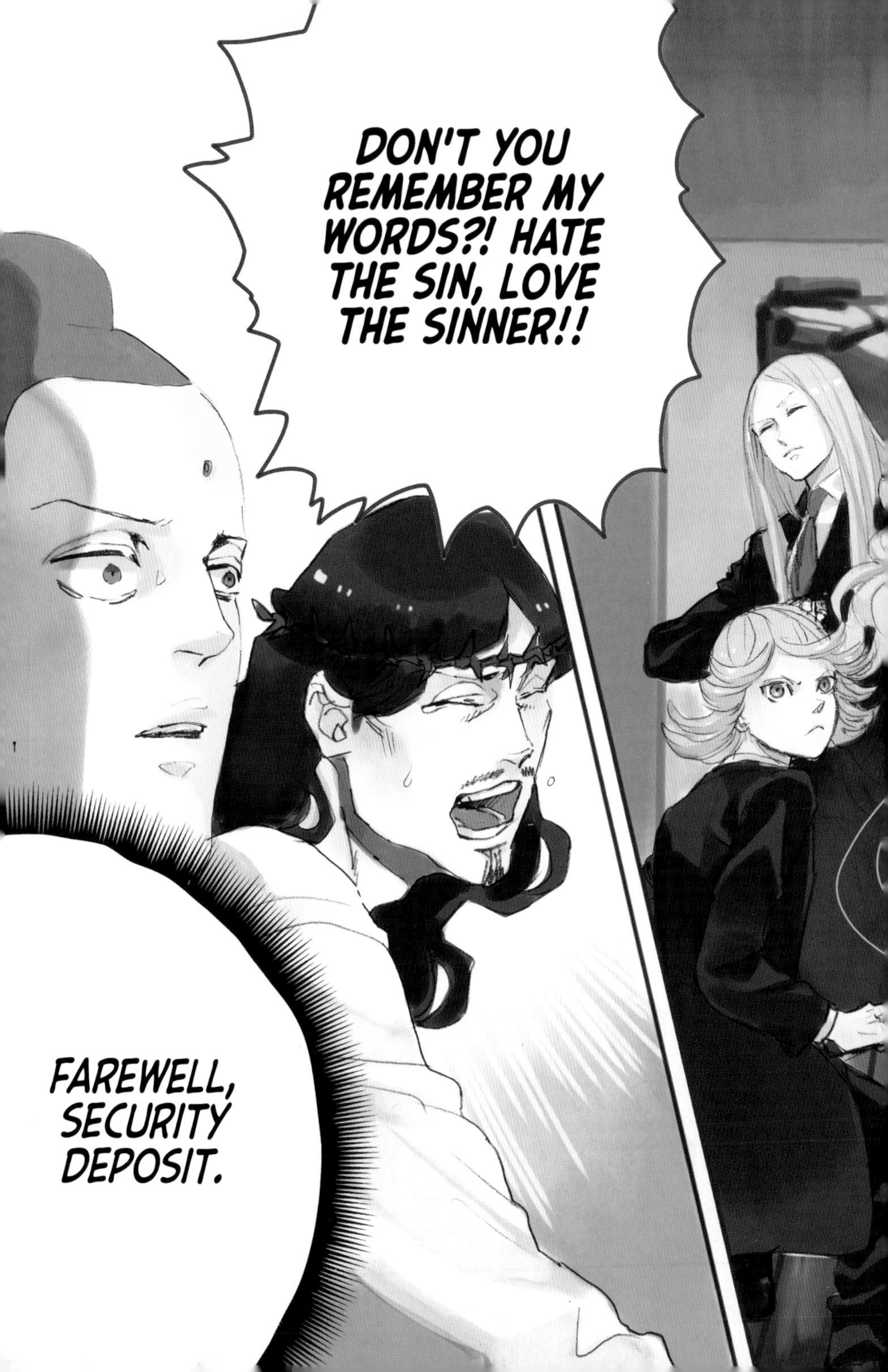
DON'T YOU REMEMBER MY WORDS?! HATE THE SIN, LOVE THE SINNER!!
FAREWELL, SECURITY DEPOSIT.

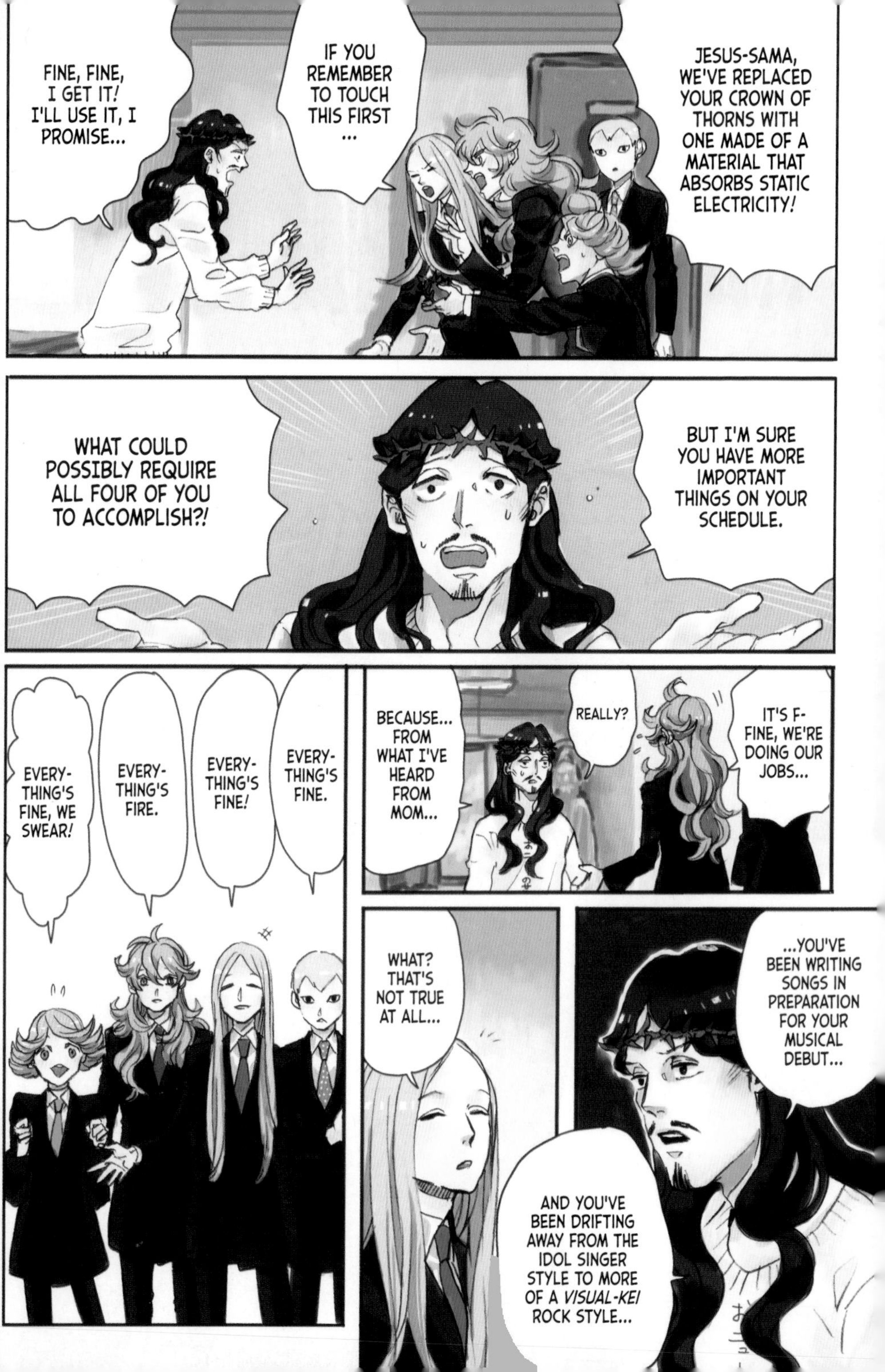
JESUS-SAMA, WE'VE REPLACED YOUR CROWN OF THORNS WITH ONE MADE OF A MATERIAL THAT ABSORBS STATIC ELECTRICITY!
IF YOU REMEMBER TO TOUCH THIS FIRST ...
FINE, FINE, I GET IT! I'LL USE IT, I PROMISE...
BUT I'M SURE YOU HAVE MORE IMPORTANT THINGS ON YOUR SCHEDULE.
WHAT COULD POSSIBLY REQUIRE ALL FOUR OF YOU TO ACCOMPLISH?!
IT'S F-FINE, WE'RE DOING OUR JOBS...
REALLY?
BECAUSE... FROM WHAT I'VE HEARD FROM MOM...
...YOU'VE BEEN WRITING SONGS IN PREPARATION FOR YOUR MUSICAL DEBUT...
AND YOU'VE BEEN DRIFTING AWAY FROM THE IDOL SINGER STYLE TO MORE OF A *VISUAL-KEI* ROCK STYLE...
WHAT? THAT'S NOT TRUE AT ALL...
EVERY-THING'S FINE.
EVERY-THING'S FINE!
EVERY-THING'S FIRE.
EVERY-THING'S FINE, WE SWEAR!

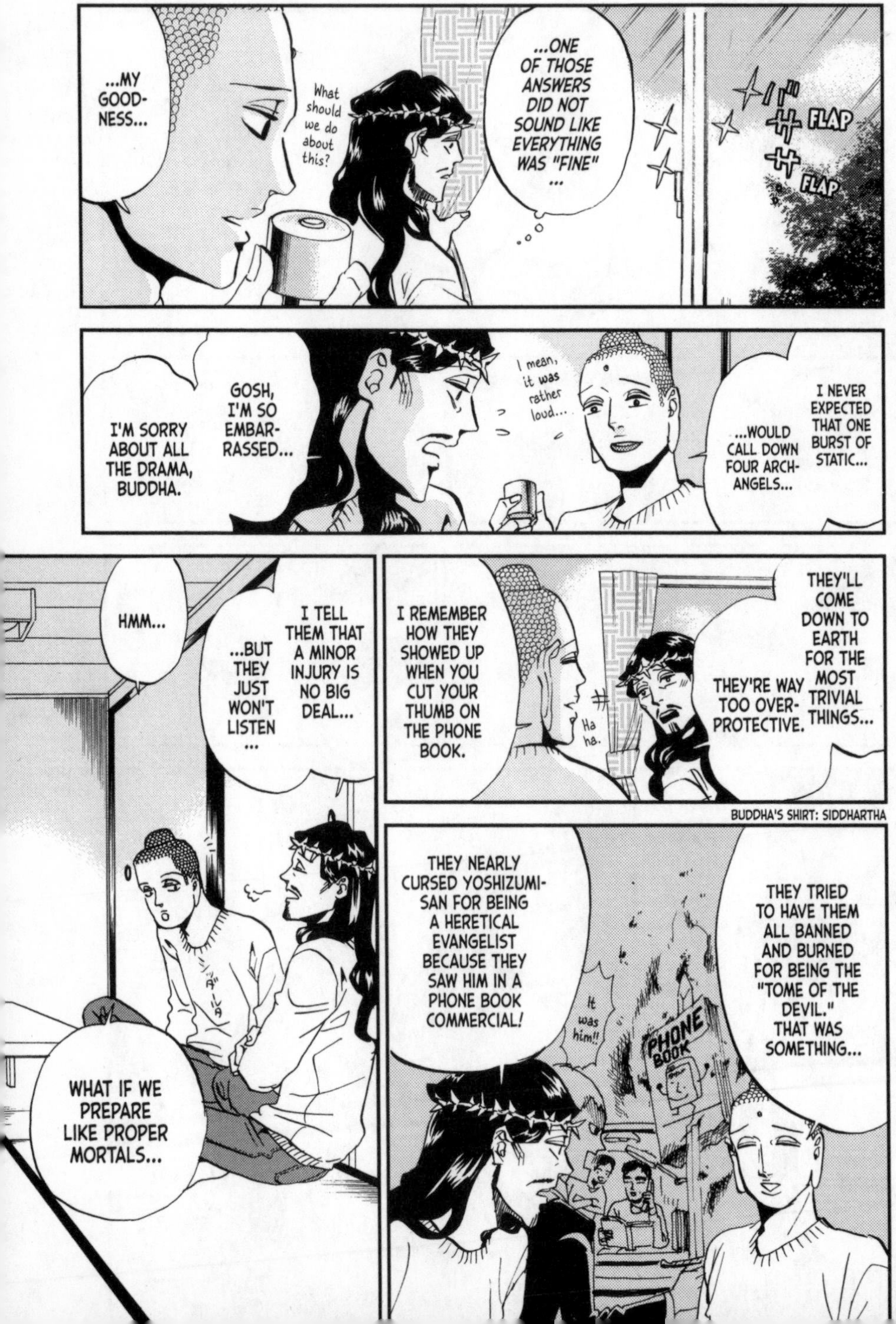
FLAP
FLAP
...ONE OF THOSE ANSWERS DID NOT SOUND LIKE EVERYTHING WAS "FINE" ...
What should we do about this?
...MY GOODNESS...
I NEVER EXPECTED THAT ONE BURST OF STATIC...
...WOULD CALL DOWN FOUR ARCH-ANGELS...
I mean, it was rather loud...
GOSH, I'M SO EMBAR-RASSED...
I'M SORRY ABOUT ALL THE DRAMA, BUDDHA.
THEY'LL COME DOWN TO EARTH FOR THE MOST TRIVIAL THINGS...
THEY'RE WAY TOO OVER-PROTECTIVE.
Ha ha.
I REMEMBER HOW THEY SHOWED UP WHEN YOU CUT YOUR THUMB ON THE PHONE BOOK.
BUDDHA'S SHIRT: SIDDHARTHA
THEY TRIED TO HAVE THEM ALL BANNED AND BURNED FOR BEING THE "TOME OF THE DEVIL." THAT WAS SOMETHING...
PHONE BOOK
It was him!!
THEY NEARLY CURSED YOSHIZUMI-SAN FOR BEING A HERETICAL EVANGELIST BECAUSE THEY SAW HIM IN A PHONE BOOK COMMERCIAL!
I TELL THEM THAT A MINOR INJURY IS NO BIG DEAL...
...BUT THEY JUST WON'T LISTEN ...
HMM...
WHAT IF WE PREPARE LIKE PROPER MORTALS...

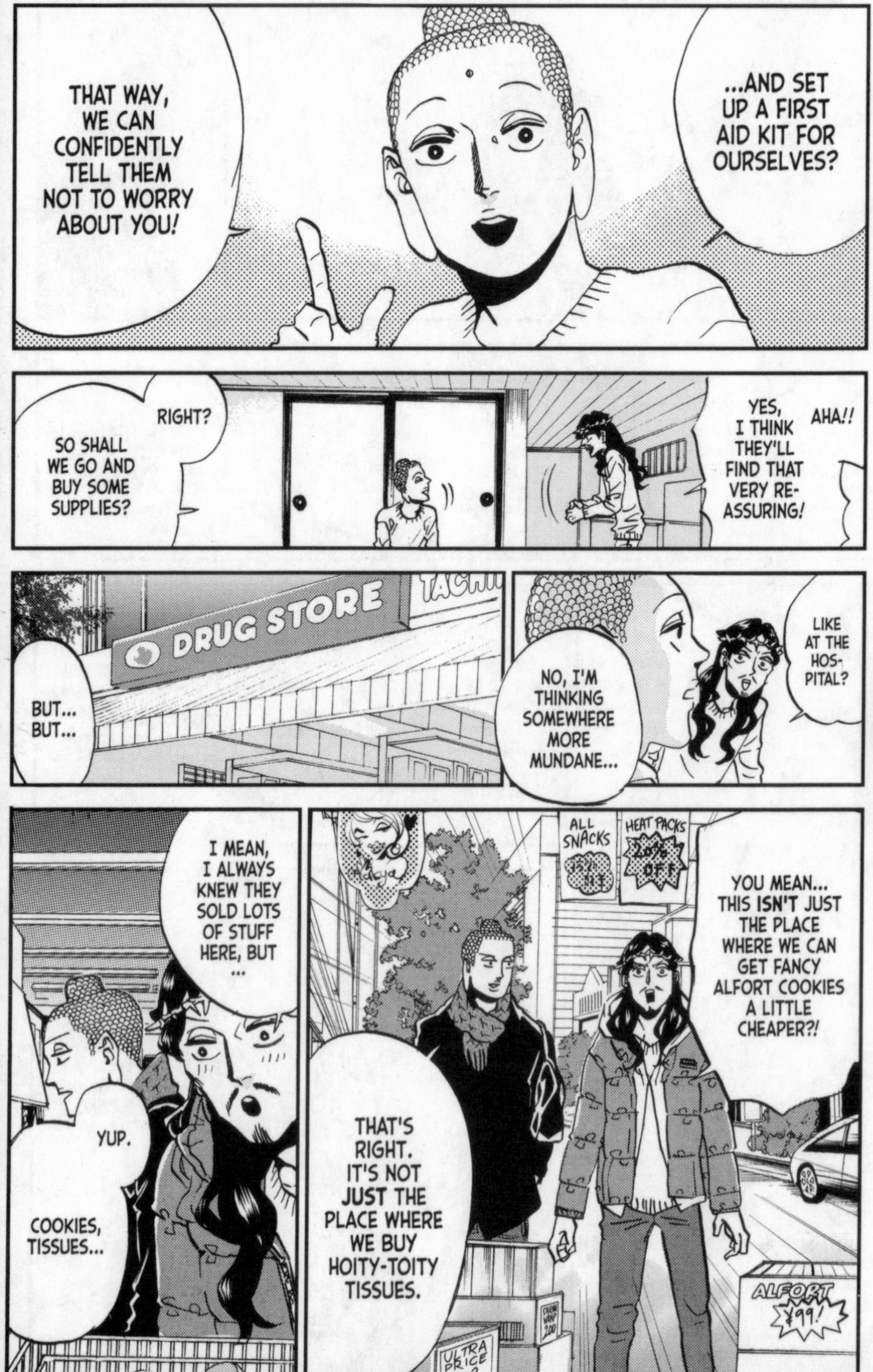
...AND SET UP A FIRST AID KIT FOR OURSELVES?
THAT WAY, WE CAN CONFIDENTLY TELL THEM NOT TO WORRY ABOUT YOU!
AHA!!
YES, I THINK THEY'LL FIND THAT VERY RE-ASSURING!
RIGHT?
SO SHALL WE GO AND BUY SOME SUPPLIES?
LIKE AT THE HOS-PITAL?
NO, I'M THINKING SOMEWHERE MORE MUNDANE...
DRUG STORE
BUT... BUT...
ALL SNACKS
HEAT PACKS 20% OFF
YOU MEAN... THIS **ISN'T** JUST THE PLACE WHERE WE CAN GET FANCY ALFORT COOKIES A LITTLE CHEAPER?!
THAT'S RIGHT. IT'S NOT **JUST** THE PLACE WHERE WE BUY HOITY-TOITY TISSUES.
ALFORT ¥99!
ULTRA PRICE ¥39
I MEAN, I ALWAYS KNEW THEY SOLD LOTS OF STUFF HERE, BUT ...
YUP.
COOKIES, TISSUES...

BUDDHA
EXACTLY HOW BIG AND HEAVY ARE BOWLING PINS, ANYWAY? IT'S SO INTRIGUING, IT KEEPS ME UP AT NIGHT.

JESUS
WHY DOES SOAP MAKE FEWER AND FEWER SUDS, THE SMALLER THE BAR SHRINKS? IT'S SO MYSTERIOUS, IT KEEPS ME UP AT NIGHT.

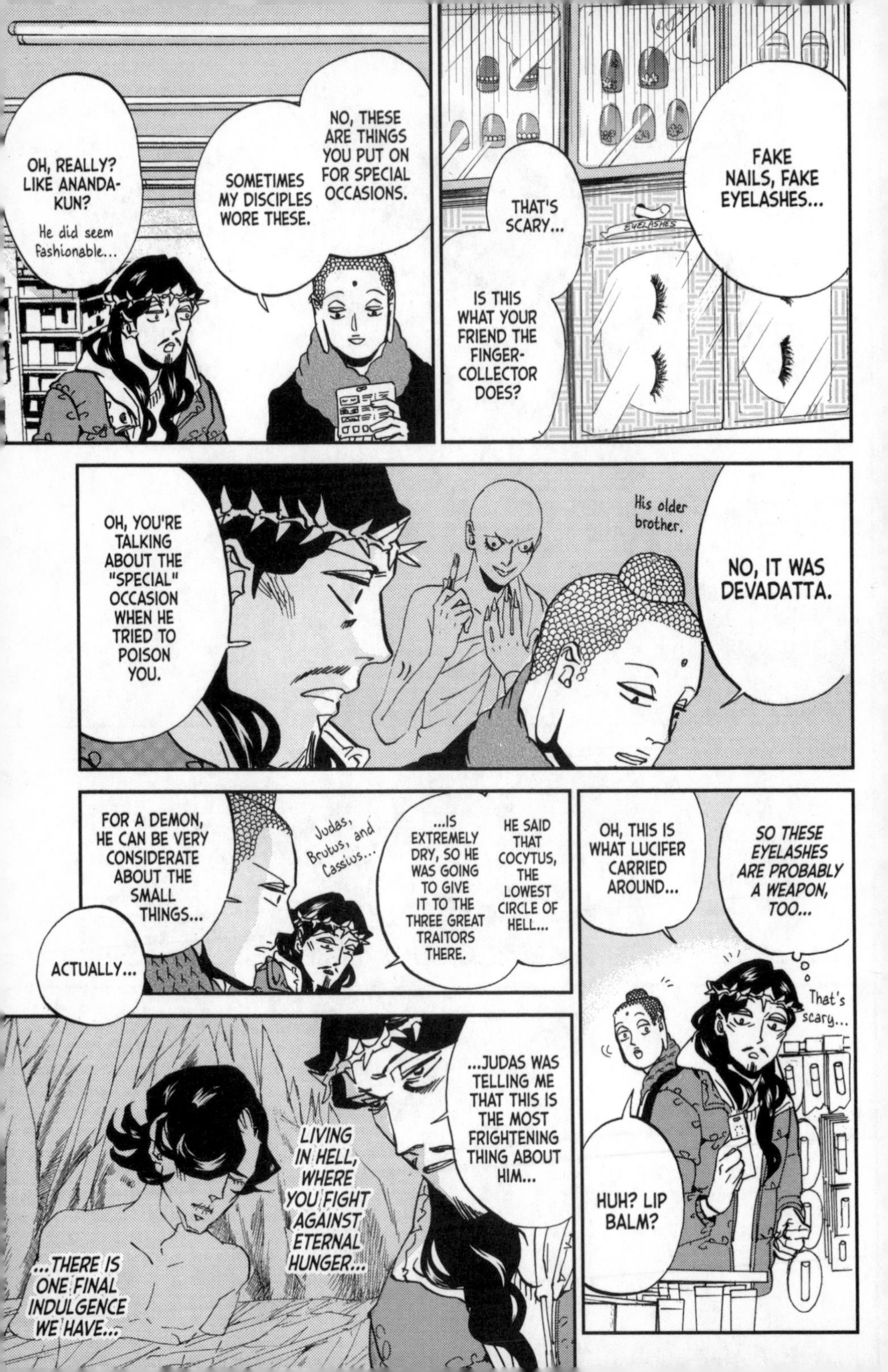
FAKE NAILS, FAKE EYELASHES...
EYELASHES
THAT'S SCARY...
IS THIS WHAT YOUR FRIEND THE FINGER-COLLECTOR DOES?
NO, THESE ARE THINGS YOU PUT ON FOR SPECIAL OCCASIONS.
SOMETIMES MY DISCIPLES WORE THESE.
OH, REALLY? LIKE ANANDA-KUN?
He did seem fashionable...
NO, IT WAS DEVADATTA.
His older brother.
OH, YOU'RE TALKING ABOUT THE "SPECIAL" OCCASION WHEN HE TRIED TO POISON YOU.
SO THESE EYELASHES ARE PROBABLY A WEAPON, TOO...
OH, THIS IS WHAT LUCIFER CARRIED AROUND...
That's scary...
HUH? LIP BALM?
HE SAID THAT COCYTUS, THE LOWEST CIRCLE OF HELL...
...IS EXTREMELY DRY, SO HE WAS GOING TO GIVE IT TO THE THREE GREAT TRAITORS THERE.
Judas, Brutus, and Cassius...
FOR A DEMON, HE CAN BE VERY CONSIDERATE ABOUT THE SMALL THINGS...
ACTUALLY...
...JUDAS WAS TELLING ME THAT THIS IS THE MOST FRIGHTENING THING ABOUT HIM...
LIVING IN HELL, WHERE YOU FIGHT AGAINST ETERNAL HUNGER...
...THERE IS ONE FINAL INDULGENCE WE HAVE...

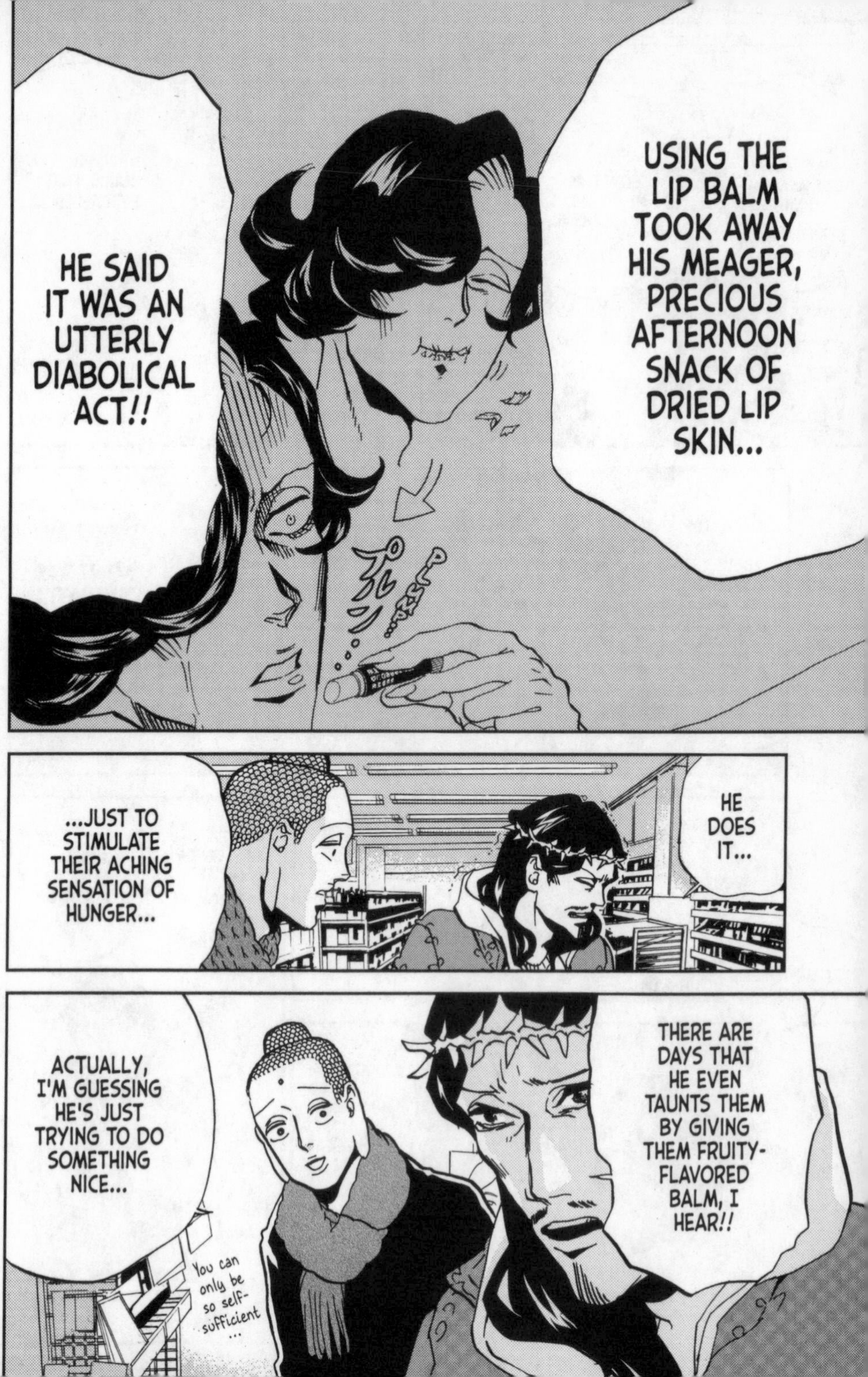
USING THE LIP BALM TOOK AWAY HIS MEAGER, PRECIOUS AFTERNOON SNACK OF DRIED LIP SKIN...
HE SAID IT WAS AN UTTERLY DIABOLICAL ACT!!
HE DOES IT...
...JUST TO STIMULATE THEIR ACHING SENSATION OF HUNGER...
THERE ARE DAYS THAT HE EVEN TAUNTS THEM BY GIVING THEM FRUITY-FLAVORED BALM, I HEAR!!
ACTUALLY, I'M GUESSING HE'S JUST TRYING TO DO SOMETHING NICE...
You can only be so self-sufficient ...

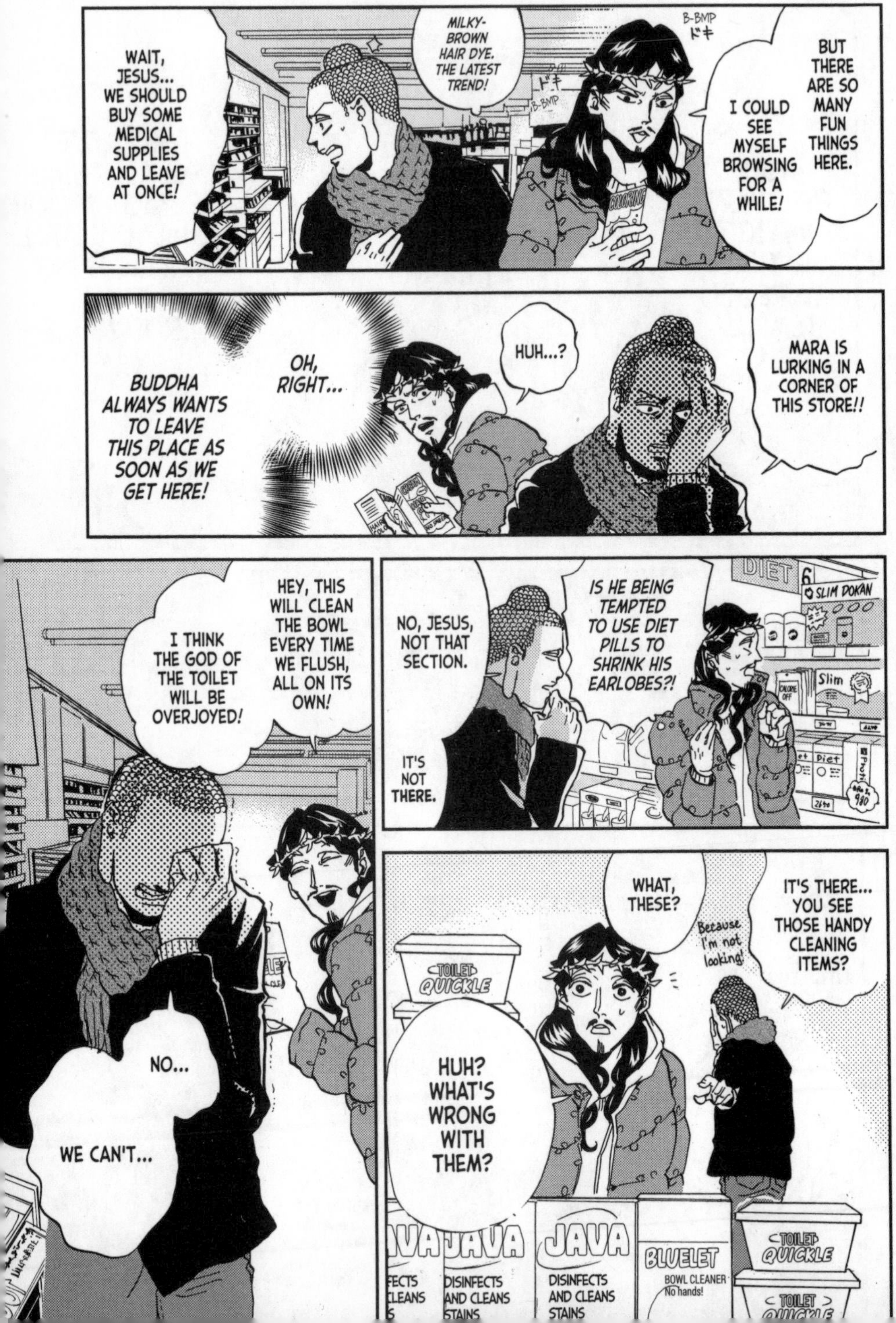
BUT THERE ARE SO MANY FUN THINGS HERE.
I COULD SEE MYSELF BROWSING FOR A WHILE!
B-BMP ドキ
MILKY-BROWN HAIR DYE. THE LATEST TREND!
ドキ B-BMP
COLORING
WAIT, JESUS... WE SHOULD BUY SOME MEDICAL SUPPLIES AND LEAVE AT ONCE!
MARA IS LURKING IN A CORNER OF THIS STORE!!
HUH...?
OH, RIGHT...
BUDDHA ALWAYS WANTS TO LEAVE THIS PLACE AS SOON AS WE GET HERE!
DIET
SLIM DOKAN
Slim
IS HE BEING TEMPTED TO USE DIET PILLS TO SHRINK HIS EARLOBES?!
NO, JESUS, NOT THAT SECTION.
IT'S NOT THERE.
IT'S THERE... YOU SEE THOSE HANDY CLEANING ITEMS?
Because I'm not looking!
WHAT, THESE?
TOILET QUICKLE
HUH? WHAT'S WRONG WITH THEM?
JAVA
DISINFECTS AND CLEANS STAINS
BLUELET
BOWL CLEANER No hands!
HEY, THIS WILL CLEAN THE BOWL EVERY TIME WE FLUSH, ALL ON ITS OWN!
I THINK THE GOD OF THE TOILET WILL BE OVERJOYED!
NO...
WE CAN'T...

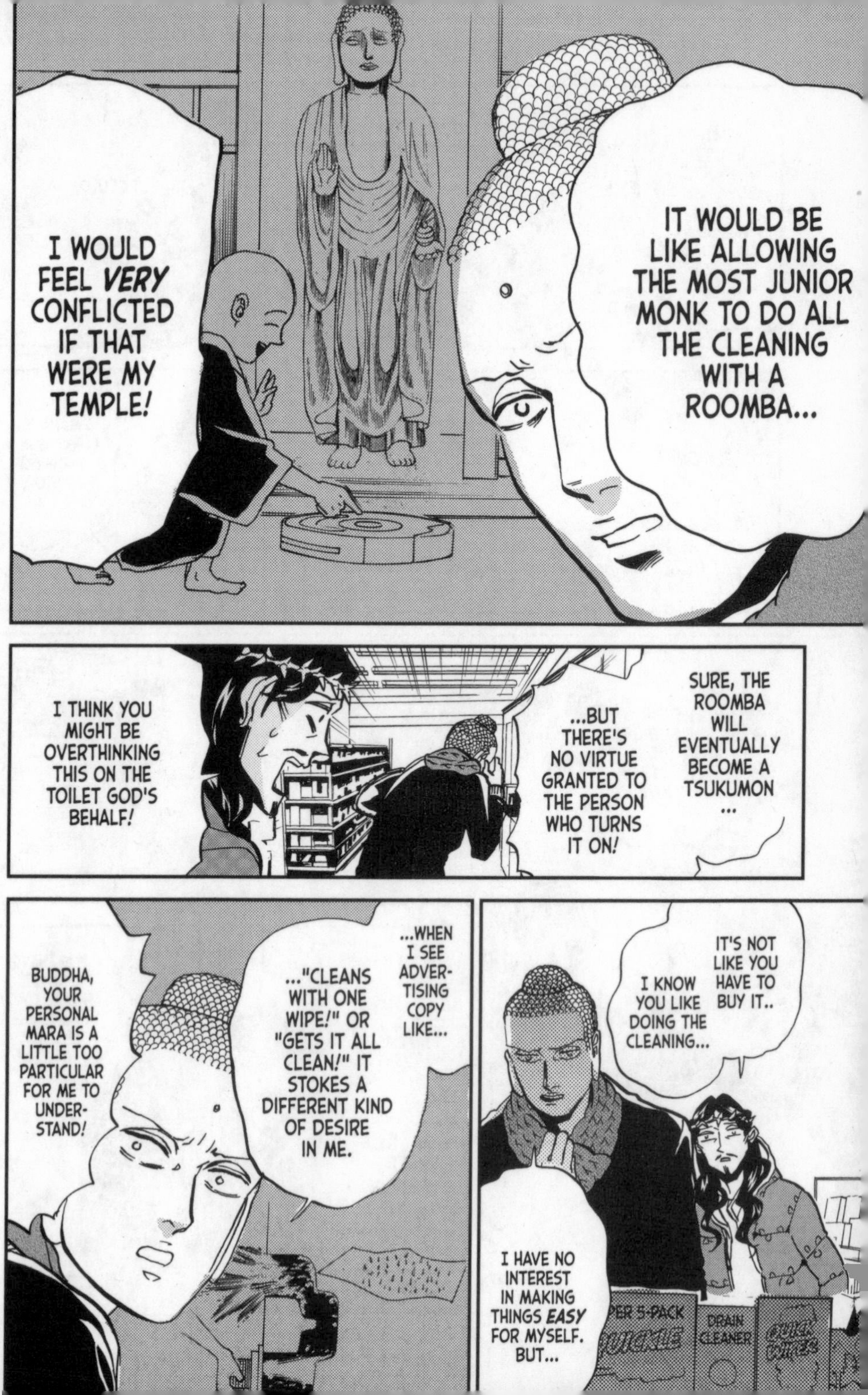
IT WOULD BE LIKE ALLOWING THE MOST JUNIOR MONK TO DO ALL THE CLEANING WITH A ROOMBA...
I WOULD FEEL *VERY* CONFLICTED IF THAT WERE MY TEMPLE!
SURE, THE ROOMBA WILL EVENTUALLY BECOME A TSUKUMON ...
...BUT THERE'S NO VIRTUE GRANTED TO THE PERSON WHO TURNS IT ON!
I THINK YOU MIGHT BE OVERTHINKING THIS ON THE TOILET GOD'S BEHALF!
IT'S NOT LIKE YOU HAVE TO BUY IT..
I KNOW YOU LIKE DOING THE CLEANING...
I HAVE NO INTEREST IN MAKING THINGS *EASY* FOR MYSELF. BUT...
PER 5-PACK
DRAIN CLEANER
...WHEN I SEE ADVER-TISING COPY LIKE...
..."CLEANS WITH ONE WIPE!" OR "GETS IT ALL CLEAN!" IT STOKES A DIFFERENT KIND OF DESIRE IN ME.
BUDDHA, YOUR PERSONAL MARA IS A LITTLE TOO PARTICULAR FOR ME TO UNDER-STAND!

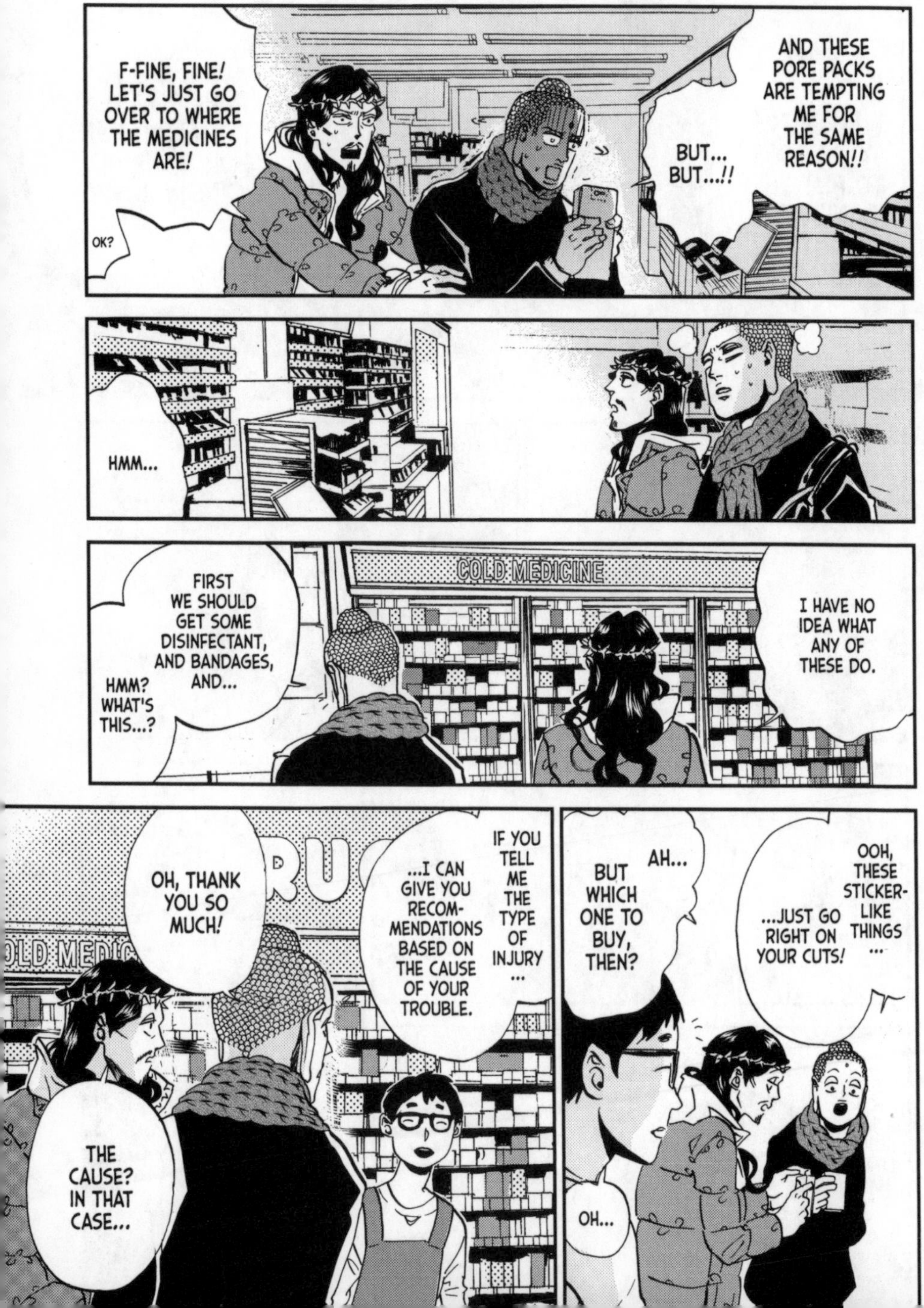

AND THESE PORE PACKS ARE TEMPTING ME FOR THE SAME REASON!!
BUT... BUT...!!
F-FINE, FINE! LET'S JUST GO OVER TO WHERE THE MEDICINES ARE!
OK?
HMM...
COLD MEDICINE
I HAVE NO IDEA WHAT ANY OF THESE DO.
FIRST WE SHOULD GET SOME DISINFECTANT, AND BANDAGES, AND...
HMM? WHAT'S THIS...?
OOH, THESE STICKER-LIKE THINGS ...
...JUST GO RIGHT ON YOUR CUTS!
AH...
BUT WHICH ONE TO BUY, THEN?
OH...
IF YOU TELL ME THE TYPE OF INJURY ...
...I CAN GIVE YOU RECOM-MENDATIONS BASED ON THE CAUSE OF YOUR TROUBLE.
OH, THANK YOU SO MUCH!
THE CAUSE? IN THAT CASE...

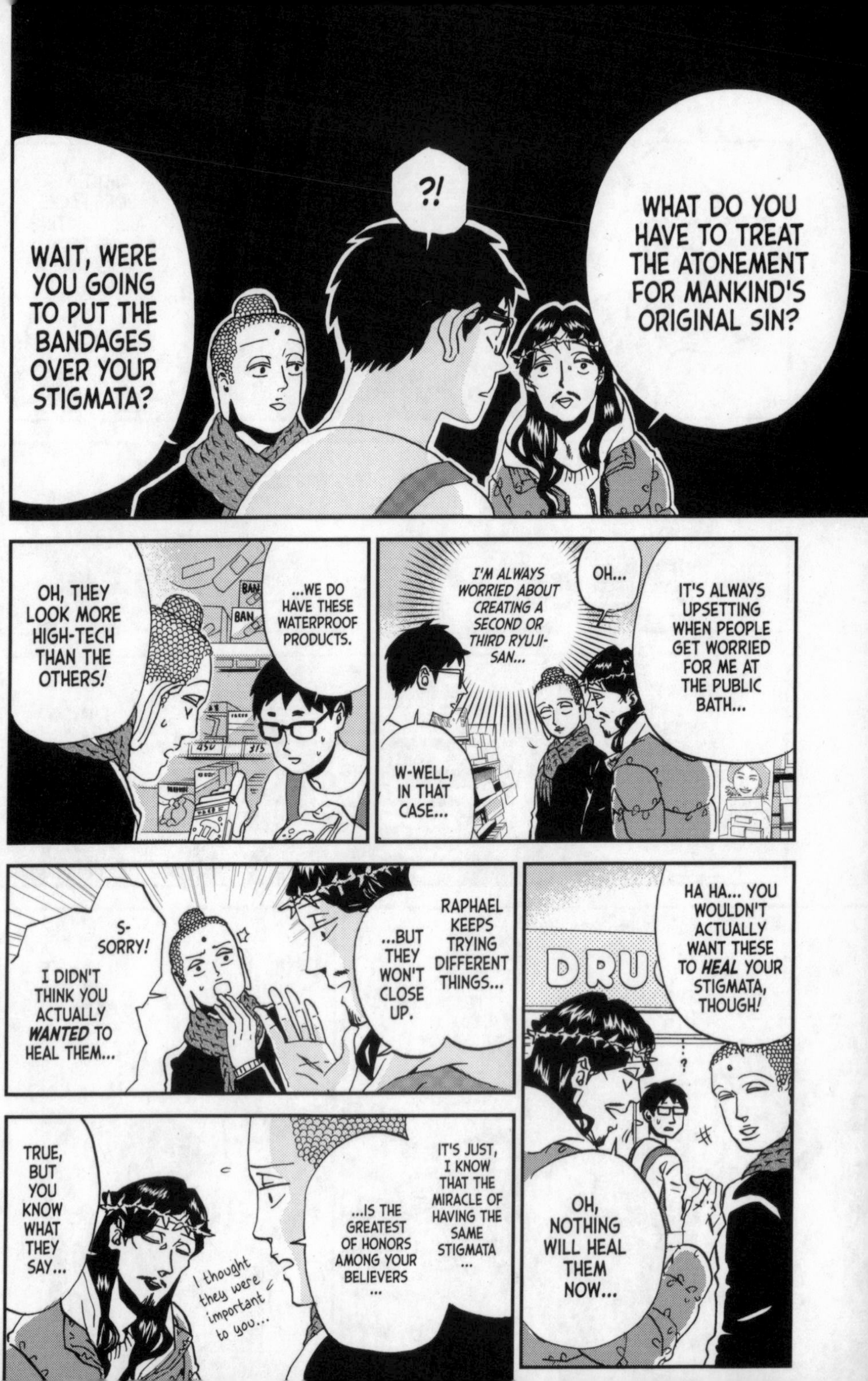
WHAT DO YOU HAVE TO TREAT THE ATONEMENT FOR MANKIND'S ORIGINAL SIN?
?!
WAIT, WERE YOU GOING TO PUT THE BANDAGES OVER YOUR STIGMATA?
IT'S ALWAYS UPSETTING WHEN PEOPLE GET WORRIED FOR ME AT THE PUBLIC BATH...
OH...
I'M ALWAYS WORRIED ABOUT CREATING A SECOND OR THIRD RYUJI-SAN...
W-WELL, IN THAT CASE...
...WE DO HAVE THESE WATERPROOF PRODUCTS.
OH, THEY LOOK MORE HIGH-TECH THAN THE OTHERS!
HA HA... YOU WOULDN'T ACTUALLY WANT THESE TO HEAL YOUR STIGMATA, THOUGH!
?
OH, NOTHING WILL HEAL THEM NOW...
RAPHAEL KEEPS TRYING DIFFERENT THINGS...
...BUT THEY WON'T CLOSE UP.
S-SORRY!
I DIDN'T THINK YOU ACTUALLY WANTED TO HEAL THEM...
IT'S JUST, I KNOW THAT THE MIRACLE OF HAVING THE SAME STIGMATA...
...IS THE GREATEST OF HONORS AMONG YOUR BELIEVERS...
I thought they were important to you...
TRUE, BUT YOU KNOW WHAT THEY SAY...

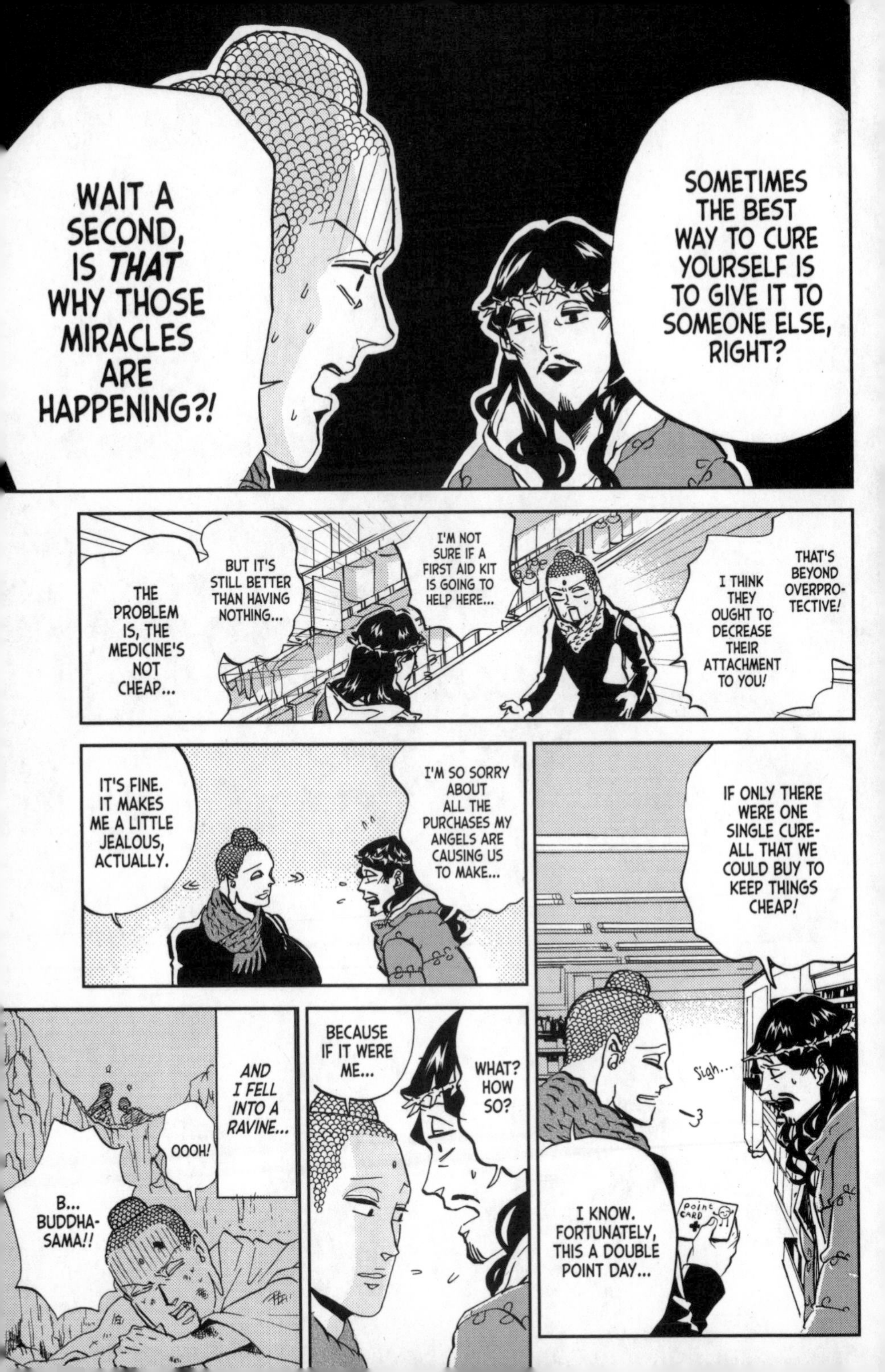
SOMETIMES THE BEST WAY TO CURE YOURSELF IS TO GIVE IT TO SOMEONE ELSE, RIGHT?
WAIT A SECOND, IS *THAT* WHY THOSE MIRACLES ARE HAPPENING?!
THAT'S BEYOND OVERPROTECTIVE!
I THINK THEY OUGHT TO DECREASE THEIR ATTACHMENT TO YOU!
I'M NOT SURE IF A FIRST AID KIT IS GOING TO HELP HERE...
BUT IT'S STILL BETTER THAN HAVING NOTHING...
THE PROBLEM IS, THE MEDICINE'S NOT CHEAP...
IF ONLY THERE WERE ONE SINGLE CURE-ALL THAT WE COULD BUY TO KEEP THINGS CHEAP!
Sigh...
I KNOW. FORTUNATELY, THIS A DOUBLE POINT DAY...
Point CARD
I'M SO SORRY ABOUT ALL THE PURCHASES MY ANGELS ARE CAUSING US TO MAKE...
IT'S FINE. IT MAKES ME A LITTLE JEALOUS, ACTUALLY.
WHAT? HOW SO?
BECAUSE IF IT WERE ME...
AND I FELL INTO A RAVINE...
OOOH!
B... BUDDHA-SAMA!!

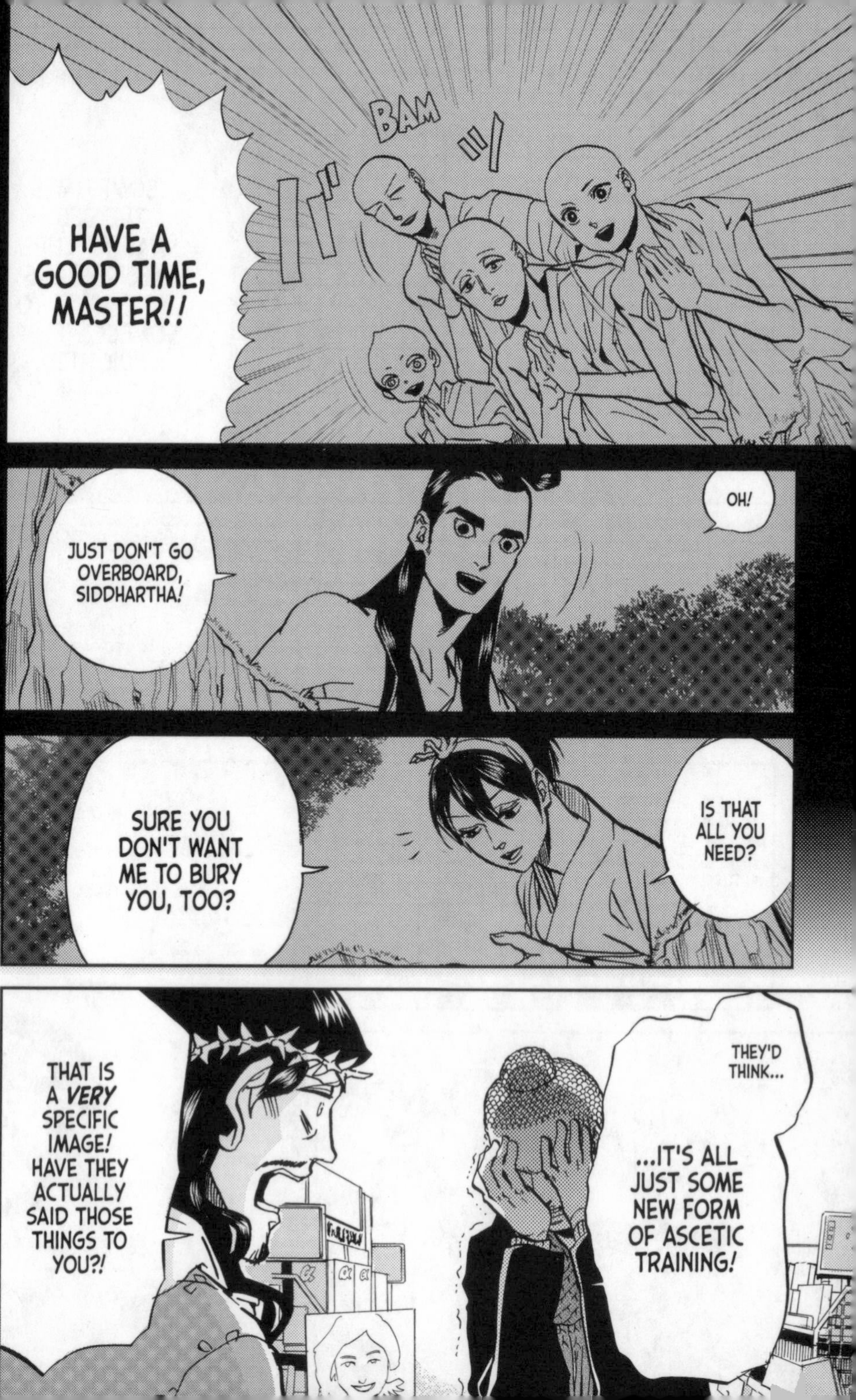
BAM
HAVE A GOOD TIME, MASTER!!
OH!
JUST DON'T GO OVERBOARD, SIDDHARTHA!
IS THAT ALL YOU NEED?
SURE YOU DON'T WANT ME TO BURY YOU, TOO?
THEY'D THINK...
...IT'S ALL JUST SOME NEW FORM OF ASCETIC TRAINING!
THAT IS A *VERY* SPECIFIC IMAGE! HAVE THEY ACTUALLY SAID THOSE THINGS TO YOU?!

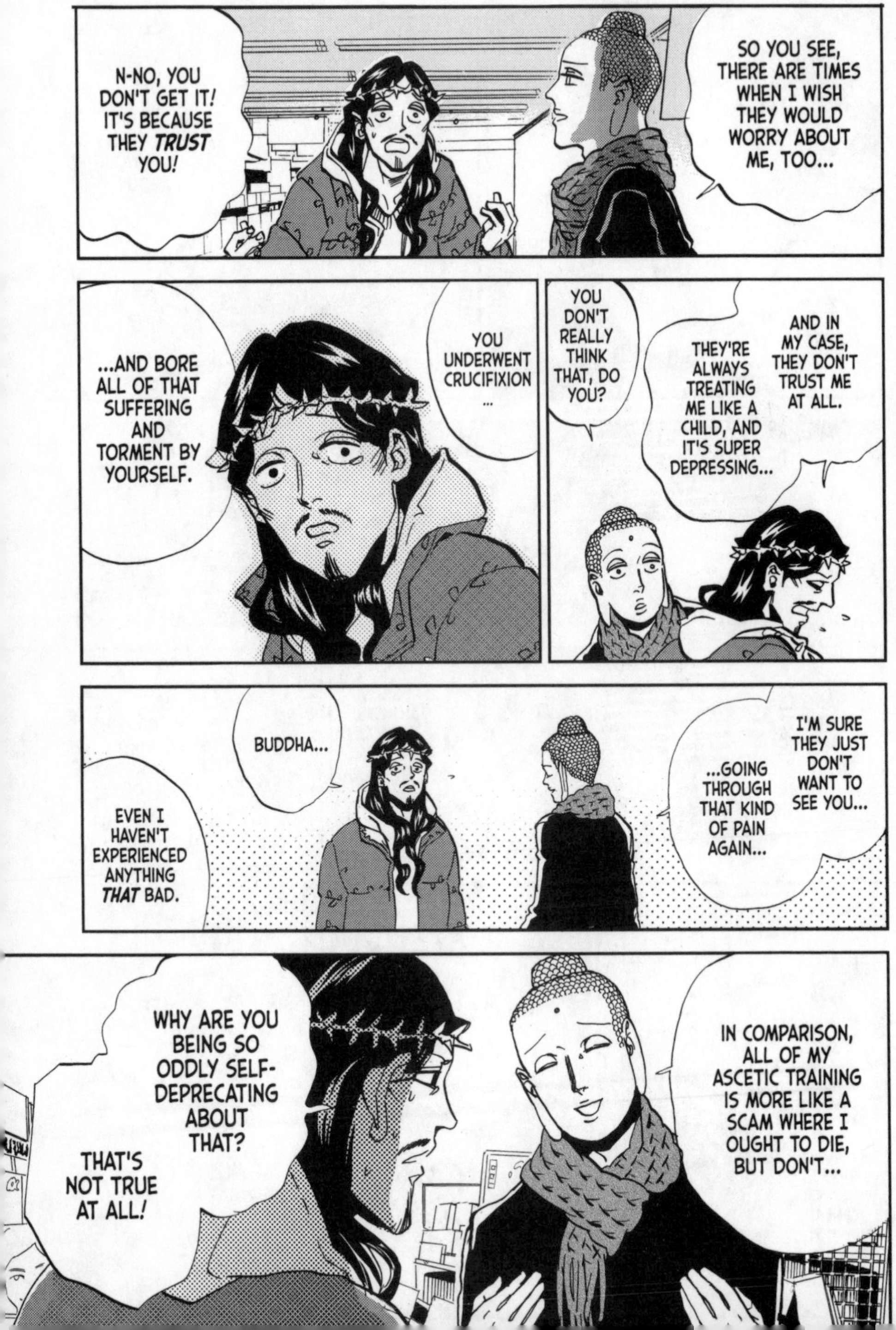
SO YOU SEE, THERE ARE TIMES WHEN I WISH THEY WOULD WORRY ABOUT ME, TOO...
N-NO, YOU DON'T GET IT! IT'S BECAUSE THEY *TRUST* YOU!
AND IN MY CASE, THEY DON'T TRUST ME AT ALL.
THEY'RE ALWAYS TREATING ME LIKE A CHILD, AND IT'S SUPER DEPRESSING...
YOU DON'T REALLY THINK THAT, DO YOU?
YOU UNDERWENT CRUCIFIXION ...
...AND BORE ALL OF THAT SUFFERING AND TORMENT BY YOURSELF.
I'M SURE THEY JUST DON'T WANT TO SEE YOU...
...GOING THROUGH THAT KIND OF PAIN AGAIN...
BUDDHA...
EVEN I HAVEN'T EXPERIENCED ANYTHING *THAT* BAD.
IN COMPARISON, ALL OF MY ASCETIC TRAINING IS MORE LIKE A SCAM WHERE I OUGHT TO DIE, BUT DON'T...
WHY ARE YOU BEING SO ODDLY SELF-DEPRECATING ABOUT THAT?
THAT'S NOT TRUE AT ALL!

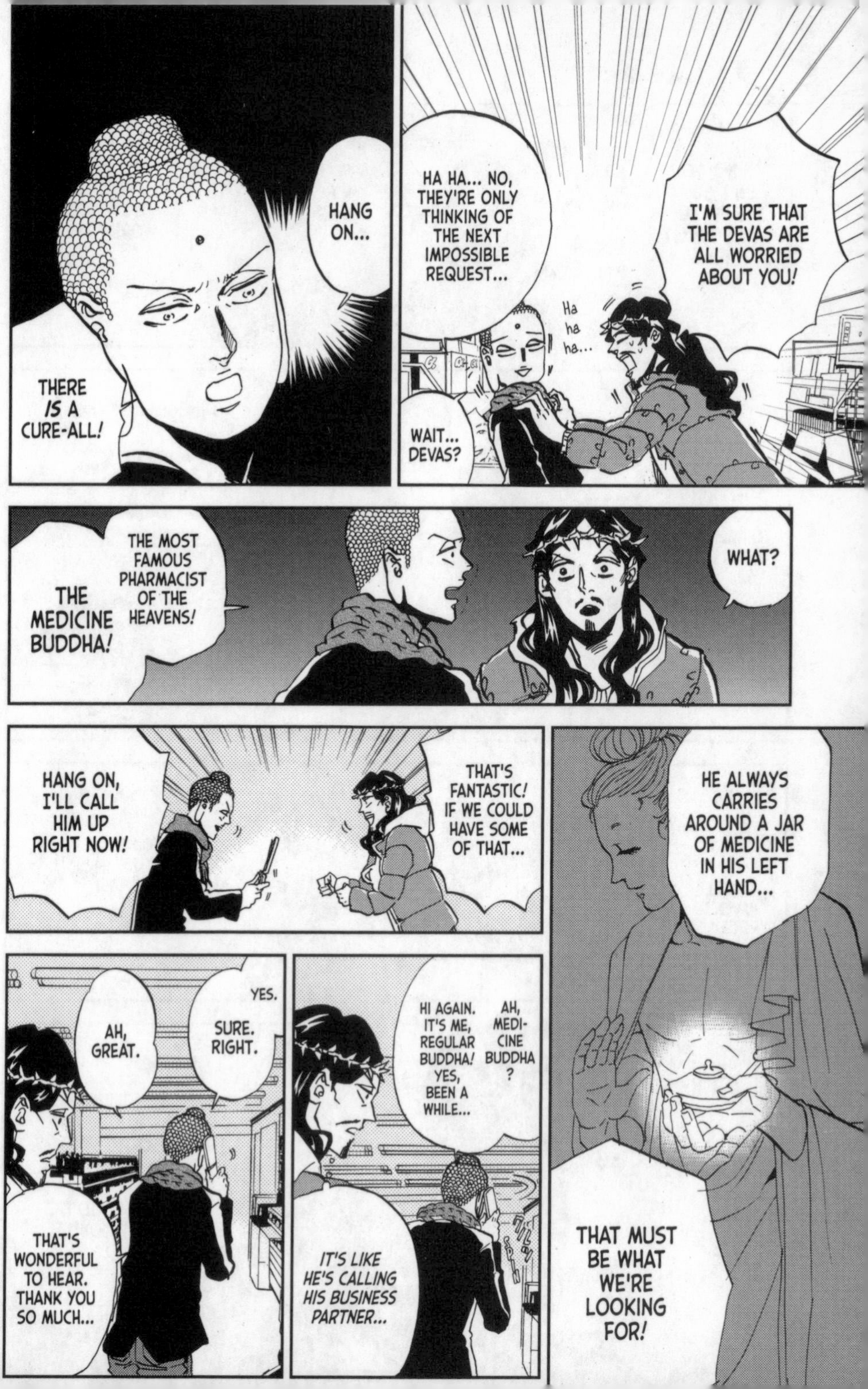
I'M SURE THAT THE DEVAS ARE ALL WORRIED ABOUT YOU!
Ha ha ha...
HA HA... NO, THEY'RE ONLY THINKING OF THE NEXT IMPOSSIBLE REQUEST...
WAIT... DEVAS?
HANG ON...
THERE *IS* A CURE-ALL!
WHAT?
THE MEDICINE BUDDHA!
THE MOST FAMOUS PHARMACIST OF THE HEAVENS!
HE ALWAYS CARRIES AROUND A JAR OF MEDICINE IN HIS LEFT HAND...
THAT MUST BE WHAT WE'RE LOOKING FOR!
THAT'S FANTASTIC! IF WE COULD HAVE SOME OF THAT...
HANG ON, I'LL CALL HIM UP RIGHT NOW!
AH, MEDI-CINE BUDDHA?
HI AGAIN. IT'S ME, REGULAR BUDDHA! YES, BEEN A WHILE...
IT'S LIKE HE'S CALLING HIS BUSINESS PARTNER...
YES.
SURE. RIGHT.
AH, GREAT.
THAT'S WONDERFUL TO HEAR. THANK YOU SO MUCH...

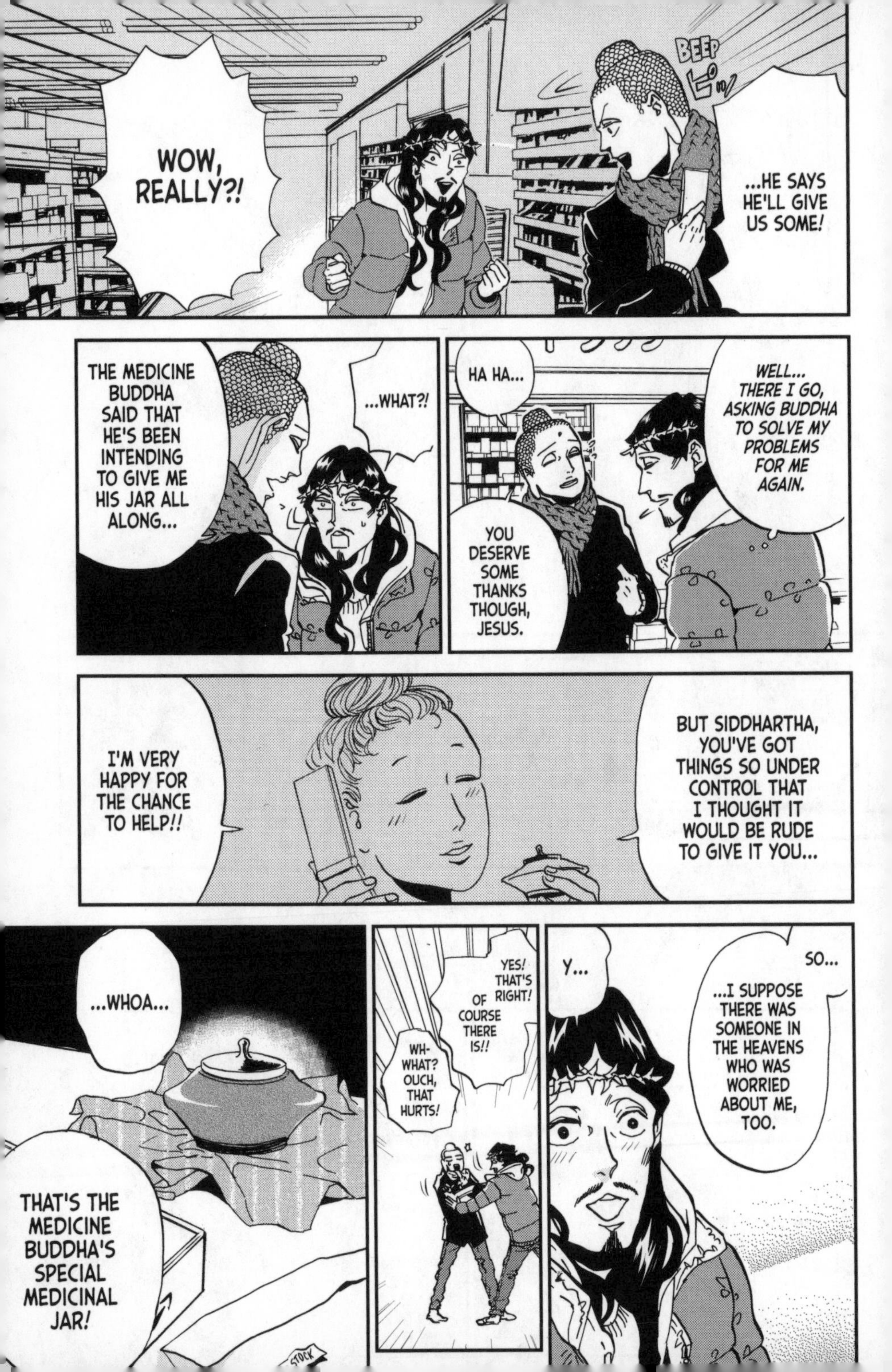
BEEP
...HE SAYS HE'LL GIVE US SOME!
WOW, REALLY?!
WELL... THERE I GO, ASKING BUDDHA TO SOLVE MY PROBLEMS FOR ME AGAIN.
HA HA...
YOU DESERVE SOME THANKS THOUGH, JESUS.
...WHAT?!
THE MEDICINE BUDDHA SAID THAT HE'S BEEN INTENDING TO GIVE ME HIS JAR ALL ALONG...
BUT SIDDHARTHA, YOU'VE GOT THINGS SO UNDER CONTROL THAT I THOUGHT IT WOULD BE RUDE TO GIVE IT YOU...
I'M VERY HAPPY FOR THE CHANCE TO HELP!!
SO...
...I SUPPOSE THERE WAS SOMEONE IN THE HEAVENS WHO WAS WORRIED ABOUT ME, TOO.
Y...
YES! THAT'S RIGHT!
OF COURSE THERE IS!!
WH-WHAT? OUCH, THAT HURTS!
...WHOA...
THAT'S THE MEDICINE BUDDHA'S SPECIAL MEDICINAL JAR!
STOCK

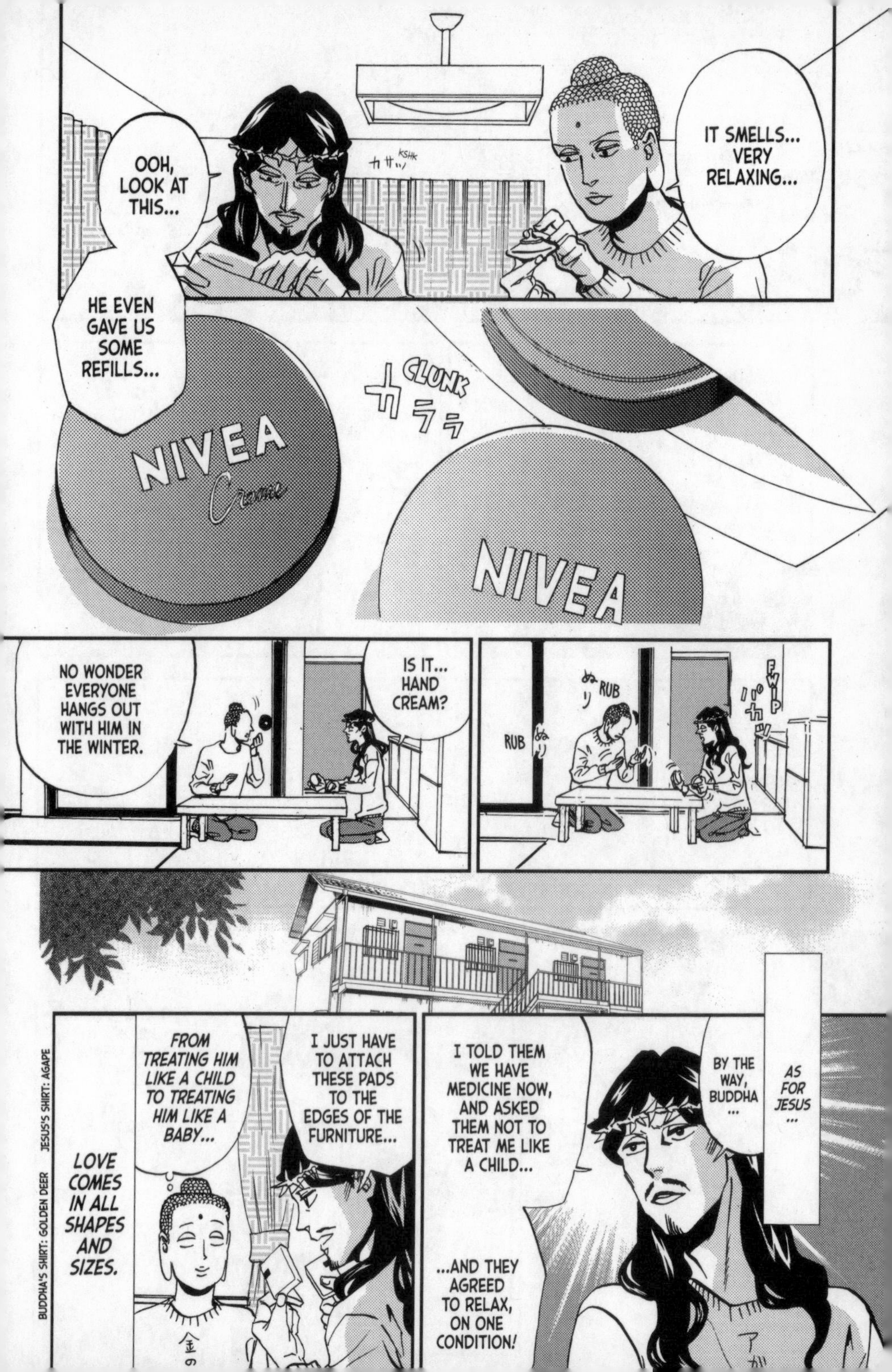
IT SMELLS... VERY RELAXING...
KSHK カサッ
OOH, LOOK AT THIS...
CLUNK カララ
HE EVEN GAVE US SOME REFILLS...
NIVEA Creme
NIVEA
FWIP パカッ
RUB ぬり
RUB ぬり
IS IT... HAND CREAM?
NO WONDER EVERYONE HANGS OUT WITH HIM IN THE WINTER.
AS FOR JESUS...
BY THE WAY, BUDDHA...
I TOLD THEM WE HAVE MEDICINE NOW, AND ASKED THEM NOT TO TREAT ME LIKE A CHILD...
...AND THEY AGREED TO RELAX, ON ONE CONDITION!
I JUST HAVE TO ATTACH THESE PADS TO THE EDGES OF THE FURNITURE...
FROM TREATING HIM LIKE A CHILD TO TREATING HIM LIKE A BABY...
LOVE COMES IN ALL SHAPES AND SIZES.
金の
BUDDHA'S SHIRT: GOLDEN DEER JESUS'S SHIRT: AGAPE

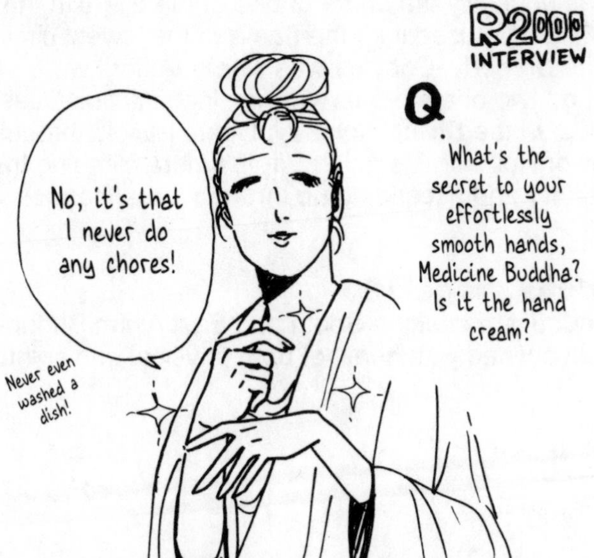
R2000 INTERVIEW
Q. What's the secret to your effortlessly smooth hands, Medicine Buddha? Is it the hand cream?
No, it's that I never do any chores!
Never even washed a dish!

CHAPTER 51 TRANSLATION NOTES

Visual-kei, page 139
A Japanese musical movement that marries hard rock genres like heavy metal and punk with a vivid "visual" element of flamboyant, glam-like fashion.

Yoshizumi, page 140
Actor and TV personality Yoshizumi Ishihara. He is typically known by his first name because he is part of the famous Ishihara family of politicians--his brothers are politicians and his father is former Tokyo governor Shintaro Ishihara. Yoshizumi has been part of a longtime commercial series for NTT's Town Page phone book, in which he visits individuals or businesses and helps them find the right phone number for the service they need.

Alfort, page 141
A brand of Japanese cookies, typically a small biscuit-type cookie set beneath a larger piece of chocolate.

Cocytus, page 142
While Cocytus was originally the name of one of the rivers in the Greek Underworld, Dante used it as the name of the lowest circle of Hell in his *Divine Comedy*. Cocytus was where traitors were sent, including Judas, and two of the primary assassins of Julius Caesar, Brutus and Cassius. In the *Divine Comedy*, Dante travels through the various circles of Hell with his guide Virgil, before climbing the mountain of Purgatory and ascending up through the sphere of Heaven.

Medicine Buddha, page 150
The Medicine Buddha is present in South and East Asian Buddhist traditions and is associated with healing, both physical and spiritual.

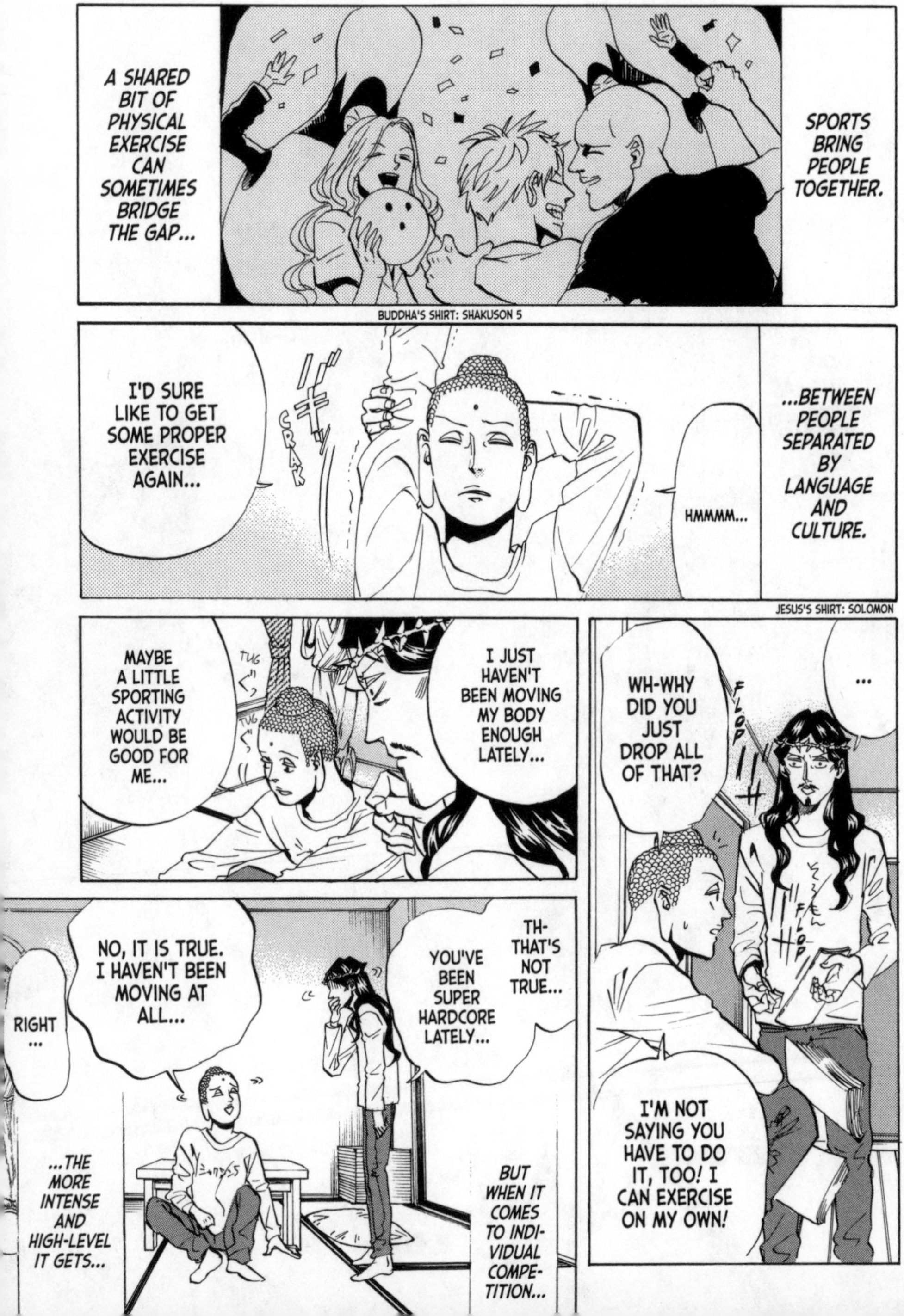
SPORTS BRING PEOPLE TOGETHER.
A SHARED BIT OF PHYSICAL EXERCISE CAN SOMETIMES BRIDGE THE GAP...
BUDDHA'S SHIRT: SHAKUSON 5
...BETWEEN PEOPLE SEPARATED BY LANGUAGE AND CULTURE.
HMMMM...
CRAK
I'D SURE LIKE TO GET SOME PROPER EXERCISE AGAIN...
JESUS'S SHIRT: SOLOMON
...
FLOP
WH-WHY DID YOU JUST DROP ALL OF THAT?
FLOP
I'M NOT SAYING YOU HAVE TO DO IT, TOO! I CAN EXERCISE ON MY OWN!
I JUST HAVEN'T BEEN MOVING MY BODY ENOUGH LATELY...
TUG
TUG
MAYBE A LITTLE SPORTING ACTIVITY WOULD BE GOOD FOR ME...
TH-THAT'S NOT TRUE...
YOU'VE BEEN SUPER HARDCORE LATELY...
NO, IT IS TRUE. I HAVEN'T BEEN MOVING AT ALL...
RIGHT...
BUT WHEN IT COMES TO INDIVIDUAL COMPETITION...
...THE MORE INTENSE AND HIGH-LEVEL IT GETS...

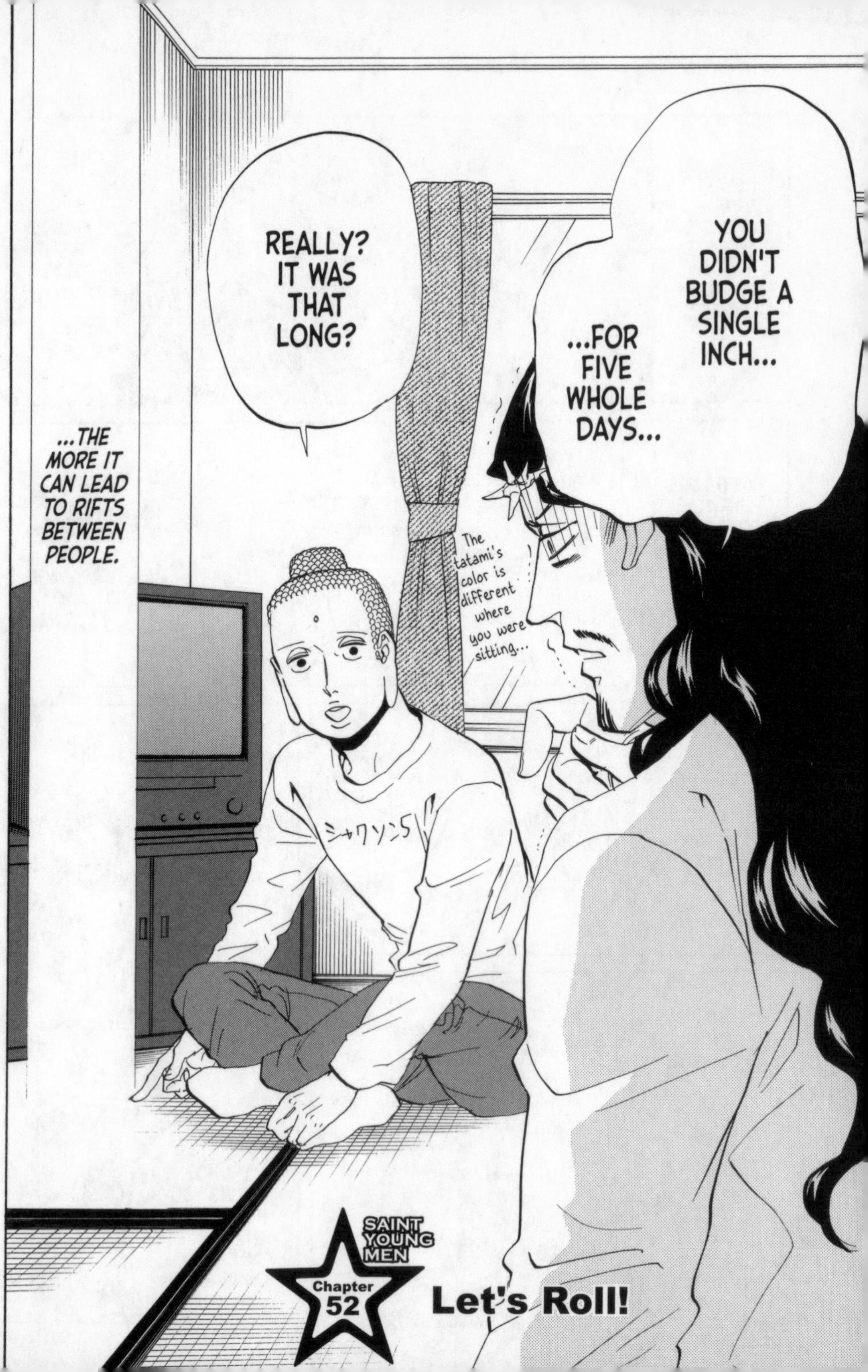
YOU DIDN'T BUDGE A SINGLE INCH...
...FOR FIVE WHOLE DAYS...
The tatami's color is different where you were sitting...
REALLY? IT WAS THAT LONG?
...THE MORE IT CAN LEAD TO RIFTS BETWEEN PEOPLE.
SAINT YOUNG MEN
Chapter 52
Let's Roll!

BUDDHA WANTS TO TRY SUMO WRESTLING IN THE OFFICIAL RING. BUT NOT BECAUSE HE'S GAINED WEIGHT OR ANYTHING.

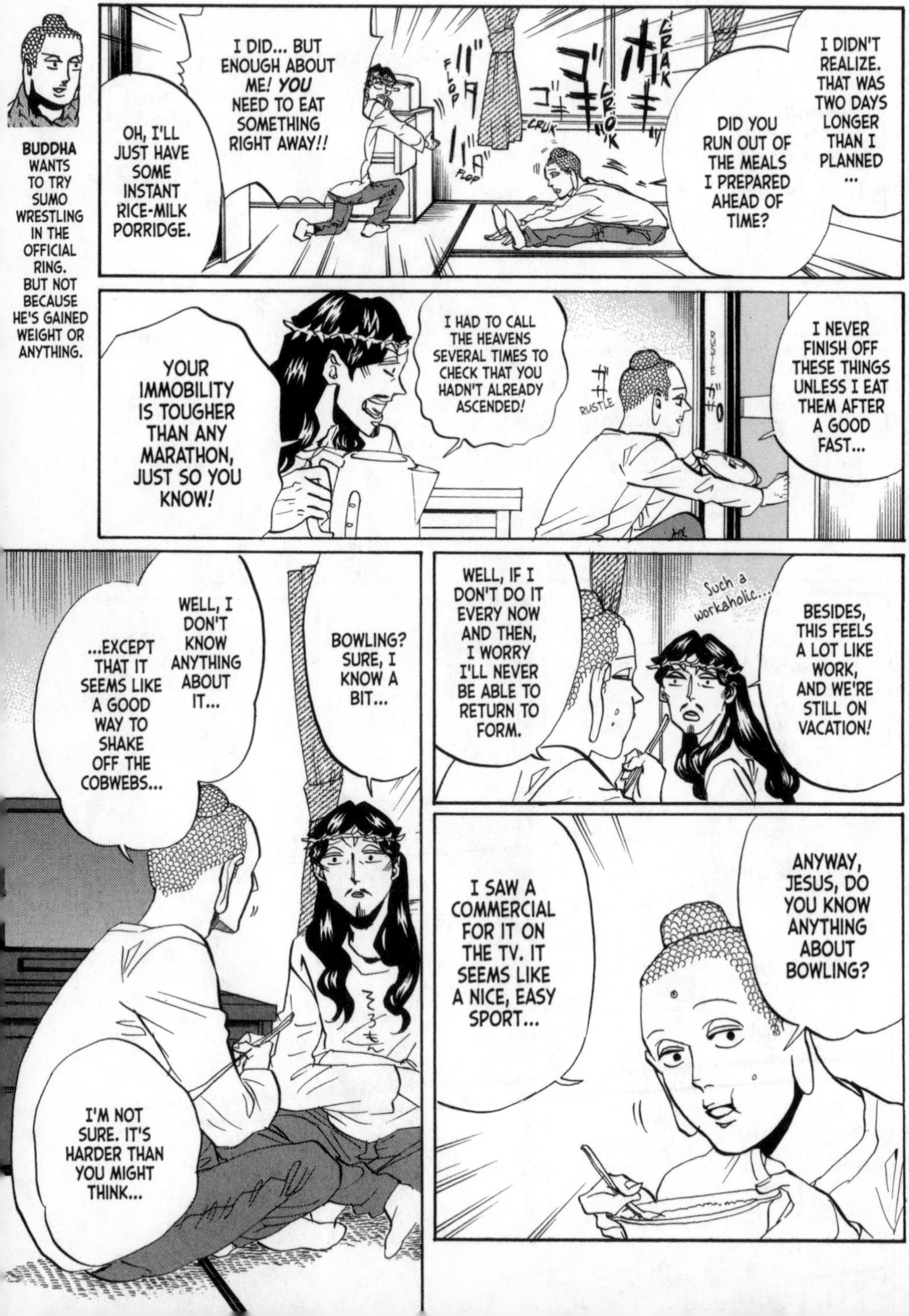
I DIDN'T REALIZE. THAT WAS TWO DAYS LONGER THAN I PLANNED...
DID YOU RUN OUT OF THE MEALS I PREPARED AHEAD OF TIME?
CRAK
CRÖK
CRUK
I DID... BUT ENOUGH ABOUT ME! YOU NEED TO EAT SOMETHING RIGHT AWAY!!
FLOP
FLOP
OH, I'LL JUST HAVE SOME INSTANT RICE-MILK PORRIDGE.
I NEVER FINISH OFF THESE THINGS UNLESS I EAT THEM AFTER A GOOD FAST...
RUSTLE
I HAD TO CALL THE HEAVENS SEVERAL TIMES TO CHECK THAT YOU HADN'T ALREADY ASCENDED!
YOUR IMMOBILITY IS TOUGHER THAN ANY MARATHON, JUST SO YOU KNOW!
BESIDES, THIS FEELS A LOT LIKE WORK, AND WE'RE STILL ON VACATION!
Such a workaholic...
WELL, IF I DON'T DO IT EVERY NOW AND THEN, I WORRY I'LL NEVER BE ABLE TO RETURN TO FORM.
ANYWAY, JESUS, DO YOU KNOW ANYTHING ABOUT BOWLING?
I SAW A COMMERCIAL FOR IT ON THE TV. IT SEEMS LIKE A NICE, EASY SPORT...
BOWLING? SURE, I KNOW A BIT...
WELL, I DON'T KNOW ANYTHING ABOUT IT...
...EXCEPT THAT IT SEEMS LIKE A GOOD WAY TO SHAKE OFF THE COBWEBS...
I'M NOT SURE. IT'S HARDER THAN YOU MIGHT THINK...

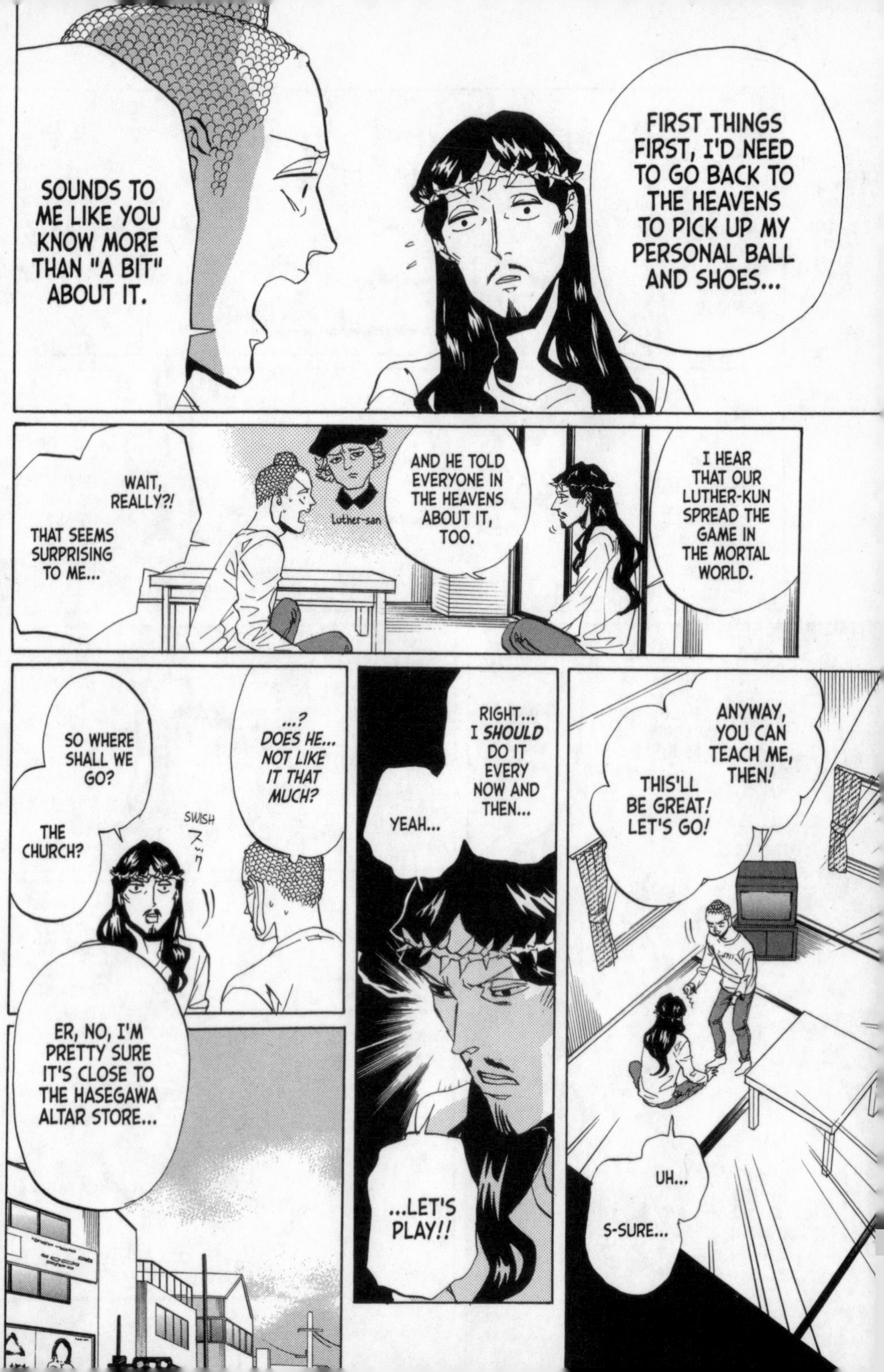
FIRST THINGS FIRST, I'D NEED TO GO BACK TO THE HEAVENS TO PICK UP MY PERSONAL BALL AND SHOES...
SOUNDS TO ME LIKE YOU KNOW MORE THAN "A BIT" ABOUT IT.
I HEAR THAT OUR LUTHER-KUN SPREAD THE GAME IN THE MORTAL WORLD.
AND HE TOLD EVERYONE IN THE HEAVENS ABOUT IT, TOO.
Luther-san
WAIT, REALLY?!
THAT SEEMS SURPRISING TO ME...
ANYWAY, YOU CAN TEACH ME, THEN!
THIS'LL BE GREAT! LET'S GO!
UH...
S-SURE...
RIGHT... I SHOULD DO IT EVERY NOW AND THEN...
YEAH...
...LET'S PLAY!!
...? DOES HE... NOT LIKE IT THAT MUCH?
SO WHERE SHALL WE GO?
THE CHURCH?
SWISH
スッ
ER, NO, I'M PRETTY SURE IT'S CLOSE TO THE HASEGAWA ALTAR STORE...

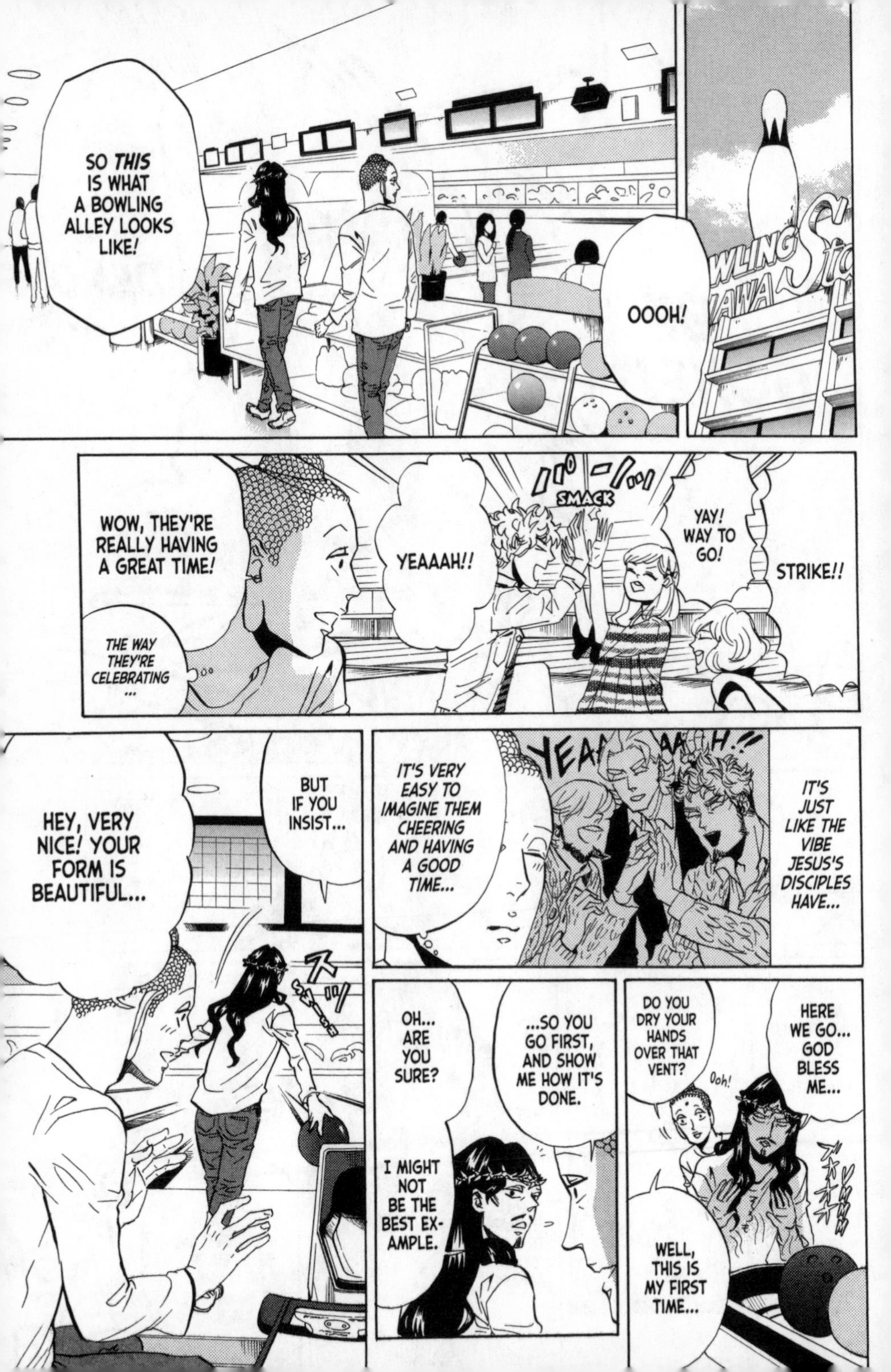
OOOH!
SO *THIS* IS WHAT A BOWLING ALLEY LOOKS LIKE!
STRIKE!!
YAY! WAY TO GO!
SMACK
YEAAAH!!
WOW, THEY'RE REALLY HAVING A GREAT TIME!
THE WAY THEY'RE CELEBRATING ...
IT'S JUST LIKE THE VIBE JESUS'S DISCIPLES HAVE...
IT'S VERY EASY TO IMAGINE THEM CHEERING AND HAVING A GOOD TIME...
HERE WE GO... GOD BLESS ME...
DO YOU DRY YOUR HANDS OVER THAT VENT?
Ooh!
WELL, THIS IS MY FIRST TIME...
...SO YOU GO FIRST, AND SHOW ME HOW IT'S DONE.
OH... ARE YOU SURE?
I MIGHT NOT BE THE BEST EX-AMPLE.
BUT IF YOU INSIST...
HEY, VERY NICE! YOUR FORM IS BEAUTIFUL...

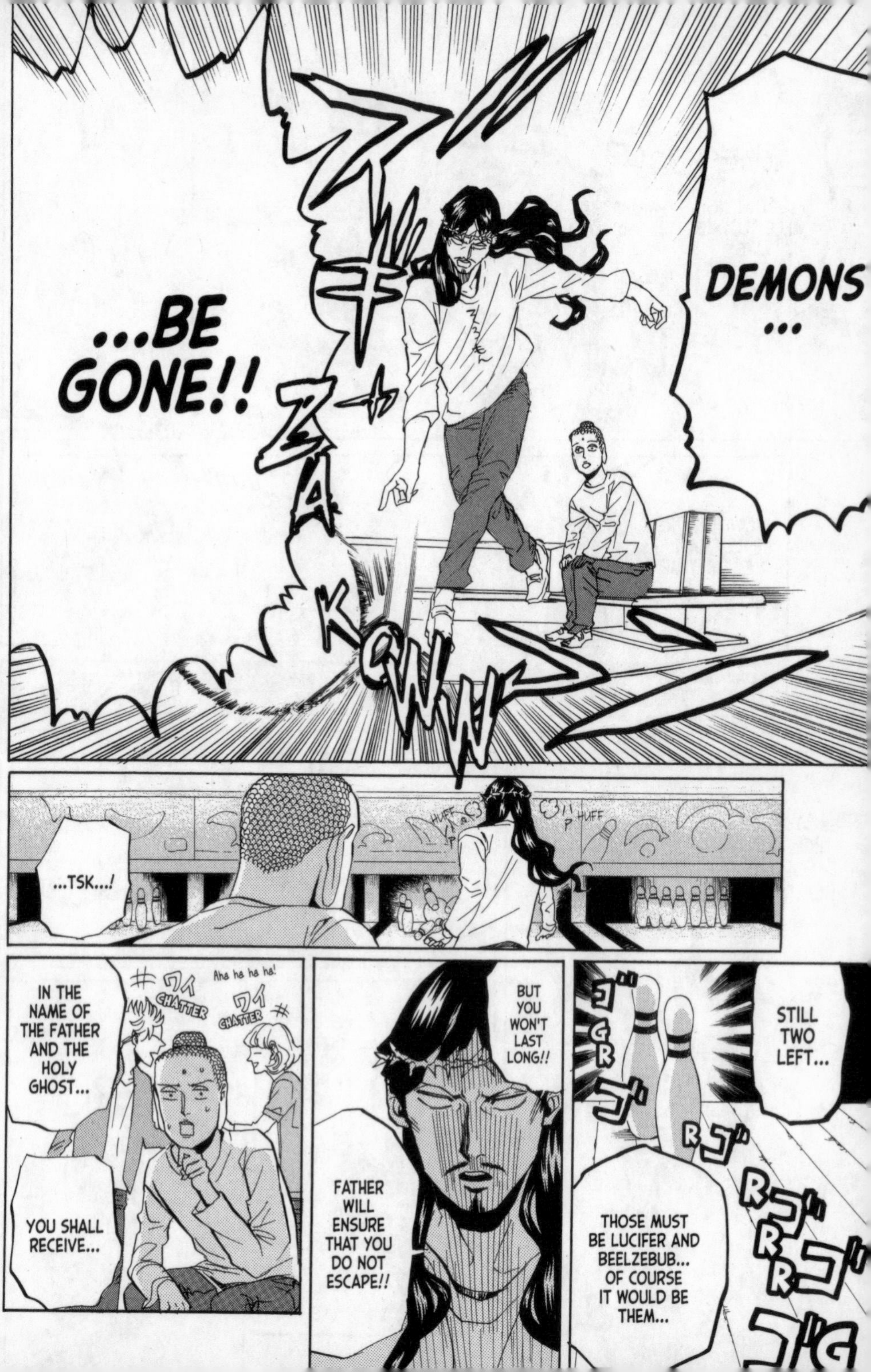
DEMONS ...
...BE GONE!!
...TSK...!
HUFF
HUFF
STILL TWO LEFT...
THOSE MUST BE LUCIFER AND BEELZEBUB... OF COURSE IT WOULD BE THEM...
BUT YOU WON'T LAST LONG!!
FATHER WILL ENSURE THAT YOU DO NOT ESCAPE!!
Aha ha ha ha!
CHATTER
CHATTER
IN THE NAME OF THE FATHER AND THE HOLY GHOST...
YOU SHALL RECEIVE...

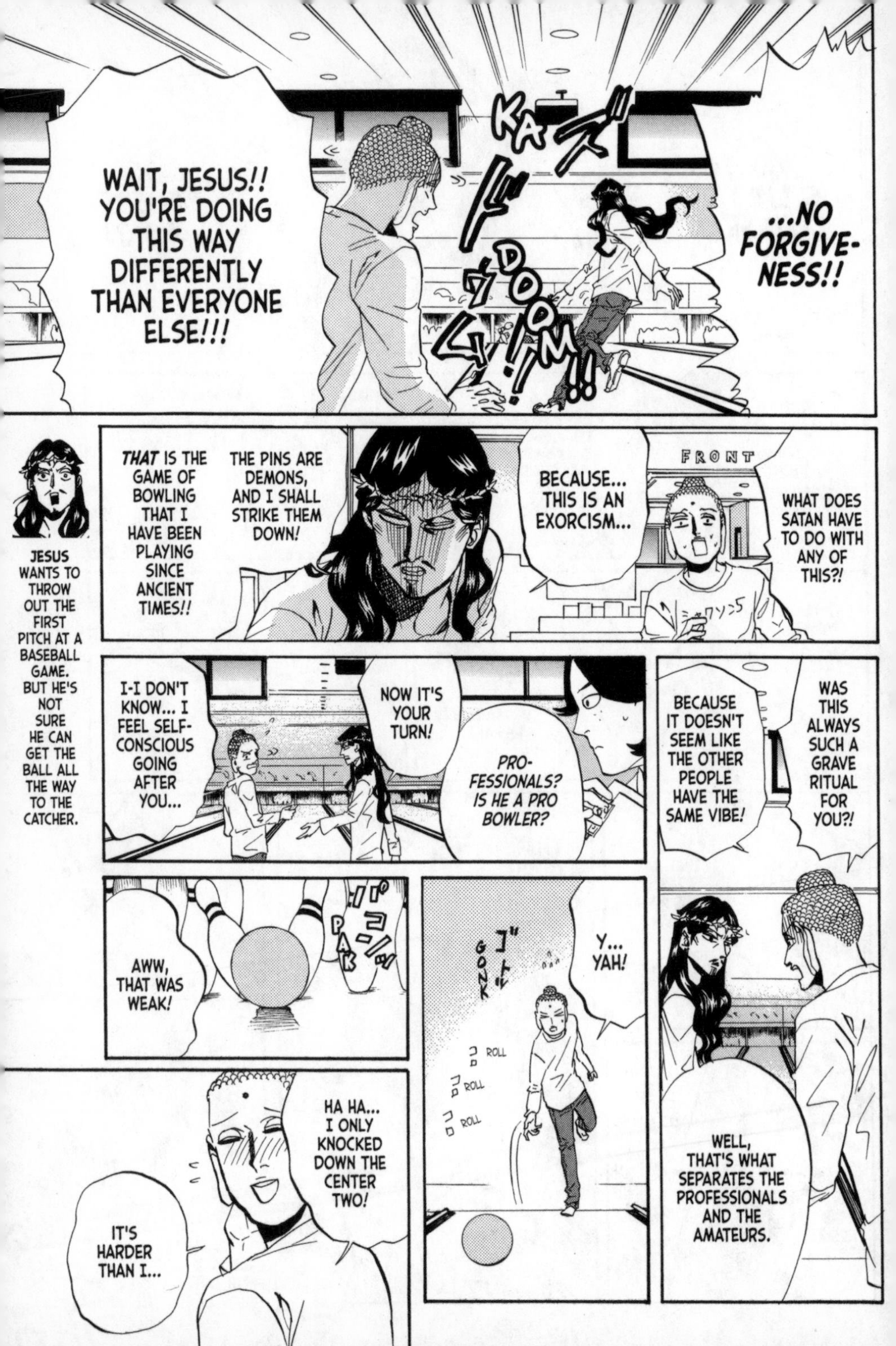
...NO FORGIVE-NESS!!
KA-DOOM!!
WAIT, JESUS!! YOU'RE DOING THIS WAY DIFFERENTLY THAN EVERYONE ELSE!!!
WHAT DOES SATAN HAVE TO DO WITH ANY OF THIS?!
FRONT
BECAUSE... THIS IS AN EXORCISM...
THE PINS ARE DEMONS, AND I SHALL STRIKE THEM DOWN!
THAT IS THE GAME OF BOWLING THAT I HAVE BEEN PLAYING SINCE ANCIENT TIMES!!
JESUS WANTS TO THROW OUT THE FIRST PITCH AT A BASEBALL GAME. BUT HE'S NOT SURE HE CAN GET THE BALL ALL THE WAY TO THE CATCHER.
WAS THIS ALWAYS SUCH A GRAVE RITUAL FOR YOU?!
BECAUSE IT DOESN'T SEEM LIKE THE OTHER PEOPLE HAVE THE SAME VIBE!
WELL, THAT'S WHAT SEPARATES THE PROFESSIONALS AND THE AMATEURS.
PRO-FESSIONALS? IS HE A PRO BOWLER?
NOW IT'S YOUR TURN!
I-I DON'T KNOW... I FEEL SELF-CONSCIOUS GOING AFTER YOU...
Y... YAH!
GONK
ROLL
ROLL
ROLL
PAK
AWW, THAT WAS WEAK!
HA HA... I ONLY KNOCKED DOWN THE CENTER TWO!
IT'S HARDER THAN I...

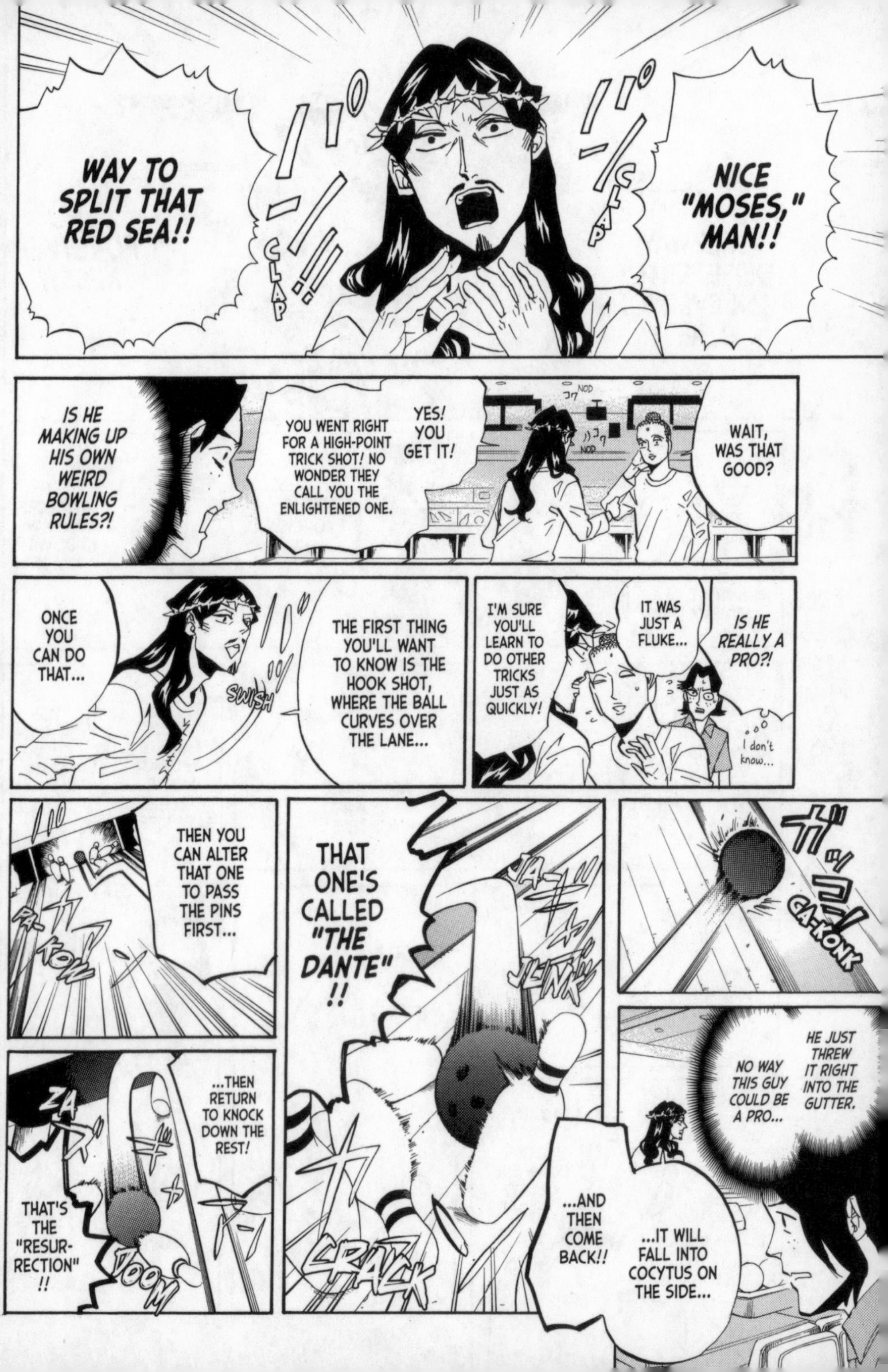

NICE "MOSES," MAN!!
CLAP
WAY TO SPLIT THAT RED SEA!!
CLAP
WAIT, WAS THAT GOOD?
NOD
NOD
YES! YOU GET IT!
YOU WENT RIGHT FOR A HIGH-POINT TRICK SHOT! NO WONDER THEY CALL YOU THE ENLIGHTENED ONE.
IS HE MAKING UP HIS OWN WEIRD BOWLING RULES?!
IS HE REALLY A PRO?!
IT WAS JUST A FLUKE...
I'M SURE YOU'LL LEARN TO DO OTHER TRICKS JUST AS QUICKLY!
I don't know...
THE FIRST THING YOU'LL WANT TO KNOW IS THE HOOK SHOT, WHERE THE BALL CURVES OVER THE LANE...
SWISH
ONCE YOU CAN DO THAT...
GA-KONK
HE JUST THREW IT RIGHT INTO THE GUTTER.
NO WAY THIS GUY COULD BE A PRO...
...IT WILL FALL INTO COCYTUS ON THE SIDE...
...AND THEN COME BACK!!
THAT ONE'S CALLED "THE DANTE"!!
JA
JLINK
CRACK
THEN YOU CAN ALTER THAT ONE TO PASS THE PINS FIRST...
PA-KOW
...THEN RETURN TO KNOCK DOWN THE REST!
ZA
THAT'S THE "RESURRECTION"!!
DOOM

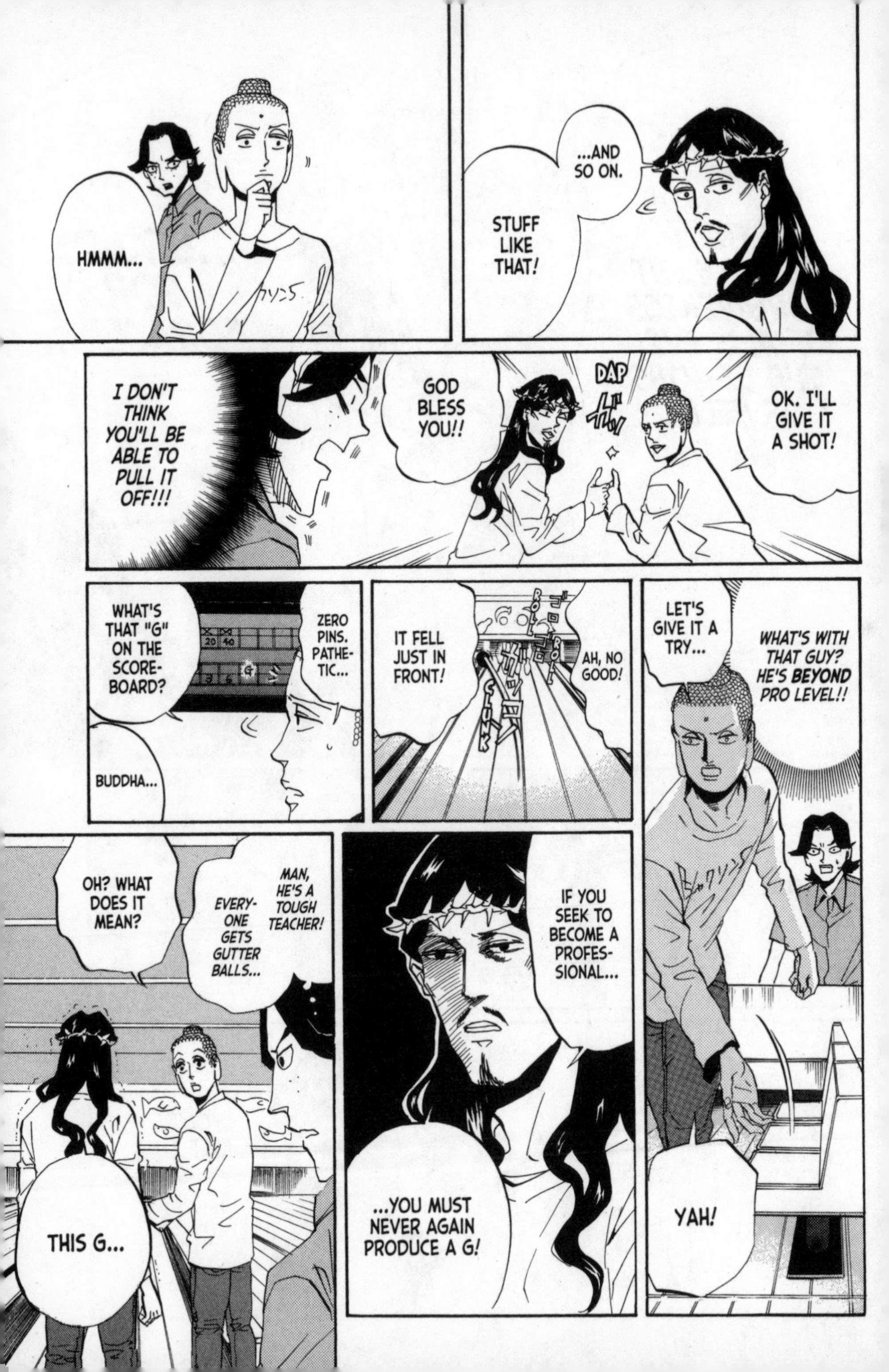
...AND SO ON.
STUFF LIKE THAT!
HMMM...
OK. I'LL GIVE IT A SHOT!
DAP
GOD BLESS YOU!!
I DON'T THINK YOU'LL BE ABLE TO PULL IT OFF!!!
LET'S GIVE IT A TRY...
WHAT'S WITH THAT GUY? HE'S BEYOND PRO LEVEL!!
YAH!
AH, NO GOOD!
ROLL
CLUNK
IT FELL JUST IN FRONT!
ZERO PINS. PATHETIC...
WHAT'S THAT "G" ON THE SCOREBOARD?
BUDDHA...
IF YOU SEEK TO BECOME A PROFESSIONAL...
...YOU MUST NEVER AGAIN PRODUCE A G!
MAN, HE'S A TOUGH TEACHER!
EVERYONE GETS GUTTER BALLS...
OH? WHAT DOES IT MEAN?
THIS G...

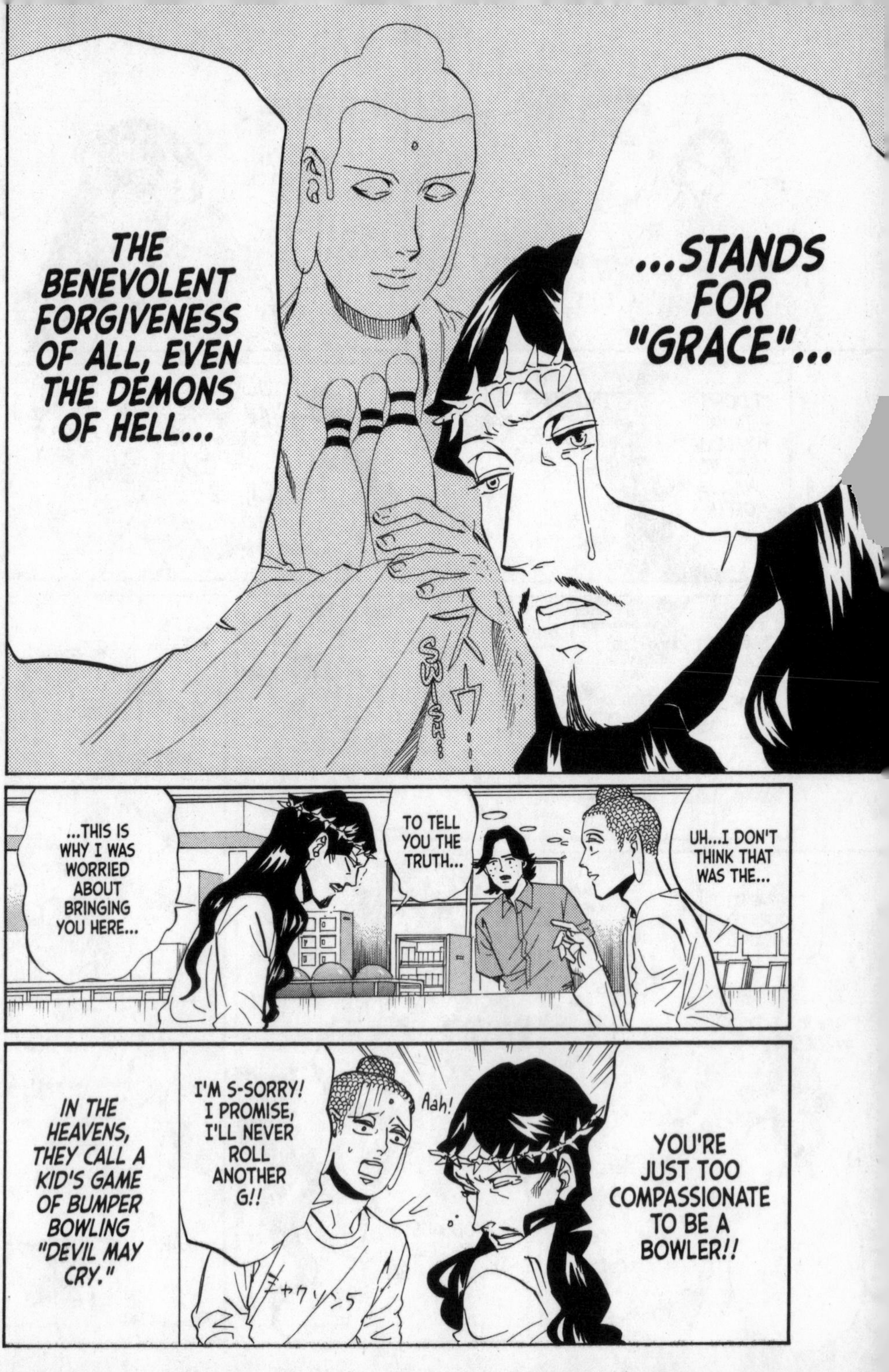
...STANDS FOR "GRACE"...
THE BENEVOLENT FORGIVENESS OF ALL, EVEN THE DEMONS OF HELL...
SWISH
UH...I DON'T THINK THAT WAS THE...
TO TELL YOU THE TRUTH...
...THIS IS WHY I WAS WORRIED ABOUT BRINGING YOU HERE...
YOU'RE JUST TOO COMPASSIONATE TO BE A BOWLER!!
Aah!
I'M S-SORRY! I PROMISE, I'LL NEVER ROLL ANOTHER G!!
IN THE HEAVENS, THEY CALL A KID'S GAME OF BUMPER BOWLING "DEVIL MAY CRY."

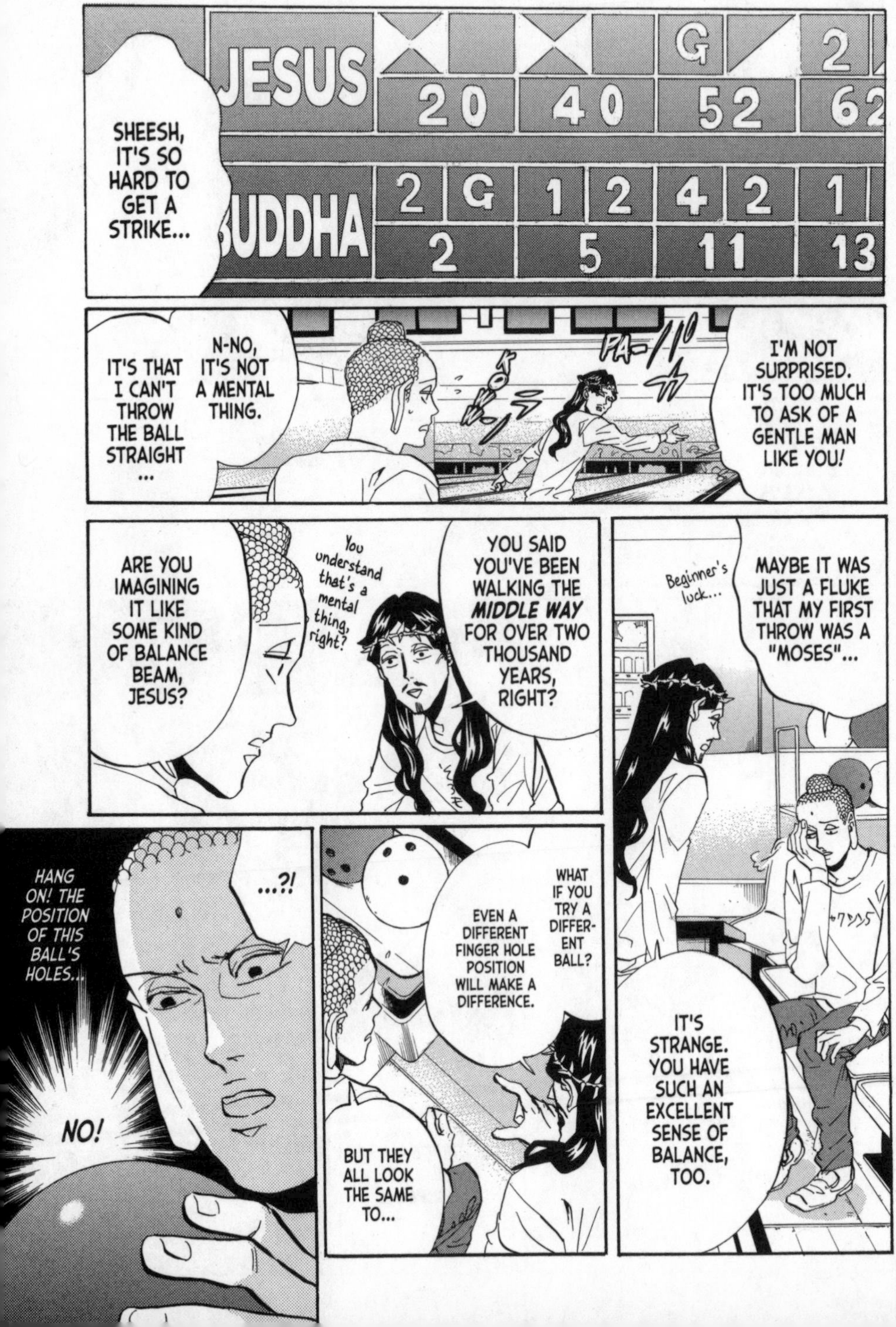
JESUS
G
2
20
40
52
62
BUDDHA
2 G 1 2 4 2 1
2
5
11
13
SHEESH, IT'S SO HARD TO GET A STRIKE...
I'M NOT SURPRISED. IT'S TOO MUCH TO ASK OF A GENTLE MAN LIKE YOU!
PA-!!
KON
N-NO, IT'S NOT A MENTAL THING.
IT'S THAT I CAN'T THROW THE BALL STRAIGHT...
MAYBE IT WAS JUST A FLUKE THAT MY FIRST THROW WAS A "MOSES"...
Beginner's luck...
IT'S STRANGE. YOU HAVE SUCH AN EXCELLENT SENSE OF BALANCE, TOO.
YOU SAID YOU'VE BEEN WALKING THE *MIDDLE WAY* FOR OVER TWO THOUSAND YEARS, RIGHT?
You understand that's a mental thing, right?
ARE YOU IMAGINING IT LIKE SOME KIND OF BALANCE BEAM, JESUS?
WHAT IF YOU TRY A DIFFERENT BALL?
EVEN A DIFFERENT FINGER HOLE POSITION WILL MAKE A DIFFERENCE.
BUT THEY ALL LOOK THE SAME TO...
...?!
HANG ON! THE POSITION OF THIS BALL'S HOLES...
NO!

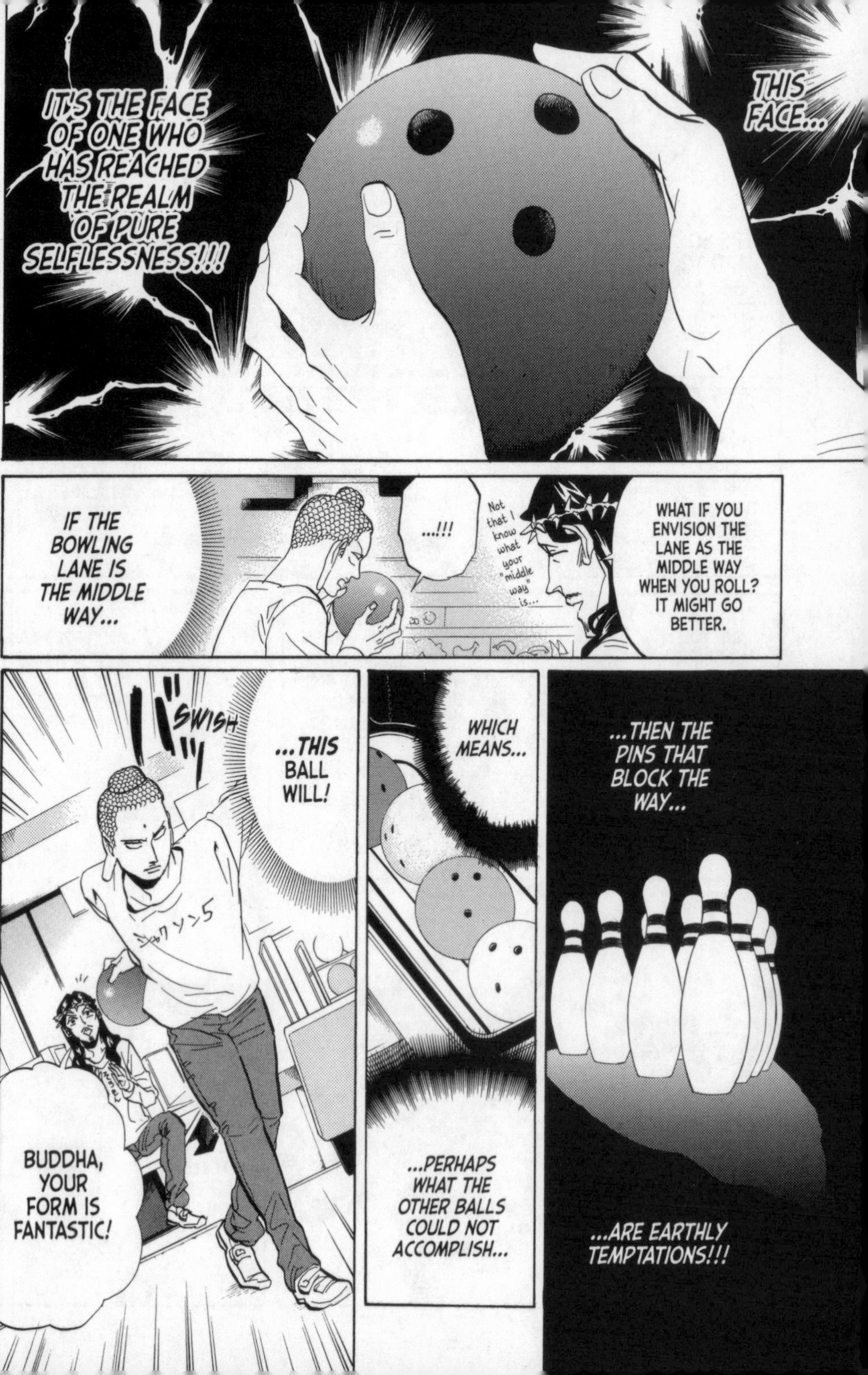
THIS FACE...
IT'S THE FACE OF ONE WHO HAS REACHED THE REALM OF PURE SELFLESSNESS!!!
WHAT IF YOU ENVISION THE LANE AS THE MIDDLE WAY WHEN YOU ROLL? IT MIGHT GO BETTER.
Not that I know what your "middle way" is...
...!!!
IF THE BOWLING LANE IS THE MIDDLE WAY...
...THEN THE PINS THAT BLOCK THE WAY...
...ARE EARTHLY TEMPTATIONS!!!
WHICH MEANS...
...PERHAPS WHAT THE OTHER BALLS COULD NOT ACCOMPLISH...
...THIS BALL WILL!
SWISH
BUDDHA, YOUR FORM IS FANTASTIC!

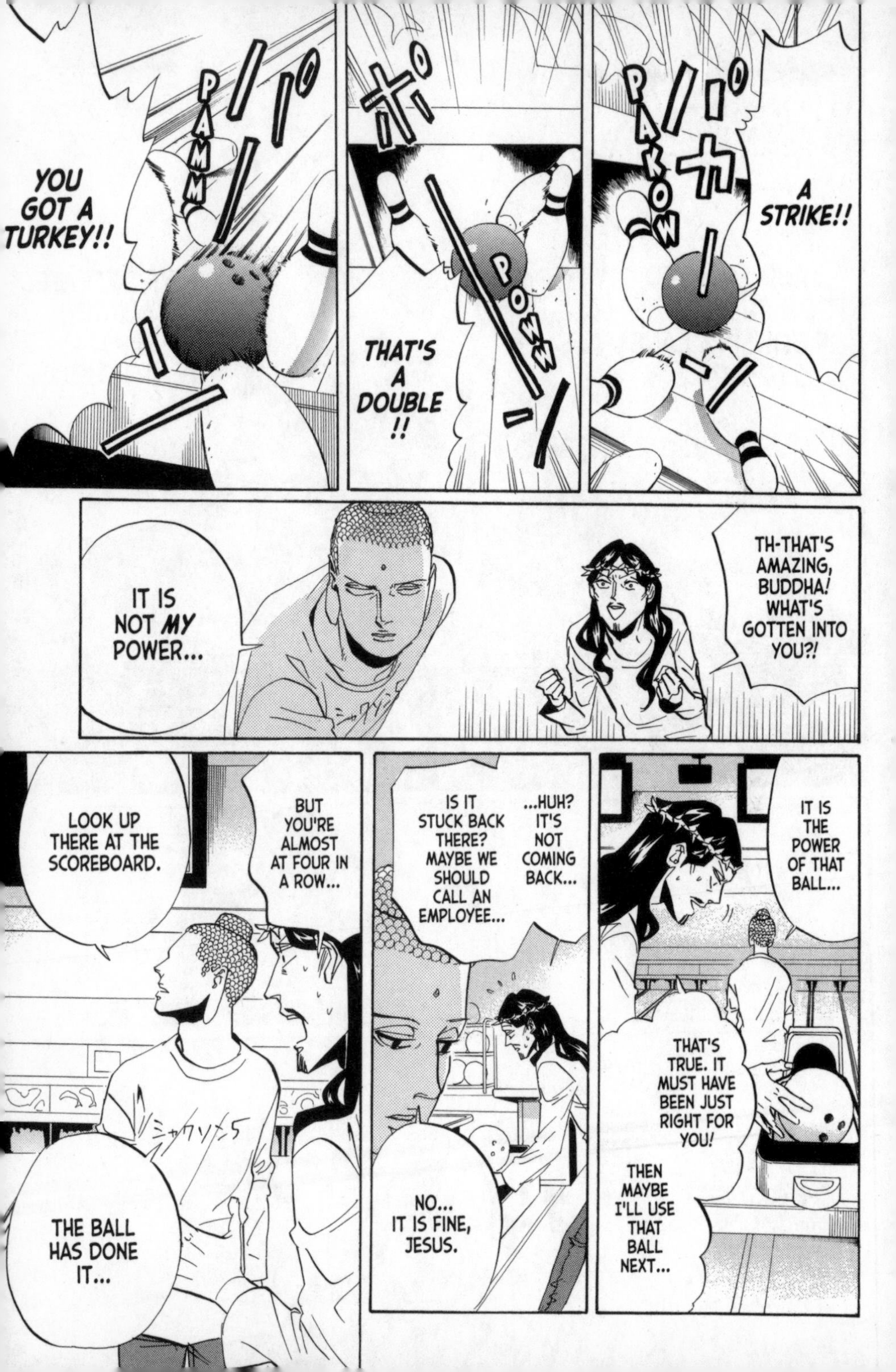
PAKOW
A STRIKE!!
POWW
THAT'S A DOUBLE!!
PAMM
YOU GOT A TURKEY!!
TH-THAT'S AMAZING, BUDDHA! WHAT'S GOTTEN INTO YOU?!
IT IS NOT MY POWER...
IT IS THE POWER OF THAT BALL...
THAT'S TRUE. IT MUST HAVE BEEN JUST RIGHT FOR YOU!
THEN MAYBE I'LL USE THAT BALL NEXT...
...HUH? IT'S NOT COMING BACK...
IS IT STUCK BACK THERE? MAYBE WE SHOULD CALL AN EMPLOYEE...
NO... IT IS FINE, JESUS.
BUT YOU'RE ALMOST AT FOUR IN A ROW...
LOOK UP THERE AT THE SCOREBOARD.
THE BALL HAS DONE IT...

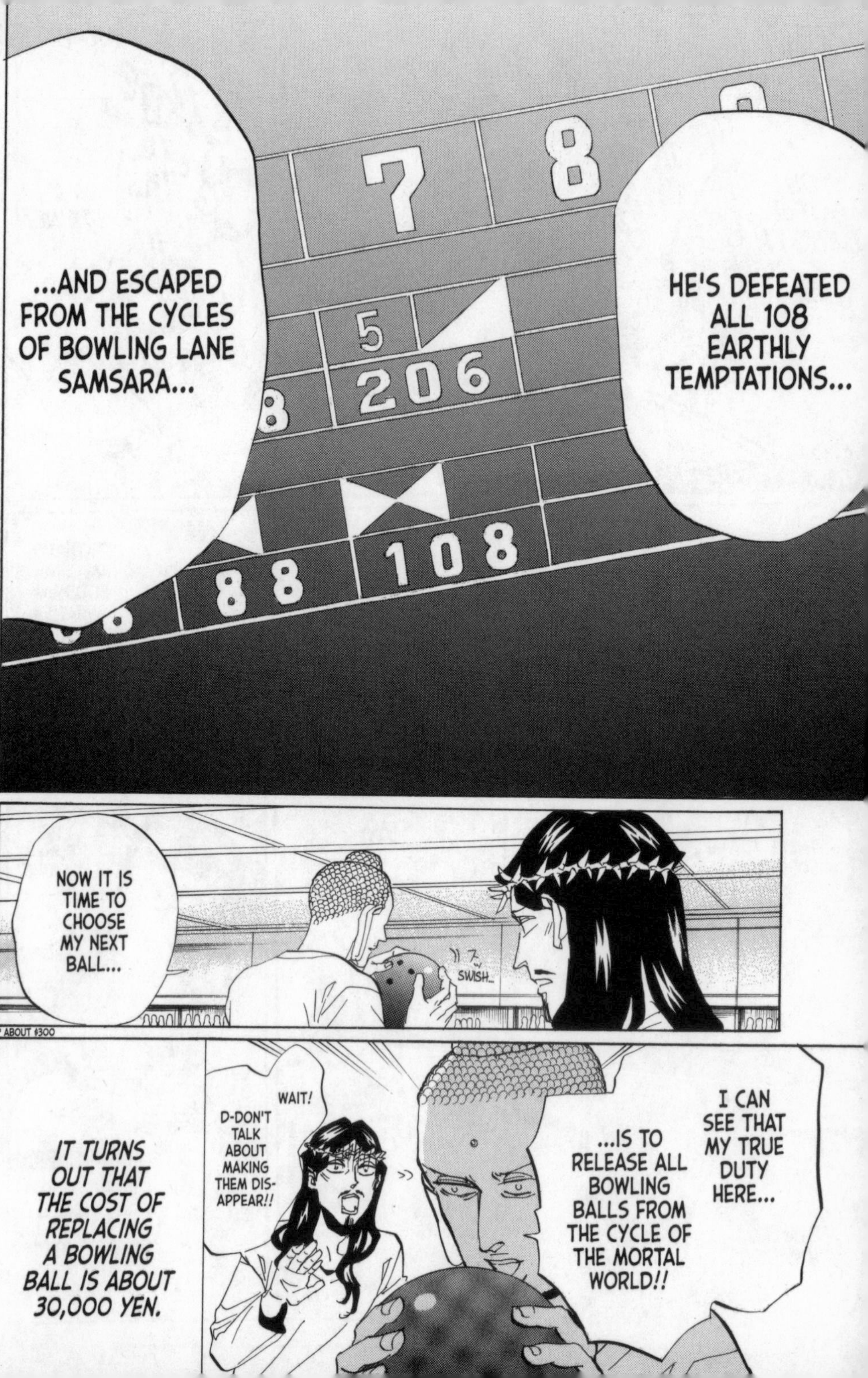
HE'S DEFEATED ALL 108 EARTHLY TEMPTATIONS...
...AND ESCAPED FROM THE CYCLES OF BOWLING LANE SAMSARA...
NOW IT IS TIME TO CHOOSE MY NEXT BALL...
SWISH...
I CAN SEE THAT MY TRUE DUTY HERE...
...IS TO RELEASE ALL BOWLING BALLS FROM THE CYCLE OF THE MORTAL WORLD!!
WAIT!
D-DON'T TALK ABOUT MAKING THEM DIS-APPEAR!!
IT TURNS OUT THAT THE COST OF REPLACING A BOWLING BALL IS ABOUT 30,000 YEN.

* ABOUT $300

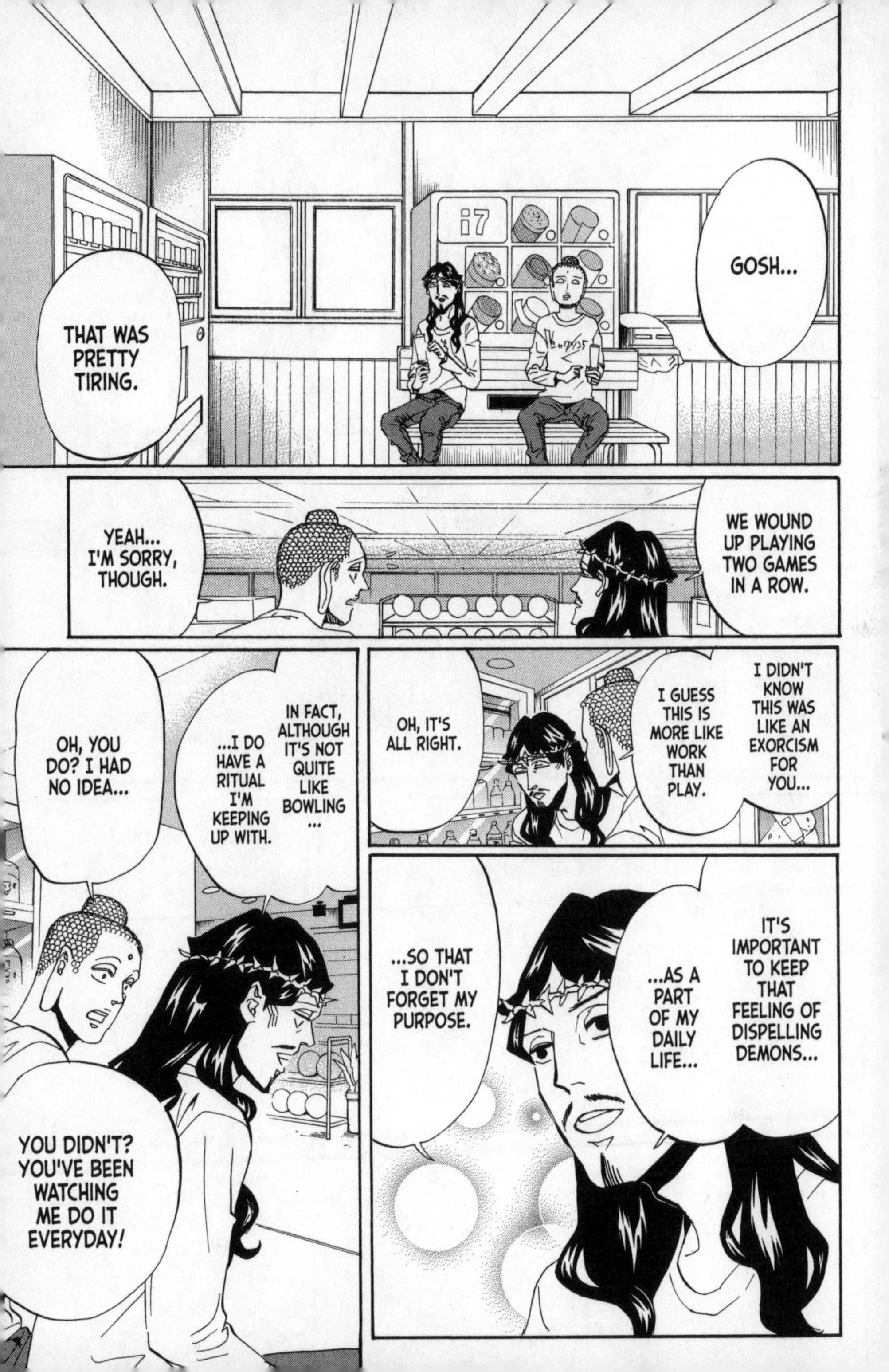
GOSH...
THAT WAS PRETTY TIRING.
WE WOUND UP PLAYING TWO GAMES IN A ROW.
YEAH... I'M SORRY, THOUGH.
I DIDN'T KNOW THIS WAS LIKE AN EXORCISM FOR YOU...
I GUESS THIS IS MORE LIKE WORK THAN PLAY.
OH, IT'S ALL RIGHT.
IT'S IMPORTANT TO KEEP THAT FEELING OF DISPELLING DEMONS...
...AS A PART OF MY DAILY LIFE...
...SO THAT I DON'T FORGET MY PURPOSE.
IN FACT, ALTHOUGH IT'S NOT QUITE LIKE BOWLING ...
...I DO HAVE A RITUAL I'M KEEPING UP WITH.
OH, YOU DO? I HAD NO IDEA...
YOU DIDN'T? YOU'VE BEEN WATCHING ME DO IT EVERYDAY!

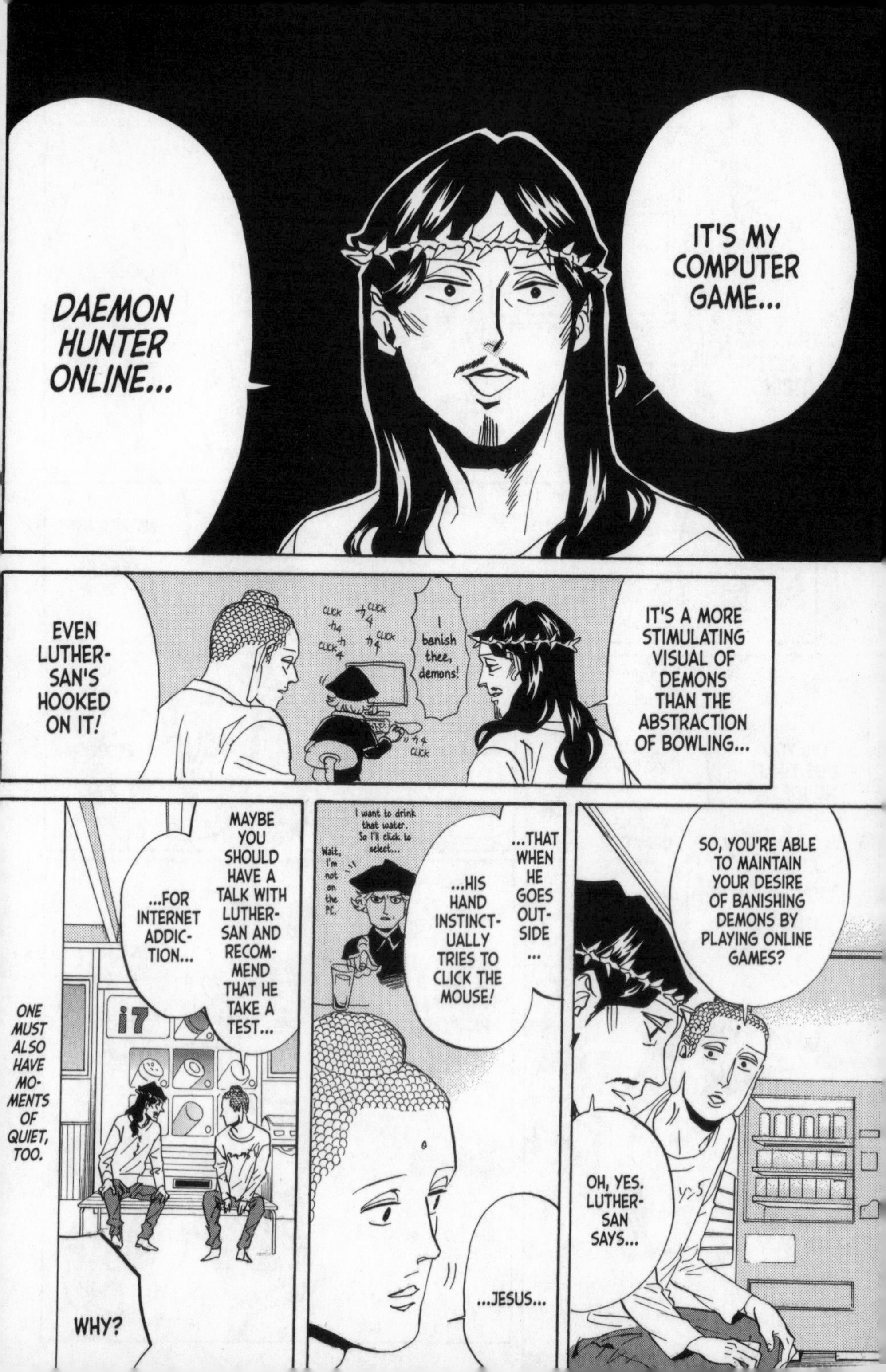
IT'S MY COMPUTER GAME...
DAEMON HUNTER ONLINE...
IT'S A MORE STIMULATING VISUAL OF DEMONS THAN THE ABSTRACTION OF BOWLING...
CLICK
I banish thee, demons!
CLICK
CLICK
CLICK
CLICK
EVEN LUTHER-SAN'S HOOKED ON IT!
SO, YOU'RE ABLE TO MAINTAIN YOUR DESIRE OF BANISHING DEMONS BY PLAYING ONLINE GAMES?
OH, YES. LUTHER-SAN SAYS...
...THAT WHEN HE GOES OUT-SIDE ...
...HIS HAND INSTINCT-UALLY TRIES TO CLICK THE MOUSE!
I want to drink that water. So I'll click to select...
Wait, I'm not on the PC.
...JESUS...
MAYBE YOU SHOULD HAVE A TALK WITH LUTHER-SAN AND RECOM-MEND THAT HE TAKE A TEST...
...FOR INTERNET ADDIC-TION...
ONE MUST ALSO HAVE MO-MENTS OF QUIET, TOO.
WHY?

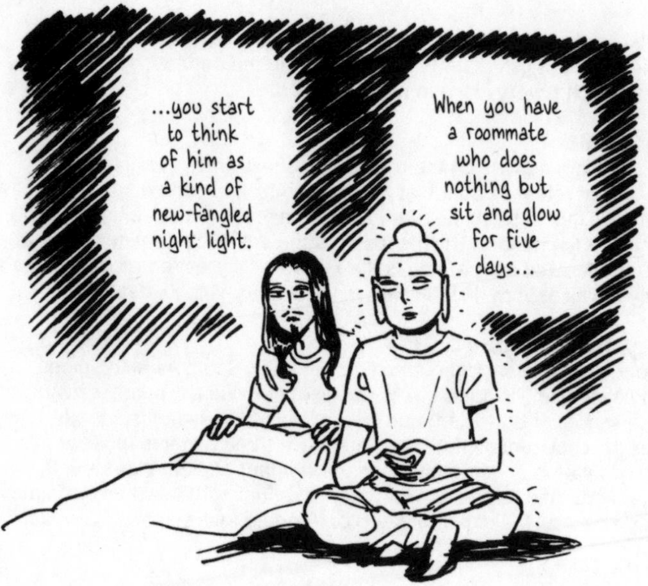
When you have a roommate who does nothing but sit and glow for five days...
...you start to think of him as a kind of new-fangled night light.

CHAPTER 52 TRANSLATION NOTES

Solomon, page 156
A king of ancient Israel and the son of David. He oversaw the most opulent period of the kingdom, and in the teachings and depictions of the Bible, he is seen as both a wise leader and an example of the sin of lavish wealth.

Shakuson, page 156
An example of one of the many Japanese titles of respect for the Buddha, thus turning this shirt into a pun on the musical group, Jackson 5.

Luther, page 159
Martin Luther, the reformer of the church who founded the Protestant movement in the 16th century AD.

Hasegawa, page 159
A retail store chain that specializes in Buddhist altars, gravestones, and other religious supplies.

Moses, page 163
The leader of the Israelites in Egypt in the book of Exodus, who became a prophet after an angel of the Lord spoke to him from within a burning bush. Moses was chosen to lead the Israelite slaves out of Egypt into Canaan, and with the Egyptians pursuing them to the edge of the Red Sea, Moses raised his staff and called upon the power of God to part the Red Sea so that the Israelites could pass safely.

Grace, page 165
In the original Japanese, the English letter G is compared to the Japanese word jihi (mercy or compassion) which is very close in pronunciation.

Middle Way, page 166
A central concept in Buddhism describing the avoidance of extremes in a variety of contexts. It commonly either refers to Buddhist practices, which in certain versions of the Buddha's biography are unique in being neither intensely ascetic nor hedonistic, or the Buddhism philosophy of reincarnation, which considers the self to be continuous as a result of the actions and effects of karma, and is the middle of the extremes of positing an eternal soul or a purely physical body, in which life ends entirely with its death.

108 earthly temptations, page 169
The number 108 appears in many sacred contexts throughout South Asian religions such as Buddhism and Hinduism. Though the methods of deriving the number might differ depending on the school of Buddhism and culture behind it, in Japan it is generally accepted that there are six root senses that can each have three aspects (positive, negative, neutral) and two states of being attached to or detached from pleasure, then three worlds of past, present, and future. All multiplied, this forms 108 distinct temptations or attachments that represent all feelings that keep one rooted to the cycle of Samsara.

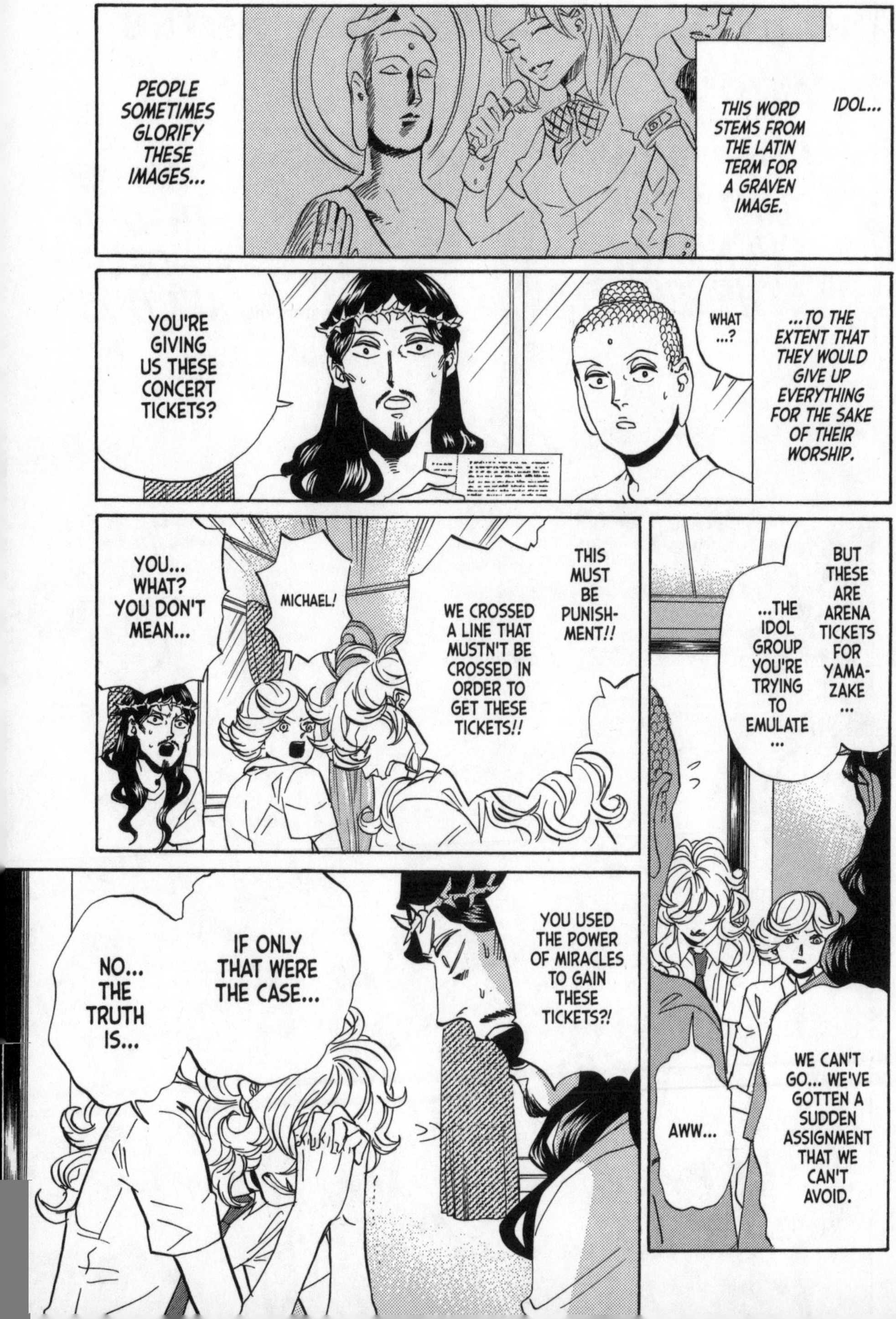
IDOL...
THIS WORD STEMS FROM THE LATIN TERM FOR A GRAVEN IMAGE.
PEOPLE SOMETIMES GLORIFY THESE IMAGES...
...TO THE EXTENT THAT THEY WOULD GIVE UP EVERYTHING FOR THE SAKE OF THEIR WORSHIP.
WHAT ...?
YOU'RE GIVING US THESE CONCERT TICKETS?
BUT THESE ARE ARENA TICKETS FOR YAMA-ZAKE ...
...THE IDOL GROUP YOU'RE TRYING TO EMULATE ...
WE CAN'T GO... WE'VE GOTTEN A SUDDEN ASSIGNMENT THAT WE CAN'T AVOID.
AWW...
THIS MUST BE PUNISH-MENT!!
WE CROSSED A LINE THAT MUSTN'T BE CROSSED IN ORDER TO GET THESE TICKETS!!
MICHAEL!
YOU... WHAT? YOU DON'T MEAN...
YOU USED THE POWER OF MIRACLES TO GAIN THESE TICKETS?!
IF ONLY THAT WERE THE CASE...
NO... THE TRUTH IS...

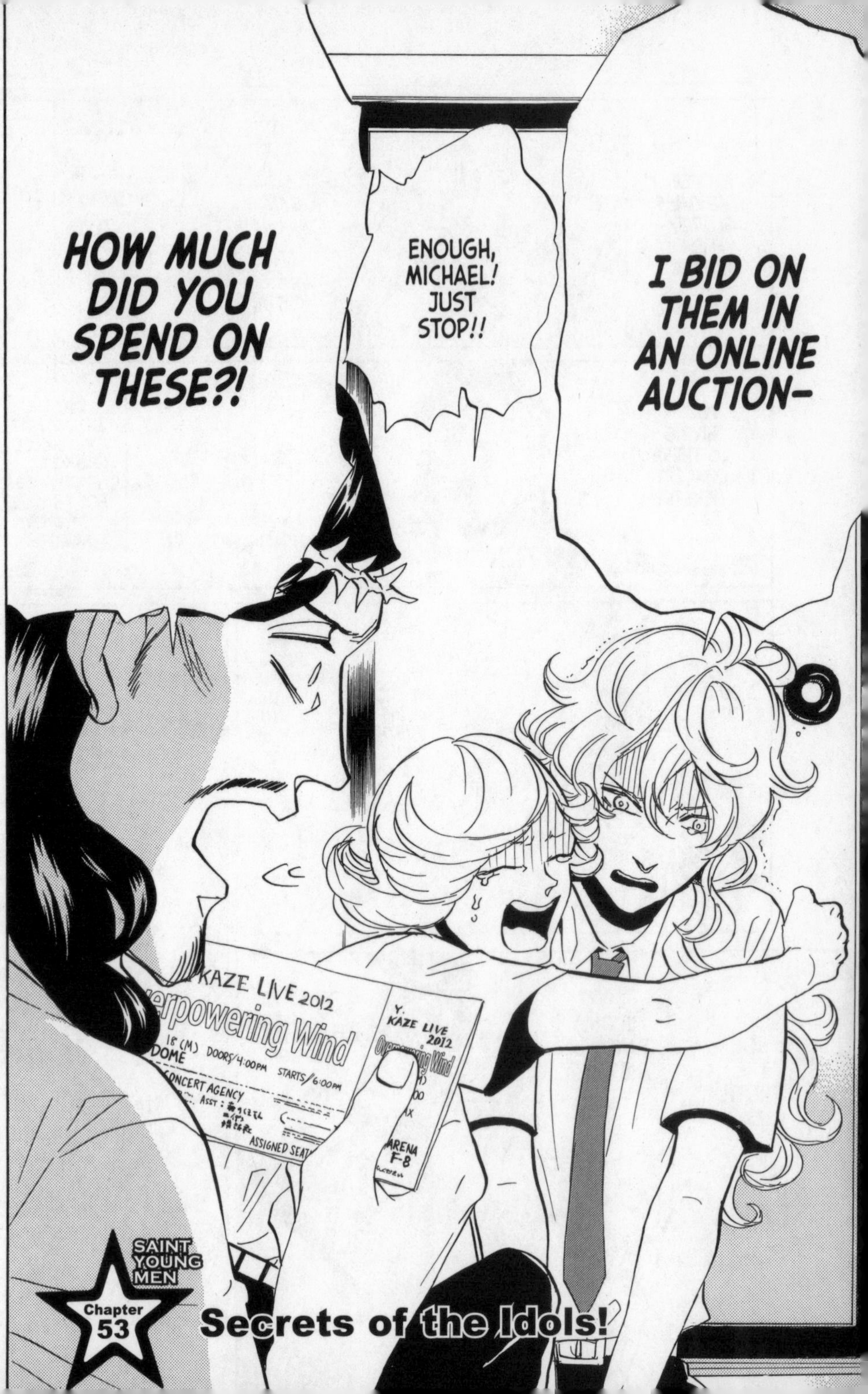

I BID ON THEM IN AN ONLINE AUCTION-
ENOUGH, MICHAEL! JUST STOP!!
HOW MUCH DID YOU SPEND ON THESE?!
Y. KAZE LIVE 2012
ARENA F-8
KAZE LIVE 2012
18 (M) DOORS/4:00PM STARTS/6:00PM
DOME
CONCERT AGENCY
SAINT YOUNG MEN
Chapter 53
Secrets of the Idols!

BUDDHA
WHEN THE SHAMPOO IS RUNNING LOW, HE SQUIRTS SOME WATER INSIDE AND SHAKES IT UP TO MAKE IT LAST. IT'S KIND OF EMBARRASSING.

JESUS
WHEN HE OPENS A CONTAINER OF ICE CREAM, HE SCOOPS THE STUFF OFF THE UNDERSIDE OF THE LID AND EATS THAT FIRST. IT'S KIND OF EMBARRASSING.

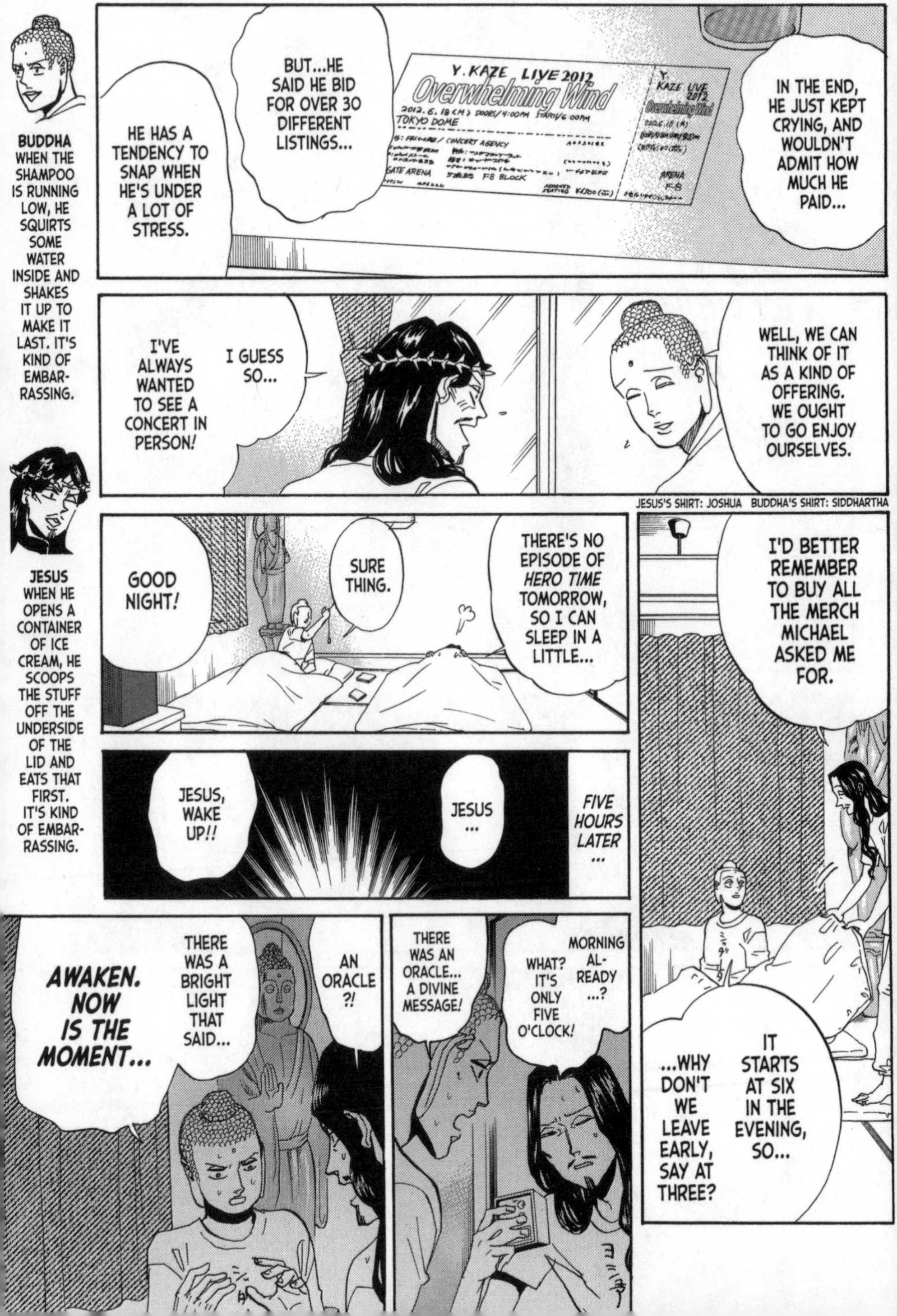
IN THE END, HE JUST KEPT CRYING, AND WOULDN'T ADMIT HOW MUCH HE PAID...
Y. KAZE LIVE 2012 Overwhelming Wind
2012. 6. 18 (M) DOORS/4:00PM START/6:00PM
TOKYO DOME
CONCERT AGENCY
GATE ARENA
F8 BLOCK
BUT...HE SAID HE BID FOR OVER 30 DIFFERENT LISTINGS...
HE HAS A TENDENCY TO SNAP WHEN HE'S UNDER A LOT OF STRESS.
WELL, WE CAN THINK OF IT AS A KIND OF OFFERING. WE OUGHT TO GO ENJOY OURSELVES.
I GUESS SO...
I'VE ALWAYS WANTED TO SEE A CONCERT IN PERSON!
JESUS'S SHIRT: JOSHUA BUDDHA'S SHIRT: SIDDHARTHA
I'D BETTER REMEMBER TO BUY ALL THE MERCH MICHAEL ASKED ME FOR.
IT STARTS AT SIX IN THE EVENING, SO...
...WHY DON'T WE LEAVE EARLY, SAY AT THREE?
THERE'S NO EPISODE OF HERO TIME TOMORROW, SO I CAN SLEEP IN A LITTLE...
SURE THING.
GOOD NIGHT!
FIVE HOURS LATER...
JESUS...
JESUS, WAKE UP!!
MORNING ALREADY...?
WHAT? IT'S ONLY FIVE O'CLOCK!
THERE WAS AN ORACLE... A DIVINE MESSAGE!
AN ORACLE?!
THERE WAS A BRIGHT LIGHT THAT SAID...
AWAKEN. NOW IS THE MOMENT...

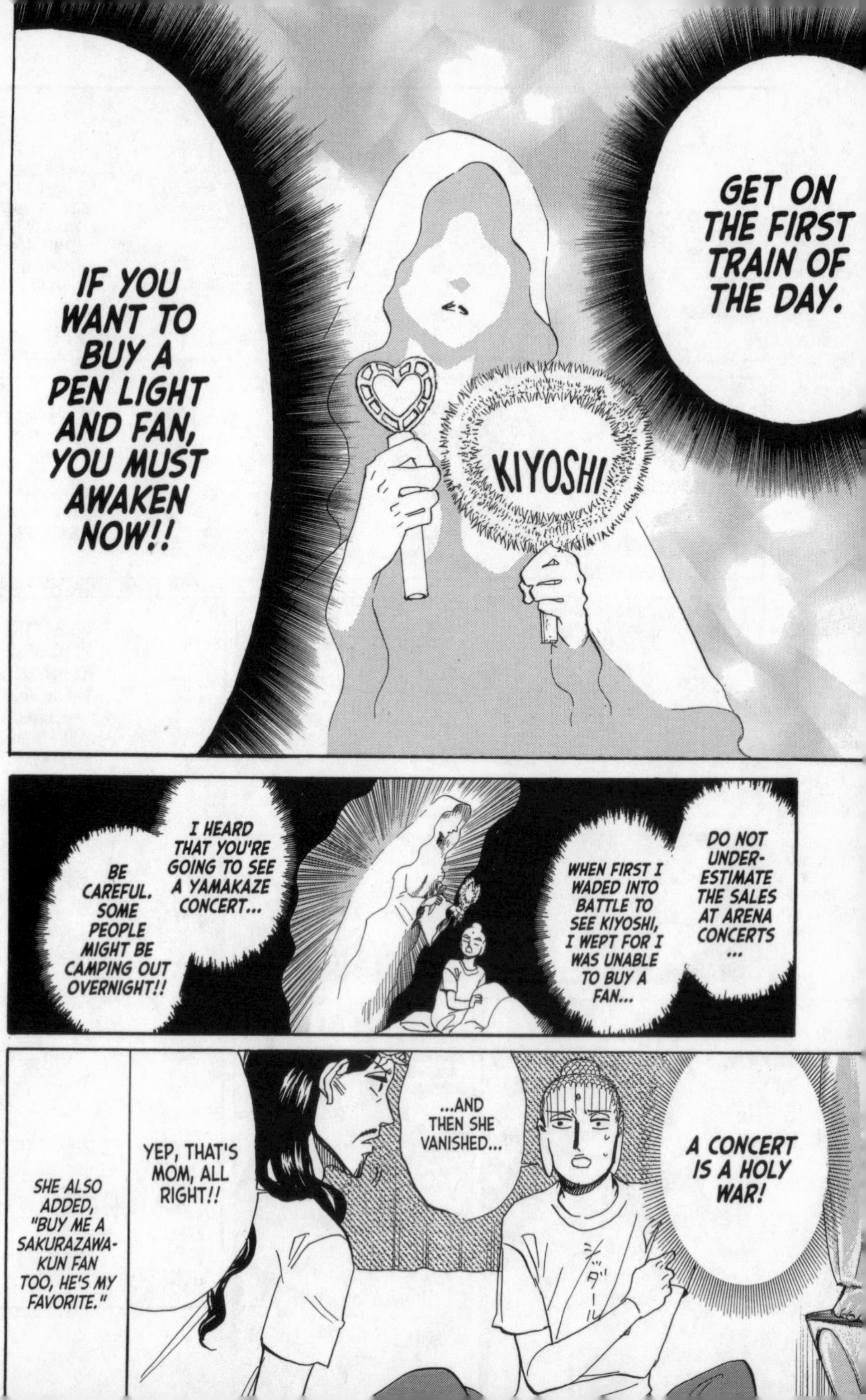
GET ON THE FIRST TRAIN OF THE DAY.
KIYOSHI
IF YOU WANT TO BUY A PEN LIGHT AND FAN, YOU MUST AWAKEN NOW!!
DO NOT UNDER-ESTIMATE THE SALES AT ARENA CONCERTS ...
WHEN FIRST I WADED INTO BATTLE TO SEE KIYOSHI, I WEPT FOR I WAS UNABLE TO BUY A FAN...
I HEARD THAT YOU'RE GOING TO SEE A YAMAKAZE CONCERT...
BE CAREFUL. SOME PEOPLE MIGHT BE CAMPING OUT OVERNIGHT!!
A CONCERT IS A HOLY WAR!
...AND THEN SHE VANISHED...
YEP, THAT'S MOM, ALL RIGHT!!
SHE ALSO ADDED, "BUY ME A SAKURAZAWA-KUN FAN TOO, HE'S MY FAVORITE."

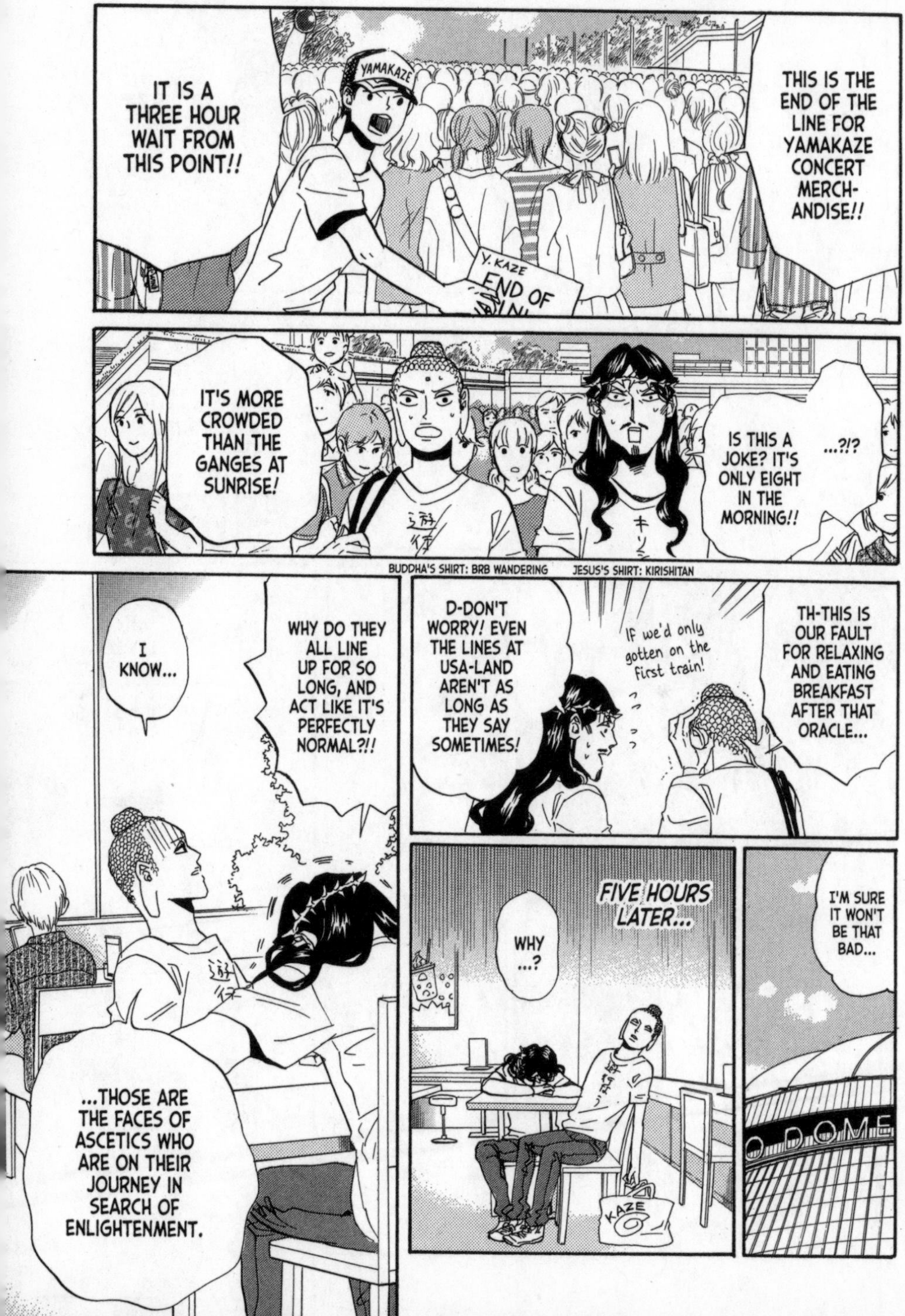
THIS IS THE END OF THE LINE FOR YAMAKAZE CONCERT MERCH-ANDISE!!
YAMAKAZE
IT IS A THREE HOUR WAIT FROM THIS POINT!!
Y. KAZE END OF
...?!?
IS THIS A JOKE? IT'S ONLY EIGHT IN THE MORNING!!
IT'S MORE CROWDED THAN THE GANGES AT SUNRISE!
BUDDHA'S SHIRT: BRB WANDERING
JESUS'S SHIRT: KIRISHITAN
TH-THIS IS OUR FAULT FOR RELAXING AND EATING BREAKFAST AFTER THAT ORACLE...
If we'd only gotten on the first train!
D-DON'T WORRY! EVEN THE LINES AT USA-LAND AREN'T AS LONG AS THEY SAY SOMETIMES!
I'M SURE IT WON'T BE THAT BAD...
DOME
FIVE HOURS LATER...
WHY ...?
KAZE
WHY DO THEY ALL LINE UP FOR SO LONG, AND ACT LIKE IT'S PERFECTLY NORMAL?!!
I KNOW...
...THOSE ARE THE FACES OF ASCETICS WHO ARE ON THEIR JOURNEY IN SEARCH OF ENLIGHTENMENT.

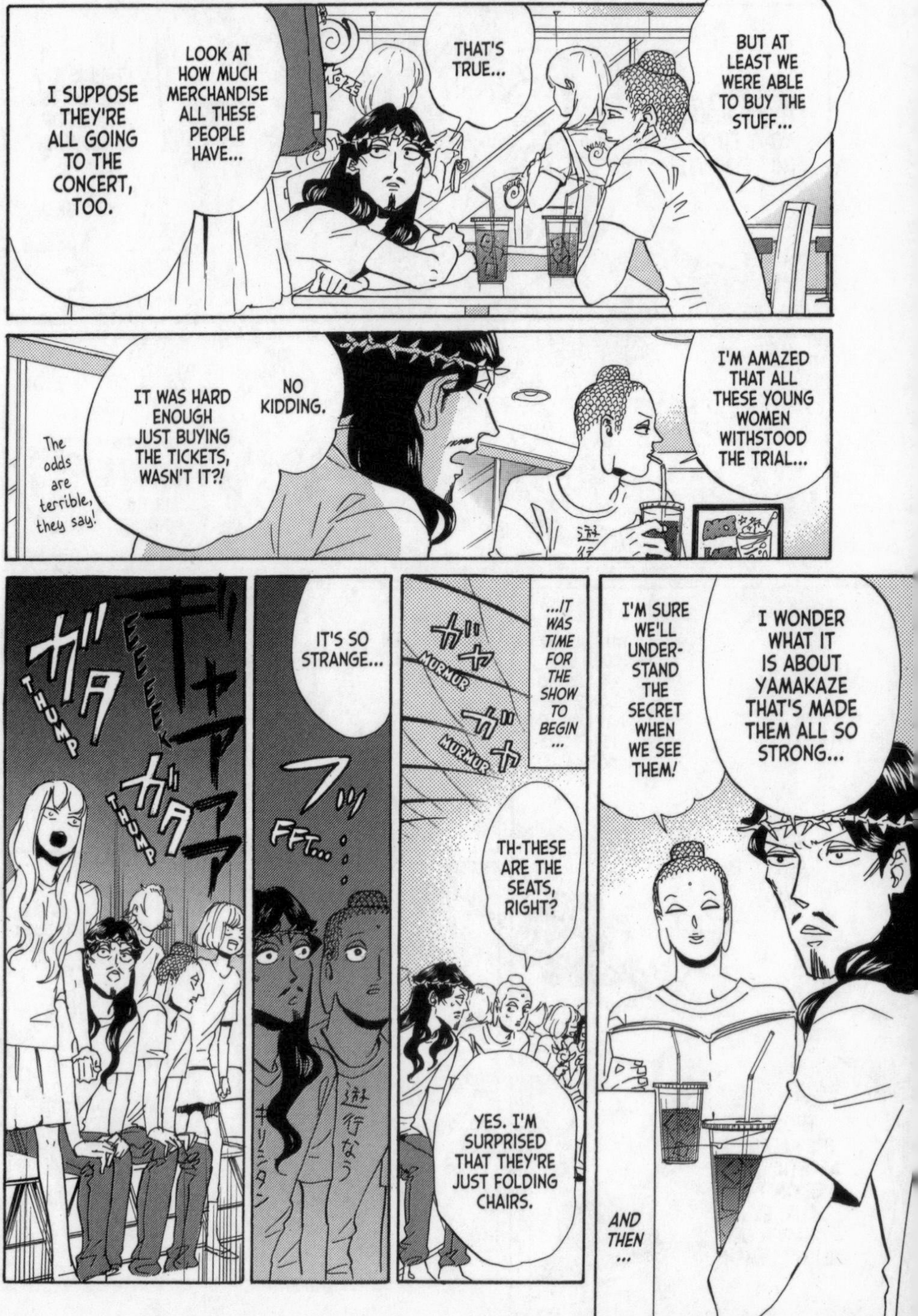
BUT AT LEAST WE WERE ABLE TO BUY THE STUFF...
THAT'S TRUE...
LOOK AT HOW MUCH MERCHANDISE ALL THESE PEOPLE HAVE...
I SUPPOSE THEY'RE ALL GOING TO THE CONCERT, TOO.
I'M AMAZED THAT ALL THESE YOUNG WOMEN WITHSTOOD THE TRIAL...
NO KIDDING.
IT WAS HARD ENOUGH JUST BUYING THE TICKETS, WASN'T IT?!
The odds are terrible, they say!
I WONDER WHAT IT IS ABOUT YAMAKAZE THAT'S MADE THEM ALL SO STRONG...
I'M SURE WE'LL UNDER-STAND THE SECRET WHEN WE SEE THEM!
AND THEN...
...IT WAS TIME FOR THE SHOW TO BEGIN...
ガヤ
MURMUR
ガヤ
MURMUR
TH-THESE ARE THE SEATS, RIGHT?
YES. I'M SURPRISED THAT THEY'RE JUST FOLDING CHAIRS.
IT'S SO STRANGE...
フッ
FFT...
逝行なう
キリシタン
ギャアアア
EEEEEK
ガタ
THUMP
ガタ
THUMP

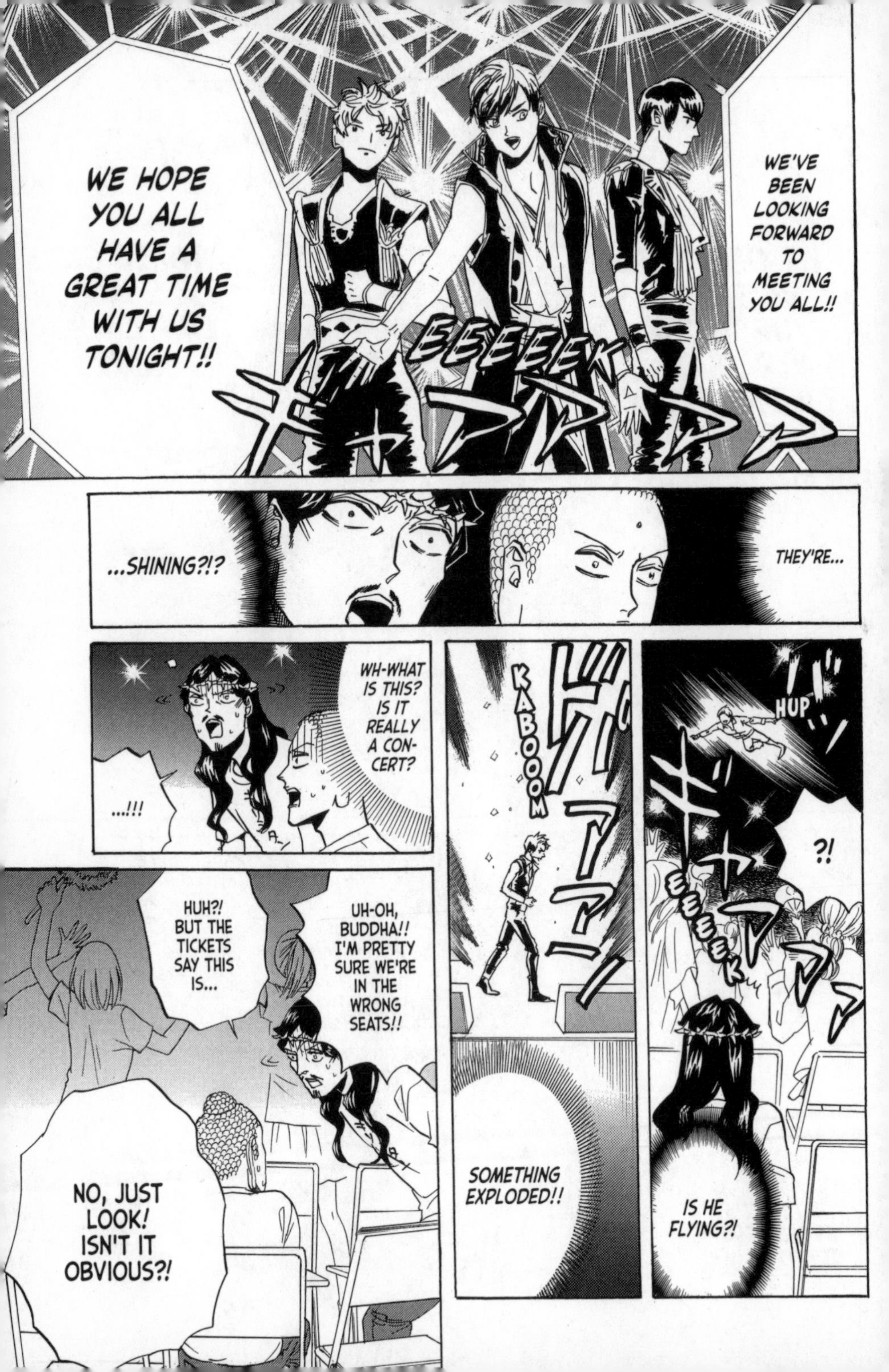
WE'VE BEEN LOOKING FORWARD TO MEETING YOU ALL!!
WE HOPE YOU ALL HAVE A GREAT TIME WITH US TONIGHT!!
EEEEEK
THEY'RE...
...SHINING?!?
HUP
?!
EEEEEK
IS HE FLYING?!
KABOOOM
SOMETHING EXPLODED!!
WH-WHAT IS THIS? IS IT REALLY A CONCERT?
...!!!
UH-OH, BUDDHA!! I'M PRETTY SURE WE'RE IN THE WRONG SEATS!!
HUH?! BUT THE TICKETS SAY THIS IS...
NO, JUST LOOK! ISN'T IT OBVIOUS?!

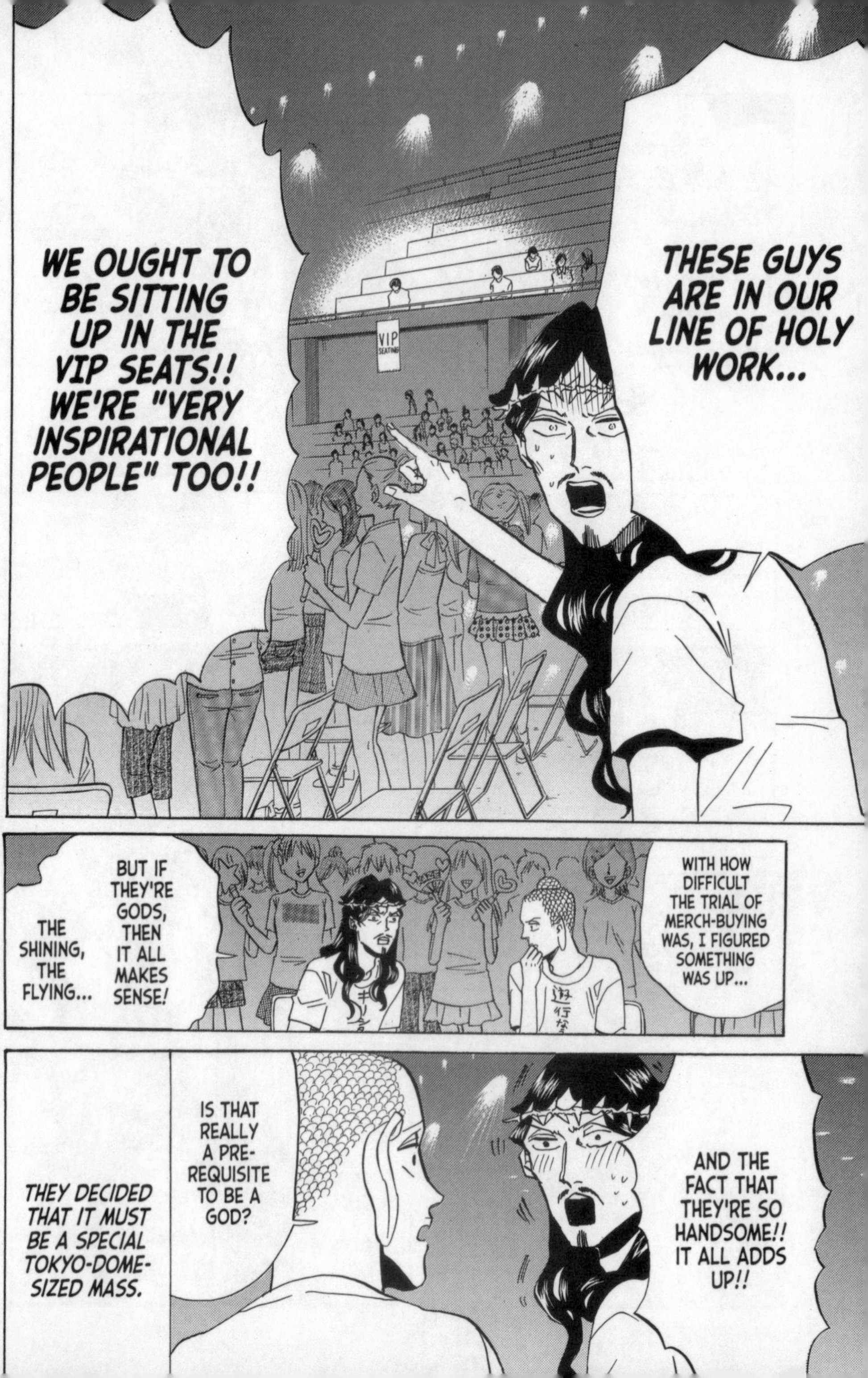
THESE GUYS ARE IN OUR LINE OF HOLY WORK...
WE OUGHT TO BE SITTING UP IN THE VIP SEATS!! WE'RE "VERY INSPIRATIONAL PEOPLE" TOO!!
VIP SEATING
WITH HOW DIFFICULT THE TRIAL OF MERCH-BUYING WAS, I FIGURED SOMETHING WAS UP...
BUT IF THEY'RE GODS, THEN IT ALL MAKES SENSE!
THE SHINING, THE FLYING...
AND THE FACT THAT THEY'RE SO HANDSOME!! IT ALL ADDS UP!!
IS THAT REALLY A PRE-REQUISITE TO BE A GOD?
THEY DECIDED THAT IT MUST BE A SPECIAL TOKYO-DOME-SIZED MASS.

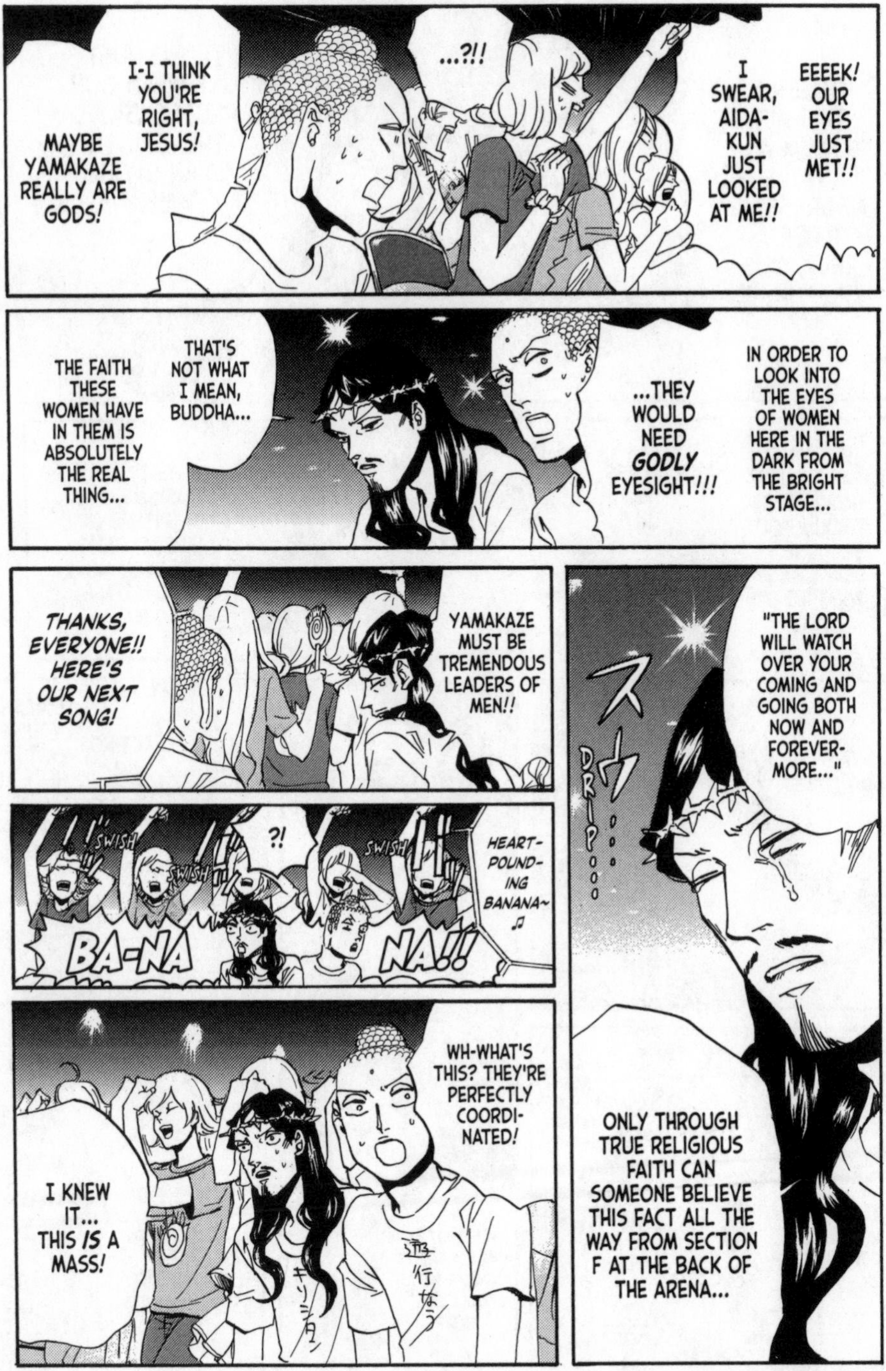
EEEEK! OUR EYES JUST MET!!
I SWEAR, AIDA-KUN JUST LOOKED AT ME!!
...?!!
I-I THINK YOU'RE RIGHT, JESUS!
MAYBE YAMAKAZE REALLY ARE GODS!
IN ORDER TO LOOK INTO THE EYES OF WOMEN HERE IN THE DARK FROM THE BRIGHT STAGE...
...THEY WOULD NEED GODLY EYESIGHT!!!
THAT'S NOT WHAT I MEAN, BUDDHA...
THE FAITH THESE WOMEN HAVE IN THEM IS ABSOLUTELY THE REAL THING...
"THE LORD WILL WATCH OVER YOUR COMING AND GOING BOTH NOW AND FOREVER-MORE..."
スゥ
DRIP...
ONLY THROUGH TRUE RELIGIOUS FAITH CAN SOMEONE BELIEVE THIS FACT ALL THE WAY FROM SECTION F AT THE BACK OF THE ARENA...
YAMAKAZE MUST BE TREMENDOUS LEADERS OF MEN!!
THANKS, EVERYONE!! HERE'S OUR NEXT SONG!
HEART-POUNDING BANANA~♫
SWISH
?!
SWISH
SWISH
BA-NA NA!!
WH-WHAT'S THIS? THEY'RE PERFECTLY COORDI-NATED!
I KNEW IT... THIS IS A MASS!

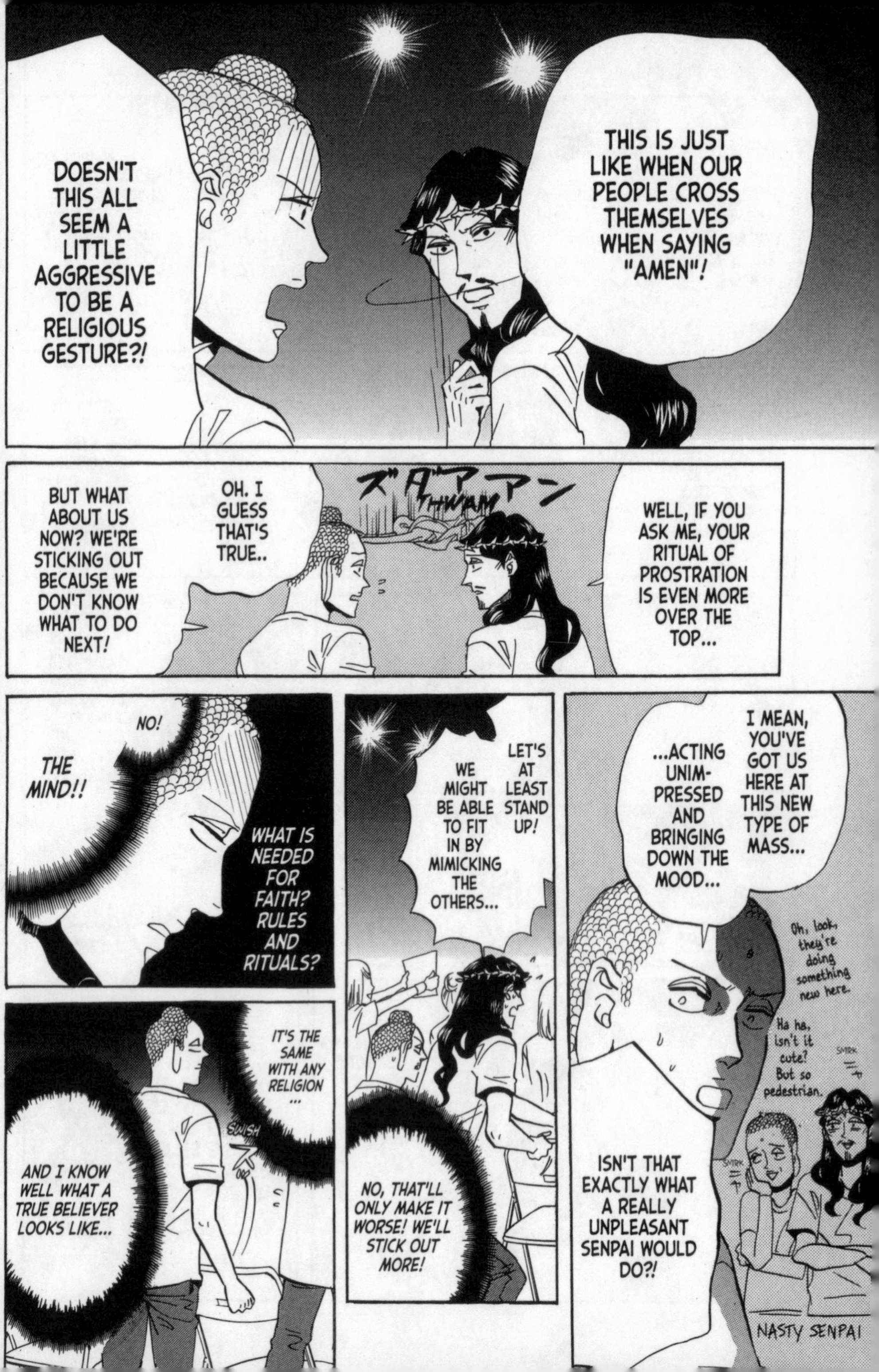
THIS IS JUST LIKE WHEN OUR PEOPLE CROSS THEMSELVES WHEN SAYING "AMEN"!
DOESN'T THIS ALL SEEM A LITTLE AGGRESSIVE TO BE A RELIGIOUS GESTURE?!
WELL, IF YOU ASK ME, YOUR RITUAL OF PROSTRATION IS EVEN MORE OVER THE TOP...
HWAM
OH. I GUESS THAT'S TRUE..
BUT WHAT ABOUT US NOW? WE'RE STICKING OUT BECAUSE WE DON'T KNOW WHAT TO DO NEXT!
I MEAN, YOU'VE GOT US HERE AT THIS NEW TYPE OF MASS...
...ACTING UNIM-PRESSED AND BRINGING DOWN THE MOOD...
Oh, look, they're doing something new here.
Ha ha, isn't it cute? But so pedestrian.
SMIRK
SMIRK
ISN'T THAT EXACTLY WHAT A REALLY UNPLEASANT SENPAI WOULD DO?!
NASTY SENPAI
LET'S AT LEAST STAND UP!
WE MIGHT BE ABLE TO FIT IN BY MIMICKING THE OTHERS...
NO, THAT'LL ONLY MAKE IT WORSE! WE'LL STICK OUT MORE!
NO!
THE MIND!!
WHAT IS NEEDED FOR FAITH? RULES AND RITUALS?
IT'S THE SAME WITH ANY RELIGION ...
SWISH
AND I KNOW WELL WHAT A TRUE BELIEVER LOOKS LIKE...

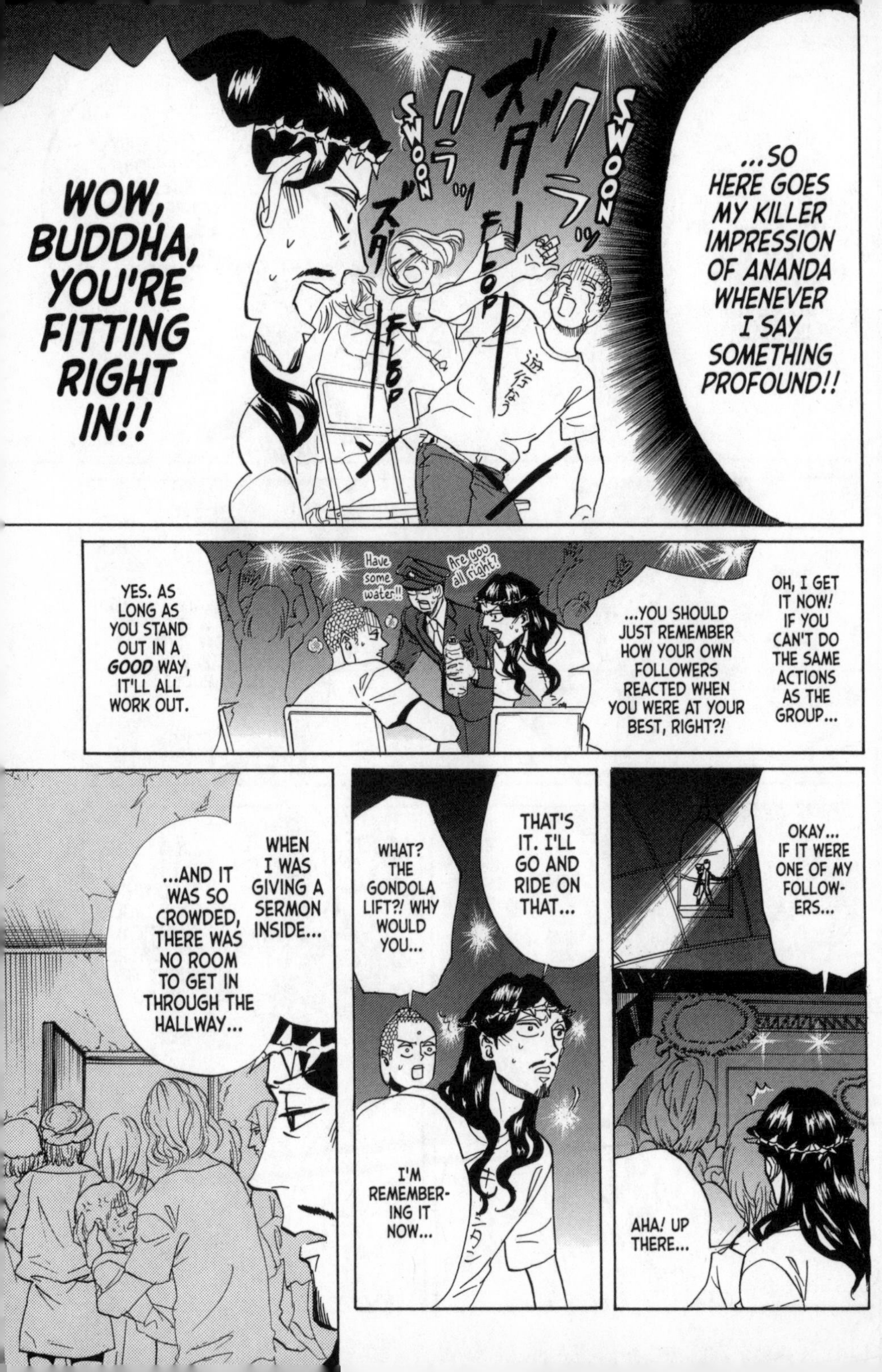
...SO HERE GOES MY KILLER IMPRESSION OF ANANDA WHENEVER I SAY SOMETHING PROFOUND!!
SWOON
SWOON
FLOP
FLOP
WOW, BUDDHA, YOU'RE FITTING RIGHT IN!!
OH, I GET IT NOW! IF YOU CAN'T DO THE SAME ACTIONS AS THE GROUP...
...YOU SHOULD JUST REMEMBER HOW YOUR OWN FOLLOWERS REACTED WHEN YOU WERE AT YOUR BEST, RIGHT?!
Are you all right?
Have some water!!
YES. AS LONG AS YOU STAND OUT IN A GOOD WAY, IT'LL ALL WORK OUT.
OKAY... IF IT WERE ONE OF MY FOLLOW-ERS...
AHA! UP THERE...
THAT'S IT. I'LL GO AND RIDE ON THAT...
WHAT? THE GONDOLA LIFT?! WHY WOULD YOU...
I'M REMEMBER-ING IT NOW...
WHEN I WAS GIVING A SERMON INSIDE...
...AND IT WAS SO CROWDED, THERE WAS NO ROOM TO GET IN THROUGH THE HALLWAY...

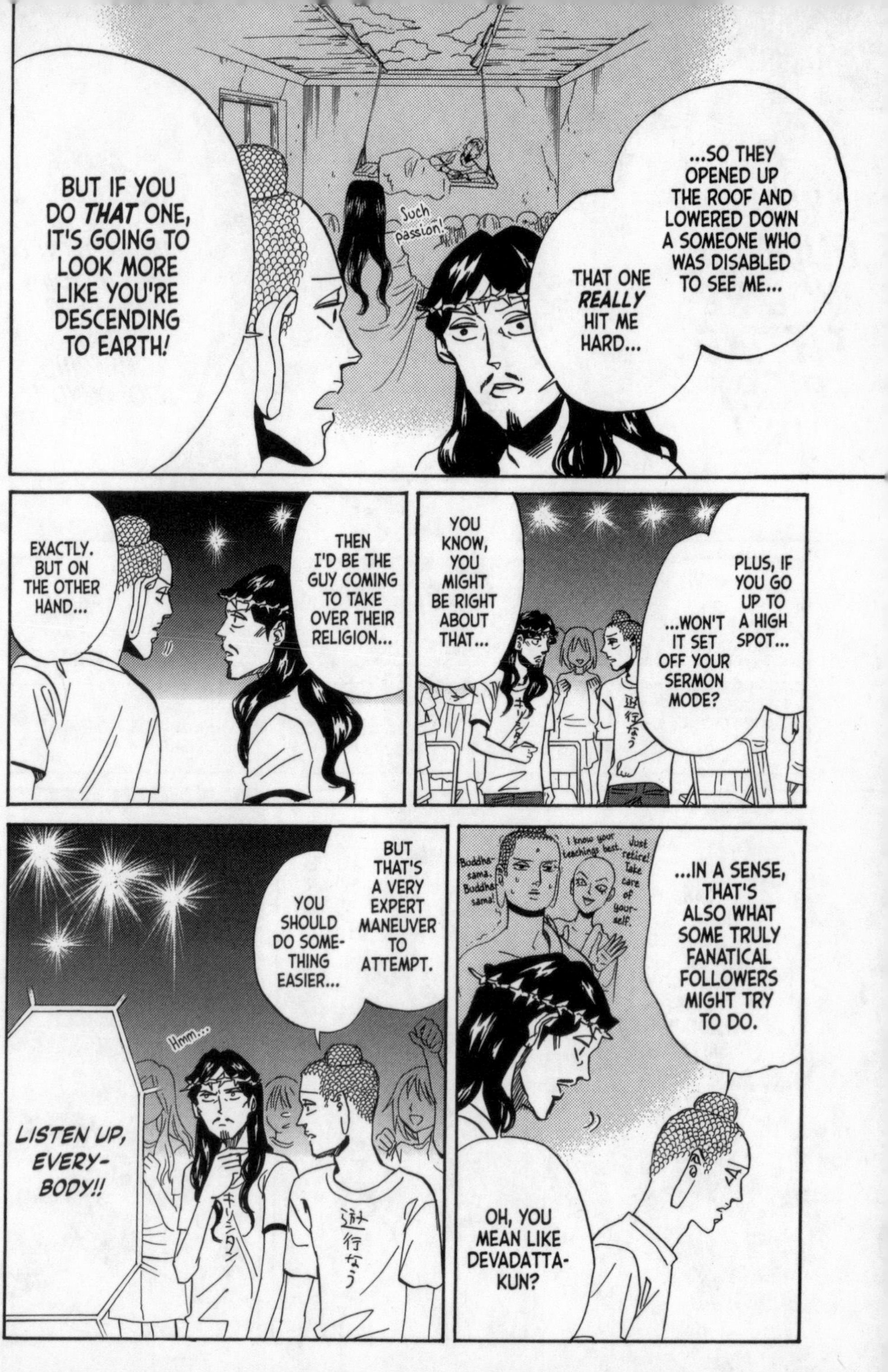
...SO THEY OPENED UP THE ROOF AND LOWERED DOWN A SOMEONE WHO WAS DISABLED TO SEE ME...
THAT ONE *REALLY* HIT ME HARD...
Such passion!
BUT IF YOU DO *THAT* ONE, IT'S GOING TO LOOK MORE LIKE YOU'RE DESCENDING TO EARTH!
PLUS, IF YOU GO UP TO A HIGH SPOT...
...WON'T IT SET OFF YOUR SERMON MODE?
YOU KNOW, YOU MIGHT BE RIGHT ABOUT THAT...
THEN I'D BE THE GUY COMING TO TAKE OVER THEIR RELIGION...
EXACTLY. BUT ON THE OTHER HAND...
...IN A SENSE, THAT'S ALSO WHAT SOME TRULY FANATICAL FOLLOWERS MIGHT TRY TO DO.
Just retire! Take care of your-self.
I know your teachings best.
Buddha-sama. Buddha-sama!
OH, YOU MEAN LIKE DEVADATTA-KUN?
BUT THAT'S A VERY EXPERT MANEUVER TO ATTEMPT.
YOU SHOULD DO SOME-THING EASIER...
Hmm...
LISTEN UP, EVERY-BODY!!

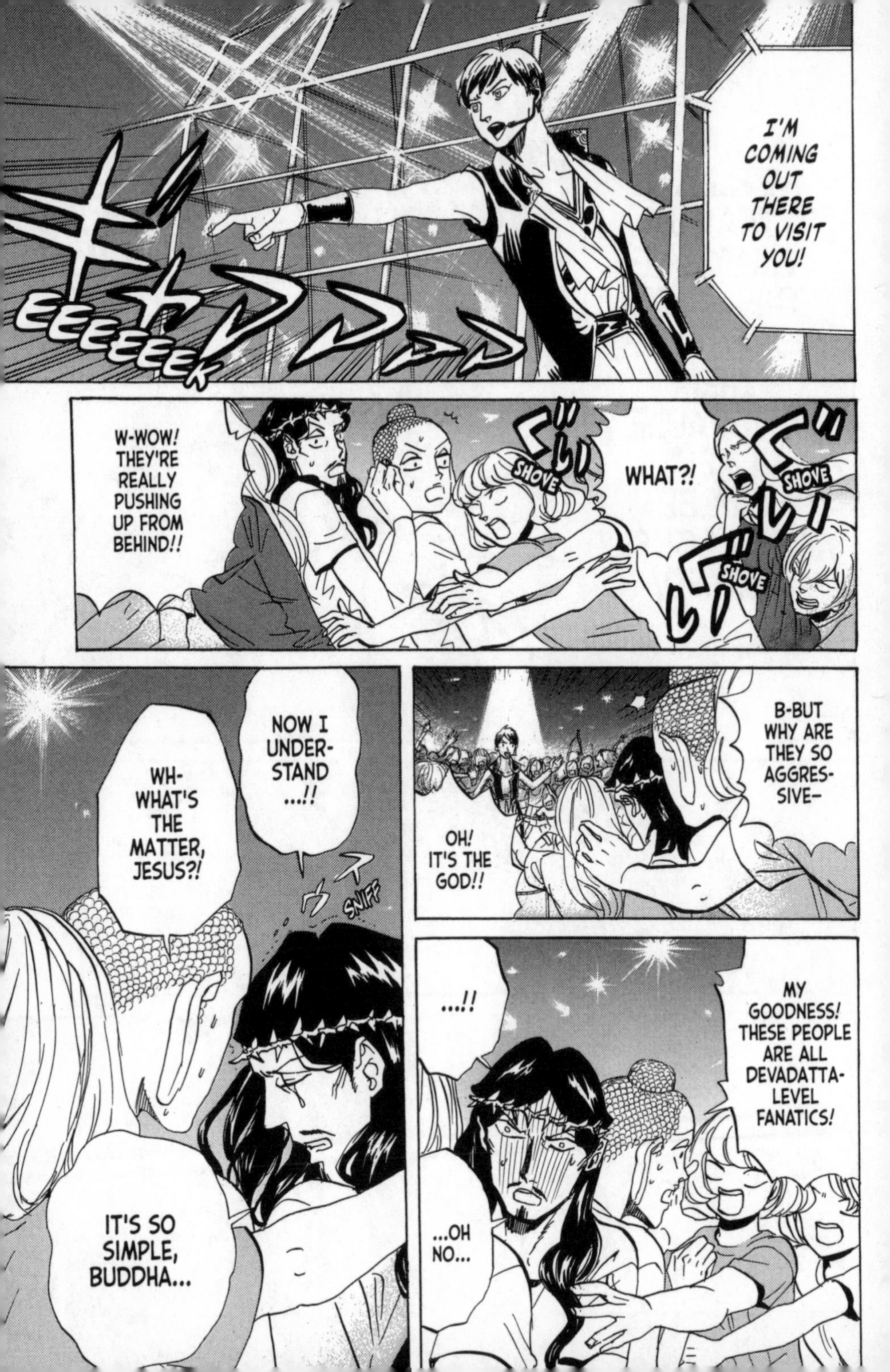
I'M COMING OUT THERE TO VISIT YOU!
EEEEEEEEK
SHOVE
SHOVE
WHAT?!
SHOVE
W-WOW! THEY'RE REALLY PUSHING UP FROM BEHIND!!
B-BUT WHY ARE THEY SO AGGRES-SIVE-
OH! IT'S THE GOD!!
MY GOODNESS! THESE PEOPLE ARE ALL DEVADATTA-LEVEL FANATICS!
...!!
...OH NO...
NOW I UNDER-STAND ...!!
WH-WHAT'S THE MATTER, JESUS?!
SNIFF
IT'S SO SIMPLE, BUDDHA...

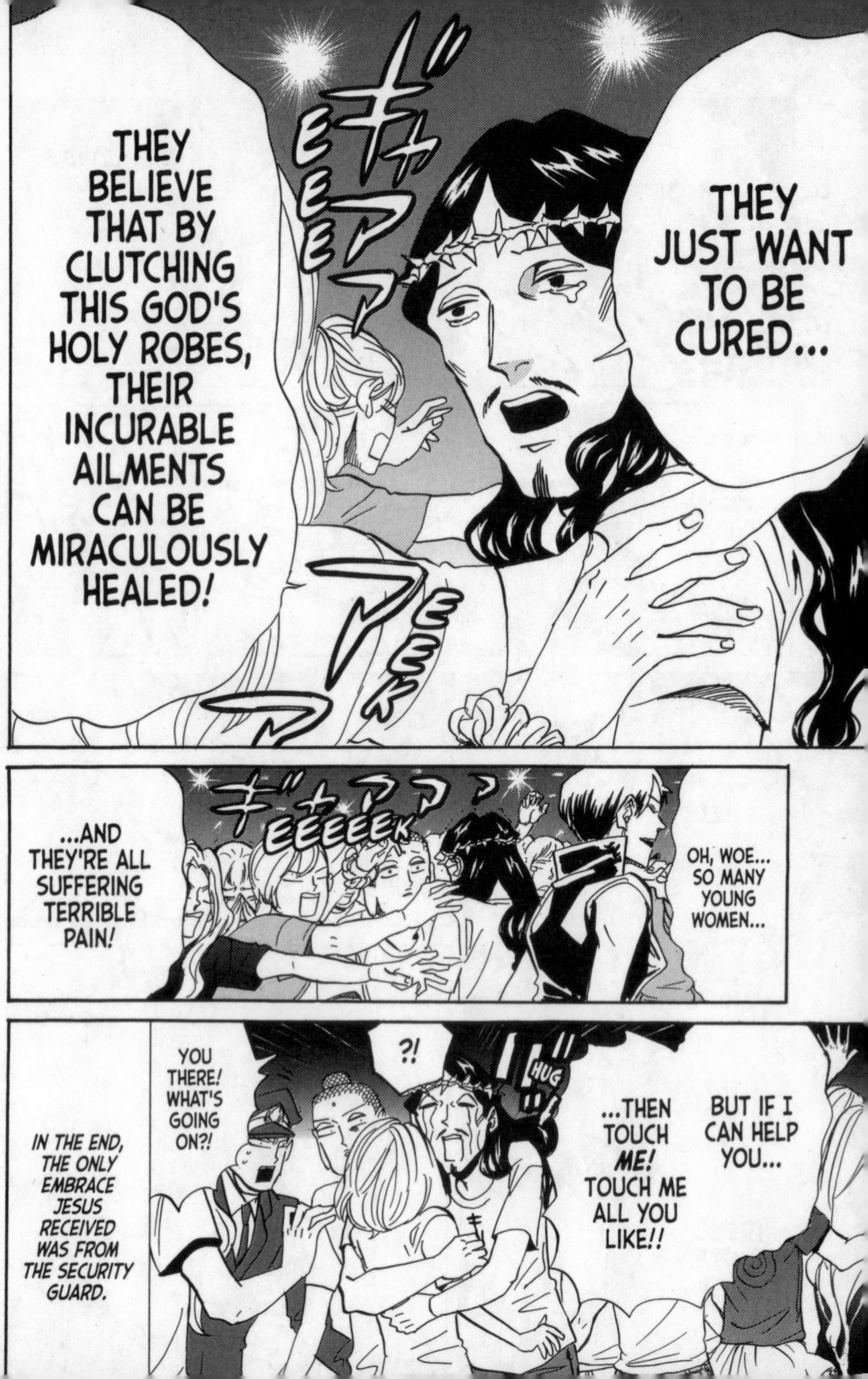
THEY JUST WANT TO BE CURED...
EEEE
EEEK
THEY BELIEVE THAT BY CLUTCHING THIS GOD'S HOLY ROBES, THEIR INCURABLE AILMENTS CAN BE MIRACULOUSLY HEALED!
OH, WOE... SO MANY YOUNG WOMEN...
EEEEEK
...AND THEY'RE ALL SUFFERING TERRIBLE PAIN!
BUT IF I CAN HELP YOU...
...THEN TOUCH ME! TOUCH ME ALL YOU LIKE!!
HUG
?!
YOU THERE! WHAT'S GOING ON?!
IN THE END, THE ONLY EMBRACE JESUS RECEIVED WAS FROM THE SECURITY GUARD.

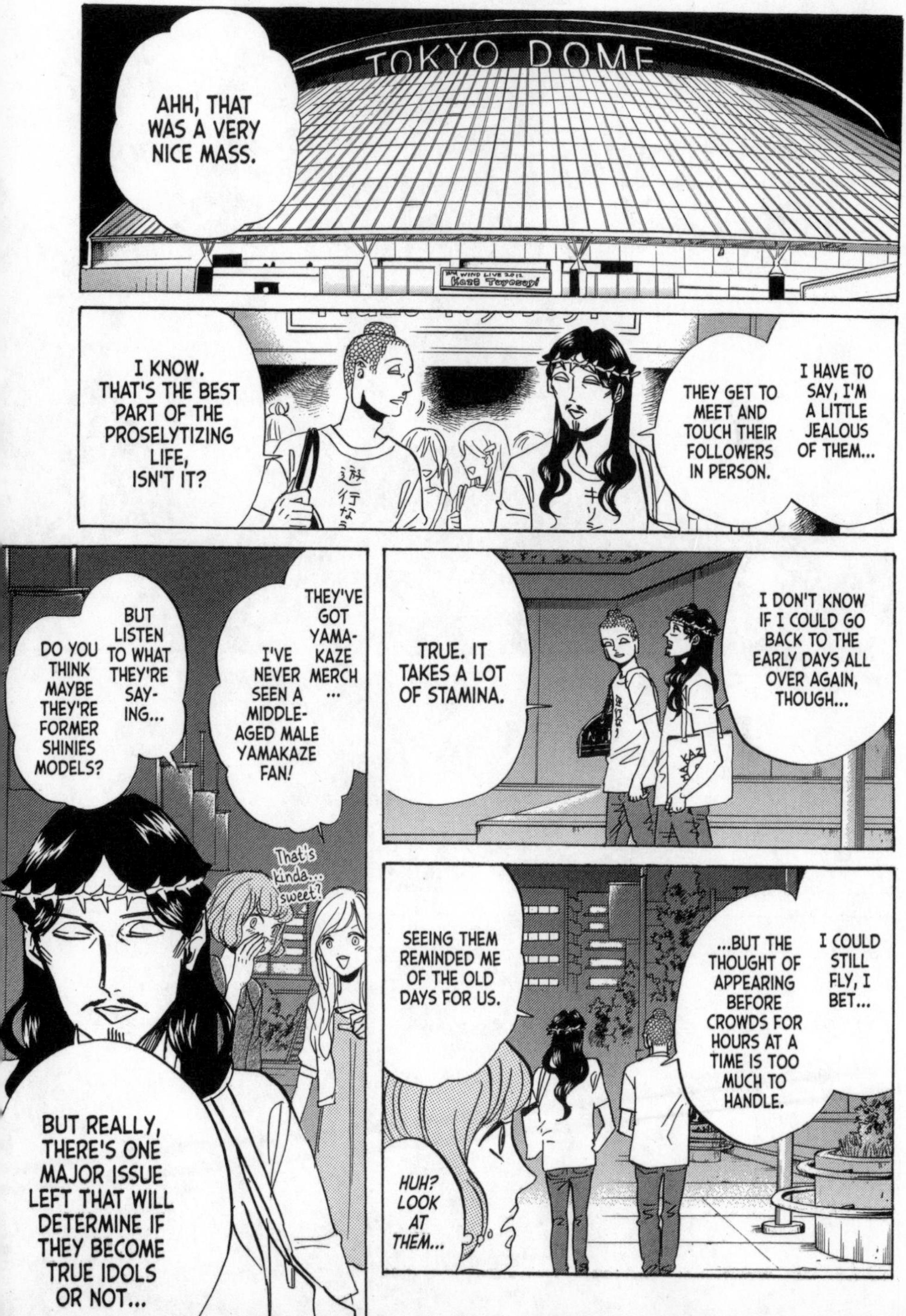
TOKYO DOME
AHH, THAT WAS A VERY NICE MASS.
I HAVE TO SAY, I'M A LITTLE JEALOUS OF THEM...
THEY GET TO MEET AND TOUCH THEIR FOLLOWERS IN PERSON.
I KNOW. THAT'S THE BEST PART OF THE PROSELYTIZING LIFE, ISN'T IT?
I DON'T KNOW IF I COULD GO BACK TO THE EARLY DAYS ALL OVER AGAIN, THOUGH...
TRUE. IT TAKES A LOT OF STAMINA.
I COULD STILL FLY, I BET...
...BUT THE THOUGHT OF APPEARING BEFORE CROWDS FOR HOURS AT A TIME IS TOO MUCH TO HANDLE.
SEEING THEM REMINDED ME OF THE OLD DAYS FOR US.
HUH? LOOK AT THEM...
THEY'VE GOT YAMAKAZE MERCH...
I'VE NEVER SEEN A MIDDLE-AGED MALE YAMAKAZE FAN!
BUT LISTEN TO WHAT THEY'RE SAYING...
DO YOU THINK MAYBE THEY'RE FORMER SHINIES MODELS?
That's kinda... sweet?
BUT REALLY, THERE'S ONE MAJOR ISSUE LEFT THAT WILL DETERMINE IF THEY BECOME TRUE IDOLS OR NOT...

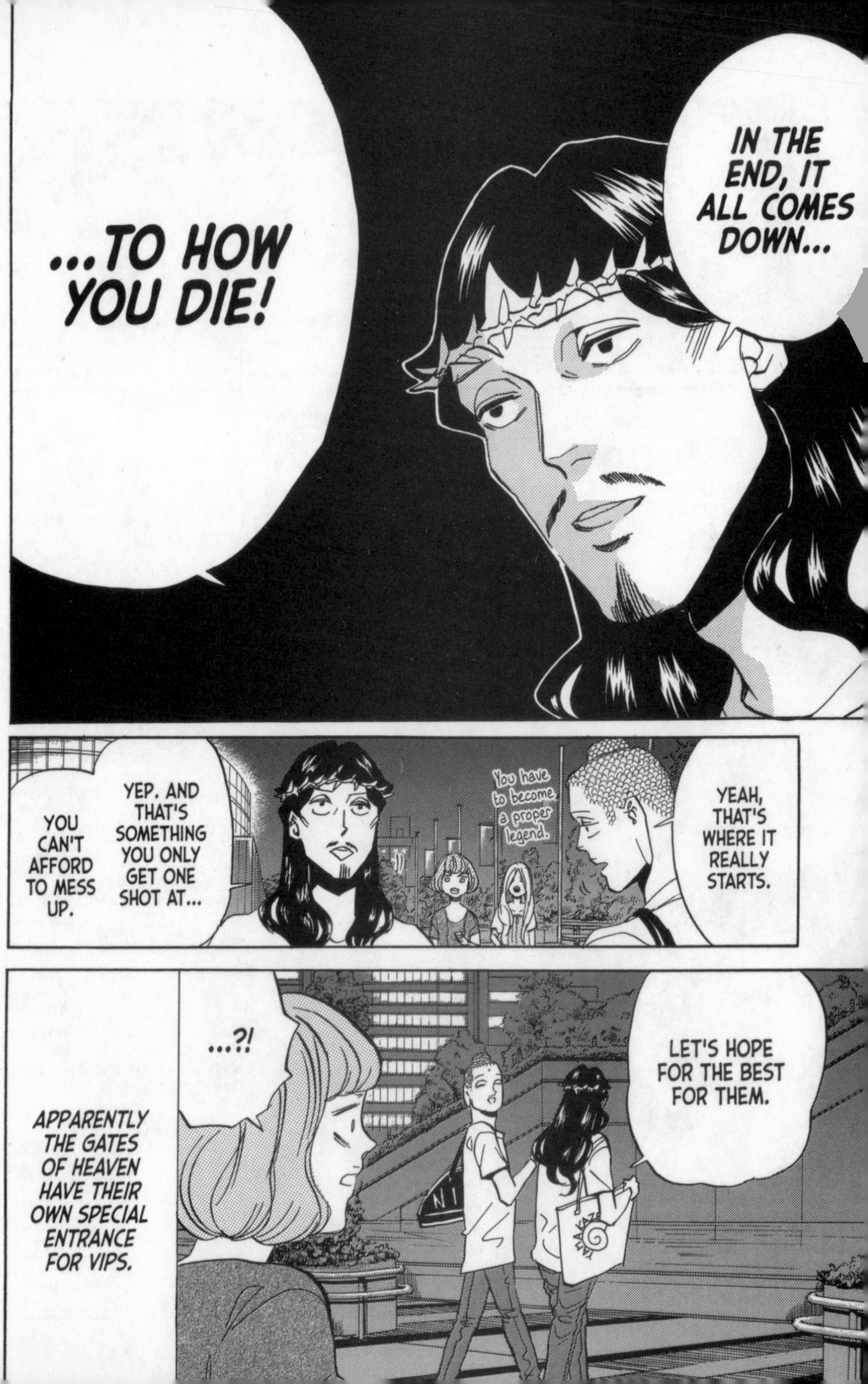
IN THE END, IT ALL COMES DOWN...
...TO HOW YOU DIE!
YEAH, THAT'S WHERE IT REALLY STARTS.
You have to become a proper legend.
YEP. AND THAT'S SOMETHING YOU ONLY GET ONE SHOT AT...
YOU CAN'T AFFORD TO MESS UP.
LET'S HOPE FOR THE BEST FOR THEM.
...?!
APPARENTLY THE GATES OF HEAVEN HAVE THEIR OWN SPECIAL ENTRANCE FOR VIPS.

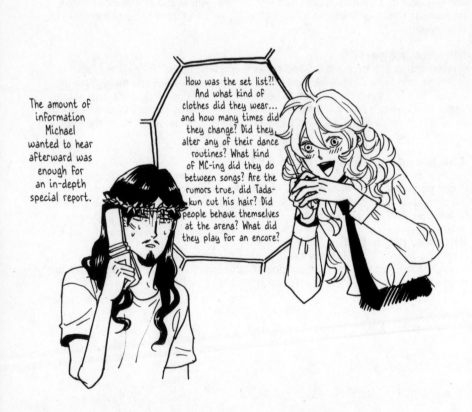

How was the set list?! And what kind of clothes did they wear... and how many times did they change? Did they alter any of their dance routines? What kind of MC-ing did they do between songs? Are the rumors true, did Tada-kun cut his hair? Did people behave themselves at the arena? What did they play for an encore?
The amount of information Michael wanted to hear afterward was enough for an in-depth special report.

CHAPTER 53 TRANSLATION NOTES

Yamakaze, page 175
A term meaning "mountain wind," and most likely a parody of the ultra-popular boy band Arashi ("storm"). Arashi were one of the most popular groups throughout the 2010s. The fictional Yamakaze members mentioned in this chapter (Sakurazawa, Aida) have similar surnames as real-life Arashi members (Sakurai, Aiba).

Kirishitan, page 178
When the Portuguese missionaries first spread Catholicism to Japan in the 16th century, the word *Kirishitan* was initially used to refer to Japanese who converted to Christianity. The more general term for Christians today would be *Kirisuto-kyôto* ("believer of Christianity") or simply *Kurisuchan* ("Christian"). In a historical sense, the use of the word Kirishitan today refers to those early Japanese Christians and the social movement of which they were a part, prior to the crackdown by the Shogunate.

USA-Land, page 178
A fictional theme park. USA is very close to "USJ," which is the commonly-used abbreviation for Universal Studios Japan, and the letters usa in Japanese could be seen as referring to usagi, or "rabbit," with the "Land" part being reminiscent of Disneyland.

Miracle, page 185
A reference to one of Jesus's miracles, as mentioned in the Gospels of Mark, Matthew, and Luke. When the crowd hearing him teach inside the house was too packed to allow the paralytic man to hear, some others opened up the roof above Jesus and lowered the man down on his mat. Jesus forgave him his sins, shocking the people who thought only God could forgive sin, and he then healed the man and told him to walk.

The bleeding woman, page 187
Another of Jesus's miracles, in which he healed a woman with a bleeding disorder. When no doctor could help her, she went to Jesus among the crowd, and in seeking his help, clutched his cloak. When he turned and saw her, he said that her faith had healed her, and she went in peace.

Shinies, page 188
A play on Johnny's, the famous talent agency for male entertainers--primarily musicians and actors. Among their most famous members, current and former, are male idol groups like SMAP, Arashi, Tokio, and Kanjani Eight.

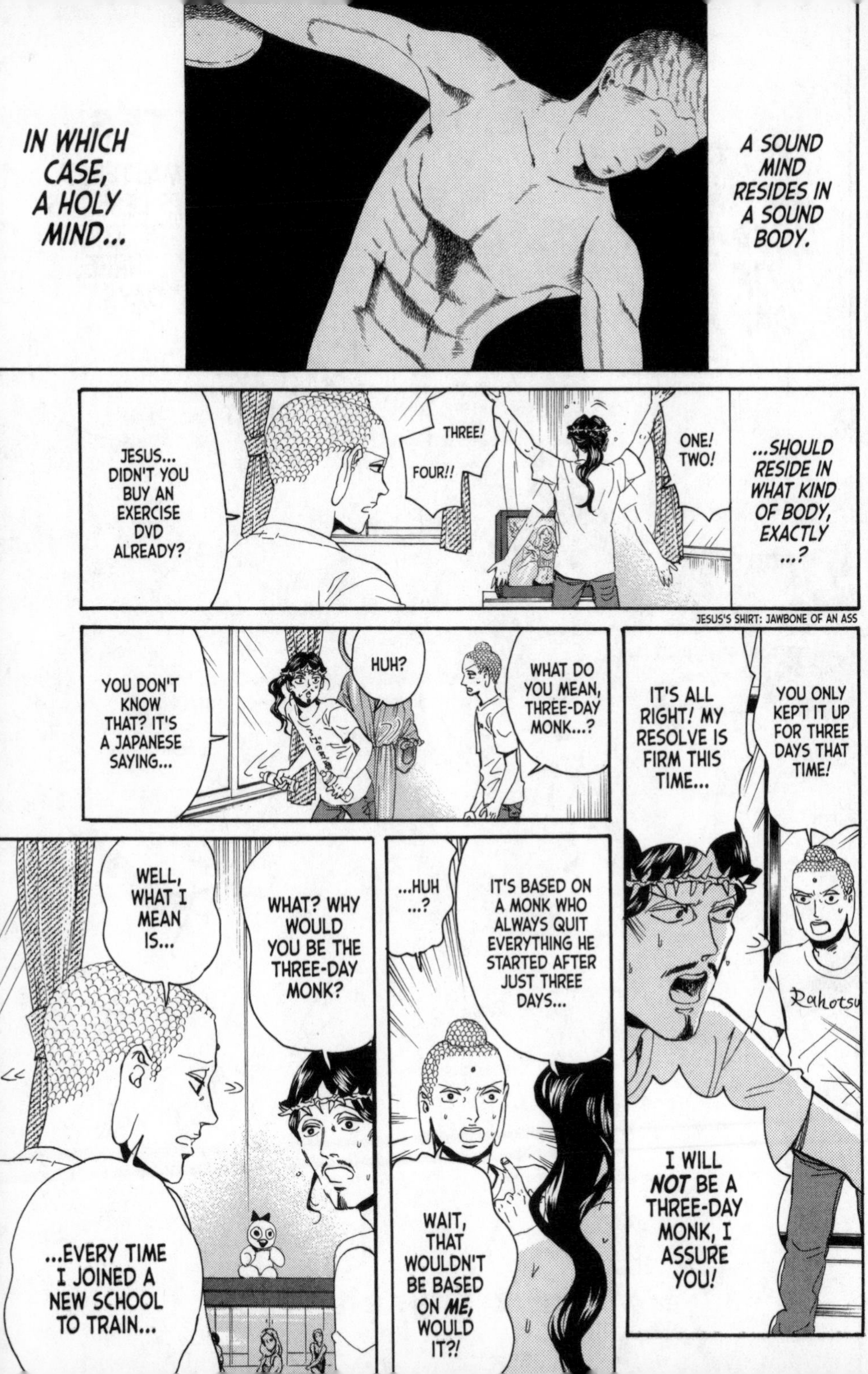
A SOUND MIND RESIDES IN A SOUND BODY.
IN WHICH CASE, A HOLY MIND...
...SHOULD RESIDE IN WHAT KIND OF BODY, EXACTLY...?
ONE! TWO!
THREE!
FOUR!!
JESUS... DIDN'T YOU BUY AN EXERCISE DVD ALREADY?
JESUS'S SHIRT: JAWBONE OF AN ASS
YOU ONLY KEPT IT UP FOR THREE DAYS THAT TIME!
IT'S ALL RIGHT! MY RESOLVE IS FIRM THIS TIME...
Rahotsu
I WILL *NOT* BE A THREE-DAY MONK, I ASSURE YOU!
WHAT DO YOU MEAN, THREE-DAY MONK...?
HUH?
YOU DON'T KNOW THAT? IT'S A JAPANESE SAYING...
IT'S BASED ON A MONK WHO ALWAYS QUIT EVERYTHING HE STARTED AFTER JUST THREE DAYS...
...HUH ...?
WAIT, THAT WOULDN'T BE BASED ON *ME*, WOULD IT?!
WHAT? WHY WOULD YOU BE THE THREE-DAY MONK?
WELL, WHAT I MEAN IS...
...EVERY TIME I JOINED A NEW SCHOOL TO TRAIN...

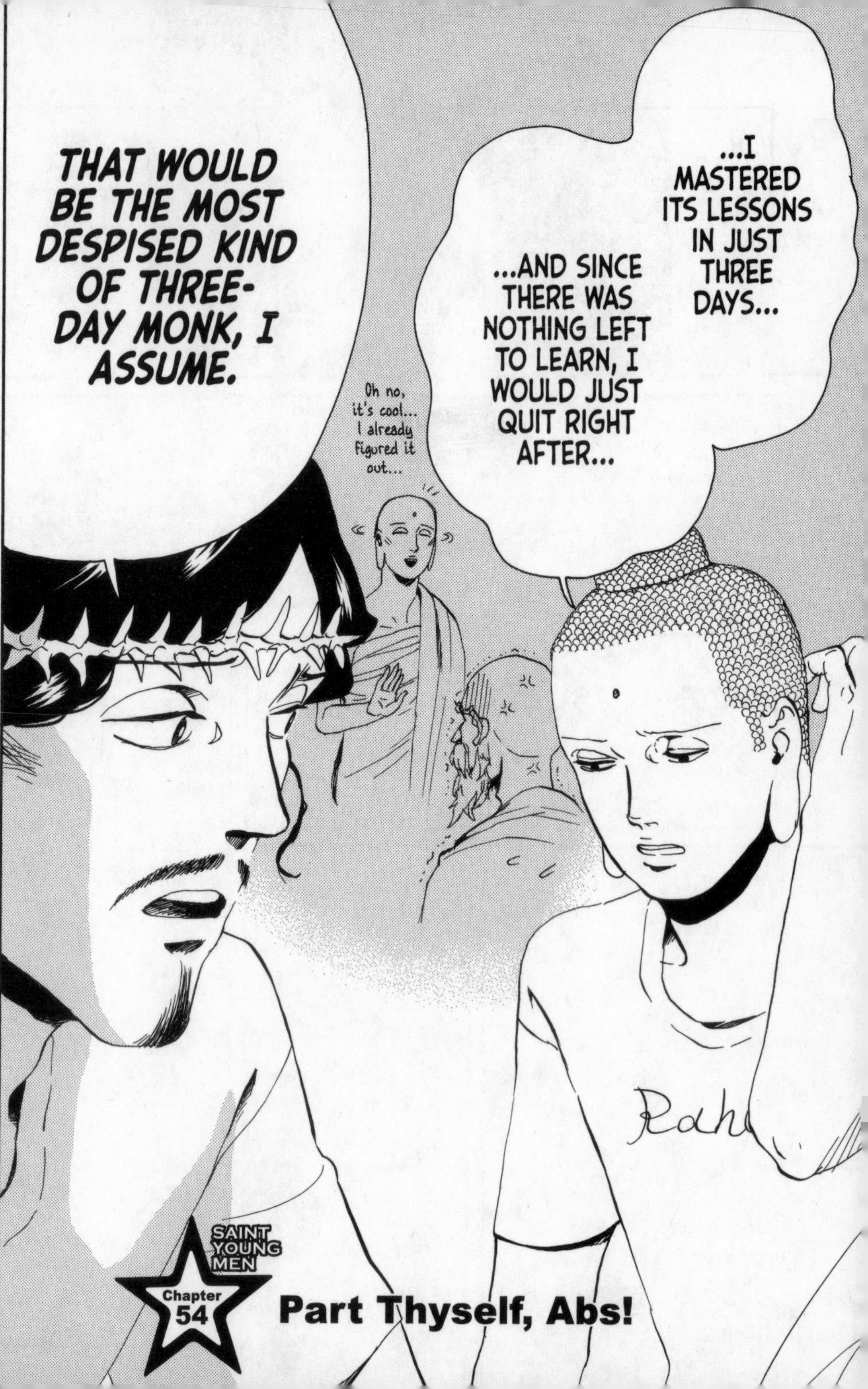
...I MASTERED ITS LESSONS IN JUST THREE DAYS...
...AND SINCE THERE WAS NOTHING LEFT TO LEARN, I WOULD JUST QUIT RIGHT AFTER...
Oh no, it's cool... I already figured it out...
THAT WOULD BE THE MOST DESPISED KIND OF THREE-DAY MONK, I ASSUME.
SAINT YOUNG MEN
Chapter 54
Part Thyself, Abs!

BUDDHA
HIS FAVORITE SUBWAY IS THE MARUNOUCHI LINE. IT'S NICE HOW IT POPS ABOVE GROUND HERE AND THERE.

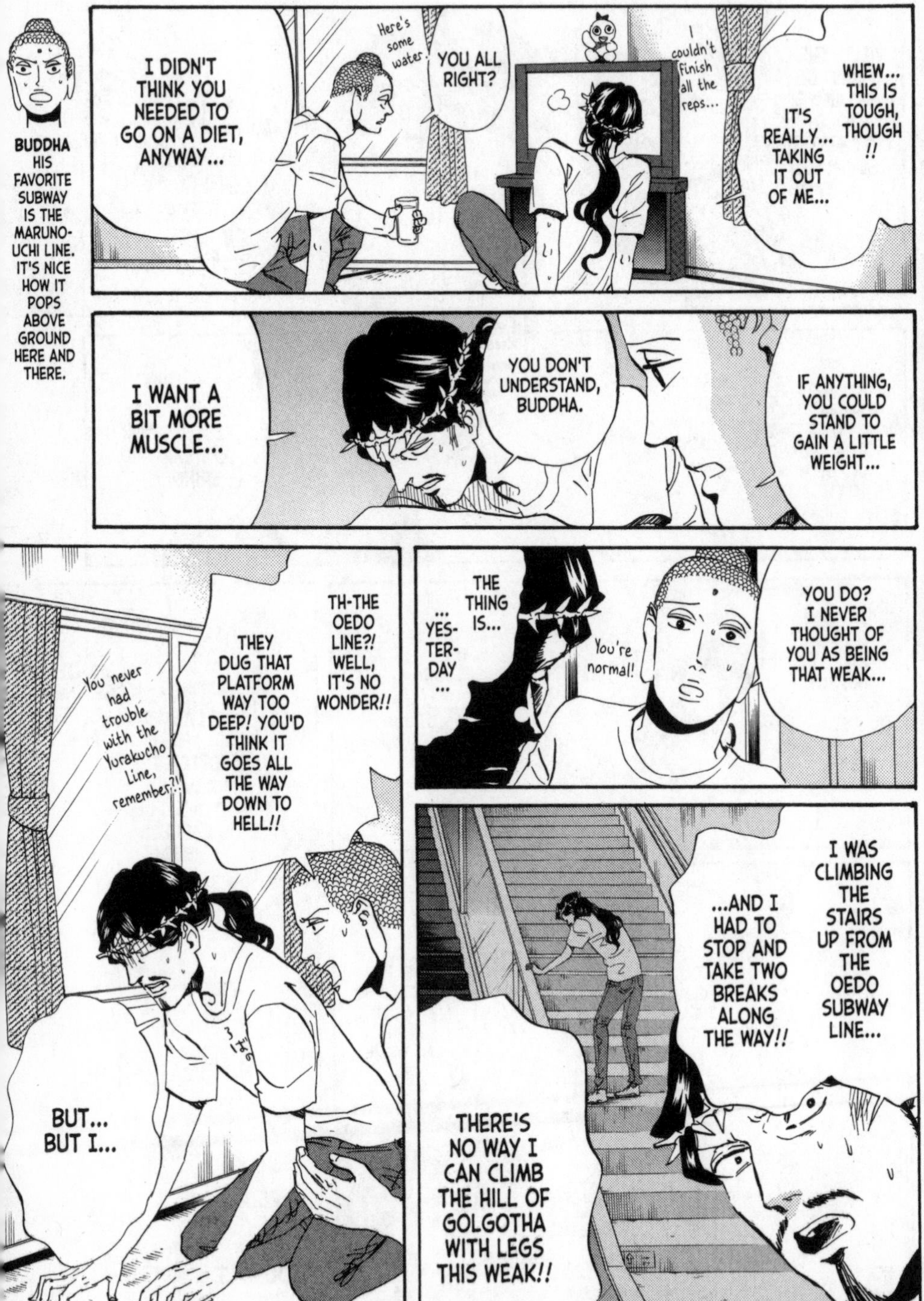
WHEW... THIS IS TOUGH, THOUGH!!
IT'S REALLY... TAKING IT OUT OF ME...
I couldn't finish all the reps...
YOU ALL RIGHT?
Here's some water.
I DIDN'T THINK YOU NEEDED TO GO ON A DIET, ANYWAY...
IF ANYTHING, YOU COULD STAND TO GAIN A LITTLE WEIGHT...
YOU DON'T UNDERSTAND, BUDDHA.
I WANT A BIT MORE MUSCLE...
YOU DO? I NEVER THOUGHT OF YOU AS BEING THAT WEAK...
You're normal!
THE THING IS...
...YESTERDAY...
I WAS CLIMBING THE STAIRS UP FROM THE OEDO SUBWAY LINE...
...AND I HAD TO STOP AND TAKE TWO BREAKS ALONG THE WAY!!
THERE'S NO WAY I CAN CLIMB THE HILL OF GOLGOTHA WITH LEGS THIS WEAK!!
TH-THE OEDO LINE?! WELL, IT'S NO WONDER!!
THEY DUG THAT PLATFORM WAY TOO DEEP! YOU'D THINK IT GOES ALL THE WAY DOWN TO HELL!!
You never had trouble with the Yurakucho Line, remember?!
BUT... BUT I...

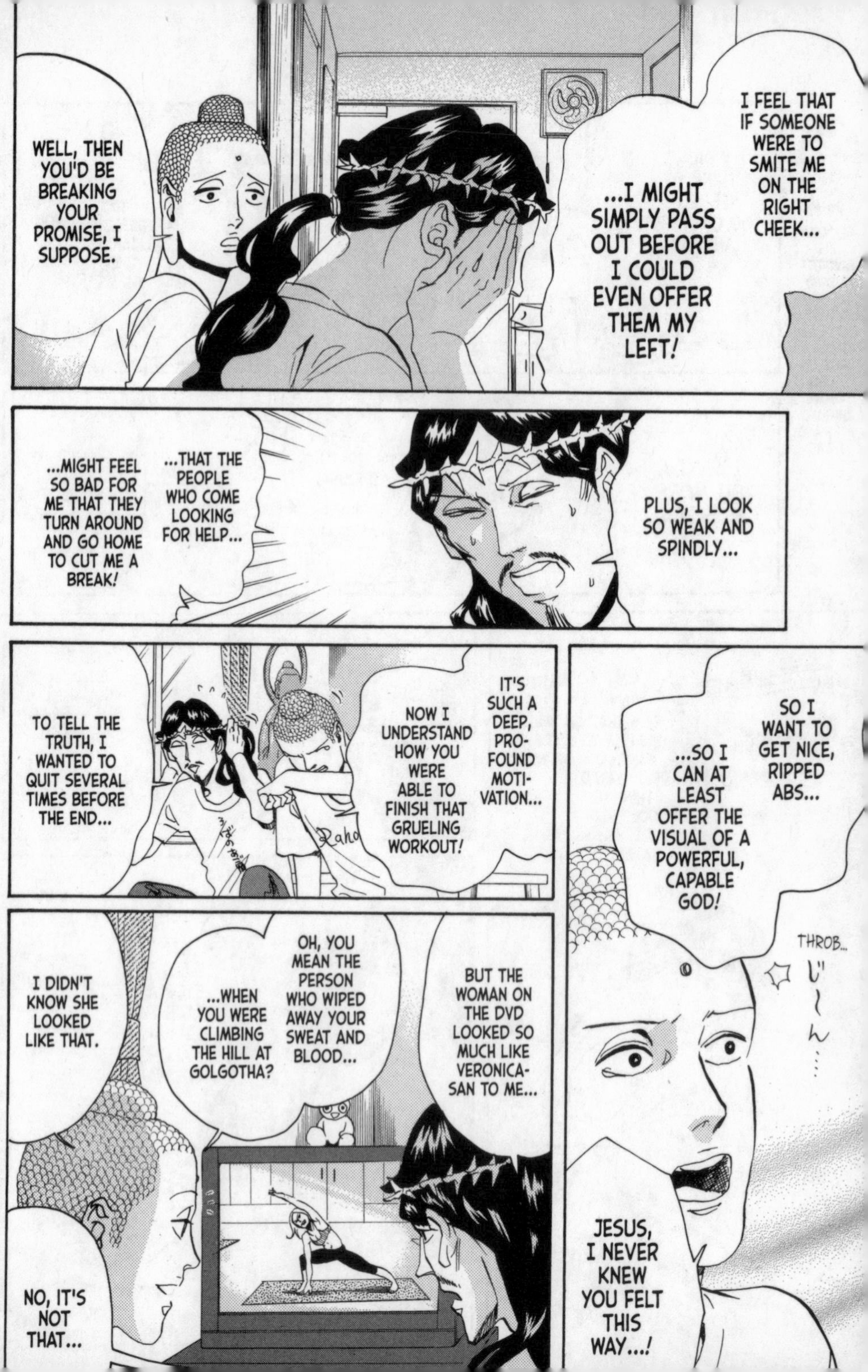
I FEEL THAT IF SOMEONE WERE TO SMITE ME ON THE RIGHT CHEEK...
...I MIGHT SIMPLY PASS OUT BEFORE I COULD EVEN OFFER THEM MY LEFT!
WELL, THEN YOU'D BE BREAKING YOUR PROMISE, I SUPPOSE.
PLUS, I LOOK SO WEAK AND SPINDLY...
...THAT THE PEOPLE WHO COME LOOKING FOR HELP...
...MIGHT FEEL SO BAD FOR ME THAT THEY TURN AROUND AND GO HOME TO CUT ME A BREAK!
SO I WANT TO GET NICE, RIPPED ABS...
...SO I CAN AT LEAST OFFER THE VISUAL OF A POWERFUL, CAPABLE GOD!
THROB...
じ〜ん…
JESUS, I NEVER KNEW YOU FELT THIS WAY...!
IT'S SUCH A DEEP, PRO-FOUND MOTI-VATION...
NOW I UNDERSTAND HOW YOU WERE ABLE TO FINISH THAT GRUELING WORKOUT!
TO TELL THE TRUTH, I WANTED TO QUIT SEVERAL TIMES BEFORE THE END...
BUT THE WOMAN ON THE DVD LOOKED SO MUCH LIKE VERONICA-SAN TO ME...
OH, YOU MEAN THE PERSON WHO WIPED AWAY YOUR SWEAT AND BLOOD...
...WHEN YOU WERE CLIMBING THE HILL AT GOLGOTHA?
I DIDN'T KNOW SHE LOOKED LIKE THAT.
NO, IT'S NOT THAT...

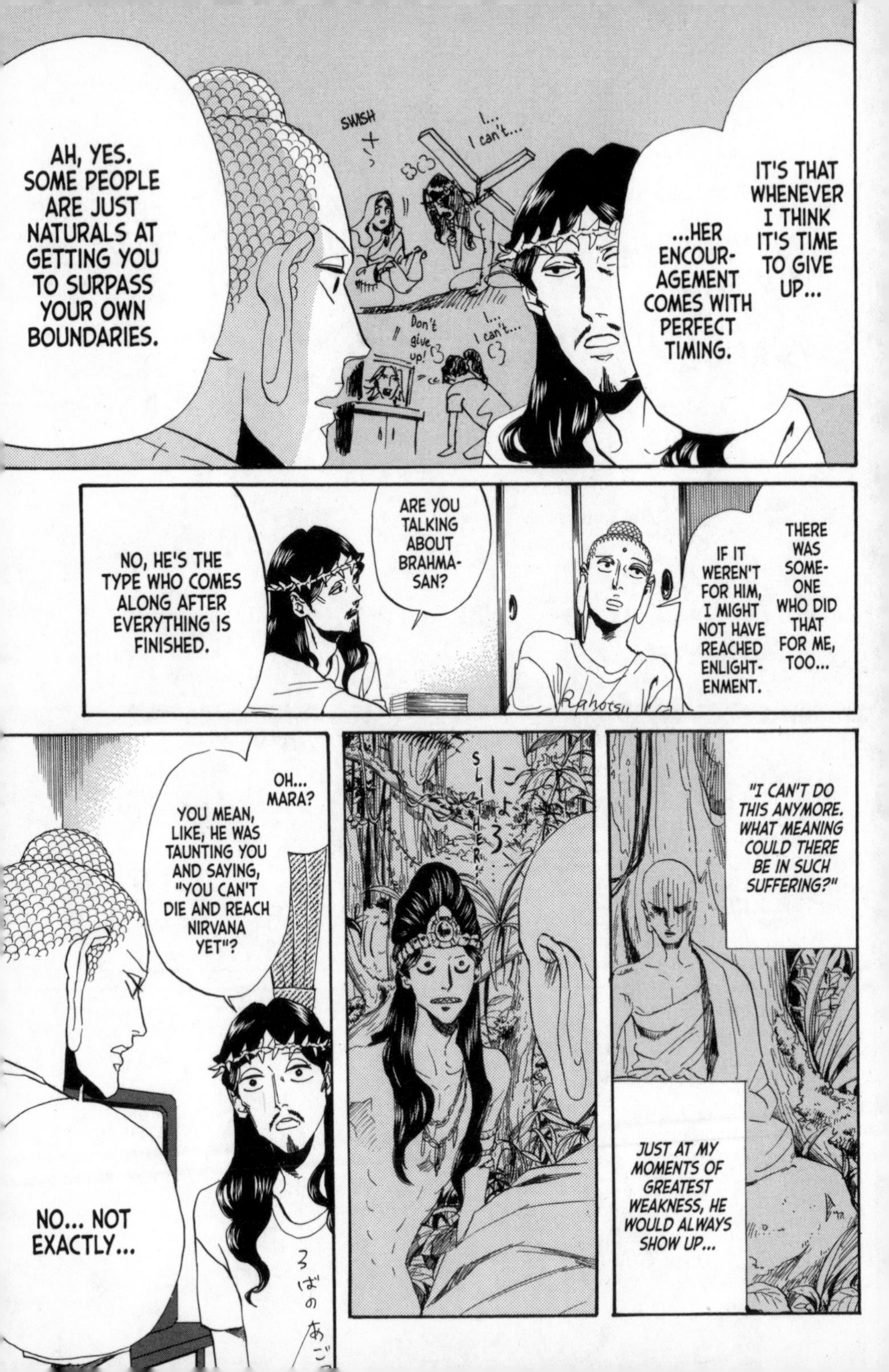
IT'S THAT WHENEVER I THINK IT'S TIME TO GIVE UP...
...HER ENCOUR-AGEMENT COMES WITH PERFECT TIMING.
I... I can't...
SWISH
Don't give up!
I... I can't...
AH, YES. SOME PEOPLE ARE JUST NATURALS AT GETTING YOU TO SURPASS YOUR OWN BOUNDARIES.
THERE WAS SOME-ONE WHO DID THAT FOR ME, TOO...
IF IT WEREN'T FOR HIM, I MIGHT NOT HAVE REACHED ENLIGHT-ENMENT.
ARE YOU TALKING ABOUT BRAHMA-SAN?
NO, HE'S THE TYPE WHO COMES ALONG AFTER EVERYTHING IS FINISHED.
"I CAN'T DO THIS ANYMORE. WHAT MEANING COULD THERE BE IN SUCH SUFFERING?"
JUST AT MY MOMENTS OF GREATEST WEAKNESS, HE WOULD ALWAYS SHOW UP...
にょろ
SLITHER
OH... MARA?
YOU MEAN, LIKE, HE WAS TAUNTING YOU AND SAYING, "YOU CAN'T DIE AND REACH NIRVANA YET"?
NO... NOT EXACTLY...

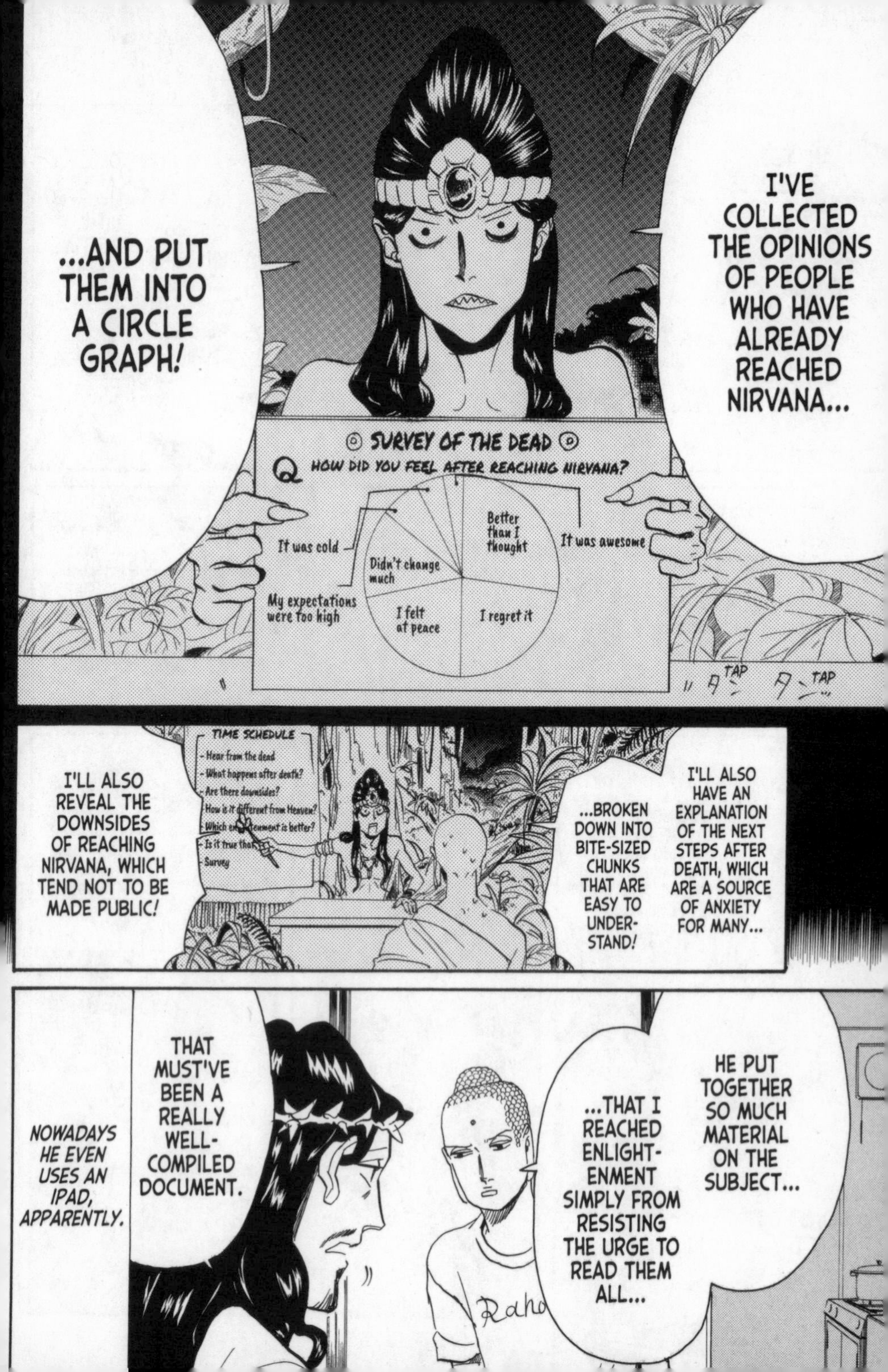
I'VE COLLECTED THE OPINIONS OF PEOPLE WHO HAVE ALREADY REACHED NIRVANA...
...AND PUT THEM INTO A CIRCLE GRAPH!
SURVEY OF THE DEAD
Q HOW DID YOU FEEL AFTER REACHING NIRVANA?
Better than I thought
It was awesome
I regret it
I felt at peace
My expectations were too high
Didn't change much
It was cold
TAP TAP
I'LL ALSO HAVE AN EXPLANATION OF THE NEXT STEPS AFTER DEATH, WHICH ARE A SOURCE OF ANXIETY FOR MANY...
...BROKEN DOWN INTO BITE-SIZED CHUNKS THAT ARE EASY TO UNDER-STAND!
TIME SCHEDULE
- Hear from the dead
- What happens after death?
- Are there downsides?
- Is it true that
- Survey
I'LL ALSO REVEAL THE DOWNSIDES OF REACHING NIRVANA, WHICH TEND NOT TO BE MADE PUBLIC!
HE PUT TOGETHER SO MUCH MATERIAL ON THE SUBJECT...
...THAT I REACHED ENLIGHT-ENMENT SIMPLY FROM RESISTING THE URGE TO READ THEM ALL...
THAT MUST'VE BEEN A REALLY WELL-COMPILED DOCUMENT.
NOWADAYS HE EVEN USES AN IPAD, APPARENTLY.
Raho

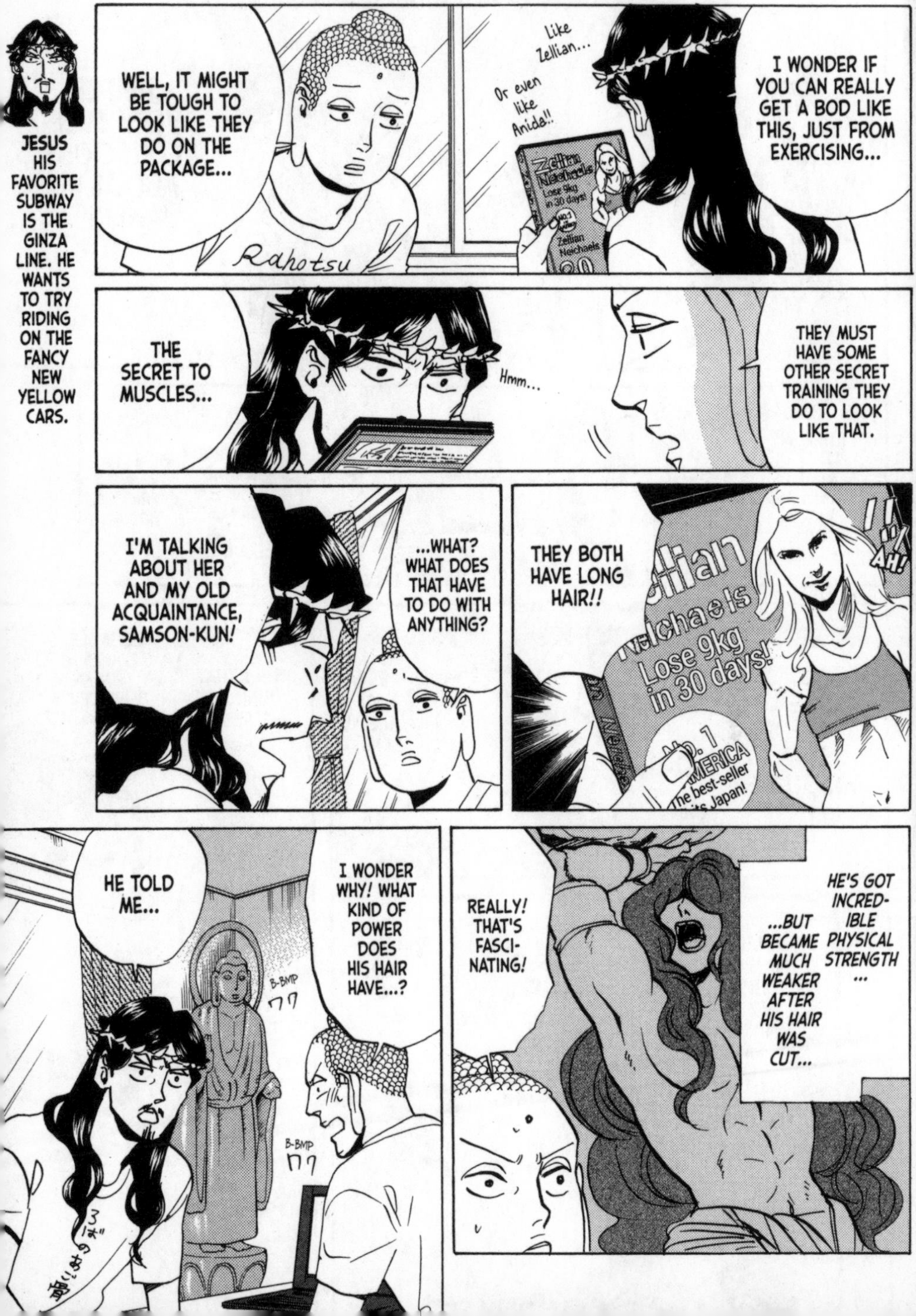
JESUS
HIS FAVORITE SUBWAY IS THE GINZA LINE. HE WANTS TO TRY RIDING ON THE FANCY NEW YELLOW CARS.
I WONDER IF YOU CAN REALLY GET A BOD LIKE THIS, JUST FROM EXERCISING...
Like Zellian...
Or even like Anida!!
Zellian Neichaels
Lose 9kg in 30 days!
WELL, IT MIGHT BE TOUGH TO LOOK LIKE THEY DO ON THE PACKAGE...
Rahotsu
THEY MUST HAVE SOME OTHER SECRET TRAINING THEY DO TO LOOK LIKE THAT.
Hmm...
THE SECRET TO MUSCLES...
!!
AH!
THEY BOTH HAVE LONG HAIR!!
Zellian Neichaels
Lose 9kg in 30 days!
No. 1 AMERICA
The best-seller hits Japan!
...WHAT? WHAT DOES THAT HAVE TO DO WITH ANYTHING?
I'M TALKING ABOUT HER AND MY OLD ACQUAINTANCE, SAMSON-KUN!
HE'S GOT INCREDIBLE PHYSICAL STRENGTH...
...BUT BECAME MUCH WEAKER AFTER HIS HAIR WAS CUT...
REALLY! THAT'S FASCINATING!
I WONDER WHY! WHAT KIND OF POWER DOES HIS HAIR HAVE...?
B-BMP
B-BMP
HE TOLD ME...

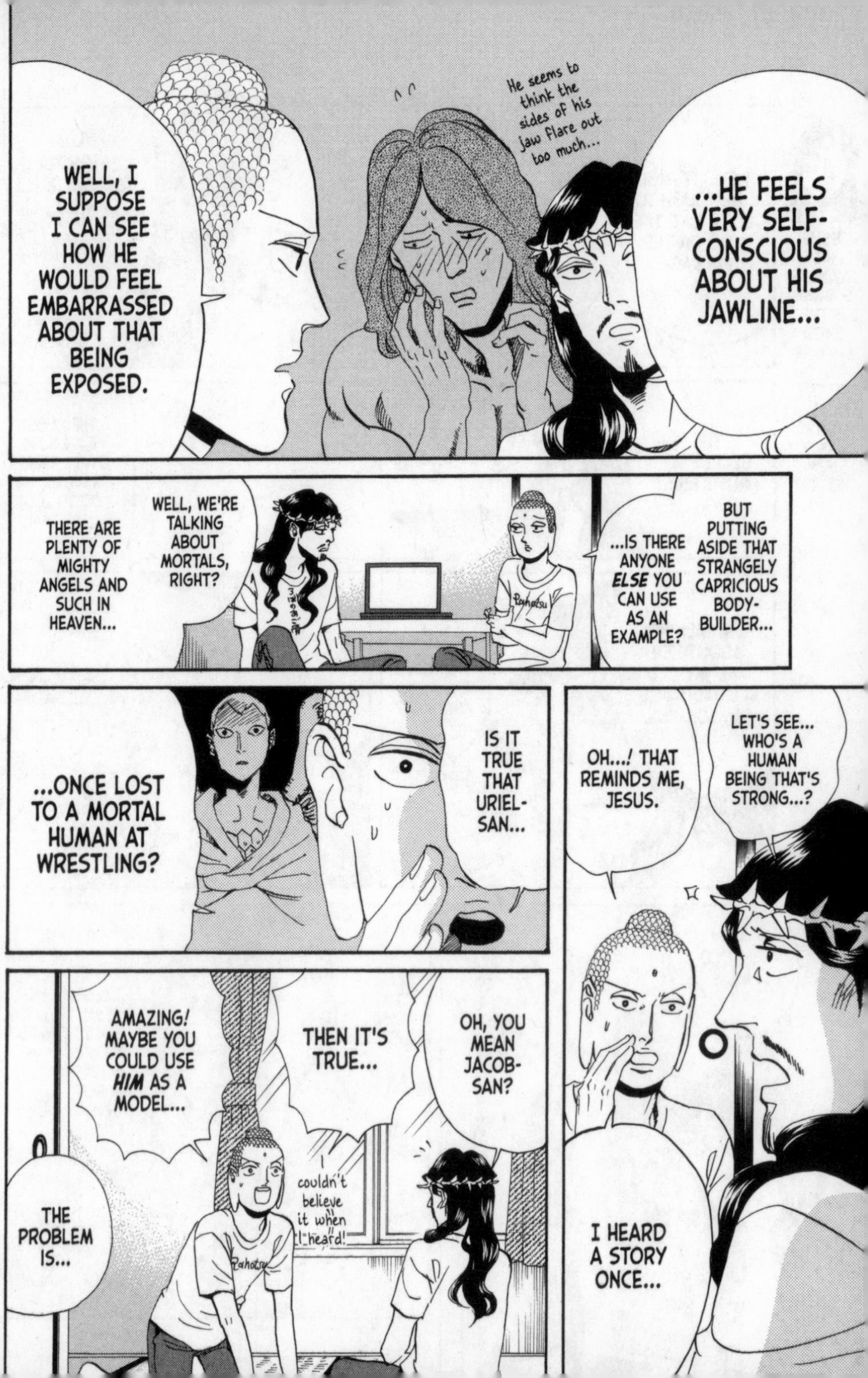
...HE FEELS VERY SELF-CONSCIOUS ABOUT HIS JAWLINE...
He seems to think the sides of his jaw flare out too much...
WELL, I SUPPOSE I CAN SEE HOW HE WOULD FEEL EMBARRASSED ABOUT THAT BEING EXPOSED.
BUT PUTTING ASIDE THAT STRANGELY CAPRICIOUS BODY-BUILDER...
...IS THERE ANYONE *ELSE* YOU CAN USE AS AN EXAMPLE?
WELL, WE'RE TALKING ABOUT MORTALS, RIGHT?
THERE ARE PLENTY OF MIGHTY ANGELS AND SUCH IN HEAVEN...
LET'S SEE... WHO'S A HUMAN BEING THAT'S STRONG...?
OH...! THAT REMINDS ME, JESUS.
I HEARD A STORY ONCE...
IS IT TRUE THAT URIEL-SAN...
...ONCE LOST TO A MORTAL HUMAN AT WRESTLING?
OH, YOU MEAN JACOB-SAN?
THEN IT'S TRUE...
I couldn't believe it when I heard!
AMAZING! MAYBE YOU COULD USE *HIM* AS A MODEL...
THE PROBLEM IS...

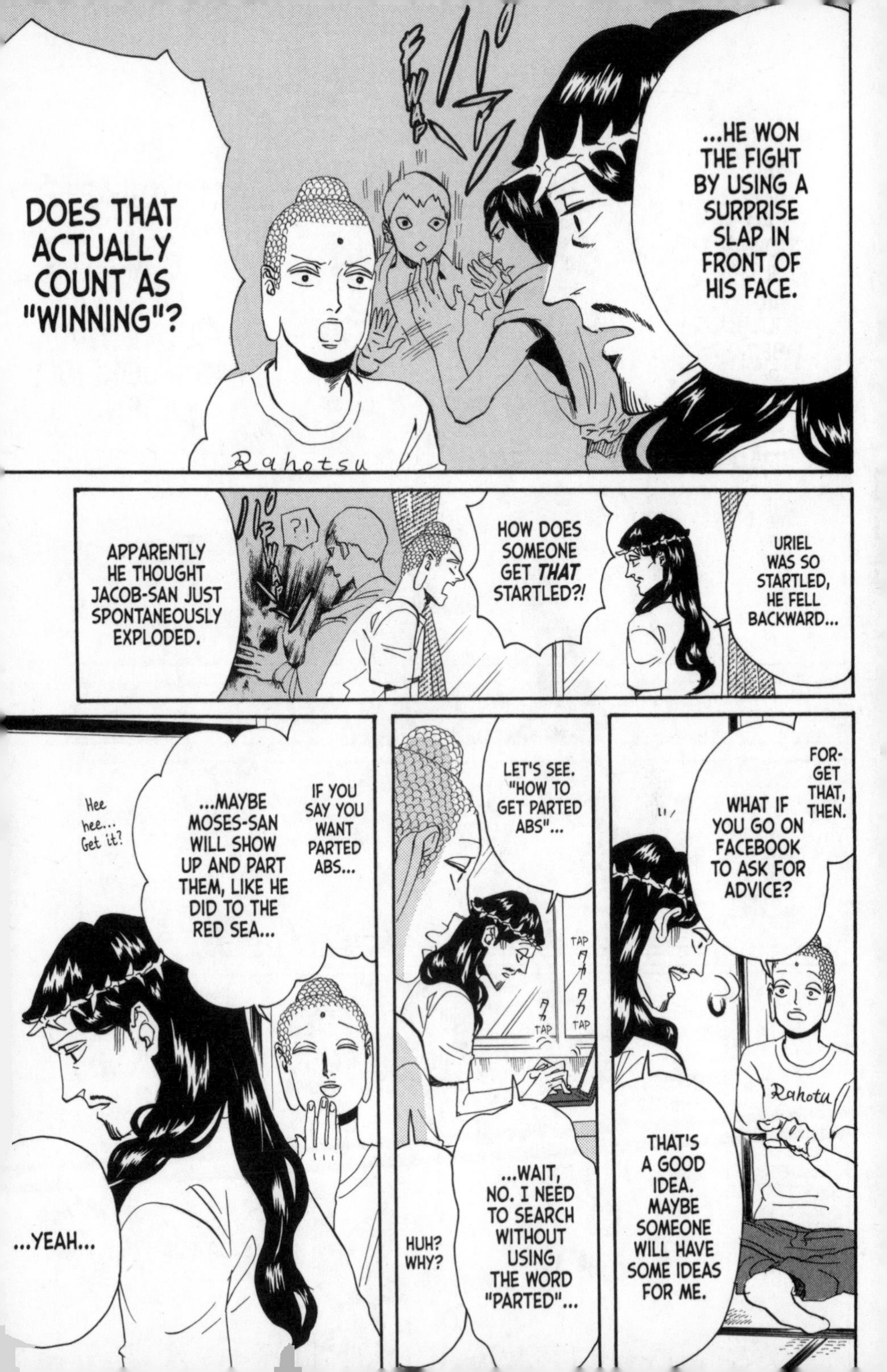
...HE WON THE FIGHT BY USING A SURPRISE SLAP IN FRONT OF HIS FACE.
FWAP
DOES THAT ACTUALLY COUNT AS "WINNING"?
Rahotsu
URIEL WAS SO STARTLED, HE FELL BACKWARD...
HOW DOES SOMEONE GET *THAT* STARTLED?!
?!
APPARENTLY HE THOUGHT JACOB-SAN JUST SPONTANEOUSLY EXPLODED.
FOR-GET THAT, THEN.
WHAT IF YOU GO ON FACEBOOK TO ASK FOR ADVICE?
Rahotu
THAT'S A GOOD IDEA. MAYBE SOMEONE WILL HAVE SOME IDEAS FOR ME.
LET'S SEE. "HOW TO GET PARTED ABS"...
TAP
TAP
TAP
...WAIT, NO. I NEED TO SEARCH WITHOUT USING THE WORD "PARTED"...
HUH? WHY?
IF YOU SAY YOU WANT PARTED ABS...
...MAYBE MOSES-SAN WILL SHOW UP AND PART THEM, LIKE HE DID TO THE RED SEA...
Hee hee... Get it?
...YEAH...

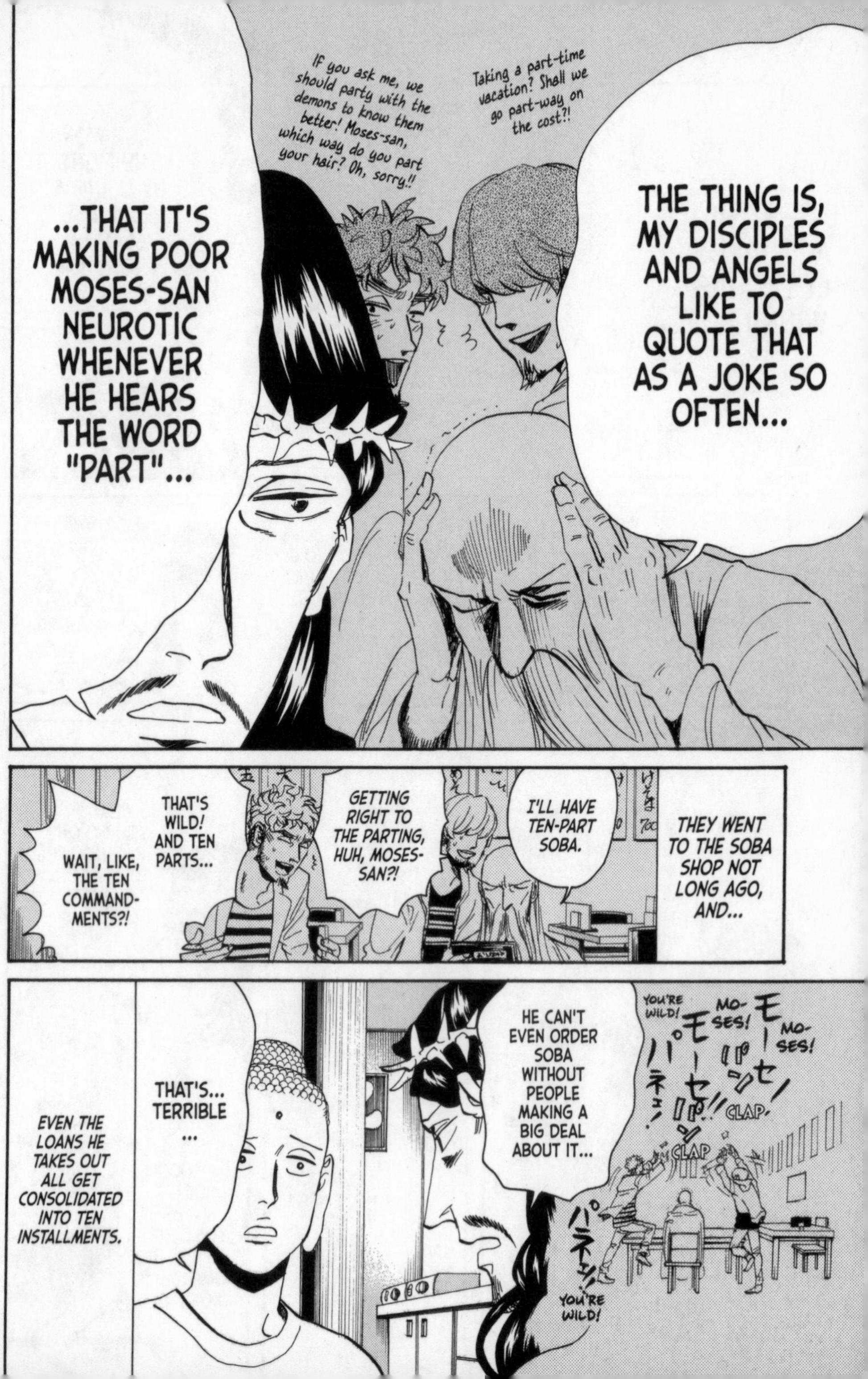
THE THING IS, MY DISCIPLES AND ANGELS LIKE TO QUOTE THAT AS A JOKE SO OFTEN...
Taking a part-time vacation? Shall we go part-way on the cost?!
If you ask me, we should party with the demons to know them better! Moses-san, which way do you part your hair? Oh, sorry!!
...THAT IT'S MAKING POOR MOSES-SAN NEUROTIC WHENEVER HE HEARS THE WORD "PART"...
THEY WENT TO THE SOBA SHOP NOT LONG AGO, AND...
I'LL HAVE TEN-PART SOBA.
GETTING RIGHT TO THE PARTING, HUH, MOSES-SAN?!
THAT'S WILD! AND TEN PARTS...
WAIT, LIKE, THE TEN COMMANDMENTS?!
MO-SES!
MO-SES!
YOU'RE WILD!
CLAP
CLAP
YOU'RE WILD!
HE CAN'T EVEN ORDER SOBA WITHOUT PEOPLE MAKING A BIG DEAL ABOUT IT...
THAT'S... TERRIBLE...
EVEN THE LOANS HE TAKES OUT ALL GET CONSOLIDATED INTO TEN INSTALLMENTS.

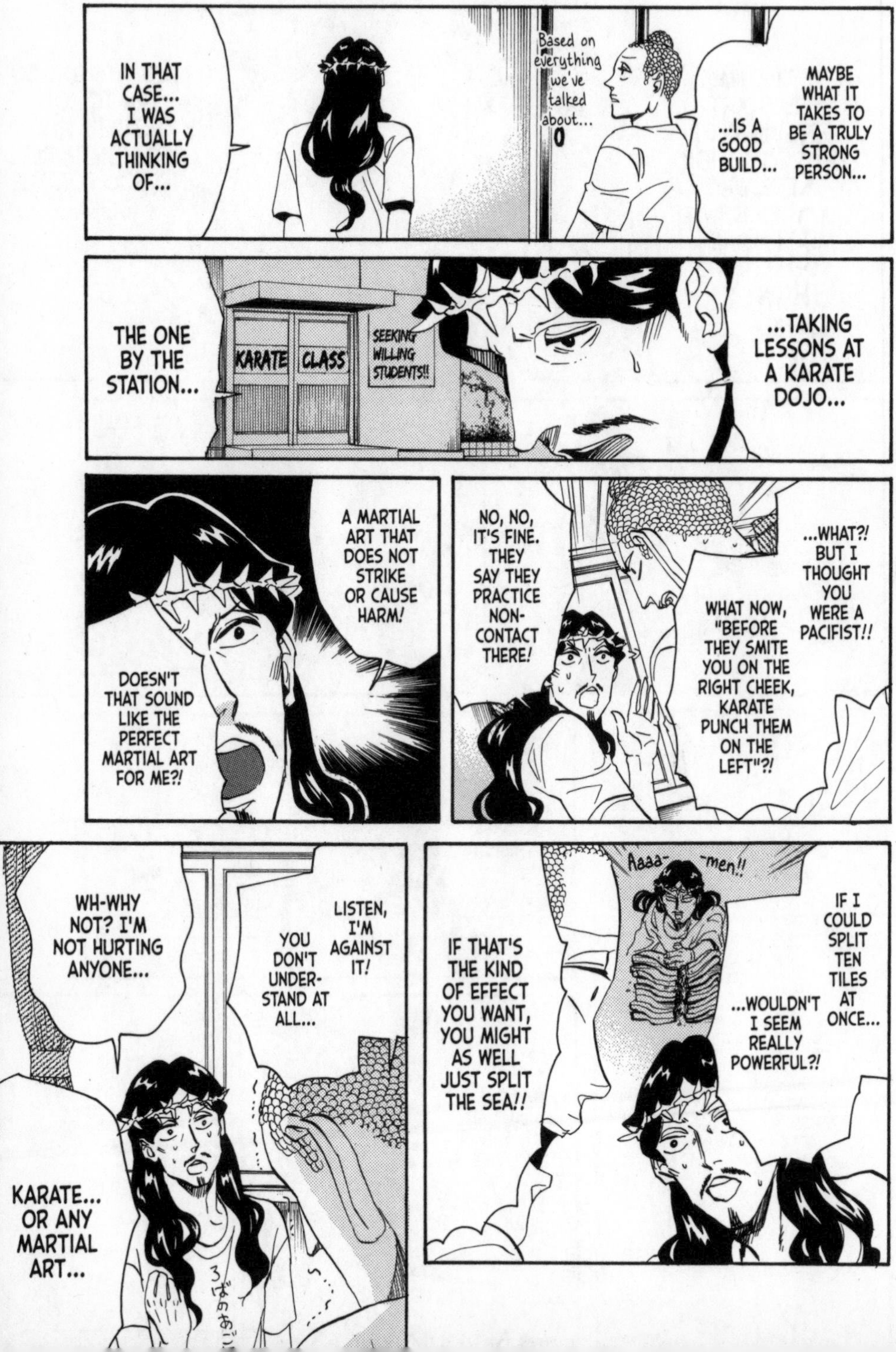
MAYBE WHAT IT TAKES TO BE A TRULY STRONG PERSON...
...IS A GOOD BUILD...
Based on everything we've talked about...
IN THAT CASE... I WAS ACTUALLY THINKING OF...
...TAKING LESSONS AT A KARATE DOJO...
SEEKING WILLING STUDENTS!!
KARATE CLASS
THE ONE BY THE STATION...
...WHAT?! BUT I THOUGHT YOU WERE A PACIFIST!!
WHAT NOW, "BEFORE THEY SMITE YOU ON THE RIGHT CHEEK, KARATE PUNCH THEM ON THE LEFT"?!
NO, NO, IT'S FINE. THEY SAY THEY PRACTICE NON-CONTACT THERE!
A MARTIAL ART THAT DOES NOT STRIKE OR CAUSE HARM!
DOESN'T THAT SOUND LIKE THE PERFECT MARTIAL ART FOR ME?!
IF I COULD SPLIT TEN TILES AT ONCE...
...WOULDN'T I SEEM REALLY POWERFUL?!
Aaaa- -men!!
IF THAT'S THE KIND OF EFFECT YOU WANT, YOU MIGHT AS WELL JUST SPLIT THE SEA!!
LISTEN, I'M AGAINST IT!
YOU DON'T UNDERSTAND AT ALL...
WH-WHY NOT? I'M NOT HURTING ANYONE...
KARATE... OR ANY MARTIAL ART...

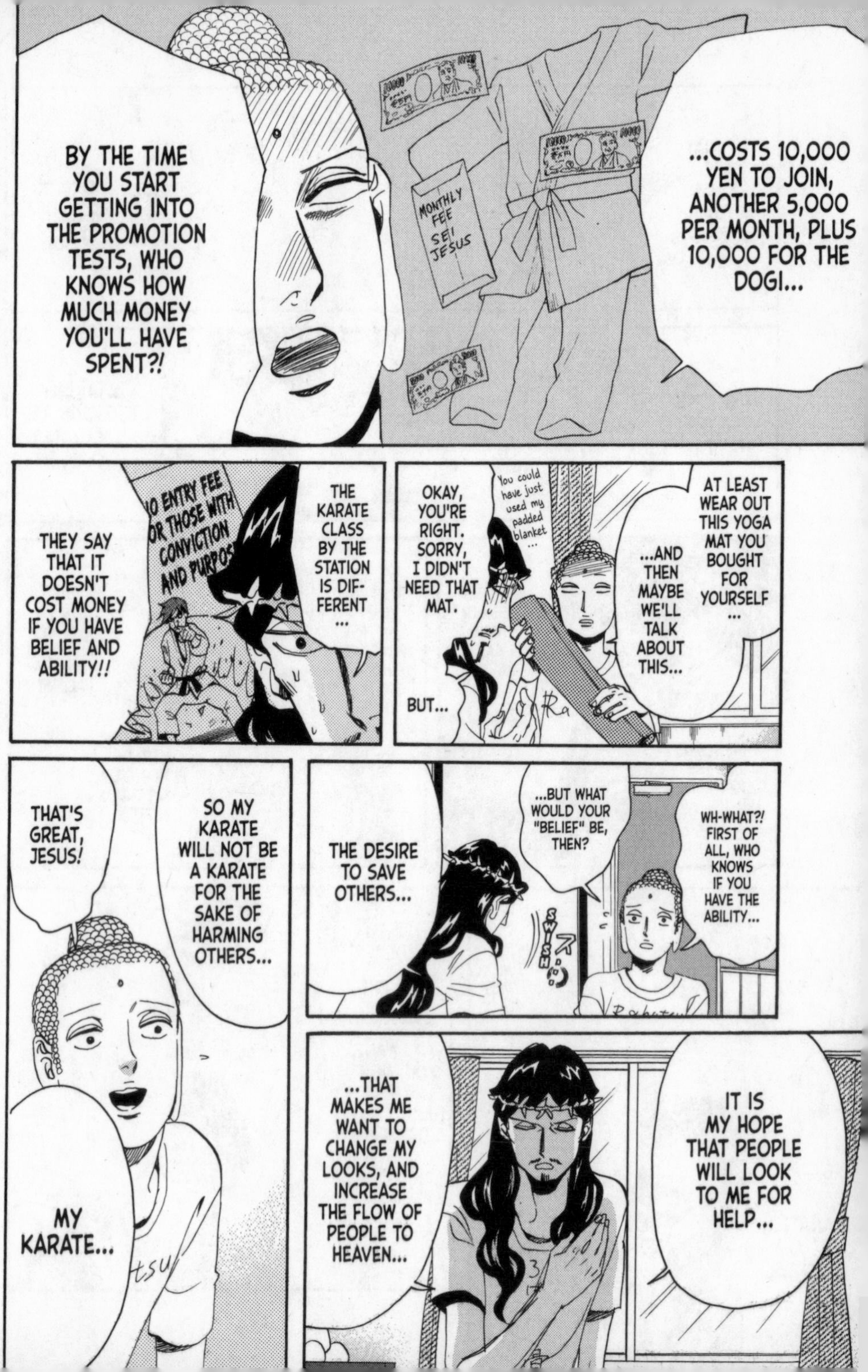
...COSTS 10,000 YEN TO JOIN, ANOTHER 5,000 PER MONTH, PLUS 10,000 FOR THE DOGI...
MONTHLY FEE SEI JESUS
BY THE TIME YOU START GETTING INTO THE PROMOTION TESTS, WHO KNOWS HOW MUCH MONEY YOU'LL HAVE SPENT?!
AT LEAST WEAR OUT THIS YOGA MAT YOU BOUGHT FOR YOURSELF...
...AND THEN MAYBE WE'LL TALK ABOUT THIS...
You could have just used my padded blanket...
OKAY, YOU'RE RIGHT. SORRY, I DIDN'T NEED THAT MAT.
BUT...
THE KARATE CLASS BY THE STATION IS DIF- FERENT...
O ENTRY FEE OR THOSE WITH CONVICTION AND PURPOS
THEY SAY THAT IT DOESN'T COST MONEY IF YOU HAVE BELIEF AND ABILITY!!
WH-WHAT?! FIRST OF ALL, WHO KNOWS IF YOU HAVE THE ABILITY...
...BUT WHAT WOULD YOUR "BELIEF" BE, THEN?
SWISH
THE DESIRE TO SAVE OTHERS...
IT IS MY HOPE THAT PEOPLE WILL LOOK TO ME FOR HELP...
...THAT MAKES ME WANT TO CHANGE MY LOOKS, AND INCREASE THE FLOW OF PEOPLE TO HEAVEN...
SO MY KARATE WILL NOT BE A KARATE FOR THE SAKE OF HARMING OTHERS...
THAT'S GREAT, JESUS!
MY KARATE...

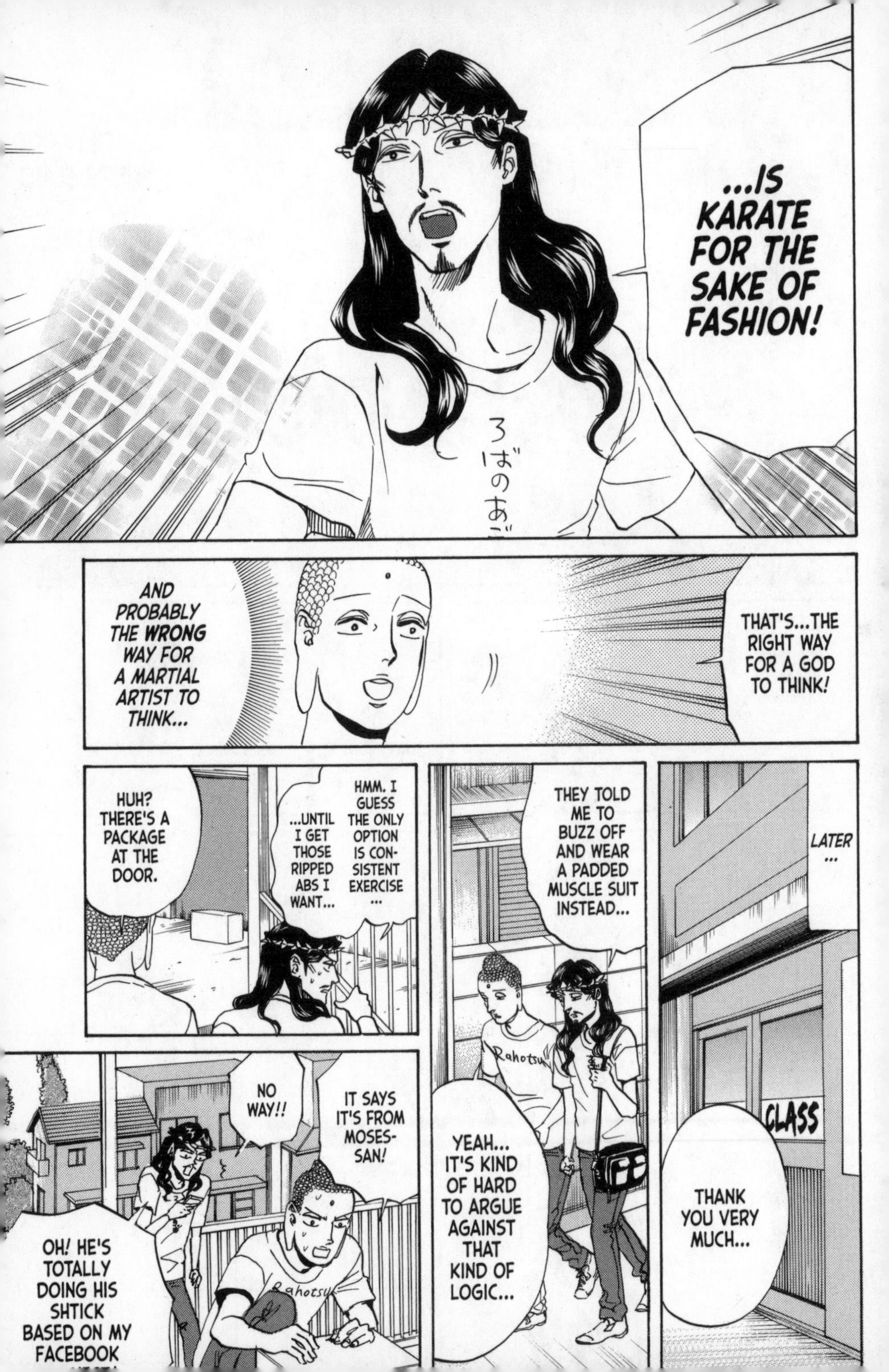
...IS KARATE FOR THE SAKE OF FASHION!
THAT'S...THE RIGHT WAY FOR A GOD TO THINK!
AND PROBABLY THE WRONG WAY FOR A MARTIAL ARTIST TO THINK...
LATER ...
CLASS
THANK YOU VERY MUCH...
THEY TOLD ME TO BUZZ OFF AND WEAR A PADDED MUSCLE SUIT INSTEAD...
Rahotsu
YEAH... IT'S KIND OF HARD TO ARGUE AGAINST THAT KIND OF LOGIC...
HMM. I GUESS THE ONLY OPTION IS CONSISTENT EXERCISE...
...UNTIL I GET THOSE RIPPED ABS I WANT...
HUH? THERE'S A PACKAGE AT THE DOOR.
IT SAYS IT'S FROM MOSES-SAN!
NO WAY!!
Rahotsu
OH! HE'S TOTALLY DOING HIS SHTICK BASED ON MY FACEBOOK

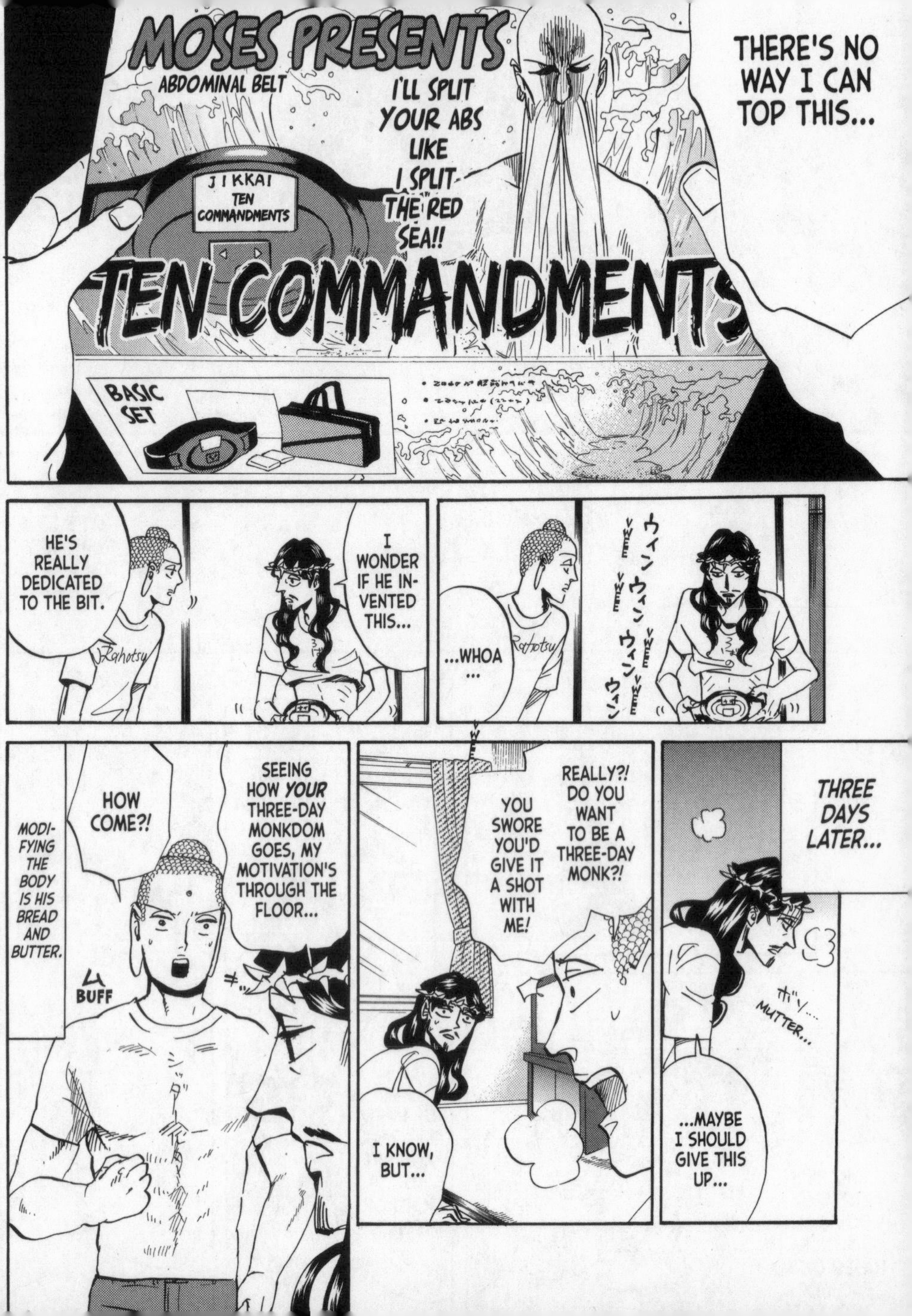
THERE'S NO WAY I CAN TOP THIS...
MOSES PRESENTS
ABDOMINAL BELT
I'LL SPLIT YOUR ABS LIKE I SPLIT THE RED SEA!!
JIKKAI TEN COMMANDMENTS
TEN COMMANDMENTS
BASIC SET
ウィン ウィン ウィン ウィン
WEE WEE WEE WEE
...WHOA...
Rahotsu
I WONDER IF HE INVENTED THIS...
HE'S REALLY DEDICATED TO THE BIT.
Rahotsu
THREE DAYS LATER...
MUTTER...
...MAYBE I SHOULD GIVE THIS UP...
REALLY?! DO YOU WANT TO BE A THREE-DAY MONK?!
YOU SWORE YOU'D GIVE IT A SHOT WITH ME!
I KNOW, BUT...
SEEING HOW *YOUR* THREE-DAY MONKDOM GOES, MY MOTIVATION'S THROUGH THE FLOOR...
HOW COME?!
MODIFYING THE BODY IS HIS BREAD AND BUTTER.
BUFF

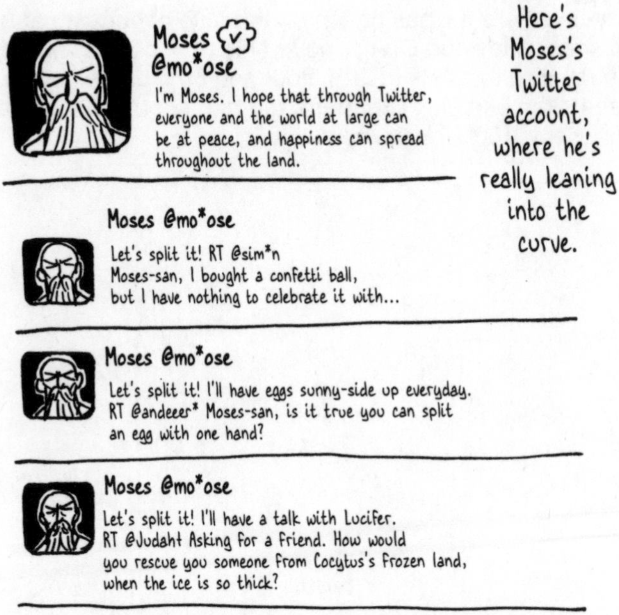
Here's Moses's Twitter account, where he's really leaning into the curve.
Moses
@mo*ose
I'm Moses. I hope that through Twitter, everyone and the world at large can be at peace, and happiness can spread throughout the land.
Moses @mo*ose
Let's split it! RT @sim*n Moses-san, I bought a confetti ball, but I have nothing to celebrate it with...
Moses @mo*ose
Let's split it! I'll have eggs sunny-side up everyday. RT @andeeer* Moses-san, is it true you can split an egg with one hand?
Moses @mo*ose
Let's split it! I'll have a talk with Lucifer. RT @Judaht Asking for a friend. How would you rescue you someone from Cocytus's frozen land, when the ice is so thick?

CHAPTER 54 TRANSLATION NOTES

Rahotsu, page 192
The Japanese word for Buddha's characteristic curls of hair.

Jawbone of an ass, page 192
In the Book of Judges, the mighty hero Samson demonstrates his strength by slaying a thousand Philistines with the jawbone of an ass (donkey).

Golgotha, page 194
The site at which Jesus was crucified. According to the Gospels, it was located just outside of Jerusalem's walls, although the exact location is disputed.

Jacob, page 199
Chapter 32 of the Book of Genesis describes Jacob's encounter with a messenger of the Lord (an angel). Jacob wrestles with the angel all night, until eventually the angel touches Jacob's hip to dislocate it, and gives him the name of Israel, which means "contends with God."

Ten-part soba, page 201
Soba noodles come in different types based on the ratio of buckwheat (the main ingredient of soba) and flour. One popular type of noodle is "two-eight" soba (ni-hachi soba) which consists of 20% flour and 80% buckwheat, where each "part" represents ten percent. Therefore, ten-part soba (juwari soba) refers to noodles made of 100% buckwheat.

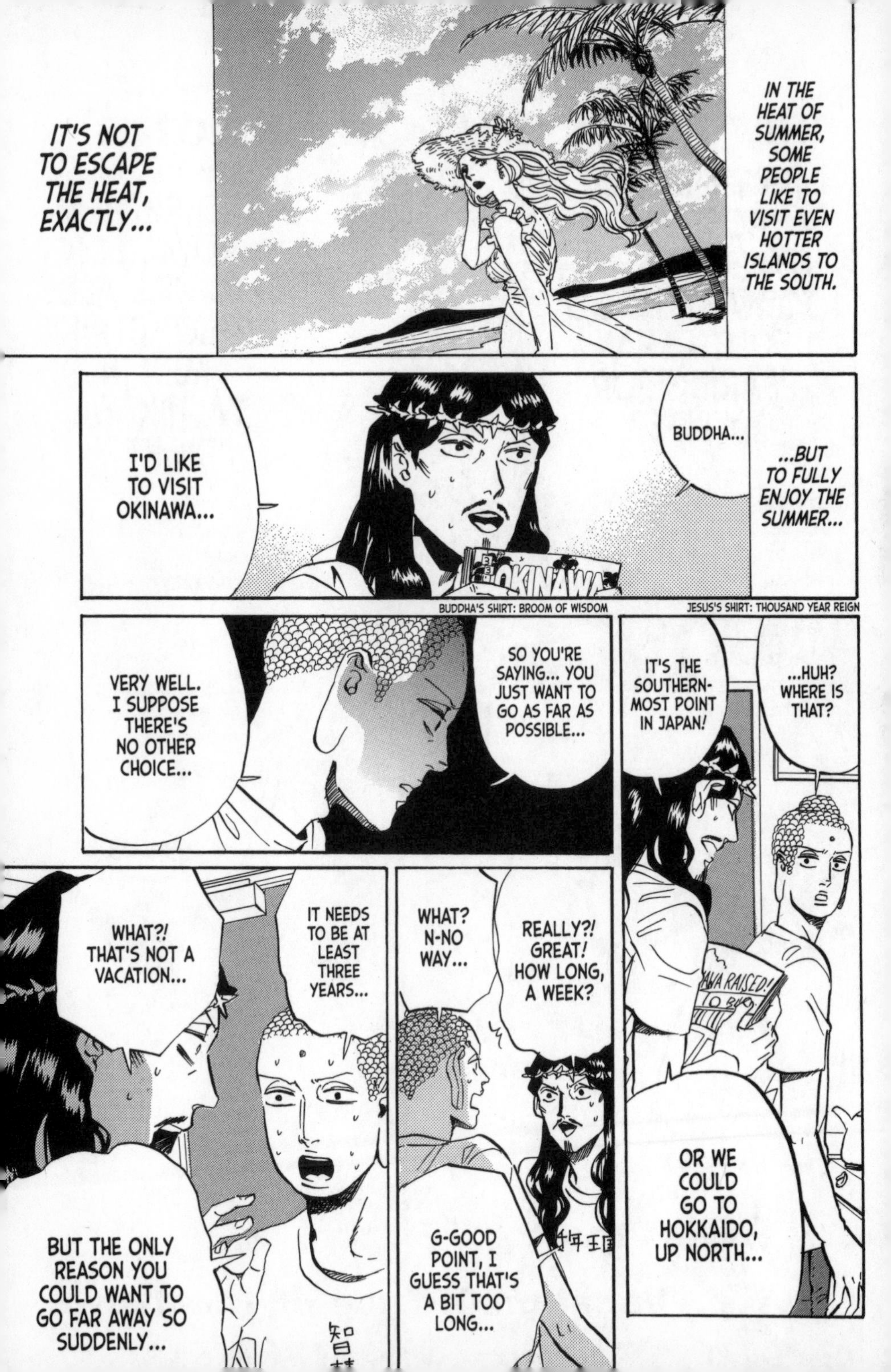
IN THE HEAT OF SUMMER, SOME PEOPLE LIKE TO VISIT EVEN HOTTER ISLANDS TO THE SOUTH.
IT'S NOT TO ESCAPE THE HEAT, EXACTLY...
...BUT TO FULLY ENJOY THE SUMMER...
BUDDHA...
I'D LIKE TO VISIT OKINAWA...
OKINAWA
JESUS'S SHIRT: THOUSAND YEAR REIGN
BUDDHA'S SHIRT: BROOM OF WISDOM
...HUH? WHERE IS THAT?
IT'S THE SOUTHERN-MOST POINT IN JAPAN!
OR WE COULD GO TO HOKKAIDO, UP NORTH...
SO YOU'RE SAYING... YOU JUST WANT TO GO AS FAR AS POSSIBLE...
VERY WELL. I SUPPOSE THERE'S NO OTHER CHOICE...
REALLY?! GREAT! HOW LONG, A WEEK?
WHAT? N-NO WAY...
IT NEEDS TO BE AT LEAST THREE YEARS...
G-GOOD POINT, I GUESS THAT'S A BIT TOO LONG...
WHAT?! THAT'S NOT A VACATION...
BUT THE ONLY REASON YOU COULD WANT TO GO FAR AWAY SO SUDDENLY...

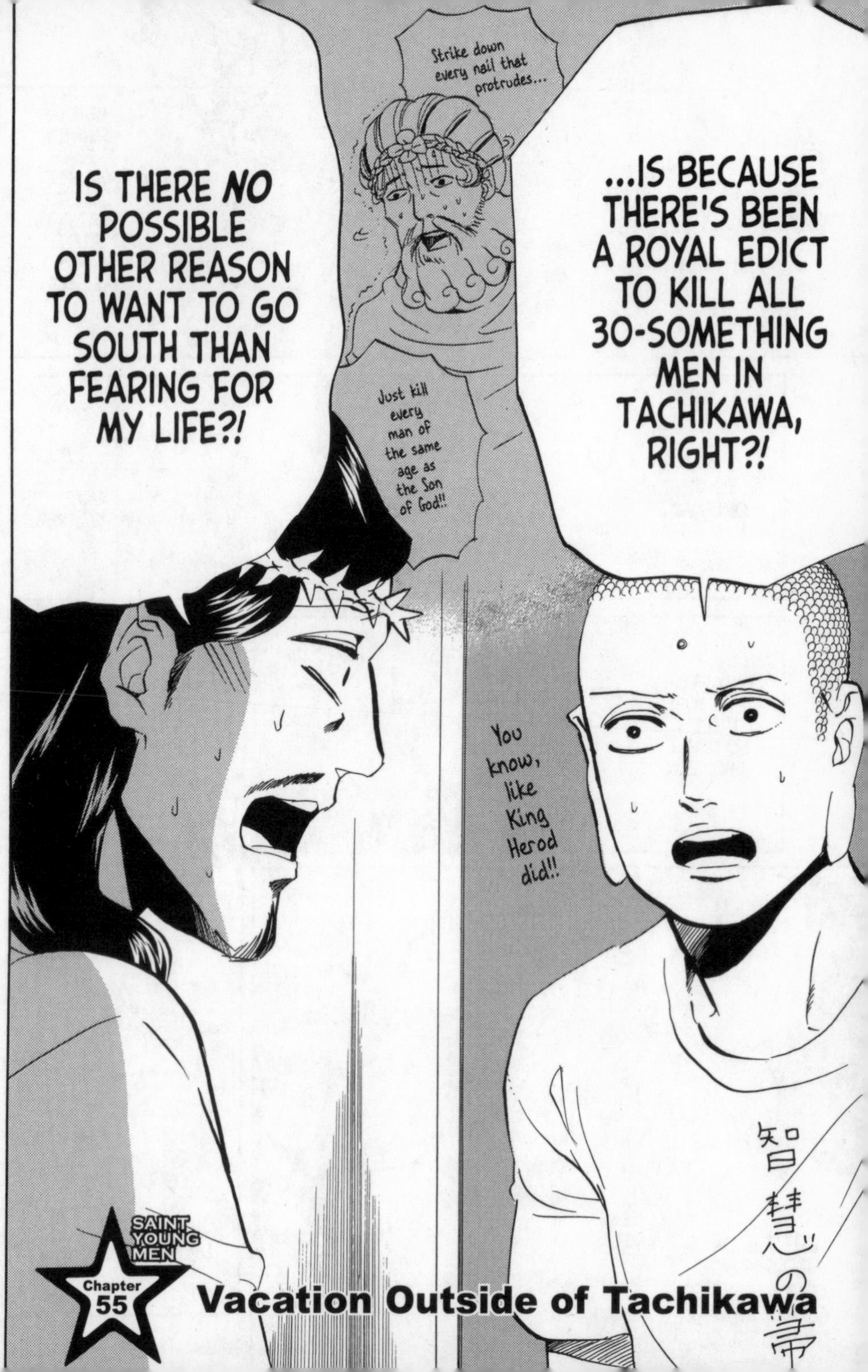
...IS BECAUSE THERE'S BEEN A ROYAL EDICT TO KILL ALL 30-SOMETHING MEN IN TACHIKAWA, RIGHT?!
You know, like King Herod did!!
Strike down every nail that protrudes...
Just kill every man of the same age as the Son of God!!
IS THERE NO POSSIBLE OTHER REASON TO WANT TO GO SOUTH THAN FEARING FOR MY LIFE?!
智慧の
SAINT YOUNG MEN
Chapter 55
Vacation Outside of Tachikawa

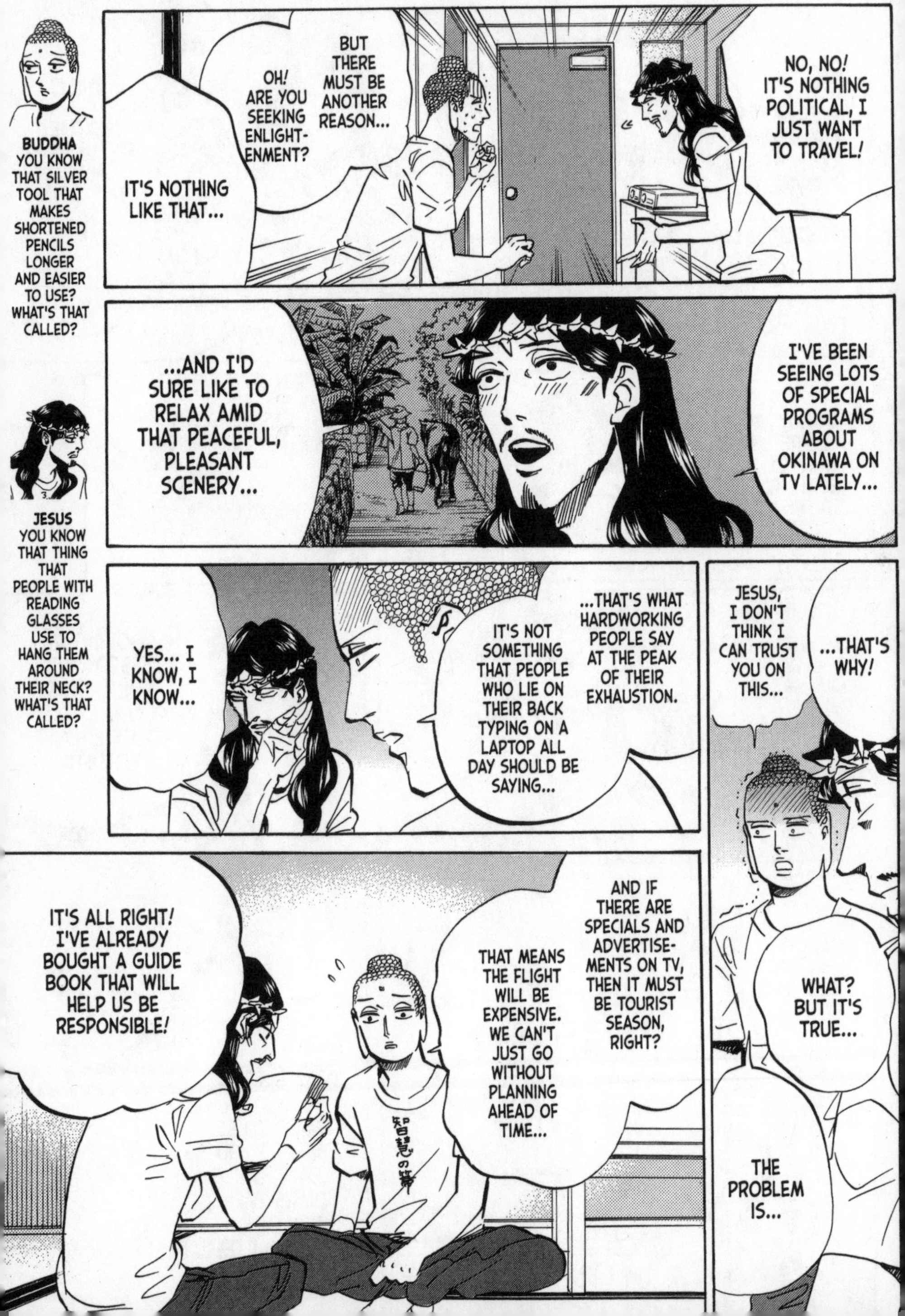
NO, NO! IT'S NOTHING POLITICAL, I JUST WANT TO TRAVEL!
BUT THERE MUST BE ANOTHER REASON...
OH! ARE YOU SEEKING ENLIGHTENMENT?
IT'S NOTHING LIKE THAT...
I'VE BEEN SEEING LOTS OF SPECIAL PROGRAMS ABOUT OKINAWA ON TV LATELY...
...AND I'D SURE LIKE TO RELAX AMID THAT PEACEFUL, PLEASANT SCENERY...
...THAT'S WHY!
JESUS, I DON'T THINK I CAN TRUST YOU ON THIS...
WHAT? BUT IT'S TRUE...
THE PROBLEM IS...
...THAT'S WHAT HARDWORKING PEOPLE SAY AT THE PEAK OF THEIR EXHAUSTION.
IT'S NOT SOMETHING THAT PEOPLE WHO LIE ON THEIR BACK TYPING ON A LAPTOP ALL DAY SHOULD BE SAYING...
YES... I KNOW, I KNOW...
AND IF THERE ARE SPECIALS AND ADVERTISEMENTS ON TV, THEN IT MUST BE TOURIST SEASON, RIGHT?
THAT MEANS THE FLIGHT WILL BE EXPENSIVE. WE CAN'T JUST GO WITHOUT PLANNING AHEAD OF TIME...
IT'S ALL RIGHT! I'VE ALREADY BOUGHT A GUIDE BOOK THAT WILL HELP US BE RESPONSIBLE!
BUDDHA YOU KNOW THAT SILVER TOOL THAT MAKES SHORTENED PENCILS LONGER AND EASIER TO USE? WHAT'S THAT CALLED?
JESUS YOU KNOW THAT THING THAT PEOPLE WITH READING GLASSES USE TO HANG THEM AROUND THEIR NECK? WHAT'S THAT CALLED?

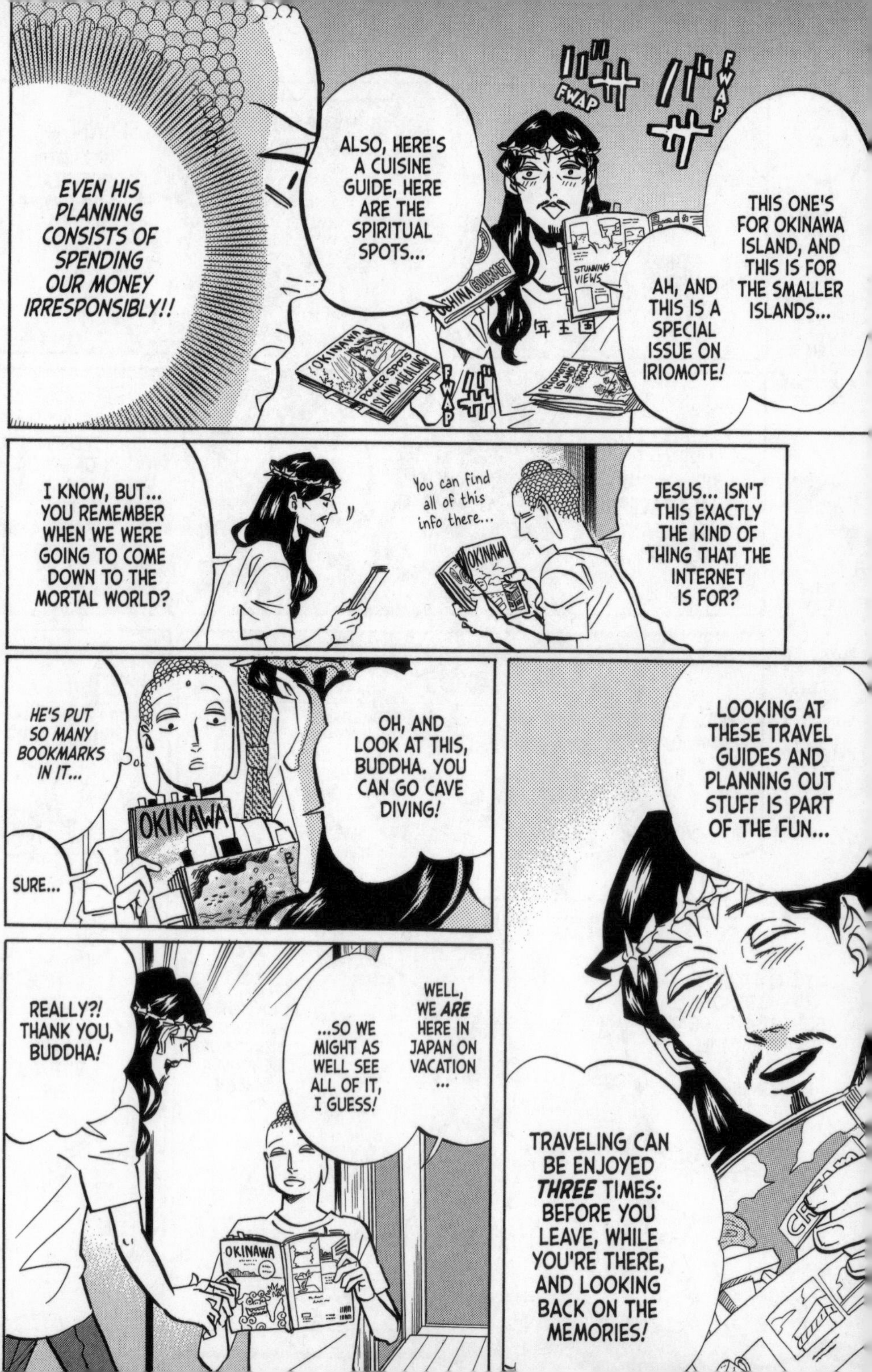
THIS ONE'S FOR OKINAWA ISLAND, AND THIS IS FOR THE SMALLER ISLANDS...
AH, AND THIS IS A SPECIAL ISSUE ON IRIOMOTE!
FWAP
FWAP
STUNNING VIEWS
IRIOMOTE ISLAND
ALSO, HERE'S A CUISINE GUIDE, HERE ARE THE SPIRITUAL SPOTS...
OKINAWA
POWER SPOTS ISLAND of HEALING
FWAP
EVEN HIS PLANNING CONSISTS OF SPENDING OUR MONEY IRRESPONSIBLY!!
JESUS... ISN'T THIS EXACTLY THE KIND OF THING THAT THE INTERNET IS FOR?
You can find all of this info there...
OKINAWA
I KNOW, BUT... YOU REMEMBER WHEN WE WERE GOING TO COME DOWN TO THE MORTAL WORLD?
LOOKING AT THESE TRAVEL GUIDES AND PLANNING OUT STUFF IS PART OF THE FUN...
TRAVELING CAN BE ENJOYED *THREE* TIMES: BEFORE YOU LEAVE, WHILE YOU'RE THERE, AND LOOKING BACK ON THE MEMORIES!
OH, AND LOOK AT THIS, BUDDHA. YOU CAN GO CAVE DIVING!
HE'S PUT SO MANY BOOKMARKS IN IT...
OKINAWA
SURE...
WELL, WE *ARE* HERE IN JAPAN ON VACATION...
...SO WE MIGHT AS WELL SEE ALL OF IT, I GUESS!
OKINAWA
REALLY?! THANK YOU, BUDDHA!

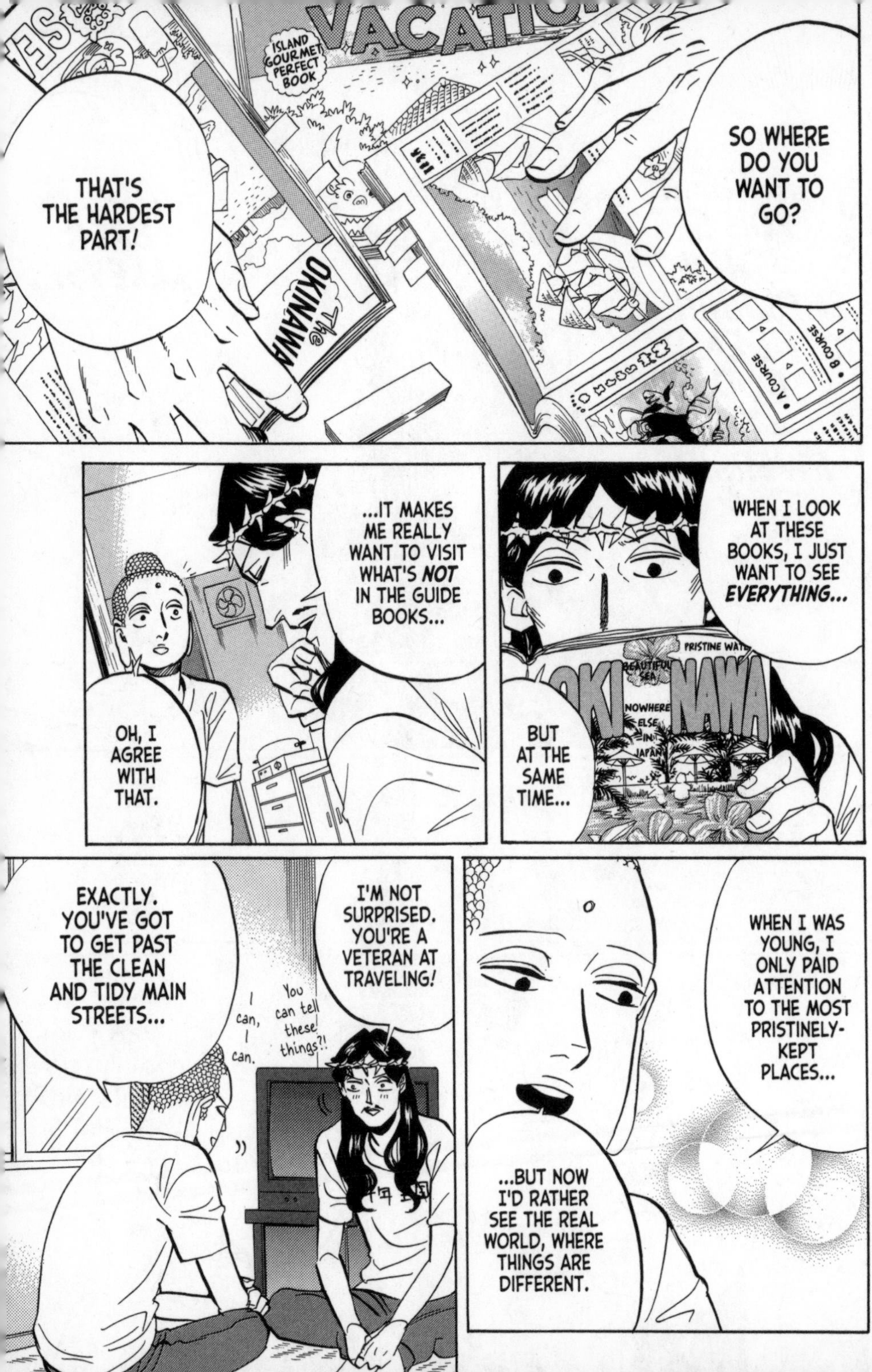
VACATIO
ISLAND GOURMET PERFECT BOOK
SO WHERE DO YOU WANT TO GO?
THAT'S THE HARDEST PART!
The OKINAWA
B COURSE
A COURSE
WHEN I LOOK AT THESE BOOKS, I JUST WANT TO SEE *EVERYTHING...*
BEAUTIFUL SEA
OKINAWA
NOWHERE ELSE IN JAPAN
BUT AT THE SAME TIME...
...IT MAKES ME REALLY WANT TO VISIT WHAT'S *NOT* IN THE GUIDE BOOKS...
OH, I AGREE WITH THAT.
WHEN I WAS YOUNG, I ONLY PAID ATTENTION TO THE MOST PRISTINELY-KEPT PLACES...
...BUT NOW I'D RATHER SEE THE REAL WORLD, WHERE THINGS ARE DIFFERENT.
I'M NOT SURPRISED. YOU'RE A VETERAN AT TRAVELING!
EXACTLY. YOU'VE GOT TO GET PAST THE CLEAN AND TIDY MAIN STREETS...
You can tell these things?!
I can, I can.

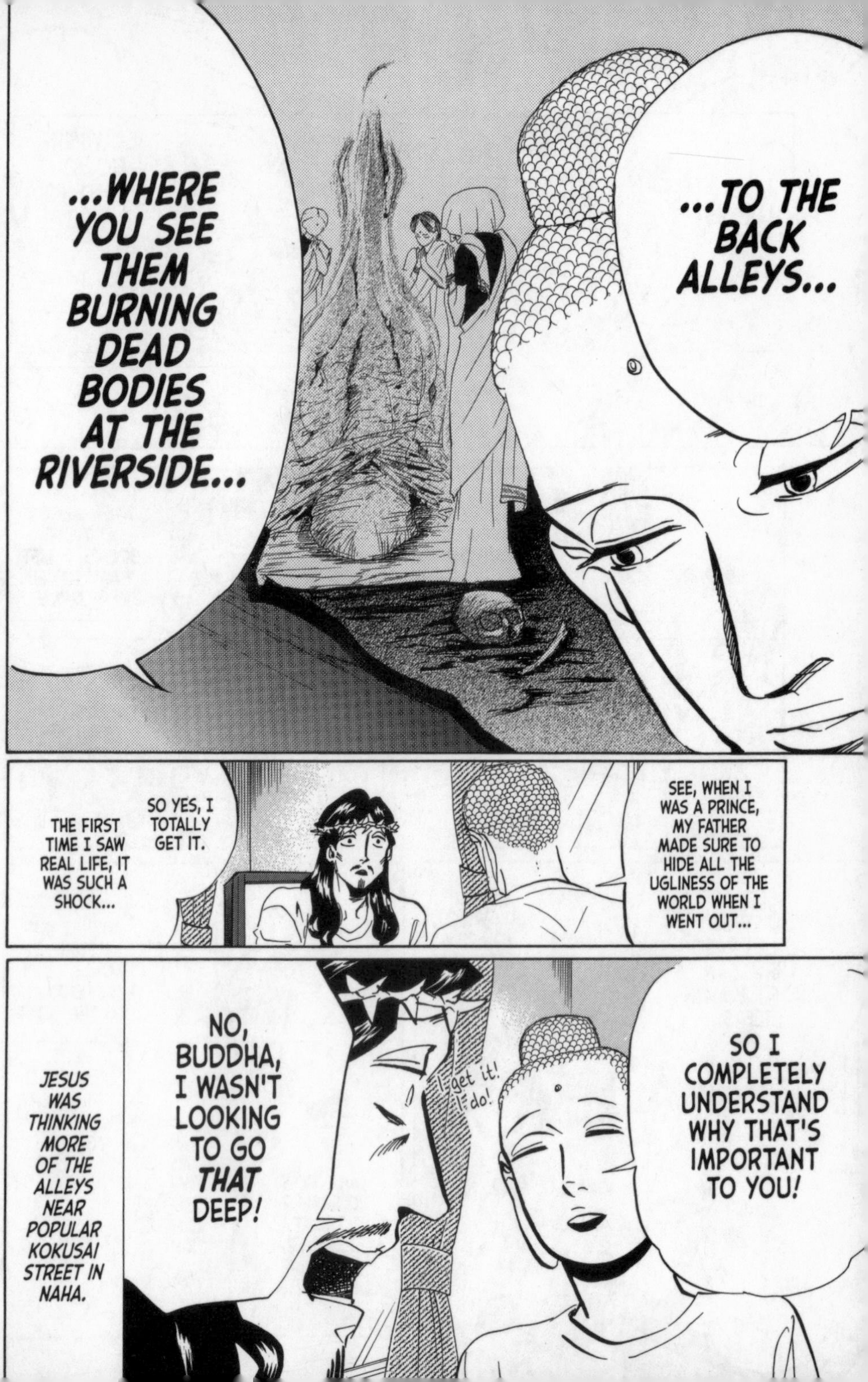
...TO THE BACK ALLEYS...
...WHERE YOU SEE THEM BURNING DEAD BODIES AT THE RIVERSIDE...
SEE, WHEN I WAS A PRINCE, MY FATHER MADE SURE TO HIDE ALL THE UGLINESS OF THE WORLD WHEN I WENT OUT...
THE FIRST TIME I SAW REAL LIFE, IT WAS SUCH A SHOCK...
SO YES, I TOTALLY GET IT.
SO I COMPLETELY UNDERSTAND WHY THAT'S IMPORTANT TO YOU!
I get it! I do!
NO, BUDDHA, I WASN'T LOOKING TO GO *THAT* DEEP!
JESUS WAS THINKING MORE OF THE ALLEYS NEAR POPULAR KOKUSAI STREET IN NAHA.

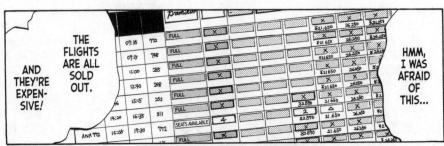

AND THEY'RE EXPENSIVE!

THE FLIGHTS ARE ALL SOLD OUT.

	07:35	7'12	FULL		X			×21,650	26,250	32,85?
	07:15	748	FULL		X			×21,650	26,250	32,85?
	11:00	285	FULL		X			×21,650	26,250	32,85?
	13:40	248	FULL		X			×21,650	26,250	32,85?
	15:15	252	FULL		X			32,870	21,650	26,250	X
16	19:20	311	FULL					2 32,870	21,650	△ 26,250	X
ANA 712	16:05	19:30	7'12	SEATS AVAILABLE	4			32,870	21,650	26,285	X
		121	FULL								× 26,25?

HMM, I WAS AFRAID OF THIS...

OH, YOU MEAN BECAUSE HE'S THE GUARDIAN ANGEL OF TRAVELERS...?

WHAT? WHY?

SHOULD I REACHED OUT TO RAPHAEL, YOU THINK?

HMM, WHAT NOW...?

OH, GOOD THINKING!

THE MAIN ATTRACTION FOR ME IS GOING DIVING!

ALSO, THIS...

...WE SHOULD RESERVE SOME TOUR EVENTS WHILE WE'RE AT IT.

IN ADDITION TO THE FLIGHTS...

WHAT? HE OWNS STOCKS?!

NO, BECAUSE HE OWNS STOCK IN ANA, AND HE COULD PROBABLY GET US SPECIAL SHAREHOLDER TICKETS.

HA HA, IT'LL BE FINE. JUST GET IN TOUCH WITH HIM!

...HE'LL WHINE FOR ME TO COME HOME BEFORE I GO TO OKINAWA...

THE PROBLEM IS, IF GABRIEL FINDS OUT...

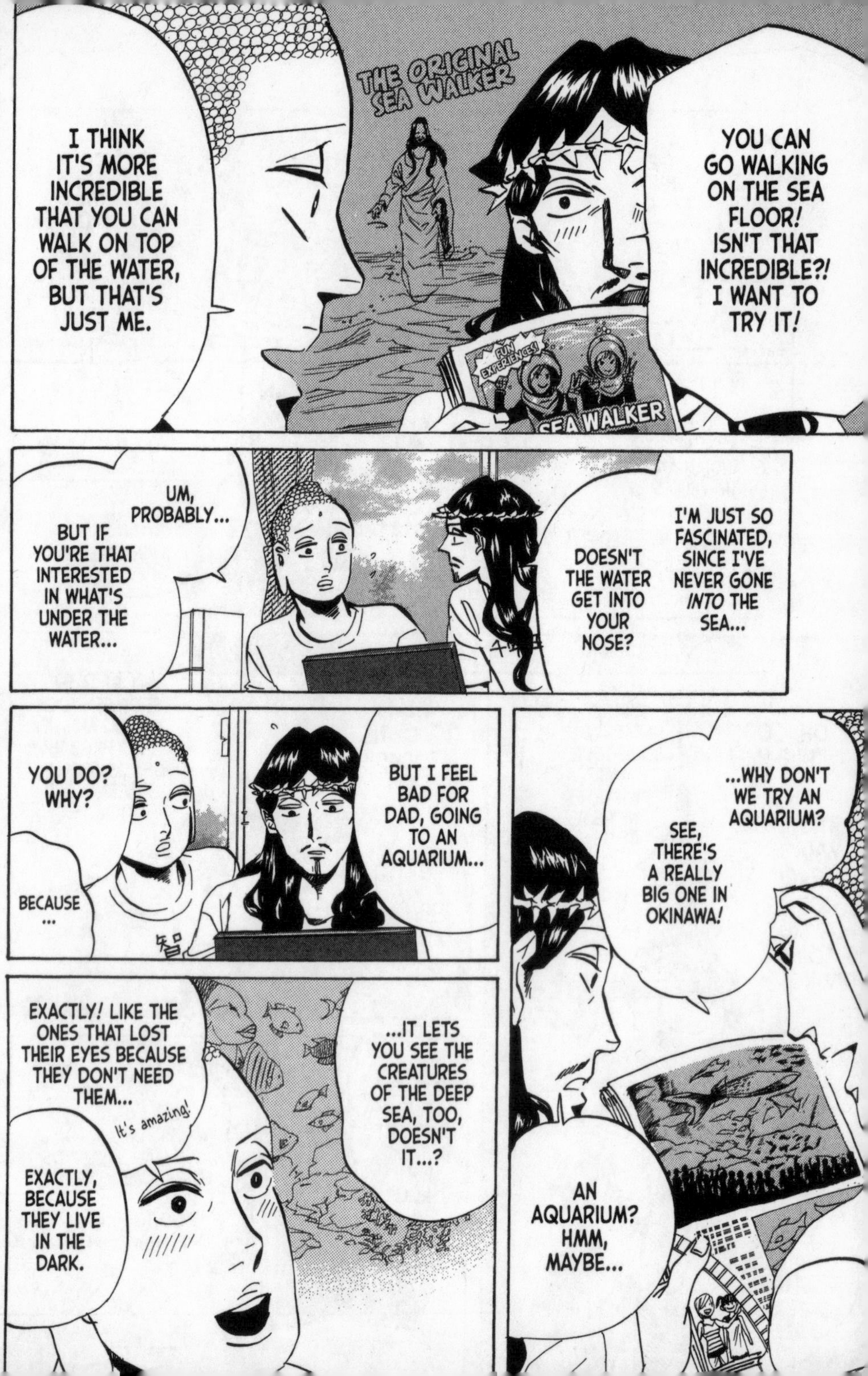
YOU CAN GO WALKING ON THE SEA FLOOR! ISN'T THAT INCREDIBLE?! I WANT TO TRY IT!
THE ORIGINAL SEA WALKER
FUN EXPERIENCES!
SEA WALKER
I THINK IT'S MORE INCREDIBLE THAT YOU CAN WALK ON TOP OF THE WATER, BUT THAT'S JUST ME.
I'M JUST SO FASCINATED, SINCE I'VE NEVER GONE *INTO* THE SEA...
DOESN'T THE WATER GET INTO YOUR NOSE?
UM, PROBABLY...
BUT IF YOU'RE THAT INTERESTED IN WHAT'S UNDER THE WATER...
...WHY DON'T WE TRY AN AQUARIUM?
SEE, THERE'S A REALLY BIG ONE IN OKINAWA!
AN AQUARIUM? HMM, MAYBE...
BUT I FEEL BAD FOR DAD, GOING TO AN AQUARIUM...
YOU DO? WHY?
BECAUSE ...
...IT LETS YOU SEE THE CREATURES OF THE DEEP SEA, TOO, DOESN'T IT...?
EXACTLY! LIKE THE ONES THAT LOST THEIR EYES BECAUSE THEY DON'T NEED THEM...
It's amazing!
EXACTLY, BECAUSE THEY LIVE IN THE DARK.

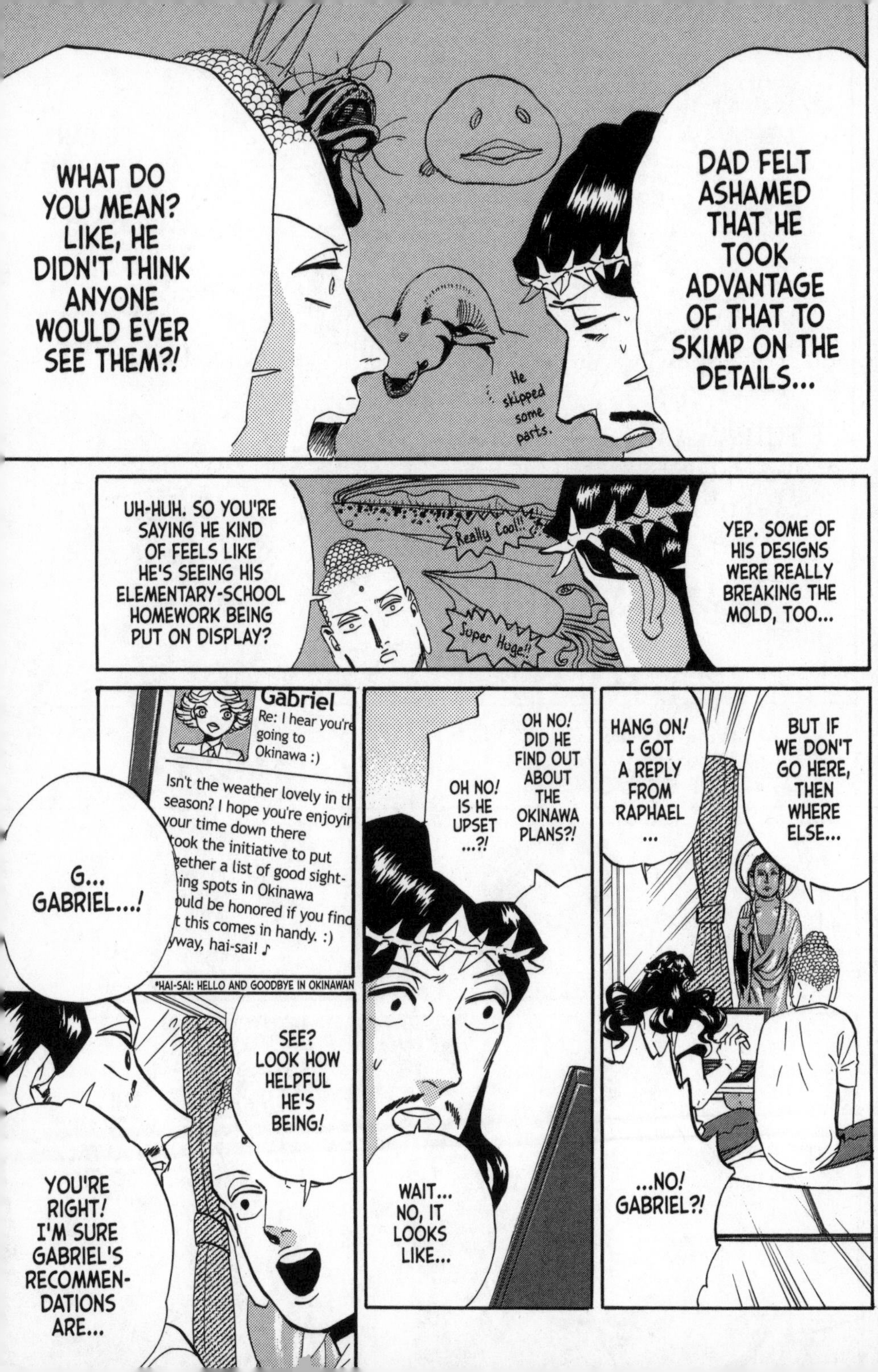
DAD FELT ASHAMED THAT HE TOOK ADVANTAGE OF THAT TO SKIMP ON THE DETAILS...
WHAT DO YOU MEAN? LIKE, HE DIDN'T THINK ANYONE WOULD EVER SEE THEM?!
He skipped some parts.
YEP. SOME OF HIS DESIGNS WERE REALLY BREAKING THE MOLD, TOO...
UH-HUH. SO YOU'RE SAYING HE KIND OF FEELS LIKE HE'S SEEING HIS ELEMENTARY-SCHOOL HOMEWORK BEING PUT ON DISPLAY?
Really Cool!!
Super Huge!!
BUT IF WE DON'T GO HERE, THEN WHERE ELSE...
HANG ON! I GOT A REPLY FROM RAPHAEL...
...NO! GABRIEL?!
OH NO! DID HE FIND OUT ABOUT THE OKINAWA PLANS?!
OH NO! IS HE UPSET...?!
WAIT... NO, IT LOOKS LIKE...
Gabriel
Re: I hear you're going to Okinawa :)
Isn't the weather lovely in th season? I hope you're enjoyir your time down there took the initiative to put gether a list of good sight-ing spots in Okinawa ould be honored if you find t this comes in handy. :) yway, hai-sai! ♪
G... GABRIEL...!
*HAI-SAI: HELLO AND GOODBYE IN OKINAWAN
SEE? LOOK HOW HELPFUL HE'S BEING!
YOU'RE RIGHT! I'M SURE GABRIEL'S RECOMMEN-DATIONS ARE...

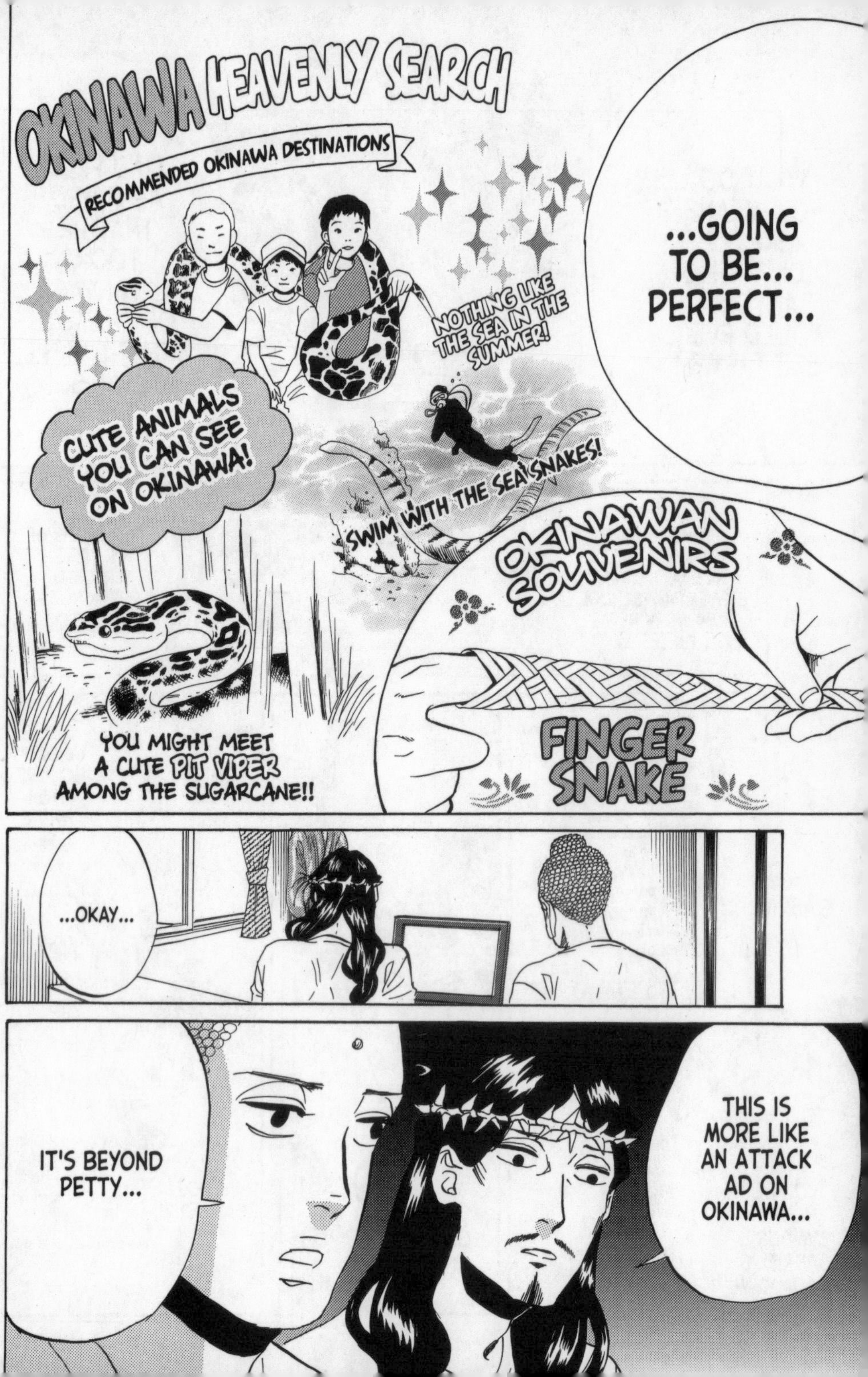
...GOING TO BE... PERFECT...
OKINAWA HEAVENLY SEARCH
RECOMMENDED OKINAWA DESTINATIONS
NOTHING LIKE THE SEA IN THE SUMMER!
CUTE ANIMALS YOU CAN SEE ON OKINAWA!
SWIM WITH THE SEA SNAKES!
OKINAWAN SOUVENIRS
FINGER SNAKE
YOU MIGHT MEET A CUTE PIT VIPER AMONG THE SUGARCANE!!
...OKAY...
THIS IS MORE LIKE AN ATTACK AD ON OKINAWA...
IT'S BEYOND PETTY...

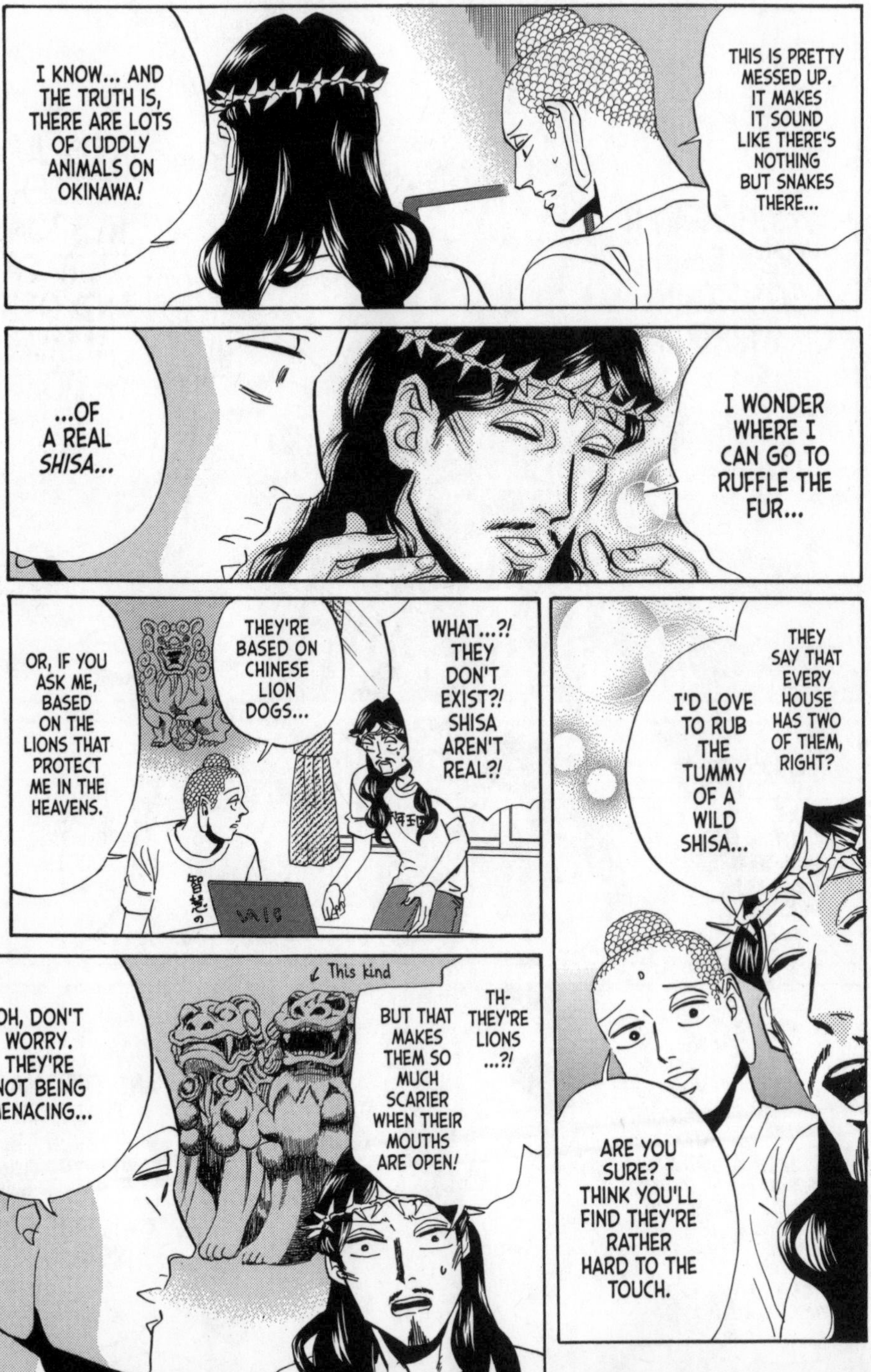
THIS IS PRETTY MESSED UP. IT MAKES IT SOUND LIKE THERE'S NOTHING BUT SNAKES THERE...
I KNOW... AND THE TRUTH IS, THERE ARE LOTS OF CUDDLY ANIMALS ON OKINAWA!
I WONDER WHERE I CAN GO TO RUFFLE THE FUR...
...OF A REAL *SHISA*...
THEY SAY THAT EVERY HOUSE HAS TWO OF THEM, RIGHT?
I'D LOVE TO RUB THE TUMMY OF A WILD SHISA...
ARE YOU SURE? I THINK YOU'LL FIND THEY'RE RATHER HARD TO THE TOUCH.
WHAT...?! THEY DON'T EXIST?! SHISA AREN'T REAL?!
THEY'RE BASED ON CHINESE LION DOGS...
OR, IF YOU ASK ME, BASED ON THE LIONS THAT PROTECT ME IN THE HEAVENS.
TH- THEY'RE LIONS ...?!
BUT THAT MAKES THEM SO MUCH SCARIER WHEN THEIR MOUTHS ARE OPEN!
This kind
OH, DON'T WORRY. THEY'RE NOT BEING MENACING...

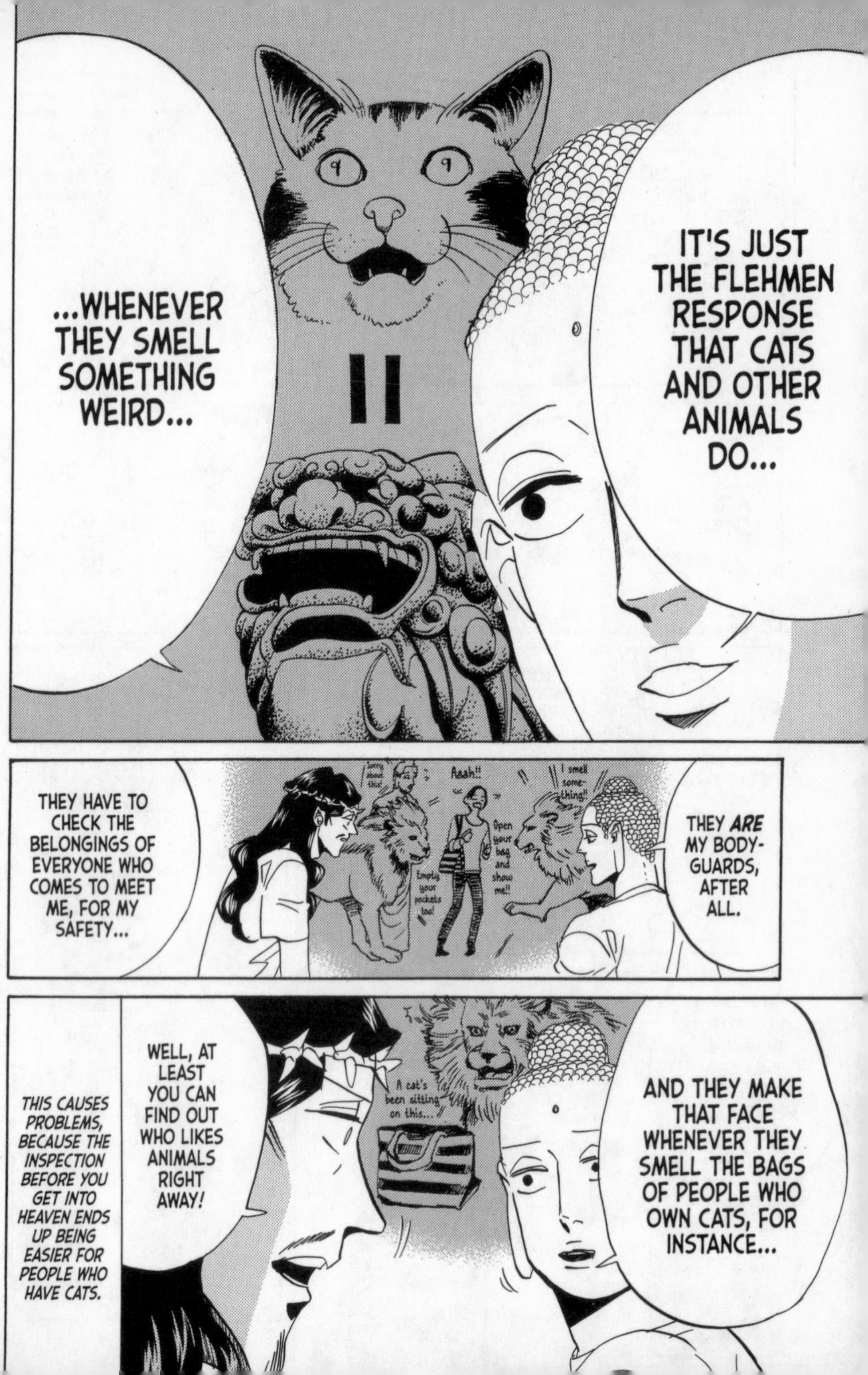
IT'S JUST THE FLEHMEN RESPONSE THAT CATS AND OTHER ANIMALS DO...
...WHENEVER THEY SMELL SOMETHING WEIRD...
THEY *ARE* MY BODY-GUARDS, AFTER ALL.
I smell some-thing!!
Open your bag and show me!!
Aaah!!
Sorry about this!
Empty your pockets too!
THEY HAVE TO CHECK THE BELONGINGS OF EVERYONE WHO COMES TO MEET ME, FOR MY SAFETY...
AND THEY MAKE THAT FACE WHENEVER THEY SMELL THE BAGS OF PEOPLE WHO OWN CATS, FOR INSTANCE...
A cat's been sitting on this...
WELL, AT LEAST YOU CAN FIND OUT WHO LIKES ANIMALS RIGHT AWAY!
THIS CAUSES PROBLEMS, BECAUSE THE INSPECTION BEFORE YOU GET INTO HEAVEN ENDS UP BEING EASIER FOR PEOPLE WHO HAVE CATS.

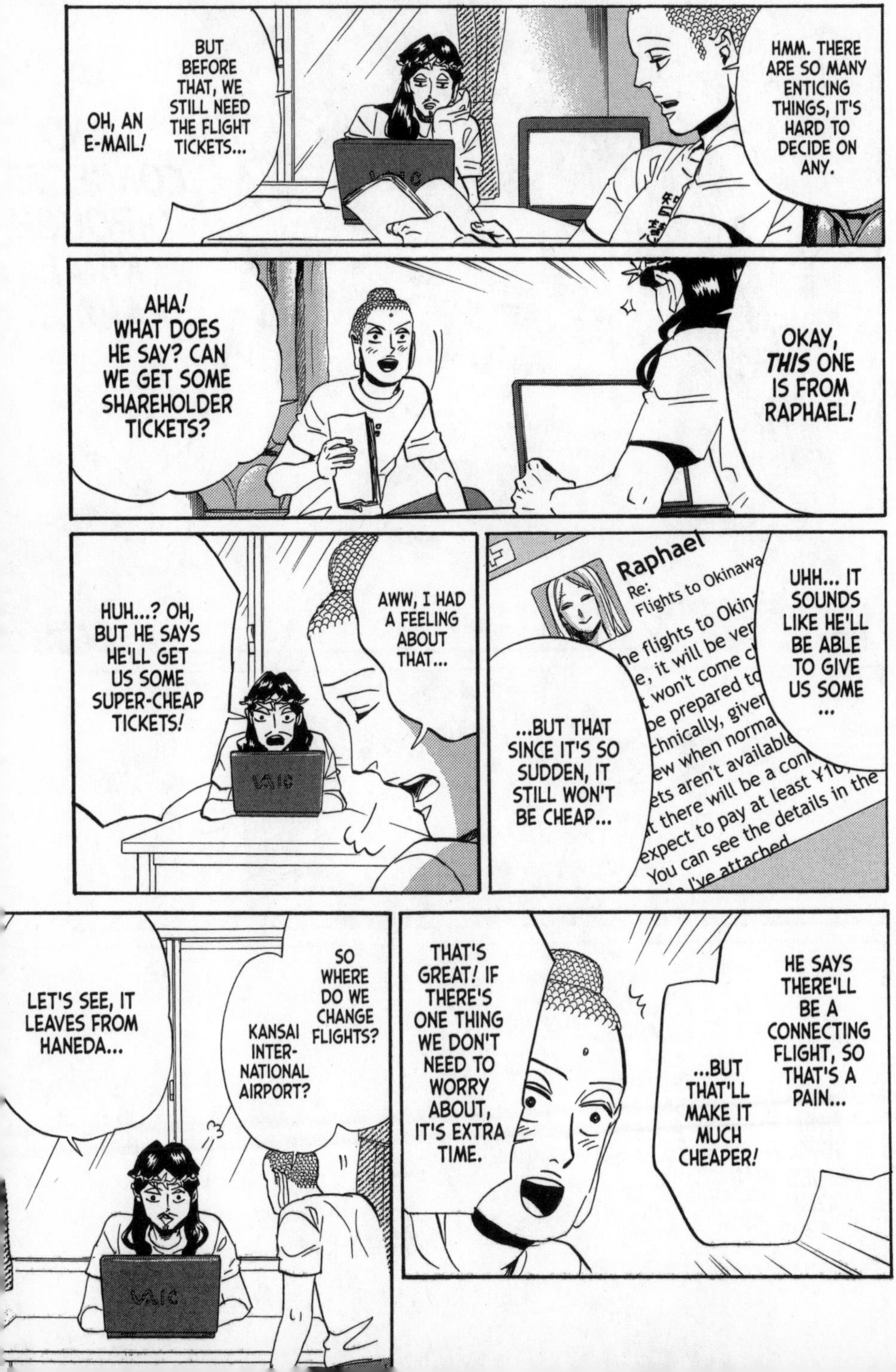
HMM. THERE ARE SO MANY ENTICING THINGS, IT'S HARD TO DECIDE ON ANY.
BUT BEFORE THAT, WE STILL NEED THE FLIGHT TICKETS...
OH, AN E-MAIL!
OKAY, *THIS* ONE IS FROM RAPHAEL!
AHA! WHAT DOES HE SAY? CAN WE GET SOME SHAREHOLDER TICKETS?
Raphael
Re: Flights to Okinawa
UHH... IT SOUNDS LIKE HE'LL BE ABLE TO GIVE US SOME ...
...BUT THAT SINCE IT'S SO SUDDEN, IT STILL WON'T BE CHEAP...
AWW, I HAD A FEELING ABOUT THAT...
HUH...? OH, BUT HE SAYS HE'LL GET US SOME SUPER-CHEAP TICKETS!
HE SAYS THERE'LL BE A CONNECTING FLIGHT, SO THAT'S A PAIN...
...BUT THAT'LL MAKE IT MUCH CHEAPER!
THAT'S GREAT! IF THERE'S ONE THING WE DON'T NEED TO WORRY ABOUT, IT'S EXTRA TIME.
SO WHERE DO WE CHANGE FLIGHTS?
KANSAI INTER-NATIONAL AIRPORT?
LET'S SEE, IT LEAVES FROM HANEDA...

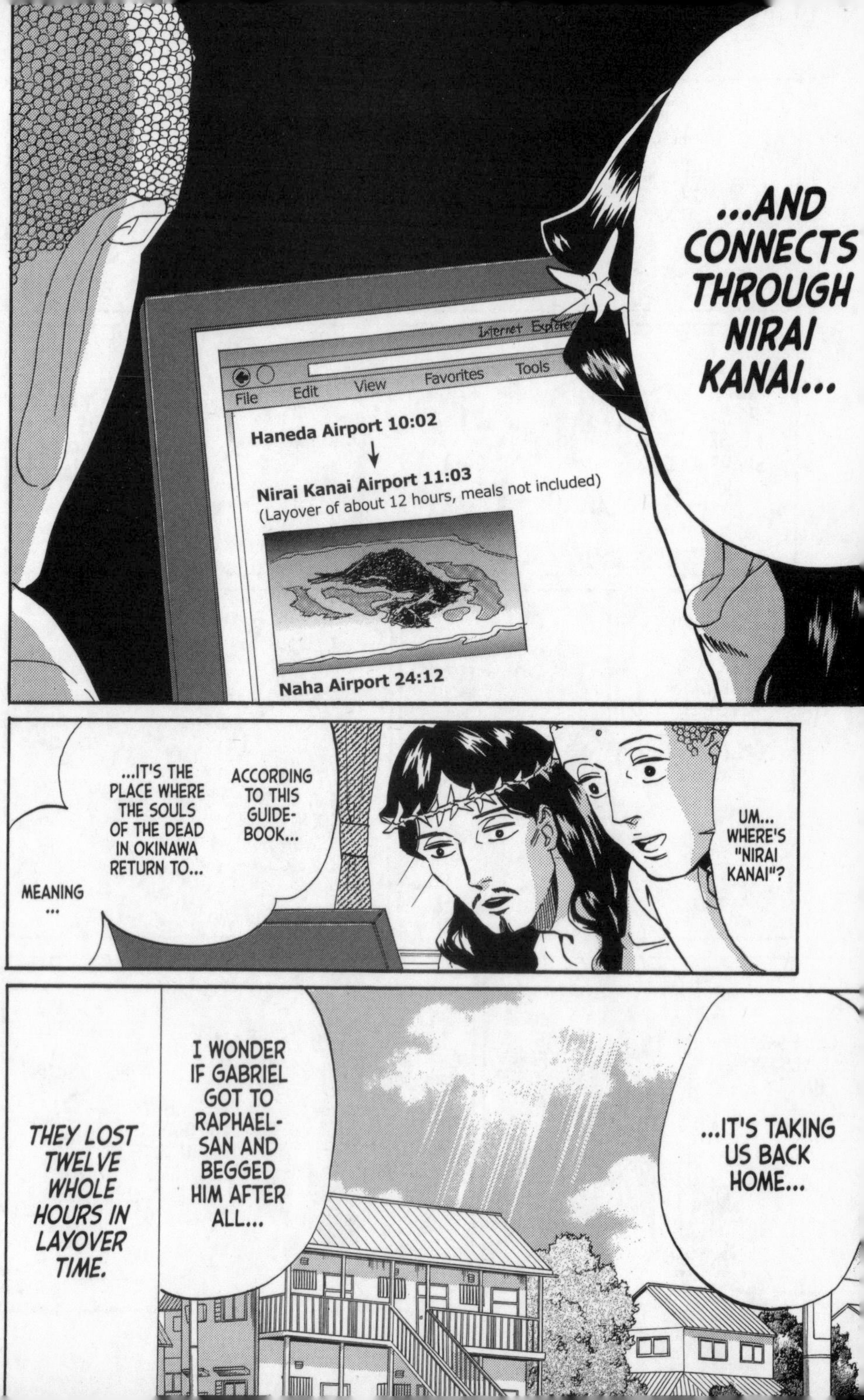
...AND CONNECTS THROUGH NIRAI KANAI...
File Edit View Favorites Tools
Haneda Airport 10:02
Nirai Kanai Airport 11:03
(Layover of about 12 hours, meals not included)
Naha Airport 24:12
UM... WHERE'S "NIRAI KANAI"?
ACCORDING TO THIS GUIDE-BOOK...
...IT'S THE PLACE WHERE THE SOULS OF THE DEAD IN OKINAWA RETURN TO...
MEANING ...
...IT'S TAKING US BACK HOME...
I WONDER IF GABRIEL GOT TO RAPHAEL-SAN AND BEGGED HIM AFTER ALL...
THEY LOST TWELVE WHOLE HOURS IN LAYOVER TIME.

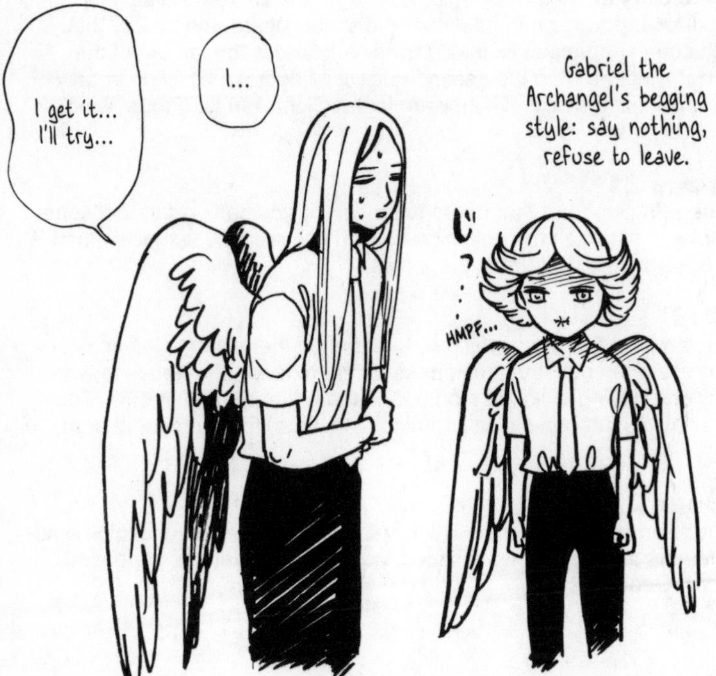
Gabriel the Archangel's begging style: say nothing, refuse to leave.
じっ...
HMPF...
I...
I get it... I'll try...

CHAPTER 55 TRANSLATION NOTES

Thousand Year Reign, page 208
In the Book of Revelation, it is stated that after Christ's return, the souls of the faithful who were killed for being faithful to him shall be resurrected and join Christ in a thousand-year reign over the earth, after which the rest of the souls of the dead will be revived.

Broom of Wisdom, page 208
An idea that stems from the story of one of the Buddha's lesser-known disciples, Suddhipanthaka, who was dull-witted and unable to learn the Buddha's teachings. Instead, Buddha taught him to sweep the floor and repeat that statement in his mind. By doing so, the broom of wisdom also swept his mind free of negative forces and allowed him to reach enlightenment.

King Herod, page 210
The King of Judea at the time of Jesus' birth. According to the 2nd chapter of Matthew, Herod heard of the prophecy of the infant Messiah, and attempted to have all newborn boys put to death to ensure that his rule could not be overthrown.

Okinawa, page 210
The southernmost territory of Japan. Much like Hawaii in the United States, it is a tourist destination for Japanese and has its own distinct culture and history that is separate from the main Japanese islands. Okinawa Island is the largest of the islands in Okinawa Prefecture, and the second-largest is Iriomote, which is largely wild jungle. The term Uchina means "Okinawan" in the Okinawan language, which is called Uchinaaguchi.

Power spot, page 211
A Japanese-invented English term that refers to any place you can visit to feel some kind of spiritual "power," although the definition of such is extremely subjective and is largely used as a designation for tourism purposes.

Shisa, page 218
A traditional Okinawan guardian spirit which is a variant on the ancient Chinese guardian lion. They are often constructed in pairs on the exterior of a house to ward off evil, traditionally one having a closed mouth, and the other an open mouth. They also have a close relative in Japan called komainu (lion dogs) that originated from the same source.

Nirai Kanai, page 221
The realm of the gods and the dead in the Ryukyuan (Okinawan) native religion, and the source of all life. It is traditionally worshipped facing east, toward its supposed location in the Pacific Ocean.

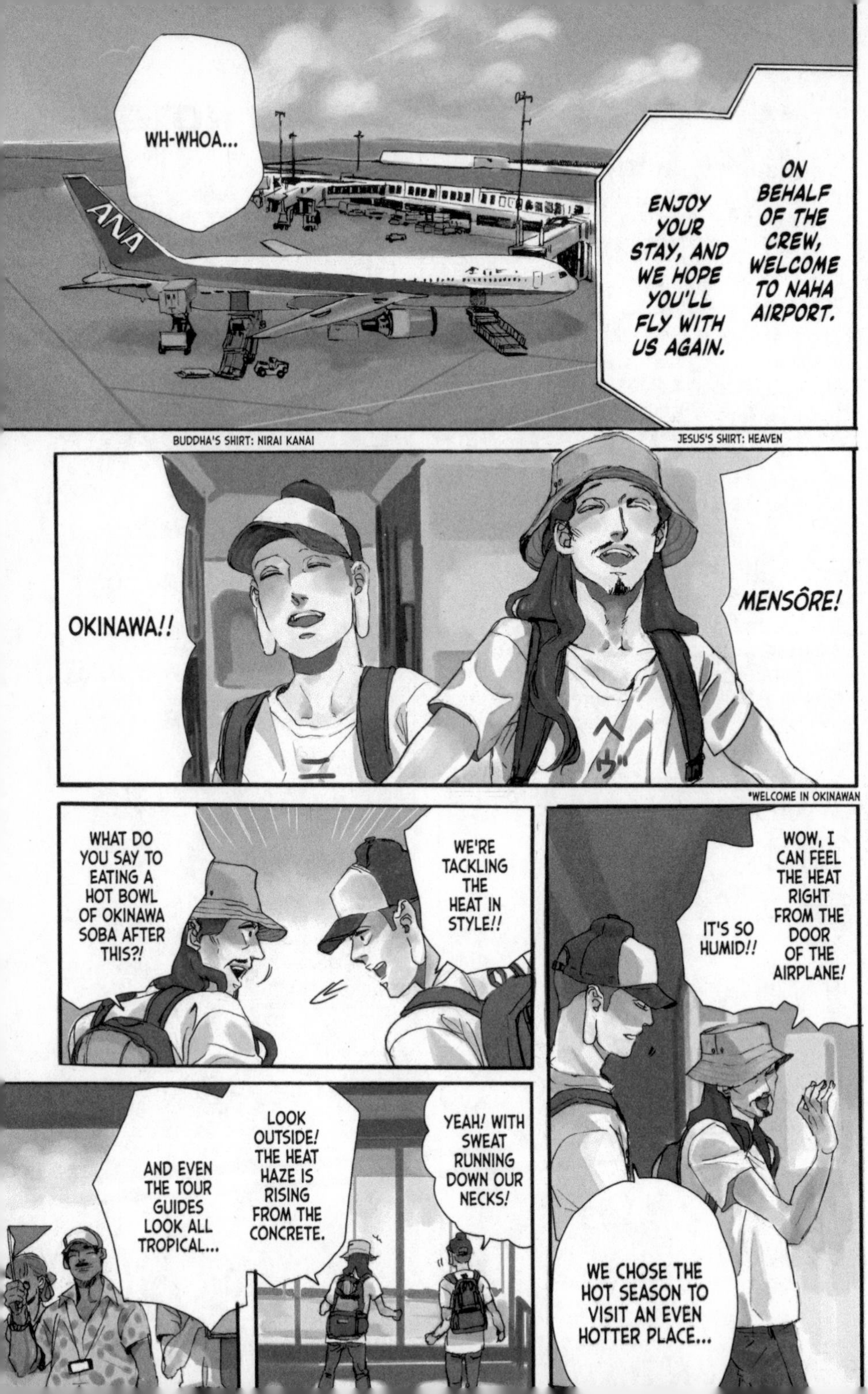
ON BEHALF OF THE CREW, WELCOME TO NAHA AIRPORT.
ENJOY YOUR STAY, AND WE HOPE YOU'LL FLY WITH US AGAIN.
WH-WHOA...
JESUS'S SHIRT: HEAVEN
BUDDHA'S SHIRT: NIRAI KANAI
MENSÔRE!
OKINAWA!!
*WELCOME IN OKINAWAN
WOW, I CAN FEEL THE HEAT RIGHT FROM THE DOOR OF THE AIRPLANE!
IT'S SO HUMID!!
WE CHOSE THE HOT SEASON TO VISIT AN EVEN HOTTER PLACE...
WE'RE TACKLING THE HEAT IN STYLE!!
WHAT DO YOU SAY TO EATING A HOT BOWL OF OKINAWA SOBA AFTER THIS?!
YEAH! WITH SWEAT RUNNING DOWN OUR NECKS!
LOOK OUTSIDE! THE HEAT HAZE IS RISING FROM THE CONCRETE.
AND EVEN THE TOUR GUIDES LOOK ALL TROPICAL...

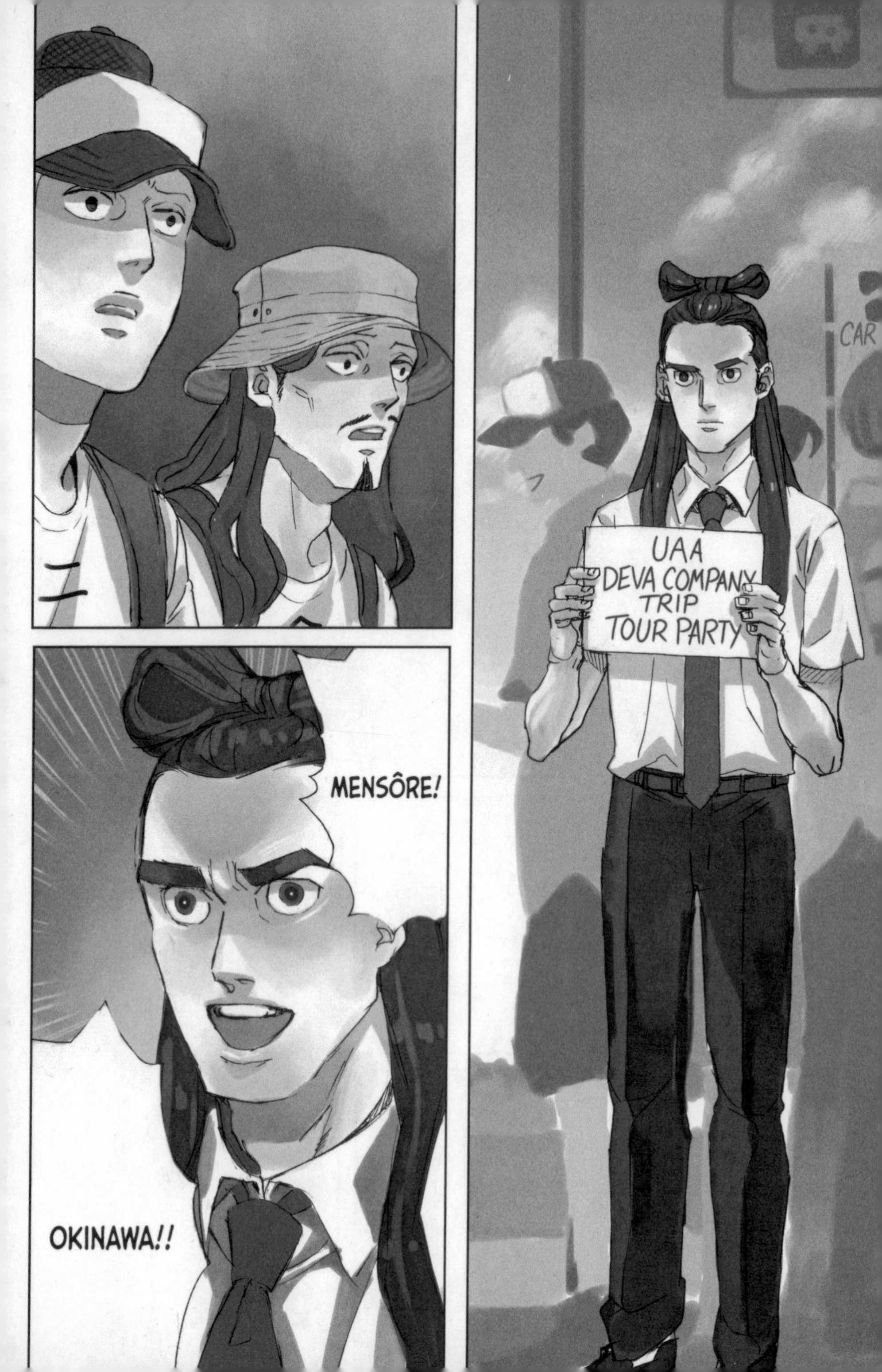
CAR
UAA
DEVA COMPANY
TRIP
TOUR PARTY
MENSÔRE!
OKINAWA!!

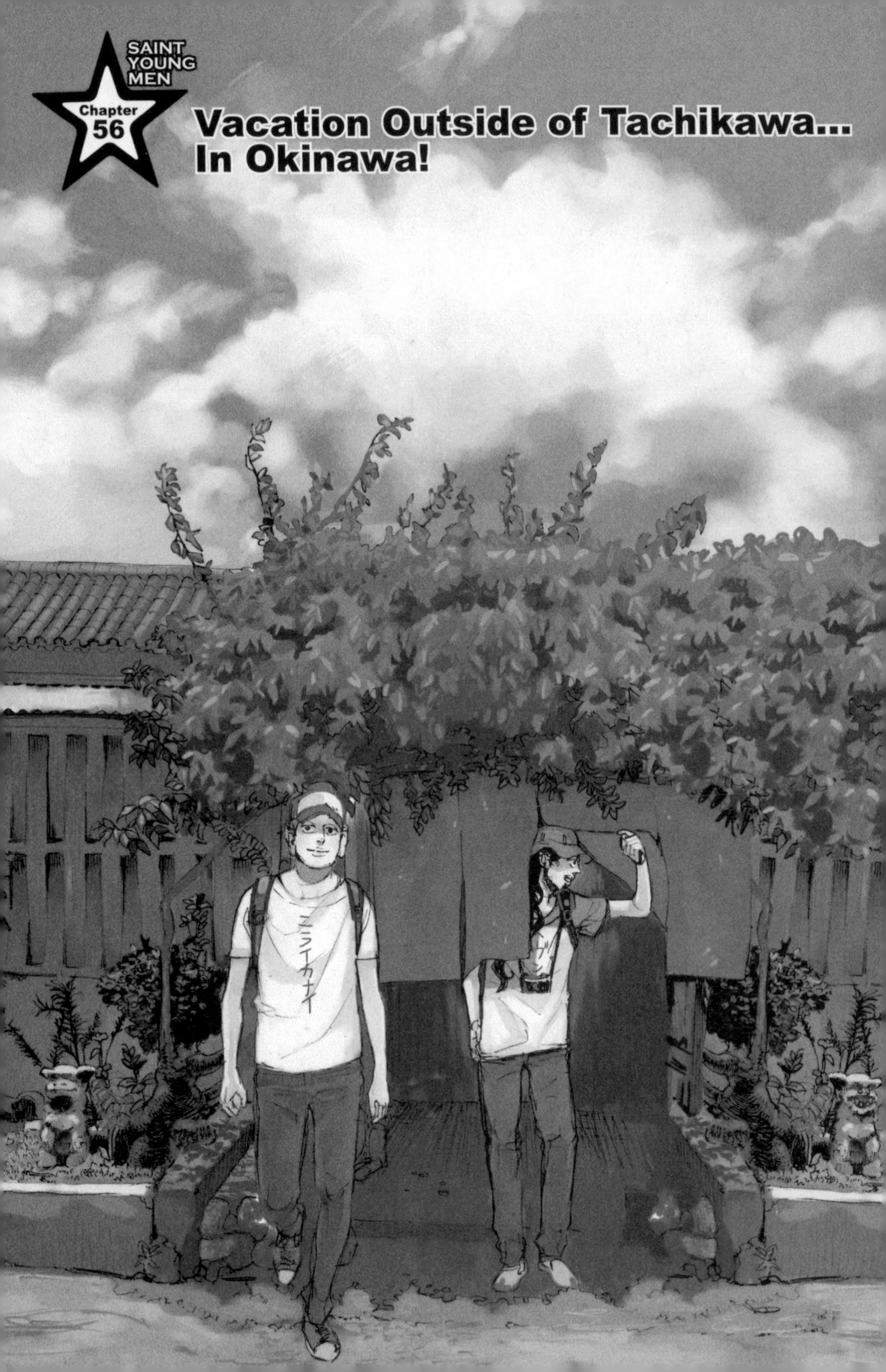
SAINT YOUNG MEN
Chapter 56
Vacation Outside of Tachikawa... In Okinawa!
ニライカナイ

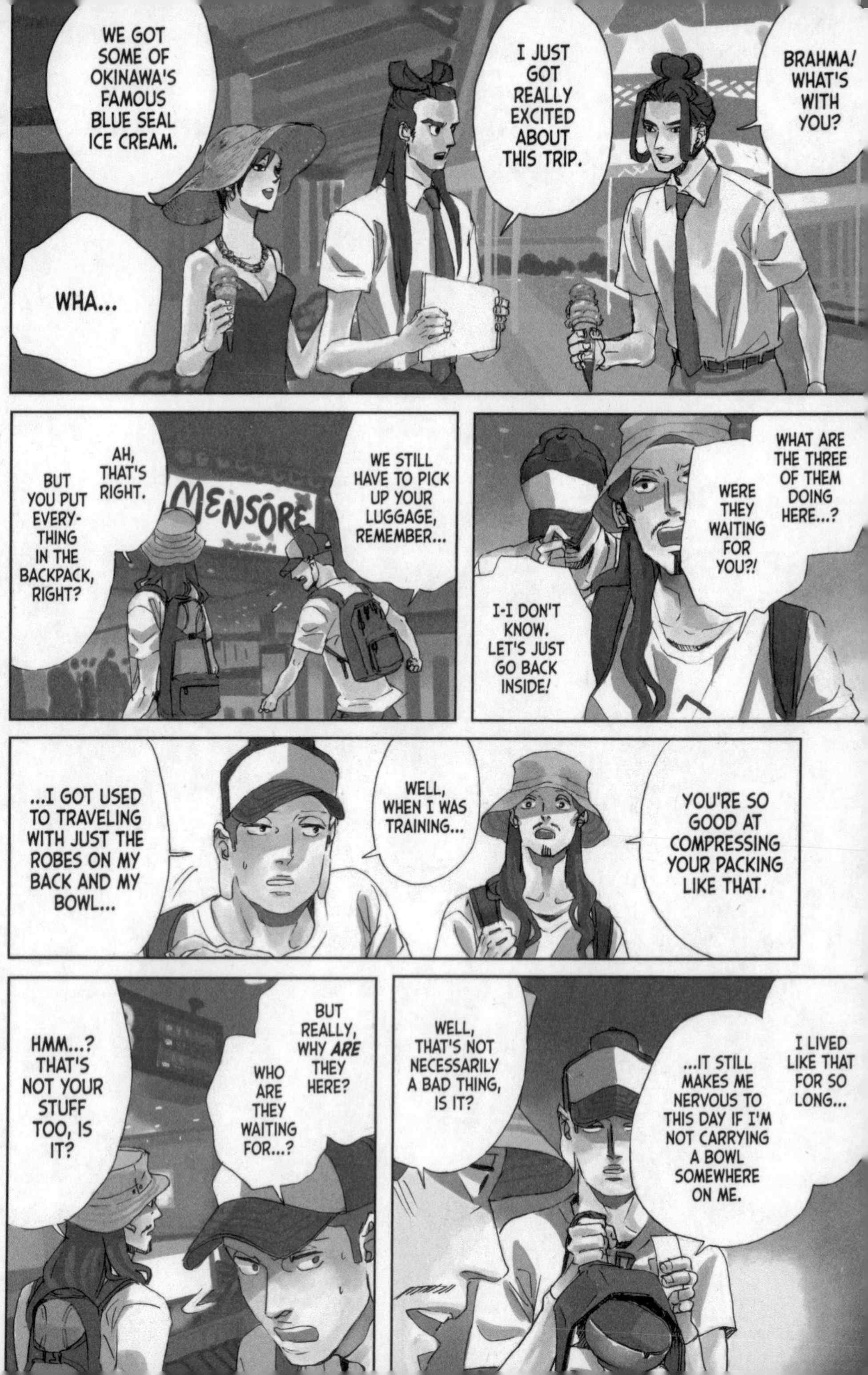
BRAHMA! WHAT'S WITH YOU?
I JUST GOT REALLY EXCITED ABOUT THIS TRIP.
WE GOT SOME OF OKINAWA'S FAMOUS BLUE SEAL ICE CREAM.
WHA...
WHAT ARE THE THREE OF THEM DOING HERE...?
WERE THEY WAITING FOR YOU?!
I-I DON'T KNOW. LET'S JUST GO BACK INSIDE!
MENSÔRE
WE STILL HAVE TO PICK UP YOUR LUGGAGE, REMEMBER...
AH, THAT'S RIGHT.
BUT YOU PUT EVERY-THING IN THE BACKPACK, RIGHT?
YOU'RE SO GOOD AT COMPRESSING YOUR PACKING LIKE THAT.
WELL, WHEN I WAS TRAINING...
...I GOT USED TO TRAVELING WITH JUST THE ROBES ON MY BACK AND MY BOWL...
I LIVED LIKE THAT FOR SO LONG...
...IT STILL MAKES ME NERVOUS TO THIS DAY IF I'M NOT CARRYING A BOWL SOMEWHERE ON ME.
WELL, THAT'S NOT NECESSARILY A BAD THING, IS IT?
BUT REALLY, WHY *ARE* THEY HERE?
WHO ARE THEY WAITING FOR...?
HMM...? THAT'S NOT YOUR STUFF TOO, IS IT?

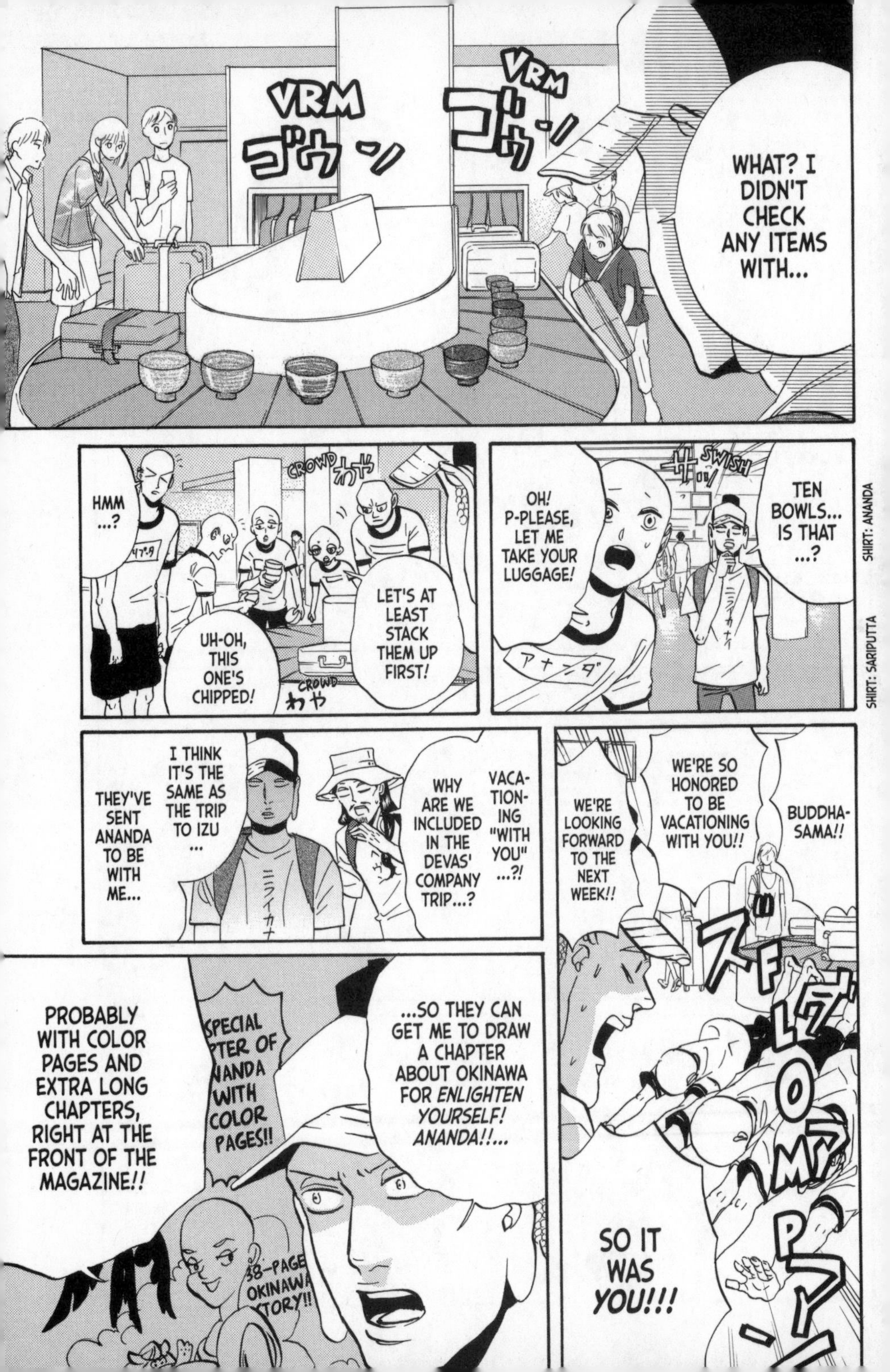
VRM
VRM
WHAT? I DIDN'T CHECK ANY ITEMS WITH...
SWISH
TEN BOWLS... IS THAT ...?
OH! P-PLEASE, LET ME TAKE YOUR LUGGAGE!
HMM ...?
CROWD
LET'S AT LEAST STACK THEM UP FIRST!
UH-OH, THIS ONE'S CHIPPED!
CROWD
SHIRT: ANANDA
SHIRT: SARIPUTTA
BUDDHA-SAMA!!
WE'RE SO HONORED TO BE VACATIONING WITH YOU!!
WE'RE LOOKING FORWARD TO THE NEXT WEEK!!
FLOMP
SO IT WAS YOU!!!
VACA-TION-ING "WITH YOU" ...?!
WHY ARE WE INCLUDED IN THE DEVAS' COMPANY TRIP...?
I THINK IT'S THE SAME AS THE TRIP TO IZU ...
THEY'VE SENT ANANDA TO BE WITH ME...
...SO THEY CAN GET ME TO DRAW A CHAPTER ABOUT OKINAWA FOR *ENLIGHTEN YOURSELF! ANANDA!!*...
SPECIAL PTER OF NANDA WITH COLOR PAGES!!
PROBABLY WITH COLOR PAGES AND EXTRA LONG CHAPTERS, RIGHT AT THE FRONT OF THE MAGAZINE!!
38-PAGE OKINAWA TORY!!

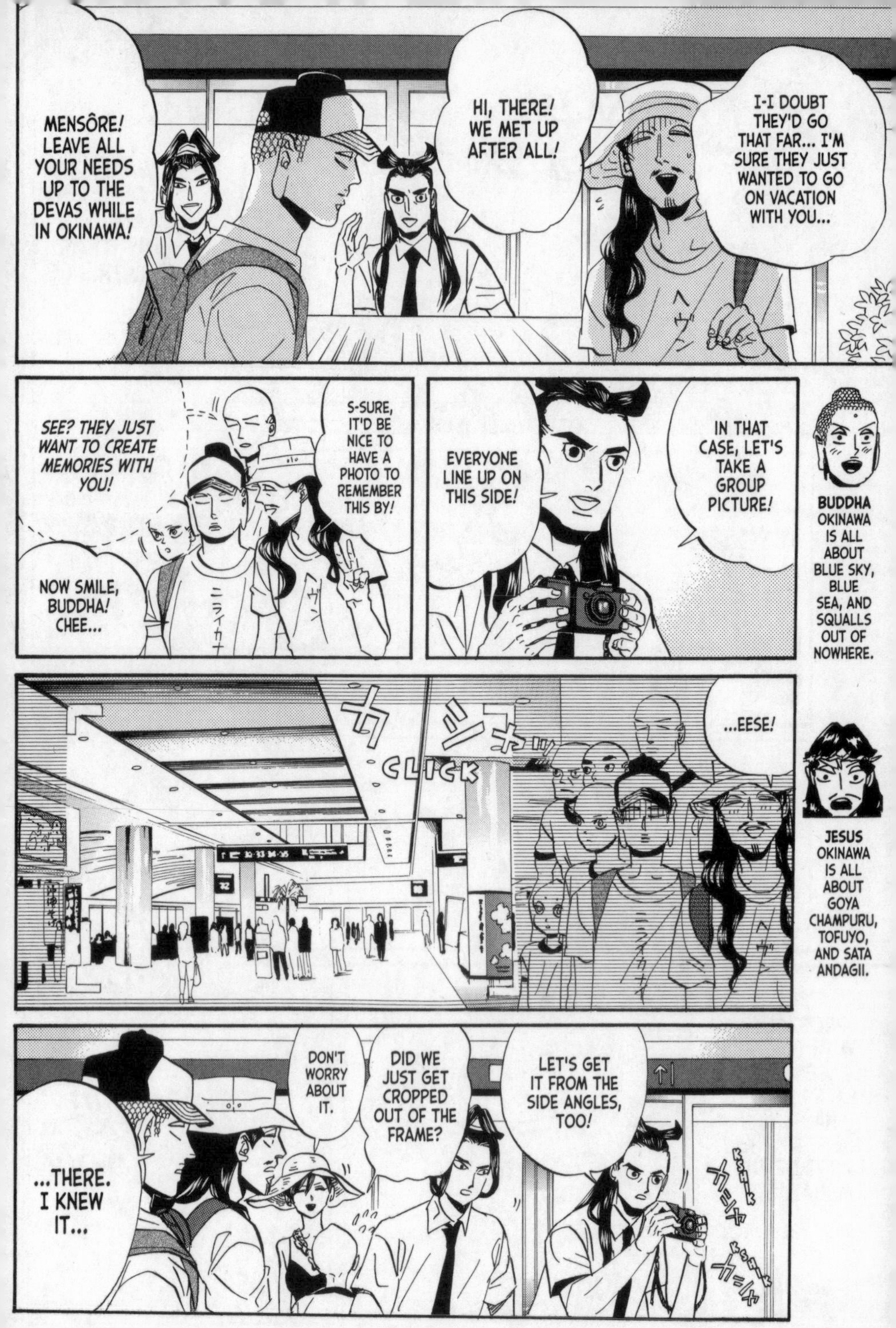
I-I DOUBT THEY'D GO THAT FAR... I'M SURE THEY JUST WANTED TO GO ON VACATION WITH YOU...
HI, THERE! WE MET UP AFTER ALL!
MENSÔRE! LEAVE ALL YOUR NEEDS UP TO THE DEVAS WHILE IN OKINAWA!
IN THAT CASE, LET'S TAKE A GROUP PICTURE!
EVERYONE LINE UP ON THIS SIDE!
S-SURE, IT'D BE NICE TO HAVE A PHOTO TO REMEMBER THIS BY!
SEE? THEY JUST WANT TO CREATE MEMORIES WITH YOU!
NOW SMILE, BUDDHA! CHEE...
...EESE!
CLICK
LET'S GET IT FROM THE SIDE ANGLES, TOO!
KSHAK
KSHAK
DID WE JUST GET CROPPED OUT OF THE FRAME?
DON'T WORRY ABOUT IT.
...THERE. I KNEW IT...
BUDDHA
OKINAWA IS ALL ABOUT BLUE SKY, BLUE SEA, AND SQUALLS OUT OF NOWHERE.
JESUS
OKINAWA IS ALL ABOUT GOYA CHAMPURU, TOFUYO, AND SATA ANDAGII.

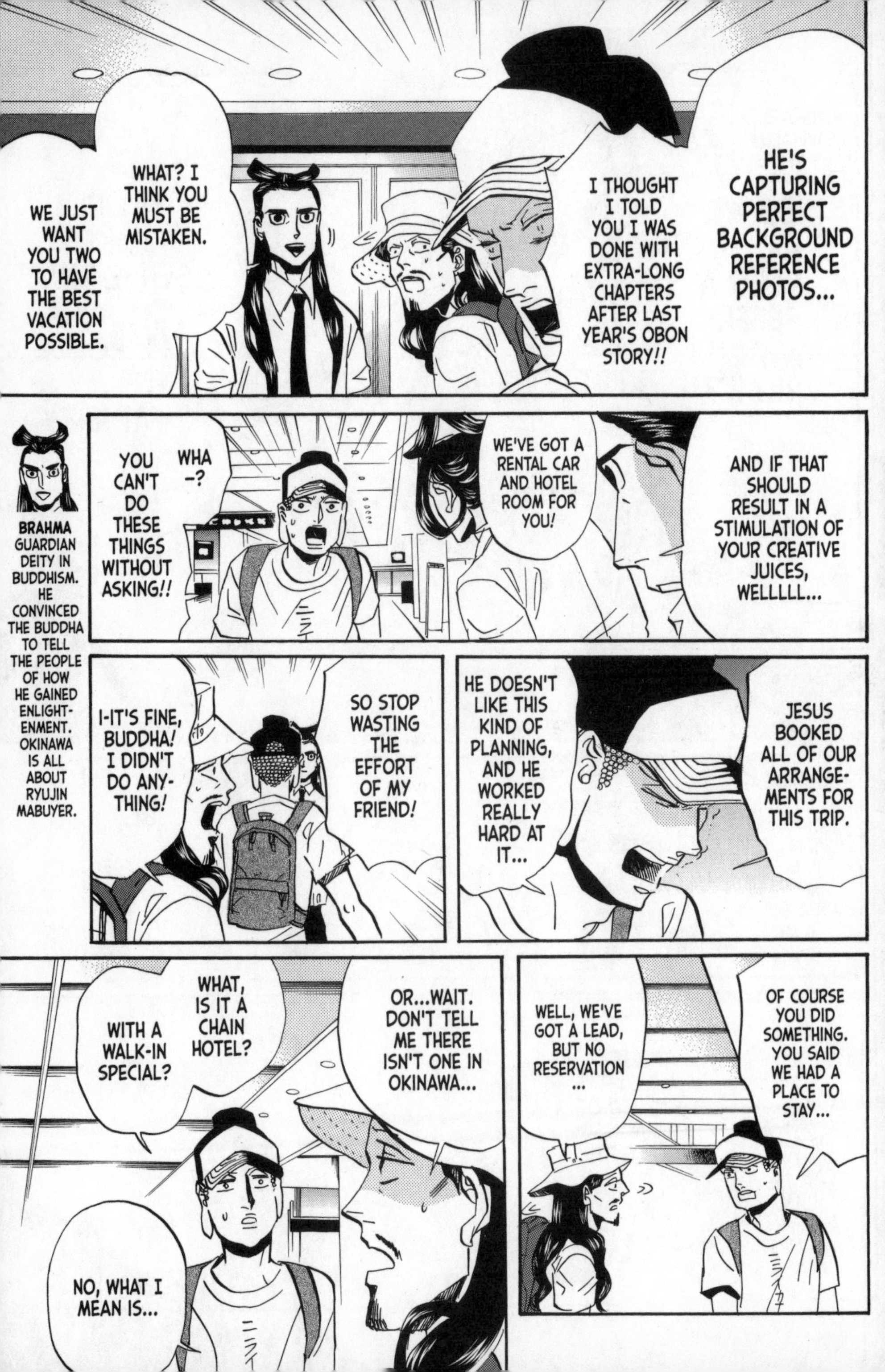
HE'S CAPTURING PERFECT BACKGROUND REFERENCE PHOTOS...
I THOUGHT I TOLD YOU I WAS DONE WITH EXTRA-LONG CHAPTERS AFTER LAST YEAR'S OBON STORY!!
WHAT? I THINK YOU MUST BE MISTAKEN.
WE JUST WANT YOU TWO TO HAVE THE BEST VACATION POSSIBLE.
AND IF THAT SHOULD RESULT IN A STIMULATION OF YOUR CREATIVE JUICES, WELLLLL...
WE'VE GOT A RENTAL CAR AND HOTEL ROOM FOR YOU!
WHA–?
YOU CAN'T DO THESE THINGS WITHOUT ASKING!!
BRAHMA GUARDIAN DEITY IN BUDDHISM. HE CONVINCED THE BUDDHA TO TELL THE PEOPLE OF HOW HE GAINED ENLIGHT-ENMENT. OKINAWA IS ALL ABOUT RYUJIN MABUYER.
JESUS BOOKED ALL OF OUR ARRANGE-MENTS FOR THIS TRIP.
HE DOESN'T LIKE THIS KIND OF PLANNING, AND HE WORKED REALLY HARD AT IT...
SO STOP WASTING THE EFFORT OF MY FRIEND!
I-IT'S FINE, BUDDHA! I DIDN'T DO ANY-THING!
OF COURSE YOU DID SOMETHING. YOU SAID WE HAD A PLACE TO STAY...
WELL, WE'VE GOT A LEAD, BUT NO RESERVATION ...
OR...WAIT. DON'T TELL ME THERE ISN'T ONE IN OKINAWA...
WHAT, IS IT A CHAIN HOTEL?
WITH A WALK-IN SPECIAL?
NO, WHAT I MEAN IS...

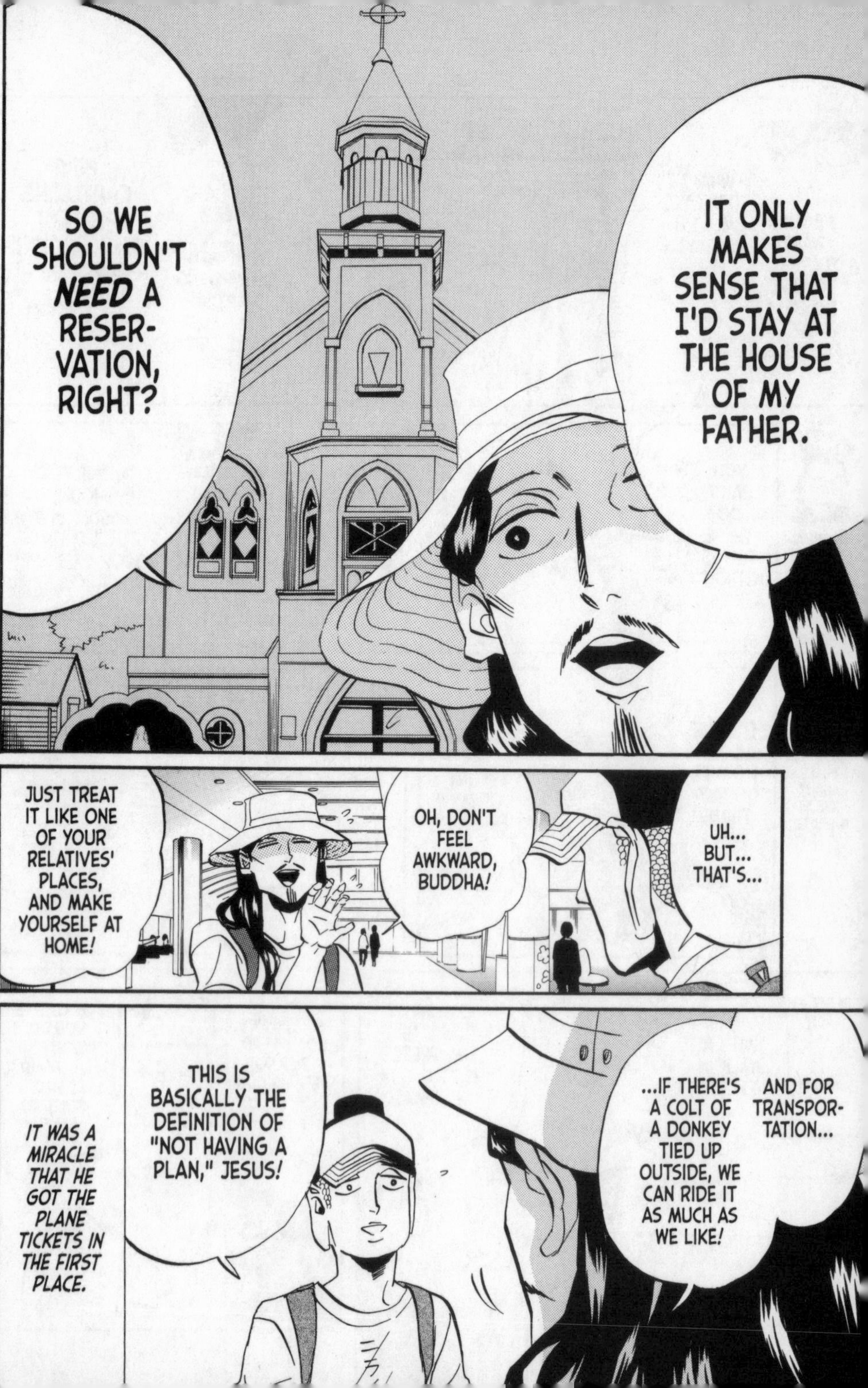
IT ONLY MAKES SENSE THAT I'D STAY AT THE HOUSE OF MY FATHER.
SO WE SHOULDN'T *NEED* A RESER-VATION, RIGHT?
UH... BUT... THAT'S...
OH, DON'T FEEL AWKWARD, BUDDHA!
JUST TREAT IT LIKE ONE OF YOUR RELATIVES' PLACES, AND MAKE YOURSELF AT HOME!
AND FOR TRANSPOR-TATION...
...IF THERE'S A COLT OF A DONKEY TIED UP OUTSIDE, WE CAN RIDE IT AS MUCH AS WE LIKE!
THIS IS BASICALLY THE DEFINITION OF "NOT HAVING A PLAN," JESUS!
IT WAS A MIRACLE THAT HE GOT THE PLANE TICKETS IN THE FIRST PLACE.

TAISHAKUTEN
GUARDIAN DEITY IN BUDDHISM. WORKED AS BRAHMA'S PARTNER TO CONVINCE THE BUDDHA TO TELL THE PEOPLE OF HOW HE GAINED ENLIGHTENMENT. OKINAWA IS ALL ABOUT CHINSUKÔ.

BENZAITEN
GUARDIAN DEITY IN BUDDHISM. GOD OF WISDOM, BEAUTY AND MUSIC. OKINAWA IS ALL ABOUT THE SANSHIN, OF COURSE.

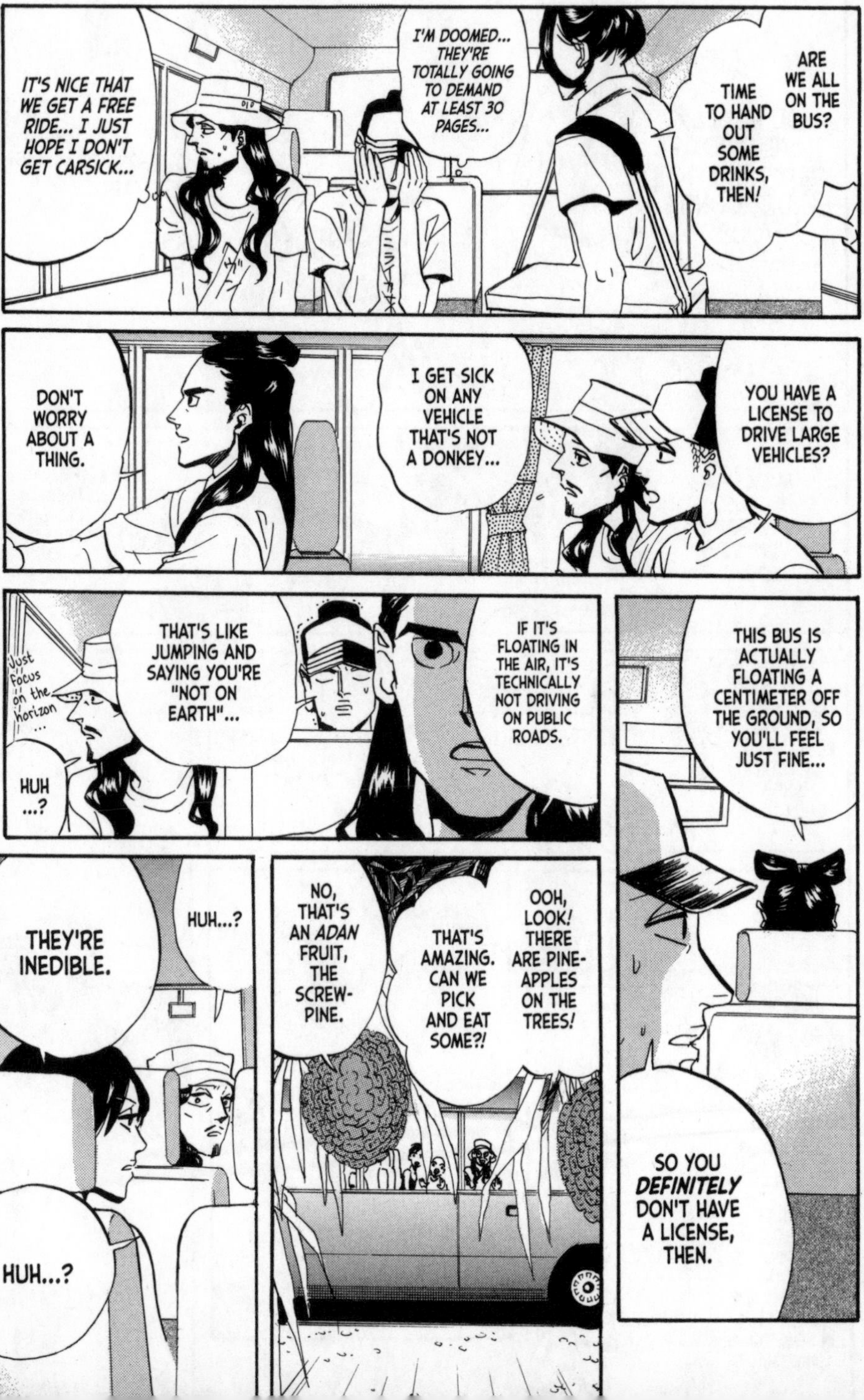
ARE WE ALL ON THE BUS?
TIME TO HAND OUT SOME DRINKS, THEN!
I'M DOOMED... THEY'RE TOTALLY GOING TO DEMAND AT LEAST 30 PAGES...
IT'S NICE THAT WE GET A FREE RIDE... I JUST HOPE I DON'T GET CARSICK...
YOU HAVE A LICENSE TO DRIVE LARGE VEHICLES?
I GET SICK ON ANY VEHICLE THAT'S NOT A DONKEY...
DON'T WORRY ABOUT A THING.
THIS BUS IS ACTUALLY FLOATING A CENTIMETER OFF THE GROUND, SO YOU'LL FEEL JUST FINE...
SO YOU *DEFINITELY* DON'T HAVE A LICENSE, THEN.
IF IT'S FLOATING IN THE AIR, IT'S TECHNICALLY NOT DRIVING ON PUBLIC ROADS.
THAT'S LIKE JUMPING AND SAYING YOU'RE "NOT ON EARTH"...
Just focus on the horizon...
HUH...?
OOH, LOOK! THERE ARE PINE-APPLES ON THE TREES!
THAT'S AMAZING. CAN WE PICK AND EAT SOME?!
NO, THAT'S AN *ADAN* FRUIT, THE SCREW-PINE.
HUH...?
THEY'RE INEDIBLE.
HUH...?

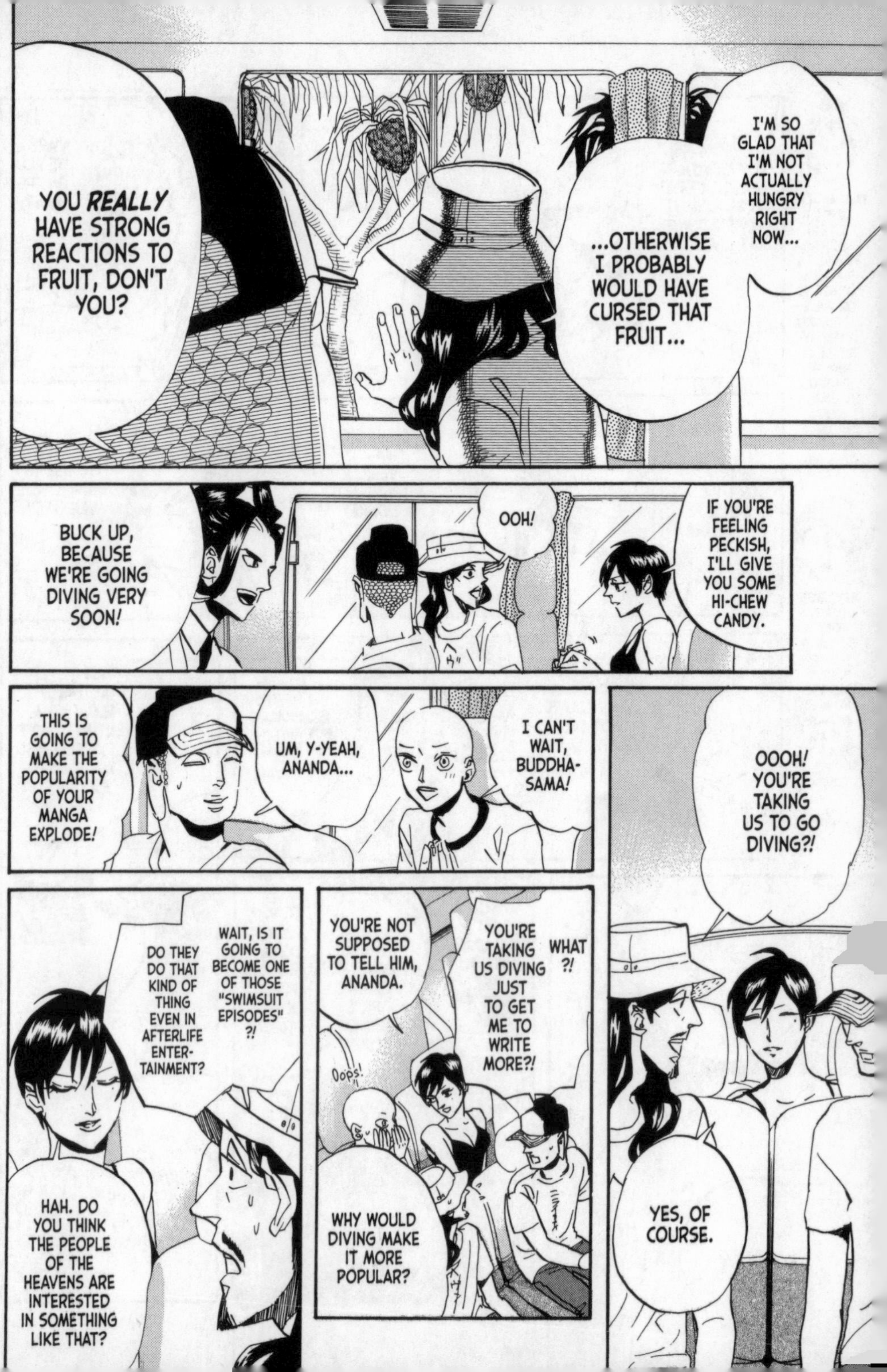

I'M SO GLAD THAT I'M NOT ACTUALLY HUNGRY RIGHT NOW...
...OTHERWISE I PROBABLY WOULD HAVE CURSED THAT FRUIT...
YOU *REALLY* HAVE STRONG REACTIONS TO FRUIT, DON'T YOU?
IF YOU'RE FEELING PECKISH, I'LL GIVE YOU SOME HI-CHEW CANDY.
OOH!
BUCK UP, BECAUSE WE'RE GOING DIVING VERY SOON!
OOOH! YOU'RE TAKING US TO GO DIVING?!
YES, OF COURSE.
I CAN'T WAIT, BUDDHA-SAMA!
UM, Y-YEAH, ANANDA...
THIS IS GOING TO MAKE THE POPULARITY OF YOUR MANGA EXPLODE!
WHAT?!
YOU'RE TAKING US DIVING JUST TO GET ME TO WRITE MORE?!
YOU'RE NOT SUPPOSED TO TELL HIM, ANANDA.
Oops!
WHY WOULD DIVING MAKE IT MORE POPULAR?
WAIT, IS IT GOING TO BECOME ONE OF THOSE "SWIMSUIT EPISODES"?!
DO THEY DO THAT KIND OF THING EVEN IN AFTERLIFE ENTERTAINMENT?
HAH. DO YOU THINK THE PEOPLE OF THE HEAVENS ARE INTERESTED IN SOMETHING LIKE THAT?

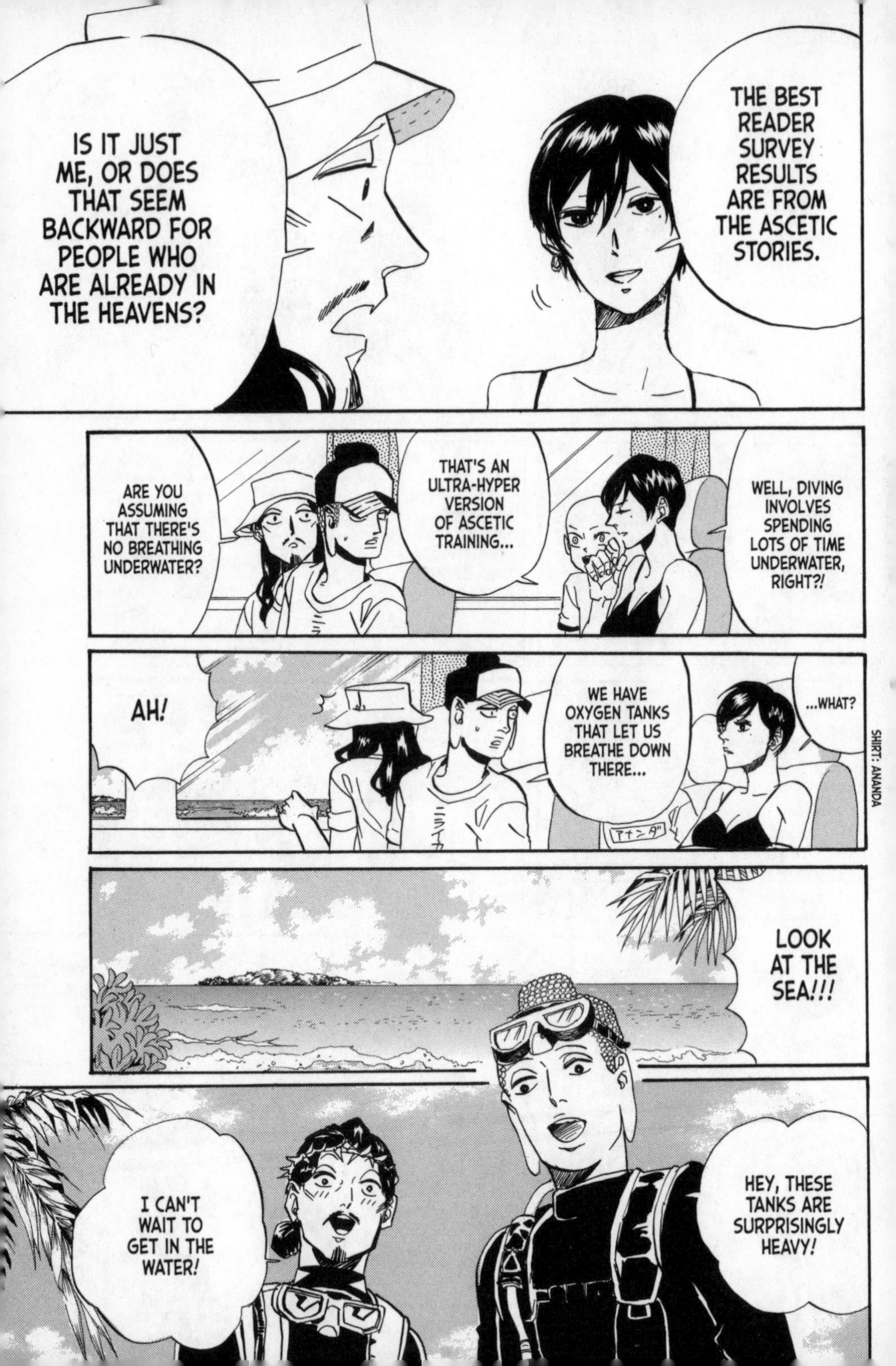
THE BEST READER SURVEY RESULTS ARE FROM THE ASCETIC STORIES.
IS IT JUST ME, OR DOES THAT SEEM BACKWARD FOR PEOPLE WHO ARE ALREADY IN THE HEAVENS?
WELL, DIVING INVOLVES SPENDING LOTS OF TIME UNDERWATER, RIGHT?!
THAT'S AN ULTRA-HYPER VERSION OF ASCETIC TRAINING...
ARE YOU ASSUMING THAT THERE'S NO BREATHING UNDERWATER?
SHIRT: ANANDA
...WHAT?
アナンダ
WE HAVE OXYGEN TANKS THAT LET US BREATHE DOWN THERE...
AH!
LOOK AT THE SEA!!!
HEY, THESE TANKS ARE SURPRISINGLY HEAVY!
I CAN'T WAIT TO GET IN THE WATER!

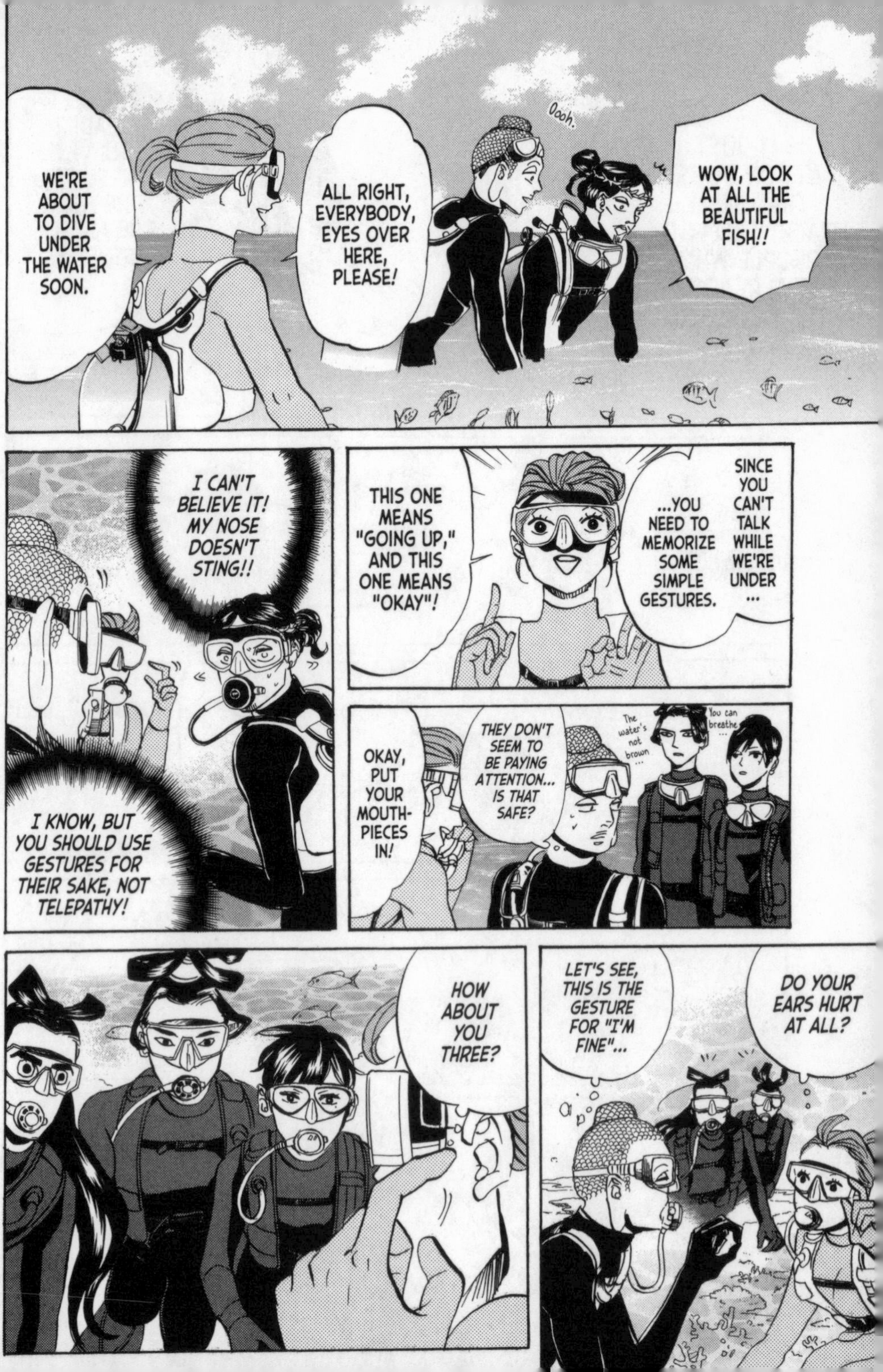
WOW, LOOK AT ALL THE BEAUTIFUL FISH!!
Oooh.
ALL RIGHT, EVERYBODY, EYES OVER HERE, PLEASE!
WE'RE ABOUT TO DIVE UNDER THE WATER SOON.
SINCE YOU CAN'T TALK WHILE WE'RE UNDER ...
...YOU NEED TO MEMORIZE SOME SIMPLE GESTURES.
THIS ONE MEANS "GOING UP," AND THIS ONE MEANS "OKAY"!
You can breathe ...
The water's not brown ...
THEY DON'T SEEM TO BE PAYING ATTENTION... IS THAT SAFE?
OKAY, PUT YOUR MOUTH-PIECES IN!
I CAN'T BELIEVE IT! MY NOSE DOESN'T STING!!
I KNOW, BUT YOU SHOULD USE GESTURES FOR THEIR SAKE, NOT TELEPATHY!
DO YOUR EARS HURT AT ALL?
LET'S SEE, THIS IS THE GESTURE FOR "I'M FINE"...
HOW ABOUT YOU THREE?

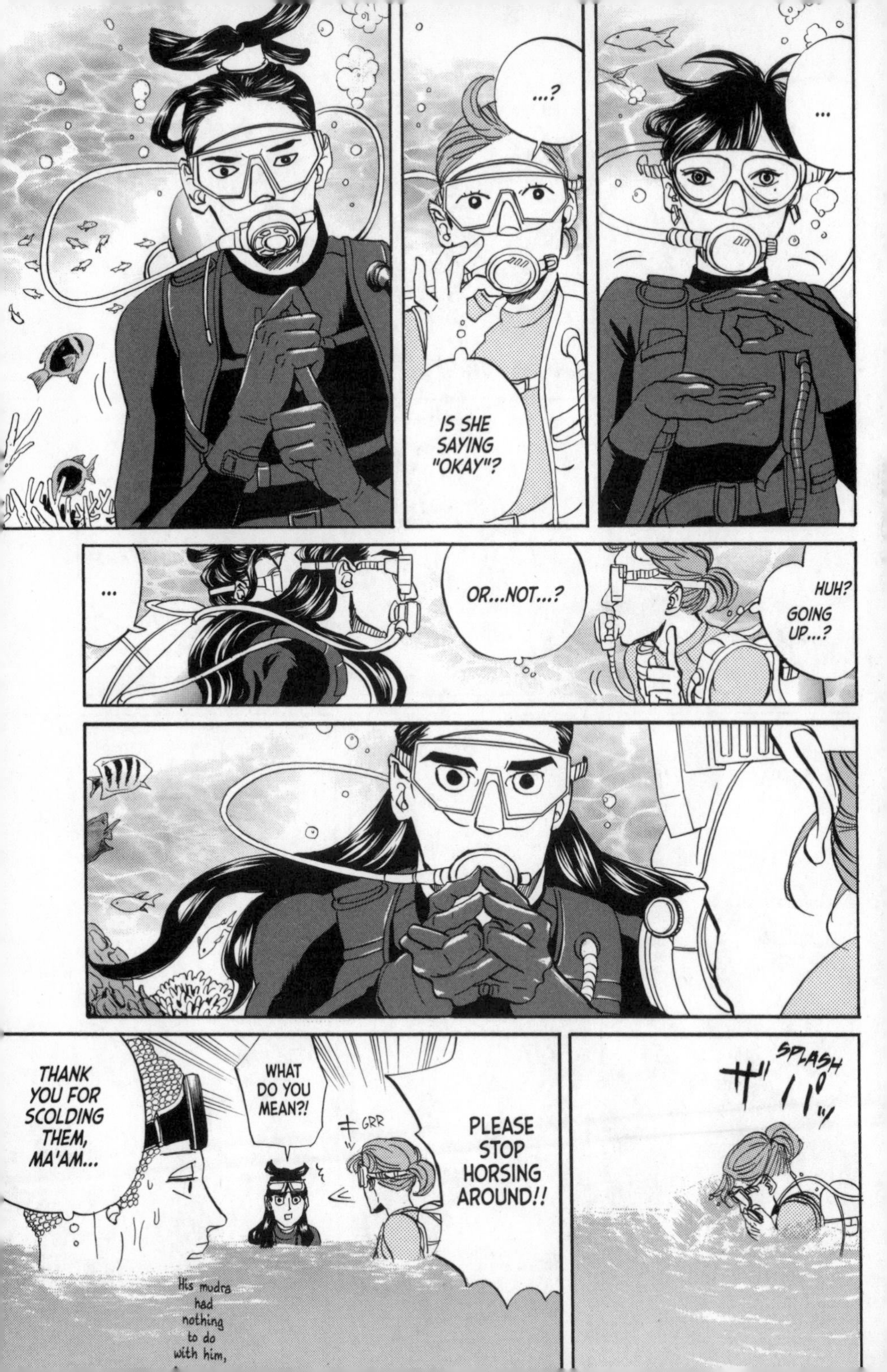
...
...?
IS SHE SAYING "OKAY"?
HUH? GOING UP...?
OR...NOT...?
...
SPLASH
PLEASE STOP HORSING AROUND!!
GRR
WHAT DO YOU MEAN?!
THANK YOU FOR SCOLDING THEM, MA'AM...
His mudra had nothing to do with him,

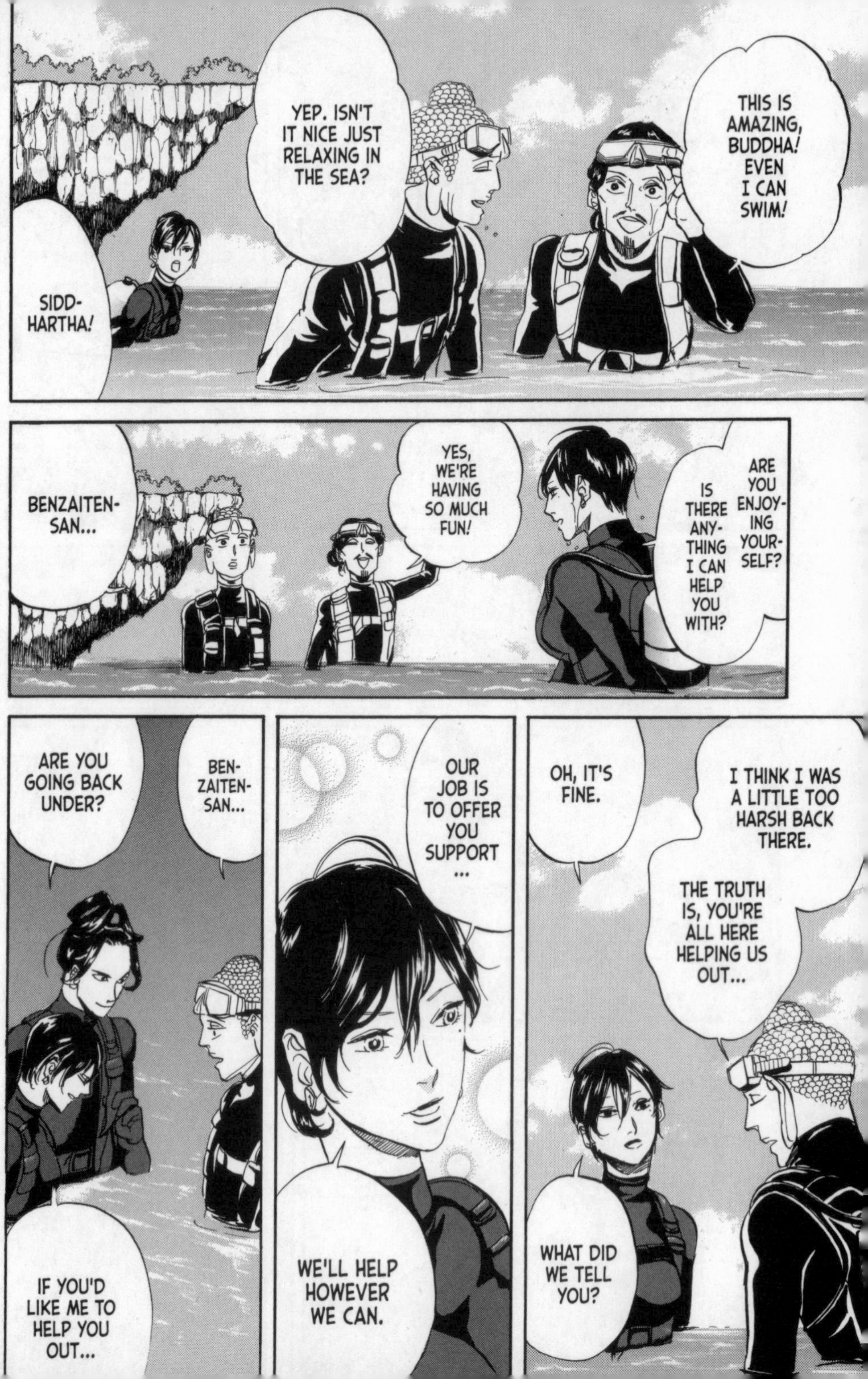
THIS IS AMAZING, BUDDHA! EVEN I CAN SWIM!
YEP. ISN'T IT NICE JUST RELAXING IN THE SEA?
SIDD-HARTHA!
ARE YOU ENJOY-ING YOUR-SELF?
IS THERE ANY-THING I CAN HELP YOU WITH?
YES, WE'RE HAVING SO MUCH FUN!
BENZAITEN-SAN...
I THINK I WAS A LITTLE TOO HARSH BACK THERE.
THE TRUTH IS, YOU'RE ALL HERE HELPING US OUT...
OH, IT'S FINE.
WHAT DID WE TELL YOU?
OUR JOB IS TO OFFER YOU SUPPORT ...
WE'LL HELP HOWEVER WE CAN.
BEN-ZAITEN-SAN...
ARE YOU GOING BACK UNDER?
IF YOU'D LIKE ME TO HELP YOU OUT...

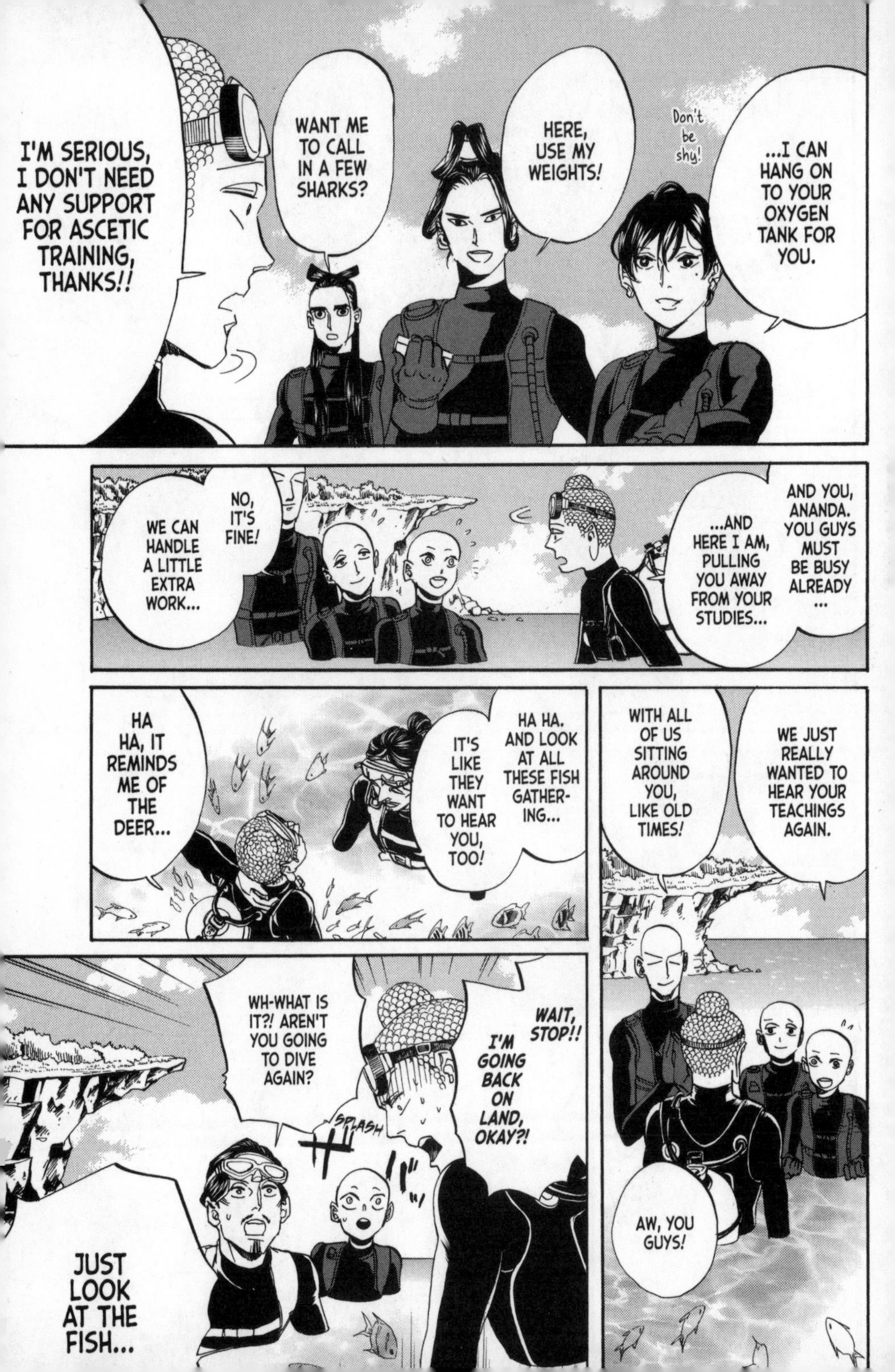
...I CAN HANG ON TO YOUR OXYGEN TANK FOR YOU.
Don't be shy!
HERE, USE MY WEIGHTS!
WANT ME TO CALL IN A FEW SHARKS?
I'M SERIOUS, I DON'T NEED ANY SUPPORT FOR ASCETIC TRAINING, THANKS!!
AND YOU, ANANDA. YOU GUYS MUST BE BUSY ALREADY...
...AND HERE I AM, PULLING YOU AWAY FROM YOUR STUDIES...
NO, IT'S FINE!
WE CAN HANDLE A LITTLE EXTRA WORK...
WE JUST REALLY WANTED TO HEAR YOUR TEACHINGS AGAIN.
WITH ALL OF US SITTING AROUND YOU, LIKE OLD TIMES!
AW, YOU GUYS!
HA HA. AND LOOK AT ALL THESE FISH GATHERING...
IT'S LIKE THEY WANT TO HEAR YOU, TOO!
HA HA, IT REMINDS ME OF THE DEER...
WAIT, STOP!!
I'M GOING BACK ON LAND, OKAY?!
WH-WHAT IS IT?! AREN'T YOU GOING TO DIVE AGAIN?
SPLASH
JUST LOOK AT THE FISH...

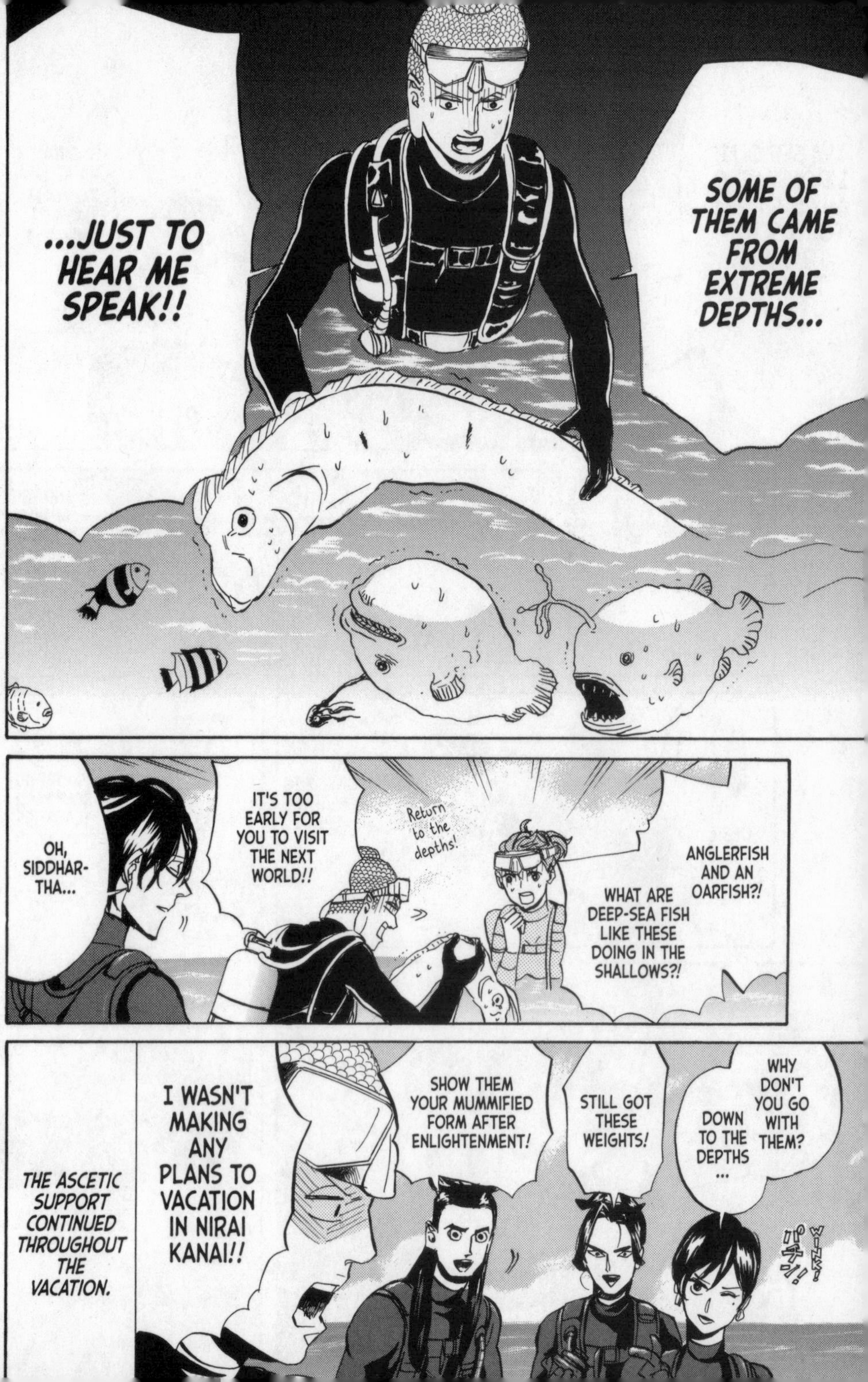
SOME OF THEM CAME FROM EXTREME DEPTHS...
...JUST TO HEAR ME SPEAK!!
ANGLERFISH AND AN OARFISH?!
WHAT ARE DEEP-SEA FISH LIKE THESE DOING IN THE SHALLOWS?!
Return to the depths!
IT'S TOO EARLY FOR YOU TO VISIT THE NEXT WORLD!!
OH, SIDDHARTHA...
WHY DON'T YOU GO WITH THEM?
DOWN TO THE DEPTHS ...
WINK!
STILL GOT THESE WEIGHTS!
SHOW THEM YOUR MUMMIFIED FORM AFTER ENLIGHTENMENT!
I WASN'T MAKING ANY PLANS TO VACATION IN NIRAI KANAI!!
THE ASCETIC SUPPORT CONTINUED THROUGHOUT THE VACATION.

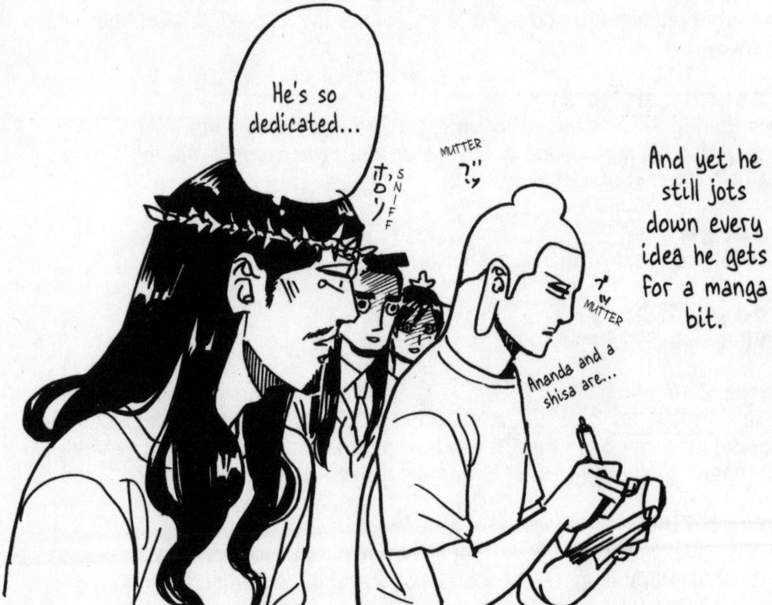
And yet he still jots down every idea he gets for a manga bit.
MUTTER
MUTTER
Ananda and a shisa are...
SNIFF
He's so dedicated...

CHAPTER 56 TRANSLATION NOTES

Mensôre, page 224
The Okinawan word for "welcome." Another terms that pops up in this Okinawa vacation story is haisai ("what's up" or "how's it going").

Blue Seal, page 227
An Okinawan ice cream shop founded by US military members shortly after occupation of Japan in the 1940s, meant to be a taste of home for the soldiers stationed there. Now it is owned by locals and features ice cream inspired by local flavors.

Okinawan food, page 229
The things mentioned in Jesus's profile are all iconic Okinawan dishes. Champuru is a kind of stir fry often made with tofu, vegetables, egg, and meat. One very popular kind is made with goya, a kind of bitter melon. Tofuyo is a fermented tofu dish with a very rich taste that is often soaked in the traditional Okinawan spirit, awamori. Sata andagi is a fried dough treat often compared to donuts.

Ryujin Mabuyer, page 230
A tokusatsu action series based on a hero in Okinawa. Ryujin means "god of Okinawa" and "Mabuyer" is a corruption of the word mabuya, a word for "soul." It's often spoken for good luck after someone falls down or is shocked, to keep the soul from slipping away.

Colt of a donkey, page 231
In the Gospels, during Jesus's triumphal entry into Jerusalem--the start of the Passion of the Christ, his final period of life--he entered the city riding humbly on a donkey and a colt, the foal of a donkey.

Chinsukô, page 232
A traditional Okinawan pastry much like shortbread, made with lard and flour.

Sanshin, page 232
An Okinawan three-stringed instrument that is the predecessor of the shamisen.

Mudra, page 236
Mudras are the symbolic hand gestures found in Buddhist art. Benzaiten's gesture is known, appropriately enough, as the "Benzaiten mudra." Taishakuten's is the Vajra Mudra, which means "Fist of Wisdom." Brahma's is known as the "Inner Lion" mudra.

Mummy, page 239
A practice called sokushinbutsu, which refers to monks and ascetics who die (reach enlightenment) while meditating, and whose bodies are left in that state without preservatives.

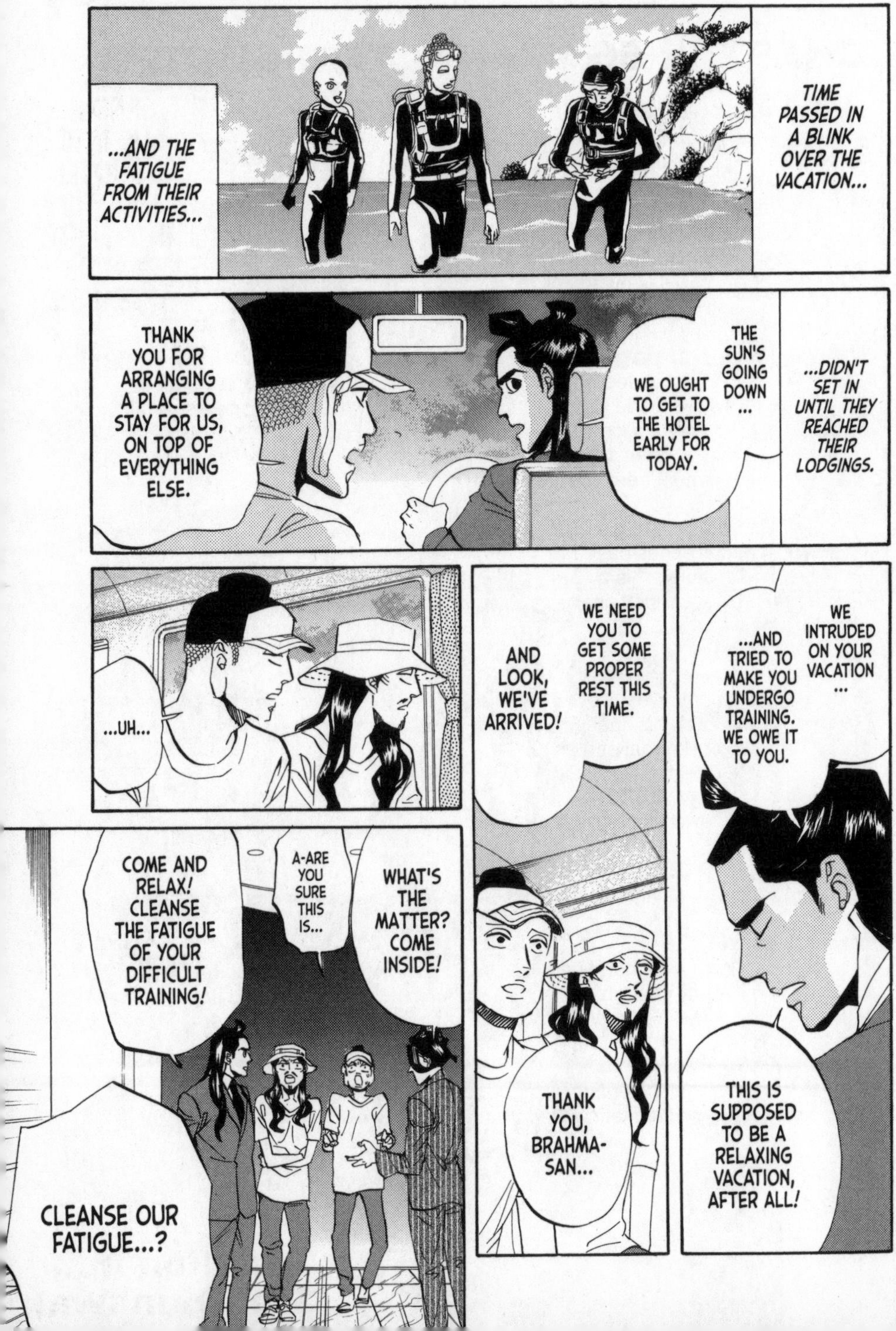
TIME PASSED IN A BLINK OVER THE VACATION...
...AND THE FATIGUE FROM THEIR ACTIVITIES...
...DIDN'T SET IN UNTIL THEY REACHED THEIR LODGINGS.
THE SUN'S GOING DOWN...
WE OUGHT TO GET TO THE HOTEL EARLY FOR TODAY.
THANK YOU FOR ARRANGING A PLACE TO STAY FOR US, ON TOP OF EVERYTHING ELSE.
WE INTRUDED ON YOUR VACATION...
...AND TRIED TO MAKE YOU UNDERGO TRAINING. WE OWE IT TO YOU.
THIS IS SUPPOSED TO BE A RELAXING VACATION, AFTER ALL!
WE NEED YOU TO GET SOME PROPER REST THIS TIME.
AND LOOK, WE'VE ARRIVED!
THANK YOU, BRAHMA-SAN...
...UH...
WHAT'S THE MATTER? COME INSIDE!
A-ARE YOU SURE THIS IS...
COME AND RELAX! CLEANSE THE FATIGUE OF YOUR DIFFICULT TRAINING!
CLEANSE OUR FATIGUE...?

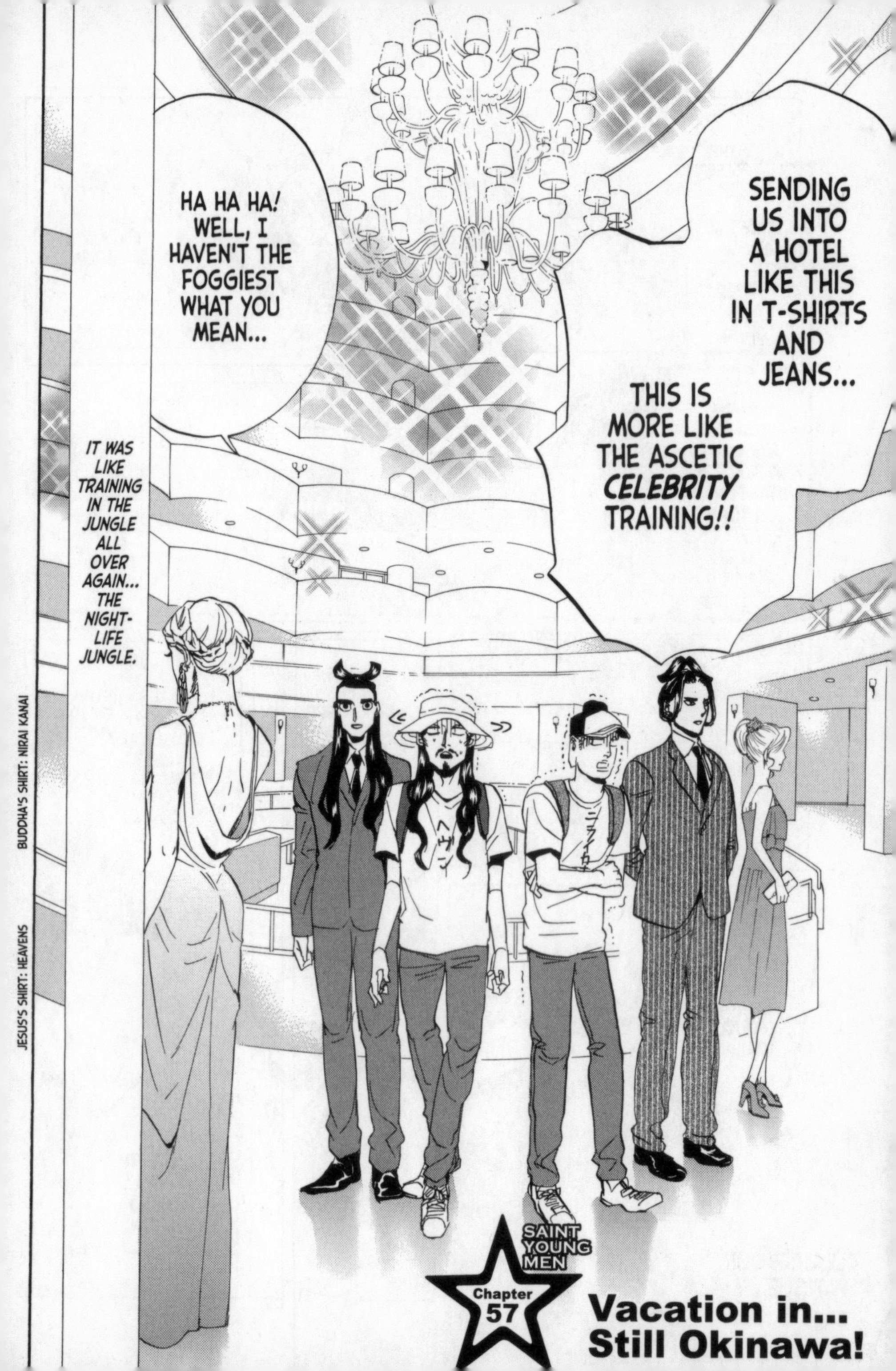
SENDING US INTO A HOTEL LIKE THIS IN T-SHIRTS AND JEANS...
THIS IS MORE LIKE THE ASCETIC *CELEBRITY* TRAINING!!
HA HA HA! WELL, I HAVEN'T THE FOGGIEST WHAT YOU MEAN...
IT WAS LIKE TRAINING IN THE JUNGLE ALL OVER AGAIN... THE NIGHT-LIFE JUNGLE.
BUDDHA'S SHIRT: NIRAI KANAI
JESUS'S SHIRT: HEAVENS
SAINT YOUNG MEN
Chapter 57
Vacation in... Still Okinawa!

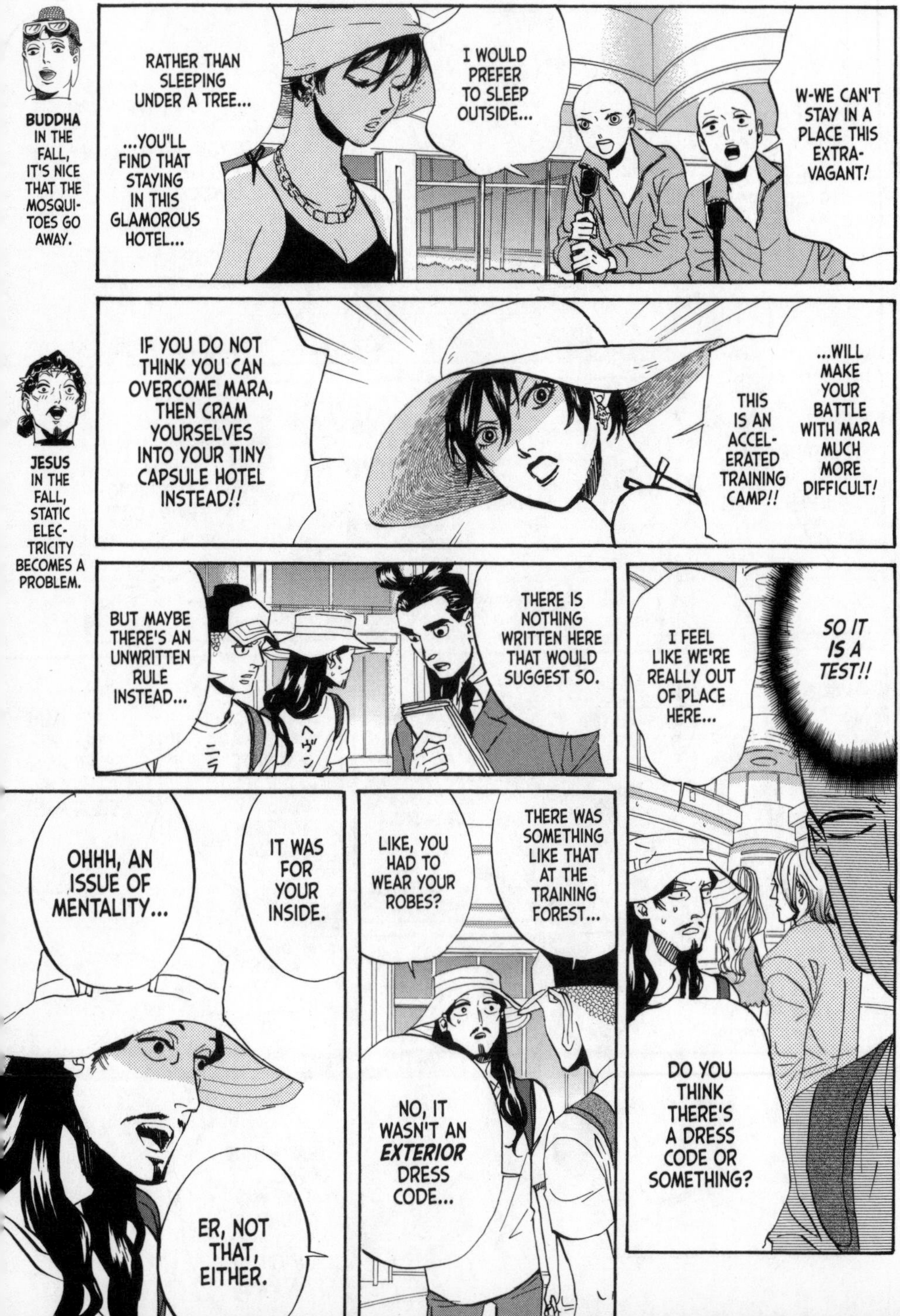
W-WE CAN'T STAY IN A PLACE THIS EXTRA-VAGANT!
I WOULD PREFER TO SLEEP OUTSIDE...
RATHER THAN SLEEPING UNDER A TREE...
...YOU'LL FIND THAT STAYING IN THIS GLAMOROUS HOTEL...
...WILL MAKE YOUR BATTLE WITH MARA MUCH MORE DIFFICULT!
THIS IS AN ACCEL-ERATED TRAINING CAMP!!
IF YOU DO NOT THINK YOU CAN OVERCOME MARA, THEN CRAM YOURSELVES INTO YOUR TINY CAPSULE HOTEL INSTEAD!!
SO IT IS A TEST!!
I FEEL LIKE WE'RE REALLY OUT OF PLACE HERE...
DO YOU THINK THERE'S A DRESS CODE OR SOMETHING?
THERE IS NOTHING WRITTEN HERE THAT WOULD SUGGEST SO.
BUT MAYBE THERE'S AN UNWRITTEN RULE INSTEAD...
THERE WAS SOMETHING LIKE THAT AT THE TRAINING FOREST...
LIKE, YOU HAD TO WEAR YOUR ROBES?
NO, IT WASN'T AN *EXTERIOR* DRESS CODE...
IT WAS FOR YOUR INSIDE.
OHHH, AN ISSUE OF MENTALITY...
ER, NOT THAT, EITHER.
BUDDHA IN THE FALL, IT'S NICE THAT THE MOSQUI-TOES GO AWAY.
JESUS IN THE FALL, STATIC ELEC-TRICITY BECOMES A PROBLEM.

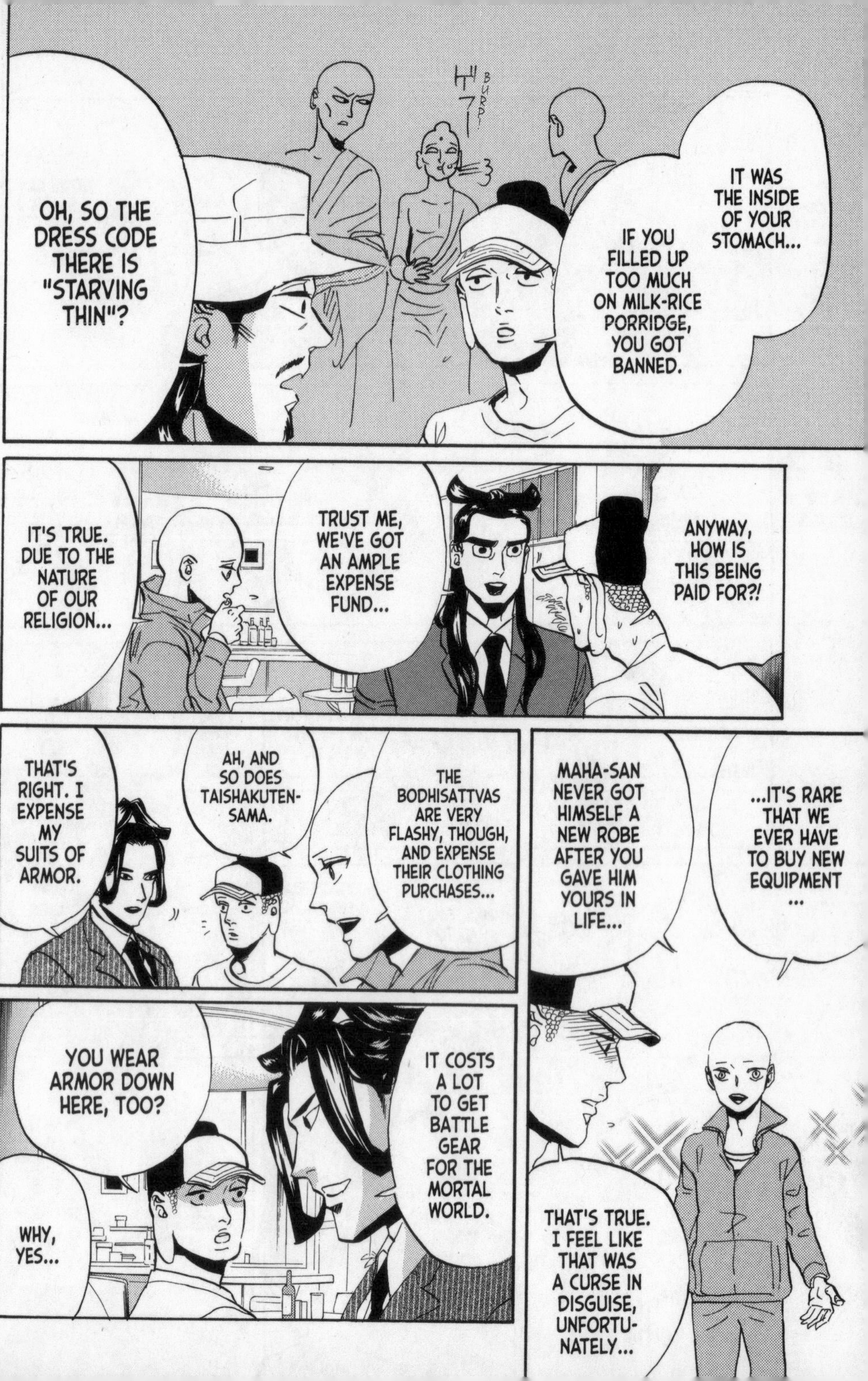

IT WAS THE INSIDE OF YOUR STOMACH...
IF YOU FILLED UP TOO MUCH ON MILK-RICE PORRIDGE, YOU GOT BANNED.
ゲフー
BURP!
OH, SO THE DRESS CODE THERE IS "STARVING THIN"?
ANYWAY, HOW IS THIS BEING PAID FOR?!
TRUST ME, WE'VE GOT AN AMPLE EXPENSE FUND...
IT'S TRUE. DUE TO THE NATURE OF OUR RELIGION...
...IT'S RARE THAT WE EVER HAVE TO BUY NEW EQUIPMENT...
MAHA-SAN NEVER GOT HIMSELF A NEW ROBE AFTER YOU GAVE HIM YOURS IN LIFE...
THAT'S TRUE. I FEEL LIKE THAT WAS A CURSE IN DISGUISE, UNFORTUNATELY...
THE BODHISATTVAS ARE VERY FLASHY, THOUGH, AND EXPENSE THEIR CLOTHING PURCHASES...
AH, AND SO DOES TAISHAKUTEN-SAMA.
THAT'S RIGHT. I EXPENSE MY SUITS OF ARMOR.
YOU WEAR ARMOR DOWN HERE, TOO?
WHY, YES...
IT COSTS A LOT TO GET BATTLE GEAR FOR THE MORTAL WORLD.

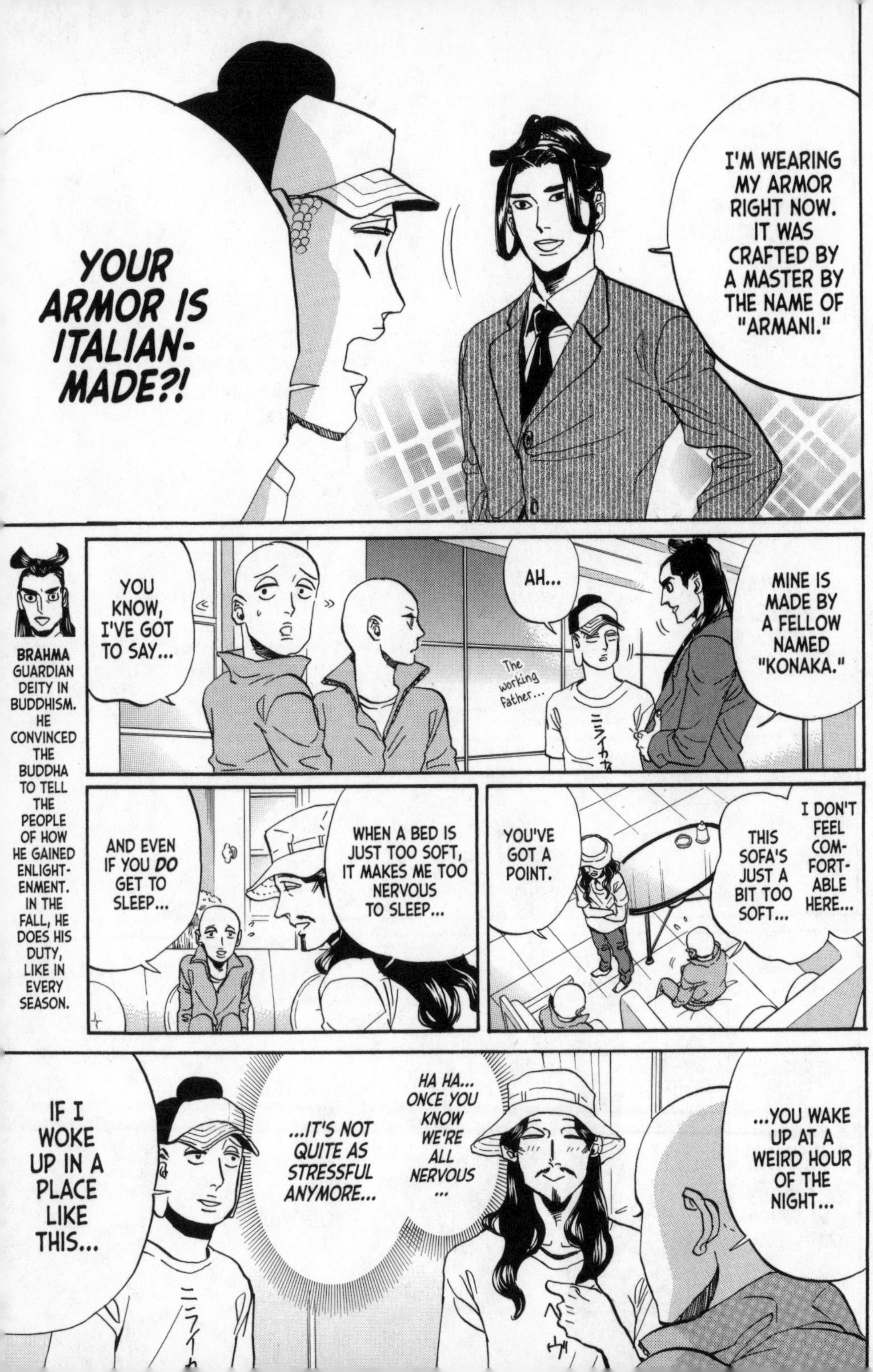
I'M WEARING MY ARMOR RIGHT NOW. IT WAS CRAFTED BY A MASTER BY THE NAME OF "ARMANI."
YOUR ARMOR IS ITALIAN-MADE?!
MINE IS MADE BY A FELLOW NAMED "KONAKA."
AH...
The working father...
YOU KNOW, I'VE GOT TO SAY...
I DON'T FEEL COMFORTABLE HERE...
THIS SOFA'S JUST A BIT TOO SOFT...
YOU'VE GOT A POINT.
WHEN A BED IS JUST TOO SOFT, IT MAKES ME TOO NERVOUS TO SLEEP...
AND EVEN IF YOU *DO* GET TO SLEEP...
BRAHMA GUARDIAN DEITY IN BUDDHISM. HE CONVINCED THE BUDDHA TO TELL THE PEOPLE OF HOW HE GAINED ENLIGHTENMENT. IN THE FALL, HE DOES HIS DUTY, LIKE IN EVERY SEASON.
...YOU WAKE UP AT A WEIRD HOUR OF THE NIGHT...
HA HA... ONCE YOU KNOW WE'RE ALL NERVOUS ...
...IT'S NOT QUITE AS STRESSFUL ANYMORE...
IF I WOKE UP IN A PLACE LIKE THIS...

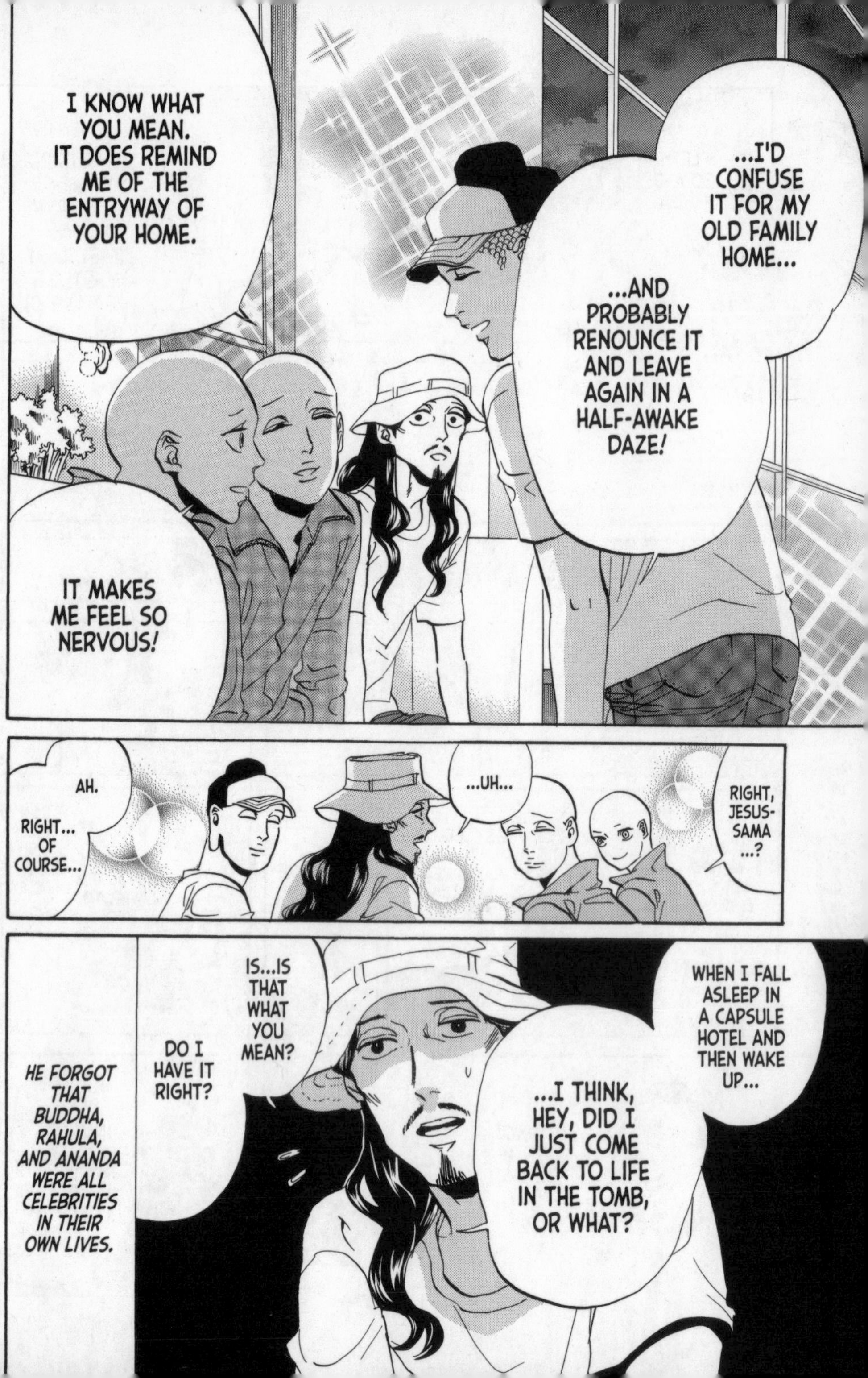
...I'D CONFUSE IT FOR MY OLD FAMILY HOME...
...AND PROBABLY RENOUNCE IT AND LEAVE AGAIN IN A HALF-AWAKE DAZE!
I KNOW WHAT YOU MEAN. IT DOES REMIND ME OF THE ENTRYWAY OF YOUR HOME.
IT MAKES ME FEEL SO NERVOUS!
RIGHT, JESUS-SAMA ...?
...UH...
AH.
RIGHT... OF COURSE...
WHEN I FALL ASLEEP IN A CAPSULE HOTEL AND THEN WAKE UP...
...I THINK, HEY, DID I JUST COME BACK TO LIFE IN THE TOMB, OR WHAT?
IS...IS THAT WHAT YOU MEAN?
DO I HAVE IT RIGHT?
HE FORGOT THAT BUDDHA, RAHULA, AND ANANDA WERE ALL CELEBRITIES IN THEIR OWN LIVES.

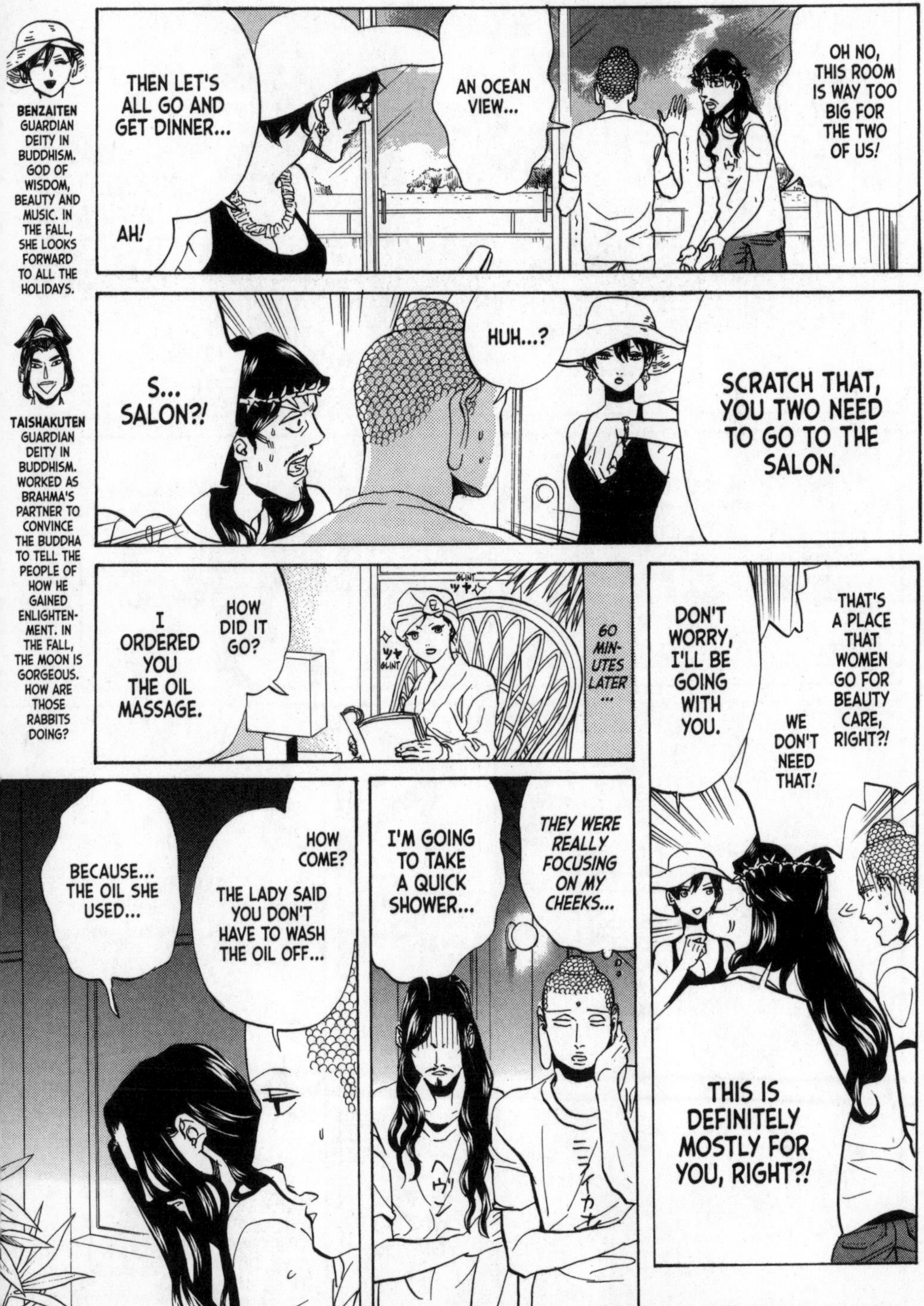
BENZAITEN GUARDIAN DEITY IN BUDDHISM. GOD OF WISDOM, BEAUTY AND MUSIC. IN THE FALL, SHE LOOKS FORWARD TO ALL THE HOLIDAYS.
TAISHAKUTEN GUARDIAN DEITY IN BUDDHISM. WORKED AS BRAHMA'S PARTNER TO CONVINCE THE BUDDHA TO TELL THE PEOPLE OF HOW HE GAINED ENLIGHTENMENT. IN THE FALL, THE MOON IS GORGEOUS. HOW ARE THOSE RABBITS DOING?
OH NO, THIS ROOM IS WAY TOO BIG FOR THE TWO OF US!
AN OCEAN VIEW...
THEN LET'S ALL GO AND GET DINNER...
AH!
SCRATCH THAT, YOU TWO NEED TO GO TO THE SALON.
HUH...?
S... SALON?!
THAT'S A PLACE THAT WOMEN GO FOR BEAUTY CARE, RIGHT?!
WE DON'T NEED THAT!
DON'T WORRY, I'LL BE GOING WITH YOU.
THIS IS DEFINITELY MOSTLY FOR YOU, RIGHT?!
60 MINUTES LATER...
GLINT
GLINT
HOW DID IT GO?
I ORDERED YOU THE OIL MASSAGE.
THEY WERE REALLY FOCUSING ON MY CHEEKS...
I'M GOING TO TAKE A QUICK SHOWER...
HOW COME?
THE LADY SAID YOU DON'T HAVE TO WASH THE OIL OFF...
BECAUSE... THE OIL SHE USED...

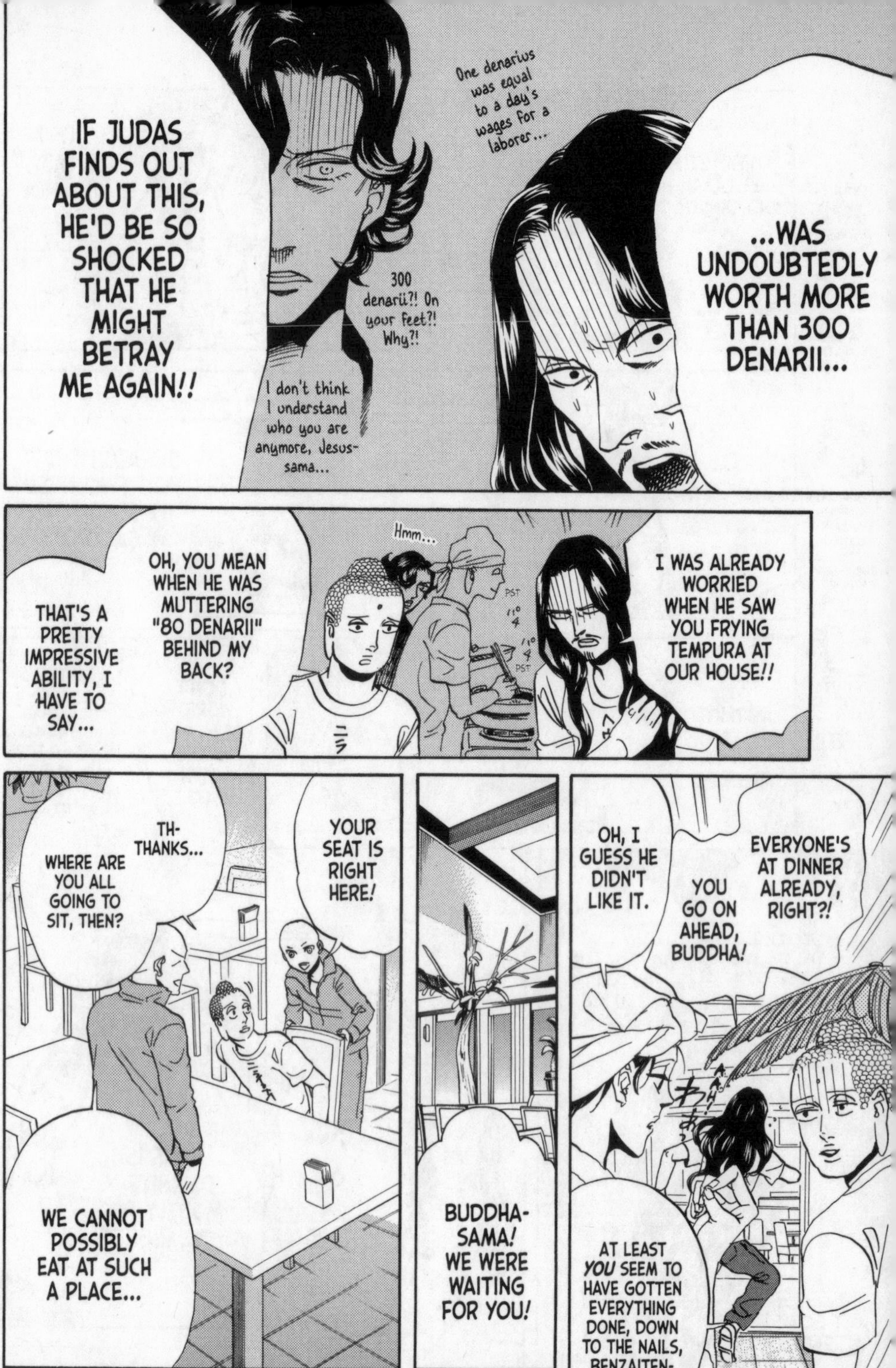
...WAS UNDOUBTEDLY WORTH MORE THAN 300 DENARII...
One denarius was equal to a day's wages for a laborer...
300 denarii?! On your feet?! Why?!
IF JUDAS FINDS OUT ABOUT THIS, HE'D BE SO SHOCKED THAT HE MIGHT BETRAY ME AGAIN!!
I don't think I understand who you are anymore, Jesus-sama...
I WAS ALREADY WORRIED WHEN HE SAW YOU FRYING TEMPURA AT OUR HOUSE!!
Hmm...
PST
PST
OH, YOU MEAN WHEN HE WAS MUTTERING "80 DENARII" BEHIND MY BACK?
THAT'S A PRETTY IMPRESSIVE ABILITY, I HAVE TO SAY...
EVERYONE'S AT DINNER ALREADY, RIGHT?!
YOU GO ON AHEAD, BUDDHA!
OH, I GUESS HE DIDN'T LIKE IT.
AT LEAST YOU SEEM TO HAVE GOTTEN EVERYTHING DONE, DOWN TO THE NAILS, BENZAITEN-SAN...
BUDDHA-SAMA! WE WERE WAITING FOR YOU!
YOUR SEAT IS RIGHT HERE!
TH- THANKS...
WHERE ARE YOU ALL GOING TO SIT, THEN?
WE CANNOT POSSIBLY EAT AT SUCH A PLACE...

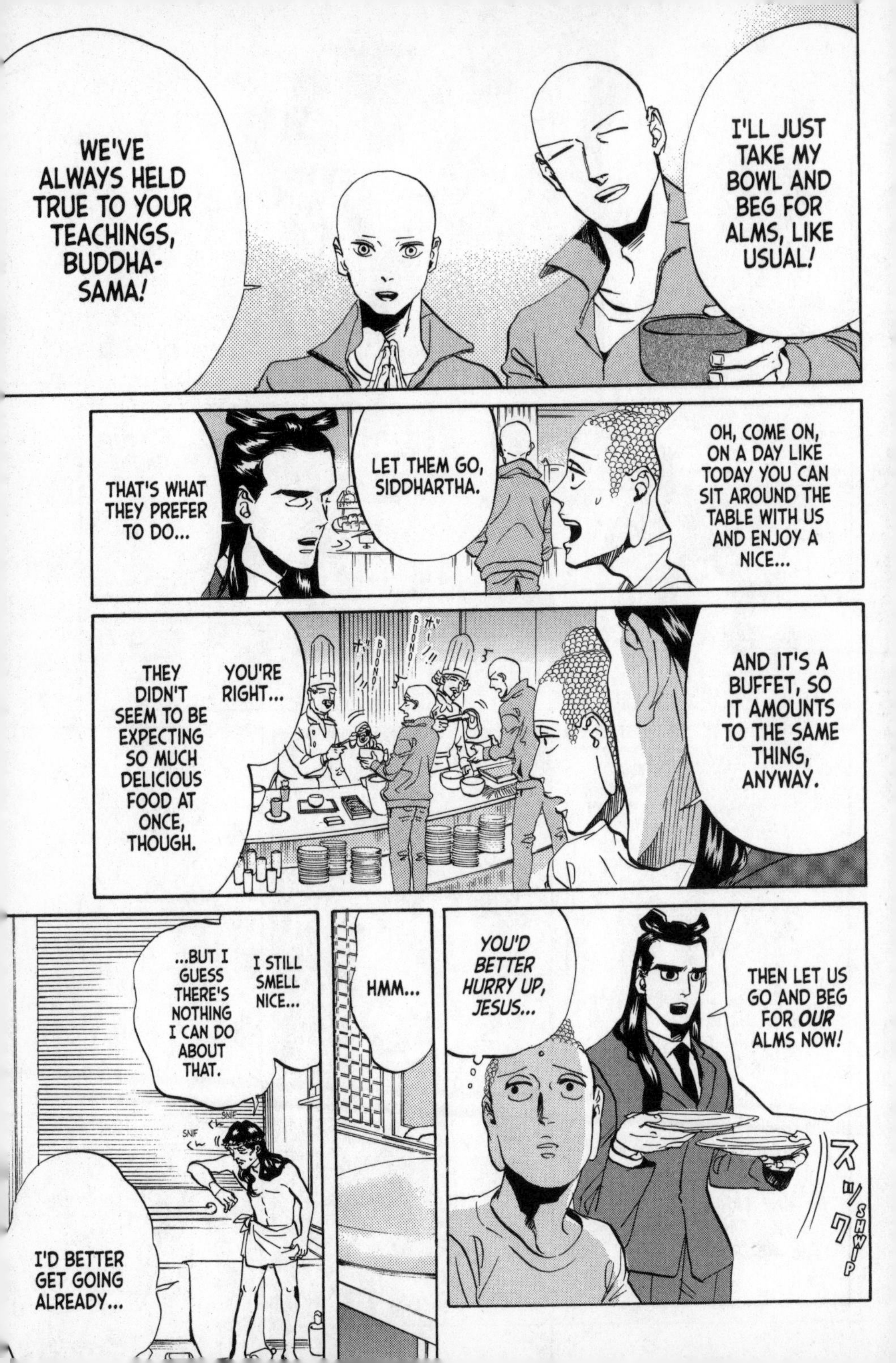
I'LL JUST TAKE MY BOWL AND BEG FOR ALMS, LIKE USUAL!
WE'VE ALWAYS HELD TRUE TO YOUR TEACHINGS, BUDDHA-SAMA!
OH, COME ON, ON A DAY LIKE TODAY YOU CAN SIT AROUND THE TABLE WITH US AND ENJOY A NICE...
LET THEM GO, SIDDHARTHA.
THAT'S WHAT THEY PREFER TO DO...
AND IT'S A BUFFET, SO IT AMOUNTS TO THE SAME THING, ANYWAY.
BUONO
BUONO
YOU'RE RIGHT...
THEY DIDN'T SEEM TO BE EXPECTING SO MUCH DELICIOUS FOOD AT ONCE, THOUGH.
THEN LET US GO AND BEG FOR *OUR* ALMS NOW!
SHWIP
YOU'D BETTER HURRY UP, JESUS...
HMM...
I STILL SMELL NICE...
...BUT I GUESS THERE'S NOTHING I CAN DO ABOUT THAT.
SNIF
SNIF
I'D BETTER GET GOING ALREADY...

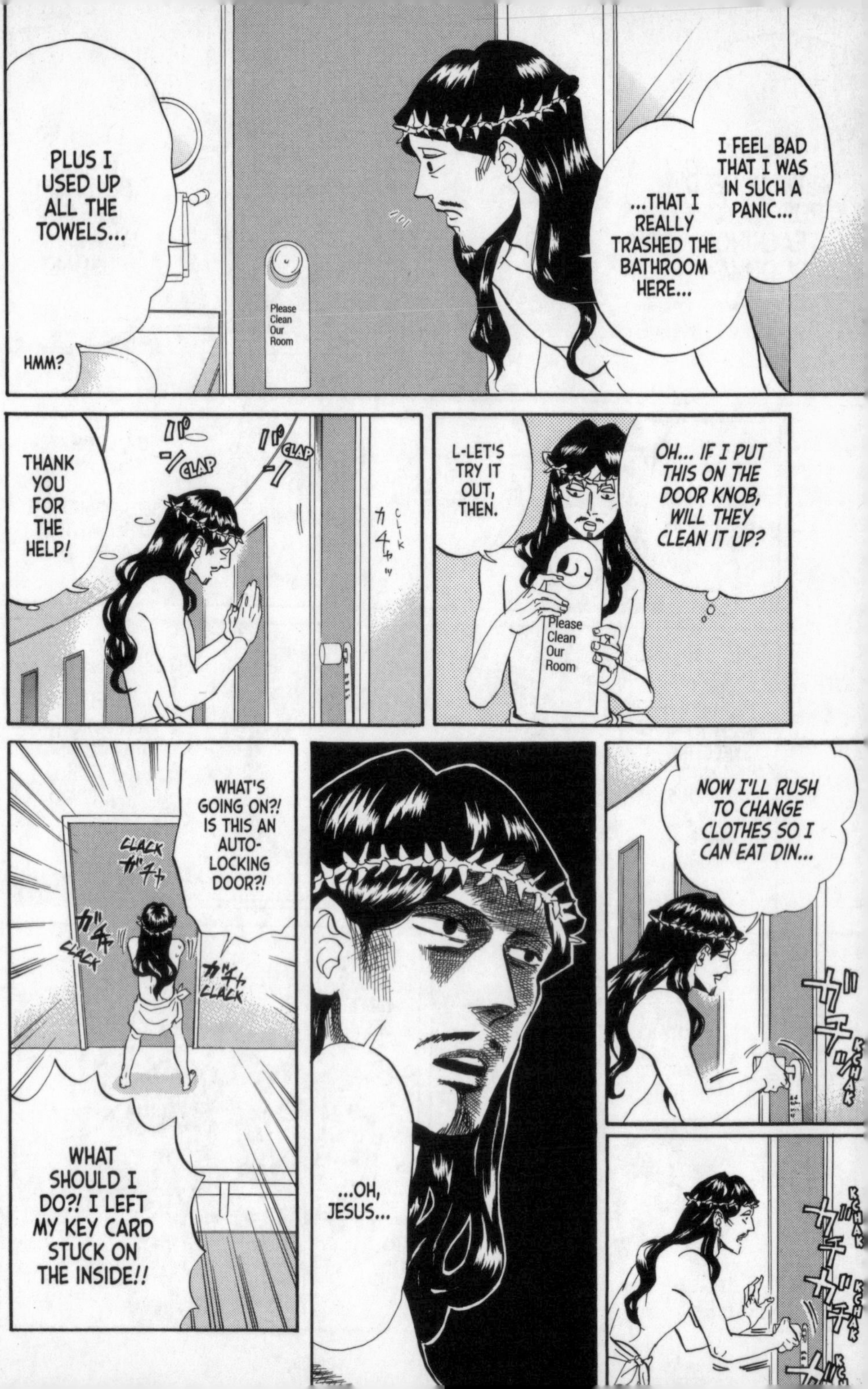
I FEEL BAD THAT I WAS IN SUCH A PANIC...
...THAT I REALLY TRASHED THE BATHROOM HERE...
Please Clean Our Room
PLUS I USED UP ALL THE TOWELS...
HMM?
OH... IF I PUT THIS ON THE DOOR KNOB, WILL THEY CLEAN IT UP?
L-LET'S TRY IT OUT, THEN.
Please Clean Our Room
CLAP
CLAP
THANK YOU FOR THE HELP!
CLIK
NOW I'LL RUSH TO CHANGE CLOTHES SO I CAN EAT DIN...
KCHAK
KCHAK
KCHAK
...OH, JESUS...
WHAT'S GOING ON?! IS THIS AN AUTO-LOCKING DOOR?!
CLACK
CLACK
CLACK
WHAT SHOULD I DO?! I LEFT MY KEY CARD STUCK ON THE INSIDE!!

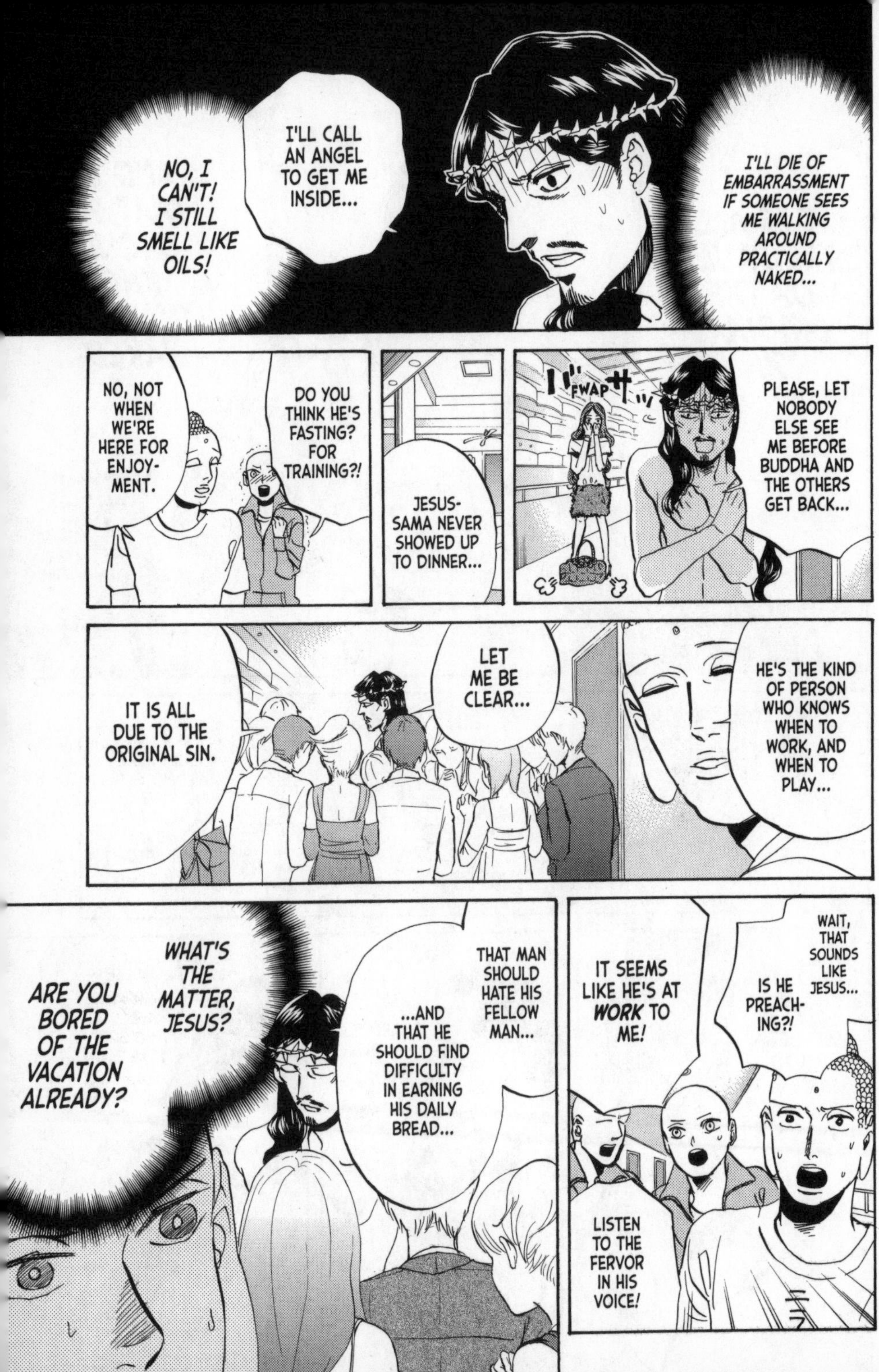
I'LL DIE OF EMBARRASSMENT IF SOMEONE SEES ME WALKING AROUND PRACTICALLY NAKED...
I'LL CALL AN ANGEL TO GET ME INSIDE...
NO, I CAN'T! I STILL SMELL LIKE OILS!
PLEASE, LET NOBODY ELSE SEE ME BEFORE BUDDHA AND THE OTHERS GET BACK...
FWAP
JESUS-SAMA NEVER SHOWED UP TO DINNER...
DO YOU THINK HE'S FASTING? FOR TRAINING?!
NO, NOT WHEN WE'RE HERE FOR ENJOY-MENT.
HE'S THE KIND OF PERSON WHO KNOWS WHEN TO WORK, AND WHEN TO PLAY...
LET ME BE CLEAR...
IT IS ALL DUE TO THE ORIGINAL SIN.
WAIT, THAT SOUNDS LIKE JESUS...
IS HE PREACH-ING?!
IT SEEMS LIKE HE'S AT *WORK* TO ME!
LISTEN TO THE FERVOR IN HIS VOICE!
THAT MAN SHOULD HATE HIS FELLOW MAN...
...AND THAT HE SHOULD FIND DIFFICULTY IN EARNING HIS DAILY BREAD...
WHAT'S THE MATTER, JESUS?
ARE YOU BORED OF THE VACATION ALREADY?

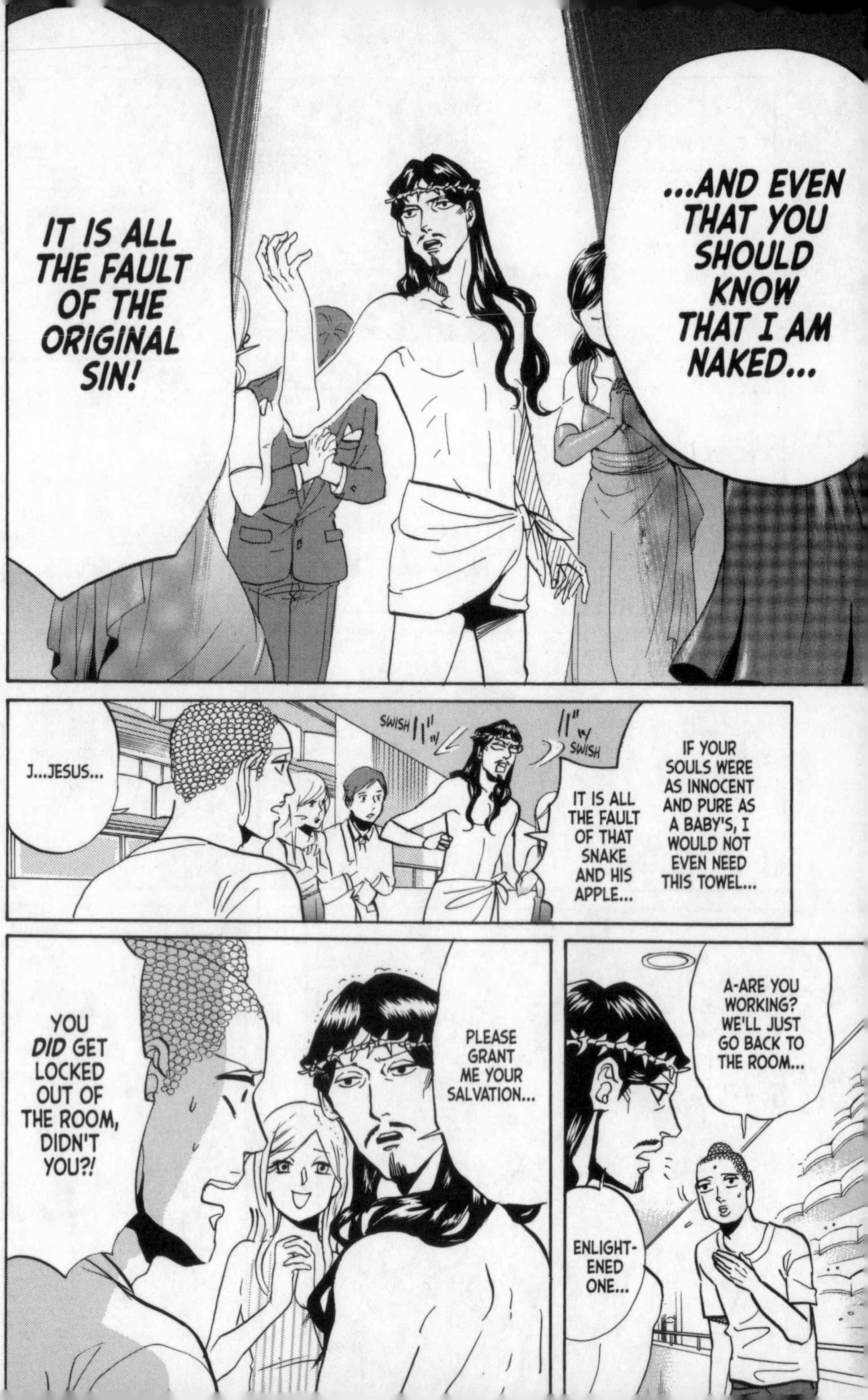
...AND EVEN THAT YOU SHOULD KNOW THAT I AM NAKED...
IT IS ALL THE FAULT OF THE ORIGINAL SIN!
IF YOUR SOULS WERE AS INNOCENT AND PURE AS A BABY'S, I WOULD NOT EVEN NEED THIS TOWEL...
IT IS ALL THE FAULT OF THAT SNAKE AND HIS APPLE...
SWISH
SWISH
J...JESUS...
A-ARE YOU WORKING? WE'LL JUST GO BACK TO THE ROOM...
ENLIGHT-ENED ONE...
PLEASE GRANT ME YOUR SALVATION...
YOU *DID* GET LOCKED OUT OF THE ROOM, DIDN'T YOU?!

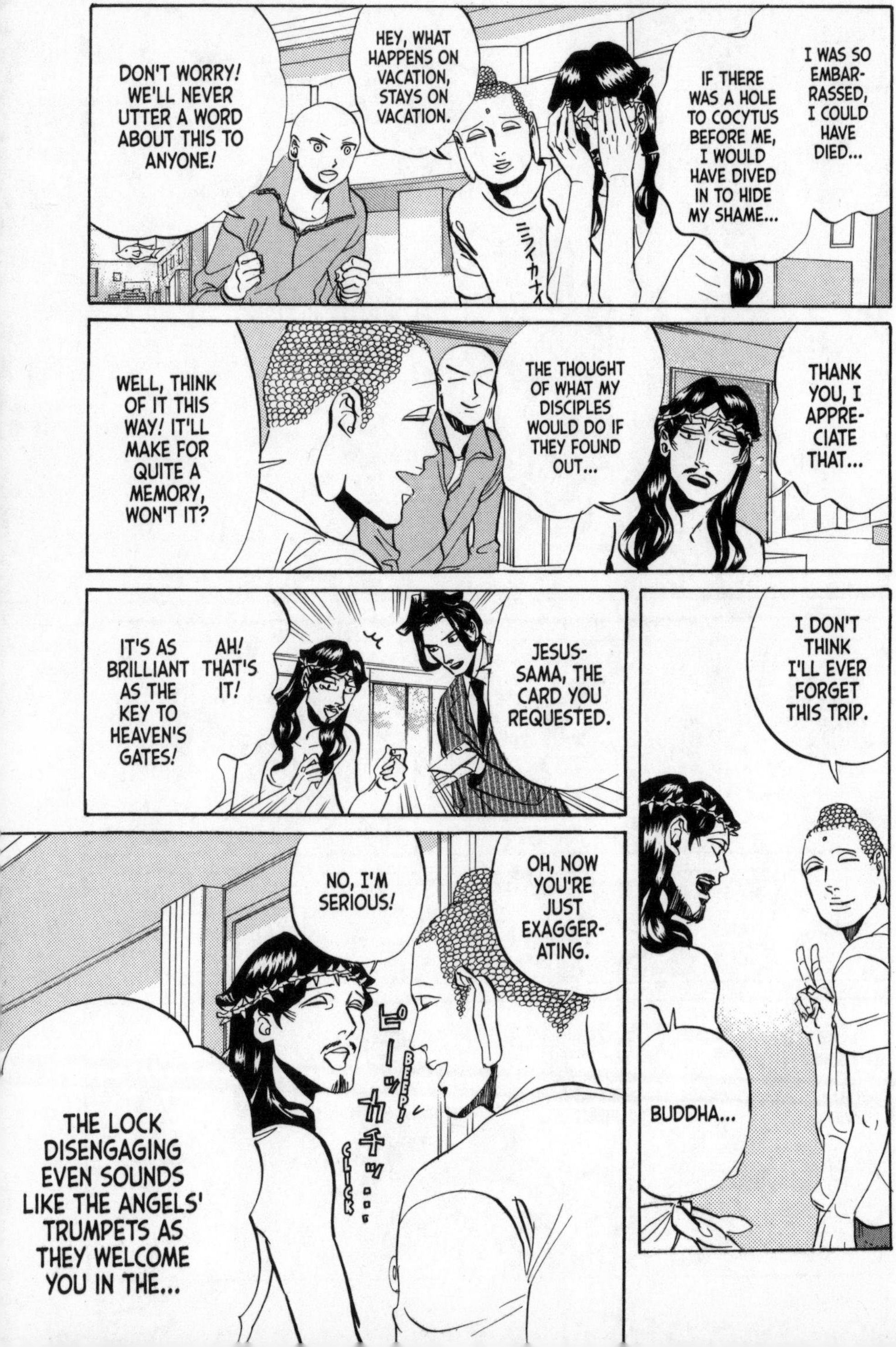
I WAS SO EMBARRASSED, I COULD HAVE DIED...
IF THERE WAS A HOLE TO COCYTUS BEFORE ME, I WOULD HAVE DIVED IN TO HIDE MY SHAME...
HEY, WHAT HAPPENS ON VACATION, STAYS ON VACATION.
ミライカナイ
DON'T WORRY! WE'LL NEVER UTTER A WORD ABOUT THIS TO ANYONE!
THANK YOU, I APPRECIATE THAT...
THE THOUGHT OF WHAT MY DISCIPLES WOULD DO IF THEY FOUND OUT...
WELL, THINK OF IT THIS WAY! IT'LL MAKE FOR QUITE A MEMORY, WON'T IT?
I DON'T THINK I'LL EVER FORGET THIS TRIP.
BUDDHA...
JESUS-SAMA, THE CARD YOU REQUESTED.
AH! THAT'S IT!
IT'S AS BRILLIANT AS THE KEY TO HEAVEN'S GATES!
OH, NOW YOU'RE JUST EXAGGERATING.
NO, I'M SERIOUS!
ピーッ
BEEP!
カチッ...
CLICK
THE LOCK DISENGAGING EVEN SOUNDS LIKE THE ANGELS' TRUMPETS AS THEY WELCOME YOU IN THE...

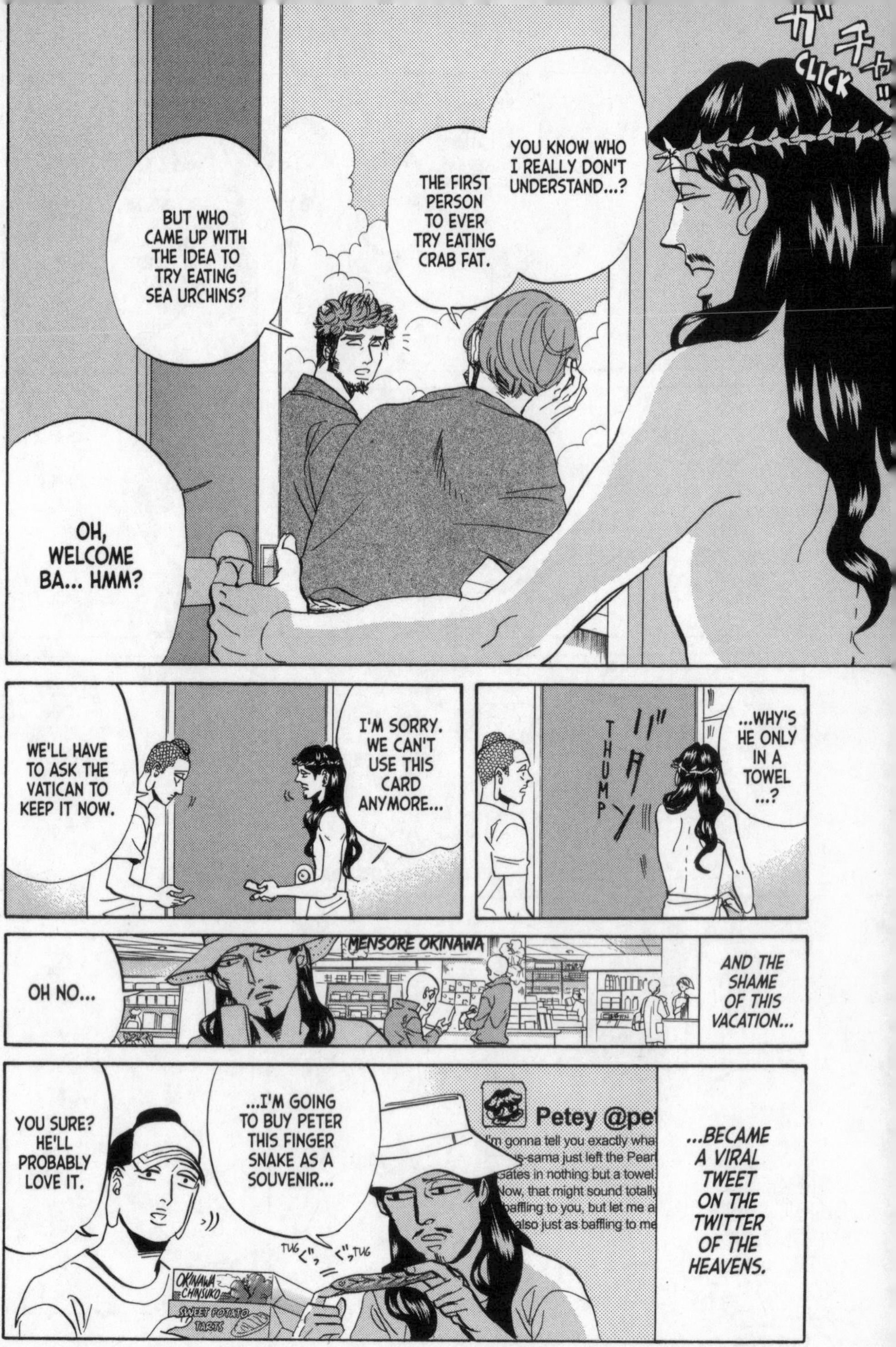
ガチャ
CLICK
YOU KNOW WHO I REALLY DON'T UNDERSTAND...?
THE FIRST PERSON TO EVER TRY EATING CRAB FAT.
BUT WHO CAME UP WITH THE IDEA TO TRY EATING SEA URCHINS?
OH, WELCOME BA... HMM?
...WHY'S HE ONLY IN A TOWEL ...?
バタン
THUMP
I'M SORRY. WE CAN'T USE THIS CARD ANYMORE...
WE'LL HAVE TO ASK THE VATICAN TO KEEP IT NOW.
AND THE SHAME OF THIS VACATION...
MENSORE OKINAWA
OH NO...
...BECAME A VIRAL TWEET ON THE TWITTER OF THE HEAVENS.
Petey @pet
I'm gonna tell you exactly wha
us-sama just left the Pear
Gates in nothing but a towel.
Now, that might sound totally
baffling to you, but let me a
also just as baffling to me
...I'M GOING TO BUY PETER THIS FINGER SNAKE AS A SOUVENIR...
TUG ぐっ ぐっ TUG
OKINAWA CHINSUKO
SWEET POTATO TARTS
YOU SURE? HE'LL PROBABLY LOVE IT.

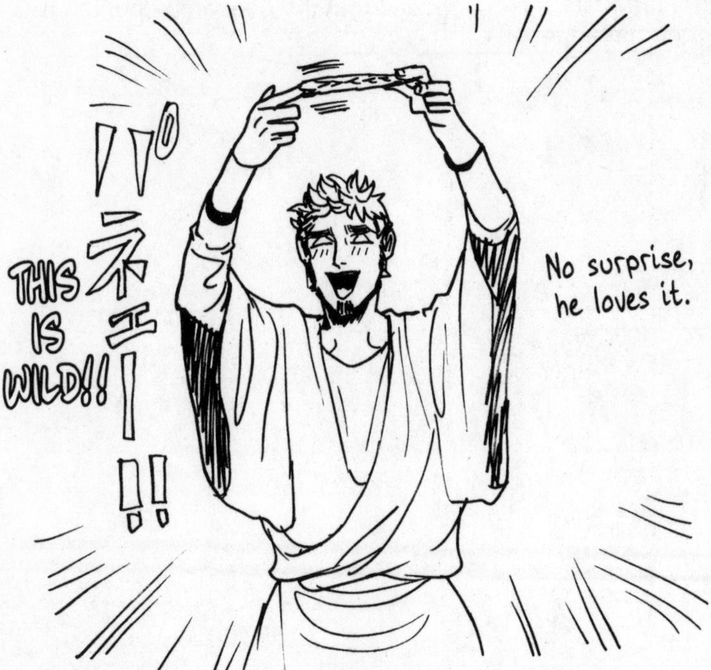
No surprise, he loves it.
パネェー!!
THIS IS WILD!!

CHAPTER 57 TRANSLATION NOTES

Capsule hotel, page 109

An infamous kind of ultra-cheap and minimalistic hotel in which the rooms are actually pods recessed into the wall with just enough space to lie down and sleep.

Konaka, page 111

A retail chain that deals primarily with men's clothing and formal wear. Not as expensive as Armani.

Denarii, page 114

A Roman silver coin often equated to a day's wages for a laborer. Mary of Bethany is said to have anointed Jesus' feet with a very fine perfumed oil worth 300 denarii, an extravagance that shocked his disciples, especially Judas.

Original Sin, page 118

When Adam and Eve committed the original sin of eating the fruit of the Tree of Knowledge, the first consequence is that they become cognizant and ashamed of their nakedness.

SAINT☆YOUNG MEN

Saint Young Men 4 copyright © 2011, 2012 Hikaru Nakamura
English translation copyright © 2020 Hikaru Nakamura

Published in the United States by Kodansha Comics, an imprint of Kodansha USA Publishing, LLC, New York.

Publication rights for this English edition arranged through Kodansha Ltd., Tokyo.

First published in Japan in 2011, 2012 by Kodansha Ltd., Tokyo as *Seinto oniisan*, volumes 7 & 8.

ISBN 978-1-63236-999-4

Original cover design by Hiroshi Niigami (NARTI;S)

Printed in the United States of America.

www.kodanshacomics.com

9 8 7 6 5 4 3 2 1
Translation: Stephen Paul
Lettering: E.K. Weaver
Editing: Nathaniel Gallant
Kodansha Comics edition cover design by Phil Balsman

Publisher: Kiichiro Sugawara

Director of publishing services: Ben Applegate
Associate director of operations: Stephen Pakula
Publishing services managing editor: Noelle Webster
Assistant production manager: Emi Lotto, Angela Zurlo